Contents

Study and examination skills

This chapter of the book is designed to aid Sixth Form students in their preparation for public examinations in History.

- Differences between GCSE and Sixth Form History
- Extended writing: the structured question and the essay
- How to handle sources in Sixth Form History
- Historical interpretation
- Progression in Sixth Form History
- Examination technique

Differences between GCSE and Sixth Form History

- **The amount of factual knowledge required for answers to Sixth Form History** questions is more detailed than at GCSE. Factual knowledge in the Sixth Form is used as supporting evidence to help answer historical questions. Knowing the facts is important, but not as important as knowing that factual knowledge supports historical analysis.

- **Extended writing is more important in Sixth Form History.** Students will be expected to answer either structured questions or to write essays.

Structured questions require students to answer more than one question on a given topic. For example:

In what ways did the New Deal aid agriculture?

To what extent did the New Deal bring fundamental change to the USA?

Each part of the structured question demands a different approach.

Essay questions require students to produce one answer to a given question. For example:

To what extent was Lyndon B. Johnson's Great Society programme a continuation of John F. Kennedy's New Frontier programme?

Similarities with GCSE

- Source analysis and evaluation

The skills in handling historical sources, which were acquired at GCSE, are developed in Sixth Form History. In the Sixth Form, sources have to be analysed in their historical context, so a good factual knowledge of the subject is important.

● Historical interpretations

Skills in historical interpretation at GCSE are also developed in Sixth Form History. The ability to put forward different historical interpretations is important. Students will also be expected to explain why different historical interpretations have occurred.

Extended writing: the structured question and the essay

When faced with extended writing in Sixth Form History, students can improve their performance by following a simple routine that attempts to ensure they achieve their best performance.

Answering the question

What are the command instructions?
Different questions require different types of response. For instance, 'In what ways' requires students to point out the various ways in which something took place in History; 'Why' questions expect students to deal with the causes or consequences of an historical question.

Are there key words or phrases that require definition or explanation?
It is important for students to show that they understand the meaning of the question. To do this, certain historical terms or words require explanation. For instance, if a question asked 'how far' a president was an 'innovator', an explanation of the word 'innovator' would be required.

Does the question have specific dates or issues that require coverage?
If a question mentions specific dates, these must be adhered to. For instance, if you are asked to answer a question on the foreign policy of USA it may state clear date limits such as 1945 to 1991. Questions may also mention a specific aspect such as 'domestic', 'religious', 'social' or 'economic'.

Planning your answer

Once you have decided on what the question requires, write a brief plan. For structured questions this may be brief. This is a useful procedure to make sure that you have ordered the information you require for your answer in the most effective way. For instance, in a balanced, analytical answer this may take the form of jotting down the main points for and against a historical issue raised in the question.

Writing the answer

Communication skills
The quality of written English is important in Sixth Form History. The way you present your ideas on paper can affect the quality of your answer. The Government, through QCA (Qualifications and Assessment Authority), have placed emphasis on the quality of written English in the Sixth Form. Therefore, punctuation, spelling and grammar, which were awarded marks at GCSE, require close attention. Use a dictionary if you are unsure of the meaning or spelling of a word. Use the glossary of terms you will find in this book to help you.

The introduction
For structured questions, you may wish to dispense with an introduction altogether and begin writing reasons to support an answer straight away. However, essay answers should begin with an introduction. These should

be both concise and precise. Introductions help 'concentrate the mind' on the question you are about to answer. Remember, do not try to write a conclusion as your opening sentence. Instead, outline briefly the areas you intend to discuss in your answer.

Balancing analysis with factual evidence
It is important to remember that factual knowledge should be used to support analysis. Merely 'telling the story' of an historical event is not enough. A structured question or essay should contain separate paragraphs, each addressing an analytical point that helps to answer the question. If, for example, the question asks for reasons why the Civil War began, each paragraph should provide a reason for the outbreak of war.

Seeing connections between reasons
In dealing with 'why'-type questions it is important to remember that the reasons for an historical event might be interconnected. Therefore, it is important to mention the connection between reasons. It might also be important to identify a hierarchy of reasons – that is, are some reasons more important than others in explaining an historical event?

Using quotations and statistical data
One aspect of supporting evidence that sustains analysis is the use of quotations. These can either be from a historian or a contemporary. However, unless these quotations are linked with analysis and supporting evidence, they tend to be of little value.

It can also be useful to support analysis with statistical data. In questions that deal with social and economic change, precise statistics that support your argument can be very persuasive.

Source analysis

Source analysis forms an integral part of the study of History. In Sixth Form History, source analysis is identified as an important skill in Assessment Objective 3.

In dealing with sources you should be aware that historical sources must be used 'in historical context' in Sixth Form History. Therefore, in this book sources are used with the factual information. Also, a specific source analysis question is included in each chapter.

Assessment Objectives

1 knowledge and understanding of history

2 evaluation and analysis skills

3 a) source analysis in historical context

   b) historical interpretation

How to handle sources in Sixth Form History

In dealing with sources, a number of basic hints will allow you to deal effectively with source-based questions and to build on your knowledge and skill in using sources gained at GCSE.

Written sources

Attribution and date

It is important to identify who has written the source and when it was written. This information can be very important. If, for instance, a source was a private letter between President Eisenhower and Secretary of State John Foster Dulles about the Hungarian Uprising of 1956, this information could be of considerable importance if you are asked about the usefulness (utility) or reliability of the source as evidence of Eisenhower's foreign policy.

It is important to note that just because a source is a primary source does not mean it is more useful or less reliable than a secondary source. Both primary and secondary sources need to be analysed to decide how useful and reliable they are. This can be determined by studying other issues.

Is the content factual or opinionated?

Once you have identified the author and date of the source, it is important to study its content. The content may be factual, stating what has happened or what may happen. On the other hand, it may contain opinions that should be handled with caution. These may contain bias. Even if a source is mainly factual, there might be important and deliberate gaps in factual evidence that can make a source biased and unreliable. Usually, written sources contain elements of both opinion and factual evidence. It is important to judge the balance between these two parts.

Has the source been written for a particular audience?

To determine the reliability of a source it is important to identify to whom it is directed. For instance, a public speech may be made to achieve a particular purpose and may not contain the author's true beliefs or feelings. In contrast, a private diary entry may be much more reliable in this respect.

Corroborative evidence

To test whether or not a source is reliable, the use of other evidence to support or corroborate the information it contains is important. Cross-referencing with other sources is a way of achieving this; so is cross-referencing with historical information contained within a chapter.

Visual sources

Maps

Maps which appear in Sixth Form History are either contemporary or secondary sources. These are used to support factual coverage in the text by providing information in a different medium. Therefore, to assess whether or not information contained in maps is accurate or useful, reference should be made to other information. It is also important to check the attribution and date of written sources. These could be significant.

Statistical data and graphs

It is important when dealing with this type of source to check carefully the nature of the information contained in data or in a graph. It might state the information in old forms of measurement such as pounds instead of kilograms. Be careful to check if the information is in **index numbers**. These are a statistical device where a base year is chosen and given the figure 100. All other figures are based on a percentage difference from that base year. For instance, if 1900 is taken as base year for unemployment in the USA it is given a figure of 100. If the index number for 1910 is 107 it means that unemployment has risen 7% since 1900.

An important point to remember when dealing with data and graphs over a period of time is to identify trends and patterns in the information. Merely describing the information in written form is not enough.

Historical interpretation

An important feature of both GCSE and Sixth Form History is the issue of historical interpretation. In Sixth Form History, it is important for students to be able to explain why historians differ, or have differed in their interpretations of the past.

Availability of evidence

An important reason is the availability of evidence on which to base historical judgements. As new evidence comes to light, historians today may have more information on which to base their judgements than historians in the past; for instance, sources for early United States history include presidential papers – correspondence between the President and individuals such as state governors, members of the Cabinet or Congressional leaders. Occasionally, new evidence comes to light that may influence judgements about early United States history.

Archaeological evidence may also be important. The archaeological study of ships – such as that used for the 'USS Monitor', which sank off Cape Hatteras during the Civil War – has produced considerable evidence about naval warfare and weapons of the Civil War.

'A philosophy of history?'

Many historians have a specific view of history that will affect the way they make their historical judgements. For instance, Marxist historians – who take their view from the writings of Karl Marx, the founder of modern socialism – believe that society has been made up of competing economic and social classes. They also place considerable importance on economic reasons in human decision making.

The role of the individual

Some historians have seen past history as having been moulded by the acts of specific individuals. President Abraham Lincoln and Dr Martin Luther King are seen as individuals whose personality and beliefs changed the course of United States' history. Other historians have tended to 'downplay' the role of individuals; instead, they highlight the importance of more general social, economic and political change. Rather than seeing George Washington, Booker T. Washington and Wendell Wilkie as individuals who changed the course of history, these historians tend to see them as representing the views of wider social, religious or economic change.

Placing different emphasis on the same historical evidence

Even if historians do not possess different philosophies of history or do not place different emphases on the role of the individual, it is still possible for them to disagree because they place different emphases on aspects of the same factual evidence. As a result, Sixth Form History should be seen as a subject that encourages debate about the past based on historical evidence.

Progression in Sixth Form History

The ability to achieve high standards in Sixth Form History involves the acquisition of a number of skills:

● Good written communication skills

● Sound factual knowledge

● Evaluating factual evidence and making historical conclusions based on that evidence

● Source analysis

● Understanding the nature of historical interpretation

● Understanding the causes and consequences of historical events

● Understanding the themes in history which will involve a study of a specific topic over a long period of time

● Understanding the ideas of change and continuity associated with themes.

Students should be aware that the acquisition of these skills will take place gradually over the time spent in the Sixth Form. At the beginning of the course the main emphasis may be on the acquisition of factual knowledge, particularly when the body of knowledge studied at GCSE was different.

When dealing with causation, students will have to build on their skills from GCSE. They will not only be expected to identify reasons for a historical event but also to provide a hierarchy of causes. They should identify the main causes and less important causes. They may also identify that causes may be interconnected and linked. Progression in Sixth Form History will come with answering the questions at the end of each sub-section, as well as with practising the skills outlined through the use of the factual knowledge contained in the book.

Examination techniques

The ultimate challenge for any Sixth Form historian is to produce quality work under examination conditions. Examinations will take the form of either modular examinations taken in January and June or of an 'end of course' set of examinations.

Here is some advice on how to improve your performance in an examination.

● *Read the whole examination paper thoroughly*
Make sure that the questions you choose are those for which you can produce a good answer. Don't rush – allow time to decide which questions to choose. It is probably too late to change your mind half way through answering a question.

● *Read the question very carefully*
Once you have made the decision to answer a specific question, read it very carefully. Make sure you understand the precise demands of the question. Think about what is required in your answer. It is much better to think about this before you start writing, rather than trying to steer your essay in a different direction half way through.

● *Make a brief plan*

Sketch out what you intend to include in your answer. Put in order the points you want to make. Examiners are not impressed with additional information included at the end of the essay, with indicators such as arrows or asterisks.

● *Pace yourself as you write*

Success in examinations has a lot to do with successful time management. If, for instance, you have to answer an essay question in approximately 45 minutes then you should be one-third of the way through after 15 minutes. With 30 minutes gone, you should start writing the last third of your answer.

Where a question is divided into sub-questions make sure you look at the mark tariff for each question. If in a 20-mark question a sub-question is worth a maximum of 5 marks, then you should spend approximately one-quarter of the time allocated for the whole question on this sub-question.

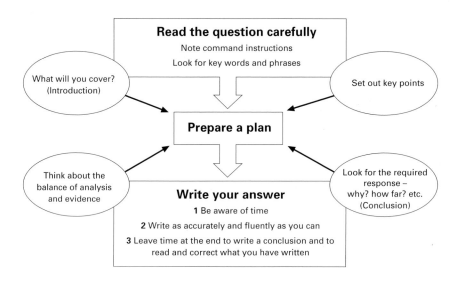

The USA, 1776–1992: a synoptic assessment

Key Issues

- *In what ways did the federal government increase its power 1789–1992?*

- *How did the USA's position in world affairs change between 1776–1992?*

- *What were the reasons for changes in US society 1776–1992?*

- How did the power of the President change between 1789 and 1992?
- What impact did westward expansion have on the USA?
- How important has immigration been to the development of the USA?
- Why have civil rights been an important feature of US history?
- How has the USA developed into a major world power?

How did the power of the President change between 1789 and 1992?

Separation of powers: The principle in the US Constitution that prevents any one institution exercising complete power. Within the federal (national) government, for instance, the power to make laws was divided between the President, Congress and Supreme Court. Political powers were also divided between the federal government and state governments.

Federal state: A state where political power is divided between a federal government and state governments. In the USA, the federal government has responsibility for foreign relations, national defence and inter-state commerce; the states have responsibility for education, law and order and welfare.

Habeus corpus: A civil right where anyone arrested for a crime must either be formally charged within 24 hours or released.

According to the historian Marcus Cunliffe, in *American Presidents and the Presidency* (published in 1970):

'The American presidency is the most important and, perhaps, most peculiar office on earth. The President is a monarch who must abdicate, a politician without a firm constituency, a man of formidable authority who is often derided and thwarted.'

Since the appointment of the first President, George Washington, in 1789, the power of the President has been an issue of debate. Part of the problem lies in the position of the President as laid down in the Constitution (see page 27). With the operation of the principle of the **separation of powers**, the President has to work with Congress. Because the USA is a **federal state**, the federal government has to work with the states. As a result, presidential power is limited.

A theme of US history has been how individual presidents have used this power. Rexford Tugwell, a close adviser to President F.D. Roosevelt in the 1930s, stated that when the Constitution was drawn up in 1787 at Philadelphia:

'none could have had any definite picture of the official they had created – except that he would be very much like [George] Washington.'

Since George Washington, individual presidents have used their authority to increase their power. The clearest example of this trend was Abraham Lincoln. During the American Civil War, Lincoln used his powers to suspend *habeus corpus*, to imprison opponents and to call up troops. Lincoln's defence was that to save the Constitution he had to ignore it occasionally. His extension of presidential power was limited to the emergency of civil war. The presidents who followed him did not possess increased power as a result. In 1885, Woodrow Wilson wrote a study of the US political system, which he entitled 'Congressional Government'.

This title reflected the authority of Presidents in the late 19th century. Nevertheless, the Civil War had decided one very important issue in US politics: the states' rights (see page 60) were reduced considerably with the triumph of the Union cause over the Confederacy.

The rise of presidential power mirrors the rise of the USA as a major industrial and military power. As an industrial power, the US government grew in size to reflect the complexity of society. As Chief Executive (Head of Government), the President began to be responsible for a larger and larger federal government. Extra departments were added: Agriculture in 1889 and Commerce and Labor in 1903 (see insert). In 1921, the Bureau of the Budget was created to aid the President in producing the annual budget. By 1939, a separate Executive Office of the Presidency was formed to incorporate all the advisory agencies to the presidency which had developed during the early 20th century.

Cabinet: The heads of government departments, such as State, Treasury, Labor, who help the President run the Administration.

Evolution of the government departments in US Cabinet

Original members:
Secretary of State, 1789
Secretary of Treasury, 1789
Secretary of War, 1789 (loses **Cabinet** status, 1947)
Attorney General, 1789 (not head of Justice Department until 1870)

Added, 1798–1813
Secretary of Navy, 1798 (loses Cabinet status, 1947)
Postmaster General, 1829 (loses Cabinet status, 1970)
Secretary of Interior, 1849
Secretary of Agriculture, 1889
Secretary of Commerce and Labor, 1903 (office divided by 1913)
Secretary of Commerce, 1913
Secretary of Labor, 1913

Added, 1947–1977
Secretary of Defense, 1947 (subordinate to him, without Cabinet rank, are secretaries of army, navy and air force)
Secretary of Health, Education and Welfare, 1953
Secretary of Housing and Urban Development, 1965
Secretary of Transportation, 1966
Secretary of Energy, 1977

The development of US military power was even more significant for the role of the President. As Commander-in-Chief, he had the power to send US troops abroad, without Congressional approval, if he felt US lives or property were in danger. Theodore Roosevelt used this power to send US troops to the Caribbean and Central America during his presidency (1901–09). Woodrow Wilson (1913–21) sent US troops into Mexico in 1916.

As the USA entered the First World War, the President's role in foreign relations increased the prestige of the office greatly. As one of the 'Big Four' at the Paris Peace Conference in 1919, President Wilson personified US military and industrial power. He became the first US President to have a major input in European affairs.

The crisis of the 1930s increased US presidential authority at home. At his **inauguration**, in March 1933, President F.D. Roosevelt asked for powers to deal with the economic depression, which would be the same as if the country were facing the crisis of war. As a result, during the New Deal, the federal government greatly increased its role in American life. Alphabet agencies were involved in industry, agriculture and regional development.

Inauguration: The official ceremony for the swearing in of a new President.

The President's position changed so much that commentators at the time were accusing Roosevelt of being a dictator.

The turning point in the rise of presidential power came with the Second World War. From 1941, the USA emerged as a world power, with its head of state as a world leader. From 1945, the USA entered the nuclear weapons age. From that day forward, the US President has had the awesome responsibility and power to authorise the use of nuclear weapons.

It is significant that the last time Congress was authorised to declare war was on 8 December 1941. Since that date, successive US Presidents have used their power as Commander-in-Chief to send large numbers of US armed forces abroad. In 1950, President Truman sent US troops to Korea. He used the defence that he was acting on behalf of the United Nations. Most significantly, Presidents Kennedy, Johnson and Nixon sent large numbers of troops to South East Asia during the Vietnam conflict.

Such a major growth of presidential power was reflected in Arthur Schlesinger's study *The Imperial Presidency* published in 1972. By that date, the office of President had become so powerful that it no longer reflected the original constitutional role of the office. As world statesman and head of the armed forces, the President of the USA became the world's most powerful politician.

However, in domestic affairs, the President's power remained limited. Without the support of Congress, it was very difficult for a president to implement a viable domestic programme. President Kennedy suffered from this problem between 1961 and 1963. Furthermore, the Supreme Court could declare government or Congressional Acts unconstitutional. President F.D. Roosevelt faced this problem in the First New Deal (1933–35).

Impeachment: The trial of a public official, especially in the USA, for a serious crime committed while in office.

In the year Schlesinger produced his book, the Watergate Scandal was developing – causing great damage to the office of President. Nixon's obstruction of investigations into White House activities during the 1972 presidential campaign and party financing led to calls for his **impeachment**. On 9 August 1974, when impeachment was almost certain, Nixon became the only US President to resign from office.

Since 1974, presidential power has not diminished in foreign and military affairs. In 1991, George Bush Senior sent US forces to fight in the Gulf War. The US President still has the personal authority to launch a retaliatory nuclear attack. Rather than seeing the power of the office changing through time, it is better to look at how individual presidents have been able to use their power. Political scientist, Richard Neustadt, states that presidential power is 'the power to persuade'. Certain presidents, because of personality, political skill and circumstance, have used the full potential of the office. Strong presidents include Washington, Jackson, Lincoln, Theodore and Franklin Roosevelt, and Lyndon Johnson. Weak presidents include Pierce, Buchanan, Hayes, Ford and Carter.

What impact did westward expansion have on the USA?

Title: To have title over land is to rule or govern it effectively.

Ever since English colonists first settled in Virginia and Massachusetts, the history of America has been one of westward expansion. The 'frontier spirit' has been an important theme in American society. In 1783, when the 13 colonies won independence from Britain, the USA had **title** over territory as far west as the Mississippi river.

During the early history of the Republic, the North American continent was the scene of colonial competition between the USA and several European powers. Britain still controlled Canada and the Oregon territory.

The French controlled the vast lands west of the Mississippi. The Russians controlled the Alaskan coast with outposts as far south as Fort Ross in northern California. In Florida and the South and West, a vast Spanish empire existed.

The history of the United States, from its creation until 1890, was to dominate much of the North American continent from the Atlantic to the Pacific. They were able to buy Louisiana from the French in 1803. The Spanish were forced out of Florida in 1819 and they defeated Mexico in a war (1846–48). They negotiated with the British over Maine and Oregon between 1842 and 1846, and they purchased Alaska from Russia in 1867.

Even though the USA had claim on these vast lands, they still had to be settled and the Native-American peoples defeated. A theme of US history is the conflict between the government and the 250 Indian tribes that inhabited the USA. Superior military technology and divisions amongst the Indian tribes were the main reasons for US success. However, successive governments from the 1830s onwards believed westward expansion was the God-given right to dominate the continent. As a result, Native Americans were treated as second class. In the early 1830s, in defiance of a Supreme Court ruling, President Jackson forced the five 'civilised' tribes of the South-East to move westward to Indian Territory, now the state of Oklahoma. During the course of westward expansion, the US government made and then broke virtually every treaty it ever had with Indian tribes.

Prairies: The large, flat areas of grassy land in North America, with very few trees.

It is clear that the westward movement of population, and the settlement and cultivation of the **prairies** were one of the greatest achievements of the 19th century. However, they were achieved at a cost. The vast herds of North-American bison (buffalo) were wiped out and Native-American society was destroyed.

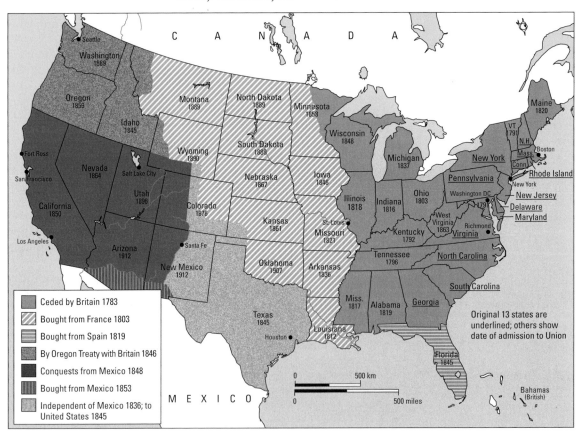

Growth of the United States of America

Admission of states into the Union

State	Date of admission	State	Date of admission
1 Delaware	12 December 1787	26 Michigan	26 January 1837
2 Pennsylvania	18 December 1787	27 Florida	3 March 1845
3 New Jersey	2 January 1788	28 Texas	29 December 1845
4 Georgia	9 January 1788	29 Iowa	28 December 1846
5 Connecticut	6 February 1788	30 Wisconsin	29 May 1848
6 Massachusetts	28 April 1788	31 California	9 September 1850
7 Maryland	23 May 1788	32 Minnesota	11 May 1858
8 South Carolina	21 June 1788	33 Oregon	14 February 1859
9 New Hampshire	25 June 1788	34 Kansas	29 January 1861
10 Virginia	26 July 1788	35 West Virginia	20 June 1863
11 New York	21 November 1789	36 Nevada	31 October 1864
12 North Carolina	29 May 1790	37 Nebraska	1 March 1867
13 Rhode Island	4 March 1791	38 Colorado	1 August 1876
14 Vermont	1 June 1791	39 North Dakota	2 November 1889
15 Kentucky	1 June 1792	40 South Dakota	2 November 1889
16 Tennessee	1 March 1796	41 Montana	8 November 1889
17 Ohio	30 April 1803	42 Washington	11 November 1889
18 Louisiana	11 December 1812	43 Idaho	3 July 1890
19 Indiana	10 December 1816	44 Wyoming	10 July 1890
20 Mississippi	3 December 1817	45 Utah	4 January 1896
21 Illinois	14 December 1818	46 Oklahoma	16 November 1907
22 Alabama	15 March 1819	47 New Mexico	6 January 1912
23 Maine	10 August 1820	48 Arizona	14 February 1912
24 Missouri	15 June 1821	49 Alaska	3 January 1959
25 Arkansas	7 December 1836	50 Hawaii	21 August 1959

The move westward also had a major impact on the East. With every new admission of a state to the Union (see map opposite and chart above), the issue of whether it should be a free state or a slave state was raised. The uneasy compromises of 1820 and 1850 prevented conflict between the 'free North' and the 'slave South'. However, it was the Kansas–Nebraska Act of 1854 – which created a new territory in the West – that began the chain of events that would lead to civil war by 1861.

By 1890 and the Battle of Wounded Knee, the Indian Wars had come to an end. In Chicago, historian Frederick Jackson Turner declared in 1893 that the Frontier had also come to an end. Yet the spirit of expansion survived. From the 1890s, many Americans began to look for expansion outside North America. This desire was an important factor behind the Spanish–American War. As a result of the war, the USA acquired a colonial empire in the Philippines and Puerto Rico. From 1898, the USA was becoming a world power.

The end of westward expansion helped to launch the USA on to the world stage. With vast mineral wealth, extensive agriculture and industry, the USA rivalled Britain and Germany. The 19th century had been based on westward expansion; the 20th century saw US influence expand across the world.

How important has immigration been to the development of the USA?

Apart from Native Americans, the entire population of the USA is descended from immigrants – people who arrive from another country or continent to live and work in a different country. Up to the time of the American War Independence, the majority of immigrants came from the British Isles and Germany. Many came for economic reasons, to acquire land and to improve their economic and social standing. Others came to avoid religious persecution – such as the Pilgrim Fathers to Massachusetts, the Quakers to Pennsylvania and the German Amish and Mennonite sects. Those who signed the Declaration of Independence came predominantly from White, Anglo-Saxon, Protestant (WASP) backgrounds.

Immigration came to the USA in two huge waves. Between the 1840s and the Civil War, the 'old immigration' came from Scandinavia, Germany and Ireland. The Irish came mainly as a result of the Great Famine of 1845–49. They were destitute when they arrived in the USA, and the vast majority were Roman Catholic. This sparked off a recurrent theme in 19th- and 20th-century American history: the reaction of WASPs or **Nativist** Americans to the different religions and cultures of the immigrants. In the 1850s, Catholic Irish immigration led to the rise of the 'Know Nothing' party which was anti-Catholic.

Nativist: A supporter of the idea that the USA should be a country of White Anglo-Saxon Protestants (WASPs).

After the Civil War, the 'new immigration' began. Not only did it include immigrants from Germany, Ireland and Scandinavia, it also included Jews from Eastern Europe, Italians, Poles and Russians.

These immigrant groups had a large impact on US society:

● They provided the cheap labour required to fuel the rapid economic growth of the USA.

● They brought with them skills that were needed for economic development.

● They also brought their own religions and culture.

Foreign immigration to America, 1840–60

Cities such as New York and Chicago developed ethnic neighbourhoods inhabited almost exclusively by Italians, Poles, Jews or the Irish.

The WASP resistance to immigration took a variety of forms. The rise of the prohibition movement (see Chapter 2) was in part due to opposition to the drinking excesses of the new immigrants. By the time of the First World War and the 1920s, Nativist opposition seemed to be triumphant. National prohibition was passed in 1918. The Ku Klux Klan was re-formed in 1915. It added Jews and Catholics to the list of groups it opposed and intimidated. Finally, in 1924, immigration was severely restricted. No longer would the words on the Statue of Liberty ring true: 'Bring me your huddled masses yearning to be free.'

Since the 1960s, a new wave of immigration has taken place. Hispanic Americans have entered the USA in large numbers, either legally or illegally. This influx has been so great that Spanish has become an important second language in California and several south-west states. In addition, Asian immigration has included the Vietnamese, Koreans and people from the Indian sub-continent.

These waves of immigration have been met by resistance, but this has not stopped the USA becoming a 'melting pot' of races. However, the 'melting pot' has found it extremely difficult to incorporate one of America's oldest ethnic minorities, African Americans.

Growth of US population and area

Census	Population	Land area (square miles)	Population/square mile	%age of population Urban	Rural
1790	3,929,214	867,980	4.5	5.1	94.9
1800	5,308,483	867,980	6.1	6.1	93.9
1810	7,239,881	1,685,865	4.3	7.2	92.8
1820	9,638,453	1,753,588	5.5	7.2	92.8
1830	12,866,020	1,753,588	7.3	8.8	91.2
1840	17,069,453	1,753,588	9.7	10.8	89.2
1850	23,191,876	2,944,337	7.9	15.3	84.7
1860	31,433,321	2,973,965	10.6	19.8	80.2
1870	39,818,449	2,973,965	13.4	24.9	75.1
1880	50,155,783	2,973,965	16.9	28.2	71.8
1890	62,947,714	2,973,965	21.2	35.1	64.9
1900	75,994,575	2,974,159	25.6	39.1	60.3
1910	91,972,266	2,973,890	30.9	45.7	54.3
1920	105,710,620	2,973,776	35.5	51.2	48.8
1930	122,775,046	2,973,965	41.2	56.2	43.8
1940	131,669,275	2,977,128	44.2	56.5	43.5
1950	150,697,361	2,974,726**	50.7	64.0	36.0
1960*	179,323,175	3,540,911	50.6	69.9	30.1
1970	203,235,298	3,536,855	57.5	73.5	26.5
1980	226,504,825	3,536,855	64.0	73.7	26.3
1990	249,975,000	3,536,855	70.3	–	–

* As measured in 1940; shrinkage offset by increase in water area.
** First year for which figures include Alaska and Hawaii.
Source: Census Bureau, *Historical Statistics of the United States*, updated by relevant Statistical Abstract of the United States

Why have civil rights been an important feature of US history?

From the creation of the United States, civil rights have been a central issue. The American War of Independence was fought to defend the rights of the colonies against action by the British government. When the Constitution was drawn up in 1787 (see page 27), several states would not accept it unless civil rights were included. The first 10 Amendments of the Constitution (passed in 1791), known as the Bill of Rights, included basic civil rights.

The most enduring issue of civil rights involves African Americans. The vast majority of African Americans in 1787 were slaves. The decision of the Founding Fathers of the Constitution to ignore slavery only put off what was to be the most divisive issue facing the country. With the country divided between free states and slave states, the issue of African-American civil rights was bound to cause conflict. Tension was increased with the westward expansion of the USA. Each time a territory requested admission as a state, the issue of free state or slave state arose. In 1819, and again in 1850, compromises were agreed which prevented conflict and kept an uneasy balance between slave states and free states in the Congress.

The issue of slavery reached its height during the 1850s. The Kansas–Nebraska Act of 1854 created the distinct possibility of conflict between pro- and anti-slavery groups in the Kansas–Nebraska territory. Kansas, in particular, engaged in a civil war years before the nation became involved in 1861.

Unilaterally: Acting on one's own without reference to others.

The outbreak of civil war in 1861 was about whether or not states could **unilaterally** leave (secede from) the USA. Lincoln initially led the North in a campaign to maintain the union of states. But in 1862, partly as a ploy to win the war, Lincoln issued the Emancipation Proclamation (see page 95), which turned the war into a moral crusade to free the slaves in the South.

The Northern victory, by 1865, should have been a turning point in the history of African-American civil rights. The Thirteenth, Fourteenth and Fifteenth Amendments of the Constitution gave African Americans full civil and political equality. However, in the years after 1877 the white-dominated state governments of the former Confederacy introduced 'Jim Crow laws', which created a society segregated between whites and blacks. For most of the period 1877 to the 1950s, African Americans in the Old South held second-class status in a divided society.

The development of a civil rights movement in the 1950s and 1960s brought the issue to national attention. Through a variety of methods, African Americans fought for and obtained civil and political equality by the end of the 1960s. Using the court system and by protesting against discrimination, African Americans forced the federal and state governments of the South to end **legal segregation.**

Legal segregation: The deliberate creation by law of separate facilities for whites and African Americans, mainly in the former Confederate states.

However, full civil and political equality did not bring social equality. Since the 1960s, African-American society has been divided between rich and poor. By 1992, large numbers of African Americans still lived in abject poverty in either the rural South or inner city North.

Although African-American rights have been a dominant theme, other issues of civil rights have become important in the 20th century. Women's rights initially involved campaigns for the vote and for national prohibition in the early part of the century. Since the 1960s, a women's movement has developed which demand full social and civil equality for women. Also in the 1960s, a campaign for gay and lesbian rights developed. By the early 1970s, the nation was affected by demands for Black Power, Gay Power and Feminist Power. It even involved Red Power when Native

Americans occupied the old Alcatraz prison in San Francisco Bay as a protest for more Native-American rights.

In the end, the history of the United States from 1776 to 1992 has been an attempt to turn into reality the Declaration of Independence, which stated:

> 'We hold these truths to be self-evident, that all men are created equal, and that they are endowed with certain inalienable rights.'

How has the United States developed into a major world power?

Today the United States is the world's greatest power. With the collapse of the USSR in 1991, the Cold War has come to an end – leaving one world superpower. However, for much of its history the United States has played only a minor part in world affairs. For most of the period 1776–1890, the US government was involved in extending its authority over the vast western territories it had acquired. Occasionally – as in 1853 – the US armed forces were used to help open up trade with Japan. Later, the USA adopted an 'open door' policy towards trade with China. In this respect, the United States seemed to stand against the trend where European powers carved up the globe into vast colonial empires.

Yet the USA did play a role outside its immediate borders. In 1823, President Monroe issued the Monroe Doctrine. It stated that the United States would look unfavourably upon any attempt by European powers to create colonies in the Americas. Its unofficial aim was to ensure that the USA would be the dominant power in the Americas. As a result, throughout the late 19th and 20th centuries, the USA has intervened in the internal affairs of Central and South American states to further its own interests.

A turning point in US relations with the outside world was the Spanish–American War of 1898. For the first time the USA acquired colonies outside the North American continent. Also, during the presidency of Theodore Roosevelt, the USA began to play a more active role in international affairs. The US 'Great White' fleet was sent on a world tour to show off US naval might. In 1905, Roosevelt acted as peacemaker between Russia and Japan to end the Russo–Japanese War. He was awarded the Nobel Peace Prize for his efforts.

Entry into the First World War in 1917 brought the USA, albeit temporarily, into the centre stage of world affairs. Woodrow Wilson's '14 Points' of January 1918 became the unofficial war aims of the Allies. At Paris in 1919, Wilson put forward his plan for a League of Nations as a guarantor of world peace (see Chapter 7). The high point of Wilson's presidency was quickly followed by its nadir (lowest point). In 1919, the Senate rejected the Treaty of Versailles. It later signed a separate peace with Germany. During the 1920s and 1930s, the USA entered a new period of isolation.

The involvement of the USA in the Second World War transformed it from a major power into one of two superpowers. The defeat of Germany and Japan and the weakening of the British Empire left the USA and USSR to dominate the post-war world. The end of the Second World War also brought the beginning of the nuclear age and the Cold War (see Chapters 8 and 9). The writer Gore Vidal regards 1947 as the beginning of the 'national security' state in the USA. The National Security Act of 1947 created the Central Intelligence Agency and the National Security Agency (see page 396). It also produced a new decision-making body in foreign and military affairs – the National Security Council. With the introduction

Communism: The political belief that the state should own and control the means of producing everything, so that all levels of society can be equal. Then everyone will do as much as they can and get as much as they need.

Armaments: Weapons and military equipment belonging to an army or a country.

Corporations: Large businesses or groups of companies that are all controlled and run together as single organisations.

1. What do you regard as the most important theme in the domestic history of the USA 1776–1992?

Explain your answer.

2. To what extent has presidential power grown as a result of the growth of US military power?

3. How far has the United States been 'a melting pot' of different races?

of selective service (compulsory military service, or the 'draft'), the USA was on a war footing in peacetime.

In 1950, the issuing of the National Security Council paper NSC-68 and the outbreak of the Korean War led to a massive arms build-up by the USA. By that date, the USA was engaged in a global military and ideological conflict with communist states. The USA developed a worldwide network of military bases and alliances in an attempt to contain **communism**.

The demand for military equipment led to the development of the 'military-industrial complex' in the USA. This term describes those groups within the USA who benefited from massive **armaments** expenditure. It included **corporations** such as McDonnell Douglas, Lockheed and Boeing. It also included politicians whose states and districts benefited from armaments contracts. Union leaders saw the armaments industry as a lucrative source of work for their union members. The rise of these mutually-interested groups even worried President Eisenhower who, in his farewell speech of 1961, warned his successor of the influence of the military-industrial complex on foreign policy. Eisenhower clearly identified the group with an aggressive, anti-communist policy which would require considerable military expenditure.

The international tension created by the Cold War resulted in periodic crises. The most serious of these crises came in 1961 and 1962, over Berlin and Cuba respectively. On both occasions, the USA came close to all-out nuclear war with the USSR.

However, the most serious Cold War conflict was a conventional war in Vietnam. From March 1965, US combat forces were dispatched to 'save' South Vietnam from communism. By 1969, the numbers had risen to 600,000. The failure to 'win in Vietnam' created a major domestic crisis, which led to Lyndon Johnson withdrawing from the presidential race in 1968. The Vietnam War also caused Nixon considerable domestic problems during his first term, when he invaded Cambodia and engaged in a massive aerial bombing offensive against North Vietnam.

By the early 1980s, the presidency of Ronald Reagan led to another massive arms build-up by the USA. A 'New Cold War' developed when the USA sited Cruise and Pershing II missiles in Europe. However, the arms race between the USA and USSR did have a beneficial effect on America's world position. The USSR was economically incapable of producing the armaments necessary to compete with the USA. By 1986, the new Soviet leader, Mikhail Gorbachev, offered the USA an agreement to cut nuclear forces.

By the time President Bush entered office in 1989, the Cold War seemed to be coming to an end. By the end of 1989, virtually all the countries of Eastern Europe had overthrown their communist governments. In 1991, communist rule came to an end with the collapse of the USSR and the division into 15 separate states.

The year 1991 seemed to be when the USA emerged as the unchallenged world power. Not only had the USSR collapsed, but also the USA led a coalition of countries in the expulsion of Iraq from Kuwait.

As the world's strongest economy, the USA had the economic power and technological expertise to develop massive armed forces. The crusade against world communism from 1945 had provided the political will.

1 The foundations of the United States, 1776–1803

1.1 Why did the American War of Independence take place?
1.2 What were the main reasons for American victory in the war?
1.3 In what ways did the Articles of Confederation fail to provide strong government?
1.4 In what ways did the Constitution of 1787 change the USA political system?
1.5 How did the Constitution and political system develop by 1803?

Key Issues

- *Why was the United States created in 1783?*
- *In what ways did the Constitution of 1787 differ from the Articles of Confederation?*
- *How was political power divided up by the Constitution of 1787?*

Framework of Events

1776	(4 July) Declaration of Independence
	(9 September) Congress resolves that name be changed from United Colonies to United States
1777	(17 October) Battle of Saratoga
	(15 November) Congress adopts Articles of Confederation
1778	France joins American colonies in the war with Britain
1779	Spain declares war on Britain
1780	Britain declares war on Holland
1781	Articles of Confederation agreed by all colonies
1783	Treaty of Paris gives 13 American colonies independence from Britain
1787	Constitutional Convention in Philadelphia
1788	(21 June) Constitution ratified by 9 states and becomes law of USA
1789	George Washington becomes first President
1791	First 10 Amendments, known as the Bill of Rights, added to the Constitution
1803	'Marbury v Madison' case decided by US Supreme Court.

Overview

DURING the last quarter of the 18th century, 13 of Britain's colonies in North America rebelled against British rule. In the course of the rebellion, a major war occurred in which France, Spain and Holland joined the American colonists in the fight against Britain. By 1783, the British agreed to American Independence.

From the war with Britain until the beginning of the 19th century, the newly independent colonies laid the foundations of the United States. Initially, the

Confederation: Alliance of smaller groups or states.

colonies were formed into a loose **confederation**. In 1787, in Philadelphia, the US Constitution was drawn up. It was ratified by nine states by 1788. In 1791, all 13 colonies had agreed to the Constitution.

The Constitution produced in 1787 has stood the test of time. It forms the foundation stone of the US political system. The subsequent history of the United States is inextricably linked to the interpretation of what was decided in Philadelphia in the summer of 1787.

1.1 Why did the American War of Independence take place?

The war that took place was the result of a growing split between Britain and 13 of its North American colonies since the British victory over the French in the Seven Years' War of 1763. An important consequence of the Seven Years' War was the removal of the French threat to the 13 colonies.

To boycott: To refuse to have any dealings with someone. The origins of the word 'boycott' lie in the nationalist agitation in Ireland in the late 1870s. During the depression of that time, tenants were frequently evicted and the land taken over by others. Often, those who took over the land from evicted tenants were treated with hostility and given no help. This fate befell Captain Boycott in County Mayo.

However, a major cause of friction between home country and colonies was the decision of Britain to tax those who created the colonies in order to pay for the upkeep of the British army in North America. The crisis initially erupted over the Stamp Act of 1765 and relations deteriorated until 1775 when fighting took place between colonists and British troops in Massachusetts.

The common opposition to British taxation brought the colonists together. In 1765, several of them attended the Stamp Tax Congress **to boycott** British goods. In September 1774, colonists met again to form the Continental Congress. This denounced British interference in the colonies. In May 1775, a second Continental Congress met in Philadelphia. This Congress helped to set up the first American army under George Washington.

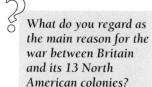

What do you regard as the main reason for the war between Britain and its 13 North American colonies?

On 7 June 1776, Richard Henry Lee of Virginia called on the Congress to declare independence from Britain. On 4 July 1776, a declaration of independence was signed. It was mainly the work of Thomas Jefferson.

The split between Britain and the colonies involved conflicts over trade and taxation. Ultimately, the colonies believed they had the right to be consulted about their affairs. This defence of individual rights became a central feature of the American Revolution.

1.2 What were the main reasons for American victory in the War?

The Continental (American) Army was led by George Washington. His ability to keep an army intact for the duration of the war was an important factor in American success (see page 25).

More important was the terrain over which the war was fought. British troops, accustomed to fighting in Europe, found it difficult to adjust to fighting in the woods and mountains of North America. This was matched by poor generalship by British officers. In addition, their supply line across the Atlantic was long and it took several months for supplies to arrive.

The turning point in the war came in 1777. American forces defeated General Burgoyne in upstate New York at Saratoga. The next year, France declared war on Britain. The involvement of Spain in 1779 and of Holland in 1790 created major problems for Britain. It faced invasion from France and lost command of the Atlantic. With the fall of Yorktown, Virginia, to the Americans and French in 1781, the war was lost.

Not all colonists supported a break with Britain. In many ways, the War of Independence was a civil war between colonists. At the end of the war, most 'loyalist' colonists moved to Canada.

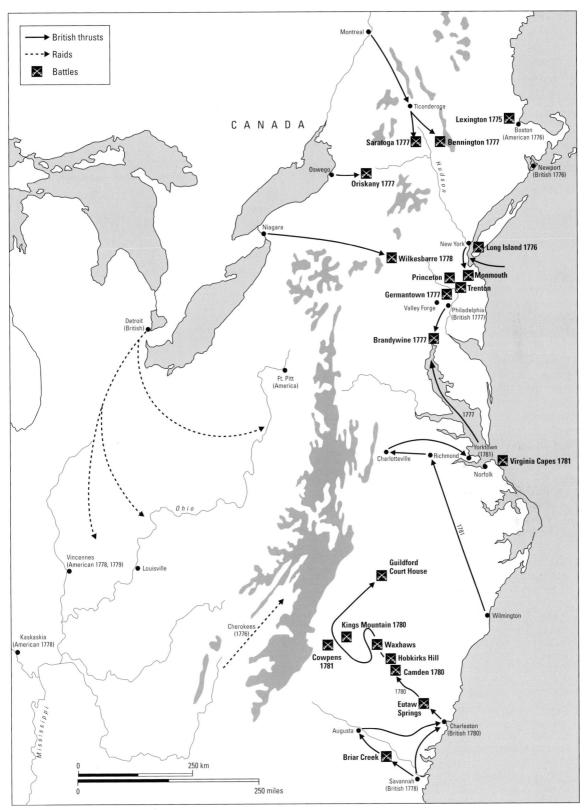

The American War of Independence, 1775–1781

The United States in 1783

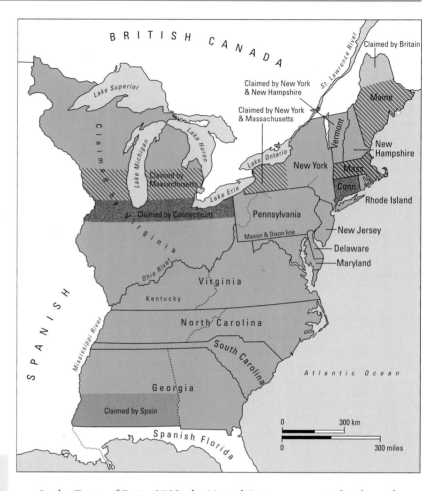

?
What was the main reason why Britain lost the American War of Independence? Explain your answer.

In the Treaty of Paris, 1783, the United States was granted independence from Britain. The land given to the new state included western lands as far as the Mississippi river, as well as the 13 colonies. British resentment against the new state still existed. Between 1812 and 1814, the two states would fight again in 'the war of 1812'.

George Washington (1732–1799)
1st President of the USA (1789–97); known as 'the father of his country'. Commander of American forces during the American War of Independence. Of British descent; largely self-taught. Began his career as a land surveyor, before inheriting an estate from his brother. In 1758 he resigned command of Virginia troops and married a rich widow, Martha Custis. The union of their plantations made George Washington one of the wealthiest men in state of Virginia. He took over as Commander-in-Chief of colonial armies on 15 June 1775.

Elected as one of Virginia's delegates to First Continental Congress. When the Second Continental Congress met in Philadelphia, the general feeling was that a Southern man should lead the New Englanders (see page 37). George Washington was that man. Although others wrote the Constitution, it was Washington who did much to smooth the way.

As President, he upset his Secretary of State, Thomas Jefferson, by accepting the economic policy proposed by Alexander Hamilton and by overseeing the payment of the foreign and domestic debts incurred by the new nation (the USA). He shaped the powers of the presidency, even assuming some powers not specified by the Constitution – including the power to create a national bank, and the power to introduce an excise tax.

Washington wanted to retire at the end of his first term, but was persuaded to stay on and was re-elected for a second term by a unanimous vote. He was widely criticised for signing the Jay's Treaty of 1794 that resolved outstanding differences with Britain, enabling trading links to be re-established.

He declined a third term as President. In his farewell address, Washington warned the people against entangling alliances and advised them to keep aloof from European quarrels.

The American War of Independence (1775–1781)

April 1775
Fighting begins between colonists and British troops – the Lexington massacre in Massachusetts is followed by more outbreaks at Concord.

17 June 1775
British control hills overlooking Charlestown and Boston, although 1,000 British soldiers are killed in Battle of Bunker Hill (three times the American casualties).

July 1776
The British leave Boston to the rebels. Instead, they use New York as their centre of operations, amply supplied by 35,000 troops and 500 ships. They easily outnumber the 18,000 men assembled by Washington.

December 1776
Defeat of the colonials at the Battle of Long Island, out of New York, only narrowly avoided becoming a rout when Washington is able to escape to Manhattan, and from there to New Jersey. The British commander, General Howe, complacently chooses not to pursue the Americans, allowing Washington's troops to cross the Delaware river on Christmas Day and attack an encampment of British soldiers on 26 December.

3 January 1777
Another American victory at Princeton. In a few weeks, General George Washington has turned around the situation and shown the British that a quick victory was far from assured.

The British focus now turns to upstate New York with an attempt to capture Albany and the river valley of the Hudson. Capturing the Hudson would divide troublesome New England from the other colonies and provide a useful link between New York and Canada. Two British forces advance from the north at the start of 1777: General Burgoyne leads the major force of 7,000 from Lake Champlain, whilst a smaller force under Colonel Barry St Leger begins an advance from the west via Lake Ontario. It is expected that Howe will advance up the Hudson from New York if needed.

August–October 1777
The action goes wrong from the start. Instead of moving up the Hudson, Howe moves south-west to Philadelphia, defeating Washington at the battles of Brandywine Creek and Germantown in October and easily capturing the rebel capital. Howe's successes in Pennsylvania mean that Washington's army is forced to endure a miserable winter at Valley Forge. It also means Burgoyne is left alone when he begins to run into difficulties by the autumn. St Leger is checked at Oriskany in August and by October Burgoyne is trapped at Saratoga. (Desperate but effective action by Benedict Arnold in October of 1776 on Lake Champlain prevents the British from retaking the fortress of Ticonderoga until 1777, so delaying Burgoyne's march south. The difficult march through inhospitable terrain is time-consuming and morale-draining with rebel militia men harassing the British as they advance.) On 17 October, Burgoyne is forced to surrender, with 5,000 men at Saratoga, to the American Horatio Gates. Any advantage gained by Howe in Pennsylvania is quickly lost. The British suddenly look vulnerable.

Saratoga is significant, for it is the American military success that prompts the French to intervene directly in the war. The French have been watching events in North America carefully, encouraged by the American ambassador in Paris, Benjamin Franklin. They have been secretly supplying the colonials since 1776, keen to see Britain weakened in its empire. France is also attracted to the ideals of liberty that the American struggle seems to represent, especially after the Declaration of Independence. However they are anxious to avoid direct help for fear that the British will declare war on France itself – a war that France cannot afford to fight.

6 February 1778
The Declaration of Independence and the Battle of Saratoga convince the French that the rebel leaders are serious in their fighting and stand a chance of victory. In such circumstances, the French Government offer to recognise the independence of the colonies as well as a military and commercial alliance (signed on 6 February 1778).

1778–1780
The British withdraw from Philadelphia to New York in 1778 and choose to concentrate on the southern states. Between 1778 and 1780, the British enjoy some success there, taking Georgia and the major ports of the Carolinas. They receive another boost, in October 1780, when rebel hero Benedict Arnold turns traitor and almost succeeds in handing over the key fortress of West Point to the British. But the tide has turned in the South and the British commander, Lord Cornwallis, despite winning most engagements, fails to gain control of the interior.

October 1781
By 1781, Cornwallis withdraws to the North, leaving the loyalists in Georgia and South Carolina to look after themselves. In the west, most Indian tribes side with the British and launch a series of attacks against American settlers of the 1770s.

Although the small American navy makes little impact against the British navy, Britain's merchant fleet suffers, especially from privateers (pirates).

The French fleet is more concerned with protecting the French West Indies from the British fleet than with helping the colonials. This changes in 1781 when the French fleet is made available to assist Washington (who also has the support of a French land force of 6,000 troops). Cornwallis' troops are withdrawn from Virginia to Chesapeake Bay, awaiting reinforcements. Surrounded by Washington and the French army on land and at sea, Cornwallis has no alternative but to surrender, which he does at Yorktown on 19 October 1781.

Fighting continues for over a year. The British remain in control of New York, Savannah and Charleston with 32,000 men stationed in the colonies, but the major fighting on the continent has come to an end.

1.3 In what ways did the Articles of Confederation fail to provide strong government?

In the summer of 1776, Congress appointed a committee to provide a framework for national government. Some of the colonial leaders, such as John Dickinson, wanted a strong central government. Instead, they produced Articles that went to the opposite extreme of preserving the rights of states and creating a weak national government.

The Articles of Confederation were finally adopted in 1781, when Maryland agreed to sign. They provided a one-chambered (unicameral) Congress in which each state, irrespective of size, would have one vote. A committee of 13 would provide the government – one delegate from each state. In order to amend (change) the Articles, all 13 states had to agree.

The government had the power to make war and to make treaties. It also had the power to admit new states. However, it did not have the power to raise taxes, raise troops or regulate commerce.

From the start, many colonists were unhappy with the form of government under the Articles. In 1783, in the Newburgh Conspiracy, some colonial leaders approached the army second-in-command, Horatio Gates, to force the states to surrender more power to the central government.

By 1785, a meeting at George Washington's house, of representatives from Maryland, Virginia, Pennsylvania and Delaware, called for a discussion on the problems of government. In September 1786, only five states sent representatives to the Annapolis Convention, but they called all states to attend a Constitutional Convention in Philadelphia in 1787 to revise the Articles of Confederation.

1. How was power divided between the state and national government under the Articles of Confederation?

2. Why do you think many Americans were dissatisfied with the Articles of Confederation?

Strengthening the Central Government

Under Articles of Confederation	Under Federal Constitution
A loose confederation of states	A firm union of people
One vote in Congress for each state	Two votes in Senate for each state; representation by population in House of Representatives
Two-thirds vote (9 states) in Congress for all important measures	Simple majority vote in Congress, subject to presidential veto
Laws executed by committees of Congress	Laws executed by powerful President
No Congressional power over trade	Congress to regulate both foreign and inter-state trade
No Congressional power to levy taxes	Extensive power in Congress to levy taxes
No federal courts	Federal courts, capped by Supreme Court
Unanimity of states for amendment	Amendment less difficult
No authority to act directly upon individuals, and no power to coerce states	Ample power to enforce laws by coercion of individuals and to some extent of states

1.4 In what ways did the Constitution of 1787 change the US political system?

Outline of the United States Constitution

Preamble
'We the people of the United States in order to form a more perfect union, establish justice, ensure domestic tranquillity, provide for the common defence, promote the general welfare, and secure the blessings of liberty to ourselves and our posterity, do ordain and confirm the Constitution for the United States of America.'

Article I: The Legislature (Congress)
Congress is divided into two parts:
1. The House of Representatives: 435 members determined by population.
2. The Senate: 100 members since 1959 – two from each state.

The House of Representatives:
- may start impeachment against a President or other high government officials.
- All bills that deal with money must begin in the House.
- Speaker of the House presides over proceedings.
- Members, known as Congressmen, are elected every two years (minimum age: 25).

The Senate:
- was originally elected by state legislatures, but since Seventeenth Amendment in 1913 they are directly elected.
- approves or rejects nominations from President for senior government officials and Supreme Court justices (Advice and Consent Power).
- approves or rejects treaties with other countries (Advice and Consent Power).
- Debate is unlimited.
- The Vice-President presides over proceedings and can only vote in the event of a tie.

- Senators are elected for six years (citizens over 30 years). A third are elected every two years.

Article II: The Executive (President and Government)
President is elected every four years. Originally elected without limit. Since the Twenty-Second Amendment, can only serve two terms. Must be native born and at least 35 years of age.

President is:
- Commander-in-Chief of the armed forces
- Chief Executive (Head of Government)
- Head of State
- Chief lawmaker.

Article III: The Judiciary
US Supreme Court created as highest court of appeal for federal and state cases. Precise composition of Courts defined by Judiciary Act of 1789.

Article IV: Inter-state relations
- All states are guaranteed a republican form of government.
- Any new state is equal to the original 13 states.
- Each state shall respect the laws of the other states.

Article V: Amending the Constitution
Amendments must receive two-thirds support from both Houses of Congress and three-quarters of the states before they become law.

Article VI: Ratification of the Constitution
Nine of the original 13 states had to accept the Constitution before it could become law.

The Constitution that was produced at Philadelphia was a compromise between the views of the delegates.

James Madison proposed the 'Virginia Plan'. This suggested that Congress should have two houses, each based on size of population. The smaller states feared they would lose influence under the plan. So William Patterson produced the 'New Jersey Plan'. This would involve keeping the one-chambered Congress of the Articles of Confederation, with equal representation for all states. He also suggested a large increase in the powers of the national government. In the end, a 'great compromise' was reached. The Congress would comprise two houses:

- In one house – the Senate – all states, irrespective of size, would have two seats.

- The House of Representatives would be based on size of population.

Another issue of debate was slavery. A compromise was reached, where the Constitution neither supported nor condemned slavery. For the purposes of calculating representation in the House of Representatives, slaves would count as three-fifths of a freeman. They did not have the right to vote.

The third compromise came over the presidency. George Washington was certain to be first President. He was trusted not to abuse his power, so the President was given control over foreign policy and the right to veto Congress's legislation. In the unlikely event of the President or senior government officially acting unlawfully, a system of removal was included. This was the impeachment process. The House of Representatives has the right to begin impeachment proceedings. Then the Senate tries the individual. If convicted, the person is removed from office. No President has been successfully impeached. Only two – Andrew Johnson in 1868 and Bill Clinton in 1999 – have been tried for impeachment.

As a result of the decisions in Philadelphia, the United States was confirmed as a federal state. This meant political power was divided between a national (federal) government and state government (see below). In 1787, such a decision was inevitable. The United States had been created out of a voluntary union of 13 separate states. As the country grew and more states were admitted, the size and geography of the USA meant that the federal system of government was the only logical form of government. No national government based in Washington DC could make laws for over 250 million people living in a country over 3,000 miles wide which embraced deserts, mountains and farmland.

Electoral college: Method of choosing a President and Vice-President. Each state votes separately. The winner in a state gets all the state's electoral college votes. These votes are calculated by adding the number of senators allotted to each state to the number of Congressmen.

To emphasise the federal nature of the political system, the President and Vice-President were chosen by an **electoral college**. In a presidential election, each state would vote separately. Whichever candidate won the state's popular vote, won all the electoral college votes. The electoral college votes

---

The separation of powers between the federal and state governments

Powers reserved for the federal government alone
- Regulation of foreign trade
- Regulation of inter-state commerce
- Minting money
- Running the post office
- Regulating immigration
- Granting copyrights and patents
- Declaring war and peace
- Admitting new states
- Fixing weights and measures
- Organising the armed forces
- Governing the federal capital, Washington DC
- Conducting foreign relations.

Powers reserved for state governments only
- Conducting elections
- Establishing voter qualifications
- Providing local government
- Regulating contracts
- Regulating trade within the state
- Providing education
- Maintaining a police force and internal law and order.

Powers shared by federal and state governments
- Taxation
- Controlling the state militia, later known as the National Guard.

1. Explain the meaning of 'federal state' as it applied to the USA.

2. What was the 'separation of powers'? Explain how it divided power between the states and federal government and between the three branches of the federal government: President, Congress and Supreme Court.

3. Explain how the electoral college is involved in electing the President and Vice-President. What are its drawbacks?

were based on the number of Senators and Congressman a state had in Congress. In 1992, for example, Wyoming had three electoral college votes because it had two senators and one Congressman; California had 53 electoral college votes because it had two senators and 51 Congressmen.

As a result, in a presidential election it was possible for a candidate to get the most popular votes but lose in the electoral college. This happened in 1876 when Samuel Tilden polled most votes, but Rutherland B. Hayes won the electoral college by one vote. It also occurred in 2000 when George W. Bush Junior became President.

To avoid the abuse of power, a central principle of the Constitution was the separation of powers. Political power was divided between federal and state government (see panel opposite). It was also divided within the federal government. For instance, in passing laws, both the Senate and the House of Representatives had to agree. Then the President had to agree. He could veto the Bill. However, Congress could override the veto if two-thirds of both Houses agreed. Even then, the US Supreme Court might declare the law unconstitutional if it believed it contravened the Constitution. Also, no member of the Executive (government) could be a member of Congress.

The Senate was given advice and consent power over the appointment of senior government officials and Supreme Court justices. The President had the right to nominate them, but the Senate had to agree. Similarly, the President negotiated treaties with foreign states but the Senate could reject them. In 1919, the Senate rejected the Treaty of Versailles with Germany.

1.5 How did the Constitution and political system develop by 1803?

Federalists: People who believe in a federal system of government (i.e. controlled by central government).

Democrats: Members or supporters of the Democratic Party in the USA. They believe in ideals of democracy, personal freedom and equality.

Republicans: Members or supporters of the Republican Party in the USA. They believe that the best system of government for a country is a republic (i.e. where everyone has equal status, so that there is no king or queen and no aristocracy).

Whigs: A political party of the 1830s and 1840s that supported social reform and opposed the extension of slavery to the West.

Supreme Court: The judicial branch of the US federal government. The President appoints the nine Supreme Court judges. Their job is to make sure that Congress (the legislative branch) and the President run the country according to the Constitution.

Although a constitution was produced in 1787, it was by no means clear whether the required nine states would agree to it before it became law. On 7 December 1787, the small state of Delaware unanimously agreed to it. It was not until 21 June 1788 that New Hampshire became the ninth state to agree. However, large states such as North Carolina, Virginia and New York had not agreed by that date. Eventually, all 13 states agreed with the Constitution provided a guarantee of civil rights was included. Therefore, in 1791, 10 Amendments (changes) were included, collectively known as the Bill of Rights (see box on page 30).

The Constitution made no mention of political parties. Yet within a short time they had begun to develop. In the debate on the Constitution in 1787 those who wanted the Constitution accepted became known as **federalists**. They eventually became associated with the idea of a strong national government.

Those who opposed the Constitution were anti-federalists. Later, from 1792, anti-federalists developed to become Democratic-Republicans, following the views of Thomas Jefferson (see page 34). He wanted the USA to be a nation of small, independent farmers with minimal government. From 1816 to the mid-1820s, party conflict subsided but reappeared with the rise of Andrew Jackson (see page 49), who transformed the Democratic-Republicans into the Democrat Party. Against the **Democrats** were National **Republicans** in the 1820s, **Whigs** in the 1830s and, from 1854, the Republican Party.

The Constitution made general reference to the court system. In the Judiciary Act of 1789, the precise organisation was created. The **Supreme Court** would comprise six justices and was given the power to decide on the validity of state law. It was also given the power to interpret the Constitution. A system of district and appeal courts was also created.

Amendments to the Constitution

Amendments 1–10, made in 1791, are known as the Bill of Rights.

1. Freedom of religion; freedom of speech; freedom of the press.
2. Right to keep arms.
3. Troops cannot be housed in private citizens' homes.
4. Protects against unreasonable searches and seizures of property.
5. Protects rights of accused in trials; no citizens can be imprisoned without 'due process of law'.
6. Guarantees a speedy trial.
7. Guarantees a trial by jury.
8. Protects against cruel and unusual punishment.
9. Rights not mentioned above are still kept by the people.
10. States have power not expressly given to federal government by the Constitution.
11. States may not be sued by individuals (1798).
12. President and Vice-President must be elected separately (1800).
13. Abolished slavery (1865).
14. Guaranteed equal protection of the law to all citizens (1868).
15. Extended voting rights to African Americans (1870).
16. Legalised federal income tax (1913).
17. Allowed senators to be directly elected (1913).
18. Outlawed the manufacture and consumption of alcohol (Prohibition) (1919).
19. Extended voting rights to women (1920).
20. Changed inauguration day from 4 March to 20 January (1933).
21. Repealed the Eighteenth Amendment (1933).
22. Limited President to two terms (1951).
23. Gave presidential voting rights to District of Columbia (1961).
24. Prohibited poll taxes (1964).
25. Outlined order of succession to the presidency (1967).
26. Extended voting rights to 18 year olds (1971).
27. Congressional pay increases could only take effect following next Congressional election (1992).

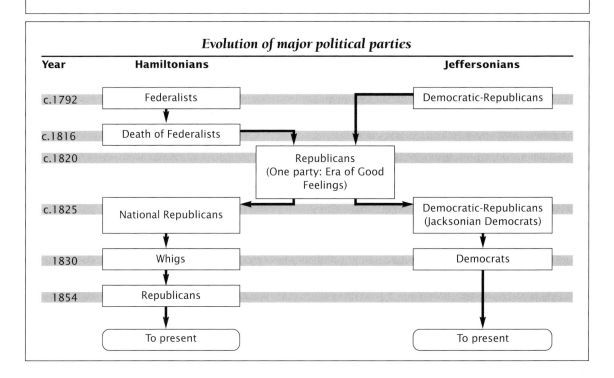

Evolution of major political parties

Year	Hamiltonians		Jeffersonians
c.1792	Federalists		Democratic-Republicans
c.1816	Death of Federalists		
c.1820		Republicans (One party: Era of Good Feelings)	
c.1825	National Republicans		Democratic-Republicans (Jacksonian Democrats)
1830	Whigs		Democrats
1854	Republicans		
	To present		To present

Secretary of State: This is an official in the American government whose job it is to take care of America's relations with other countries. See Chapter 8 for a list of US Secretaries of State in the post-war period.

1. How did political parties develop in the USA?

2. What is judicial review and how did it increase the power of the US Supreme Court?

Even after the Judiciary Act of 1789, the role of the US Supreme Court was not clear. However, under the first Chief Justice, John Marshall, the Court developed its position within government. In 1803, Marshall and the Court decided the 'Marbury versus Madison' case. Just before President John Adams gave up office in 1801, he had made several individual justices of the peace (JPs), but did not issue them with commissions. William Marbury was one of these. The new **Secretary of State**, James Madison, refused to make him a JP, so Marbury sued the Supreme Court. Chief Justice Marshall declared part of the Judiciary Act of 1789 unconstitutional. This established the principle of 'judicial review', which gave the Supreme Court the right to declare Acts of Congress unconstitutional. This became the foundation of the Supreme Court power to act as a check on both Government and Congress.

Western expansion in the 19th century

Key Issues

● Why did so many Americans move west in the 19th century?

● What were the consequences of the western expansion?

● Why was Plains Indian society destroyed?

2.1 Why did it become possible to move west?

2.2 Who went west, and why?

2.3 What are the reasons for the destruction of Native-American society?

2.4 What was the extent of federal government involvement in western expansion?

2.5 How did western expansion affect American attitudes?

Framework of Events

1803	Louisiana Purchase
1804–1806	Lewis and Clark Expedition to Pacific North-West
1811	Tecumseh's Confederacy defeated at Battle of Tippecanoe
1819	Adams–Onis Treaty cedes Florida to USA from Spain
1820	Missouri Compromise
1825	Completion of Erie Canal
1830	Indian Removal Act: removal of south-east Indians to Indian Territory
1832	Oregon Trail becomes main route West
1836	War between Mexico and Texan settlers; leads to independence of Texas following Battle of San Jacinto
1846	Mexican Wars begin
	Brigham Young leads Mormons on trek to Utah
1848	Treaty of Guadeloupe-Hidalgo ends Mexican War: USA acquires California, Nevada, New Mexico, Arizona, Utah and parts of Colorado
	Gold is discovered in California
1849	California Gold Rush
1853	Gadsden Purchase
	Kansas–Nebraska Act
1858	Comstock Silver Lode is discovered in Nevada
1860	Pony Express
1862	Homestead Act provides cheap land in West
1867	Indian Peace Commission establishes Indian reservation policy
1868	Laramie Treaty between USA and Sioux
1869	First transcontinental railroad is completed at Promontory Point Utah where Union Pacific meets Central Pacific railroads
1876	Battle of Little Big Horn between US army and Sioux/Cheyenne
1890	Battle of Wounded Knee; end of Indian Wars
	Turner Thesis on West.

Overview

THE development of the West is a major theme in the history of the United States of America. It helped to transform the country from a small state clinging the eastern seaboard to a vast continental power stretching from the Atlantic Ocean to the Pacific.

The process of expansion was partly achieved through the clever purchase of land. In 1803, Jefferson purchased the vast Louisiana territory for $15 million from Emperor Napoleon I of France. In 1853, the USA acquired the Gadsden Purchase of land in the Gila Desert, from Mexico, as a possible route for a transcontinental railroad.

However, land was also acquired through war. In 1819, the USA acquired Florida from Spain and, in 1848, large areas in the South-West and West from Mexico.

Even though the USA had acquired large areas of land, there had to be reasons for Americans wanting to move westward. Part of the reason lay in the vast mineral wealth of the West. Gold and silver led to thousands heading west to become rich. Others went west to farm. The Mormons were forced west because of religious persecution.

To aid movement west, Americans used a variety of transportation. River travel took them part of the way, usually to St Joseph or Independence, Missouri. To get further west, they organised themselves into wagon trains. From the end of the Civil War, the main way west was by train. The nation was joined from Pacific Ocean to Atlantic Ocean by a transcontinental railroad in 1869. This allowed tens of thousands to move west.

In the process of moving west, Americans came into conflict with Native-American society. The story of westward expansion is the history of armed conflict between whites and Indians. To provide the basis for the destruction of Native-American society, many believed it was the 'Manifest Destiny' of the USA to conquer and colonise the whole continent.

Many Indian tribes were initially moved west of the Mississippi river, in the 1830s, to occupy Indian Territory (later the state of Oklahoma). However, after the Civil War, open conflict occurred between the USA and the Plains Indians. It took until 1890 for the Plains Indians to be defeated. That date stands out as the end of westward expansion – the end of the 'Frontier'. In 1890, in Chicago, the historian Frederick Jackson Turner provided an interpretation of American history in which the desire to move westward was a central theme. Once the Frontier had come to an end, many Americans looked outside the continent for further expansion of American influence.

2.1 Why did it become possible to move west?

In the half-century from 1803 to 1853, the USA was transformed. Within a period of 50 years, the United States changed from a republic of 16 states to the east of the Mississippi into the major regional power that stretched from the Atlantic to the Pacific – three times the size and almost five times as populous. The number of American citizens living west of the Appalachian mountain range went from 2.5 million in 1820 to over 5 million in 1830; from 25% to 40% of the total population. This significant territorial increase was, of course, important for population expansion westward. So, before one investigates why so many Americans moved west, one must first understand why it became possible to do so. The answer lies in a combination of the territorial expansion of the growing republic and changes in transport and communications that made moving out west increasingly viable.

Territorial expansion

The Louisiana Purchase, 1803

In 1803, President Thomas Jefferson supported the purchase of the Louisiana territory for the bargain sum of $15 million. In doing so, the size of the United States doubled overnight, adding 828,00 square miles to the **republic**. The whole process came about rather unexpectedly. In 1800, Spain ceded (gave) the territory to France whose leader, Napoleon Bonaparte, had dreams of restoring a colonial empire in North America. Jefferson, though generally a supporter of Republican France, was well aware of the importance of New Orleans to American trade, situated as it was at the mouth of the Mississippi river (down which frontier farmers transported their produce) and already a major port.

Suggestions, in 1802, that the rights of Americans to trade through New Orleans might be limited, prompted Jefferson to send James Monroe to France to negotiate the purchase of the port and any lands to the east. By the time of his arrival in France, Napoleon had already abandoned his colonial plans and informed the American Minister in Paris, Robert Livingston, that he was willing to sell the whole of Louisiana for $15 million. Livingston and Monroe, having been authorised to spend up to $10 million on New Orleans and lands to the East, were now being offered almost half of the remaining continent in the West, of which New Orleans was a tiny but significant part. Without time to consult and fearing Napoleon might change his mind, they quickly signed the Treaty. The **Senate** ratified this in October. It led to the formal transfer of this vast tract of land by the end of the year.

The **Louisiana Purchase** was a significant moment in American history. Overnight the idea of a nation stretching from the Atlantic to the Pacific coasts of America suddenly seemed possible and the foundations of a major power were laid. Furthermore, the United States now controlled both banks of one of the most fertile river valleys in the world. Jefferson's ideal of a republic of self-sufficient farmers could now spread down this 'Valley of Democracy'.

During the following decades, the rush for further territorial expansion died down, although there were always some voices keeping the issue

Republic: A country whose system of government is based on the idea that every citizen has equal status, so that there is no king or queen and no aristocracy.

Senate: The smaller and more important of the two councils that form the law-making part of the government in some countries, e.g. the USA and Australia.

Louisiana Purchase: This was the biggest land sale in history. In April 1803, the size of the USA doubled when the federal government bought the whole of the Mississippi Valley up to the Rocky Mountains from France – an area of 828,000 square miles (2,144,522 square kilometres or 2,145 hectares). The US government paid $15 million for this land. The American Minister in Paris, Robert Livingston, and the future President, James Monroe, negotiated the treaty.

Thomas Jefferson (1743–1826)
3rd President of the USA (1801–09), founder of the Democratic-Republican Party. As a member of the Continental Congress (1775–76), Jefferson was largely responsible for drafting the Declaration of Independence. He was the first President to be inaugurated in Washington DC. Jefferson supported the French Revolution and spent 4 years in France (1785–89). Upon his return to the United States, he was Secretary of State (1789–93) and Vice-President (1797–1801). His political philosophy of 'agrarian democracy' placed responsibility for upholding a virtuous American republic mainly upon the yeoman farmers. Ironically, his two terms as President saw the adoption of some of the ideals of his opponents, the Federalists. This period also witnessed the Louisiana Purchase (1803) and the abolition of the slave trade (1808).

'**Manifest Destiny**': The belief of many white Americans in the early 1800s that all land could be owned. Expansion westwards was seen as a natural right. The ideology of 'Manifest Destiny' was used to justify forcing Indians off their ancient lands, and thus allowing the white occupation of the American West.

Expansionism: Seeking to enlarge the area of the world under your control, not always by internationally acceptable means.

alive. The 1840s, especially after the election of James Polk as President in 1844, saw renewed interest in western expansion. Indeed, by the end of the decade, US territory extended to the Pacific coast, justified and encouraged by the popular idea of '**Manifest Destiny**'. This expansion was due to diverse policies regarding Texas, Oregon and Mexico that had the common theme of seeking to extend American influence and power westwards (see map below).

Florida, 1819

Under the colonial control of the Spanish, Florida was always going to be vulnerable to US **expansionism**. Already, during the war of 1812 when Spain had been allied with Britain, Americans had seized the opportunity to take control of the most westerly parts of Florida around Mobile and Baton Rouge. As Spain was forced to deal with a series of revolts in its South American colonies, troops were removed from Florida and the area became a centre for outlaws and runaway slaves, as well as the Seminole Indians (see page 48). In 1817, General Andrew Jackson was asked by the federal government to pursue these groups, after a series of raids over the border in Georgia and the Mississippi territory. Although the government had not ordered Jackson to attack Spanish posts, this is what the triumphant general did when he seized Pensacola and St Mark's in 1818. Spain could do little to resist and, struggling to maintain its empire elsewhere, it gave up Florida in 1819, as well as abandoning any claims to the Oregon territory in the North-West.

Texas, 1836–1845

The future of Texas was the source of many political debates following its securing of a tenuous independence from Mexico in 1836. Although

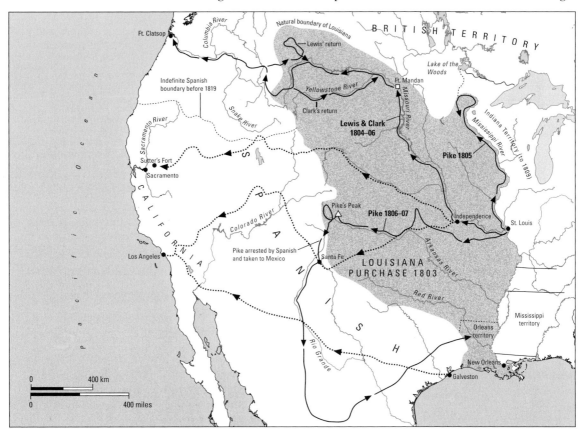

Explorations in the West

Mexico's **dictator**, Santa Anna, had accepted Texan independence when captured by Sam Houston in 1836, at the Battle of San Jacinto. Since that time, he had refused to accept Texan independence. Texans feared it was only a matter of time before Mexico sought to retake the province. President Andrew Jackson recognised Texan independence in 1837. Ever since then, there had been support for Texas to be annexed to the United States, not least from the Texans themselves (who hoped for greater security from Mexico). There was also support from most southerners and expansionists who feared that an independent Texas might be susceptible to British influence and act as a block to western expansion of the United States. Many in the North feared Texan annexation, however. Many of those who had moved to Texas when it was part of Mexico had gone from the South with their slaves. The admission into the Union of a territory the size of Texas would significantly extend slavery in the Union, especially if it broke up into several states. This might well lead to war with Mexico.

In 1844, a treaty for **annexation** was supported by the Texans but defeated in the Senate. With the election of James Polk as a committed 'annexer' the same year, it seemed only a matter of time before Texas joined the Union. A joint resolution (a constitutional device, since a joint resolution does not need a two-thirds majority, as a treaty does) was put to Congress. Reassuring some northerners by insisting that Texas would not be divided up, so only adding two slave-state votes to the Senate, the resolution passed Congress in just three days. By the end of the year, Texas had entered the Union as the 28th state.

Oregon, 1846

When James Polk was elected President in 1844, he made clear his desire to secure Oregon – an area in the North-West that had ill-defined boundaries. It had been occupied jointly by Britain and the USA since 1818, when attempts to divide the region had failed. At the time the territory had been largely empty of settlers from either nation, but since 1830 there had been considerable settlement by American **pioneers** who followed the 'Oregon Trail' as **missionaries** and farmers. By 1845, around 5,000 Americans were living in Oregon, compared with less than 1,000 British. In the 1844 election, Polk had called for the occupation of all of Oregon up to the 54° 40′ line of latitude North (see map) and there was talk of war if the British did not cooperate. In the end, a compromise was worked out that saw the territory divided at the 49th Parallel, which then formed the northern border of the USA with Canada. There was some discontent with Polk for compromising on his tough campaign line over Oregon, especially from some northerners who felt that the President was favouring expansion to the South over the North. However, the advantages of securing a route to the Pacific without a single shot having been fired, and without upsetting the world's strongest power, suggests the Oregon Treaty of 1846 suited the United States well. The fact that by the time the Senate approved the treaty the USA was already at war with Mexico may well have encouraged a spirit of compromise in the North-West.

War with Mexico, 1846–1848

President Polk, with his firm belief in 'Manifest Destiny', could not help but be tempted by the vast territories still held by Mexico. Calculating that the United States could easily win a conflict with Mexico and secure significant territorial prizes, he put pressure on the Mexicans from the start in the hope of provoking a conflict or securing concessions.

California was the most attractive prize Mexico had to offer. Many Americans were aware of its possibilities as a gateway to the Pacific, as well as its being a lush agricultural prospect. There were some Americans living in California, as there had been in Texas before the revolt there, but it seemed unlikely that they would rise up against Mexico as the Texans had done. Besides, Spanish Mexicans and Native Americans easily out-numbered them. Polk's hopes that he might settle the issue peacefully came to nothing, despite sending a minister to Mexico City, in 1845, with the offer of up to $25 million for California and the territory that would link it to Texas. The Mexicans were still upset over Texas and were not about to negotiate away more territory.

Polk now became deliberately provocative. In 1846, he sent 4,000 troops under General Zachary Taylor to a disputed area around the Rio Grande, which both Mexico and Texas claimed was theirs. He had already positioned a US naval squadron off the Californian coast and had sent an expeditionary force under Captain John Fremont into California to make 'topographical and scientific observations'. Polk was anxious to maximise support for war by having the Mexicans make the first attack. He moved quickly when, in May 1846, news reached Washington that General Taylor's troops had been attacked by Mexican troops who had crossed the Rio Grande on 25 April.

Topographical and scientific observations: A study of the area for producing maps.

Polk issued a war message to Congress which, with minimal opposition, authorised the President to raise 50,000 men to fight Mexico and voted him $10 million for the campaign. He had deliberately provoked a war with Mexico in a determined effort to secure California by force, once it became clear the Mexicans would not sell. It was, in the words of the historian Hugh Brogan, a 'disgraceful affair'. The action faced severe criticism from many **New Englanders** who saw it as a southern adventure.

New Englanders: Those Americans who lived in the six north-eastern states of Vermont, New Hampshire, Massachusetts, Maine, Rhode Island and Connecticut.

Polk now intended to fight a war as quickly as possible. Quick victories by Taylor in 1846 saw the United States capture the port of Matamoros. The area south of the Rio Grande was all in US hands by February 1847 with the capture of Buena Vista, despite being outnumbered 4 to 1. Meanwhile, Santa Fe had been captured in the north and Fremont had done his work in California, working with local Americans to overthrow Mexican rule there by the end of 1846. Polk was determined to force the Mexicans to retreat. He sent a second army under General Winfield Scott to attack Mexico City in November 1846.

A brilliant campaign saw the Mexican capital fall by September 1847 and a treaty was quickly drawn up – the Treaty of Guadalupe-Hidalgo – in February 1848. Polk secured the approval of the Senate in March by a majority of 38 to 14, with opposition from both southern expansionists who clamoured for all of Mexico and anti-slavery Whigs who feared the spread of slavery and had been uncomfortable with the war from its start.

The 1848 Treaty of Guadalupe-Hidalgo was an extraordinary triumph for Polk. For an **indemnity** of $15 million, America was confirmed in Texas and secured the entire area to the West, including California. Mexico had lost almost half its land mass overnight, whilst the USA increased by a further third, incorporating territory even larger than the Louisiana Purchase. That it had been achieved in rather dubious circum-stances, and the way in which it now opened up the slavery issue and paved the way for the sectional strife of the 1850s, were of little immediate consequence to the expansionists around Polk. They could rejoice in the final achievement of 'Manifest Destiny', as the still young republic now stretched from coast to coast and was the undoubted power in the region.

Indemnity: Amount of money or goods received by someone or some nation as compensation for some damage or loss they have received.

The Gadsden Purchase, 1853
The final piece of the jigsaw was inserted in 1853 when James Gadsden, a **railroad magnate** from South Carolina, was sent by the government to negotiate the purchase of some land to the south of New Mexico that would allow the construction of a southern transcontinental railroad to

Railroad magnate: An owner of a large number of railroads (railways).

California. Although arousing some opposition in the North, where attempts to get the first transcontinental railroad built would soon lead to the troubles of Kansas–Nebraska (see page 66), Gadsden found the Mexicans eager for the $10 million on offer. The purchase was made in a treaty of 1853 that was approved by the Senate in the same year.

Taming the wilderness

Although a number of hardy individuals were always likely to move out west, it is hard to imagine any major western settlement without the improvements in technology and communication that made life on the frontier a manageable family experience. As well as acquiring the western territories, governments, settlers and **entrepreneurs** set their minds to making western movement a viable option for the growing American population.

Entrepreneurs: People who set up business deals in order to make a profit for themselves.

Exploring and opening up the West

As soon as Jefferson had secured the Louisiana Purchase, he was keen to explore the new territory and consider its viability as land for settlement. In 1804, he secretly secured $2,500 from Congress to fund an expedition into the new territory led by his private secretary, Meriwether Lewis, and a young army officer, William Clark. The men, accompanied by the Shoshone princess Sacajawea and a party of 50, explored the territory for the next two and a half years. They learnt much about the terrain and inhabitants of the land and found the route to the Pacific via Oregon that would open up the 'Oregon Trail' in the ensuing decades. They were the best known of several explorers who opened up the interior and came back with vital intelligence and a love for the rich lands to the West that aroused the passion of potential pioneers. In 1805, Lieutenant Zebulon Pike explored the upper Mississippi and, in 1806, trekked to the eastern Rockies of modern-day Colorado.

Communications

If the West was to attract anything more than explorers and trappers, an effective and secure route to the area had to be opened up. Trails such as that to Oregon saw forts spring up along their course as protection from Indian tribes. Supply centres also developed and the routes out west became increasingly well worn. In 1811, the **federal government** began the construction of the Cumberland road – a highway that, by its completion in 1852, stretched almost 600 miles from Maryland to Illinois and which opened up the Mid-West to relatively easy settlement.

Federal government: The central government of a country (or group of states) which deals with things concerning the whole country, such as foreign policy. Each state within the Union has it own local powers and laws.

By the time of the American Civil War (see Chapter 3), there were numerous trails across the West (see map on page 35), carrying horse-drawn stagecoaches as pioneers headed west. By the end of the Civil War, the stagecoach entrepreneur Ben Holladay had built up 5,000 miles of stage routes across America. The stagecoaches also formed the basis of the earliest communication and postage systems. In 1857, the federal transcontinental mail contract was awarded to a **syndicate** headed by John Butterfield who, for an annual subsidy of $600,000, provided a twice-weekly mail service in each direction linking St Louis in the East with San Francisco in the West – a distance of 2,800 miles. The first service ran in 1858. Despite considerable costs, overland communication with California had superseded sea transport in popularity by 1860.

Syndicate: A group of people or organisations that is formed for business purposes or in order to carry out a project.

More dramatic was the Pony Express service, established in April 1860, that ran from St Joseph, Missouri, to Sacramento – a distance of 2,000 miles which was covered in a staggering ten days as intrepid horsemen galloped between stations about ten miles apart. The service only lasted 18 months, suffering from a lack of funding and from the arrival of the

Pony Express, in 1861

telegraph. In October 1861, the first transcontinental telegraph line was established. Thereafter, communications between East and West would be less dramatic but far more immediate, reliable and affordable. With the widespread development of the telegraph, pioneers could now set forth west without a sense that they would never be heard of again. The plains would still be wild, but less lonely from now on.

The development of the steamboat also did much to open up the West, especially around the Mississippi and its tributaries. The first steamboat was launched by Robert Fulton in 1807, and by 1860 there were over a thousand chugging up and down the Mississippi. The steamboats were not subject to the tides and currents of the major rivers. With a speed of around ten miles per hour, they became reliable for transporting goods, especially timber and minerals, from the West to the markets of the East.

The impact of the railroads

For all the importance of stagecoach routes, trails, telegraph lines and steamboats, nothing could compare with the importance of the railroads in opening up the western lands of the USA. Westerners had to wait some time for their coming for, despite the acknowledgement that a transcontinental route was desirable as early as the 1840s, the vast expense in construction meant that only one line could be contemplated initially. There was also hot competition over where the terminal should be. The development of California and the Gadsden Purchase were pursued by Southerners anxious to compete with the expanding North, whilst Douglas' ill-fated Kansas–Nebraska Act (see page 66) had its origins in the desire to settle territory that would allow the construction of a line to terminate in Chicago. In the end, the matter could only be settled once the southern states had seceded and Congress could easily pass a bill that would see the construction of a northern transcontinental line. On 1 July 1862, the First Pacific Railroad Act chartered two companies to start building: the Union Pacific Railroad, westward from Omaha; and the Central Pacific Railroad, eastwards from Sacramento. The incentives were in the form of very large land grants, giving the companies a 400-feet (122-metre) right of way and alternate sections of land for each completed mile of track. Thus an incentive was created for the two companies to build as much track as they could.

Even then, investment was slow and construction only began in 1864 when the land grant was doubled and government money was provided as a loan to attract further investors. Construction was difficult with all the raw materials, plus food and supplies for thousands of workers, having to be transported out west. As well as significant natural obstacles such as the 7,000-feet (2,134-metre) Sierra Nevada mountains to contend with, the railroad builders also faced Indian attacks and a hostile environment. Many of those constructing the railroad arrived as **immigrants**: Chinese contract workers in the West, Irish immigrants to the East. In the end, the track was completed in the spring of 1869 at Promontary, Utah, with the Union Pacific laying 1,086 miles of railroad to the Central Pacific's 689 miles. The speed with which the line was constructed meant that in places it was not especially secure, but the rapid use made of the line encouraged the quick construction of other lines.

By the end of the century, there were four more transcontinental lines: the Northern Pacific; Southern Pacific; Atchison, Topeka and Santa Fe; and the Great Northern. These major lines spawned a major network across the West. Western railroad mileage had increased from 3,000 miles of track west of the Mississippi in 1865 to 87,000 miles by 1900 (see page 127). Following a series of scandals involving financing the railroads, the government stopped making loans to companies. However, the land grants remained significant, with the federal government giving 131 million acres away in all and a further 48 million acres being offered by the states' governments.

Immigrants: People who arrive to live and work in a country from another country or continent.

1. *Explain why the USA was able to acquire so much land in the West between 1803 and 1854.*

2. *Explain the changes in transport that allowed Americans to move West after 1803.*

Construction of the Union Pacific Railroad on the Nebraska plains in 1867.

2.2 Who went west, and why?

The lure of the West

At the start of the 19th century, the area to the West of the Mississippi was unknown and in the possession of European powers. Apart from the Native-American tribes who roamed the plains, the only humans who ventured there were traders, trappers and explorers. Even by mid-century the vast majority of western lands were unexplored and uninhabited, with the exception by then of California, which had suddenly filled with gold prospectors in 1849, and the Mormon base at Salt Lake City in modern-day Utah. The farming frontier was slowly advancing, however. The development of communications and of improved farming methods (as mentioned above) saw settlers move into the 1,500-mile wilderness in the subsequent decades.

Many pioneers were motivated by the prospect of financial gain, though others were escaping the growing urban centres of the East and of Europe. The move west was encouraged by politicians and writers in the East who saw the West as the place where real American values continued to survive, where the Jeffersonian ideal of an **independent yeomanry** was most likely to flourish. Expansionist presidents such as James Polk and Franklin Pierce were keen to see their newly-acquired lands inhabited. Indeed, Polk deliberately encouraged the rush to California in 1849 with his announcement of the discovery of gold there. Writers like Mark Twain told of the liberation of life on the frontier with his popular accounts of Huckleberry Finn and Tom Sawyer. The influential New York journalist, Horace Greeley, used his 'New York Tribune' to publicise stories of frontier life following his journey from New York to San Francisco. 'Go West, young man, and grow up in the country', he urged in 1859 and published an account, 'The Plains as I Crossed Them', in 1869. Settlers were not only attracted by romantic notions of the wilderness and of self-advancement, there were also numerous incentives offered by both federal and state governments and by railroad companies eager to get people to settle on the land they had acquired from the government during construction. Indeed, a number of railroad companies had agents actively recruiting immigrants in Europe by the end of the 19th century. For the most part, people went west as farmers or miners, establishing mining, cattle and homestead frontiers, with the exception of the Mormons who had fled West to escape persecution in the East.

The Mormons go west

The Mormons, or Church of Jesus Christ of Latter-Day Saints, was a new, American-born religion founded in 1830 by Joseph Smith after he reported receiving golden plates from an angel that translated into the Book of Mormon. Many religious groups and **sects** have established themselves before and since in the USA, but the Mormons suffered serious prejudice in mid-19th-century America. It was more to do with their social practices than their religious beliefs. The Mormons operated as cooperatives, voting as a unit, establishing their own **militia** and practising **polygamy**. Other Americans could not accept such a group. Congress passed an anti-polygamy law in 1862.

The Mormons increasingly settled together and, although this was a way of surviving, it only served to emphasise their distinctiveness still more. In 1844, Joseph Smith and his brother were killed by a mob in Carthage, Illinois, near to their settlement of Nauvoo. Smith's successor, Brigham

Independent yeomanry: Farmers who owned, rather than rented, a small plot of land.

Joseph Smith (1805–1844)
Founder of the Mormon religious sect. He received his first religious call in 1820, and in 1827 claimed to have been granted the revelation of the 'Book of Mormon' (an ancient American prophet), inscribed on gold plates and concealed a thousand years before in a hill near Palmyra, New Jersey. Smith founded the Church of Jesus Christ of Latter-day Saints in 1830 in Fayette, New York. The Mormons were persecuted for their beliefs. Smith and his brother were killed by an angry mob in Illinois in 1844.

Sects: Groups of people that have a particular set of religious beliefs. Many sects have separated themselves from a larger group in order to follow their strongly held, or some would say, extreme beliefs.

Militia: Organisation that operates like an army but whose members are not professional soldiers.

Polygamy: The custom in some societies of marriage to more than one person at the same time.

Brigham Young (1801–1877)
Mormon religious leader who succeeded Joseph Smith. He joined the Mormon Church in 1832 and was appointed an apostle three years later. After a successful recruiting mission to Liverpool, England, he returned to the USA. He led the Mormon migration to the Great Salt Lake in Utah (1846), where he headed the colony until his death.

Young, proved to be a more vigorous and charismatic leader. In 1846, he persuaded the Mormons to leave their settlements and head West to set up a new republic free from their hostile neighbours. The great Mormon trek of 1846–47 saw pioneer Mormons march 1,300 miles westwards and settle in the desert valley of the Great Salt Lake, then part of Mexico. They quickly established themselves in the Utah territory. By the end of 1848, 5,000 Mormons had established themselves in their colony of Deseret (see map below). With strong leadership and a cooperative approach to farming, the Mormons prospered. Many thousands of Mormons, from Europe and the Mid-West, trekked westward to join Deseret and the settlements that spread out from the Salt Lake down to southern California.

America's acquisition of the territory in 1848 saw Young being made territorial governor of Utah in 1850, though the community still did not fit in with American society. In 1857, a federal army was sent against the Mormons before an accommodation was reached. The Mormons, nonetheless, maintained their cooperative and polygamous practices (Young had almost 30 wives) and so Utah did not achieve statehood until 1896. The Mormon settlements in the Utah desert developed largely independently of any other movements out West, as the hostile territory made the area unsuitable for cultivation or hunting.

The mining frontier

Perhaps the best known of all western pioneers are the 'Forty-niners' who flocked to California in search of gold, following its discovery and the announcement by Polk in 1848. Many prospectors for precious metals went west in the earliest days of the frontiers. The 'Forty-niners' were the

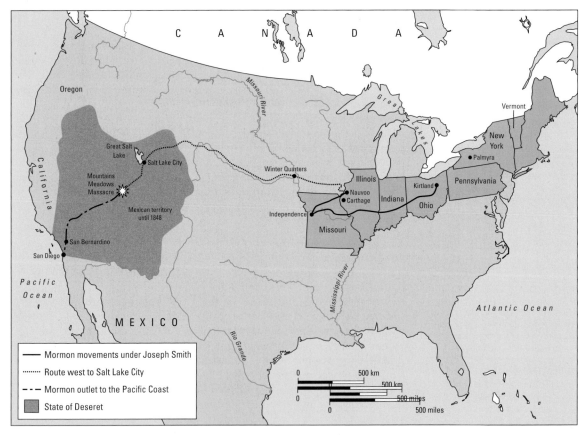

The westward route of the Mormons

first discernible group to head west and settle. There were a series of strikes in the 1860s and 1870s: the largest deposit of precious metals was found at Comstock Lode, Nevada, in 1859 and the last major strike provoked a gold rush to Dakota in 1874.

The development of mining towns followed a similar pattern across the West. An initial, disorderly rush of prospectors, usually men, would establish camps around gold deposits. Early mining would consist of the basic 'placer mining', which involved washing the surface-deposit gold out of the rocks. These camps would soon attract a collection of hangers-on who sought to exploit the predominantly male and lawless pioneers. Saloons, brothels and gambling dens quickly sprung up to give the hard-living miners an outlet for their money and energy. A good example is Virginia City which emerged from the discovery of the Comstock Lode in 1859. From nowhere, the town had a population of 38,000 by 1878, complete with four banks, six churches and 150 liquor stores (off-licences).

Mining towns often lived up to their reputation for being the 'Wild West'. Gunfights, vigilante action and stagecoach robberies were frequent, though the more established towns had to develop their own rudimentary justice systems quickly in order to rule in mining disputes and to administer basic law. Many of the towns were home to European and Mexican immigrants. Almost a third of Cornwall's tin miners left Britain in search of western gold in the 1860s. Of the 1,966 miners at Comstock Lode in 1880, 1,234 were of British origin. As the deposits dried up, miners would simply pack up and move on, leaving a trail of 'ghost towns' in their wake.

Gradually, the surface deposits dried up and more ambitious deep-level mining developed. Such mining required machinery, skill and capital outlay. This was not likely to develop on an individual basis. By the end of the 19th century, the traditional miner became obsolete, as large-scale businesses developed out West – the most significant of which was the Anaconda Mining Corporation of Montana.

The early pioneers either moved on to new areas, such as those of the gold rushes in Canada at the end of the century, returned to the East or found themselves working as more skilled labour with the new, large-scale companies. The mining frontier opened up stretches of the United States that were not likely to develop agriculturally and, in that sense, was crucial in the settlement of the mountainous West. Most significant of all was the major movement and development of California. Within two years of the discovery of gold, 90,000 settlers had moved to California. It became a state in 1850, without going through the process of organising itself as a territory.

The cattle frontier

The decades immediately after the Civil War marked the 'golden age' of the cowboy, who ranged across the plains of the South-West driving his cattle to the developing railroad towns of the Mid-West. In the 1860s, there were around five million longhorn cattle roaming wild in Texas (they had been introduced by the Spanish in the 18th century). Worth only $3 or $4 per head in Texas, they could fetch ten times as much in the northern meat markets, centred on Chicago. The issue was how to get them there. In 1866, a group of Texans herded some cattle 1,000 miles to the terminus of the Missouri–Pacific railroad at Sedalia, Missouri. Heavy losses en route made them change routes the following year and herd to Abilene, Kansas, where the cattle were loaded on to the Kansas–Pacific railroad at its western terminus and transported to Chicago. It was the beginning of a major trade for Abilene, which saw 35,000 cattle pass through in 1867,

Quarantine: Period of time during which animals that may have a disease are kept separate from other animals. This prevents the disease spreading to other animals.

rising to 700,000 by 1871. Abilene was a popular choice, due to the decision of lifestock dealer Joseph McCoy (the real 'Real McCoy') to run a line from Chicago to Abilene and to the liberal **quarantine** laws in Kansas that allowed transport of live cattle. This practice of ranging cattle over two or three months from Texas to the Mid-West railheads spread quickly. Soon 'cow towns' such as Abilene, Dodge City in Kansas and Miles City in Montana emerged as the transportation centres for cattle. Between 1866 and 1888, almost ten million cattle were driven by cowboys to these stations, and America became a beef-eating nation.

Not all cowboys herded cows. There was considerable sheep-herding too in the north around Oregon and Montana, and about a quarter of the herders were former black slaves finding a free life out West. In many ways, cowboy life is the most potent image of life on the frontier, but cowboys lived a dangerous yet predictable life with wages rarely going beyond $30 per month. Two-month journeys entirely outdoors with little comfort and facing natural hazards as well as rustlers and Indian attacks were the standard lifestyle. Then at the end the cow towns were rarely as wild as their mining cousins. Indeed, Kansas adopted **prohibition** as early as 1880.

Prohibition: A rule or law, which states that a particular thing is not allowed. It usually refers to the sale and consumption of alcohol.

The ranging lifestyle did not last long, however. The spread of railroads made it easier for cattle farmers to transport cattle from nearer home. The invention of barbed wire, in 1873, allowed the formation of large ranches where cattle could roam free without drifting off. Moreover, a series of outbreaks of splenic fever in cattle yards and severe winters in the mid-1880s – that saw cattle exposed to other herds and to the elements respectively – encouraged farmers to protect their cattle with winter shelter. As ranches developed and water supplies were fenced off, so it became harder to maintain a ranging lifestyle at all. By the 1880s, almost all cowboys found themselves working on ranches as little more than farmhands. Just as mining opened up California, so the range and ranch systems brought settlement and identity to Texas and the South-West. The 'Lone Star' state of Texas was soon integrated into the US system.

The farming frontier

By far the least glamorous, but most significant, settlement out West was that of the farmers who gradually cultivated the western lands around and then beyond the Mississippi. They created a wheat belt which, by the end of the American Civil War, was set to supply not only the United States but a hungry global market too. Land could be acquired by several methods: straightforward private purchase; grants from federal or state governments; or land from the railroads, keen to establish settlement alongside their own lines. Initially, the federal government had sold land in large plots allowing **land speculation**. There was growing pressure by mid-century for a homestead act that would allow families to purchase affordable plots of land that would sustain one farm. This was finally achieved by the Homestead Act of 1862 which was passed whilst Congress was free of southerners, who rightly feared that small-scale farming would prevent the development of plantations and so slavery. The Act allowed farmers to acquire 160 acres in one of two ways:

Land speculation: Where people who buy land sell it again for a profit.

1. either a settler could stake a claim and live on the land for five years, after which it was his;

2. or the settler could live there for six months and then pay $1.25 per acre.

Between 1862 and 1900, 600,000 settlers claimed their homesteads and, although it was subject to widespread abuse with speculators and companies putting in numerous dummy applications, the Homestead

Act did allow small-scale settlement to develop. Problems linked to the inappropriate size of the homesteads in areas where the terrain was poor were resolved by the Desert Land Act of 1877, and the Timber and Stone Act a year later. The former Act allowed the purchase of 640 acres at $1.25 per acre provided the homesteader established an **irrigation** scheme. The Timber and Stone Act of 1878 allowed the purchase of land unfit for cultivation for mining and lumbering. Although these federal land acts did stimulate settlement, most homesteaders still purchased their land from the states or railroad companies.

Perhaps of greater significance was the Morrill Act, also passed in 1862, which granted public land to states to provide for agricultural colleges that might help farmers learn new and improved techniques. Life on the farms was hard, made more difficult by the start-up costs which, at around $1,000 for an average homestead, meant many farmers faced chronic debts. Life was wild and frequently homesteaders lived many miles from their nearest neighbours. The treeless and dry region saw homesteaders living in houses scraped from the earth and resorting to animal dung for fuel. Railroads and the telegraph made life more bearable as the century wore on, but farmers were highly vulnerable to drought, fire, tornadoes and grasshopper plagues, as well as Indian attacks in the early years. There were even occasional battles to be fought against rangers who resented the fencing off of the plains and water supplies they had traditionally used.

Most of the early farmers in the West began as subsistence farmers and struggled to break the virgin soils of the plains. A series of new inventions and techniques allowed this to change dramatically as farming became more mechanised. Farmers could cultivate wider areas and achieve higher yields than they needed for themselves or even, by mid-century, the needs of the entire United States.

The breakthrough came in the 1830s, most notably with the development of the first steel plough by John Deere of Illinois in 1837 and the patenting of the McCormick Reaper in 1834 by Cyrus McCormick.

McCormick's reaper provided a mechanical means of harvesting that replaced the **sickle and scythe**. It allowed two men with horses to harvest 20 acres of wheat per day, covering five times as much ground as was the case previously. Deere's plough opened up new soils to planting as it became possible to cut through soil formerly resistant to the wooden plough. This was further strengthened by the chilled-iron plough invented by James Oliver in 1868 and known as the 'sod buster' for its ability to cut through the toughest soil.

One of the most significant inventions was barbed wire, invented by Joseph Glidden in 1873 and popularised by John Gates. Barbed wire provided a cheap and efficient means of fencing off vast tracts of less productive grazing land in the South-West and Texas. It encouraged settled livestock farming, as opposed to the ranging that had featured previously. Other new techniques included 'dry-farming' – the practice of deep ploughing and frequent harrowing that checked evaporation and so helped cultivation in drier climates – and the development of spring and winter wheat harvests. Irrigation schemes did not emerge effectively until the 20th century, though awareness of the need to preserve moisture and the potential for irrigation was growing from the 1870s onwards.

Such inventions and developments in technique lightened the load for farmers, but they added further to the need for capital outlay that was often beyond the resources of the small-scale farmer. Increasingly large farms developed, known as 'bonanza farms', out in the prairies of Minnesota and the Dakotas. Farming there became a large-scale industry and small-scale farmers found themselves bought out. They either moved away or became employed as farmhands.

There was a pattern to western settlement that can be seen in all three accounts above. Initial small-scale enterprises of individual pioneers developed by the end of the century into large-scale productions. The independent-minded yeoman farmer or miner, although he existed, did not dominate the Valley of Democracy as Jefferson and others had hoped.

Who were the settlers?

Traditionally, there had been an assumption that many of those who went west had come from the towns in the East and so eased the tensions of the cities, meaning America avoided much of the urban unrest that characterised urban Europe in the 19th century. This theory does not stand up to critical examination. Determining exactly who was moving west in the 19th century is not as easy as working out what they were doing there. Certainly, the West was a more diversely populated region than popular films and television suggest. Up to a quarter of cowboys may well have been former slaves, whilst the construction of the railroads brought thousands of Irish and Chinese workers into the western states. Many of the farmers were already farming in the Mississippi Valley and were simply trying their luck elsewhere; the environment was not suited to city-dwellers with no farming experience. Many, of course, moved directly west having arrived as immigrants; some specifically recruited by the railroad companies. These foreign-born farmers tended to settle in national groups, so that a traveller through the mid-West in the 1840s might well hear as much Swedish or German spoken as English, especially in states such as Wisconsin and Michigan.

Nor did the population grow uniformly. Although the number of white settlers living in the wheat-belt states of Kansas, Nebraska, the Dakotas, Iowa and Minnesota increased from one million to seven million between 1860 and 1900, the population of Nebraska actually fell between 1890 and 1900. Many westerners – farmers, ranchers or miners – moved around constantly. Of the settlers who entered Kansas in the 1850s, only 35% of them were still there in 1865.

Finally, the western states were overwhelmingly male. In 1880, Colorado had twice as many men as women and Wyoming three times. This was especially the case in the mining towns of the Rockies where the climate was not suited to women in their traditional roles. As a result, those women who did live out West tended to be treated more as equals than their eastern sisters. The daily fight for survival and the rudimentary conditions were not conducive to the maintenance of separate spheres. It is not surprising that the first states to introduce female suffrage were in the West.

1. Explain the religious and economic reasons why some Americans went west in the 1840s.

2. What do you regard as the main reasons why many Americans wanted to settle in the West? Explain your answer.

2.3 What are the reasons for the destruction of Native-American society?

Early federal responses to the Native Americans

Early encounters between Native Americans and settlers had been varied. Tribes had responded in various ways to the arrival of the Europeans – from cooperation and integration to outright hostility and warfare. Whatever the course of action, the Europeans had nonetheless had the best of it in the long term for, at the start of the 19th century, the Native Americans found themselves pushed westward into the territories of the **North-West Ordinance**, safely out of the way of the original 13 colonies. There were a few exceptions to this, where Indian tribes were more settled in their farming habits, such as the Cherokee of Georgia. These Indians lived in protected areas, agreed by treaty and beyond the jurisdiction of state or

North-West Ordinance: A law passed by Congress on 13 July 1787. It allowed north-west territories – including Ohio, Indiana and Illinois – acquired from Britain in 1783 to be colonised and later admitted as states.

federal authority. The North-West Ordinance had made it clear that the Native Americans were to be left to their own devices in the territories.

> 'The utmost good faith shall always be observed toward the Indians; their land and property shall never be taken away from them without their consent, and in their property, rights and liberty, they shall never be invaded or disturbed, unless in just and lawful wars authorised by Congress.'

There was a clear warning in the final phrase that the United States might not be forever persuaded to ignore the Indians, but it was clear that the federal government had no intention of allowing individual settlers to take matters into their own hands.

Early government policy, under the Federalists and later Thomas Jefferson, had hoped that the Indians might gradually be integrated into settler society via a programme of education and persuasion. Organisations such as the Society for Propagating the Gospel Among Indians, founded in 1787, sent missionaries into Indian villages, and Congress voted money to promote literacy and European farming practices. Jefferson's liberalism encouraged him to be interested in and to study the various tribes. However, it did not extend so far as to see them as the white man's equals. His Secretary for War, Henry Deerborn, was happy to write, in 1803, that 'the government consider it a very important object to introduce among the several Indian nations within the United States the arts of civilisation'.

Tecumseh's Confederacy

Hopes of a gradual and peaceful 'civilisation' of the tribes were dashed in the early 19th century. The Louisiana Purchase meant that millions of acres of land had been acquired by the United States. Substantial settlement was likely to begin in the area between the Appalachians and the Mississippi river, especially in the lush farming areas around modern-day Kentucky and Ohio. Jefferson might continue to talk of **assimilation** and civilisation but, as President, he was as clear as anyone else that Indian claims to hunting grounds in the North-West Territory were illegal. If the tribes were to reject 'civilisation', then their only alternative was to move to the West.

As tribal leaders saw white settlers move further and further into their traditional hunting grounds, a resistance movement began to take shape which would culminate in the most united resistance the Native Americans ever managed against the settlers – **Tecumseh's Confederacy**. The Shawnee chief Tecumseh, together with his **shaman** brother Tenskwatawa (the 'Prophet') concluded that this was the last opportunity for the Indians to resist settler encroachment for good. They managed to unite the many tribes to the east of the Mississippi in a pan-Indian alliance against the white man. Tecumseh used his organisational skills and eloquence to put together the largest concerted resistance the Americans were ever to face. He told the governor of Indiana territory, William Henry Harrison, how the 'paleface' intruders had 'driven us from the sea to the lakes – we can go no further'. As well as being a respected warrior, Tecumseh was aware of the difficulties and importance of maintaining Indian unity. He argued passionately that the tribes should renounce those elements of European life which some had adopted. Textile clothing and alcohol were to be discarded and negotiation over land rejected. Land was a general commodity, not subject to specific ownership in the American sense.

The uprising soon found itself entangled with the war of 1812 against the British. Indeed, British arming of the Indians was partially a cause of the

Assimilation: Learning ideas from other people and making use of them.

Tecumseh's Confederacy: A union of Eastern Indian tribes, formed in 1811 to stop the westward advance of Americans. It included Shawnees, Kaskaskias and Cherokees. They were defeated by Governor of Indiana, William Henry Harrison, at the Battle of Tippecanoe on 6 November 1811.

Shaman: A medicine-man of some of the north-west American Indians.

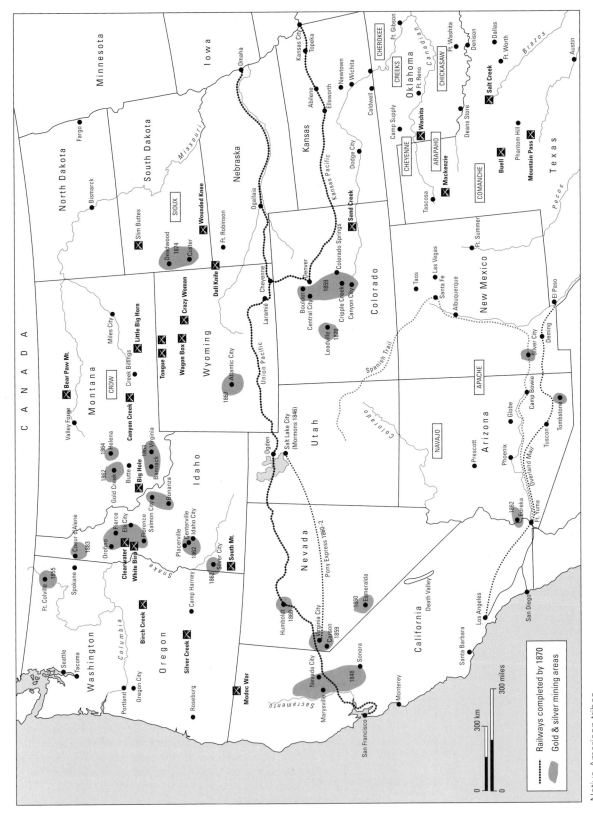

Native-American tribes

Legend:

········· Railways completed by 1870

Gold & silver mining areas

300 km

300 miles

Anglo–American conflict. Before war against the British had broken out, Henry Harrison had managed to destroy the Shawnee base at Tippecanoe, in November 1811, forcing Tecumseh to abandon the village. Tecumseh himself, having been appointed Brigadier General in the British army, was killed fighting alongside the British at the Battle of the Thames in 1813.

With Tecumseh dead, the Confederacy died with him, though several tribes fought on for several more months. Andrew Jackson was active on the southern frontiers, defeating a Creek army at the Battle of Horseshoe Bend in 1814 before turning his attention to the Spanish and the British. Tecumseh's revolt and the support the Indians gave to the British ensured that, thereafter, American attitudes to the Native Americans would be more hostile. Several treaties were drawn up, forcing the Indians in the North to move west of the Mississippi, whilst in the South the First Seminole War (1817–18) saw action against the Seminoles in the marshes of Florida. As Jefferson wrote ruefully in 1813:

> 'They would have mixed their blood with ours and been amalgamated and identified with us within no distant period of time [but] the cruel massacres they have committed on the women and children of our frontiers taken by surprise will oblige us now to pursue them to extermination or drive them to new seats beyond our reach.'

Andrew Jackson and Indian Removal

Andrew Jackson (1767–1845)
7th President of the USA (1829–37), a Democrat. Major General in the war of 1812, he defeated a British force at New Orleans (1815) and was involved in the war that led to the purchase of Florida (1819). Elected President, at the second attempt, in 1829 – the first election in which electors were chosen directly by voters rather than state legislators. He demanded loyalty from his Cabinet members. The political organisation he built was the basis of the modern Democratic Party. Known as an expansionist and the scourge of the Creeks and Seminoles.

Those Indians who remained east of the Mississippi now found themselves as small islands surrounded by covetous settlers. By 1830, most territory east of the Mississippi had been settled as states – for example, Illinois joined in 1818 and Alabama in 1819. It was unlikely that the 125,000 Native Americans still living in the East could survive much longer, especially following the election of Andrew Jackson as President in 1829. Jackson is traditionally seen as one of the Presidents most hostile to the Indians, but his attitude is more complex than seems at first, since he adopted an Indian boy. He respected Indian values, even if he did not see how the tribes could continue to exist within the civilised borders of the United States. On his election, he championed the idea of removal, which came to fruition with the Indian Removal Act of 1830. The Act allowed for the removal out west of all Indians living to the east of the Mississippi. In 1834, modern-day Oklahoma was designated Indian territory (see map opposite). There they were to be left 'permanently free' in an area no one expected the white man to penetrate.

In a sense, Jackson's policies were more progressive than Jefferson's. Although he was no more prepared than his predecessors to see Indians denying land to white settlers, he did acknowledge and respect the Indian way of life and genuinely assumed that it could be continued after their removal. The subsequent removals were not always accepted peacefully by the Indian tribes. In Illinois, the Sauk and Fox Indians under Chief Black Hawk fought unsuccessfully against the militia in the Black Hawk War of 1832. The federal government was forced into a long and not totally successful war against the Seminoles in Florida between 1835–42, which saw 1,500 US casualties and which cost the Treasury $30 million. Most significantly, the removal policy saw the forced march of the 'five civilised tribes' of the Cherokees, Chickasaws, Choctaws, Creeks and Seminoles out of their southern lands to the Indian reservation in Oklahoma. The Cherokees, in particular, had reason to be unimpressed. Having adopted a settled agricultural life in Georgia, that even saw them owning several hundred black slaves in the 1820s, the state of Georgia tried to move them out in 1828.

Despite the Supreme Court, under the Chief Justice John Marshall, ruling in their favour on three occasions, the Cherokees were eventually forced out by federal troops, who marched 15,000 of them over the winter of 1838–39 to the Indian territories. The conditions on the march – known to history as the Trail of Tears – were so terrible that a quarter died on route. Jackson had made his own views on the Cherokees perfectly clear. On hearing that the Supreme Court had supported the Cherokees, he is reported to have replied, 'John Marshall has made his decision; now let him enforce it.'

By 1840, almost all Indians had been moved to the 'Great Desert' beyond the Mississippi. There, supplies and rations were administered by the Bureau of Indian Affairs, established in 1836 and supported by the US army.

The Indian Wars of the 1860s and 1870s

By mid-century, around 300,000 Indians lived on the Great Plains. Some of the tribes had always lived there, whilst others had been moved there during the removals of the previous decades. These Indians maintained their tribes and, for the most part, their traditions. Thus, with the exception of the 'civilised tribes' of the South, most operated in bands. There were tribal subdivisions of between 300 and 500 who lived a nomadic lifestyle, living off the buffalo herds and hunting on horseback. They would be as likely to fight one another as the settlers. Until 1850, they could for the most part ignore the settlers who passed through on trails to Oregon, California and Utah.

This began to change as mineral discoveries, improvements in farming techniques and the development of the Texas cattle industry opened up the central plains of America, previously written off as the Great American Desert, to settlers. The 'permanent freedom' of the Indians began to look less secure. Treaties continued to be made – such as the agreements at Fort Laramie in 1851, when the major Indian chiefs agreed to accept certain fixed tribal boundaries in return for goods and supplies. However, Indian chiefs treated such agreements with growing distrust. Many would agree with the words of Chief Spotted Tail of the Sioux when he observed, in the 1870s, that '… since the Great Father promised that we should never be removed we have been removed five times … I think that you had better put the Indians on wheels and you can run them about wherever you wish.'

Although Spotted Tail tended to support peaceful coexistence with the white men, there now erupted a series of wars in the West as Indian tribes became frustrated. These were not coordinated uprisings, like Tecumseh's, but occurred across the frontier from the 1860s to the 1880s. Although the Indians managed to secure some short-term victories, they were no match in the long term for the superior technology of the settlers, state militias and the US army. A number of conflicts broke out during and immediately after the Civil War when, because of the absence of the US army in most places, Indians felt emboldened and local militia less observed. Several conflicts followed (see opposite).

There were a few sporadic outbursts across the Plains and Rockies in the final years of the 19th century, but it was clear to the Native Americans that the battle had been lost. The Blackfoots and Crows were pushed out of Montana, the Utes lost their lands in Colorado after a brief war in 1879. Geronimo, chief of the Apaches, was caught in 1886 after 15 years of fighting. The Nez Perces were finally pushed out of Idaho when, despite a brilliant campaign by their chief Joseph, he was captured in 1877. His surrender speech eloquently reflects the resignation of the proud warriors:

'I am tired. My heart is sick and sad. From where the sun now stands I will fight no more forever.'

Major conflicts of the Indian Wars

● In 1862 an uprising of the eastern Sioux, led by Little Crow, saw 500 settlers massacred in Minnesota before the militia re-established control and hanged the ringleaders.

● In 1864 the Cheyennes, who had been launching occasional raids in Colorado, were persuaded to gather at Fort Lyon on Sand Creek to discuss peace terms. There, 450 men, women and children were massacred by Colonel John Chivington, a Methodist minister who took delight in exhibiting the scalps he collected from the massacre. The massacre, one of the most notorious events of the Indian Wars, did lead to the survivors giving up their lands the following year.

● Between 1865 and 1867, the western Sioux harassed soldiers building a road through their hunting territory in Montana. This led, in December 1866, to the Fetterman Massacre when 82 soldiers under Captain Fetterman were ambushed and murdered.

● The Red River War of 1874–75 marked southern tribal hostility to the reservation policy being implemented at the time. A winter campaign under General Sheridan saw the Indians eventually forced to accept the terms.

● Perhaps the most famous incident of the Indian Wars was part of a campaign against the Sioux in the Black Hills of Dakota in 1876. The Sioux were resisting settler encroachment into their territories because of the discovery of gold there. During the campaign, General Custer found the main Sioux encampment on the Little Big Horn river in Montana. In June, he and his small band of 265 men were surrounded and totally destroyed by 2,500 Sioux Indians led by Sitting Bull and Crazy Horse. Even then, the Sioux did not capitalise on their victory. The following year, the Sioux were forced to give up their hunting grounds, despite having been promised them less than a decade earlier.

Reservations and Americanisation

Whilst the wars were taking place in the West, the federal government was trying to work out a new policy to deal with the fact that, with western settlement across the continent, removal was no longer an option. In 1867, an Indian Peace Commission was established that was to set up and police a reservation policy. This led to Indians being moved to protected federal lands in modern-day Dakota and Oklahoma, the latter already established as a place of Indian settlement. Indians, not surprisingly, were unhappy about the reservation policy and a number of the wars documented above were the result of resistance to removal to the reservations.

The later decades of the century saw a return to Jefferson's assimilationist ideas. Eastern **humanitarians**, horrified at the accounts of the physical destruction, turned their well-meaning but culturally arrogant minds to policies collectively known as 'Americanisation'. Boarding schools, such as the Carlisle Institute in Pennsylvania, were established to teach Indians civilised ways, before sending them back to the reservations to educate their

Humanitarians: People concerned about the welfare of other people. The aim of humanitarianism is to improve life for people and to lessen their pain and suffering.

elders. Indian practices and dress were outlawed and instruction in the virtues of independent farming and private ownership encouraged. In 1887, the Dawes Act broke the reservation lands up into family holdings and granted citizenship to all property holders after 25 years. In 1901, the five civilised tribes of Oklahoma received citizenship automatically.

Most of these policies were motivated by genuine liberal sentiment, but they resulted in the loss of millions of acres by Indians who were tricked into surrendering their land by fraudsters before they understood the concept of ownership. Between 1887 and 1934, Native Americans lost almost two-thirds of the land they had been granted. More to the point, their way of life and customs were being gradually destroyed. They may not have been physically destroyed but in terms of the Indian way of life it was as much a cultural **genocide** as the massacres of settlers on the plains.

Genocide: The deliberate and systematic killing of an ethnic or national group.

Why was Native-American society destroyed?

The destruction of the Native Americans has tended to be seen as inevitable once the settlers began to move West, but it is important to consider the factors at work in order to decide if the destruction of the native culture, and triumph of the European/American culture, was really unavoidable. Several factors can be identified.

● **The incompatibility of nomadic and settler cultures**

It is important to establish first of all that, once settlers moved west, a clash of some kind between settlers and Native Americans was inevitable. That is not to say that the settlers were bound to win that struggle, but the nomadic lifestyle of the Indian tribes could not really exist side by side with settlers who were fencing off land and so depriving tribes of traditional water and hunting resources. Some tribes did adapt, such as the Cherokees, and there are examples of white traders accepting elements of Indian culture too. However, it is difficult to see how this could have operated on a wide-scale basis without the Indians effectively ceasing to operate as an independent nation.

● **The development of transport and farming methods that opened up the frontier**

It is clear that some easterners assumed that the removal method was a long-term solution. This was based on an assumption that the Indians were being moved to territory that no settler would want to inhabit. New agricultural techniques, developments in transport and communications, and the expansion of the USA to the Pacific changed this. It made the idea of two fundamentally opposed social systems co-existing on one continent impossible to sustain.

● **The lure of Indian lands to settlers**

Not only were settlers moving into the Great Desert, but also the lands set aside for Indian reservations were not secure for the Indians. This was most graphically illustrated in the 1870s when the discovery of gold in the Dakota hills, though part of the northern reservation, drew numerous white settlers into the territory and the US army did nothing to protect Indian rights there.

● **The destruction of the buffalo**

The destruction of the buffalo dealt a serious blow to the Indians who depended on them not just for food but for clothing, fuel, hunting and cooking utensils. A craze for buffalo robes and leather in the East, together with railroads opening up the hunting of the buffalo (William Cody, or Buffalo Bill, was reputed to have killed over 4,000 buffalo in 18 months), saw their numbers decline rapidly. From an estimated 13 million buffalo on the plains in 1865, they were almost extinct by the end of the century. It is unclear if the extinction policy was deliberate, but federal officials were well aware of the implication of their destruction for the Indians. For example, General Sheridan commented, 'let them kill, skin and sell until the buffalo is exterminated as it is the only way to bring lasting peace and allow civilisation to advance'.

● **Indian divisions**

After the death of Tecumseh in 1813, there was no further coherent Indian resistance to settler advance and at times tribes were fighting one another rather than the Americans.

● **Broken promises and assurances**

Inevitably, some Indian chiefs only realised too late that the treaties they drew up were worthless. Even when there was an attempt to get them enforced – as seen with the Cherokees in Georgia – it required executive or army support to see justice done. That was unlikely given the general attitude of the federal government to Indian policy. As the western states secured representation in Congress and enjoyed political influence, this became even less likely. At times, the federal army intervened explicitly on the side of the settlers, even sometimes in the face of instructions from back east. The Civil War helped further, as eastern minds were turned elsewhere.

● **Technological advantages of the settlers**

For all their bravery, speed and skills, the Indian tribes could not match the impact of the telegraph and railroad that the settlers could use for transport and communication, nor the repeating Winchester rifle and Colt revolver that they could use in the field.

● **The cultural destruction of assimilation and Americanisation**

Even those Americans who sympathised with the plight of the Native Americans saw the solution in terms of assimilation or Americanisation. Thus the best the Indians could hope for was to survive physically: once the western lands were coveted by the settlers, their only alternative was to fight or adapt.

1. How did President Andrew Jackson deal with Native Americans in the 1830s?

2. Why did it take so long to defeat the Plains Indians?

3. Draw a spidergram showing the reasons why Native-American society was destroyed.

4. Did the Americans engage in genocide against Native Americans?

2.4 What was the extent of federal government involvement in western expansion?

For the most part, the federal government encouraged western expansion and did much to facilitate the movement west.

In some obvious ways, the government helped settlement. The North-West Ordinance, for example, established a clear and encouraging system to allow states to join the Union easily. The actions of Presidents generally favoured settlement, from the Indian removal policies of Andrew Jackson to the deliberately expansionist actions of James Polk over Mexico and Texas. The federal government also passed a number of Acts to encourage people to move West, most notably the Homestead Act and the Morrill Land Act of 1862. Financial assistance and substantial land grants were made to transcontinental railroad companies and Butterfield's stagecoach route was also subsidised by the federal government. In some ways, government inaction was as telling as any legislation passed, not least the blind eye that was turned to some settler actions against Native Americans in the middle decades, and even the specific collaboration of federal army units and posts out West from time to time. There was a general mood of encouragement and support for 'Manifest Destiny' that became even easier after the sore of slavery had been removed by the Civil War and the free/slave state tensions of western expansion had long since gone.

However, there were moments and issues that saw the federal government at least putting a brake on expansion. Certainly, some settlers came to resent the unhelpful interference, as they saw it, of the federal government in their affairs. There were three areas in particular where, from time to time, the federal government got in the way of settler desires:

● slavery disputes and sectional opposition to expansion

● Native American policy

● conservation.

We will now look at these three areas in some detail.

Slavery disputes and sectional opposition to expansion

Sectionalism: The idea that different parts of the USA have a strong regional identity (such as North and South).

The most obvious check on expansionism came in the period before the Civil War, when growing **sectionalism** and fears of either slave or free states dominating Congress meant that some of the more expansionist instincts of Presidents and settlers had to be put on hold. The best example of this is the northern restraint on Polk and Pierce in their plans for expansion southwards in the 1840s and 1850s. This manifested itself most clearly in 1854 when Pierce was involved in secret negotiations with his **ambassadors** to offer $120 million for Cuba. If Spain refused, they were to go to war over the sugar- and slave-rich colony. Details of the secret plotting – the Ostend Manifesto – leaked out and Pierce was forced to abandon his plans before even making them public, when he was faced with northern anger and opposition. Awareness of such opposition also explains Polk's decision not to press for more territory off Mexico and to secure California and New Mexico quickly, before northern opposition grew.

Ambassadors: Important officials who are sent by their government to live in a foreign country and to represent their own country's interests there.

Earlier in the century, the Federalists had similarly acted as a restraining force on westerners clamouring to take Canada in the war of 1812, fearing most the further growth of Mid-West farming states, which tended to be attracted to the radical politics of Jeffersonian Republicanism. As long as sectionalism pervaded the federal institutions, then expansionism would always be viewed with a wary eye by one section or the other. This was also seen with policies towards the western settlement. The Homestead and the Transcontinental Railroad Acts, both essential to the substantial population movement westward in the later half of the century, had to wait until the southern secession ensured their passage through Congress.

Native American policy

Although the federal government tended to turn a blind eye to settler violence against Native Americans, and on occasion federal troops played an overt role in moves against them, there were certain policies that at times thwarted, or tried to thwart, anti-Indian moves. Some politicians sought to accommodate Indian concerns or to humanise policy towards them. For instance, President Grant attempted to staff the Indian Affairs

Office with pacifist **Quakers**. Also, President Hayes' admitted in 1877, in seeking to strengthen treaties drawn up with the tribes, that 'many, if not most, of our Indian wars have had their origin in broken promises and acts of injustice on our part'. The Supreme Court did, on occasion, intervene in support of treaties when states or individuals seemed to break them, most famously in the 1830s cases when Chief Justice Marshall repeatedly ruled in favour of the Cherokees in their battles against Georgia. For the most part, these interventions were insignificant in the overall scheme of things. However, the federal government did act at certain times as a restraint on the wilder excesses of settlers in their dealings with Native Americans, even if there was fundamental collaboration in the slow extinction of their way of life.

Conservation

As the last stretches of wilderness began to disappear at the end of the century, so the issue of conservation became significant as some Americans began to wake up to the possibility that the West was not inexhaustible. The destruction of wildlife, woodland and mineral wealth, as well as the exhaustion of the soil, became an issue and there were several federal attempts to preserve lands and resources out West. Pressure grew after the Civil War for some action to protect American timber reserves. In 1873, the Timber Culture Act acknowledged the issue when it offered 160-acre plots to settlers prepared to plant a quarter of their land with trees. Attempts to introduce a forest management system, as existed in Canada, were resisted until 1897 when the Forest Management Act established the Bureau of Forestry, initially under the Swiss expert Gifford Pinchot. By 1910, the Bureau managed 149 protected national forests, after a process of setting aside public lands initiated by President Benjamin Harrison in the Forest Reserve Act of 1891.

The setting aside of land for preservation and public enjoyment had received a boost several decades earlier when, in 1872, two million acres of Wyoming were set aside to create Yellowstone National Park for 'the benefit and enjoyment of the people'. Yellowstone was the first of several national parks, with three being established in California alone in 1890: Yosemite, Sequoia and General Grant. Initially, it was difficult to ensure that the national parks and national forests were policed and protected from indignant settlers who saw the land as theirs. Hence the creation of the Bureau of Forestry and later the National Park Scheme, complete with rangers, in 1916.

Irrigation was a policy more likely than the national parks to secure the support of westerners. Though even here there was a reluctance to take the issue seriously until a series of droughts, in the 1880s, gave greater credence and urgency to the warnings of soil erosion issued by geologists such as Major John Wesley Powell. He urged the federal government to develop water reserves out West before the soils were eroded and exhausted for good. It was not until 1902 that the appropriately named Senator Newlands secured the passage of the National Reclamation Act. This established the principle of federal management of the waterways and authorised the federal government to build and maintain irrigation projects out West. The resulting Bureau of Reclamation acted quickly. By 1914, over a million acres had been reclaimed for farmland from schemes such as the Buffalo Bill Dam in Wyoming and the Theodore Roosevelt and Boulder (later Hoover) dams in Arizona. Conservation was one of the major achievements of the Progressive era, but it was done for the most part against the instincts of western settlers, who generally resented federal interference and ownership of lands which they viewed as their own.

1. Why are there differing views on why the federal government became involved in westward expansion?

2. What do you regard as the most important reasons why the federal government became involved in westward expansion? Explain your answer.

Without federal action – through territorial expansion, military protection and financial support – the rapid western expansion of the USA could not have taken place. Nevertheless, the federal government did not always act in unison and there were times when settlers had to force the issues themselves. It is also important to recognise that, for all the support and encouragement the federal government might have given, it still required brave pioneers and risk-taking entrepreneurs to act upon the opportunities the federal government presented.

2.5 How did western expansion affect American attitudes?
A CASE STUDY IN HISTORICAL INTERPRETATION

The Turner Thesis

The impact of the major population movement westwards in the 19th century was not limited to the western lands themselves. Historians have been concerned ever since with the extent to which western expansion and 'Manifest Destiny' have shaped the modern American mind. Certainly, writers concerned with American 'exceptionalism' have been attracted to the idea of a frontier mentality affecting American social and political attitudes which make them distinct from European attitudes. It is also the case that the West has produced more than its fair share of American myths, most often promoted by Hollywood and the 'spaghetti western'. The individualistic, anti-government streak in the American character has been well fed by tales of Custer's Last Stand, Wyatt Earp, Buffalo Bill and Davy Crockett.

The first historian to consider these issues directly was Frederick Jackson Turner in his lecture 'The Significance of the Frontier in American History' delivered to the American Historical Association in 1893. Turner, a historian at Wisconsin University, presented his thesis ('The Turner Thesis') following the announcement by the Census Bureau, in 1890, that the frontier had effectively ended and that all western regions were sufficiently inhabited not to be seen as wilderness. It is worth quoting Turner:

'It is to the frontier that the American intellect owes its striking characteristics. That coarseness and strength combined with acuteness and inquisitiveness; that practical, inventive turn of mind, quick to find expedients; that masterful grasp of material things, lacking in the artistic but powerful to effect great ends; that restless, nervous energy; that dominant individualism, working for good and for evil, and with all that buoyancy and exuberance which comes with freedom – these are the traits of the frontier, or traits called out elsewhere because of the existence of the frontier.'

Turner was thus suggesting that the frontier had been the source of a number of what might be seen as American values, including democratic ideals, an open society, rugged individualism and unrestricted economic activity. He was also proposing that American characteristics commented upon by Europeans, such as individualism, inventiveness and expansionism, had their roots in the frontier. Turner suggested that the frontier had acted as a safety valve for America, in times of potential economic strife, by providing an escape from urban centres for otherwise discontented citizens. He concluded by seeing the ending of the frontier as a significant turning point in American history:

> 'The frontier has gone and with its going has closed the first period of American history.'

Turner's Thesis has its merits. One can see, for instance, the ideals of Jeffersonian democracy functioning far better in the West, and it is true that certain movements in US history – such as temperance reform, populism and women's rights – all had their origins in the West. However, historians have since raised objections to the thesis.

Whilst the earliest settlement did tend to involve pioneering individuals acting alone, most western expansion gradually involved whole communities working together; for example, the development of ranches and mining enterprises. Farmers increasingly formed alliances, such as the Granger and Populist movements, to work together. The most distinct group to move west, the Mormons, actually went because their community-style society did not fit with American values in the East.

Individual democratic ideals can be seen as having their origins in the Whiggism of 17th-century England. The values of the Declaration of Independence and the Constitution – developed when the USA essentially looked East – were certainly dominated by the elites of New England and Virginia.

The idea of western expansion as a safety valve for urban dwellers does not stand up to scrutiny when one notes that most of those moving West were already farmers, either in Europe or in the Mississippi Valley. The attraction of moving west was that of better lands on which to continue farming, not to start up a farming life from scratch.

The ideal that Turner's Thesis suggests ignores the vast diversity of cultures and backgrounds that were to be found out West. Not only did Native Americans play their role out West, but the West saw Mormons, Hispanics, free blacks, Irish labourers, Scandinavian farmers and Chinese immigrants all bringing their unique cultures and identities into the western melting-pot. The idea of the hard-living, white male pioneer is a legitimate stereotype, but cannot be seen as typifying all western settlers.

If Turner was correct, then one ought to detect a change after 1890 in the direction of US history, but that does not seem to have occurred and there remain today distinct differences in the attitudes of Americans living in different sections of the Union. There may then have been a western frame of mind, but the idea that it shaped the views of others is exaggerated.

However, just as it is perhaps best not to accept all that Turner had to say as an all-embracing philosophy, so it is fair to see some elements of truth in his observations. It is certainly possible to argue that it is no coincidence that shortly after the closing of the frontier, Americans began to look further west still. They began the process, hesitant at first but confident later, of acquiring an overseas empire. 'Manifest Destiny' had seen the Americans overwhelm colonial powers and native settlers in the space of less than a century. Western expansion had given America status as a world power. The USA, and the world, would spend much of the next century trying to come to terms with that reality.

1. Explain Frederick Jackson Turner's Thesis on the role of the West in American history.

2. Using information from this chapter, how far do you think Turner's views on the role of the West are correct?

? Source-based questions: The causes of the Mexican War of 1846–1848

SOURCE A

Care has been taken – that all our military and naval movements shall be strictly defensive. We will not be the aggressor upon Mexico – but if her army shall cross the [Rio Grande] del Norte and invade Texas, we will if we can drive her army – to her territory. We invite Texas to unite her destinies with our own.

Letter from President James K. Polk to William H. Haywood, August 1845

SOURCE B

Sir, I am directed by the President to instruct you to advance and occupy with the troops under your command, positions on or near the east bank of the Rio [Grande] del Norte as soon as it can be conveniently done with reference to the season and the routes by which your movements must be made.

It is not designed, in our present relations with Mexico, that you should treat her as an enemy; but, should she assume that character by a declaration of war, or an open act of hostility towards us, you will not act merely on the defensive.

Order from Secretary of War, William L. Marcy, to General Zachary Taylor of the US Army, 13 January 1846

SOURCE C

The strong desire to establish peace with Mexico on liberal and honourable terms, and the readiness of this Government to regulate and adjust our boundary induced me last September to seek a reopening of diplomatic relations between the two countries. An envoy of the USA [went] to Mexico with full powers to adjust every existing difference. His mission was unavailing. The Mexican government not only refused to receive him or listen to his propositions, but have at last invaded our territory and shed the blood of our fellow-citizens on our own soil.

President Polk's War Message to Congress, 11 May 1846

---

1. Study Sources A and B.

How far do these two sources agree on the role of the US army in possibly starting a war with Mexico?

2. Study Source C.

How reliable is this source as evidence of the reason why the Mexican War took place in 1846?

3. Study Sources A, B and C, and use information from this chapter.

'The USA went to war with Mexico out of self-defence.'

Assess the validity of this statement.

3 The causes and course of the Civil War, 1840–1865

Key Issues

- Why were there growing sectional tensions in the 1840s and 1850s?

- Why did civil war break out in 1861?

- Why did the North win the Civil War?

3.1 How did slavery cause problems during western expansion?
3.2 Why did sectionalism grow in the 1850s?
3.3 Why did Lincoln win the presidential election of 1860?
3.4 How did the election of Lincoln lead to the outbreak of war?
3.5 What were the strengths of the two sides on the eve of war?
3.6 How did the two sides perform in the military campaigns?
3.7 What opposition did the political leadership face during the Civil War?
3.8 How did foreign powers respond to the war?
3.9 What was the importance of the Emancipation Proclamation?
3.10 Historical interpretation: Why did the North win the Civil War?
3.11 To what extent was the Civil War the 'first modern war'?

Framework of Events

1820	Missouri Compromise
1844	Polk is elected President
1846	Start of Mexican War
	Wilmot Proviso
1847	Calhoun Doctrine
1849	California ratifies a free state constitution
1850	Compromise measures pass Congress
1851	*Uncle Tom's Cabin* is published
1852	Pierce is elected President
1854	Kansas–Nebraska Act
	Emergence of Republican and 'Know Nothing' parties
1854–1856	'Bleeding Kansas'
1856	Beating of Sumner; Buchanan is elected President
1857	Dred Scott decision in Supreme Court
	'Panic of 1857'
	Kansas elects a free state legislature and Lecompton slave constitution
1858	Lincoln–Douglas debates in Illinois
1859	John Brown's Raid
1860	Lincoln is elected President
	Secession of South Carolina
1861	(February) Deep South secedes; establishment of Confederacy
	(April) Shots fired at Fort Sumter
	Secession of the Upper South
	First Manassas (Bull Run)
1862	(April) Battle of Shiloh
	(2 June) Robert E. Lee takes command of Army of North Virginia
	McClellan's Penisula Campaign
	Second Manassas
	(September) Battle of Antietam
	Lincoln issues Emancipation Proclamation
	(13 December) Battle of Fredericksburg

1863	Battle of Chancellorsville
	(July) Battle of Gettysburg
	(April) Grant is appointed General-in-Chief of all Union forces
	(4 July) Union captures Vicksburg
	Riots in New York over the draft
	Battle of Chickamauga
1864	(November) Union capture Atlanta
	Lincoln is re-elected President
	(December) Sherman's 'March through Georgia'
	Battle of Nashville
1865	(9 April) Lee surrenders at Appomattox
	(15 April) Assassination of Abraham Lincoln.

Overview

Cotton gin: A machine invented by Eli Whitney in Georgia, in 1793. It consists of two rollers: one, covered in spikes, tears the cotton-wool away from the seed; the other, covered with bristles, brushes the cotton off the first roller.

Constitution: A legal statement of limitations upon the power of the government, and upon the rights and freedoms of the governed.

Secession: The formal separation of a region or state from a larger group or country. In this instance, the southern states of America wanted to break away from the Union (i.e. the USA) and form their own group of states (to be known as the Confederacy).

Confederacy: The name given to the breakaway southern states of America, under the presidency of Jefferson Davis, during the period of the Civil War.

States' rights: Belief that the state government rather than the federal government had the final say in policy and decision making.

T HE war between North and South came as a surprise to many. It had its origins in several decades of growing tensions between the two sections of the young republic. For economic and geographical reasons, slavery remained the dominant economic system in the plantation South long after it had died out in the northern states. It was given a further boost by the invention of the **cotton gin** in 1793. Whilst both sections could accept different systems in the old states, tensions grew over the spread of slavery as the United States expanded westwards. The extent to which slavery could continue to grow in the newly acquired territories was an issue that kept raising its ugly head. Initially, the issue was resolved by compromise; in the **Constitution**, in the 1820 Missouri Compromise and the Compromise of 1850. However, by the 1850s the two sections were growing increasingly uneasy about one another's intentions. The Wilmot Proviso and the Calhoun doctrines – both issued in the late 1840s – raised the stakes on both sides and the work of northern abolitionists became more prominent, most notably with the publication of *Uncle Tom's Cabin*.

A series of events in the 1850s saw both sections move to more extreme positions, made more likely by the decline of the national two-party system. The emergence of the sectional Republican Party, which only sought support in the North, as well as the increasing domination of the Democratic Party by southerners (followed by its formal split in 1860), meant that the forum and will for compromise was diminished. Clashes over the future of Kansas–Nebraska territory gave rise to civil war in the area between 1854 and 1856. There was also violence on the Senate floor when an angry southern Congressman, Charles Sumner, was beaten up by a northern senator. Matters came to a head in 1860 when Republican Abraham Lincoln was elected President without a single southern state supporting him. South Carolina led the way for a southern **secession** from the Union and for the formation of the **Confederacy**, which Lincoln refused to recognise. The failure of compromise in 1861 led to Lincoln resorting to violence in order to force the southern states back into the Union, which in turn caused four more slave states to secede in the cause of '**states' rights**'.

Neither side expected the ensuing war to last the four years it did (1861–65). In fighting it, the United States introduced to the world the horrors and destruction of modern warfare. Initial southern successes were not enough to overcome northern morale or resources, strengthened by Lincoln's determination to win. A series of northern victories on the battlefield in 1863, and the appointment of Ulysses Grant to overall military control in 1864 (the same year as Lincoln's re-election), saw the tide turn in the North's favour. The exhausted South was forced to surrender to the North in April 1865. The Civil War had transformed the **Union** forever, causing some historians to refer to it as the Second American Revolution. Slavery disappeared following Lincoln's Emancipation Proclamation and the northern success marked a victory for the proponents of strong central power over the supporters of states' rights. It also marked the beginnings of further westward expansion and the development of a more industrialised economy and society.

Union: The name given to the northern states of America, under President Lincoln, during the Civil War.

3.1 How did slavery cause problems during western expansion?

In a sense, the American Civil War was caused neither by slavery nor by western expansion, but rather by the way in which these two key issues of the 19th century intertwined. Slavery had existed initially throughout the United States, but had gradually been abolished in the northern states so that by the beginning of the 19th century it was concentrated in the southern part of the USA. Although there were active campaigners against slavery, known as **abolitionists**, the majority of Americans were happy to accept that there were different economic and social systems existing within their country. A number expected slavery gradually to die out as, state by state, planters would come to prefer different systems. However, this hope was destroyed by the invention of the cotton gin by Eli Whitney in 1793. The cotton gin made possible a massive expansion inland of cotton production and the figures for cotton production rose dramatically:

Abolitionists: People who are in favour of abolishing a particular system or practice. In this instance, the abolitionists wanted to abolish slavery.

1790	3,000 bales (one bale is 500 lb/227 kg)
1801	100,000 bales
1820	400,000 bales
1860	c. 4,000,000 bales

The close relationship between cotton production and slavery was encouraged further by the development of effective labour systems which made slavery a highly productive way of working the southern economy. With the purchase of the vast Louisiana territory from France in 1803, the pattern of slave distribution also changed. In the 18th century, half of the slaves in the USA were in Virginia. By the 1850s, the largest concentrations were to be found in eastern Virginia and the Deep South, in a belt stretching from South Carolina across to the Mississippi and the state of Louisiana (see map on page 80).

The abolition of the slave trade in 1808 did not lead to a decline in slavery. Instead, the value of slaves increased as the supply from Africa ceased. The value of the average slave hand increased from $300 in the 1790s to almost $2,000 by the 1850s. The majority of southerners were not slave-holders. In 1860, there were almost 400,000 slave-holders out of a white population of around eight million in the South, but only about 50,000 of them could be called planters (i.e. owning more than 20 slaves on a plantation). Despite this, most people living in the South accepted slavery as part of their way of life. They might well have aspired to own slaves even if they did not do so themselves.

The existence of slaves also acted as a reminder to poorer whites that there was a social class below them in society. Slavery was thus seen very much as part of the Southern way of life – its 'peculiar institution' as it was later referred to. Attacks on slavery were seen as attacks on the South as a whole.

Discrimination: The practice of treating one person or group of people less fairly than others.

Not that slavery came under much attack in the early decades of the 19th century. The American Colonisation Society had been founded in 1817 with the aim of returning freed slaves to Africa. The first group arrived in Liberia in 1822, but by 1860 only 15,000 black Americans had actually made the journey. In 1831, the northern radical William Lloyd Garrison first published a weekly abolitionist newspaper, 'The Liberator'. A year later, he founded the New England Anti-Slavery Society. The American Anti-Slavery Society was established by Arthur and Lewis Tappan in 1833. However, neither organisation attracted mainstream support in the North or the South until the 1850s, and the movement was initially troubled by divisions. Northerners were no less racist than their southern brothers and there are plenty of examples of **discrimination** against freed and escaped slaves in the northern states. Workers, especially immigrants, feared the economic competition of freed blacks, and abolitionists were the subject of attacks in their own states throughout the 1830s. That is not to say that there were not important voices speaking out against slavery, on both moral and economic grounds, during the period. It is simply that their influence can be exaggerated.

The Missouri Compromise

Congress: The elected group of politicians that is responsible for making the law in the USA. It is the American parliament and has two houses: the House of Representatives and the Senate (see page 27).

Tallmadge Amendment: In 1819 it was proposed that the territory of Missouri be admitted to the Union as a slave state. Congressman James Tallmadge of New York proposed an amendment that Missouri should be accepted as a slave state only if it undertook to forbid further slave immigration and to free its slaves gradually, as the northern states had done earlier. Tallmadge and his associates had two objectives: to reserve as much as possible of the Louisiana Purchase (see page 34) for free, white labour; and to weaken the political ascendancy in the Union which the South had enjoyed since independence.

Emancipation: The freeing of people from the social, political or legal restrictions that are considered to be degrading or unnecessary. In this instance, it refers to the freeing of slaves.

Whilst few northerners felt the need to abolish slavery, this tolerance did not extend to agreeing to the expansion of slavery into the western territories. The first tensions were seen in 1819, as **Congress** considered the entry of the southern territory of Missouri into the Union. Missouri easily qualified for statehood but, when it applied to join the Union, the House of Representatives passed the **Tallmadge Amendment**. This called for a ban on any more slaves entering Missouri and anticipated gradual **emancipation** by stating that any children born to slaves should be free. This was not acceptable to the slave-holding Missourians, nor to southerners generally, so the Amendment was defeated in the Senate. The issue went beyond Missouri, however.

As the USA developed, the North was emerging as the more populous, more economically diverse and more wealthy section, whilst the South identified itself more and more with slavery and plantation agriculture. As a consequence, the North began to dominate in the House of Representatives, which was constituted according to population. In 1819, there were 11 free states and 11 slave states, so the balance in the Senate – where each state had two senators regardless of size – was even. Southerners became concerned that, with the Tallmadge Amendment, the North might at some point begin to use its population advantage to limit or even abolish slavery in the South and certainly in the expanding territories. For this reason, they were determined to maintain the slave/free state balance in the Senate as a counterweight to northern dominance of the House. In the end, a compromise was found – the Missouri Compromise of 1820. This stated:

> 'Missouri would be admitted as a slave state. Maine, a free-soil area that had been part of Massachusetts, would be admitted as a separate state, so preserving the balance in the Senate.
>
> Slavery would not be permitted in the future in any territories that were created out of the Louisiana Purchase above the line of 36 degree-30 – which constituted the whole of the territories of the USA as existed in 1820.'

Although neither side was entirely happy with the solution, both houses of Congress accepted it (although a majority of southern Congressmen opposed it). Wiser heads were not convinced that the issue had been resolved. Former President John Quincy Adams saw the issue as 'a title-page to a great tragic volume', whilst Thomas Jefferson feared the Compromise as 'the most [portentous] question which ever yet threatened our Union'.

The impact of the expansion of the 1840s

The slavery issue went quiet in the 1820s and 1830s, but by the end of the 1840s it was threatening to destroy the Union altogether. Between 1836 and 1848, three slave states and three free states had been admitted to the Union, so preserving the sectional balance in the Senate achieved in the Missouri Compromise. However, the acquisition of Oregon in 1846 and of California and New Mexico in 1848, the discovery of gold in California in 1848 and migration of the Mormons to Utah ensured that there would soon be large populations out West. This forced the issue of whether the new states should be free or slave. A number of northern Congressmen were already concerned that the Democratic President, James Polk, appeared to be favouring the South (he had compromised with Britain over Oregon in the North-West, but was fighting a provoked war against Mexico). This would mean more territory susceptible to slavery was likely to be added to the Union. The northern Congressmen were anxious to prevent slavery from spreading into the new territories. In August 1846, David Wilmot, a Democrat from Pennsylvania, proposed an amendment to a war bill that became known as the 'Wilmot Proviso'.

The Proviso proposed to exclude slavery from any territory acquired from Mexico, whether from war or purchase. The House of Representatives passed it but it was defeated in the Senate, with voting more on sectional than party lines – the majority of northern Congressmen voted for the proposal; all but two southerners voted against.

Senator John Calhoun of South Carolina most eloquently expressed the southern response to the Wilmot Proviso and growing sectional tensions. He issued a series of resolutions, in February 1847, that later came to be known as the 'Calhoun Doctrine' or 'The **Platform** of the South'. The main points were:

Platform: Collection of policies put forward by a political party during an election; otherwise known as a manifesto.

- Territories were the common property of all the states.

- Any US citizen should be able to settle in any territory with their property (including slaves) as guaranteed by the Constitution.

- Each state was sovereign and had the right to leave the Union (secede) if it chose to do so.

- If northerners continued to ignore southern interests and threaten slavery, then the South would be justified in leaving the Union.

Between the two extremes of the Wilmot Proviso and the Calhoun Doctrine lay a large group of talented and moderate politicians who were committed to the Union and who were determined to find a solution to the controversy. They were helped by the fact that the two main political parties, the Whigs and the Democrats, contained members from both sections of the Union. The two most likely solutions were:

Popular sovereignty: This would allow the people living in a territory to decide whether they wished to become a slave or free state at the point of applying for statehood.

- either to extend the 36 degree-30 line agreed in the Missouri Compromise to the Pacific coast and so include any new territory secured;

- or to adopt the doctrine of **popular sovereignty**, proposed by the northern Democrat Lewis Cass.

Democracy: A political system in which there are many parties and the people get to choose their government through voting. There is free speech and a free press. The United States and the United Kingdom are democracies.

Popular sovereignty was a solution that fitted in with the commitment to federalism and **democracy**. It provided enough ambiguity so that southerners could feel that slavery was permitted to expand, whilst northerners could be reassured that, given the terrain out west and nature of the settlers, a vote for slavery in the new territories was unlikely. Cass, as Democratic Presidential candidate in 1848, campaigned on the idea. His Whig opponent, Zachary Taylor, expressed no views on the subject – a conscious decision by the Whigs, who wanted to avoid the divisive issue arising during the campaign.

Ominously, a third party – the Free Soil Party – also contested the election and secured 10% of the popular vote, on a platform supporting the Wilmot Proviso and calling for resistance to southern influence and slavery expansion. Taylor won the election and carried states equally in the North and the South, but the issue of slavery expansion remained there for Congress to resolve. Within weeks, the House of Representatives had reaffirmed the Wilmot Proviso and condemned the slave trade in Washington DC, whilst Calhoun had issued another statement supporting slavery that was signed by a third of slave-state representatives.

Tensions were given a specific focus in 1849 when both Californian gold prospectors and Mormons around Salt Lake City applied for statehood. Taylor encouraged them to establish constitutions and apply immediately for statehood. Despite being a southerner and slave-owner himself, Taylor alienated most of his Whig supporters in the South by his refusal to seek compensation for the South if the two states were to be admitted as free states. By the autumn of 1849, the situation was looking very tense. In October of that year, Mississippi urged all slave states to send representatives to a convention to discuss some way of resisting 'Northern aggression'.

When Congress met in December 1849 many southerners were talking openly of secession and invoking the Calhoun Doctrine. Northerners began to raise the stakes over slavery in Washington DC and southerners complained of the non-enforcement of the Slave Fugitive Law (see box).

The 1850 Compromise

The situation in 1850 needed all the reserves of skill and diplomacy that could be mustered if secession or war was to be avoided. Over the next few months, politics was dominated by the 'Great Debate' which finally led to the 'Compromise of 1850'. This was an acceptance by the two main parties and the majority of the country of its 'finality'. In the debate, three of the key political figures of the previous decades were to make their final contributions to American politics:

- 72 year-old Henry Clay, who proposed the Compromise

- 68 year-old Daniel Webster, who provided important northern support

- 68 year-old John Calhoun, who made his last great speech against compromise.

Within two years they were all dead.

Compromise of 1850

Concessions to the North

- California should be admitted as a free state.

- Territory disputed by Texas and New Mexico to be surrendered to New Mexico.

- Abolition of the slave trade (but not slavery) in the District of Columbia.

Concessions to the South

- The remainder of the Mexican Cession area to be formed into the territories of New Mexico and Utah, without restriction on slavery – hence open to popular sovereignty.

- Texas to receive $10 million from the federal government as compensation.

- A more stringent Fugitive Slave Law, going beyond that of 1793.

The Omnibus Bill tried to provide something for all sections of the Union. Clay and Webster made eloquent appeals to both sides to compromise for the sake of the greater cause, the Union. Nevertheless, the Bill was defeated as a single package in the Senate, in July 1850. Clay returned to his home state of Kentucky, ill and dejected. This was not the end of the Bill though. The convention called by Mississippi the previous year went ahead, but it soon became clear that the South did not yet have the appetite to fight. Also, President Taylor died suddenly in July 1850 and his successor, Vice-President Millard Fillmore, appointed Webster Secretary of State and threw himself behind the proposals that had just been defeated. The Democratic senator, Stephen Douglas of Illinois, now took up Clay's cause. Douglas recognised that an omnibus bill would attract the opposition of both southern and northern extremists. Instead, he divided the Bill into its five parts and was able to pass each section by combining the support of one section with the moderates who had supported the Omnibus Bill. Thus by September 1850 all of Clay's original proposals had been passed into law. The Compromise of 1850 resolved all the immediate issues that the late 1840s had thrown up. Douglas rejoiced in its passing: 'Each section has maintained its honour and its rights and both have met on the common ground of justice and compromise.'

In the election of 1852, both national parties agreed to accept the 'finality' of the 1850 Compromise and avoided discussing the slavery question. The Free Soil Party polled over 100,000 fewer votes than in 1848, as a spirit of unionism spread across the country.

The confidence of the unionists can, however, be seen as misplaced. After all, the Compromise was only achieved through political skill, rather than through a genuine acceptance of the legitimacy of each section's view by the other. There were no guiding principles established for the future and the South had certainly not abandoned the central beliefs of the Calhoun Doctrine, even if popular support had taken the wind out of secession for the moment. With the admission of California as a free state the North now had a balance in their favour in the Senate. The main sop to the South, the Slave Fugitive Law, was untested and would need the support of northerners to work.

Thus the 1850 Compromise may have been effective in preventing violence in 1850, but it could only be a permanent solution if subsequent events could be controlled and if the Union had time to establish a spirit of cooperation. It is for these reasons that the historian David Potter has described the Compromise of 1850 as 'an armistice rather than a compromise'. It is also why studying the events that followed is now so critical.

1. How did expansion westward create problems between North and South?

2. Explain why the North and South were able to avoid conflict in the period to 1850?

3.2 Why did sectionalism grow in the 1850s?

The Compromise of 1850, however faulty it may have been, did manage to keep a kind of peace for the next ten years. However, some fighting did break out during the Kansas–Nebraska issue and violence increasingly became a tool the two sections were prepared to employ. John Brown's Raid on Harper's Ferry and the beating of Charles Sumner on the Senate floor (see page 68) demonstrated this. The 1850s were an unhappy decade for the USA. What was needed after the patched-up peace of 1850 was a period of stability and calm. What America got instead was a series of events that polarised opinion between North and South. This led to a growing sense of sectionalism, in which the two sections identified more with the North or South than they did with the Union and came to view almost all the actions and pronouncements of the other section as hostile. As this notion grew on both sides, so perceptions became blurred with reality, while perceived slights became actual ones.

The Kansas–Nebraska Bill

Kansas–Nebraska was a large and unsettled region in the early 1850s, although interest in the area was growing in the period as agricultural and irrigation improvements meant that it had agricultural possibilities. The territory covered the likely route that a northern transcontinental railroad might follow.

Senator Stephen Douglas, the chairman of the Senate Committee on Territories and a prominent Northern Democrat from Illinois, proposed the settlement of the territory in his Kansas–Nebraska Bill to Senate in 1854. Ever since the 1840s, Douglas had been a prominent supporter of western expansion and believed such expansion should not be held up because of sectional disputes. He had been a key figure in getting the 1850 Compromise through Congress and now believed that the last major unsettled territory in the West could be settled with minimal sectional conflict. Douglas also stood to gain personally from the Bill, hoping to strengthen his presidential chances by appearing as the champion of western expansion and improving his position in his home state of Illinois by bringing the transcontinental railroad terminus to Chicago.

In proposing the Bill, Douglas was aware that southerners in Congress were unlikely to be enthusiastic. The area was north of the 36° 30′ line (see map on page 80) and so forbidden to slavery under the Missouri Compromise (the land was unlikely to suit slavery anyway, at least in the northern part). A number of southerners were pushing for a southern transcontinental link. They recognised that the Bill would open up the northern route more effectively. Douglas thus proposed that the whole territory should be admitted as just one state (so avoiding a major free state/slave state imbalance in the Senate) and that the issue of slavery should be settled according to the principle of popular sovereignty (i.e. the Bill ignored the Missouri Compromise). In seeking southern support for what Douglas saw as an essentially northern bill, he accepted two southern amendments that included a rejection of the Missouri Compromise. It was agreed that the territory should be divided into two states – Kansas and Nebraska – since southerners felt that there was at least a possibility of voters choosing to introduce slavery in Kansas, the southern part of the territory. Unfortunately for Douglas, his concessions to the South provoked a hostile reaction among the North who saw southern demands as evidence that they did not accept the terms of the 1850 Compromise. Douglas was branded a traitor to the section and various groups united against the Bill.

The South now took up the Kansas–Nebraska Bill as a cause to fight for, assuming that northern hostility confirmed that it was in the southern interest. They campaigned equally energetically against the North and for its passage.

The Bill dominated congressional debates in 1854. As President, Franklin Pierce faced significant pressure to come down on one side. In the end, recognising the importance of the southern votes to the Democratic Party, he tried to make it a party issue and put pressure on some northern Democrats to support Douglas' Bill. The Bill was passed in May 1854, but the section from which a Congressman came was more significant than the party he belonged to in determining his vote. Ninety per cent of all southern Congressmen voted in favour of the Bill and 64% of all northerners, with the northern Democrats in the House split 44 in favour and 43 against.

Stephen Arnold Douglas (1813–1861)

Democrat who served in the House of Representatives (1843–47) and as a senator for Illinois (1837–61). He urged a compromise on slavery. After losing the presidential race to Abraham Lincoln (1860), Douglas pledged his support to Lincoln's Administration (see definition on page 109). He earned the nickname 'Little Giant' for his support for western expansion.

Franklin Pierce (1804–1869)

14th President of the USA (1852–56), a Democrat. Served in the New Hampshire legislature (1829–33), before holding office in the House of Representatives (1833–37) and the Senate (1837–42). Pierce saw action in the Mexican War of 1846–48. Despite his expansionist foreign policy, North–South tensions grew more intense during his Presidency.

The Kansas–Nebraska Bill thus served to re-ignite the sectional tensions of 1849–50 and confirmed northern fears of a 'slave power' at work. Perhaps most importantly, the Bill weakened the national reputation of the Democrats and encouraged politicians in voting according to section rather than party. Coming as it did just as the national Whig Party went into decline, it meant that one of the reasons why sectional tensions tended to be overcome – the non-sectional appeal of the two-party system – had been undermined. As if to confirm this, the 1854 elections were a disaster for the Democrats in the North where they controlled only two northern **legislatures** after the elections, having controlled all but two before. Furthermore, the number of Democrats from free states fell from 91 to 23, compared to a fall from 67 to 63 in slave states. The Democratic Party was becoming a party that increasingly depended on, and appealed to, the South.

Legislatures: The group of people in a particular state who have the power to make and pass laws.

Growing northern concerns

Before the Kansas–Nebraska Bill, many in the North and the South were prepared to accept the terms of the 1850 Compromise even though they disliked certain elements of it. The abandonment of the Missouri Compromise in 1854 changed all that, and mass meetings appeared in the North to protest against elements of federal policy that seemed to favour the South. Already, northerners had felt uneasy about the expansionist policies that Pierce and the Democrats seemed to be supporting:

● in Cuba (which would almost certainly have joined the union as a slave state);

● the Gadsden Purchase in 1853, where the federal government purchased some land off Mexico for $10 million that would allow a transcontinental railroad to run through the southern states.

A poster advertising *Uncle Tom's Cabin*.

Southerners had opposed attempts to annex Canada and to bring Hawaii into the Union for fear it would have strengthened the free states in Congress, which had also frustrated northerners. As a consequence, arguments that there was a 'slave-power conspiracy' – initially only argued and put about by abolitionists – gained credibility among more moderate northerners, who were prepared to tolerate slavery but did not want to see it spread to the North and threaten the free-labour system there.

The popularity of Harriet Beecher Stowe's anti-slavery novel, *Uncle Tom's Cabin* (which sold 300,000 copies in its first year of publication in 1852), showed a growing concern in the North. It helped to develop the view of slavery as an unacceptable and immoral system that diminished the USA. Northerners were increasingly reluctant to accept the Fugitive Slave Law, especially the requirement that all citizens had to help in the capture and return of runaway slaves. A number of states passed personal liberty laws that prevented local gaols from being used for runaway slaves. There were several outbreaks of violence where mobs tried to prevent federal law officers from returning slaves, especially in the more radical cities such as Boston.

Perhaps the most dramatic illustration of the growing tension between the two sections occurred on the Senate floor itself in May 1856. A southern representative, Preston Brooks, beat unconscious the abolitionist senator Charles Sumner in revenge for a savage verbal attack that Sumner had launched on Senator Andrew Butler, a relative of Brooks. Although fined, Brooks was not expelled and became something of a popular hero in the South. He was re-elected and sent numerous canes with the invitation to hit harder next time. There could have been no clearer image for the North of a brutal southern 'slave power' silencing free speech and challenging the essence of democracy.

'Bleeding Kansas'

It was not long before the simmering tensions boiled over. It was perhaps unsurprising that it should be events in Kansas that were responsible. The settlement of Kansas proceeded far from smoothly and popular sovereignty was found to have delayed, rather than solved, a problem. When it came to voting on a constitution for Kansas, pro-slavery and anti-slavery forces mobilised support both inside and outside the territory to try and influence the outcome. The result was that two different governments and constitutions were established: a pro-slavery one at Shawnee Mission and a free-soil government in Topeka.

Within Kansas, a minor civil war erupted with extreme forces from outside the territory getting involved. Most notorious was the attack on Lawrence, when an attempt to arrest anti-slavery leaders led to several deaths. This was followed by a retaliatory attack on a pro-slavery camp at Pottawatomie Creek by John Brown, who led a small band that murdered five pro-slavery men. The pro-slavery faction now arranged a rigged election for the convention that drew up the constitution of the state, which was boycotted in protest by the anti-slavery faction. As a consequence, the

Lecompton Constitution:
A constitution drawn up in 1857 by settlers in Kansas which would have allowed slavery if Kansas became a state. Anti-slavery settlers refused to take part in a referendum on the Lecompton Constitution, but it was theoretically accepted. In 1858, Congress refused to admit Kansas as a state and the Lecompton Constitution was rejected.

constitution that was drawn up – the **Lecompton Constitution** – protected slave property. By now it was clear to almost everyone that the slavery faction was a minority in the state – a fact supported by both federally appointed governors and by Senator Douglas, the author of the original distress.

Nevertheless, the new Democratic President, James Buchanan, insisted on supporting the Lecompton Constitution and recommended that Kansas enter the Union as a slave state. He was supported in the Senate but the bill failed to pass the House of Representatives and, in a direct referendum in Kansas in 1858, the Constitution was defeated. The troubles within Kansas now died down (Kansas was eventually admitted to the Union in 1861 as a free state, after many southern states had seceded), but a great deal of damage had been done. The issue aroused passions on both sides and created a great deal of anger that now sought outlets. Also, the Democratic Administrations of Pierce and Buchanan had so favoured the slavery view that the Democrats were seriously weakened in the North and looked even more like a party of the South.

The emergence of the Republican Party

By the time of the presidential election of 1856, many northern Democrats were no longer prepared to support their party, especially in the North-West. The Democrat James Buchanan managed to get elected, helped no doubt by his absence while a diplomat in Britain during the Kansas dispute. He did not receive a majority of the popular vote and was helped by the existence of two new parties that had emerged to replace the Whigs: the 'Know Nothing' (American) Party and the Republicans. Both parties began life as single-issue groups that attracted significant support in the North.

The 'Know Nothings' were a nativist party, concerned at the threat they perceived the new immigrants posed to the traditional American way of life. At first, they seemed the most likely to emerge to challenge the Democrats. By 1854, they had over one million members. The Republicans, formally

**James Buchanan
(1761–1868)**
15th President of the USA (1857–61), a Democrat. Member of the House of Representatives (1821–31) and US minister to Russia (1832–34) when he was elected to the Senate. He left his Senate seat to serve as US Secretary of State during the Mexican War (1846–48). When elected President, he could do little to avert the secession of the South over the issue of slavery. This led to the outbreak of Civil War in 1861.

Free-soilers: People who opposed the extension of slavery westward.

created in 1854, were a disparate group of abolitionists, **free-soilers** and former Whigs and northern Democrats who shared a common concern at the spread of slavery and who feared its expansion out west where it might threaten the capitalist system of 'free labour'. They were increasingly convinced that there was a 'slave power' at work and that southerners had gained control of the Democratic Party and were now using it for their own ends in expanding slavery.

In the 1854 elections, both parties fielded candidates but it is unclear precisely which party best commanded the anti-Democratic vote as a number of candidates simply stood as anti-Democrat or actually supported the agenda of both parties. By 1856 though, the Republicans emerged as the stronger group, helped by sectional divisions that now plagued the 'Know Nothings' too. Republicans also expressed concern over the expansion of slavery at the moment that immigration was declining as an issue. Events in Kansas, and Pierce's responses, seemed to confirm the views of the party to the wider and more moderate electorate. Despite the party only having existed for two years, the Republican candidate for President, John Fremont, polled 33% of the vote, 45% in free states, and gained 114 electoral college votes.

The Republicans now emerged as the only serious challengers to the Democrats and began to prepare for a victory in 1860. The 1856 result was important not only because it marked the emergence of the Republicans but also because it showed that they could win an election without winning any votes in the South at all. Fremont had only won 1,196 votes in all the slave states combined. However, because the free states had far greater populations (and therefore more votes in the electoral college), Fremont only needed to win two or three of the five free states Buchanan had won in 1856 (Pennsylvania, New Jersey, Indiana, Illinois and California) to be elected President. None of this was lost on the Republicans, who now set out to broaden their appeal across the North, or the South.

At this point, it is important to avoid seeing the conflict that followed as inevitable. The Democrats had clearly maintained strong pockets of support in the North, and the Kansas dispute was likely to be the last major issue of western expansion. Although tensions were running high in 1856, and each section was seeing the extremists increase their influence as their claims became more believable, the Republicans depended for their support on northerners continuing to believe in the threat of slavery expansion from the South. If Buchanan could defuse the tensions, then the Republicans would be without an issue. Alas for the Union, Buchanan was not only lacking in ability, but events were to occur that would test him still further.

The Dred Scott Case

Within days of Buchanan's inauguration, the Dred Scott decision raised the controversy over slavery to new heights. Dred Scott was a slave from Missouri who had moved with his owner to the northern part of the western territories, where slavery was forbidden under the terms of the Missouri Compromise. Scott sued for his freedom and the Supreme Court, under Chief Justice Taney, ruled on 6 March 1857 that:

> 'No black slave or descendant could be a US citizen and therefore Scott could not bring a case to a federal court. Since a slave was the property of his master, Congress had no constitutional right to deprive that master of his property in the territories.'

The clear implication was that the Missouri Compromise was unconstitutional. Slavery was protected in all federal territories, allowing slave owners to take their slaves anywhere across the territories and to settle with them. This was a clear victory for the South, though it allowed the Republicans to claim that not only the Presidency but also the Supreme Court was controlled by 'slave power'. With five of the nine justices from slave states, and coming at the same time as the controversy over the Lecompton Constitution, such claims were all the more credible. Moderate opinion became increasingly tuned in to Republican claims.

Economic divisions and arguments

In order to secure victory across the North in the next presidential election, the Republicans recognised that they needed to broaden their appeal to include workers in the major industrial cities who did not see slavery expansion as the main issue to determine their vote. Republicans therefore sought to become a fully sectional party of the North, rather than only concerned with the expansion of slavery. They developed a clear economic programme that included higher tariffs to protect northern manufacturing industry from foreign competition, a transcontinental railroad to link Chicago with California and support for internal improvements in communications and transport. They were helped by responses in the South to abolitionist attacks on slavery – the most worrying of which had been Hinton Rowan Helper's contemporary book *The Impending Crisis in the South, How to Meet It*. Helper was a North Carolinian who argued that small-scale farmers and workers suffered from slavery. His arguments threatened the internal stability of the South. Southerners responded by attacking the northern 'factory system' for making 'industrial slaves' of the workers who were disposable once they had been drained of their energy. They contrasted it with a southern slavery system that provided welfare in return for work. Thus the controversy was being elevated to a clash between two economic systems.

The dispute became more dramatic in 1857 when a financial crisis (the 'Panic of 1857') was followed by an economic depression for northern industry. Republicans were quick to blame the low tariffs of the Democrats for the problem. The South, on the other hand, did not suffer in the depression and felt that their system was even more vindicated. 'King Cotton' became the rallying cry. Southerners became dangerously confident that their economic system was better than the North's and that they could easily survive alone if they had to. Just as the northern Republicans were beginning to convince mainstream opinion of the dangers of the 'slave power', so were southern extremists ('Fire-eaters') making the case for secession if it should come to that.

The Lincoln–Douglas debates of 1858

Until 1858, Abraham Lincoln had been a relatively unknown lawyer and politician from the frontier, serving in the Illinois Legislature but only

**Abraham Lincoln
(1809–1865)**

16th president of the USA, a Republican. He was President at a very difficult time. During the Civil War (1861–65), he coordinated the Union campaign against the South, leading the North to victory. He fought hard to end slavery, which was finally abolished in 1865. Lincoln also played a vital role in the 1862 Homestead Act, which was to have a huge impact on settlement in the West (see page 44). He displayed considerable skills in working with people in his government with different beliefs and opinions. Following an announcement that he favoured some blacks having the vote in one state, Lincoln was assassinated by an actor and Confederate sympathiser, John Wilkes Booth.

once (1846–48) in the House of Representatives in Washington. He came to national prominence in 1858 as the Republican candidate standing against Senator Douglas in the senate race for Illinois. With Douglas' national reputation, the contest received national coverage. This was made more dramatic by a series of debates – seven in all – that took place during the contest. Douglas won the election, but the contest and the debates had an important impact on national politics.

Lincoln came to national prominence as a result. In attacking a skilled and prominent figure, he attracted supporters who saw him as a potential Republican candidate for the Presidency. Supporters began to put forward his name as a challenger and he was sure of good 'name-recognition' when it came to the Republican Convention in 1860.

Douglas' attempts to portray Lincoln as an abolitionist and supporter of racial equality (both clearly untrue when one looks at the speeches) made southerners fear the election of Lincoln as President in 1860 more than they need to have done. Although Lincoln never denied his personal disapproval of slavery, he did not support abolition in the South. Yet the very name of Lincoln became associated, because of press reporting in the South, with the more violent extremes of northern abolitionism.

In order to win moderate votes in Illinois, Douglas was forced to claim that the Dred Scott decision did not mean that slavery could exist in the territories. This view – known as the Freeport Doctrine because the debate took place there – played well in Illinois. It would have been soon forgotten but, because the contest was being watched nationally, it under-mined Douglas' standing with southern Democrats, who were now unlikely to endorse him for President.

John Brown and Harper's Ferry

The attack on a **federal arsenal** at Harper's Ferry, Virginia, in October 1859 by abolitionist John Brown became a defining event of the last year of peace and union. Brown's attack ended in failure and he was hanged, along with other members of his group, in December 1859, having been found guilty of treason. He had hoped to gain enough weapons from Harper's Ferry to launch a slave rebellion in the Upper South. However, he was caught too early and, anyway, there were few signs of slave revolt. Although the Republican leaders, including Lincoln, made clear their opposition to Brown, it became evident that he had received financial support from various prominent abolitionists. Brown was transformed into a martyr by northern abolitionists and writers. For southerners, despite the position of the Republicans, it became further evidence of northern hostility to slavery. The 'fire-eaters' were able to present the incident as proof that the North was committed to the abolition of slavery across the South and not just to the limiting of its expansion.

John Brown (1800–1859)
US slavery abolitionist. On the night of 16 October 1859, with 18 men, he seized the government arsenal at Harper's Ferry in West Virginia. His apparent intent was to distribute weapons to runaway slaves who would then defend a stronghold that Brown hoped would become a republic of former slaves. On 18 October, US marines under Colonel Robert E. Lee stormed the arsenal. Brown was tried and hanged on 2 December, becoming a martyr. He is the hero of the song 'John Brown's Body' (written in about 1860).

Federal arsenal: A place for storing ammunition and weapons to be used by the US Army.

1. **What impact did the Kansas–Nebraska Act of 1854 have on the conflict between North and South?**

2. **To what extent was civil war inevitable by the end of the 1850s?**

3.3 Why did Lincoln win the presidential election of 1860?

The election of Abraham Lincoln as the first Republican President, in November 1860, was very much the trigger for the secession of the Deep South. It set in motion events that would lead directly to the Civil War itself. Within two months of the results being known, South Carolina had passed a resolution for secession. Thus, of all single events that can be seen as a cause of the Civil War, this is in many ways the most critical.

Lincoln had not been favourite to get the Republican nomination, but a determination to prevent the front-runner, William Seward, from being nominated, saw Lincoln emerge as the stop-Seward candidate. He was certainly helped by the Republican Convention being held in Lincoln's home state of Illinois. By the third ballot, Lincoln had overtaken Seward and secured the nomination.

He now faced three rivals for the top job:

● Stephen Douglas, the candidate of the Northern Democrats and his old rival from 1858;

● John Breckinridge, the Southern Democrat and current Vice-President from Kentucky;

● John Bell, fighting for the Constitutional Union, an organisation dedicated to saving the Union by means of compromise.

The Democrats divided

The Democrats needed to be united to have a hope of winning. However, it was clear from the beginning of the year that this last, great, cross-sectional institution was likely to go the way of the Whigs under the strain of an election campaign. Southern Democrats could not stomach the favoured and obvious candidate of most Northerners, Stephen Douglas. Despite his high-profile victory over Lincoln in the 1858 Senate race in Illinois, southerners associated Douglas with the hated Freeport Doctrine voiced in the Kansas–Nebraska dispute. Many in the Deep South were determined to have a specific commitment on slavery in the party programme. These divisions led ultimately to a walkout by many Southern delegates at the Democratic Convention at Charleston in April 1860. Following this, no candidate secured victory to become the presidential candidate despite 57 ballots.

The remaining delegates agreed to meet again, which they did in Baltimore, Maryland, in June. Tempers had not cooled. The Southern delegates, increasingly assertive and determined to defend their 'peculiar institution', were in no mood to accept a Northern candidate, particularly Douglas. They were equally determined to see defence of slavery on the platform. There was another Southern walkout, which at least made it easy for the remaining Democrats to agree on Douglas as their candidate. They quickly adopted popular sovereignty and a defence of the Slave Fugitive Law as their platform. The southern Democrats now held their own convention, also in Baltimore, at which they nominated John Breckinridge of Kentucky. They adopted a platform protecting property (slavery) in the territories and calling for the annexation of Cuba, a slave-holding Spanish colony.

By the summer of 1860, the Democrats had clearly weakened themselves and their chances of victory seemed slim. However, a Republican victory was by no means certain. Breckinridge was not as limited sectionally as one might have thought. Indeed, former Democrat Presidents Pierce and Buchanan and the majority of Northern Democrat Congressmen supported him. Douglas, too, could still win the race. The split of the more extreme southerners actually made him a more effective candidate in the North, whilst it was by no means certain that he could not win some of the border slave states, such as Missouri and Delaware. The Republicans could not be sure of victory just because the Democrats were divided, and it was certainly a possibility that no candidate would get a majority in the electoral college. If that happened, then the decision would go to the House of Representatives – where anything might happen.

The appeal of the Republicans

The Republicans had learnt two important lessons from the 1856 presidential election: that they could win without taking a single slave state and that they would have to broaden their appeal beyond being an anti-slavery expansion party if they were to carry free states that traditionally voted Democrat. In 1856, the only free states that the Republicans did not win were Pennsylvania, Illinois, Indiana, New Jersey and California.

The party platform of the Republicans was deliberately moderate. There was a specific promise not to interfere with slavery where it already existed, and Republican speakers throughout the campaign repeated this. The Republicans even took care to criticise John Brown's raid and one of their leading politicians confirmed his party's opposition to 'hostile aggression upon the constitutional rights of any state'. Lincoln himself was a model moderate for the Republicans, taking mainstream opinions on slavery expansion, prohibition and immigration.

Given our knowledge of what followed, there is a danger of overplaying the importance of slavery and constitutional issues in the election. The Republican Party developed an economic position that deliberately appealed to targeted voters in the critical states. A pledge to introduce free 160-acre homesteads was included with the slogan 'Vote yourself a farm'. A commitment to building, with federal subsidy, a transcontinental railroad was designed to appeal to the two states likely to be at either end – Illinois and California. A programme of higher tariffs was promised and was a vote-winner in the industrial cities of New Jersey and Pennsylvania. Furthermore, a deliberate attempt was made to associate Douglas and Breckinridge with the sleaze and corruption of the previous Buchanan Administration. 'Honest Abe' was an important symbol of a cleaner and fresher start in politics, even if in reality the Republicans had a good number of corruption scandals to keep covered themselves.

Certainly, by the time it came to vote, it could be said that the Republicans had fought a clear and united campaign that appealed to all opinion in the North – not just to radical opponents of slavery and its extension.

The campaign

The actual campaign of 1860 was a strange affair. There were four candidates nationally but it was in fact a contest between Lincoln and Douglas in the North, Bell and Breckinridge in the South. Douglas hoped that he could hold on to the states won by the Democrats in the North in 1856, whilst reassuring the Southern states that he posed no threat to slavery and so securing their vote as the only candidate to stop Lincoln. He even chose as his vice-presidential candidate Herschel V. Johnson, the former Governor of Georgia. Unfortunately, he succeeded in neither aim. As Brian Holden Reid writes, in *The Origins of the American Civil War* (1996), 'the polarisation of voters around sectional issues resulted in Douglas falling through the middle'. Douglas was in danger of coming second everywhere, and therefore not getting the crucial electoral college votes.

Lincoln played the election traditionally, by not entering the fray and by allowing his supporters to present him as the westerner who had risen from the log cabin and was on his way to the White House. Both sides presented the other as extreme and a danger to the other section. Republicans talked again of the dangers of a 'slave power', whilst Democrats spoke of the 'black Republican, free love, free Nigger Party'.

When it seemed, from state elections in October, that the Republicans might win, Douglas all but acknowledged the result and 'went South to save the Union'. He urged Southerners to support Lincoln's inauguration and made a passionate case for maintaining the Union. His campaigns for election and against secession were both in vain.

How big was Lincoln's victory in 1860?

In the electoral college, Lincoln won a convincing victory; there would be no need to resort to the House of Representatives. With 180 votes, he was well ahead of Breckinridge with 72 votes. Douglas had indeed fallen 'through the middle', achieving 30% of the popular vote but securing the electoral college votes of only Missouri and three votes of New Jersey's seven.

However, Lincoln was a minority President. He won only 40% of the popular vote. His victory was also confined to the North. In 10 states he secured no popular votes at all and he achieved miserly numbers in Kentucky, Virginia and Maryland. Even in the free states his vote was not conclusive. He got 54% of the vote in the Northern states to Douglas' 36%. Even Breckinridge gained 5% of the votes in the free states. The combined votes of Breckinridge and Douglas, the two Democratic candidates, was 47%, compared with Lincoln's 40%.

Whilst this may give the impression that Lincoln only won because of the split Democratic vote, some historians have been quick to point out that Lincoln would have won in the electoral college even if the Democratic votes had been added together. Lincoln only won three states – New Jersey, Oregon and California – because of split votes and the other states would have been enough to give him victory, albeit by a smaller margin. This is a fair point, but not totally convincing since we must assume that a united Democratic Party would have gone into the election with greater confidence and may well have won more popular votes in such circumstances. The truth is that we will never know. What we do know is that Lincoln now found himself a minority and sectional President. For those in the South who favoured secession, the chance now presented itself.

That the election made secession automatic is not a fair conclusion. The election was not a particularly sectional affair. Breckinridge did not secure a majority of the votes in the slave states; 55% had voted for pro-Union candidates, mainly Bell with 593,000 votes. Anyway, the results when taken as a whole did not spell disaster for the South. The Southerners still controlled the Supreme Court and neither House of Congress had a Republican majority. Secession and civil war may have been brought closer, but there was nothing inevitable about either in November 1860.

> Explain why the Republicans won the 1860 presidential election.

3.4 How did the election of Lincoln lead to the outbreak of war?

It is generally thought that Lincoln's election led to Southern Secession and that that led inevitably to war itself. Such an assessment will not, however, do. There were three phases to secession:

1. The decision of South Carolina to secede, which happened within weeks of Lincoln's election.

2. The decisions of six further slave states to join with South Carolina, which happened in the early weeks of 1861.

3. This led to the formation of the Confederacy in February 1861 and to the secession of a further four states in May/June 1861.

It was only in April 1861, six months after Lincoln's election, that the first shots of the Civil War were actually fired. During that six-month period there had been serious attempts at compromise, most significantly the Crittenden proposals, and much soul-searching from men on both sides of the conflict. America had dealt with crises like this before in 1850, 1819 and 1832, and most citizens assumed it would deal with it again. The purpose of this section is to see how events between Lincoln's election and the final secession led to the outbreak of fighting and then to all-out war. It is interesting to consider how much the conflict might, even at this stage, have been prevented.

The early secessions and formation of the Confederacy

The response of South Carolina was probably no surprise to anyone. The much-publicised threats to secede were quickly followed through. Within four days of Lincoln's election, the Legislature of South Carolina had voted unanimously to secede. This was confirmed, again unanimously, at a special convention held at Charleston in December. Thus, on 20 December 1860, South Carolina became the first state to leave the USA. That did not, of course, mean that any other would follow suit. The South Carolinians had already made their reputation for defiance in the Nullification Crisis in the 1830s. Then, South Carolina had been left to stand alone by the other southern states. It could easily have happened again. The South Carolinians were themselves aware of this. At the same time as they voted to secede, they appointed commissioners to lobby elsewhere and to prepare for a general convention of seceded states in the new year.

A debate now raged through the South. Through the winter of 1860–61, secessionists debated with **cooperationists** throughout the southern states. The pattern in all six seceding states was similar: in all but Texas elections were held for a convention to decide on whether to secede (Texas called a referendum to confirm a decision made by the Legislature). Even where the voting was close, as in Georgia for example, the conventions voted overwhelmingly for secession. Once the decision was taken, most southerners then pledged themselves to the decision. By the beginning of February 1861, Mississippi, Florida, Alabama, Georgia, Louisiana and Texas had all voted to join South Carolina in seceding. The seven rebel states met in Montgomery, Alabama on 4 February 1861 and declared their intention to form a new country, the Confederate States of America.

The Constitution, ratified by April, was modelled on the USA with more explicit protection of slavery and states' rights. The Stars and Bars were adopted, a new army and currency established, and Jefferson Davis was adopted as President (inaugurated on 18 February). Davis was a former Senator and cabinet member, as well as being a graduate of West Point (US military academy). His Vice-President, Alexander Stephens of Georgia, had been a leading anti-secessionist. From the start, the majority of Confederate leaders were anxious not to provoke the North. They sought a moderate reputation in the hope they might eventually entice the less enthusiastic Upper South states to join them. Thus, in his inauguration speech, Davis asked that the Confederacy be left alone. But Lincoln had no intention of doing that.

Attempts at compromise

Crises over the Union had been faced before, and the customary attempts at compromise now began again. Politicians had solved the problem in 1819 and 1850, surely they would do so again. Some historians have argued that this was still possible in 1861 and that it was the poor quality of the politicians at the time that allowed a crisis to escalate into war. This idea of 'blundering politicians' focuses on several figures, not least the President at the time, James Buchanan, whose inactivity in dealing with the rebels or taking a lead in finding compromise has been criticised both then and since. Lincoln, too, can be blamed. He would have nothing to do with the most

Cooperationsts: Those who supported a compromise solution with the northern states.

Jefferson Davis (1808–1889)
US politician; President of the short-lived Confederate States of America (1861–65). Served in US Army before becoming a cotton planter in Mississippi. Davis was leader of the Southern Democrats in the Senate from 1857. He was a defender of 'humane' slavery. In 1860, he issued a declaration in favour of secession from the USA. During the American Civil War, Davis showed strong leadership. He was imprisoned for two years after the War. Known for his fiery temper. His call for conscription in the South raised protests that he was a military dictator.

serious attempt at compromise – the one led by Senator John Crittenden of Kentucky. Crittenden was in a strong position to find compromise. He was a slave-owning unionist from a border state and had sympathy with southern views whilst disapproving of secession. In December 1860, Congress met and Crittenden's proposals were put forward in a Senate which now excluded delegates from the states of the Lower South.

These Crittenden Proposals were clearly designed to reassure the South. They extended the Missouri Compromise line of 36 degree-30 to the Pacific, so allowing slavery below the line in all present territories plus those 'hereafter to be acquired'. This would give slave-owners protection in all southern territories while prohibiting slavery north of the line. It also meant that the possible expansion of the USA southwards into Mexico and Cuba could see slavery expanding as a force in the Union. A constitutional amendment was added, guaranteeing slavery where it existed, even in Washington DC, with federal compensation awarded to slave-holders if slaves escaped.

These proposals were flatly rejected by the Republicans, including Lincoln, and the amendments were defeated 25–23 in the Senate and 113–80 in the House of Representatives. It is hard to see how Lincoln could have supported such proposals given the platform he had been elected on, but it is clear that his outright opposition to them did nothing but bring the conflict closer. There were other attempts at reform. For example, in February 1861 a Peace Convention was called in Washington, but after three weeks' deliberations a compromise remarkably similar to Crittenden's proposals was defeated in Congress. One is probably forced to agree with historian David Potter when he wrote, 'given the momentum of secession and the fundamental set of Republicanism, it is probably safe to say that compromise was impossible from the start'.

Attitudes in the North

Northerners who had feared slavery expansion suddenly had a new issue to debate, secession. Some Northerners believed that the South was better left alone – let the Confederates go it alone and have a state free of the cancer of slavery. Most Southerners had expected the North to take this view too. But this was not the view of the President-elect, nor of the majority of people in the northern states. Northerners had seen the Union as perpetual – individual states had surrendered their sovereignty when they joined the Union. If states could simply secede whenever they felt like it, then the result would be **anarchy** and coherent government could never take place. The attitude of the 'Cincinnati News' is typical when they wrote:

> 'The doctrine of secession is anarchy. If the minority have the right to break up the Government at pleasure, because they have not had their own way, there is an end of all government.'

The majority might have agreed on their determination not to accept secession, but that did not mean they agreed on how they should now respond. Only a minority wanted an immediate dispatch of troops to the South. Most supported the deliberate inaction of both Buchanan and later Lincoln, who spent most of the weeks before and after his inauguration (on 4 March 1861) worrying about appointments rather than an impending war.

Most Northerners believed the South had over-reached itself, that once it became clear that the Upper South would not join them in their Confederacy they would return, tail between legs, to the union. It was probably that thinking which persuaded them not to take compromise solutions seriously. It was also that thinking which meant events were

Anarchy: Where nobody pays attention to any rules or laws. Anarchists advocate a society based upon free association and voluntary cooperation between groups and individuals.

allowed to drift regarding federal property. Yet again, the mistaken perceptions of both sides were going to lead to an increase in rage. The South was serious about secession, just as the North was serious about not tolerating it. Neither side yet appreciated the intent of the other but, for the sake of saving time and of keeping the Upper South on side, neither said anything yet about it.

What happened at Fort Sumter?

Confederates: Supporters of the Confederate States of America, which were created in Montgomery, Alabama in February 1861.

Garrisons: Groups of soldiers whose job is to guard the town or building in which they live.

As the crisis deepened over the winter of 1860–61, most federal forts and arsenals that were based in the South were taken over by the **Confederates** without any trouble. The exceptions to this were Fort Pickens off the coast of Florida and Fort Sumter in Charleston Harbour. Both forts continued to have **garrisons** loyal to the Union. Fort Sumter became the focal point of tensions between North and South that eventually led to the first shots of the Civil War itself.

After December 1860, the garrison at Fort Sumter lost all contact with the federal government but its commander, Major Robert Anderson, was determined to defend federal property from the South Carolinians despite having fewer than 100 men. He withdrew from other federal fortifications in the harbour in order to concentrate on Fort Sumter. Initial attempts by President Buchanan to send supplies and reinforcements to Sumter led to a stand-off in January 1861. By March, Anderson was forced to send a message to Lincoln saying that he only had four to six weeks of supplies left. This was a critical moment. The Confederates could not allow the continuation of a northern-held fortress in the middle of one of their major ports. So they would not let reinforcements through. However, Lincoln knew that if he did not supply the fortress then he would look weak, only days into his Presidency. Yet a conflict with South Carolina might encourage the Upper South states to join with the Confederates, if they felt Lincoln was forcing the Union on the South.

Lincoln's Cabinet was divided. His generals advised withdrawal on the grounds that they could not hold the fort if South Carolina chose to become hostile. Lincoln dithered and changed his mind at least once, but by the end of March he had taken the fateful decision that he would re-provision (not reinforce) Forts Sumter and Pickens. On 4 April, Anderson was told by Lincoln to stay firm and on 9 April a naval expedition set out to relieve Fort Sumter. On 11 April, the Confederate Commander in Charleston, General Beauregard, acting under orders from Jefferson Davis, demanded Anderson's surrender. Anderson's refusal meant that, at 4.30 a.m., the two sides opened fire on one another and continued to do so for the following 33 hours. By the end of that time, Anderson was forced to surrender and he withdrew to Washington. However, the moment of truth had arrived. Although no one was killed in the exchanges at Fort Sumter, the period of tension had come to an end. The first shots of a four-year war had been fired.

How did the Upper South respond?

Both Lincoln and Davis issued calls to arms in the wake of the attack on Fort Sumter and both were overwhelmed with support and volunteers. However, immediate attention focused on what the Upper South would now do. Lincoln declared, on 19 April, that he was dealing with a rebellion and ordered an immediate blockade of the Southern rebel states. This put the Upper South on the spot. Slave states which had chosen, until that point, to remain in the Union, had to decide which side they would take. Most significantly, this applied to Virginia – the oldest state, possessing more industrial strength than the rest of the Confederacy combined. Most of the inhabitants of the Upper South preferred to remain in the Union themselves, but accepted the principle of the Calhoun Doctrine which said that their fellow Southerners had the right to secede. Now Lincoln was requiring them to take arms and support a war to force fellow southern states back into the Union. The debate in the Upper South took place reluctantly against a feeling that Lincoln had pushed them into an unnecessary corner.

The Upper South took stock. Four states – Virginia, North Carolina, Arkansas and Tennessee – now followed the Lower South into the Confederacy. The four remaining slave states stayed in the Union with varying degrees of enthusiasm. Delaware was always likely to support the Union, with only 2% of its people holding slaves. The situation was more tense and uncertain in Maryland, Missouri and Kentucky. Kentucky tried for a time to remain neutral, while Missouri remained in the Union despite its pro-Confederate governor. Generally pro-Confederate, Maryland had voted for Breckinridge in 1860 and, on 19 April, riots had broken out in Baltimore when volunteer troops from Massachusetts had passed through (causing, incidentally, the first casualties of the Civil War when four soldiers and 12 civilians were killed).

Lincoln could not, however, afford to lose Maryland. Had he done so, he would have been forced to abandon Washington as a capital since it was between Virginia and Maryland. Working with the pro-Union Governor, Lincoln took drastic action, arresting potential rebels and suspending *habeas corpus*. By the summer, Maryland had been secured for the North. It is hard now to underestimate the importance of the decision of these states. Had the Confederacy remained the Lower South only, it is difficult to see how an effective war could have been waged, certainly over a sustained period of time. Equally, the decisions of Maryland, Kentucky and Missouri not to join the South deprived the Confederates of an extra 45% white population and a massive 80% increase in manufacturing capacity.

Why did the southern states secede?

There was no single motive behind the decision of the southern states to secede. It is important to distinguish between the motives of the Deep South, who seceded in the aftermath of Lincoln's election, and the Upper South who only seceded after the President had declared war. Several key issues can nonetheless be identified:

● The determination of South Carolina to leave the Union on the election of Lincoln but to ensure that this time they would not be left alone meant that South Carolinians actively canvassed the other southern states. Certainly, states were emboldened by the feeling that they were not alone and the Confederacy existed as a home to go to.

● A feeling that anti-slavery Northerners were beginning to dominate the Union was in many ways the main concern of the Deep South. It was not that Lincoln himself threatened slavery immediately (though many accepted his demonisation that had started with the debates against Lincoln), but the fact that a northern anti-slaver could be elected without any southern votes was an ominous sign for the future. The powers of a Republican president could be used against the South in other ways, such as in the appointment of Supreme Court judges and postmasters in the South.

● A confidence grew – encouraged by the 1857 crisis and King Cotton – that the South could survive alone, especially if it had control over its tariff levels. In some cases, southerners actually felt that their economy was being held back by northern economic concerns and they expected not only to survive but also to experience economic growth.

1. Did President Lincoln's election make civil war inevitable?

2. Why did the states of the Upper South secede after the attack on Fort Sumter in April 1861?

- The work of the 'fire-eaters' created a sense of momentum that carried a number of southerners along.

- The feeling that compromise had finally resolved sectional tensions in 1819 and 1850 meant that a number of moderates were slow to wake up to the seriousness of intent of southern secessionists until it was too late.

- There was a genuine belief in the Calhoun Doctrine that particularly motivated the Upper South. Although they did not necessarily share the concerns about Lincoln that the Deep South felt, they were not prepared to fight to force the Deep South to return to the Union. They respected the right of those states to secede, though many in the Upper South hoped for a subsequent compromise to allow them to return.

3.5 What were the relative strengths of the sides on the eve of war?

Historians have tended to look at the formidable balance of resources between North and South in 1861 and conclude that the defeat of the South was almost inevitable from the start. Indeed, the historian Shelby Foote writes, in *The Civil War* (1991), of the North winning 'with one hand behind its back'. This was not, however, how contemporaries from either side, or abroad, saw things at the time. It was only as the Civil War drew on that the resource advantage of the North became clear.

What advantages was the South seen to have at the start?

The Confederacy was seen to have several advantages at the start:

- They expected to be able to rely on cotton exports – at an all-time high in 1860 – to sustain them. It was expected that those European states that relied on cotton imports from the South, most significantly Britain, would be encouraged to recognise and support the Confederate Government.

- The nature of the Civil War was that the Union had to fight in the South in order to enforce federal authority, while the Confederates only had to defend their territory. Since the Confederacy was large (750,000 square miles), warfare favoured the defender.

- There were no obvious targets for the North to attack (except perhaps the capital, Richmond). This was a much greater task than that facing the South, who simply had to resist for long enough to convince the North to abandon their struggle.

- The South had a more obvious cause to fight for: they were defending their way of life, as they saw it. Almost all southerners, including those who had opposed secession, supported the fight against the North in 1861. Morale and determination were higher among ordinary southerners than in the North, where the cause of **federalism** was an abstract battlecry.

Federalism: Belief or support for a federal system of government (i.e. central government rather than state control).

- There was a feeling that the South and southern men were more suited to a military campaign. The assumption was that farmers, who were used to guns and the outdoors, would make better soldiers than factory workers. In addition, there was a strong military tradition in

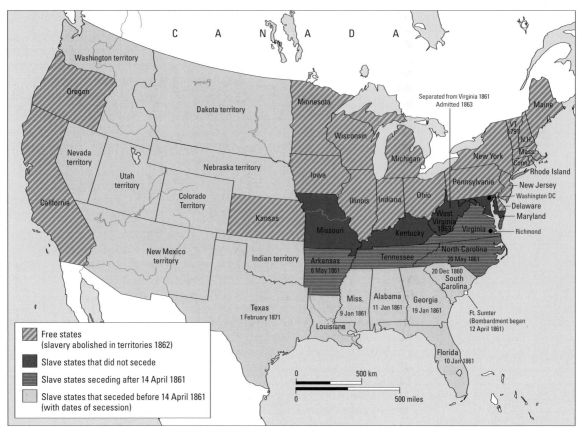

The United States on the eve of
the Civil War

the South. Southerners dominated the military colleges and the higher
ranks of the US Army. Many southerners had fought successfully in
the recent war with Mexico.

● The North had only 44% of its male population in military service in
1864, compared with 90% in the South.

● The slavery system also meant that a greater proportion of men from
the South could fight without having such a detrimental effect on
agricultural production.

In addition to these advantages, there were plenty of examples from military
history of smaller, less well-resourced nations beating larger powers.
Southerners could thus start the campaign in better heart than most later
commentators gave them credit for (hindsight is a wonderful thing!). For
the South the crucial thing was to induce war-weariness in the North as
early as possible, so that pressure could be put on the northern leadership to
abandon the campaign to coerce the southern states into the Union. Firm
defence and resilience was what was needed, rather than any dramatic
capture of major northern centres such as New York and Boston.

What advantages did the North have at the start?

There is, however, no doubting that the North had significant advantages
over the South, especially in the longer term.

● The North had an overwhelming superiority of numbers. The
population of the northern states was 22 million, compared with the
southerners 9 million. The South was restricted further by their refusal

to use slaves as soldiers. The superiority of numbers was not only a matter of troop numbers, it also meant that industrial and agricultural production would be able to sustain wartime levels more easily.

● The South had fewer major cities than the North (only New Orleans had a population greater than 50,000) and industry was confined to the mining area around the Appalachian mountains. By contrast, in 1860 the North produced 94% of US pig iron and over 90% of coal and firearms, as well as 80% of the country's wheat. With twice as much railroad mileage too, the North could clearly arm, supply and transport its forces far more effectively than the Confederacy.

● The North also dominated at sea, both in terms of the navy and merchant navy. With the industrial imbalance, the South needed to import wheat and food but the northern blockade – even though it was never 100% effective – severely limited such opportunities. Also, the South was unable to export its main product, cotton, which it needed in order to get foreign currency and foreign goods.

● Abraham Lincoln's political skill managed to keep three states – Maryland, Missouri and Kentucky – on the side of the Union, or at least out of the Confederate camp. This came about despite strong sentiment from large parts of these three slave states. (The allegiance of Delaware was always likely to be to the North and slavery had all but died out there.) A combination of firm action when needed and gentle treading at other times worked effectively in keeping all three states officially in the Union. This was important for resources (they would have greatly helped the Confederacy industrially), population balance (Missouri, in particular, had a large population of southern migrants) and geography. If Maryland had become part of the Confederacy then the Union capital in Washington DC would have been surrounded by enemy territory (see map opposite). Similarly, Kentucky and Missouri were critical to the campaigns out west. They acted as a buffer to any southern attempts to reach the Mid-West grain belt.

1. What do you regard as the most important advantage the North had at the start of the Civil War? Explain your answer.

2. Given the advantages of the North over the South, how do you account for the long duration of the Civil War?

Most of the advantages that the North had in terms of resources would only become apparent as the Civil War went on. Although both sides set out in 1861 anticipating and planning a short campaign, it was the South that was most likely to suffer from the stalemate of 1861–62. Even though actual casualties in the early battles were, on the whole, worse for the North than the South, the Confederacy often lost a greater proportion of their available troops. Thus the apparent early victories of the South were often won at a greater cost in the long term. This imbalance between the two sides did not mean that the North was guaranteed victory, but it did dictate southern strategy, for Generals Lee and Davis were aware from the start that they needed to deliver quick blows that might destroy the morale of northern voters; hence the ill-fated attacks on Antietam (September 1862) and Gettysburg (July 1863). Lincoln, on the other hand, had to worry more about sustaining morale than victory in the field (though, of course, the two were linked). Both sides were well aware of attrition favouring the side with the greater numbers and resources.

3.6 How did the two sides perform in the military campaigns?

Early Confederate successes

Both sides anticipated a quick war. Lincoln only requested men to enlist for three months when they signed up. It seemed that the decisive battles would take place in northern Virginia as the two capitals, Richmond and Washington, were only 98 miles apart. The aim of Lincoln and his advisers was to capture Richmond quickly and then force the Confederates to seek peace. The Confederates, however, were highly effective at preventing a Union breakthrough in the early years of the Civil War. They were able to make their own attacks on the North in September 1862.

The first major battle of the war, Bull Run (or First Manassas) on 21 July 1861, saw a Union army of 30,000 repulsed as they tried to march south to Richmond. They were forced to retreat back to Washington DC. It was at this battle that the southern officer Thomas 'Stonewall' Jackson earned his nickname for the brave way in which he and his troops held their ground 'like a stonewall'. Although the Confederates did not follow up the northern retreat with an attack on Washington, it was an important southern victory which showed Lincoln that he could not expect to force the South to return quickly to the Union.

Lincoln appointed George B. McClellan (at only 34) to head the Army of the Potomac for the planned attack on Richmond the following year, 1862. McClellan set about using the winter to restore morale and to create an effective and organised army of 150,000. He had learned his tactics from the Crimean War, and was determined to avoid full frontal assaults. He had learned sooner than most that modern warfare was increasingly favouring the defender. Determined to avoid a repeat of Bull Run, which he put down to over-confidence, McClellan's campaigning in 1862 ended up being over-cautious and indecisive. Urged on by Lincoln, he finally moved against Richmond in April 1862, when he decided to attack from the **peninsula** to the south of the city. With this in mind, McClellan ferried his troops down river to Fortress Monroe and laid siege to Yorktown.

Whilst McClellan was besieging Yorktown, the Confederates had time to reinforce and defend Richmond. By the time McClellan took Yorktown (which the Confederates had by then evacuated, happy to have delayed the Union attack) and began to move northwards up the peninsula, he had lost the initiative. By May 1862 he was within 20 miles of Richmond, but he preferred to wait for reinforcements despite outnumbering Confederate forces 2:1. The reinforcements, however, did not come for

---

Thomas 'Stonewall' Jackson (1824–1863)
Confederate general in the American Civil War. He acquired his nickname at the First Battle of Bull Run (21 July 1861), from the firmness with which his soldiers resisted the attack by northern troops. In 1862, Jackson organised the Shenandoah Valley campaign and assisted Robert E. Lee's invasion of Maryland. He also helped to defeat General Joseph Hooker's Union army at the Battle of Chancellorsville, Virginia (1863), but was fatally wounded by one of his soldiers in the confusion of battle.

Peninsula: A body of land surrounded on three sides by water.

George B. McClellan (1826–1885)
Civil War general, commander-in-chief of Union forces (1861–62). He was first dismissed by President Lincoln after retreating from the planned attack on Richmond in May 1862. He was asked by Lincoln to resume command of Union forces after his successor, John Pope, suffered heavy defeats at the Second Battle of Bull Run. McClellan was dismissed for a second time by Lincoln after he delayed for five weeks in following up his victory over the Confederate General Lee at Antietam. McClellan was the Democrat Presidential candidate against Lincoln in 1864.

Robert E. Lee (1807–1870)
Confederate general in the American Civil War. Earlier he had served in the Mexican War and was responsible for suppressing John Brown's raid on Harper's Ferry in 1859 (see page 71). At the outbreak of the Civil War he joined the Confederate army of the South. In 1862, as commander of the army of North Virginia, he won the Seven Days' Battle, defending Richmond (Confederate capital) against General McClellan's Union forces. He also won victories at Fredricksburg and Chancellorsville (1863) and at Cold Harbor (1864). He was besieged in Petersburg (June 1864–April 1865) and surrendered to General Grant at Appomattax courthouse on 9 April.

'Stonewall' Jackson had been busy in the Shenandoah Valley with 18,000 men, diverting 60,000 Unionist soldiers in a series of battles.

When the Confederates began to counter-attack in June, under the new leader of the Confederate Army of North Virginia, General Robert E. Lee, McClellan decided he could not succeed. He retreated back down the peninsula. President Lincoln, frustrated at the lack of action, took the opportunity to replace McClellan with General John Pope.

Pope was, however, no more successful than McClellan. At the end of August 1862, he suffered a heavy defeat at the hands of Confederate generals Jackson and Longstreet in the Second Battle of Bull Run (or Second Manassas). Lincoln, faced with little alternative, asked McClellan to resume command.

General Lee now decided to follow up his victories by taking the war into the North. He invaded Maryland with 40,000 troops early in September, leaving Jackson to capture the federal arsenal at Harper's Ferry with a smaller force. Lee hoped that by marching into Maryland he would take the fight out of Virginia (thus protecting the harvest there). He would be moving the fighting away from Richmond and could perhaps gain some support from Confederate sympathisers in Maryland. Lee was also aware that control of Maryland would threaten Washington DC. The people of the North were more likely to become demoralised if fighting was taking place on their own soil.

The Confederates were very confident but, unfortunately, Lee's battle plans fell into McClellan's hands. Discovering that Lee and Jackson were divided, McClellan blocked Lee's path at Antietam. Battle ensued, on 17 September 1862. The Battle of Antietam saw the highest casualties for a single day of the Civil War. At the end of it, neither side was a clear victor. Lee retreated into Virginia for the winter. So, in the sense that the South failed to meet their objectives, Lincoln was able to claim it as a northern victory. McClellan failed to follow up the victory by pursuing Lee, despite a 2:1 numerical advantage. President Lincoln, complaining that McClellan had 'the slows', replaced him again – this time with General Ambrose E. Burnside.

Burnside was more no successful than his predecessors. A further attempt on Richmond was stopped at the Battle of Fredericksburg in December 1862, when Lee easily outwitted Burnside. The Confederates suffered 4,000 casualties to the Union's 11,000. Lincoln's replacement for Burnside, the fiery Joseph Hooker, suffered an even greater disaster the following spring at the Battle of Chancellorsville. Lee, despite having to divide his troops and having fewer than half the numbers the North could rely on, inflicted a humiliating double defeat on the Unionists at Chancellorsville and Fredericksburg. Chancellorsville was probably Lee's greatest victory of the Civil War, but he lost a key commander when Jackson was fatally wounded. More importantly, it was clear to Lee (and to Jefferson Davis) that the imbalance of resources meant that the South could not keep on fighting indefinitely, even if they won the battles. At Chancellorsville, a significant Confederate victory and with fewer actual casualties, Lee lost 22% of his men, compared with Hooker's 15%.

Lee believed it was now essential to head north in order to try to inflict a devastating defeat on the North on their home territory. The hope was that this might convince enough people in the North to abandon their coercion of the South, or at least to force the Union to move troops over from the West, where the Confederates were not enjoying so much success. So, when Lee headed north in June 1863 to face the Army of the Potomac, now commanded by yet another general, George C. Meade, he was well aware of the significance of the battle he aimed to fight.

Gettysburg, Pennsylvania (1–3 July 1863)

If any battle can be seen as the turning point in the Civil War, then that fought at Gettysburg on 1–3 July 1863, is the one. Indeed, the combatants themselves recognised its importance. Lee, determined to force some movements in the war, commented after the first day that, 'I am going to whip them here, or they are going to whip me.'

The result of the battle hung in the balance and could easily have gone either way. It is one of the great 'what ifs' of military history. Gettysburg was a small town through which a number of main roads passed. It was here that the forward units of the Confederate Army encountered a small band of Unionists on 30 June. Both sides began pouring troops into the town and by the end of the first day of battle (1 July), the Confederates seemed likely to secure a victory. They had taken the town and pushed Meade and his 85,000 troops on to a ridge (Cemetery Ridge) to the south.

The following day, Longstreet attacked the left flank of Meade's troops. He sustained heavy damage whilst taking the areas known as the Peach Orchard and Devil's Den. Crucially, Longstreet did not take a small hill known as Little Round Top. It was a chance moment and quick thinking on the part of a northern officer which saved the hill for the Union. From Little Round Top, the Unionist troops on Cemetery Hill would have been exposed to Confederate fire without having to launch a frontal assault.

By the end of day two, the situation had reached stalemate, with Meade's men having had a full day to dig in on the ridge and fortify their position. On 3 July, it was up to Lee to force events. He took the ill-fated decision to launch a direct attack on the centre of Unionist lines on Cemetery Ridge. After a lengthy artillery bombardment, in an attempt to weaken northern defences, the charge was led by General Pickett and his 15,000 men. The infamous 'Pickett's Charge' was to end in disaster, with 6,500 casualties in under an hour. The Confederates almost broke through, despite their appalling losses. General Lee, having lost 28,000 men in the three-day battle, was forced to return to Virginia. Any hopes of invading the North that year went with him.

In direct contrast to President Lincoln's tendency to remove his unsuccessful commander after each defeat, Jefferson Davis refused to accept Lee's resignation. 'To ask me to substitute you by someone in my judgement more fit to command … is to demand an impossibility', Davis wrote in response to Lee's letter. The Confederacy was helped by Meade's decision not to follow Lee into Virginia. That this was disastrous for the Confederacy was not in doubt, especially given the fall of Vicksburg in the West on the same day. Southern morale had taken a knock and Lee's aura of invincibility had been diminished. Further, it seemed that, while the South could hold off northern attacks in Virginia, the battles of Antietam and now Gettysburg suggested that the South could not deliver the knockout blow that might persuade the North to consider peace. It does not mean that a Confederate victory at Gettysburg would have guaranteed overall victory in the Civil War, but Confederate defeat made a victory seem much more remote. In confirming that the advantage lay with the defender, Gettysburg suggested that the Civil War would drag on for a few more months or years as each side

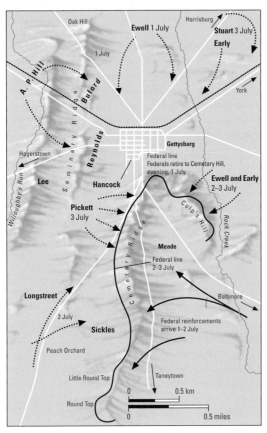

Battle of Gettysburg, 1–3 July 1863

tried to break the other's defences. The problem for the South was that the balance of resources did not favour them in a drawn-out war. Gettysburg meant that the American Civil War would not end in 1863, and a war that went beyond the winter was more likely to be won by the North.

The western theatre

Although much of the focus of the first two years of the Civil War was in Virginia, important developments were taking place further west, where Albert Sidney Johnston was in overall command of 40,000 Confederate forces defending a long and difficult border. Little movement took place until 1862, when Union troops launched an offensive to take some of the key river forts controlling the important waterway network that linked the Confederacy together. In the spring of 1862, 15,000 Union troops, under the command of General Ulysses S. Grant and supported by **gunboats**, captured Fort Henry and Fort Donelson. They gained control of the Cumberland and Tennessee rivers that flow eastwards into Tennessee. Confederate counter-attacks at Shiloh in April 1862 and in Kentucky in the summer and autumn had some success. However, Johnston was killed at Shiloh and Union reinforcements forced a Confederate retreat. In Kentucky, the new Confederate commander, General Braxton Bragg, was forced back into Tennessee because of supply problems.

In 1863, attention switched out west to the battle for the Mississippi port of Vicksburg, under siege by the Union since August of the previous year. Although the Union had captured the South's largest port, New Orleans, at the mouth of the Mississippi, in April 1862, Confederate control of Vicksburg prevented the Union from using the river. The Unionists were determined to capture a symbolic town that Davis referred to as 'the nailhead that held the South's two halves together'. Grant was charged with taking the town.

He succeeded in doing so on 4 July 1863, after a long and inspired campaign. The campaign involved crossing the Mississippi south of Vicksburg in **ironclads** that had sailed past the town in the night and then attacking two Confederate armies, marching 200 miles and fighting several battles before defeating Confederate armies in May 1863. Vicksburg then faced a serious and effective siege that came to an end with its surrender on 4 July, the day after the Battle of Gettysburg. The fall

Gunboats: Small ships that have several large guns fixed to them.

Ironclads: Ships of war cased with thick plates of iron or steel, as a defence against shot. See photo.

Federal ironclad river gunboat

of Port Hudson five days later meant the Mississippi now became a 'Union highway' and the Confederacy was split in two.

Towards the end of 1863, fighting flared up again in Tennessee – this time in the east of the state, around the important railroad junction of Chattanooga. General Bragg, still commanding the western Confederate forces, had won a costly engagement at Chickamauga Creek in September 1863. The Unionists had been forced to retreat into Chattanooga itself. Bragg, however, refused to follow up the success with an attack on the main Union force and simply set up a siege that lasted several months, much to the anger of his officers. In November 1863, General Grant, fresh from his victory at Vicksburg and now appointed by Lincoln as Commander-in-Chief throughout the West, advanced quickly to Chattanooga. He destroyed the Confederate position in a stunning manoeuvre, forcing them to withdraw to Georgia. Davis now replaced Bragg, but the damage had been done. The South began 1864 looking very vulnerable.

1864: Grant takes charge

There had been three major defeats for the South in 1863, at least two of which – Gettysburg and Chattanooga – might well not have happened as they did. That counted for little in 1864, when the South found itself under attack from all sides. In March, Lincoln assembled a team that finally looked like an effective and proven command. Grant was now General-in-Chief of all Union armies, supported by Meade, who headed the Army of the Potomac, and Grant's close friend, William Sherman, who took control of the forces in the West.

Grant instructed Meade to pursue Lee wherever he went, while Sherman was to capture Atlanta (capital of Georgia) and then march into the heart of the Confederacy. At the same time, smaller campaigns were launched in Louisiana, the peninsula below Richmond – where McClellan had fought two years earlier – and in the Shenandoah Valley (the key to northern Virginia). These smaller campaigns had limited success and impact, but the major campaigns in Virginia and Georgia were crucial in 1864.

In Virginia, Meade and Grant were determined to draw Lee into open combat. Meanwhile, Lee sought the opposite: trying to keep the Union forces away from Richmond and drawing them into well-fortified positions, hoping to prolong the war. Lee was hoping that a prolonged campaign would encourage northern defeatism in time for the presidential elections in November, when the North might turn Lincoln out of office and seek a negotiated peace.

The consequence was a confusing and bloody series of battles throughout May and June. There were serious casualties on both sides, but especially the Unionists who sustained 50,000 casualties in the first month. By the end of July, the constant flanking of one another had settled down to a siege of Petersburg, an important railroad junction 20 miles south of Richmond. Although Grant had lost considerably more men than Lee, by the end of the 'Virginia campaign' he still had more men than Lee had started with. Lee, however, was seeing his numbers continually reduced. He found himself on the defensive by the end of the year. He could not hope for reinforcements from the Shenandoah Valley, because Union successes there in the autumn had secured the area for the Union.

Meanwhile, Sherman had moved into northern Georgia. By September, after a series of disputes and misjudgements within the Confederate defenders, Sherman had taken Atlanta. This was an important boost to northern morale in advance of Lincoln's campaign for

Ulysses S. Grant (1822–1885)
18th President of the USA (1869–77), a Republican. Born Hiram Ulysses Grant. He was general-in-chief for the Union during the American Civil War. As President, he reformed the civil service and ratified the Treaty of Washington with the UK (1871). He carried through a liberal Reconstruction policy in the South. However, he failed to suppress extensive corruption within his own party and Cabinet, which tarnished the reputation of his second term.

William Tecumseh Sherman (1820–1891)
Union general in the American Civil War, renowned for smoking cigars. He had served in the Mexican War and then became a banker. Early in the Civil War, he served at the First Battle of Bull Run (1861) and at Shiloh (1862). He replaced General Grant as commander of the West (1864) and launched his 'Georgia campaign'. After capturing and burning Atlanta, he waged an economic campaign against the civilian population of Georgia and the Carolinas, laying waste to the countryside and driving the Confederates northwards. After the war, he was appointed commander of the army (1869–83).

re-election. In November, Sherman set out on his infamous 'March through Georgia'. He cut a 60-mile wide front through the state, destroying all in his path and doing damage worth $100 million to Georgia in the process. Sherman reached Savannah on the coast in December and set about planning to join up with Meade by marching north to Petersburg. The Confederate Army that had been defending Atlanta – under the young, brave but impetuous John Bell Hood – did not pursue Sherman. Instead, they attacked a Union army under General Thomas in Tennessee. The attack came to nothing and Thomas convincingly destroyed Hood's forces at the Battle of Nashville in December 1864.

The final months

With Lincoln triumphantly re-elected and the South demoralised after Sherman's march and under attack from all sides, northern victory seemed certain to come early on in 1865. The Confederacy was desperately short of men and resources. It resorted to desperate measures, offering at various times: a negotiated surrender, full emancipation and, in March 1865, the raising of slave regiments who could be offered freedom in return for fighting.

It was all in vain. Sherman marched north to Richmond, devastating South Carolina and capturing the last major southern ports on the way. Lee's lines defending Petersburg and Richmond were broken on 2 April. Lee headed westwards where he fought his last battle at Sayler's Creek on 6 April. On 9 April, Lee surrendered the Army of North Virginia to Grant at Appomattox. Within weeks, the final shots of the Civil War had been fired. Jefferson Davis initially fled from Richmond, urging the Confederacy to fight on, but there was no heart left in the Confederacy. Davis was captured on 10 May, with the last engagement of the war ending on 13 May in Texas.

The naval campaign

There may have been some doubt in 1861 as to the strongest army section militarily, but there was no question over the North's domination in naval terms. With a strong naval tradition, almost 300 ships in operation and more commissioned, the industrial capacity for quick manufacture and repair, and the majority of naval officers remaining loyal to the Union, the Confederacy could not have started at a greater disadvantage. Lincoln's strategy of blockading the South and the many inland waterways which allowed the easy movement of troops, meant that this, too, was a useful advantage to have. The Union's Secretary of the Navy, Gideon Welles, made good use of these advantages. This was seen most notably in the Peninsular Campaign of 1862 and the fall of Vicksburg in 1863.

The northern naval strategy had three elements to it:

● maintaining the blockade and capturing the southern sea port

● using ships to transport troops and supplies

● controlling the inland waterways, particularly in the West.

The South had no navy to speak of, and could not hope to outbuild the North. So the Secretary of War for the Confederacy, Stephen Mallory, had to resort to tactics of **sabotage** and raids, rather than set-piece battles. This was not as defeatist an approach as it might sound. The North had 3,500 miles of coastline to patrol and Southern ships might well break through the blockade and inflict considerable damage, if they wished. Mallory made some major innovations in naval warfare so that, even if the North

Sabotage: The deliberate damaging or destruction of railroad lines, bridges etc., as a way of weakening the enemy.

did have the better of it, the Confederates certainly kept the Unionists on their toes. Mallory's most important innovations were:

● The development of the 'ironclad' – a new vessel first used in March 1862 ('The Virginia'), but the North were quickly able to outproduce the South.

● Fast raiders, purchased in Britain by James Bullock to get round the neutrality laws. The most famous – 'The Alabama' and 'The Florida' – did inflict significant damage on Union shipping, sinking or damaging 200 merchant vessels.

● Torpedoes – which damaged or sank around 40 Union ships.

● The submarine – sank one boat in 1864, then sank itself.

It is hard to think what else Mallory might have done. Ultimately, the resource imbalance was unanswerable; the South never had more than 40 vessels in service at any one time. In all three areas – transport of troops, control of the inland waterways and sustaining the blockade – Northern naval dominance was a major factor in military success and planning.

How important were the military campaigns to the final outcome?

In recent years, historians have tended to neglect military factors. Instead, they have looked to economic, social and political issues to explain the outcome of the American Civil War, and wars generally. Although there were important domestic issues that had an impact on the war, the military campaigns do deserve serious study. For a start, there were moments when decisive battles, such as Gettysburg, the Peninsular Campaign and Antietam, might well have gone the other way. Also, it is clear that the prolonging of the war worked to the disadvantage of the less well-resourced South. Thus the military failure of Lee to break through in 1862 and 1863 is important. It is only by studying the battles that we can understand the difficulties General Lee faced. Similarly, the ability of the South to defend Richmond successfully in 1861–62 prevented a quick Union victory that might well have produced different consequences for the USA, if the greater slaughter of 1862–65 had not occurred.

It is also worth remembering that Lincoln was not only elected President in 1860 on a minority of the votes cast, but his re-election in 1864 was by no means certain. A Democratic President might well have been tempted to sign a negotiated peace. Confederate victories at Gettysburg, Vicksburg and Chattanooga could easily have encouraged defeatism in the North. Although many of the military problems facing the South were to do with inferior resources, there are plenty of examples in history of the better-resourced side being defeated. You only need to think of the Americans in Vietnam and the British in the War of Independence. It is thus significant that the tide really turned for the North with the appointment of Grant. Also, an early failure to break through by the South lengthened the Civil War and so diminished the chances of the Confederacy.

Raising and supplying troops
The North had a clear numerical advantage of troops. Around 2,000,000 northerners served in the armed forces during the War, compared with around 900,000 Confederates. Both sides originally relied on volunteers, and there were many of them in the early weeks. Initially, a number of volunteers were actually turned away. Local state militias were the main source of volunteers. After July 1862, Lincoln was able to call state militias into federal service for up to nine months.

Conscription: Making people in a particular country join the army, navy or air force. In America it worked like a form of lottery.

Draft: The practice of ordering people to serve in the armed forces, usually for a limited period of time. The term originated in America.

As it became clear that the Civil War was likely to drag on and was not going to be the romantic adventure that many early volunteers had expected, both the North and the South had to resort to **conscription**. The Confederacy passed the first **draft** law in April 1862 and the North followed in July 1863. The laws were unpopular and were resisted in both sections, most notably in New York, where the first draft selections caused riots in the summer of 1863, resulting in the deaths of several hundred people, especially blacks. The fact that rich people could avoid the draft by hiring a substitute or paying $300 was especially unpopular. Although conscription only accounted for around 10% of the troops who fought in the Civil War, there were certainly a number of men who volunteered only when the threat of conscription was raised.

Both sides were initially reluctant to use black troops. General Lee had urged Davis to establish slave regiments, but it was only in the final, desperate weeks of March 1865 that the Confederacy agreed to such a measure, with the promise of freedom in return. In the North, there was also resistance to the idea of black troops. Even when they did use blacks it was in segregated regiments, usually in non-combat roles and, until 1864, for lower pay. There were some regiments before 1863, but the majority enlisted after the Emancipation Proclamation (see section 3.9) and at a time when whites were reluctant to volunteer. Of the 46,000 black men eligible to fight in the North, 33,000 enlisted. The rest of the black soldiers were slaves – about 100,000 from the Confederacy and a further 42,000 securing their freedom from the Union slave states of Kentucky, Missouri, Delaware and Maryland. By the end of the war, blacks were a major part of the Union army – around 180,000 had served.

War supply was less easy, especially for the South. In 1863, the South passed the Impressment Act, which allowed the seizure of goods in order to supply the troops. They were also helped by 'taxation-in-kind' that provided agricultural resources from the summer of 1863. Transportation was vitally important in supplying and moving troops. This was, in many ways, the first war in which railroads played a key part. The North had an advantage here for they not only had a larger railroad system but they could destroy the Southern network by tearing up rails in areas they controlled and they could more easily repair their own network.

The North was unable to blockade the South effectively, especially at first. Blockade-running was a highly profitable, if risky, venture that the Confederate Government became involved in by 1863. It required all blockade-runners to carry one-third of government cargo – that is, cotton exports and war supply imports. As a result, until the last weeks of the Civil War, the South secured the majority of its weapons from overseas.

Financing the war

Both governments adopted unprecedented policies to raise money. The South suffered particularly because of the decline in trade due to the northern blockade. It had to raise money centrally by demanding levies on individual states. Whilst both sides lacked full credit systems, the North was able to reform banking laws and to draw upon reasonable gold reserves, whereas in the South most capital was tied up in land and slaves.

The North passed a federal tax on incomes over $800 in August 1861. The Internal Revenue Act of 1862 saw significant taxation across the board. A similar policy was followed in the South where income tax and a 10% tax 'in kind' was levied on agricultural produce after 1863 (i.e. agricultural goods rather than cash were handed over). Because each southern state was responsible for raising taxation for the federal government, a number of states did so reluctantly and inefficiently. Only 8% of

Greenbacks: American banknotes such as dollar bills.

Inflation: An increase, sustained over a period of time, in the general level of prices. It can be caused by an increase in the cost of raw materials which is then passed on to the consumer, or by a shortage of goods the demand for which pushes the prices up.

Hoarding/riots/black marketeering: These are all common in times of shortages, especially when there is a war going on. Shortages of food and manufactured items may lead to riots as people cannot get essential items. Hoarding also occurs when items are in short supply. By stockpiling, the aim is to create a shortage, thereby pushing up prices and thus making a large profit for the hoarders when they decide to sell. 'Black marketeering' is the buying and selling of goods illegally. Usually it is conducted on a cash or barter basis. Although the 'black market' generates a large proportion of national income, the fact that it is not recorded in any accounting records means that no tax is paid on the transaction. This makes black marketeering attractive to those buying and selling in the 'black market'.

Confederate income was raised through taxation, compared with 20% in the North.

The main method of raising funds for both sections was through borrowing. In the North around 70% of the money raised for the war was borrowed ($2.6 billion), much in the form of war bonds bought by ordinary citizens hoping to establish a stake in northern victory. The Confederacy was able, initially, to raise money through loans and bonds secured on cotton. As the war went on and people became less convinced of a southern victory, loans became harder to raise and the last major loan was secured in January 1863.

In both North and South, the government issued paper money (**greenbacks**) that was not redeemable in gold or silver, so soon lost its value. The situation was bad in the North, where $450 million greenbacks were produced and where **inflation** ran at 80% during the Civil War. In the South, where individual states also issued notes, inflation was rife. The shortage of goods and the ineffectiveness of other methods of raising money made this worse. Inflation destroyed the southern currency, with prices rising over 5,000% during the Civil War. By 1865, the Confederate government was $800 million in debt, with state governments having run up equally unmanageable amounts.

Economics of war
Northerners in Congress took advantage of the absence of southern votes to pass various pieces of economic legislation that favoured the North. They had been struggling to get these through Congress in the years prior to the Civil War. Much of the legislation helped the expansion of northern industry after the war. Such acts included federal support for a transcontinental railroad, higher tariffs, the easing of immigration rules, improved banking laws and the 1862 Homestead Act. While most of the Acts needed some time before their full impact was felt, northern industry responded well to the demands of war placed upon it. There was:

● a significant increase in production of both agricultural and manufactured goods

● an expansion of communications and transport

● mechanisation that improved agricultural yields and industrial output.

Many speculators and investors could make considerable amounts out of wartime contracts. Although wages lagged behind prices, it was a time of general prosperity, especially as the need for soldiers helped to increase the demand for workers. Overall, economic growth was not as great as one might expect, but much of this was down to the decrease in population (not only war deaths but immigration also declined during the period) and to the loss of southern markets and capital. In areas of war demand, growth was dramatic. The inflationary impact of war finance helped companies to pay off debts and to invest in new techniques and machinery.

In the South, of course, it was a different story. The northern blockade, and the previous dependency on the northern states as a market and on northern transport for exporting meant that the South struggled to find a market for its agricultural goods, especially cotton. It therefore lacked the wherewithal to purchase necessary materials for war – a situation that got worse as the fighting went on. Furthermore, whole areas of the South – especially Virginia and Tennessee, and Georgia and South Carolina after 1864 – saw most of the fighting. These areas suffered the physical destruction that war brought. **Hoarding, riots and black marketeering** were rife, especially given the inflation rate. The Confederate Government interfered more directly in the southern economy than was the case in the

North. This caused some historians to talk of 'Confederate Socialism'. The Confederate Government exercised considerable control over railroads, communications and private industry, as well as encouraging planters to shift from cotton to agricultural production. The longer the fighting went on:

● the more the northern economy was stimulated and responded to the demand positively;

● the more desperate the situation in the South became, so that, when the end of the war came, many at home were grateful for peace in whatever circumstances.

3.7 What opposition did the political leadership face during the Civil War?

Scapegoat: Someone is blamed publicly for something that has happened, although it may not be their fault, just because other people are angry about it and need to have someone they can blame and punish.

Jefferson Davis faced criticism over his leadership from the start. Historians have continued to criticise the way in which he governed and led the Confederacy. Some of these claims have some validity, though there is no doubt that a lot of colleagues and southern writers made Davis into something of a **scapegoat** after the war. Similarly, Lincoln is remembered today as the 'great emancipator', the man who won the war; but at the time he faced criticism for his actions and decisions, and his re-election in 1864 was far from certain.

Davis did not work with colleagues easily and there was a high turnover of personnel in his Cabinet. He had a number of disputes with his commanders. He was not good at delegating and yet struggled to make quick and effective decisions. Cabinet meetings in the Confederacy dragged on and on. Davis was also accused of meddling in military affairs. In his defence, he did have a military background. He was also firm in his defence of General Lee, refusing to accept his resignation after Gettysburg. This contrasts with Lincoln, who chopped and changed his top commanders throughout the first few years of the Civil War, before settling on Grant in 1864. Lincoln, however, was a consummate manager of men. He was not afraid to have in his Cabinet men with widely differing views who had experience of government far ahead of himself. He got a lot out of some very talented men. Lincoln had good working relations with Congress. He also had a knack of knowing, for example, when he could and when he could not try to abolish slavery.

Lincoln's other great advantage over Davis was his ability to make inspirational speeches that captured the mood of the nation. He had great self-confidence and an unswerving conviction that what he was doing was right, and he was able to communicate this to the public and to the northern troops. Lincoln maintained unity in the North despite facing loyal but wary opposition. In the early years, he countered the growing defeatism that took hold as the war dragged on and the South inflicted embarrassing defeats. Davis, on the other hand, was not a great communicator. He did not build a national spirit of optimism and sacrifice which became necessary as the war turned against the South.

On the question of war powers and use of executive control, there is no doubt that Lincoln went much further than Davis. A number of contemporaries felt that Lincoln exceeded his powers, beyond a level that was constitutionally acceptable. On the other hand, some historians have criticised Davis for acting too cautiously. The historian David Donald, in *Lincoln* (1995), suggests that the South 'died of democracy' because Davis did not take a strong enough line against dissent and was too concerned with liberties. Davis made a virtue of this at the time, proclaiming in

February 1862 that, by comparing himself with the Northern command, 'there has been no act on our part to impair personal liberty of the freedom of speech, of thought or of the press'.

Lincoln showed little concern for the civil liberties of individuals in the North during the Civil War. He supported the suspension of the writ of *habeas corpus* and agreed that anyone could be tried in a military court for preventing conscription or helping the enemy. A number of cases that ensued were highly suspect and many people suffered arbitrary arrest that Lincoln did little to oppose. In the early months, he took decisions before Congress met in July 1861 that included instituting the naval blockade, suspending basic freedoms of speech and association, removing *habeas corpus* in Maryland, raising troops and spending money on arms and supplies. Lincoln justified all this on the grounds of 'war powers' – a new phrase in America. It is clear that these actions played a significant role in saving the **border states** (see map on page 97) for the Union. Throughout the Civil War, Lincoln was not afraid to use direct powers if he felt they were necessary. He would worry about the clashes with Congress and the courts later.

Border states: Slave states that stayed loyal to the Union during the Civil War. They were Missouri, Kentucky, Delaware and Maryland.

It is possible to exaggerate the differences between North and South in terms of political control. After all, if Lincoln had been as tyrannical as his opponents claim, he would hardly have allowed the continued political debate that even saw him fighting for re-election in 1864. Similarly, Davis' concern for individual rights did not prevent him from supporting conscription when it came. However, it is fair to say that Lincoln did provide better and clearer leadership for the Union than Davis achieved for the Confederacy. This is not going as far as historian David Potter has in suggesting that if Davis and Lincoln had swapped roles, then the South might have won.

Internal opposition

Both Lincoln and Davis had to deal with critics on the home front during the Civil War. Some opposed the war altogether. Most southerners supported secession, or were at least happy to abide by the decision of the states to secede. However, a sizeable number of white southerners – around 90,000 – fought in the Union army. Western Virginia and eastern Tennessee, where slavery was not prevalent and economic conditions were closer to those in the North, showed substantial support for the Union. Indeed, West Virginia actually seceded from Virginia and became a free state of the Union in 1873. Support for war in the North was more solid in 1861. Douglas, the defeated northern Democratic candidate, called on all Democrats to rally round Lincoln. The President helped matters by promoting a number of Democrats to positions in the Administration and army, including McClellan (the commander of the Army of the Potomac). The few who opposed war initially were labelled 'Copperheads' by their opponents, and Republicans later tried to smear all Democrats with the label.

Even if northern Democrats were prepared to support the war, that did not mean they supported Lincoln's policies. Lincoln was attacked for his alleged abuses of presidential power and the Democrats were keen to criticise Republican economic policies, as well as more radical war measures like conscription and emancipation. In 1862, the Democrats enjoyed considerable success in the Congressional elections under the slogan 'The Constitution as it is: the Union as it was: the **Negroes** where they are'.

Negroes: People with black skin who came from Africa or whose ancestors came from Africa. In America, this term was used for slaves, which many people now find offensive.

Republicans had some success in discrediting the Democrats by claiming that they tacitly supported the Confederacy. In early 1863, with a series of defeats behind him, Lincoln had to take the arguments of leading peace Democrats seriously. His two greatest crises of internal opposition occurred in the summer of 1863.

Military tribunal: A court that usually deals with cases within the armed forces.

1. Lincoln supported General Burnside who had tried a leading peace Democrat, Clement Vallandingham, by **military tribunal**. As a civilian making speeches condemning the war and calling upon soldiers to desert, Vallandingham was clearly undermining the war effort. However, to try a civilian in a military court for making a speech was clearly taking things beyond the law. Although Lincoln backed Burnside, he set Vallandingham free afterwards but insisted he left the Union.

2. More serious for Lincoln were the anti-draft riots in New York in July 1863. Partially encouraged by the public opposition to the draft by the Democratic Governor, Horatio Seymour, over a hundred people were killed by a protesting mob. Lincoln acted swiftly, sending in 20,000 troops who shot rioters dead, where it was deemed necessary to restore order.

Lincoln's greatest personal test came in his campaign for re-election in November 1864. He had looked vulnerable at one point to a challenge from the more radical Republicans, who rallied round John Fremont (the Republican candidate in 1856). They wanted a stronger line on reconstructing the Union and handling the South than Lincoln favoured. However, the war began to turn in the North's favour again that autumn. Lincoln campaigned on a National Union platform in the hope of attracting War Democrat votes (i.e. Democrats who supported the Civil War; as opposed to peace Democrats who did not). This was made more likely by his choice of Andrew Jackson, a War Democrat from Tennessee, as his running-mate (vice-presidential candidate). The re-election of Lincoln looked more secure as a result.

The Democrats called for a negotiated peace and promised to preserve states' rights, although their candidate, the Union commander George McClellan, made it clear that he would keep fighting. The South saw the 1864 presidential election as their last hope of victory. They were hoping that the northern voters would be tired of the Civil War and would vote Lincoln out in the hope of getting some form of negotiated settlement. McClellan secured a respectable 45% of the vote, but Lincoln's victory on a platform of unconditional surrender and destruction of slavery paved the way for the final collapse of the Confederacy.

Jefferson Davis found that, as the war dragged on and looked less promising, so opposition increased. As in the North, opposition to the draft was the major cause of discontent in 1862–63. Opposition was widespread across the South, made worse by exemptions that favoured the rich and the planters. The extent to which class conflict followed can be exaggerated, but it does seem that at least some of the resentment stemmed from a perception that it was a 'rich man's war but a poor man's fight'. Small-scale farmers, in particular, found themselves heavily taxed and suffering inflation and shortage of goods. As the northern troops advanced, **refugees** moved into cities. These cities became a centres of discontent, with food riots in Atlanta and Richmond in 1863 and a growing number of strikes. Davis had to threaten striking workers with the draft.

Refugees: People who are forced to leave their country because there is a war or because of their political or religious beliefs.

More generally, Davis had to face the dilemma that the Confederacy had been formed on the principle of states' rights and so many of his fellow southerners resisted any attempts at creating a strong Confederate identity that would mean a lessening of state powers. Some state governors, such as Zebulon Vance in North Carolina and Joseph Brown in Georgia, protested at times against what they saw as the

1. Who do you think faced greater opposition during the Civil War: Abraham Lincoln or Jefferson Davis? Explain your answer.

2. Who was the more effective political leader: Lincoln or Davis? Give reasons for your answer.

unnecessary centralisation of the Richmond government. Vance often prevented supplies reaching Confederate troops in north Virginia because he was concerned to maintain the defences of North Carolina. Brown opposed conscription and managed to prevent thousands of Georgians from fighting by granting exemptions.

Davis also faced opposition from the Confederate Congress where, although there was no official opposition, he found factions working against him, especially after 1863. He also lacked the support of his Vice-President, Alexander Stephens of Georgia, who described his President as 'weak and vacillating, timid, petulant, peevish, obstinate, but not firm'.

Although both leaders – Lincoln and Davis – could rely on the support of the majority of the people in their section, they both had to govern in the knowledge that such support had to be maintained with care. Davis had the added difficulty of having to maintain morale in the final two years when southern defeat looked increasingly likely.

3.8 How did foreign powers respond to the war?

The Confederacy was well aware that their best hopes of success lay in getting early recognition from major international powers, most importantly Britain. Recognition would not only establish international legitimacy, but it might also encourage some limited European involvement in the conflict, at least in helping to break the blockade. The Confederacy had reason to be hopeful too, for there were strong links between the southern states and the Lancashire cotton mills of northern England. The blockade might well threaten unemployment in the mill towns if their raw material supply dried up. It was also not lost on British policy-makers that if north America were divided into two separate states, Britain would be less likely to see a strong commercial rival emerge on the other side of the Atlantic.

Radicals: People who believe that there should be great and extreme changes in society.

Liberals: Moderates who favour gradual progress by the changing of laws, rather than by revolution.

The cause of states' rights was also taken up by a number of **radicals** in Britain who supported the nationalist claims of the southerners. On the other hand, a larger number of radicals and **liberals** were unwilling to back an uprising which was partly to do with preserving slavery. The British were aware that direct involvement in support of the South could easily lead to attacks on Canada or central American possessions. Although ties with the cotton-producing South were important, Britain also imported large amounts of grain from the North.

It was not surprising then that Britain chose to remain neutral during the American Civil War. Once Lincoln had issued the Emancipation Proclamation (see next section) and made slavery a main issue, that position became more fixed. Neutrality did not mean that Britain was not prepared to allow private trade between British military suppliers and Confederate agents. In fact, both sides made many military purchases in Europe. However, attempts at forcing British intervention by placing a voluntary embargo on cotton exports from the South failed, and probably made British politicians and industrialists look less favourably on the South.

There was a decent stockpile of supplies at the start of the American Civil War and, by the time the blockade had started to bite, Britain had found alternative supplies in India and Egypt. There was always a danger that Britain and the USA might find themselves at war accidentally. However, since neither side wanted that to happen, when the situation did look fragile – most notably over the Trent Affair in November 1861 – there was a flurry of diplomatic activity and face-saving compromises.

The French Government was instinctively more sympathetic to the Confederacy and would certainly have recognised the Richmond government if Britain had. Napoleon III had committed French troops to the Mexican War and hoped that he might get support from the Confederacy for increasing French involvement in Mexico in return for recognition. However, the French were not in a position to act alone and needed British naval support before getting involved in a fight with the Union.

Thus European involvement in the American Civil War was kept to a minimum, though the Confederacy in particular gained from Britain's liberal interpretation of neutrality when it came to providing weapons and commerce. British and French recognition of the Confederacy would have been a big boost to southern fortunes, but ironically such recognition was unlikely to come until Confederate victory seemed likely. One of the Confederacy's greatest political cards was never played.

> *Explain why Britain and/or France might have intervened in the Civil War.*

3.9 What was the importance of the Emancipation Proclamation?

On 23 September 1862, Lincoln issued his Emancipation Proclamation. The proclamation stated that, as from 1 January 1863, any slaves in conquered enemy territory would be 'forever free'. Although this meant that slaves living in states that were loyal to the Union, or already conquered by it, did not get their freedom (something that earned the scorn of foreign commentators), most campaigners both for and against emancipation saw it as an important move. The Democrats opposed the proposals and made gains at the November 1862 elections when campaigning on the issue, while opponents of slavery saw it as an important first step. Lincoln won the support of prominent abolitionists who had been frustrated by his reluctance to move sooner. On 1 January 1863, Lincoln announced that the securing of freedom for all slaves in the Confederacy was a Union war aim.

Lincoln's motives in issuing the proclamation have been debated since the moment it occurred. He certainly felt that the time was right to add some ideological fervour to the war. He believed that commitment to the war cause in the North was sufficiently strong to survive the inevitable opposition that would come from the Democrats and some of the pro-Union border states. Lincoln was also forced into some kind of decision because of the course of events. As the North conquered areas in the South, the question of what to do with the slaves and their ambiguous position as human property was being resolved differently by different commanders. Lincoln himself was unhappy with slavery. Although he would not have split the Union to secure its abolition, it was unlikely that Lincoln would not take the opportunity to abolish slavery if it presented itself. He also felt that slavery was a lingering sore, having remarked that 'A House divided amongst itself cannot stand'. If slavery survived the war, then the Union would be condemned to new tensions later.

The consequences of the announcement and then the carrying out of the Emancipation Proclamation were significant.

- Most importantly, Lincoln had raised the stakes of the Civil War. There could now be no compromise peace, for the South would not accept the northern war aim.

- It also made it more difficult for the South to secure foreign backing. While liberals in Europe were prepared to support a fight for **nationalism** and states' rights, they could not bring themselves to support a fight to maintain slavery.

Nationalism: The growth and spread of loyalty towards a nation, rather than to an individual ruler.

1. Why did Lincoln choose September 1862 to issue the Emancipation Proclamation?

2. How did the Emancipation Proclamation help the northern war effort?

- A northern war aim was now adopted that was a simple rallying cry and put the Union on the high moral ground. Although there would be some people in the North who did not accept abolitionism, the new war aim certainly energised the soldiers in the field, as well as making Lincoln's position in the Republican Party stronger. Given his importance to northern victory, this was a great bonus.

- It helped to tip the population imbalance further in the North's favour by encouraging slaves to flee to the North. Black regiments now began to be accepted by northern troops, too.

3.10 Why did the North win the Civil War?
A CASE STUDY IN HISTORICAL INTERPRETATION

Historians are likely to argue for many years more about the relative importance of certain factors in the northern victory – and the extent to which the South could ever have anticipated victory. There are, though, several key areas which everyone accepts should be considered and which played some role in the eventual outcome. The emphasis put on one or the other may vary from writer to writer.

Superiority of numbers and resources

The idea that the South was condemned almost from the start given the advantages that the North had in resources and manpower was voiced as early as 19 April 1865 when Robert E. Lee reflected that: 'The Army of Northern Virginia has been compelled to yield to overwhelming numbers and resources.' This argument was certainly convincing, especially when you consider the extraordinary imbalance between the two sides. It is important, though, to look at current expectations which did not acknowledge Confederate defeat as inevitable. Remember also that resources alone have not determined the results of war in a number of other conflicts. Perhaps it is better to see resources as playing an increasingly important role as the fighting went on and developed into a **war of attrition**. Certainly by 1864 southern troops were being overwhelmed by sheer force of numbers, but it cannot explain why the South did not manage to make breakthroughs earlier in the war.

War of attrition: A conflict in which victory is gained by slowly wearing down the resources and resistance of the opposing power.

Political leadership

In a point by point comparison, it is probable that Lincoln would come out ahead of Davis as a wartime leader. He was more eloquent, more decisive, more inspiring. He managed his ministers better and was prepared to delegate wherever others were up to the job. There are also specific occasions when Lincoln played a crucial and cunning role, such as keeping the border states in the Union in 1861 and managing not to alienate opinion over the slavery issue. Instead, he managed to galvanise northern morale in 1862. Lincoln came to symbolise the northern war effort and the voters endorsed his total commitment to victory in 1864. Davis certainly made mistakes, but he did have the more difficult job to do and he had to manage colleagues who made his job harder, rather than easier. Both Administrations had good and bad ministers. However, it is probably fair to say that, on balance, Lincoln was better served, and he managed his ministers better.

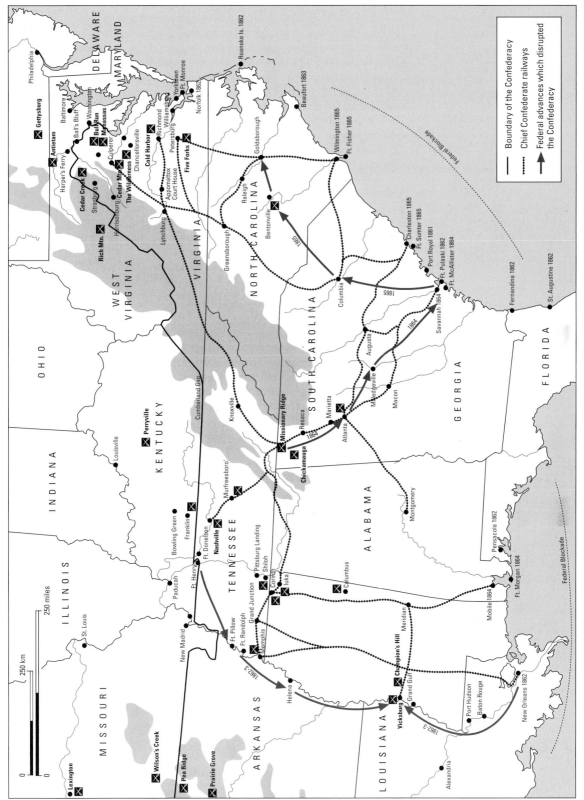

The American Civil War, 1861–1865

Military actions and leadership

Initially, the war was fought better by the South. Robert E. Lee was recognised, both then and since, as one of the great commanders. Lincoln struggled to find his equal in the early years of the Civil War. However, it is clear that the appointment of Grant – first in overall command in the West and then, in 1864, to full command of all Union forces – finally brought an outstanding general into the Union war effort. There has been criticism of Lee for concentrating on Virginia and so losing the West early in the war, and for an attacking strategy at a time when war did not favour the attacker. This was demonstrated most clearly during Pickett's Charge at Gettysburg. However, it is hard to see how the Confederacy could have done anything but defend Richmond, and Lee proved a masterful commander in Virginia. His only major offensives were at Antietam and Gettysburg. These came when he was trying to force an end to the war by effecting a crushing defeat on the North in the North – a strategy hard to criticise, given the need to finish things quickly if the South was to have a hope of victory. If military acts did play a role, it is probably better to look at the effectiveness of northern tactics under Grant and Sherman. Here the concept of total war and the determination to take the fighting into the heart of the Confederacy did much to destroy southern morale in the later years.

Internal problems and strengths

The economy was better managed and finance more easily raised in the North than in the South. This was not just a question of the competence of the ministers involved, but also of the circumstances in which they operated. States' rights and a fear of provoking internal dissent made the Confederacy more timid than it needed to be in focusing the section on all-out victory. Lincoln was not without critics, but the economy and society saw things get better in the North, while the South had to cope with rampant inflation, growing shortages and, later, the consequences of destruction. Certainly, by the later years of the Civil War, southern morale had taken a beating and the Confederacy was beginning to collapse internally.

It is not easy to see any one factor as being solely, or even largely, responsible for northern victory, but it is useful to recognise the importance of different issues as different times in the conflict. For example, after Gettysburg it was unlikely the South would now win, but it was not until Lincoln's re-election in November 1864 that it became obvious that the North would not give up. Since the South only had to survive to win the conflict, it was really a matter of whether the North would give up the attempted coercion of the South that determined when the war would end and who would be the victor. Then the failure of the South to break through in 1862 and 1863, the determination of Lincoln and his confirmation as President in 1864 and the collapse of southern morale after that, all played their roles. Also, there remain doubts as to whether the South ever really possessed the resources and internal strengths to last out longer than the North.

1. What do you regard as the most important reason why the North won the Civil War? Explain your answer.

2. Why have historians argued about the reasons why the North won the Civil War?

3.11 To what extent was the Civil War the 'first modern war'?

The American Civil War is almost equidistant in time between the battles of Waterloo (1815) and the Somme (1916–17). As such, the Civil War can be seen either as the last of the Napoleonic-style wars, or as the first of the modern era. Certainly, generals preparing for the carnage of the trenches in the First World War would have been well advised to study the battles of the American Civil War. Similarly, Wellington and Napoleon would have found much to remind them of their encounters. The truth is that the civil war in America bridges the gap between the two eras. A consideration of the civil war reveals several things.

Developments in military technology

These developments increasingly favoured the defender. From 1863, most infantry on both sides had rifle-muskets that could be loaded more quickly and were accurate at a greater distance. As a result, defending armies could fire several shots successively at an advancing army. The digging of trenches became commonplace as well, making it very difficult for an enemy to attack unless by surprise. This was especially so since opponents soon got wise to the likely attack on the flanks of a line and so defended these positions as effectively as elsewhere. The defender won almost all of the battles of the Civil War, until the final months. It did mean that, once the defender had won a battle, he could not easily follow up a victory. Consequently, war quickly developed into a process of wearing the opposition down.

Cavalry were rarely used on the Civil War battlefields as a charge by them stood little chance of success. More and more, the cavalry were used for reconnaissance and disruption of enemy supply lines.

Developments in tactics

Although, in the early stages of the Civil War, the traditional rules of etiquette were obeyed, later stages saw commanders such as Grant and Sherman taking their troops into the heart of enemy territory. They were not afraid to make civilians and their property legitimate targets. Sherman formulated the view that as war was terrible whatever the circumstances, it was best to bring it to as swift a conclusion as possible by making it as nasty but effective as was necessary. Although his 'March through Georgia' in 1864 and his attacks up the coast through the Carolinas in 1865 were not as destructive as much of 20th-century warfare, the deliberate aim of destroying civilian morale demonstrated a knowing cruelty that is a sign of the modern warfare. It is also recognition that, in an age of total warfare, all opponents – civil as well as military – are legitimate targets.

Union soldiers in camp at Harper's Ferry during 1862

Saltpetre: Potassium nitrate – a substance that is used in making gunpowder, matches and fertilisers.

1. *What do you regard as the features of 'a modern war'?*

2. *Which aspects of the American Civil War make it 'a modern war'?*

Increased importance of industrial supply

A third way in which the American Civil War can be seen as heralding modern developments is in the increased importance of industrial supply. As technology developed and weapons became more technically advanced, so it became more important to have an effective supply of iron, coal, **saltpetre** etc. Railroads and other forms of communication also assumed greater importance in ensuring that armies were kept in the field and were well supplied. Also, the growth of mass recruit armies, as opposed to the old professional bodies, made supply of food and uniforms all the more important. They also increased the civilian experience of war as families with no previous military experience could well find relatives and friends directly involved in the conflict.

For all the modern developments during the American Civil War, much fighting still took place on horseback or according to tactics learned during the Mexican Wars. However, there is no doubt that, with the benefit of hindsight, important trends in 20th-century warfare can be traced back to those conflicts. The idea of total war – one that involved home fronts as well as the military theatres – was clearly demonstrated between 1861 and 1865 in America.

Source-based questions: Origins of the American Civil War

SOURCE A

(The non-slaveholding states) have assumed the right of deciding upon the propriety of our domestic institutions; and have denied the rights of property established in 15 of the States and recognised by the Constitution; they have denounced as sinful the institution of Slavery ... They have encouraged and assisted thousands of slaves to leave their homes; and those who have remained have been incited by emissaries, books and pictures, to servile insurrection ... A geographical line has been drawn across the Union, and all the States north of that line have united in the election of a man to the high office of President of the United States whose opinions and purposes are hostile to slavery.

24 December 1660, South Carolina defends its decision to secede in the Declaration of Causes of Secession.

SOURCE B

If I could save the Union without freeing any slave, I would do it; and if I could save it by freeing all the slaves, I would do it; and if I could save it by freeing some and leaving others alone, I would also do that. What I do about slavery and the colored race I do because I believe it helps to save this Union ... I have here stated my purpose according to my view of official duty, and I intend no modification of my oft-expressed personal wish that all men everywhere could be free.

Letter from Lincoln to Horace Greeley's 'New York Tribune', 22 August 1862

SOURCE C

One-eighth of the whole population was colored slaves ... These slaves constituted a peculiar and powerful interest. All knew that this interest was somehow the cause of the war. To strengthen, perpetuate and extend this interest was the object for which the insurgents would rend the Union even by war, while the government claimed no right to do more than to restrict the territorial enlargement of it.

Abraham Lincoln speaking publicly in March 1865.

SOURCE D

[The Confederates fought] for the defence of an inherent, unalienable right to withdraw from a Union which they had, as sovereign communities, voluntarily entered ... The existence of African servitude was in no way the cause of the conflict, but only an incident.

Jefferson Davis, writing in his memoirs after the war.

---

1. Study Source A.

Explain what is being referred to in the highlighted phrases.

(a) 'denied the rights of property established in 15 of the States and recognised by the Constitution'

(b) 'assisted thousands of slaves to leave their homes'.

2. Using Source A, you need to be aware of the motives of the South Carolinians in publishing this declaration.

How far does it affect its reliability and usefulness?

3. Study Sources A and B.

How far do these two sources agree on what Lincoln's views regarding slavery were?

4. Does the fact that both sources B and C are public statements by Lincoln affect how far we can trust them as reflecting his views?

5. Study Source D.

(a) Is it possible that Davis would have written differently if this had been produced at the start of the War?

(b) How reliable are accounts written by eye-witnesses quite a long time after the events?

6. Study Sources C and D. How useful are these sources for understanding why the Civil War broke out?

7. Using the sources and the information in this chapter, do you agree with Lincoln's view in Source C that slavery was 'somehow the cause of the war'?

'The Gilded Age' to the First World War, 1865–1919

Key Issues

- *How effectively did politicians deal with the problems facing America during industrialisation and expansion?*

- *Why did the American economy expand so quickly after 1865?*

- *How did the social and economic changes affect the lives of Americans, 1877–1914?*

4.1 How did American society change in the period 1869–1896?

4.2 What were the key features of American politics, 1877–1896?

4.3 Who were the Populists and what did they believe?

4.4 What factors lay behind the economic expansion of the USA after 1865?

4.5 How did people respond to industrialisation?

4.6 What were the patterns of immigration during this period?

4.7 What was the impact of immigration on the USA?

4.8 What were the origins and aims of the Progressive movement?

4.9 What impact did Woodrow Wilson have on domestic affairs, 1913–1919?

Framework of Events

1876	Disputed Presidential election
1877	Compromise sees Rutherford Hayes accepted as President and end of Reconstruction period
1879	Rockefeller organises Standard Oil Trust
1880	Garfield is elected President
1881	Garfield assassinated; Arthur becomes President
1883	Pendleton (Civil Service reform) Act
1884	Cleveland is elected President
1886	American Federation of Labor (AFL) founded
1887	Cleveland vetoes Dependent Pensions Bill
	Interstate Commerce Act
1888	Harrison is elected President
1890	McKinley Tariff Act
	Sherman Anti-Trust Act
1892	Populist Party founded – Omaha Platform launched
	Ellis Island opened as a major immigrant clearance centre
	Cleveland is elected President for second time
1893	'Panic of 1893'
1894	Pullman Palace Car Company workers' strike
1896	McKinley is elected President, defeating Bryan, Democrat/Populist candidate
1898	Spanish–American War begins
1899	Treaty of Paris
1900	McKinley is re-elected President
1901	McKinley assassinated; Roosevelt becomes President
1902	Newlands Act
1903	Elkins Act
1904	Roosevelt is elected President
1905	Industrial Workers of the World (IWW) founded
1906	Hepburn, Meat Inspection and Pure Food and Drugs Acts
1907	More than 500,000 immigrants pass through Ellis Island
1908	Taft is elected President

1909	Payne–Aldrich Tariff
	Disputes between Ballinger and Pinchot
1910	Mann–Elkins Act
1911	Dissolution of Standard Oil Company ordered by Supreme Court
1912	Founding of Progressive Party
	Wilson is elected President after three-way battle with Taft and Roosevelt
1913	Underwood Tariff
	Federal Reserve Act
	Sixteenth and Seventeenth Amendments ratified
1914	Clayton Anti-Trust Act
1916	Federal Farm Loan, Keating–Owen, Adamson and Seamen's Acts
	Wilson is re-elected President
1917	Increased government control of the economy
	USA declares war on Germany
1919	Eighteenth Amendment is passed, introducing national prohibition.

Overview

THE end of the Civil War and victory for the Union in 1865 heralded a new age in American history. Before the Civil War, both northern and southern sections were predominantly agricultural, although the industry that there was was concentrated in the North and East. All this was to change in the following decades as America went through a process of industrialisation similar to that experienced in Britain, but at a much greater pace. By the end of the 19th century, the United States was the leading industrial power in the world. This chapter looks at the reasons for this economic transformation and expansion in the 'Reconstruction' period. It also looks at the wide-ranging effects that such dramatic and rapid change brought to American society and politics.

The rapid industrialisation was matched with significant urbanisation and the emergence of major urban centres such as New York, Chicago and Cleveland. Hundreds of thousands of immigrants flocked to these cities, not arriving from the traditional points of origin in western and northern Europe, but from Italy, Greece, Poland and Russia. These 'new immigrants' not only had a major impact on population growth in the USA (41% of population growth in the 1880s was due to immigration), they also brought very different cultures and attitudes with them. Major cities quickly found themselves with Italian, Jewish and Polish quarters. These immigrants represented major challenges, as well as a source of cheap labour. Many met the hostility and fears of the native-born Americans who felt threatened and feared for the future of their protestant and individualistic Republic.

Politicians had to confront change that they could not keep up with. Initially, this was the 'Gilded Age', in which corruption and disconnection characterised the political system. In the cities, political bosses exercised ruthless and self-interested control, whilst nationally politicians often lined their own pocket and the two political parties offered little to choose between them. Slowly, reform came – sometimes from the politicians themselves, as in the Pendleton Act and the Sherman Anti-Trust Act – more often as a result of external pressure. Farmers and small-scale businessmen in the West and the South increasingly felt isolated from the politicians in the East, who seemed to be in the pockets of the emerging 'big business' men, such as the self-made millionaires Rockefeller and Carnegie.

Protest movements emerged which developed firstly into the Populist campaigns of the 1890s and later into the Progressive movement of the early 20th century. Although the Populists failed to win power nationally, they gained control of several states and cities. They formed the basis for the Progressive movement that saw major reforms in politics, economy and society in the first two decades of the 20th century, under Presidents Roosevelt, Taft and Wilson. Thus, in the 40 years between the end of Reconstruction and America's entry into the First World War, the country was transformed into a major economic power with a modern political system and a diverse and reformed society.

4.1 How did American society change in the period 1869–1896?

During the period between the Civil War and the First World War, American society changed dramatically. The USA became a major industrial and international power during this period and through immigration, urbanisation and western expansion became the society we recognise today. However, the Presidents that governed during that period are far from household names today – few Americans would recall much, if anything, of Presidents Garfield and Arthur, Hayes and Harrison. During the period after Reconstruction, Congress provided the main focus for federal politics. The battle for control of the Congress and the Presidency dominated party politics between the Democrats and Republicans. By the end of the period, third parties were increasingly challenging the stranglehold that the two main parties had on politics. Though the Republicans and Democrats saw off that challenge, by the 20th century the adoption of elements of progressive legislation by both parties showed a recognition that the politics of the 'Gilded Age' needed to come to an end.

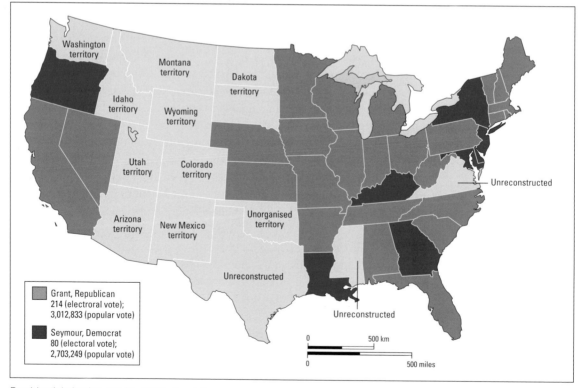

Presidential election results, 1868 – by states

Presidential and Congressional election results, 1868–1900

Year	Candidate	Party	Votes	Electoral college
1868	Grant	Republican	3,013,421	214
	Seymour	Democratic	2,706,829	80
1872	Grant	Republican	3,596,745	286
	Greeley	Democratic	2,843,446	63*
1876	Hayes	Republican	4,036,572	185
	Tilden	Democratic	4,284,020	184
	Cooper	Greenback	81,737	
1880	Garfield	Republican	4,453,295	214
	Hancock	Democratic	4,414,082	155
	Weaver	Greenback-Labor	308,578	
	Dow	Prohibition	10,305	
1884	Cleveland	Democratic	4,879,507	219
	Blaine	Republican	4,850,298	182
	Butler	Greenback-Labor	175,370	
	St John	Prohibition	150,369	
1888	Harrison	Republican	5,447,129	233
	Cleveland	Democratic	5,537,857	168
	Fisk	Prohibition	249,506	
	Streeter	Union Labor	146,935	
1892	Cleveland	Democratic	5,555,426	277
	Harrison	Republican	5,182,690	145
	Weaver	People's	1,029,846	22
	Bidwell	Prohibition	264,133	
1896	McKinley	Republican	7,102,246	271
	Bryan	Democratic	6,492,559	176
	Palmer	National Democratic	133,148	
	Levering	Prohibition	132,007	
1900	McKinley	Republican	7,218,491	292
	Bryan	Democratic	6,356,734	155
	Wooley	Prohibition	208,914	

* Greeley died between the election and the meeting of the electoral college, so his votes were distributed between four other Democrats.

How successful was the presidency of Grant, 1869–1877?

When the Republicans selected Ulysses Grant as their candidate for President in 1868, it was not because of his political record. Indeed he did not have one. He was chosen on the assumption that his war record would ensure that he was elected. Not only that, but the Radicals who dominated the party during the Reconstruction period saw in Grant someone who would be easy to influence. They also thought that Grant saw the role of President as essentially ceremonial and symbolic. Thus, his convincing victory in 1869 (winning 26 of the 34 states – see map) and re-election in 1872 gave Congress the opportunity to run the country essentially as it liked. Most of that time was spent on Reconstruction policy and later economic policies, while Grant surrounded himself with cronies, which did much to discredit the Presidency even further.

Reconstruction

The clashes that occurred under Lincoln and Johnson between the Presidency and Congress over the nature of Reconstruction policy and who was in charge, had been largely resolved by the time of Grant's election, and in favour of Congress. Thus Congress carried out the radical reconstruction favoured by men such as Thaddeus Stevens and Charles Sumner, with the

Carpetbaggers: Northerners who entered the Old South during Reconstruction (1865–1877) in order to exploit the area for profit.

Scallywags: Southern whites who cooperated with the federal occupation authorities in the Old South during the Reconstruction period.

support but minimal involvement of both the President and the Supreme Court. The mixture of **carpetbaggers**, **scallywags** and local blacks that dominated the Reconstruction governments of the South achieved mixed results, but their financial extravagance and corruption was little different from what was accepted elsewhere at the time. By 1870, all the former rebel states were back in the Union and the Fourteenth and Fifteenth Amendments to the US Constitution had been passed. When there appeared to be substantial white resistance to reconstruction, the federal government was initially prepared to get involved. It passed a series of Enforcement Acts, in 1870 and 1871, empowering the President to use military power to suppress southern violence and to use Congress to control federal elections.

This determination to enforce radical reconstruction gradually waned. By the mid-1870s, with the Supreme Court restricting the application of the Fourteenth Amendment and with the 1872 General Amnesty Act seeing Congress restore political privileges to thousands of former Confederates, there was little enthusiasm to pursue a vigorous policy ten years after the Civil War had ended. The 1876 election results were disputed, which led to a settlement that saw all federal troops withdrawn from the South in 1877 and the quick restoration of Democratic governments in the South.

Scandals and corruption
Although Grant was not personally corrupt, his time in office was marked by a series of scandals that undermined him, his office and the party to the extent that the term 'Grantism' emerged as an accepted word for corruption. By 1870, Senator James Grimes of Iowa was moved to describe the Republicans as 'the most corrupt and debauched political party that has

---

Scandals in the Grant Administration

Gold scandal, 1869
Two friends of the President – Jay Gould and Jim Fisk – devised a scheme to corner the market in gold. By spreading rumours that the President would not allow the Government to sell its own gold and by buying up much of the remaining gold themselves, they forced the price of gold up before selling when its price was at its highest.

Credit Mobilier scandal
The Credit Mobilier company had been founded by the stockholders of the Union Pacific Railroad Company to divert profits from the Railroad Company to themselves. An investigation by Congress in 1873 revealed that shares had been distributed among various Congressmen, including Vice-President Schuyler Colfax, in order to influence railroad legislation and keep Congress out of any unhelpful investigations.

The 1873 salary grab
Congress voted major salary increases across the federal government, including a 50% rise for Congressmen that was retrospective for two years. Public protest actually caused Congress to change its mind on the retrospective element, but the damage had been done to its reputation.

The Stanborn contracts of 1874
Secretary of the Treasury, William A. Richardson, was forced to resign after allowing a friend, John D. Stanborn, to claim exorbitant commissions for collecting unpaid revenues on Department taxes.

The Whisky Ring
Grant's private secretary, General Orville Babcock, was part of a conspiracy in St Louis that saw a combination of officials and distillers defrauding the Government of millions in tax revenues on the sale of whisky.

The Belknap Scandal of 1876
Secretary of War, William Belknap, was forced to resign in order to escape impeachment for accepting backhanders worth $25,000 for granting rights to sell supplies to Indian tribes.

A summary of presidential actions

President	Dates in office	Main issues of presidency
Ulysses S. Grant	1869–77	Reconstruction
		Series of corruption scandals
Rutherford B. Hayes	1877–81	Ending of Reconstruction
		Clashes with Congress over currency reform
		Clashes with Conkling over appointments in New York
James A. Garfield	1881	Assassinated by frustrated office-seeker
Chester Arthur	1881–85	Civil Service Reform
Grover Cleveland	1885–89	Dawes Act 1887
		Inter-state Commerce Act 1887
		Clashes over vetoes of pension and pork-barrel bills
		Conflict with Congress over tariffs
Benjamin Harrison	1889–93	Billion Dollar Congress
		McKinley Tariff Act
		Dependent Pensions Act
		Sherman Anti-Trust Act
		Sherman Silver Purchase Act
Grover Cleveland	1893–97	'The Panic of 1893'
		Intervention in 1894 Pullman Strike
		Continued growth of Populists
William McKinley	1897–1901	Spanish–American War
		Development of an empire

Bourbons: The white ruling class in the former Confederate states.

?
1. What were the major issues that faced Grant as President?

2. Was the presidency of Ulysses Grant little more than a period of corrupt government? Explain your answer.

ever existed'. Businessmen were able to buy off legislators and dominate political decision-making. There was virtually no civil service reform, much wasteful spending of government money and little achieved for it. Furthermore, the federal government set the standards for the rest of the country. The Reconstruction governments in the South were notoriously corrupt and gave the **Bourbons** the excuse they wanted to fight back. The political machine heavily controlled state government. At a local and city level, police would turn a blind eye to petty crime, such as gambling and prostitution, for a fee.

4.2 What were the key features of American politics, 1877–1896?

Politics was based on patronage, not principle

> 'The interests are in the main the interests of getting or keeping the patronage of government. Tenets and policies, points of political doctrine and points of political practice, have all but vanished. All has been lost, except office or the hope of it.'

Lord James Bryce's comments on the American Commonwealth in 1888 are appropriate for the whole period 1877–96. Elections were run ruthlessly, as a business, by the party bosses who organised local election machines. The most infamous of these was Tammany Hall, the New York City Democratic Party organisation. The party bosses were especially powerful in the cities where the large number of immigrants, the size of the electorate and the frequency of elections favoured party ticket voting. They were also helped by voting not being by secret ballot until 1890. Party bosses would instruct voters how to cast their votes, in return for help finding jobs, homes etc.

With the growth of the cities, there were many contracts to be handed out and many businesses found themselves depending on political supporters to get work. Many paid jobs, such as customs officials and postmasters, were in the gift of politicians from the President down. A change of party would lead to a whole-scale redistribution of jobs. The most notorious, the Democrats' Tweed Ring in New York, distributed 60,000 posts between 1869 and 1871, increasing city debts by $70 million in the process. Indeed, the assassin who killed President James Garfield in 1881 was a disgruntled office-seeker who shot the President as he was leaving Washington DC to escape the office-seekers who had plagued him since his election six months before. With little dividing the main parties politically, this may explain the relatively high turnout in elections during this period (80% of the electorate voted in the 1888 presidential election, compared with only 55% a hundred years later).

Lack of clear party divisions on the main issues

Although there were many issues that caused political debate during the period, the debate often took place within the two parties, rather than between them. Although the Republicans and Democrats tended to attract different types of supporters, it is best to see the two parties as coalitions rather than tightly organised and disciplined parties we are used to in today's politics. Wilson referred to the Democrats and Republicans as 'two empty bottles that differed only in their labels'. Indeed, on the main issues of the day – such as currency reform, big business, farming, civil service reform, immigration and the role of government – the area a Congressman came from was more likely to influence his vote than the party to which he belonged. Thus the Democratic President Grover Cleveland, coming from the east coast, was as opposed to cheap money policies as his Republican opponent in 1888, Benjamin Harrison. The Republican Chester Arthur spent much of his presidency reforming the civil service, in the teeth of the opposition of his previous Republican sponsor, Roscoe Conkling.

No party was able to dominate nationally during the period

The winning margin in all presidential elections fought between 1876 and 1892 was very close, less than 1% in three of the five elections. In 1880, Garfield won the popular vote by only 9,000 votes out of nine million cast; whilst in 1888, Grover Cleveland actually got more votes than Benjamin Harrison but lost in the electoral college. The political balance in Congress was also very close, with the Republicans tending to win in the Senate and the Democrats in the House of Representatives. On only one occasion between 1889 and 1891 did the same party (Republicans) control the presidency, Senate and House of Representatives. Because of this, party leaders found it hard to sustain a party programme. Inevitability, this led to compromise and **bipartisanship**. It also encouraged the development of **pork-barrel politics**, as Presidents and party leaders were forced to buy off supporters to get legislation through.

Bipartisanship: Both parties having to put aside their differences for a while (e.g. in a war or over a piece of legislation on which they both agree).

Pork-barrel politics: Term to describe the way in which politicians went to Washington DC to gain benefits for their home state and district.

There was an absence of a strong presidency

Although generally decent and honest, few of the Presidents sought the powers or influence of Lincoln. The Presidency had been damaged during the Reconstruction period when Congress had established its predominance

Administration: The presidential or executive branch of US government. The Administration consists of the President and his advisors, notably the secretaries of the various departments, such as Justice or Labor.

Patronage: Help and financial support given by someone to a person or a group.

over Johnson during the impeachment trial – predominance confirmed by the Supreme Court. There was a general acceptance that the President's role was as a figurehead who presided over the **Administration** rather than being particularly proactive – an idea encouraged by Grant's deliberate lack of engagement from the major issues of the day. With real control being in the Congress, party officials were keen to find cooperative, friendly types as President who would be unlikely to upset too many people and would dispense the **patronage** as the parties hoped. Presidents did not always live up to this expectation. Chester Arthur played an important role in civil service reform, for example, but recent politics had tended to work against any President trying to increase his powers within the balances of the federal government.

How did the two main parties differ from one another?

There were only two national parties that had developed in, and survived, the Civil War and Reconstruction period: the Republicans and the Democrats. Parties existed most actively on a local level and only really acted nationally at election time, especially when it came to choosing a presidential candidate. The main role of the party organisations was to nominate candidates, raise funds, conduct election campaigns and, perhaps most importantly in this period, distribute patronage via government jobs and contracts. On many issues, there was little to distinguish one party from the other. The reasons for getting heavily involved in party politics were more to do with getting some of the spoils of office if your man won. It is, however, possible to see some pointers to party affiliation, even if the following suggestions are a serious generalisation and there are many regional exceptions.

The main issues in American politics, 1877–1896

Although the positions of the parties, personalities and electorate varied according to time and place, there were five major issues that occupied the federal government during the period 1877–1896. It is worth considering the issues involved in each of them, before assessing the attitudes and actions of the leading politicians.

The money issue – greenbacks, gold and silver

Bimetallism: Using both gold and silver as currency.

Since the 1790s, the United States had supported **bimetallism**. In 1834, a ratio of 1:16 in the value of gold to silver was agreed – that is, one ounce of gold would be worth 16 ounces of silver. The consequence of this was that silver was undervalued (i.e. it was actually worth more than the currency rates suggested, so silver ore would fetch more on the open market than the Mint would pay). This became worse as more gold was discovered in California in 1848. As a result of this, instead of altering the ratio of gold to silver, silver was 'demonetised' in the 1873 Coinage Act, in other words it was no longer to be used as currency. At the same time, the price of silver began to fall and western silver miners immediately denounced the 'Crime of 1873'. They saw it as an east coast and gold miners' conspiracy. They demanded a repeal of the Coinage Act, so that silver could again be used. Unlimited circulation of silver would have had the consequence of putting more money into circulation (for there was a shortage of gold). This would, in turn, have had inflationary consequences (putting up prices). This was something that attracted farmers who were eager to get more money for the products that they sold internally. At the time they felt that keeping only gold kept prices down on internally produced goods, so they supported the silver miners. Others who supported inflationary measures were those who had to borrow money (often farmers) and exporters. An inflationary policy made money worth less over time and so made the cost of debts lower. Exporters would be able to sell their goods abroad more easily, as other countries would get more dollars for their own currencies and so be able to buy more with fewer pounds, francs or whatever.

This approach was opposed by those who called for an inflationary policy of sound money. They argued that increasing the amount of money in circulation would raise prices for ordinary consumers, undermine the value of pensions and savings, and make people less likely to invest in the American economy.

The debate not only took place in the arguments between gold and silver, but also between the use of coins and banknotes (known as greenbacks). It was not possible to follow an inflationary policy if all transactions had to take place in gold – for by definition you could only then have as much currency as you had gold. However, if you had banknotes, the notes did not cost as much to produce and a government could produce more of them if they wished to, making the dollar worth less. The 1875 Resumption Act made all greenbacks redeemable in gold, so that the Government could not do this. Thus campaigners for an inflationary policy could also campaign for the repeal of the 1875 Act, allowing for the printing of more notes.

The currency battle that was fought throughout this period was between those who supported 'sound money' policies and wanted to stick with gold and those who wanted to see inflationary measures that could either be brought about through the printing of more 'greenbacks' or by returning to bimetallism.

Corruption and civil service reform

Civil service: This consists of all the government departments that administer the affairs of the country and all the people who work in them.

Meritocracy: A social system in which people have power or prestige because of their abilities and intelligence, rather than because of their wealth or social status.

Most of the positions in the **civil service** were in the gift of the President (or the governors of states for that matter) and so tended to go to friends and supporters of the main political parties, regardless of whether they were the best people for the jobs. In 1881, the Civil Service Reform League was formed to campaign for an end to this patronage and the creation of a non-partisan civil service based on **meritocracy**, in which positions would be given on the basis of competitive examination rather than simply by presidential appointment. In this way, reformers hoped they could end corruption, the extravagance of the number of appointments and the size of salaries given, and the inefficiency and inadequacy of so many office holders.

This campaign was always likely to be difficult to convince politicians to support. It was all very well convincing politicians of the need for reform when they were out of government, if as soon as they were in government they were likely to want to reward their own supporters and suddenly be less interested in change. Nevertheless, improvements were gradually made during this period. It became especially significant when the assassination of President Garfield was seen as partly caused by the frustrations of office-seekers.

The tariff

This was one of the few issues that clearly separated the Republicans from the Democrats. There was also a regional and occupational distinction, with southerners and farmers tending to favour lowering tariffs, and easterners and industrialists favouring higher tariffs. Tariffs were used for two purposes: to raise government revenue and to protect American industry. Industrialists argued that American industry could not begin to compete with the more advanced industrial nations, especially Britain. So it was necessary to make American goods more attractive to American consumers by taxing foreign products coming into the country (i.e. tariffs). However, those who exported most of their items, especially farmers and cotton producers, felt that higher tariffs made their goods harder to sell abroad. This was both because of the likelihood that some countries would respond by taxing imports themselves, as well as because if Americans did not buy foreign goods then foreigners would not get the dollars they needed to buy American. It was also argued that tariffs added to the costs of imported goods in America and so allowed domestic producers to charge more, which meant farmers and consumers generally were out of pocket.

High tariffs throughout the period diminished the argument for tariffs as a money-raising measure, since the Government was regularly running a budget surplus. This meant that more money was going into the Treasury than was going out. Thus westerners and southerners increasingly came to see the government's tariff policy as one that discriminated in favour of industry over agriculture.

Pensions

Pressure group: An organisation that wishes to influence political decision-making but does not wish to gain political power.

One of the ways in which the Government dispensed of its ever-increasing surplus was through pensions. This was encouraged by the powerful **pressure group**, The Grand Army of the Republic, which represented war veterans. Pensions after the Civil War and from previous conflicts such as the Mexican Wars had generally been limited, both in the numbers claiming and the amounts claimed. However, the Arrears of Pensions Act of 1879 granted back-payment for disability connected with war service. Later the law was changed to allow pension payments for anyone unable to work and who had previously served in the army. By 1885, there were 350,000 names on the pension list and lawyers encouraged the number to grow. When the Bureau of Pensions did not award a pension to someone, lobbying of a representative usually led to a private pension bill being passed in Congress. In this way, the issue of pensions became crucial during the period and pensioners became an important pressure group, most closely identified with the Republicans as the 'party that saved the Union'.

Big business and regulation

The power of big business to dominate politicians became increasingly resented by individual producers and workers during this period. It was hard to counter given the financial support big business was able to give to secure the legislation and handbacks wanted. Increased pressure was put on governments to regulate some of the worst excesses of big business. This was initially on a local level and then developed upwards. On occasion, appeals were made to the courts – such as the '1877 Munn versus Illinois' ruling which said that states could regulate property in the interests of the public good where that property was operating in the public interest. This meant, for example, that they could prevent railroads from charging different prices to farmers and to large companies for the same journeys.

Trusts: Groups of people that have control of, and invest, amounts of money, property etc. usually on behalf of other people.

At other times, the federal government did take a lead with acts such as the Interstate Commerce Act of 1887 which created a regulatory body on railroads and the 1890 Sherman Anti-Trust Act which tried to limit the growth of large and powerful industrial **trusts**. Inevitably though, most politicians of both major parties depended on the support of big business and most of the legislation enacted lacked credibility.

How did the Presidents and Congresses deal with these issues?

The presidency of Rutherford Hayes, 1877–1881

Hayes was a modest and decent man, prouder of his Civil War record than anything he achieved as President. He himself said afterwards, 'I know my place was a very humble one – a place utterly unknown in history. But I

White House: Where the President of the USA resides when in office. It is in Washington DC and lives up to its name.

Rutherford Birchard Hayes (1822–1893)
19th President of the USA (1877–81), a Republican. Major general on the Union side in the Civil War. During his presidency, federal troops were withdrawn from southern states (after the Reconstruction period) and the civil service was reformed. Noted for his honesty and integrity.

Vetoed: To become law a bill is passed through various stages in Congress and then signed by the President. The President can refuse to sign. This is called the veto.

Stalwart faction: A section within the Republican Party that supported President Grant, a radical policy towards the South and the spoils system.

James A. Garfield (1831–1881)
20th President of the USA (1881), a Republican. Served in the Civil War with the Union forces. He held office for only four months before being assassinated in a Washington DC railway station by frustrated office-seeker, Charles Guiteau. His short term in office is marked by struggles within the Republican Party over influence and Cabinet posts.

---

am also glad to know that I was one of the good colonels.' Hayes' **White House** could not have been more different from that of Grant as he was determined to make the Republicans the 'party of morality'. There were morning prayers and nightly 'hymn sings'. Swearing, tobacco and alcohol went out with the corruption, with Mrs Hayes earning the nickname 'Lemonade Lucy' because of her insistence on strict teetotalism throughout the White House. Despite all this, Hayes could not escape the fact that his election in 1876 was marred by controversy. The Democrats never accepted a result that had required the disputed votes of three states to give Hayes a singe-vote victory in the electoral college. 'His Fraudulency' or 'Rutherfraud' Hayes had to accept from the start that his would be only a one-term Presidency.

Hayes remained faithful to the placation of the South as established in the 1877 Compromise. Troops were withdrawn from the remaining occupied states and Hayes appointed a Southern Democrat, David Key of Tennessee, to his Cabinet as Postmaster General. He was not going to abandon the Southern Republicans and blacks altogether though, and he **vetoed** Congressional attempts to repeal the Force Acts.

Hayes found himself in some conflict with Congress over appointments, immigration and currency reform. This indicated likely problems for some of his successors. Hayes found himself vetoing a bill designed to forbid Chinese immigration into California. He also vetoed the Bland–Allison Act of 1878 (although it was passed, amended) – an inflationary Act that tried to increase the amount of silver in circulation. Hayes thus associated himself firmly with those who supported currency stability and he also supported the Specie Act of 1879, which insisted that all greenbacks should be redeemed in gold after January 1879.

The most controversial aspects of Hayes' Presidency were his attempts to insist on a meritocratic system of appointments and his preference for civil service reform. Such policies were not easy to implement, for those who supported him in reaching the White House now expected their reward. In particular, he found himself in conflict with Senator Conkling of New York. Conkling was the powerful head of the **Stalwart faction** within the Republican Party and it was clear that the New York Customs House had been used by Conkling to reward Stalwarts with lucrative positions at the House. In 1877, Hayes dismissed two such officials, Chester Arthur and Alonzo Cornell. Hayes found himself in a massive struggle with Conkling. Although the President finally got his replacements through Congress, it was not without a real tussle and internal Republican bitterness. Hayes was scared off any further attempts at civil service reform.

James Garfield and Chester Arthur, 1881–1885
Tensions within the Republican Party were evident when it came to choosing the candidates for the 1880 election. Roscoe Conkling and the Stalwarts, determined to avoid another Hayes, pushed for the return of the freer and more corrupt days of the early 1870s and for the adoption of Grant to run for a third term. A faction that rallied around Senator James Blaine of Maine opposed them. They were known as the Half-Breeds, because their more liberal Republicanism (favouring Hayes' conciliatory policy towards the South and civil service reform) seemed only half-hearted. With the Stalwarts pushing for Grant and the Half-Breeds for Blaine, the Republican Convention was deadlocked. On the 36th vote, the anti-Grant factions united behind Senator James Garfield, a less prominent Half-Breed, who promptly chose Chester Arthur as his running-mate as a sop to the Stalwarts.

In a bitter and contentious election campaign against Democrat

**Chester A. Arthur
(1830–1886)**
21st President of the USA
(1881–85), a Republican. Had
never held an elected office
until he was made Garfield's
Vice-President in 1880.
Became Garfield's successor
when the President was shot
by an angry office-seeker.

Dogma: System of beliefs which is
accepted as true and which people
are expected to accept, without
questioning it.

**James Gillespie Blaine
(1830–1893)**
A charismatic and loyal party
man. Elected to the House of
Representatives (1862), he
became Speaker in 1868. He
was unsuccessful in gaining
the Republican presidential
nominations (1876 and 1880).
Served briefly as Garfield's
Secretary of State. Gained the
Republican presidential
nomination in 1884, but was
defeated by Grover Cleveland.
During the Harrison
Administration (1889–93),
Blaine again served as
Secretary of State.

General Winfield S. Hancock (Union commander at Gettysburg), Garfield triumphed by a majority of only 9,000 votes (though his victory in the electoral college was rather more convincing). Garfield immediately made it clear that he would favour his own Half-Breed faction. Blaine was the power behind the throne as Secretary of State, while appointments deliberately ignored the Stalwarts. Garfield even provoked the resignation of Conkling over his appointments to the New York Customs House – an action which, when Conkling failed to get the backing in New York he had expected, led to the Stalwart's leader retiring from politics altogether. His dealings with the Stalwarts were, however, to be his undoing. On 2 July 1881, Garfield was shot by a frustrated and unbalanced office-seeker, Charles Guiteau, who cried 'I am a Stalwart and Arthur is President now.' Guiteau was not quite right, for Garfield lingered on until September before dying of his wounds, but it meant that by the autumn the 'spoilsman's spoilsman' was in the White House with almost a full term to run.

Chester Arthur was quite different from his more austere predecessors. He threw out the sideboard presented to 'Lemonade Lucy' by the Women's Christian Temperance Union (it found its way into a saloon) and approached his unexpected task in a more relaxed and hospitable mood. However, the new President had never held an elected office until the Vice-Presidency, and it was only as a compromise that he had got that job. Closely associated with Conkling, he had been sacked by Hayes from the New York Customs House and virtually admitted his use of 'soap' in politics (i.e. 'you scrub my back and I'll scrub yours'). However, in office, Arthur was to be a disappointment to his former colleagues, so much so that Conkling found himself lamenting the end of the Hayes Administration. Arthur surprised almost everyone by the independence he showed, especially in his support for both civil service and tariff reform. In tariff reform he could not overcome the Republicans' unquestioning support for the **dogma** of high tariffs. The 'Mongrel Tariff' passed in 1883 was a measly reform worth a reduction of only 2%, with some prices actually rising.

In tackling fraud and civil service reform, however, Arthur was far more successful. He supported the prosecution of former cronies in the Star Route Fraud cases. In 1882, he vetoed an $18 million river and harbour development bill because of its pork-barrel elements (though Congress overturned his veto). Most significantly, Arthur used the general public revulsion at the assassination of Garfield, at least partially because of the spoils system, to justify his cooperation with Congress and the Civil Service Reform League to pass the Pendleton Civil Service Act of 1883. He also appointed a reformer as its first chairman. Thus, the man sacked by Hayes as a corrupt customs official, established as President the basis for a merit-driven civil service that by 1900 had 40% of its posts listed as 'classified services'.

Arthur sought the Republican nomination for the 1884 election but, although he was popular enough with the public, his own party did not look kindly on someone who had blocked so many of their appointments and schemes. Instead they plumped for Conkling's old rival, James Blaine, as their candidate.

A Democrat in the White House – Grover Cleveland, 1885–1889
While most Republicans supported Blaine, a small but significant group objected to his association with the spoils system, especially over his involvement with an alleged scandal (The Mulligan Letters). It seemed that Blaine had accepted money for securing a land grant for an Arkansas railroad. This group, known as the Mugwumps, supported the Democratic

(Stephen) Grover Cleveland (1837–1908)

22nd and 24th President of the USA (1885–89 and 1893–97). A beer-drinking, 18-stone, 'ugly-honest' man from Buffalo. Mayor of Buffalo (1881) and Governor of New York. First Democratic President elected after the Civil War, and the only President to hold office in two non-consecutive terms. Within a year of taking office for the second time, four million were unemployed and the USA was virtually bankrupt. Cleveland attempted to check corruption in public life.

Probity: High standard of correct moral behaviour.

candidate, Grover Cleveland. The Democrats had chosen well, for Cleveland had already established a reputation as an honest, practical opponent of the spoils system in his positions as Mayor of Buffalo and Governor of New York. As mayor, he had refused to accept 'pork-barrel bills', earning the title 'the veto mayor'. He also gained a good number of enemies in the process – something that seemed to do him no harm in the eyes of the ordinary voter: 'We love him for the enemies he has made,' wrote General Edward Bragg in 1884.

The election was another colourful one, with allegations about Blaine's financial **probity** being answered by the Republicans with rumours that Cleveland had fathered a child in his wilder bachelor days. In the end, the result was another close one, with Cleveland winning by a margin of 60,000 in the popular vote. There is no doubt that the Republicans were harmed by the Mugwumps' support for Cleveland. A late controversy in New York, where Catholic Irish took exception to the Republicans' claims that the Democrats were a party of 'rum, Romanism and rebellion', saw a late swing to the Democrats in this closely-fought state.

In office, Cleveland did bring to government the probity he promised. In the West, 81 million acres of public land were restored to the federal government after misappropriation by the 'cattle barons'. Various suits were brought against those interests that Cleveland saw as exploiting Indian lands and railroad deals. He vetoed 413 bills, more than twice that of all previous Presidents combined, believing government should be both honest and minimal. 'Though the people support the government, the government should not support the people,' he said when vetoing a bill, in 1887, to give $10,000 to relieve drought in Texas. Various Acts, passed in an unusual burst of bipartisanship, made government more efficient and balanced (see panel).

- The Tenure of Office Act, dating from Reconstruction days, was repealed in 1887.

- The Presidential Succession Act made it clearer who succeeded should the Vice-President also be incapacitated.

- The Electoral Count Act of 1887 helped to improve the procedure for disputed elections.

- The Interstate Commerce Act of 1887 created the first federal regulatory board with inter-state jurisdiction – a reform Cleveland only signed reluctantly – his instincts were for big business not big government, as we have seen.

- In 1889 the Agricultural Department was improved and upgraded.

- The Dawes Act of 1887 brought a solution (the success of which is dealt with elsewhere) to the question of Indian/Settler relations.

In spite of all that, those that anticipated significant civil service reform were to be disappointed. As the first Democratic politician to be elected since 1856, there were a lot of people expecting jobs and rewards from him. Although Cleveland extended the list of protected civil service jobs to 27,000, he essentially followed the party line and two-thirds of all federal office holders were Democrats by the time Cleveland left office.

The main issues occupying Cleveland when in office were concerned with pensions and tariffs. The cost to the government of pensions had grown rapidly throughout the period, so that by 1885 there were 350,000 names on the pensions' register and costs had risen to $80 million a year. Cleveland vetoed over 200 private pensions bills. The biggest clash with Congress came, however, in 1887 over the Dependent Pension Bill. This was passed by Congress but vetoed by Cleveland. In the Bill, the need to have been disabled 'in war' was removed and it became simply the case that anyone 'unable to work for any reason' qualified for a pension. The issue had not been resolved by the 1888 election and it gave the Republicans the opportunity to campaign on a promise to boost the finances of Union war veterans.

Initially, Cleveland had done little regarding tariffs, although it was a traditional Democratic issue to try and reduce them. At the end of 1887, he finally moved and proposed a reduction in tariffs that would reduce the average level from around 47% to 40%. The Bill was supported in the House of Representatives but floundered in the Senate. Like pensions, this was another issue that clearly separated the Democrats and Republicans when it came to the 1888 presidential election. Cleveland was not, in any sense, arguing for **free trade**. He was keen to point that out, stressing that he was not ideological about it: 'It is a condition which confronts us, not a theory.'

Thus the 1888 presidential election was the first since the Civil War with a clearly-defined issue dominating it: tariffs. The Democrats campaigned for Cleveland to be re-elected, relying on his record in office as a sound, efficient and honest President. The Republicans responded with Benjamin Harrison, grandson of a former President and a senator from Indiana. The campaign was hard-fought and dirty, with big business pouring substantial money into the Republican campaign to defend higher tariffs. There were rumours of bribery and personal scandals circulating throughout the campaign. The Republicans made a pitch for the veterans' votes with their promises on pensions and took the opportunity to remind voters of which side they had been on in the Civil War, over 20 years after its conclusion. In the end, Cleveland got the most votes but it was Harrison who carried the day, winning the key marginal states of Indiana and New York.

Benjamin Harrison and the 'Billion-dollar Congress', 1889–1893

On his election, Harrison rejoiced that 'Providence has given us the victory'. To which the Republican National Chairman privately responded to a journalist friend, 'Think of it. He ought to know that Providence hadn't a damn thing to do with it.' If he had not realised it initially, Harrison soon discovered how many promises had been made to get him to the White House. Although personally uncorrupt, he was soon lamenting: 'I could not name my own Cabinet. They had sold out every place to pay the election expenses.' The earnest and conservative President saw his Administration dominated by James Blaine, who returned as Secretary of State, Thomas Reed, the Speaker of the House and William McKinley, the powerful Chairman of the 'Ways and Means Committee' in the House. It soon became clear that Congress would be calling the shots.

With Republicans controlling both Houses of Congress and the Presidency – a rare moment in this period – they were determined to pass through a Republican agenda. They were helped significantly by Speaker Reed's rule changes, which he forced through the House to increase his own power and to minimise the impact of the Democrat minority. The Congress was quickly named the 'Billion-dollar Congress'. It was soon passing legislation to help its supporters, not least its big business paymasters.

In Harrison's first year, 31,000 of the 55,000 postmasters in the USA

Free trade: Agreements with trading partners by which each state accepted the products of the other without taxing them, confident that they would both benefit from the arrangement. The benefits of free trade were felt to be considerable: wider markets for domestic products, cheaper goods from elsewhere for the country's consumers, and possible stimulation of domestic industries through competition with strong foreign industries.

Benjamin Harrison (1833–1901)
23rd President of the USA (1889–93), a Republican. He called the first Pan-American Conference, which led to the establishment of the Pan-American Union, aimed at improving inter-American cooperation. It was also intended to develop commercial ties. This became the Organisation of American States in 1948.

were replaced with Republican sympathisers. Over $1 billion was spent on pork-barrel measures to improve harbours, rivers and transport systems and in generous payments to bond-holders. The Dependent Pension Act of 1890 was similar to that vetoed by Cleveland in 1887 and saw the number of pensions rise from 490,000 in 1889 at a cost of $89 million to 966,000 and $175 million by 1893. The appointment of a leading veteran as the Pension Commissioner only served to further the generosity with which pensions were awarded. The most blatant sop to their supporters came in the Republicans' attitude to tariffs with the McKinley Tariff Act of 1890. The tariff reached new prohibitive heights of around 49.5% by 1890. It allowed the President to put duties on goods kept on the free list if he felt it would pressurise them into a reciprocal tariff reduction. This time, the tariff was fixed so high that it did have an impact on prices. The perception that Republicans were favouring businessmen at the expense of consumers became widespread.

The Administration did pass some legislation that was more bipartisan in spirit. In 1890 the Sherman Anti-Trust Act marked the first attempt at limiting the powers of the Trusts, although it was only as effective as the courts and the President wanted it to be. In the same year, the Sherman Silver Purchase Act was passed which was, at least partially, inflationary. It pleased the silver miners in the West by committing the Treasury to buying 4.5 million ounces of silver a month, using notes redeemable with gold. This Act was passed in the hope of getting support for the Tariff Act and may also have been a response to the growing influence of the western states. This was best shown by the admission of six new states into the Union: North and South Dakota, Montana and Washington in 1889 and Idaho and Wyoming in 1890.

These more conciliatory measures were not enough, however, to save the Republicans from the voters' wrath. In the 1890 mid-term elections, the Republicans were dramatically turned out of the House, losing nearly half their seats, including McKinley's. Two years later, Cleveland was back as President, defeating Harrison in a rerun of 1888. Much of this was to do with successful Democratic attacks on the 'Billion-dollar Congress' and on the higher prices which were blamed on the high tariffs. There was also something of a Democratic revival as traditional supporters took exception to local Republican attempts at prohibition (six states went 'dry' in the 1880s) and anti-immigration policies – such as Wisconsin's law in 1889 which insisted that only English be used in schools in a state with large German and Scandinavian minorities. There was also something else going on in the early 1890s when rural discontent in the South and the West was beginning to make itself felt at the ballot box. In 1890, nine Congressmen were elected as 'Alliance-Populists'.

It is necessary now to look back and trace the development of a movement known as **Populism** that would dominate and determine the politics of the 1890s.

Populism: Beliefs based on the interests and opinions of the ordinary people. This sometimes involves the use of people's fears to achieve political success.

1. In what ways was national politics corrupt in the period 1877–1896?

2. How far was the political system reformed between 1877–1896?

3. Explain why there was so much debate over tariffs and the currency in the period 1877–1896.

4.3 Who were the Populists and what did they believe?

Jefferson's vision of the yeoman farmers acting as the mainstream of the American Republic, his 'chosen people of God', had become somewhat tarnished by the later decades of the 19th century. The victory of the North in the Civil War, and the domination of the Republicans with their industrial and East Coast agenda since then, had made farmers and westerners feel marginalised by the political elites. Several movements emerged in the 1870s and 1880s to reflect the farmers' growing sense of isolation. This reached its peak in the 1890s when various strands of opinion were united, first in the Populist Party which won over one million votes in 1892 and carried four states, and later behind the populist Democratic candidate for President, William Jennings Bryan, in 1896.

The situation for western farmers was far from easy. Life was harsh and lonely on the frontier (see Chapter 2). Many were vulnerable to fluctuations in nature, such as the drop in rainfall levels between the mid-1880s and mid-1890s which caused extensive droughts, and the plagues of grass-hoppers that frequently wreaked havoc on the plains. Things were made worse by the dramatic fall in prices that occurred during the period, as the table shows.

Price of crop per bushel

	1866	1893–1894
Wheat	$1.45	49c
Corn	75c	28c
Cotton	31c	6c

The fall in prices was primarily due to a significant increase in domestic production (with new acreage, agricultural and transport improvements and the natural response of farmers facing falling profits to produce more) and a major increase in overseas competition. There was a general global increase in production as new techniques were developed. The USA faced serious competition for their goods from Argentina, Canada, Australia and Russia, all of whom could transport agricultural goods further afield with improvements in refrigeration and canning. Although tariffs generally protected the American market, agriculture had relied on exports for a major part of its income (wheat producers exported around 40% of production and cotton 70%). American agriculture now faced markets closed or limited by cheap competition. Although many of these factors were beyond the control of federal government, inevitably farmers facing ruin looked for something or someone to blame. They soon found themselves attacking the system.

Tariffs were an obvious target. Even Cleveland's proposals to cut tariffs in 1887 would only have reduced average levels to 40%. Farmers resented a situation in which they bought protected products manufactured in the USA and so kept at an artificially high price, while they were expected to sell unprotected agricultural products, both at home and abroad. They also faced the possibility that foreign markets would retaliate for their goods being taxed as they entered America by putting tariffs on American exports, often agricultural. The McKinley Tariff of 1890 was thus the last straw for many western farmers, who saw the government as significantly alien to their interests.

Railroad costs also caused resentment. Individual farmers were faced with higher charges than big business were, for using the same route. This was a consequence of the 'discriminatory system' by which railroad companies would negotiate special concessions for companies regularly using their lines or travelling on certain routes. It meant that travel between certain stretches of railroad, such as New York to Chicago or Baltimore, was significantly cheaper than in more rural areas where farmers found themselves charged two or three times as much. Naturally, farmers felt that they were paying disproportionately to the profits of the railroad companies.

The government's preference for a deflationary economic policy made the situation worse. Low commodity prices were encouraged and credit was tight, in an attempt to prevent significant inflation, with the consequence

Mortgaged: Land or property is used as a guarantee to a company in order to borrow money from them.

Crop-lien system: Ownership of the crops produced and sold is retained by the farmer until payment for the crops is received.

that money was expensive and interest rates high. Although much of this was to do with the governments, Republican and Democrat, an easier target for blame was the banks who charged high interest rates and considerable commission and service charges. Farmers often had to borrow and found much of their land **mortgaged** in the West or operating under the **crop-lien system** in the South. Failure to meet mortgages in the West saw farmers lose their land and become tenants or workers on the new bonanza farms that were springing up across the prairies. The currency issue was thus highly relevant to farmers who saw the continued determination to stick to gold and to avoid the inflationary implications of greenbacks or silver as another example of putting business interests in the East ahead of agricultural concerns in the South and West.

How do you account for the rise of Populism?

Despite these growing concerns, farmers did not immediately pose a serious political threat. Their physical isolation from one another, as well as a psychological sense of independence and 'rugged individualism', made farmers reluctant to come together, as workers tended to form unions. It was also difficult to focus on precisely what grievances farmers felt needed addressing and what it was within the powers of government – national and local. Nevertheless, there were early movements which began a tradition of rural protest and combination that eventually grew into the major political party that was the Populists.

The Granger Movement

Founded in 1867 by Oliver Kelly, the Granger Movement was initially a social and economic organisation that tried to create a sense of community among isolated farmers who could not tackle the problems that they faced alone. The National Grange of Patrons of Industry, as it was officially known, sought to promote farmer-owned cooperatives for buying and selling goods, so removing the middleman. The Granger Movement sponsored the creation of a whole host of companies and businesses owned cooperatively by farmers and run for farmers. By 1875, there were 800,000

Cartoon from 1873 entitled 'The Grange Awakening the Sleepers', showing a Granger attack on railroad practices.

Cartoon drawn for 'Harper's Weekly' in 1886 entitled 'The Senatorial Round-House'.

members in 21,000 local parties (or lodges). Increasingly, the Granger Movement turned to political action to try and promote its members' interests. By 1873–74, there were Granger representatives in varying levels of control in 11 state legislatures, five of which passed so-called Granger Laws aimed at limiting the powers of railroad companies and big business generally in their state. Several cases went to court and the most famous ('Munn v Illinois' in 1877) marked the high point of Granger influence. As the economy began to improve in the later 1870s, membership tailed off. However, initial noises had been made to show that, when working together, the farmers could achieve something and a number of its members moved into the growing Greenback Party.

The Greenbacks
The Greenback Party had been established in 1875 and contested the 1876 presidential election. In 1878, they merged with the National Labor Reform Party to form the Greenback Labor Party and got more than a million votes and 14 representatives elected in 1878. Presidential candidate James Weaver secured 308,578 votes in the closely-fought 1880 election, though they had tailed off by 1884. The Greenback Party called for an inflationary economic policy that would, by printing paper money and increasing the amount of silver in circulation, make the dollar cheaper and so help farmers deal with their debts while improving their competitiveness when selling abroad.

The Farmers' Alliances
These alliances sprang up in the 1880s. They were a series of farmers' groups that had coalesced into three main areas by the end of the 1880s: the North-western Alliance in the Mid-West, the Southern Alliance and the Colored Farmers' Alliance, all of which had a majority of about one million. The Southern Alliance, under the leadership of Dr Charles W. Macune, soon became the dominant organisation from which the others took a lead. In some ways, the alliances were similar to the Granger Movement of the 1870s, with attempts at cooperative movements and a strong sense of community. However, they also presented a clear political agenda. In 1899, the Northern and Southern alliances, though maintaining independence from one another, adopted similar programmes which included a graduated income tax, nationalisation of transport and communications, and free unlimited coinage of silver. They were thus reflecting the farmers' concerns over the previous decades for an inflationary monetary policy and checks on the discriminatory powers of big business. The movements were especially attracted to Macune's subtreasury plan, presented to but rejected by Congress in 1890.

Macune proposed that: the Treasury give loans at 80% of the value of a farmer's stock; those crops be stored in a federal warehouse at 1% interest; these loans be paid in legal-tender notes. The policy would combine several aims of the alliances – it would be inflationary, it would solve farmers' credit problems and it would allow farmers to choose when to resell their crops, letting them control market prices to some extent. Its rejection by Congress was hardly surprising, but it did galvanise many farmers into seeking their own political party as they felt that the rejection of the Macune Plan showed that they could not hope for their objectives to be met by the traditional parties.

Increasingly, farmers were calling for easier credit, inflationary fiscal policy and regulation of big business, especially railroads. They met some success in local politics. In the 1890 elections, Alliance candidates took control of the Legislatures of Kansas (where they also won the governorship) and Nebraska, and held the balance of power in South Dakota and Minnesota. In the South, the situation was more complex as many feared that if the Populists were to challenge the dominant Bourbon Democrat groups, they might split the white vote and let in black Republicans. This fear was not eased by the high profile of Tom Watson of Georgia, who urged the blacks and whites to fight together against the Bourbons. Most whites who might have been attracted to the Alliance movements did not share Watson's progressive views and preferred to try and influence Democratic politicians to accept some of the Alliance demands in return for their electoral support.

Thus, in 1890, we can detect four pro-Alliance governors and seven pro-Alliance Legislatures in the South. The experience of the Granger Movements, the Greenback Party and the Farmers' Alliances were important in raising issues and in encouraging farmers to see that they shared a common interest against the main parties dominated by eastern politicians and money. The basis for the emergence of the Populists had been set.

What was the importance of the 1892 and 1896 elections?

The Omaha Platform and the 1892 election
The Populists were formally created at a meeting in St Louis in February 1892, where a combination of Greenbackers, farmers' alliances, Knights of Labor and reform groups came together as the People's Party. They agreed to meet at Omaha on 4 July to adopt a platform and a presidential candidate for the November elections. At the July meeting, they selected James Weaver, a former Greenbacker and a respectable figure, as their presidential candidate and adopted what came to be known as the 'Omaha Platform', written by Ignatius Donnelly of Minnesota. The opening paragraphs illustrate the dramatic style and tone of the document:

> 'The conditions which surround us best justify our cooperation; we meet in the midst of a nation brought to the verge of moral, political and material ruin. Corruption dominates the ballot-box, the Legislatures, the Congress, and touches even the ermine of the bench [judges]. The people are demoralised; most of the States have been compelled to isolate the voters at the polling places to prevent universal intimidation or bribery. The newspapers are largely subsidised or muzzled, public opinion silenced, business prostrated, homes covered with mortgages, labor impoverished, and the land concentrating in the hands of capitalists.'

The platform combined the old concerns of Greenbackers and Farmers' Alliances with new attempts to secure rights for their 'fellow producers', the industrial workers. Thus the Populists were going one step beyond the previous pressure groups in trying to combine workers from the land and the country in one campaign against **capitalism** as represented by big business and big government. Not surprisingly, many eastern conservatives were terrified by, as they saw it, the wild excesses of the Populist platform and their colourful figures. Businessmen were keen to make their workers see that their future lay in a successful capitalist system. In the election of 1892 the Populists made little progress among the industrial workers of the East Coast. They also failed to make gains in the old Granger states of the Mid-West, where improvements in the economic situation made farmers less tempted by extremes and less likely to view the system as fundamentally against them.

Extreme parties tend to flourish in extreme circumstances. The South was not at this stage ready to abandon the Democrats either – the Democrats were in the process of dismantling the systems set up under Reconstruction and race remained the top priority for Southern Whites at

Capitalism: A system of economics that allows private ownership of land, factories etc., rather than ownership by the government. People can get very rich and also become very poor. Most capitalist countries are also democracies.

this time, even the poorest. So, the Populists failed to make as much ground as they might have hoped, although Weaver did get more than a million votes and carried four western states – Colorado, Kansas, Nevada and Idaho.

Cleveland's Second Administration, 1893–1897

Cleveland's Second Administration was an unhappy one, dominated by the money issue. His actions as President confirmed to many that he was the tool of **Wall Street** and that there was little to choose between the Democrats and the Republicans when it came to the fundamental issues in politics. In the first year of the Administration, Cleveland had to deal with the 'Panic of 1893' – a serious depression caused by a drain on gold reserves which resulted in bankruptcies, closed banks and job losses. Cleveland's attitude remained *laissez faire* throughout, insisting that he could do little to promote recovery and that the recovery would be delayed if he succumbed to demands for public spending. Prudent financial measures to restore investors' confidence in the economy were what was needed, not financial irresponsibility through extra spending and an inflationary fiscal policy. Thus Cleveland repealed the Silver Purchase Act (though only with Republican support), negotiated a deal with J.P. Morgan's Syndicate for a $62 million loan, took out an injunction (against the Governor's wishes) to prevent a strike of the Pullman workers in 1894 and did little to change the tariff passed by McKinley back in 1890. The money issue became increasing dominant in political debate, with the Republican leaders and the Democratic President clearly '**gold-bugs**'. But there were 'free silver' factions in both parties and the Populists were pushing for inflationary policies too.

The 1896 Campaign

The Republicans made it quite clear where their views lay in the debate when they chose William McKinley of Ohio – the man who had been most associated with the 1890 Tariff and a friend of big business – as their presidential candidate. They ran a typical Republican campaign with calls for a protective tariff, generous Union pensions, a deflationary economic policy and naval enlargement. The Democrats had a far more difficult time of it. At their Convention, there were lively debates between the gold-bugs, keen to support Cleveland's policies and actions, and the 'Silverites' who dominated the western and southern delegations. In the end, they adopted the brilliant orator, 36 year-old William Jennings Bryan of Nebraska as their candidate (causing a walkout by some of the pro-Cleveland easterners). They supported a platform that rejected the prudence of the Cleveland Administration and offered, for the first time since the 1860s, a genuine alternative to the Republican platform.

Wall Street: The location of the New York Stock Exchange – a central market in a country for dealing in freely transferable stocks, shares and securities of all types.

'Gold-bugs': Those who supported the idea that the US currency should be based on gold.

Elements of the Democratic Programme in 1896

- Free, unlimited coinage of gold and silver at 16:1.

- Lower tariffs so that their only function was to raise federal revenue and not as instruments of economic policy.

- Attacks on the use of injunctions in labour disputes.

- An enlargement of the powers of the Interstate Commerce Commission to prevent discriminatory abuses in transport.

Bryan set the Convention alive with his famous 'Cross of Gold' speech, delivered after a series of speakers had defended Cleveland's Administration

Gold Standard: A monetary system under which national currencies have a fixed value in gold.

Egalitarian: A belief that all people are equal and should have the same rights and opportunities.

and suggested that maintaining the **Gold Standard** was critical. Bryan invoked the spirit of the Constitution and the Revolution, attacked heartless capitalism and reminded the Democrats of the **egalitarian** principles of Democrat hero Andrew Jackson. The delegates received his speech with rapturous applause. A sense of its power and vision can be gained from his final sentences:

> 'If they dare to come out in the open field and defend the Gold Standard as a good thing, we will fight them to the uttermost. Having behind us the producing masses of this nation and the world, supported by the commercial interests, the laboring interests and the toilers everywhere, we will answer their demand for a gold standard by saying to them: "You shall not press down upon the brow of labor this crown of thorns, you shall not crucify mankind upon a cross of gold."'

Nationalisation: Changing the ownership of a company or industry so that it is no longer private but owned by the state and controlled by the government.

The Populists, meeting in St Louis, now faced a dilemma. The Democrats had adopted the most popular policy, but not all the elements, of the Omaha Platform. If they supported the Democrats, then they would lose some parts of their programme, such as **nationalisation**, but if they put up their own candidate then the anti-gold-bug vote would be split and the Republicans would be likely to win easily. The period 1893–96 had seen some gains for them – for example, the Populists now controlled the legislature in South Carolina – but the big breakthrough had not occurred. Now they had the best chance ever of seeing one of their major policies adopted. However, in doing so they would lose their identity. In the end, they decided to compromise: they chose to support Bryan for President but put forward their own candidate, Tom Watson, for Vice-President.

The 1896 campaign was one of the most exciting, dramatic and polarised in American history. Bryan did not pretend that the battle was anything other than sectional, referring to the East as 'the enemy's country' and embarking on a whirlwind campaign that had him travelling 18,000 miles and making 600 speeches in 29 states. His revivalist, preachy style saw him contrasting the toiling masses against the evils of capitalist Wall Street and he certainly energised his supporters. However, whilst his style may have played well with his supporters, it horrified opponents who feared the radical **demagoguery** of both Bryan and Tom Watson. The 'New York Times' described Bryan as an 'irresponsible, irregulated, ignorant, prejudiced, pathetically honest and enthusiastic crank'.

Demagoguery: The style of leadership where the leaders try to win support by appealing to people's emotions rather than by rational arguments.

McKinley deliberately played a restrained and traditional campaign and left the arguments to his close friend and politically shrewd campaign manager, Marcus Alonzo Hanna. The Republicans built up huge funds of $16 million from horrified industrialists. Hanna used committees to help galvanise the various groups in the East which they needed to win. Trade unionists, blacks, religious and ethnic groups all had their own campaign committees.

William McKinley (1843–1901)
25th President of the United States (1897–1901). McKinley was a lawyer who entered politics as a Republican. He was a member of the House of Representatives from 1877 and Governor of Ohio from 1892. He was elected for two terms, but was shot and killed by an anarchist in 1901. It was under his presidency that the USA fought and won the Spanish–American War.

In the end, with the highest number of votes cast in US history, McKinley won 7,111,000 votes and 271 electoral college votes to Bryan's 6,509,000 and 176. As the map opposite shows, this does not reflect the full implications of the victory. McKinley won every state east of the Mississippi and north of the Ohio, while Bryan carried most of the South and the West. The Democrats and Populists had convinced their rural voters, but had failed to make inroads into the industrial workers in the East who had accepted Hanna's arguments that inflation would diminish their pay packets. Indeed, the Republicans did better among urban workers in 1896 than they had done in 1892. Some of the traditional farming states, such as Wisconsin and Iowa, also stayed Republican, where some improvements in the harvest diminished Bryan's apocalyptic warnings.

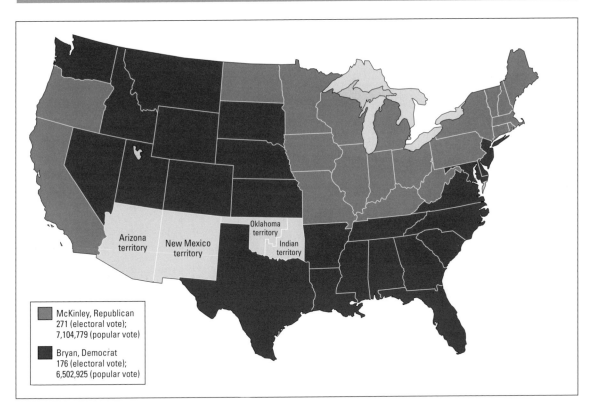

McKinley, Republican
271 (electoral vote);
7,104,779 (popular vote)

Bryan, Democrat
176 (electoral vote);
6,502,925 (popular vote)

1896 presidential election results – by states

What, if anything, did the Populists achieve?

The 1896 election marked a high watermark for the Populists and their policies. McKinley's Administration adopted the traditional policies of sound money and of supporting the interests of business. The 1897 tariff was the highest ever and the 1900 Currency Act put the USA firmly on the Gold Standard. There followed a period of prosperity across the nation and new issues, such as imperialism (see Chapter 7) and progressivism (see section 4.8) dominated politics in a period that saw Republican Presidents for the next 16 years. Agricultural problems elsewhere helped US farmers regain the international market, while gold discoveries in Canada, Alaska and South Africa meant that the Gold Standard was not as deflationary as it had been before.

The 1900 election was a rerun of 1896 but its defining issue was imperialism, not silver, and Bryan had a new issue to get steamed up about. The Populists slowly lost their distinctive position and were subsumed into the larger parties, particularly the Democrats.

That is not to say that the Populists achieved nothing. One or other of the main political parties later adopted many of the reforms they proposed. The 1890s can be seen as having paved the way for the more significant reforms of the Progressive era that followed. The American political system, particularly with the electoral college, made it difficult for third parties to break through. However, the influence that the Populists had in changing the direction of the Democrats and in bringing to the fore issues that the two East Coast-dominated parties preferred to forget cannot be ignored. In many ways, the determination with which the Republicans and their East Coast supporters fought the 1892 and 1896 elections was a compliment to the Populists in recognising the seriousness of the threat they posed.

1. What do you regard as the most important reason for the rise of Populism? Explain your answer.

2. What changes did the Populists hope to make to politics and the economy?

3. To what extent was Populism a failure?

4.4 What factors lay behind the economic expansion of the USA after 1865?

The period after the Civil War saw a major transformation of the American economy and society as massive industrialisation took place on an unprecedented scale. Although the Civil War is sometimes seen as a struggle between the industrial North and agricultural South, the North itself was still essentially an agricultural section in 1865. By 1900, though, the USA was producing 30% of the world's manufactured goods and those employed in manufacturing, mining, construction and services had risen from four million to 18 million. The USA had also become the centre of industrial and commercial inventiveness. In the 1850s, there were an average of 2,000 patents granted each year; by the 1890s, that had reached a staggering 21,000. What lay behind this growth, and what were the consequences of it?

The Civil War

Increase in pig iron production in the USA	
1855–1860	17%
1860–1865	1%
1865–1870	100%

The Civil War inevitably played a key role in the economic expansion of the United States, but it would be wrong to see it as the key factor. Actually, economic growth during the American Civil War was lower than before or after, as the figures for pig iron production show. That does not mean the Civil War did not play a major role, but it is better to see the importance in terms of the significance of the Northern victory, rather than simply the stimulation of demand brought about by the needs of war.

The absence of the South in Congress meant that a number of Acts could be passed that had been held up because of sectional disagreements before that time. The Banking Acts established a system of credit that made it far easier for businessmen to get loans, while the inevitable inflation that the Civil War had caused (with demand outstripping supply in most industries) allowed industrialists to free themselves of debts. Acts such as the Homestead Act, the Land Grant College Act and the Transcontinental Railroad Act encouraged western expansion and the development of a national market and supply system. A federal bureau was established to encourage immigration and tariffs were increased to raise taxes, but it would also protect American industrial development. All these acts and policies were to establish the foundations for economic growth in the following decades.

As well as this, war-time savings and the needs of reconstruction meant that, in the immediate aftermath of war, there was likely to be an economic boom. The triumph of the North was seen as in some way responsible for the triumph of manufacture and industry and the War had rewarded successful entrepreneurs and encouraged innovation. These businessmen and industrialists went out into the post-war world emboldened, with government policies largely on their side and with the financial powers to invest for further success.

Factors causing the post-war economic growth

So many factors were at play that it is difficult to pinpoint which should be seen as the key ones, though historians have inevitably tried and examiners will want students to do the same (see diagram opposite).

Capital

Corporations: Large businesses or groups of companies which are all controlled and run together as single organisations.

The availability of capital for investment had already improved before the Civil War with the growth of **corporations** chartered under state law. These allowed businesses to attract individual investors who would purchase shares in the companies and so provide them with start-up and investment capital. The War created an accumulation of capital as many people tended to save their earnings until the fighting was over, while the banking reforms encouraged investment. Also, a number of entrepreneurs had made significant profits out of the Civil War and were now looking to channel those profits into new economic enterprises.

Raw materials

The USA was almost self-sufficient in natural resources, especially following the expansion westwards. Huge deposits of coal, iron, lead, copper and timber were later supplemented by oil. Although natural resources alone were not sufficient to guarantee economic expansion – as the experience of states such as Russia and China in the same period show – and while developments in transport were also essential to be able to get access to these raw materials, an abundance of natural resources provided the raw materials for expansion. It is also significant that, because America possessed such resources within its borders, tariffs could be raised to protect industry without increasing the costs of raw materials (as would happen in countries that had to import some of them).

Workforce

A major increase in production could not occur without a similar increase in population, to provide a major source of labour as well as a growing market. The population increase of America during this period was significant.

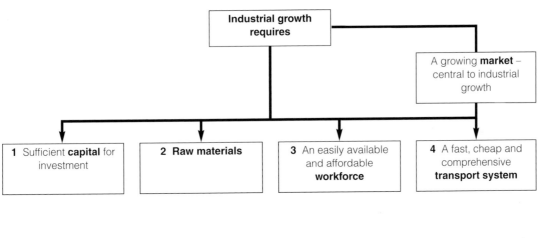

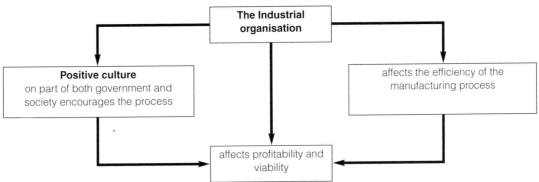

Industrial growth in the USA after the Civil War was dependent on a number of factors. The USA between 1865 and 1917 possessed all of these advantages.

Growth of population in the USA

Year	Population	% increase on previous decade
1860	31,443,321	35.6
1870	39,818,449	26.6
1880	50,155,783	26.0
1890	62,947,714	25.5

Much, but not all, of this was due to a major increase in immigration – the details of which are explained in a later section. These immigrants tended to concentrate in the growing industrial centres of America, such as Chicago and New York. They provided an unending supply of cheap and eager labour, though it is important to remember that among them were also men and women of considerable skill who brought with them managerial and technological experience from the Old World.

Industrial organisation

Holding companies: Companies that own other companies that manufacture goods or produce services.

It is significant that the dominant economic organisation of the major industries was in large-scale enterprises often in the form of trusts or **holding companies**. Although this created some tensions politically (see below), in economic terms it allowed for coordination, sustained development and heavy investment in new technology that encouraged speedy growth.

Market

Population growth, western expansion and improvements in transport and communications meant there was a massive continental market which provided internal demand for American goods. This could be protected from overseas competitors via tariffs because industry did not, at this stage, need to compete in the overseas market.

Positive culture

'Yankee ingenuity': The belief that people in the North-East USA had the ability to invent and develop industrial and manufacturing processes.

Although it is hard to quantify, there were social and cultural attitudes that tended to favour economic enterprise and to look kindly on material achievement in the United States. These attitudes did not necessarily prevail in all European states, where dominant social groups often looked down on those whose wealth came from industry. This was helped by the triumph of the North in the Civil War and the consequent admiration for **'Yankee ingenuity'**. This belief in hard work, thrift and individualism was taken up by immigrants who bought in to the American dream. They often accepted that hard work at the bottom of society might well one day see them, like Andrew Carnegie and John D. Rockefeller, as dollar millionaires. This support for entrepreneurship was also seen in the governments, at federal and local level, not only through specific acts, such as the support for tariffs and banking, but also through their instincts to favour management in labour disputes.

Transport and communications systems

Perhaps most central of all was the development of the transport system. This not only provided the links that allowed the creation of a national market and access to raw materials, but also the building of railroads was a stimulus to industrial development in itself. By 1890, the revenue from railroads was more than $1,000 million, double that of the federal government. Mileage of track had increased from 30,000 miles in 1860 to over 190,000 miles by 1900 (see map on page 129). By 1880, 90% of all rolled steel manufactured in America was going to the railroads.

Railroads created a national market that allowed mass production to

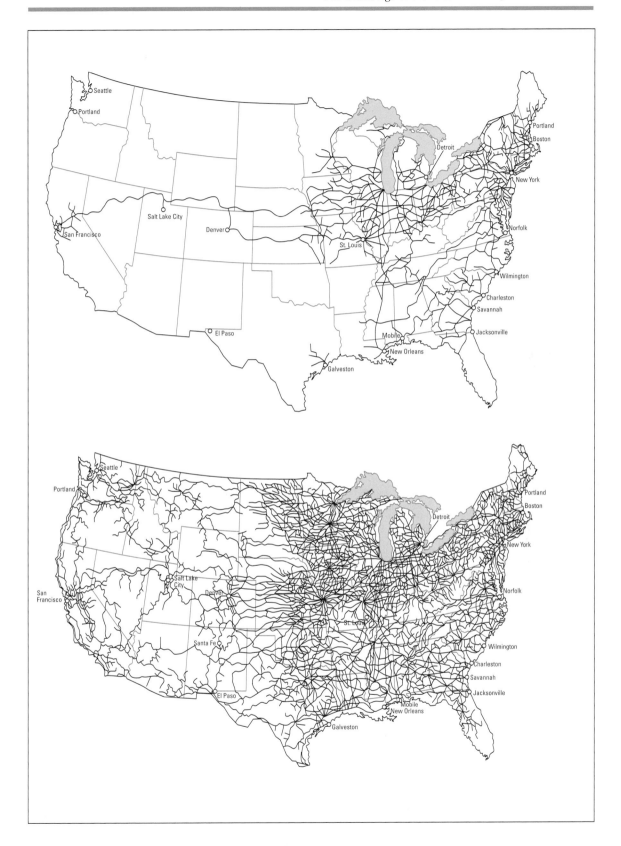

The network of railroads in the USA (top) in 1880; (bottom) in 1900.

1. What impact did the Civil War have on the economic growth of the USA?

2. Was the availability of abundant raw material the reason for the rapid growth of the US economy after 1865? Explain your answer.

develop. This meant that industries such as steel manufacture could get access to both iron and coal – previously steel could only really be manufactured in areas which had easy access to both raw materials. Production costs were also substantially lowered with rail transport being something like 10% the cost of transportation by road. Railroads were also central in allowing the growth of cities, for major urban areas needed to be able to rely on fresh food being brought in from the surrounding farms.

As well as railroads, there were also important developments in communications: the telegraph in 1844 and the telephone in 1876. Such developments allowed large-scale management to spring up across the states. Companies could establish operations across the country and could coordinate industrial development, sales and purchases. These developments also led to wide-scale marketing and advertising across the West.

4.5 How did people respond to industrialisation?
A CASE STUDY IN HISTORICAL INTERPRETATION

Big business and the critics

One of the most interesting features of America's industrialisation was the rise of entrepreneurs, who dominated the organisation and development of certain industries and ended up controlling the majority of the industry in large-scale units. Men such as John D. Rockefeller, Andrew Carnegie and Cornelius Vanderbilt provoked controversy in their lifetimes, and have continued to do so ever since. Were they the 'robber barons' who ruthlessly exploited their workers and drove competitors over the edge? Or were they the key to American industrialisation and prosperity?

They certainly dominated the fields in which they operated. Carnegie reigned supreme over the US steel industry; Vanderbilt made his fortune in railroads; and Rockefeller controlled 90% of US oil refining through his Standard Oil Company of Ohio by 1879. Rockefeller developed the idea of a trust, whereby companies acquired by the main company could be held in trust so that what appeared to be independent companies were actually controlled and regulated by a central group of trustees. In this way, by 1882, Standard Oil controlled, through trusts, 77 oil companies which produced 90% of all refined oil. Rockefeller could thus control the supply and price of oil across the USA. These business barons also developed the

Philanthropist: Person who freely gives money and other help to people who need it.

Andrew Carnegie (1835–1919)
Industrialist and **philanthropist** born in Scotland. Invested successfully in railroads, land and oil, before developing the Pittsburgh iron and steel industries – making the USA the world's leading producer. Having built up a vast industrial empire, Carnegie sold it off to the US Steel Trust in 1901. A New York music hall, which opened in 1891, was renamed the

Carnegie Hall seven years later in honour of the contribution Andrew Carnegie had made to its construction.

William Henry Vanderbilt (1821–1885)
Financier and railroad promoter. Son of financier Cornelius Vanderbilt, he became the head of a railroad trust and was strongly opposed to government regulation of the industry. Vanderbilt was given control of the

Staten Island Railroad in 1857; was named vice-president of the New York and Harlem Railroad in 1864 and acquired other railroad companies, before taking over as president of the New York Central Railroad in 1877. He is famous for his phrase, 'The public be damned'.

John D. Rockefeller (1839–1937)
Founder of Standard Oil (which had control of 90% of US refineries by 1882),

making Rockefeller a millionaire. The activities of the Standard Oil Trust led to an outcry against monopolies (see below) and the passing of Sherman Anti-Trust Act 1890. Although the Trust was dissolved in 1892, it was refounded as a holding company in 1899. He founded the Rockefeller Foundation in 1913, to which his son, John Jnr, devoted his life.

Vertical integration: Process whereby a businessman can get control of an industry. For instance, a brewer could buy barley and malt, as well as public houses. He then has complete control of the industry, from initial production through to sales.

idea of **vertical integration** in order to ensure that, in Rockefeller's words, they need 'pay no one a profit'.

The methods employed by such men to acquire rival companies left much to be desired morally. They were widely attacked, especially by the competitors they drove out of business. These 'robber barons' did much, however, to stabilise the market for the products of these staple industries. For example, before Rockefeller the oil industry had been seriously undermined by gluts, followed by periods of scarcity. Companies using oil could never rely on a consistent price for their raw materials. Rockefeller could control this. Also, large-scale investment could go into developing new techniques and methods of production which made America highly competitive in the global market. Carnegie wrote his own justification, in *Gospel of Wealth* (1889), when he stated that: 'Not evil, but good, has come to the race from the accumulation of wealth by those who have the ability and energy that produces it.'

Social Darwinism: 19th-century belief that people and societies operate in the same way as the animal kingdom, and that, as Charles Darwin argued, only those best fitted to their circumstances survive. The weak perish.

This philosophy, which was backed up by philosophers such as Herbert Spencer in England and William Sumner at Yale University, came to be known as **social Darwinism**, in which philosophers applied the laws of 'survival of the fittest' in nature to society at large. The great captains of industry (the 'naturally selected agents of society', in Sumner's words) were creating the wealth and jobs that benefited America and should be left to their own devices. This justification did have a catch, according to Carnegie, for the truly wealthy had a social responsibility to use their wealth for the public good. Carnegie was keen to use his money to promote the welfare of others. He did this not through handouts to the poor, which would encourage dependency and discourage a healthy work ethic, but rather through providing the means for self-improvement via institutions such as libraries, hospitals and public parks. 'The man who dies rich dies disgraced,' Carnegie added to his gospel.

Although the worship of big business and the 'rags-to-riches' stories were widespread, that did not mean there were no critics of this approach. By the 1880s, many were questioning the wisdom of unbridled capitalism.

Monopoly: A situation where the producer of particular goods or services controls the market, having eliminated all competitors.

- Some were afraid of the effective **monopoly** which many businessmen had and which would allow exploitation of consumers and workers by their ability to control prices and wages.

- Trade unionists felt it was harder to protect the interests of workers when there was a growing distance between manager and worker and an imbalance of power.

- Small-scale businessmen felt threatened by the undue influence their richer rivals had and by the deals they were able to strike with suppliers because of their greater purchasing power.

- Farmers resented the discriminatory practices that saw railroads charging individual farmers more to use their routes than they charged major companies which could negotiate bulk reductions.

- Many people felt that the emergence of powerful industrialists threatened the democratic institutions. Ironically, those same individuals who had used the opportunities the USA presented for upward mobility were now, by controlling the market and ruthlessly driving out competitors, undermining those opportunities for others.

Various journalists and political commentators began to attack the 'robber barons' and the culture of government *laissez-faire* that went with it. Political organisations sprang up, particularly in the West, which tried to limit the power of big business. (See section 4.3 above.) Henry George sold over two million copies of his book *Progress and Poverty* (published in 1882) that argued that industrial progress did not necessarily guarantee prosperity. For many, it brought quite the opposite. Henry Demarest Lloyd attacked Standard Oil in 1894 and called for public ownership of the major economic monopolies.

Some of these criticisms did lead to political action, initially at a local level and later nationally. The Granger Movement managed to pass various laws in some of the western states in the 1870s, which sought to restrict railroad companies by fixing maximum rates, forbidding discriminatory practices that saw different prices for different consumers, and establishing commissions to monitor and enforce the policies. When these were challenged in the courts, the Supreme Court intervened to confirm that, when private property was for public use, the states had the right to regulate public utilities ('Munn v Illinois', 1876). When state regulation still proved to be ineffective (largely because Congress continued to control matters of inter-state commerce, so action could only be taken against companies that operated within a state), the Interstate Commerce Act of 1887 was passed by Congress, albeit reluctantly. The Act prohibited pooling (a method by which individual companies worked together to control prices etc.), rebates for major consumers, discriminatory practices and higher charges for short hauls, and urged as well that all charges be 'reasonable and just'. Furthermore, it created an Interstate Commerce Commission of five members which had the powers to investigate railroad management.

Of course, commerce only dealt with transport and major industrial manufacturers continued with their monopoly practices. Where states tried to pass laws controlling trusts or combinations, many companies simply transferred their headquarters to less restrictive states. Some states deliberately encouraged this in order to attract industry. In 1890, the federal government bowed to pressure and passed the Sherman Anti-Trust Act. This declared that 'every contract, combination in the form of trust or otherwise, or conspiracy, in restraint of trade or commerce among the several states or with foreign nations, is illegal'. It allowed for suits to be brought by federal prosecutors, or individuals or firms who felt they had suffered by a trust. Those found guilty were liable to a $5,000 fine and a year in gaol.

Although the Interstate Commerce Act and the Sherman Anti-Trust Act did bring some control to industry, the odds were still stacked firmly in favour of big business and little was done to enforce either Act effectively. The laws were loosely phrased, which allowed courts to interpret them very much as they wished. Most notoriously, in 1895 the Supreme Court ruled in 'United States versus E.C. Knight' that, despite the defendant controlling 98% of the manufacture of refined sugar, he was not violating the terms of the Sherman Anti-Trust Act because manufacture was not trade. With this attitude in the courts, and no desire on the part of the government to take on the vested interests who poured money into the party organisations anyway, it is not surprising that there were only 36 suits brought under the Act between 1890 and 1901. None of these suits was against the really big corporations; and of the cases tried only 12 were won.

1. Why were the methods used by businessmen such as John D. Rockefeller criticised?

2. Why are there differing views on the impact of industrial-isation on the USA?

4.6 What were the patterns of immigration during this period?

Immigration: The movement of foreign nationals attracted by the prosperity and stability of the country or region.

Between 1820 and 1900, around 20 million people arrived as immigrants into the United States, with by far the majority arriving in the final decades. Nine million arrived in the years 1900–10 alone, with a further six million the following decade. Between 1900 and 1910, 41% of the increase in urban population was due directly to **immigration**. It is estimated that, in 1890, 80% of New Yorkers had been born abroad. New York had twice the number of Irish that Dublin had, as many Germans as lived in Hamburg and more Italians than lived in Naples. Chicago had the largest population of Czechs living anywhere in the world and the third largest number of Poles, after Warsaw and Lodz. It was not only the case that immigration increased dramatically between 1880 and 1920, but also that immigrants came from different parts of the world. Thus in this period, the 'New Immigration' changed the pattern of immigration into the USA, both in scope and nature.

Before 1880, the vast majority of immigrants came from the north and west of Europe: Germans, British, Irish, French and Scandinavians made up over 80% of immigrants in the 1860s, and most arrived in family groups with the intention of settling for good. This changed after 1880, when the majority came from southern and eastern Europe, were single men and often went back to Europe after a prolonged stay. The exception to this was Jewish immigration in which, facing **persecution** in Russia and eastern Europe and with no homeland to go to, most came to settle permanently in family groups. There is a problem establishing precisely where all these immigrants came from. Jews would be registered according to their country of birth. Poles were not listed separately between 1899 and 1918 and many of the Slavic groups coming from the Austro-Hungarian Empire, in particular, were labelled incorrectly as Germans or Austrians. One can say fairly confidently, however, that there was a major shift in immigration patterns during the period.

Why did people emigrate to the USA?

One would need to talk to immigrants to have a full idea of why they came. Also, each immigrant could tell a different story. However, most immigration can be seen as a combination of push and pull factors (i.e. there were reasons why they wanted to leave the countries in which they were born and lived, and there were specific reasons why, having decided to leave their homelands, it was the United States where they chose to settle).

Push factors (why people left their homelands)

● Socio-economic changes at home

With most European populations rising and a significant growth in **urbanisation**, many traditional communities in eastern Europe and Russia were facing disruption to their traditional lifestyles. Although many left home to settle in the urban centres of America, not all did. A number found it easier to continue their traditional farming lifestyles out in the American West, or at least even if they did stay in the cities when they arrived they had planned otherwise. Even those who had always intended to settle in cities such as New York and Chicago found it easier to make such a dramatic decision to change their lifestyles if they were going to be changing anyway.

● Religious, political and racial persecution

Many groups who left Europe had been facing persecution at home. Jews faced severe and growing persecution at the end of the 19th century, particularly in Poland and Russia where a growth of nationalism and **pan-Slavism** saw an increase in physical attacks on Jewish villages and businesses, often with the support of the authorities. Some ethnic groups also faced persecution, such as the Armenians in Turkey, from where there was a dramatic increase in immigrants in the 1900s. Ethnic groups in multi-ethnic empires, especially the Austro-Hungarian Empire, felt they could sustain their cultural identity better

Persecution: A time when a group or people are treated cruelly and unfairly, especially because of their political or religious beliefs.

Urbanisation: Making a country area more like a town, with more buildings, industry, business etc.

Pan-Slavism: A doctrine that advocates the political union of all Slav peoples. This was widely viewed in other European states as a cover for the political ambitions of Russia.

elsewhere. There was also a growing intolerance in European capitals of anarchists and socialists, a number of whom chose to leave and plan their revolutions from afar.

● Economic problems

The most dramatic example of economic emigration is the Irish, who left in their thousands during the potato famine of the 1840s. Much emigration can be traced very specifically to moments of economic collapse in various European countries, particularly in southern Europe. For example, an outbreak of cholera and a collapse in the international fruit and wine market in the 1880s in southern Italy saw a sudden rise in Italian immigration in the mid-1880s. Crop failure and a decline in the currant market may explain a major Greek exodus in 1907. Many of these immigrants were young men who went to the USA with the intention of returning. Many sent money back to their families in Europe or returned having made enough money to establish a business at home. It is interesting to note that 1,800,000 Hungarians were recorded as having entered America between 1880 and 1914, but in 1910 there were only 500,000 there – evidence indeed that the majority of immigrants returned home.

Pull factors (why people chose to settle in the USA)

● Economic opportunities

The most obvious reason why people settled in America was because of its reputation, largely justified, as a 'land of opportunity'. The economic expansion of the USA was both a cause and a consequence of mass immigration and the nature of the industrialisation meant that there was plenty of demand for unskilled labour, which the majority of immigrants represented. What appeared to be pitiable pay rates in America, seemed like small fortunes to the immigrants coming from severe poverty or **subsistence agriculture** in Europe and Russia.

Subsistence agriculture: This is the production of food solely for those that produce it and not for sale at market.

● Direct recruitment by American agents

A special bureau to encourage immigration had been established during the Civil War and many American companies sent agents to recruit cheap labour. This was known as contract labour – where workers had to agree to work for a company at a fixed price for a period of time – and was legal until 1885. Many of those arriving in America had had their passage paid for in advance and there was widespread advertising across Europe.

● America's spirit of toleration

At a time when most Europeans were denied the vote and when governments, particularly in the East, were highly authoritarian, the political freedom and liberties offered by the United States were highly attractive. Europeans would have been made aware of the Declaration of Independence that stated that 'all men are created equal', while the poem on the base of the Statue of Liberty called forth all those immigrants 'yearning to breathe free'.

The 'New Colossus'

Not like the brazen giant of Greek fame,
With conquering limbs astride from land to land
Here at our sea-washed, sunset-gates shall stand
A mighty woman with a torch, whose flame
Is the imprisoned lightning, and her name
Mother of Exiles. From her beacon-hand
Glows world-wide welcome, her mild eyes command
The air-bridges harbour that twin-cities frame.

'Keep, ancient lands, your storied pomp!' cries she,
With silent lips. 'Give me your tired, your poor,
Your huddled masses yearning to breathe free,
The wretched refuse of your teeming shore;
Send these, the homeless, the tempest-tost to me,
I lift my lamp beside the golden door!'

By Emma Lazarus (1849–1887)

Sonnet written on 2 November 1883. It is inscribed on a plaque at the foot of the Statue of Liberty. The Statue of Liberty is the first thing that immigrants see as they sail into New York Harbour.

1. Draw a spidergram and show on it the various reasons why people emigrated to the USA after 1865.

2. What do you regard as the main reason why people emigrated to the USA after 1865? Explain your answer.

As in the case with economic opportunities, some of this may have been exaggerated, but compared with the political situation in Russia or Turkey, America really was a 'land of liberty'.

● Influence of relatives and friends

Inevitably, many families followed early pioneers from their extended family or village. Indeed these cousins in the States would often pay the passage to be joined by their relatives or friends.

● Developments in transport

The transition from sail to steam allowed many more people to make the journey across the Atlantic. Also, railroads opened up the continent once immigrants arrived there. Indeed, many of the agents working to encourage immigration came from the railroad companies.

4.7 What was the impact of immigration on the USA?

The development of distinct ethnic neighbourhoods

Whatever their motives had been in moving to America, most immigrants on arrival did not get beyond the cities. Most lacked the capital to start up farming and were either attracted by the wages or quickly dragged into a system that saw influential figures from ethnic groups, often Italian or Greek, arrange the entire life for arriving immigrants, from housing to job and even the way they would vote. As a result, and because many were joining family or friends, certain nationalities were attracted to certain cities. Within cities, different neighbourhoods developed in one particular ethnic style. With everything else new, living in an ethnic neighbourhood also helped to provide some certainties and security at what could be a difficult time. Thus the Irish dominated Boston, Czechs and Poles flocked to Chicago, and the Italians took over Brooklyn, New York.

Economic impact

As the Government had clearly realised when it set up an immigration bureau in the Civil War to help fill the factories, the opportunities that immigration presented in providing a constant supply of cheap, unskilled labour were significant. Immigrants were desperate for work and often coming from a rural background, with little idea of employment law or working rights, they were easily exploited with contractors quickly signing up whole families and sending them off to various mid-West cities. Although a significant amount of urban growth was due to Americans moving from country to town, the largest factor in urban growth was immigration. In 1910, one-third of the population of the 12 largest cities in the USA was immigrant and a further third was composed of the children of immigrants. It is hard to imagine how the US economy could have grown in the way it did without this important supply of labour which was prepared to work for a rate most local workers would not accept. Inevitably, this led to some tensions between immigrants and local-born Americans who saw the immigrants as either threatening their job opportunities or depressing wage levels. There was strong working-class resentment of the new immigrants.

Political impact

The immigrants had had very little, if any, experience of politics in their previous lives and tended to vote in the same way in the cities in which they settled. Because they tended to live in ethnic neighbourhoods, they could easily dominate certain political districts and the local politicians exploited this. City bosses would provide a network of economic and social support and in return could rely on the votes of these grateful immigrants. Naturally, this concerned many Americans who were wedded to the **Jeffersonian ideal** of the individual yeoman exercising his carefully considered right to vote and casting it wisely for the good of the whole.

Jeffersonian ideal: Belief that society should be made up of independent small-scale farms and businesses.

Some concerns were also expressed that, as many of these new immigrants were Catholic, they owed their loyalties to the foreign Pope and the local priest, and were thus easily swayed and not always for patriotic reasons. The immigrants tended to be attracted to the Democratic Party, especially since the Republicans became increasingly associated with the Prohibition Movement which to some extent had racial overtones as the temperance reformers blamed much of the drink problems on the Catholic, German and Irish immigrants. As a consequence, the Democratic Party looked to immigrants in the northern cities to provide a balance to the continued domination of the Republican Party among native-born Americans in the North and East. The combination of white southerners, western farmers and urban immigrants was the coalition that helped the Democrats fight back, politically, in the decades after the Civil War.

Racial tension and discrimination

Perhaps inevitably, native-born Americans tended to use the immigrants as scapegoats to blame for the ills of society. By living in their own districts and making little attempt to integrate, the new immigrants made themselves easier targets than the old immigrants of north and west European extraction. Labour violence often erupted from immigrant slums, while the growth of anarchy and socialism among urban workers was blamed on European influences.

Immigration was seen as leading to a more corrupt and unpleasant society, less homogeneous and more violent. Although there were not the formal moves against immigrants that one saw in the 1850s, with the formation of the 'Know Nothings', and in the 'Red Scare' of the 1920s, there were outbreaks of violence and some discriminatory legislation was passed. Newspapers record stories of attacks on Greeks in Nebraska, Slavs in Utah and Chinese on the West Coast. In 1891, 11 Italians were lynched in New Orleans after a local jury acquitted them of murder. The reformation of the Ku Klux Klan in 1915 in Georgia was an ominous sign of what was to come. In 1887, the America Protective Association was formed with the aim of countering the impact of Catholics on public schools and immigrants in political life. The Asiatic Exclusion League was formed in 1905 to try and limit the numbers of Japanese who worked for lower wages. However, given the vast numbers of immigrants arriving in the USA in this period these examples are relatively few, especially when one looks at other periods of American history. It is a sign of how dramatically America was expanding and changing that the vast majority of immigrants seem to have settled quickly and effectively into the American nation.

1. Did the new immigrants have a greater impact on the economy or on politics? Explain your answer.

2. Did the new immigrants have a beneficial impact on the USA? Explain your answer.

4.8 What were the origins and aims of the Progressive movement?

Although there was a Progressive Party that contested the 1912 presidential election, Progressives were politicians and writers involved in both political parties, or neither. Who were the Progressives and what was

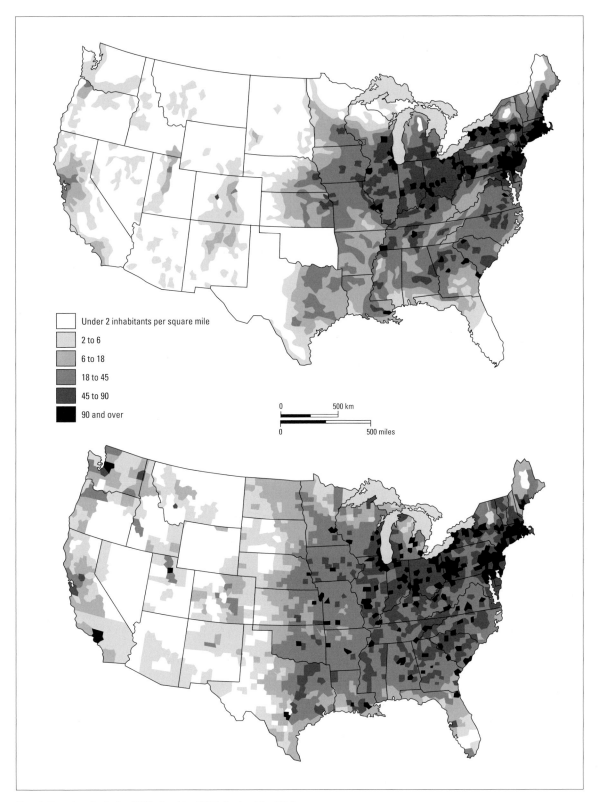

Population density in the USA: (top) in 1880; (below) in 1910.

Progressivism: An attitude to government that crossed political boundaries and was concerned with improving American politics and society in the light of the major upheaval that had transformed America since the Civil War.

Progressivism? Progressives looked on the 'Gilded Age' with distaste and were keen to end or reform the political corruption, monopolistic practices of the large firms and urban deprivation that had characterised the period. In many ways, they took on the role vacated by the Populists, although they were far more successful in bringing about changes, perhaps because they worked from within the existing political parties rather than challenging them from outside. This action took place at all levels in government, from President to city mayor. It included reforms such as limiting maximum working hours, improving working conditions and extending the franchise (vote). There was no specific programme that can be said to be progressive so what was done in its name of Progressivism varied according to the local circumstances. It is also important to remember that this did not mean that there was a sudden break with the old practices because for every progressive politician there was still one operating the old politics of graft and influence.

The Progressive movement was initially encouraged by a group of writers and journalists writing at the turn of the century. President Roosevelt christened them the 'muckrakers'. They used their books and articles to bring to the attention of the public various abuses in politics and business which stirred public opinion into demanding some regulation and change. Certain popular magazines, such as 'McClure's', 'Cosmopolitan' and 'Collier's' provided these writers with a forum for their disclosures, which were often presented in a sensationalist way.

Among the most influential were:

● Upton Sinclair, *The Jungle* (1906) – about conditions in Chicago's meat-packing industry.

● Lincoln Steffens, *Shame of the Cities* (1904) – about corruption in city governments across the USA.

● Frank Norris, *The Octopus* (1901) – attacking the Southern Pacific Railroad – and *The Pit* (1903) – attacking the Chicago grain market.

● Ida M. Tarbell, *History of the Standard Oil Company* (1904) – attacking monopolistic practices.

Although at times these 'muckrakers' claimed rather more significance for themselves than was justified, they played an important role in forcing the agenda of politicians or in providing moral and factual support for those who tried to pass some reform. Much of the work though was down to individual politicians appealing to the electorate over the heads of **vested interests**. They often acted from a genuine sense of justice and a feeling that, in industrialisation and urbanisation, America had somehow lost its way and had abandoned its guiding principles.

Vested interests: Strong reasons that someone has for acting in a particular way e.g. to protect their own money, power or reputation.

District attorney: A lawyer in the USA who works for the state and who prosecutes people on its behalf. Often referred to as 'DA'.

What did the Progressives achieve locally?

Progressivism tends to be viewed in the context of the achievements of three Presidents at federal level: Theodore Roosevelt, William Taft and Woodrow Wilson. Before looking at the work of these three men, it is important to consider the actions of politicians and activists at a local level where much of the early work was done and where reforms were pioneered.

Among the progressive governors and mayors, a small number stand out as men who became national figures and so promoted not only themselves but the ideas they were bringing to government. Perhaps the most influential of these was the Republican governor of Wisconsin, Robert M. La Follette, whose programme of reform both received national attention and became known as the 'Wisconsin Idea'. In particular, he

---

Robert M. La Follette (1855–1925)
He served as **district attorney** (1880–94) and as a member of the House of Representatives (1885–91). He was elected Governor of Wisconsin in 1900. As leader of the national progressive reform movement, he ran unsuccessfully for President in 1924.

took on the powerful vested interests in business, especially railroads, and politics. Other key progressive governors were the Republicans Charles Evans Hughes of New York and Hiram Johnson of California and Democrat Woodrow Wilson who gained a national name that would later help him secure the Presidency during his time as Governor of New Jersey. There were also a number of key figures at city level, most significantly Democrat Tom L. Johnson of Cleveland, Ohio, who was admired across the country for the work he did in cleaning up both the politics and social abuses of the city.

Much of the work of these men was concerned with breaking the powers of the political vested interests and trying to involve the people more directly in government action, whilst reforming the structure and administration of city government to make it more efficient and professional. The methods used varied and were tested and copied across the states. We will look briefly at some of these methods.

The initiative and the referendum

Both of these were first used in South Dakota in 1898 and allowed voters to have a direct say in proposing a particular law. Usually the support of around 10% of the voters was required to sign a petition calling for a particular law, which was then submitted to the state legislature or to the people for approval. If passed, it became law.

The recall

This plan, first used in Los Angeles in 1903, allowed for the removal of an office-holder before his/her term ended if a sufficient proportion of the voters (usually around 25%) was in favour and could start the process by a petition.

The direct primary

The party bosses had traditionally pre-selected the candidates for election well in advance and used the nominating conventions to great effect to impose their will and influence. The direct primary was first introduced by La Follette in Wisconsin in 1903. It was a preliminary election in which voters can nominate directly the candidate they would like to see run for their party in the general election that would follow.

Direct election of senators

Senators had not previously been elected directly, but had been nominated by their state legislatures – a practice that inevitably led to charges of influence and election-rigging. Gradually, more and more states introduced popular elections to determine who the voters wanted as their senatorial candidate, which the legislatures had little option but to accept. Eventually, the whole process became fully constitutional with the passage of the Seventeenth Amendment, a major progressive achievement, in 1913 (passed by Congress in 1911 but not ratified until 1913). This required the direct election of senators. It is a good example of a reform, eventually adopted at federal level, which had its origins in the actions of individual states.

The commission and city-manager plans

Pioneered by the city of Galveston, Texas, in 1900, the commission plan was a reorganisation of city government in which all the city functions were controlled by a small group of elected citizens (the commission), each of whom was responsible for one particular department, and which collectively made overall policy. All commissioners were, theoretically, equal with one serving as a ceremonial head, so diminishing the possibilities of one over-powerful figure dominating the city as mayor.

In some places, this developed further into the city-manager plan, pioneered in 1908 by Staunton, Virginia, and popularised by Dayton, Ohio, in 1914. In this plan, the elected commission acted more as a board of directors and appointed a non-political city manager who would hopefully have the skills and expertise to manage the city as a business rather than political fiefdom.

Although these plans did not work everywhere where they were tried, they marked an attempt to end the old days of the powerful city bosses who could easily act as a magnet for corruption. They showed early attempts at professionalising city management.

Female suffrage

The campaign for women's suffrage was also one taken up by a number of progressives. Various states gave the ballot to women before Congress passed the Nineteenth Amendment in 1919, which granted nationwide votes. Wyoming was the first state to do so, in 1890. This was followed by eight other states by 1913. All of them were in the West, reflecting the strength of the progressive movement there and the more egalitarian spirit of the frontier, where women were less likely to operate in separate spheres from men and were treated more as equals.

Welfare

Local progressives were not just concerned with political reforms. Several states and cities pioneered work in such areas as:

- slum clearance

- development of better services, such as educational and leisure facilities, in dealing with the urban growth

- improvements in employment legislation, especially for women and children, over issues such as hours and wages

- health and safety standards at work

- basic welfare for widows, orphans and the destitute.

How progressive were Presidents Roosevelt and Taft?

Although the work done at local level was significant, the man most associated with Progressivism was the Republican President from 1901–09 who dominated the political debate of his era – Theodore Roosevelt. He and his chosen successor, William H. Taft, used the position of President to bring about a number of progressive reforms in the federal government whilst simultaneously pursuing an aggressive foreign policy (see Chapter 7).

Theodore Roosevelt (1858–1919)
26th President of the USA (1901–09), a Republican. 'Teddy' or 'TR', as he was often known, was Assistant Secretary of the Navy (1897–98) and during the Spanish–American war he commanded a volunteer force of 'rough riders'. As McKinley's Vice-President he took over as President when McKinley was assassinated in 1901. At only 42, he was the youngest president. He already had a long record in public office, having been a Civil Service Commissioner, Police Commissioner and Governor of New York. When in office, he became more liberal. In 1906 he was awarded the Nobel Peace Prize for his part in ending the Russo–Japanese war. Writer of several historical works, including *The Naval War of 1812* (published in 1882) and *The Winning of the West* (1889–96). The 'teddy' bear was named after Theodore 'Teddy' Roosevelt.

William H. Taft (1857–1930)
27th President of the USA (1901–13), a Republican. Although his first interest was the judiciary, he accepted a post as governor of the Philippines and took responsibility for the construction of the Panama Canal (see page 217). He was Secretary of War (1904–08) in Theodore Roosevelt's Administration. His single term as President was noted for the struggles against the Progressives. As chief justice of the Supreme Court, Taft supported the minimum wage.

Party elders: Senior members of a political party who have influence over policy.

Roosevelt was not elected to office initially but became President when William McKinley was assassinated in September 1901. Many Republican leaders feared the young, dynamic Roosevelt. His progressive ideas did not sit comfortably with many of the **party elders**. Throughout his first Administration, Roosevelt feared that Mark Hanna – a leading industrialist and close friend of McKinley who had played a key role in getting his friend the nomination and was now the leading figure on the conservative wing of the Republicans – might stand against him for the nomination. Hanna died in 1904, Roosevelt easily secured the Republican nomination and was convincingly re-elected in 1904. He was thus able, over seven years, to bring to the Presidency a degree of progressivism that marked a considerable change from his Republican predecessors. Although some of the measures fell short of what many progressive campaigners had hoped for, Roosevelt's energy and determination that his fellow citizens should take their civic responsibilities seriously helped to bolster the progressive cause. There were also several specific measures that he helped enact. In his State of the Union address in 1901, Roosevelt called for:

- more meritocracy in the civil service

- conservation of natural resources

- greater control of businesses and interstate transport by the federal government.

Although he reassured Republicans by initially keeping the Cabinet he inherited from McKinley, he was a dominant President who knew what he wanted.

The square deal

In order to give coherence and a philosophy to his policies, Roosevelt talked of a 'square deal' that would help all Americans – businessmen, farmers, consumers and workers. He got actively involved in a dispute involving the coal miners of eastern Pennsylvania, calling the mine owners and union leaders to the White House during a strike in 1902 and attempting mediation. When talks broke down and the mine owners refused to accept his proposals for an independent board of arbitration to resolve the issue, Roosevelt threatened to use federal troops to run the mines. He started putting private pressure on the mine owners. In the end, the employers agreed to submit to such a board and a decision was reached, in March 1903, that saw a 10% wage increase and a nine-hour day, but no union recognition. Roosevelt's direct intervention was highly unusual but it paid off and became the basis of a settlement that lasted to the end of the First World War.

Roosevelt used his position to popularise the movement for better conservation of America's natural resources which were being threatened by the large-scale transfer of public land to private ownership, especially in the West. He put his authority behind the Newlands Act of 1902 which raised money from land sales to finance irrigation projects, and he gave strong support for the establishment and preservation of national parks – areas of outstanding natural beauty that could not be developed. He was behind the establishment of a national conservation commission in 1908 to oversee conservation in the West and to set aside 148 million acres of forest to protect timber reserves.

Roosevelt was not opposed to big business but he was keen to regulate to ensure fair competition and consumer-friendly practices. He supported the Pure Food and Drug Act of 1906 which outlawed the adulteration or false labelling of food and drugs as well as the Meat Inspection Act of 1908 that sought to improve conditions in the meat-processing industry, largely as a response to the 'muckraker' Upton Sinclair's research and writing. He also enforced more vigorously the terms of the 1890 Sherman Anti-Trust Act (see page 111) that had tended to be ignored by Cleveland and McKinley. Roosevelt established the Bureau of Corporations in 1903 which had the power to investigate allegations against trusts. He secured from Congress a special fund of $500,000 to allow the government to prosecute suits against companies. As a result, 24 **indictments** were secured against the trusts during Roosevelt's presidency, twice as many as under previous administrations. He was also a prominent supporter of the successful case against the Northern Securities Company, a holding company that controlled stock in several railroad companies in the North and was found guilty of 'restraint of trade' by the Supreme Court in 1904. Roosevelt also encouraged legislation to strengthen the terms of the Interstate Commerce Act of 1877 through the Elkins Act of 1903 and the Hepburn Act of 1906 (see panel below).

Indictments: Official charges made against a person.

The Elkins Act 1903

● Secret rebates on railroads were confirmed as illegal, but now the recipient of the rebate could be prosecuted as well as the grantor.

● The agent of the railroad company was liable for any change in the published rates.

The Hepburn Act 1906

Strengthened the power of the Interstate Commerce Commission by:

● increasing its membership to seven (from five)

● giving it power to reduce rates deemed by it to be too high or discriminatory

● placing the burden of proof on the carrier rather than the Commission where there was legal challenge

● forbidding railroads to carry goods they had been involved in producing

● establishing a uniform system of accounting

● extending the authority of the Commission to pipelines, ferries and express companies.

Although the courts remained likely to favour big business, there was a growing tendency, supported by the Supreme Court, to uphold the Commission's judgements.

Much of Roosevelt's contribution to Progressivism was in encouraging reforms, although his commitment to conservation in particular was very real and significant. He chose not to stand again for President in 1908, though there was nothing to stop him from doing so. Instead, he supported William Taft, who easily won the Republican nomination and then beat the

Democratic candidate, William Jennings Bryan, who was standing and losing for the third time.

Although Taft lacked the energy of Roosevelt (he weighed over 20 stone), he was more conciliatory than 'Teddy' Roosevelt. He remained committed to the progressive programme of his sponsor and he continued to encourage the prosecution of big business, the reservation of public lands and the extension of the merit system in the civil service.

- An eight-hour day was introduced for all employees on government contracts.

- The departments of Labor and Commerce were established in 1913 – the former to help workers secure decent working conditions and the latter to supervise America's commercial development.

- The Sixteenth Amendment was ratified in 1913, permitting the imposition of a graduated income tax.

- In 1910, the Mann–Elkins Act strengthened the powers of the Inter-state Commerce Commission still further, giving it authority to supervise telephone, telegraph and wireless companies, allowing it to institute its own legal proceedings and creating a new Commerce Court to speed up proceedings.

It was also during Taft's Presidency that two important suits took place against companies, using the anti-trust legislation. In 1911, the Standard Oil Company of New Jersey was dissolved for holding an illegal monopoly in oil refining. In the same year, the American Tobacco Company was ruled an illegal combination and forced to reorganise.

Taft was more cautious when it came to matters concerning tariffs, conservation and government procedure. In 1907, Roosevelt had argued that the tariff should be reduced and Taft indicated his support for this in the 1908 campaign. The tariff was at its highest level ever, at an average of 57% in 1908, and was attracting considerable criticism, especially in the West, among workers and farmers who saw prices rising faster than wages. In 1909, there were long debates in Congress and eventually Taft intervened to encourage Congress to pass the compromise Payne–Aldrich Bill which reduced rates to a 40% average. Although this did mark a reduction, it disappointed many progressive Republicans who had been arguing for a much greater reduction. They now feared Taft might be less amenable to their ideas than Roosevelt.

In conservation, Taft also upset many of Roosevelt's supporters by taking the side of his Secretary of Interior, Richard Ballinger, when he ruled that Roosevelt had taken too much power away from private interests out West. The decision was to restore various lands to private ownership in Wyoming and Montana, as well as to open up parts of Alaska to private claims for coalmining areas. When Ballinger was criticised by Louis Glavis and Gifford Pinchot, federally employed conservationists promoted by Roosevelt, Taft dismissed them in 1909 and 1910 respectively. Pinchot, in particular, accused Taft of abandoning Roosevelt's commitment to conservation – an unfair exaggeration but one that stuck. Then, in a series of struggles in 1910 between the conservative speaker in the House of Representatives, Joseph Cannon, and an alliance of Democrats and progressive Republicans, Taft found himself supporting Cannon who had not only identified himself as an opponent of progressive reforms, but had also lost the struggle to maintain his power over important House committees. It thus became clear that Taft did not have the support of the progressive Republicans and was losing his grip on the party in Congress.

Although Taft continued many of the policies associated with Roosevelt,

1. What were the aims of the Progressives?

2. How successful were the Progressives in introducing reform by 1912?

and in many ways was more directly responsible for progressive legislation and actions, a number of progressive leaders began to feel that he was not as committed to the cause as they would have liked. They began to plot against him.

4.9 What impact did Woodrow Wilson have on domestic affairs, 1913–1919?

Woodrow Wilson (1856–1924)
28th President of the USA (1913–21), a Democrat. President of Princeton University (1902–10); Governor of New Jersey (1911–13). As President, he kept the USA out of the First World War until 1917, and in January 1918 issued his 'Fourteen Points' as a basis for a peace settlement. Awarded the Nobel Peace Prize in 1919 but was forced to retire from politics through illness.

What were the issues in the 1912 presidential election?

The 1912 election was a dramatic and unusual one in that the three candidates were all Progressives of a sort and all had been President at some point. It also marked the election of Woodrow Wilson, who was the only Democrat to be elected President between 1892 and 1932.

The Democrats
Woodrow Wilson, the liberal and progressive Governor of New Jersey, was selected as the Democratic candidate after 46 ballots, crucially winning the backing of William Jennings Bryan who changed his vote as he felt that Wilson offered the best hope of challenging the powers of big business. Wilson was far more liberal than either of the two previous progressive Presidents. Although he described himself as a 'progressive with the brakes on', he fought a campaign that called for a full attack on political and economic privilege. He made it clear that he saw the trusts and business monopoly as an evil that needed destroying. The Democrats also made their traditional pledges on tariffs, though Wilson went further than the previous Democratic President (Grover Cleveland) and called for a new tariff that would be used for revenue purposes only. This was a pledge that, in reality, meant a substantial reduction.

The Republicans
The Republicans selected Taft as their candidate for re-election but only after a hotly contested convention in which Theodore Roosevelt, after some hesitation, offered himself as candidate again. Roosevelt made it clear that he felt Taft had not sustained progressivism in office as much as he would have liked. It was clear from the way that delegate voted that Roosevelt was the more popular with the rank-and-file Republicans, but that Taft was the choice of the Republican leaders. So, with the party leaders controlling the convention and the majority of delegations, Taft emerged as Republican candidate. He fought the election promising much of the same, calling for a reduced but nonetheless protectionist tariff and for tougher regulation of the trusts.

The Progressives
Since January 1911, a number of Republican senators had formed the Progressive Republican League with the idea of ensuring that progressive ideas continue to influence Republican policy making. In particular, they called for nationwide political reforms, such as the direct election of senators, direct primaries and the use of the initiative, referendum and recall. Disappointed by the actions of Taft in government, encouraged by comments by Roosevelt and his supporters such as Pinchot and some of the muckraking journalists, the League decided, in October 1911, to field

a presidential candidate. It adopted Senator Robert La Follette of Wisconsin who had won a name for himself and his Wisconsin Idea as an early progressive governor.

Although Roosevelt initially failed to support the plans of the Progressive League, his rejection by the Republicans at their convention led him to get involved with the Progressive Party which met in Chicago in August 1912. Although there to support La Follette many delegates felt that, in Roosevelt, they had someone who could win and he was nominated for President. The Progressives – known also as the 'Bull Moose' party because of Roosevelt's frequent use of the term (which means someone energetic) – thus found themselves splitting the Republican vote. The position taken by the Progressives on issues such as the tariff and trusts differed little from Taft's. In the end, a voter deciding between the Republicans and the Progressives was really faced with a choice of personalities and image rather than specific policy issues.

The split in the Republican Party gave the Democrats their first presidential victory since 1892, with Wilson winning 40 states and Taft trailing in a poor third, though the combined votes of Roosevelt and Taft outnumbered Wilson by over a million. Clearly, the results of 1912 were a consequence of Republican splits rather than of any popular enthusiasm for Wilson, although the Democrats did gain control of both the Senate and the House of Representatives. What is important about the 1912 election though is that it marked a clear victory for progressive policies. All three candidates clearly felt that in order to ensure victory they had to support political reform, lower tariffs and control of big business. In that sense, the election of 1912 marked the final confirmation that the 'Gilded Age' was well and truly behind Americans.

Results of the 1912 presidential election

		Popular vote	Electoral college
Woodrow Wilson	Democrat	6,296,547	435
Theodore Roosevelt	Progressive	4,118,571	88
William H. Taft	Republican	3,436,720	8
Eugene V. Debs	Socialist	900,672	0
Eugene W. Chafin	Prohibition	206,275	0

How progressive a president was Wilson?

In government, Wilson brought to a conclusion many of the reforms begun by Roosevelt and Taft. He was a passionate believer in justice and brought his liberal ideas to both domestic and foreign policy, although in foreign policy he struggled to stay true to his ideals in practice. In domestic affairs, he had more notable successes and played a proactive role in encouraging Congress to pass legislation he favoured. Most of the legislation passed was enacted in the early years of his Presidency, before the First World War came to preoccupy him.

The Administration supported several pieces of legislation to help farmers and workers:

● Smith–Lever Act (1914) – helped farmers learn new agricultural techniques by the introduction of home instruction.

● Federal Farm Loan Act (1916) – provided a federal farm loan bank in local districts so that farmers could get long-term mortgage loans at a lower rate than they would from commercial banks.

- Adamson Act (1916) – established an eight-hour day and overtime pay for railroad workers who were involved in interstate commerce (Congress could not get involved constitutionally in internal state employment law).

- Keating–Owen Act (1916) – banned articles produced by children under 14 from being traded or transported between states (although this was later deemed unconstitutional because it interfered with powers reserved by the states to regulate employment law).

- La Follette Seamen's Act (1915) – helped to improve safety, payment and conditions for sailors and merchant seamen.

Picketing: The standing outside a factory or other place by a group of workers, especially trade union members, in order to protest about something. The intention is often to prevent people from going in or from leaving.

Injunctions: Instructions or orders that are given officially and formally by a court of law. They are often to stop something from happening, such as an injunction to prevent people striking.

Congress also produced a new anti-trust Act to supersede the inadequate Sherman Act of 1890 when it introduced the Clayton Anti-Trust Act of 1914. The Act contained certain provisions to help workers and farmers by making it clear that strikes, boycotts and **picketing** were not illegal under federal law (some courts had declared them so because they acted 'in restraint of trade') and limited the use of **injunctions** to prevent strikes. It also made it clear that agricultural and industrial trade unions were not classified as trusts. The Act clarified, too, several restrictions on business practice that had not been explicit in the Sherman Act, namely:

- price discrimination in interstate trade

- major holding of one corporation's stock by another (aimed at limiting the powers of holding companies)

- directorates that interlocked in big businesses involved in interstate trade.

In addition, an Act of 1914 established the Federal Trade Commission – a board of five members with the power to oversee businesses involved in interstate trade by requiring the preparation of annual reports and by investigating practices such as advertising, labelling etc.

Wilson was also keen to bring a more effective banking and credit system to the USA. There had been problems in the USA where rigid credit and money supply systems had prevented easy cash flow when necessary, and Wilson was keen to ensure that money flowed more easily. He was helped by a report, in 1913, of the Pujo Committee that had looked into the financial power of a small group of bankers. It concluded that there was on Wall Street a 'money trust' that abused its control of money as much as big business did their industrial power. In 1913, Congress passed the Federal Reserve Act that created a nation-wide system of credit administered by an independent Federal Reserve Board that regulated the rates of interest and currency circulation in 12 different districts of the USA. This not only brought currency under the central control of government, it also allowed the Board to create variations in the amount of currency flowing in different parts of the country so that some districts could have mildly inflationary policies whilst other areas maintained tight monetary control.

Not surprisingly, the Democrats used their control of both Houses of Congress and of the Presidency, to make a substantial reduction in the tariff. This was achieved in the Underwood Tariff of 1913, which included:

- a reduction of rates on almost 1,000 items

- an increase of rates on around 100 luxury items

- an increase in the number of free-items (not taxed at all) to include iron, wool and steel

- the introduction of a graduated income tax (to maintain federal revenues).

Wilson played a key role in getting the tariff reduction through Congress and in overcoming **lobbying** that sought to protect individual items.

Thus, Wilson's first term in office saw the completion of much of the progressive agenda of his Republican predecessors. Government became more efficient, business more regulated and the currency more flexible, whilst the interests of workers were protected as much as was possible at federal level, given the limitations on the power of the federal government by the Constitution. Although the Republicans, largely at Roosevelt's insistence when he turned down the chance to run as a Progressive again, reunited in the 1916 presidential election, Wilson managed to secure re-election and a popular **mandate** for his progressive domestic reforms.

What impact did the First World War have on the Home Front in the USA?

Even before the USA formally entered the First World War, in April 1917, preparations had taken place. In August 1916, Congress had set up a Council of National Defense. In January 1917, the US Shipping Board was created to increase shipbuilding.

The biggest problem the USA faced was raising an army. Unlike most of the major European powers, the USA did not have conscription (compulsory military service). In April 1917, the Army numbered only 120,000 men. Under the Selective Service Act of May 1917, conscription was introduced. The Secretary of War, Newton Baker, efficiently organised the implementation of the Act. By the end of the war, in November 1918, 24 million men had been registered to join the armed forces and 3 million were called up to fight. In an unprecedented move, 11,000 women served in the navy during the First World War.

To ensure the US economy was prepared for world war, the War Industries Board was created in 1917 to organise purchases for the armed forces. From March 1918, Bernard Baruch ran the War Industries Board. To save fuel, a fuel administration was created.

On the agricultural front, a food administration was created in August 1917, under the leadership of Herbert Hoover. Hoover ensured food production was able not only to meet the requirements of the USA, but could also be shipped to Britain. He exhorted the US public not to waste food and he organised such public relations acts as 'Meatless Mondays' and 'Porkless Thursdays'.

One of the casualties of war was civil liberties. On 14 April 1917, President Wilson created the Committee on Public Information. Under the leadership of George Creel, this committee engaged in propaganda against Germany. Anti-German opposition aided the prohibition campaign because Germans dominated the US brewing industry.

The Espionage Act of June 1917 and the Sedition Act of May 1918 outlawed criticism of the war effort. Socialist leader and presidential candidate, Eugene Debs, was imprisoned under these laws. Also targeted was the extreme left-wing trade union organisation, the International Workers of the World – or 'Wobblies'. In total, over 1,500 people were imprisoned under the Acts.

These laws received support from the US Supreme Court in 1919 after the war. In 'Schenk versus the United States' the Court upheld the conviction of a man for distributing anti-call-up pamphlets during the war.

By the end of the war, the role of the federal government in the lives of ordinary Americans had increased significantly. US involvement in the war had cost $35.5 billion: $24.3 billion in expenditure on the US

Lobbying: A group of people try actively to persuade a government that a particular law should be changed or that a particular course of action should be taken.

Mandate: Political term for having the backing for a particular course of action as a result of an electoral win.

1. **Explain why Wilson won the 1912 presidential election.**

2. **How successful was Wilson in domestic affairs during his first term, 1913–1917?**

3. **How did the First World War affect life in America between 1917 and 1919?**

war effort and $11.2 billion in loans to allied countries. In addition, the war provided the final push for the achievement of national prohibition. As millions of men went off to fight, most of their jobs were temporarily filled by women. Shortly after the war, Congress also introduced a constitutional amendment (Nineteenth Amendment) which finally gave women the vote.

 Source-based questions: Immigration

SOURCE A

Decade	Population at end of decade	Population increase over decade	No. of immigrants	% of population increase due to immigration
1861–1870	39,818,449	26.6%	2,314,824	27.6%
1871–1880	50,155,783	26.0%	2,812,191	27.2%
1881–1890	62,947,714	25.5%	5,246,613	41.0%
1891–1900	75,994,575	20.7%	3,687,564	28.3%
1901–1910	91,972,266	21.0%	8,795,386	55.0%

Statistics showing figures relating to immigration and population in the USA, 1861–1910

SOURCE B

Immigrants work for almost nothing and seem to be able to live on wind – something which I cannot do.

I came to America because I heard the streets were paved with gold. When I got here I found out three things: first, the streets weren't paved with gold; second, they weren't paved at all, and third,
I was expected to pave them.

Comments from two workers in America in the 1890s – the first a native American, the second an Italian immigrant.

SOURCE C

After 1840 waves of immigrants contributed to economic growth and demand, whether the newcomer took up land or went into the city. By meeting the demand for cheap, unskilled labor, immigrants made a two-fold contribution: they moved into jobs vacated or bypassed by those who went into the factories, and they themselves made up the pool of labor from which in time factory workers were drawn.

This is a secondary source from a modern textbook (America by George Tindall and David Shi), describing the links between immigration and the economy.

Source-based questions: Immigration

SOURCE D

Europeans were sometimes blamed for the ills and conflicts of the cities and rapid industrialisation. When strikes and labor-management disagreements led to violence in the late 19th century, old-stock Americans said that foreigners brought radical and alien ideas to America and that the immigrants, not working conditions,

caused trouble. Following the assassination of President William McKinley, Congress banned anarchists. While blaming foreigners for labor problems, Americans also said that the newcomers supported corrupt political machines in the nation's growing cities. Some reformers understood that immigrants voted for the machines because the bosses helped their adjustment to the new country, but other Americans equated mass immigration with political corruption and insisted that urban crime would not subside until immigration was curbed.

Another secondary source – this time from the book Natives and Strangers *published in 1996 – talks of the social and political impact of immigrants.*

1. Study Source D.

Explain what is being referred to in both of these highlighted phrases.

(a) 'old-stock Americans'

(b) 'corrupt political machines in the nation's growing cities'

2. Study Sources B and C.

How far do the contemporaries in Source B provide support for the arguments of the historians in Source C?

3. Study Source A.

How useful is this source for understanding the nature and impact of immigration into the USA between 1860 and 1910?

4. *Using all the sources and the information in this chapter, do you agree with the view that 'immigration in the late 19th century had a negative impact on American society'?*

5 Boom and Bust: the United States, 1919–1933

Key Issues

- Why did the United States' economy change between 1919 and 1933?

- What impact did national prohibition have on the USA?

- How far were the 1920s a period of intolerance?

Framework of Events

1918	(November) First World War ends
1919	(January) Eighteenth Amendment ratified by states
	(May) Attacks on socialists and communists across USA
	(June) Congress agrees to Nineteenth Amendment of Constitution – giving women the right to vote (ratified by states in August 1920)
	(July) Race riots across USA
	(October) Volstead Act passed, over President Wilson's veto, enforcing Eighteenth Amendment introducing national prohibition
1920	(January) Palmer Raids against communists
	(May) Sacco and Vanzetti case
	Beginning of economic recession (which lasts until 1922)
	5 million become unemployed by 1921
	(November) Republican Harding defeats Democrat Cox for the Presidency. Republicans also dominate Senate and House of Representatives in Congress.
1921	(May) President Harding approves limitations on immigration
	Budget and Accounting Act establishes Office of Director of Budget
	(November) Revenue Act cuts taxes
1922	(July) Ku Klux Klan begin winning elective office across the USA
	(September) Fordney–McCumber Tariff Act raises taxes on imports
1923	(August) President Harding dies; succeeded by Vice-President Coolidge
	(October) Senate investigations begin into corruption during Harding Administration
1924	(January) First attempt to introduce McNary–Haugen bill to aid farmers
	(February) Corruption scandals of Harding Administration begin to emerge as result of Congressional investigation
	(May) Immigration Quota (National Origins) Act becomes law
	(November) Republican Coolidge defeats Democrat Davis for Presidency
1925	(July) The Scopes (Monkey) Trial in Tennessee
1926	(February) Revenue Act cuts taxes
	Florida land deals collapse

1927	(February) President Coolidge vetoes attempt to introduce McNary–Haugen Bill (vetoes it again in May 1928)
	(August) Sacco and Vanzetti are executed
1928	(November) Republican Hoover defeats Democrat Smith for Presidency
1929	(April) Hoover calls a special session of Congress to deal with farm price crisis
	(October) Wall Street Crash: collapse of prices on New York Stock Exchange
1930	(June) Hawley–Smoot Tariff raises taxes on imports
	(November) Mid-term elections: Democrats gain control of House
1931	Economic crisis spreads to Europe; economic crisis in USA deepens
1932	(January) Reconstruction Finance Corporation is created: first direct attempt by federal government to offer economic aid in Depression
	(July) Relief and Reconstruction Act provides $1.5 billion extra for public works
	Federal Home Loan Bank Act creates home loans with $125 million to prevent homeowners losing their homes
	(November) Democrat Roosevelt defeats Republican President Hoover in Presidential election; Democrats control Congress
1933	(March) Roosevelt becomes President. Beginning of New Deal.

Overview

Economic recession:
A temporary decline or setback in economic activity or prosperity. A modern term for slump, or 'depression'.

THE period 1919 to 1933 was one of rapid change within the USA. After a short **economic recession** following the First World War, the decade was associated with lively economic growth. The United States became the world's first consumer society. The product most closely associated with the 1920s is the motor car. In the second decade of the century, Henry Ford, based in Detroit, Michigan, began producing cars through the assembly-line method of production. This greatly increased production and lowered the cost of motor cars. His 'Model T' Ford became the 'people's car' of the 1920s.

The growth of the car industry stimulated other industries, such as electrics, rubber and engineering. It also led to the development of the US road system.

The 1920s were also associated with other consumer goods such as refrigerators, washing machines, sewing machines and the radio. The radio became a major addition to the media. By the early 1930s, almost every US family possessed a radio. It was a major source of entertainment and news.

The economic boom of the 1920s created thousands of new jobs in industrial and commercial centres in the North, such as Chicago, Detroit and New York. Women took many of these new jobs, such as secretaries and telephonists. In 1920 women had also received the right to vote. Female fashion reflected the change in women's political and economic status.

Although the 1920s are associated with economic prosperity, many social groups and areas missed out. African Americans were treated as second-class citizens across the USA. They received the lowest-paid jobs.

Federal: A system of government consisting of a group of states controlled by a central government. The central government deals with things concerning the whole country, such as foreign policy, but each state has its own local powers and laws.

Farmers also suffered. The war period (1914–1918) had been a period of high farm prices. With the coming of peace and the mechanisation of farming, over-production led to lower farm prices. In the South, the boll weevil devastated the cotton crop forcing many farmers out of business.

Even though industry boomed, trade unionists faced a hard time. The Supreme Court and governments, both **federal** and state, tended to support employers in strikes and over working conditions. Several major strikes occurred in the period, such as the New Jersey textile strike of January 1926.

The 1920s was also a period when White, Anglo-Saxon Protestant (WASP), small-town America attempted to reassert itself. This process took many forms. One aspect was the introduction of immigration controls. The end of mass immigration was an attempt to prevent the USA being 'overrun' with people from eastern and central Europe. These immigrants were associated with 'un-American' ideas such as socialism and communism.

WASP America also asserted itself through the introduction of national prohibition. The Eighteenth Amendment to the Constitution was the culmination of a generation of campaigning by groups such as the women's Christian Temperance Union and the Anti-Saloon League. It was a religious, social and political campaign to enforce the views of WASP America on the whole nation. National prohibition – 'The Noble Experiment' – was a complete failure. Not only was it widely ignored, even in the White House, it also led to the rise in influence of organised crime. The 1920s was not only an era of prosperity, it was also the era of the gangster.

WASP intolerance of other groups reached its height with the re-emergence of the **Ku Klux Klan**. From 1915, the new KKK was not only anti-African American but also anti-Semitic and anti-Catholic. Its former heartland of the Old South was expanded to cover the entire nation. However, just as it rose rapidly, it also declined spectacularly from 1925. This followed several well-publicised scandals involving Klan members in Indiana.

Intolerance towards religious and racial groups was matched by opposition to new ideas. The Scopes Trial in Tennessee, in 1925, received national attention when a schoolteacher challenged state law which banned discussion of Darwin's theory of evolution in schools.

Ku Klux Klan: The original group was set up in the South in 1866 under the leadership of former Confederate general Nathan Bedford Forest. It aimed to terrorise black Americans freed from slavery. With their white outfits, covered faces and burning crosses, their appearance was intended to frighten. Their lynching of 'uppity niggers' was all too successful. The Ku Klux Klan (KKK) carried out 70 lynchings in 1919; the number declined to 11 by 1928. In the 1920s, a revived KKK's updated list of hate-figures included not only blacks but also Catholics, Jews and divorcees. They defended the values of rural WASPs.

How a federal bill becomes an act

1 A proposal for a change in federal law is called a Bill. It is usually introduced simultaneously into the Senate and the House of Representatives. The two sponsors of the Bill (a Senator and a Congressman) usually give their names to the proposal. Hence, Johnson–Reed Immigration Act, Glass–Steagall Banking Act.

2 The Bill is then discussed by a Senate Committee and a House Committee. The Chair of the Ways and Means Committee in the House has considerable influence over which Bills will become law. He/she has the power to assign a bill to a particular committee. For instance, bills on agriculture go to the Senate and House Agriculture Committees.

3 Committee membership reflects the proportion of seats held by Republicans and Democrats in Congress. The chairman of a committee is always from the majority party in that house.

4 Once both committees have discussed and amended the Bill, it goes to a joint committee of both houses where a compromise agreement is made.

5 The Bill is then presented to the President for signature before it can become an act. The President can veto the Bill by refusing to sign it. The President's veto can be overridden if two-thirds of both houses of Congress agree.

6 Even after the Bill has been signed by the President it can be declared unconstitutional by the US Supreme Court. An example is the decision in 1935 to declare unconstitutional the National Recovery Administration set up by the National Industrial Recovery Act of 1934.

Wall Street Crash: On 24 October 1929 nearly 13 million shares changed hands on the New York Stock Exchange. Shock waves from the 'Crash' were felt all around the world. Many people lost a lot of money.

Stock Market: A place where stocks (shares) in companies are bought and sold.

Hobos: American word for the tramps or 'bums' who travelled round looking for work, especially during the Depression.

Hoovervilles: Developments in the USA made up of up to 100 or so small dwellings, often made out of wooden boxes, metal cans, cardboard etc.

1. In what ways did American society and the economy change between 1919 and 1933?

2. To what extent was the USA 'a land of intolerance' during the 1920s?

This opposition to modern trends stood in marked contrast to the development of the cinema industry. The USA led the world in the 1920s in the production of films. Hollywood became the centre of national and world attention as the home of film stars. Douglas Fairbanks Snr, Charlie Chaplin and Rudolf Valentino were stars of the 'silent screen'. Even here, by the end of decade, the 'Hay's Code' laid down strict guidelines on what was allowed in films in terms of male–female relations.

The turning point in the period was the onset of Depression from October 1929. Even before the **Wall Street Crash**, signs of an economic downturn were apparent. Share prices stopped rising, overproduction was taking place and workers were being 'laid off'. The **Stock Market** crash merely speeded up what was already happening. By 1930, the USA and the western world had entered the most serious economic depression the world had seen. The period 1929 to 1933 was characterised by widespread social and economic misery. **Hobos** and **Hoovervilles** spread across the country. By 1932, 25% of the workforce were unemployed.

Faced with this national emergency, President Hoover seemed to be doing nothing. However, Hoover faced an economic crisis never before seen in the USA. In retrospect, it is easy to regard his efforts at dealing with the depression as too little too late.

By 1933 the USA was, in many ways, very different from what it had been in 1919. It had witnessed major social and economic change. This was most apparent in the changing role of women. It saw the USA brought closer together with the development of the motor car, radio and cinema. However, when President Roosevelt took the oath of office, in March 1933, the USA faced a crisis it had not seen since the Civil War.

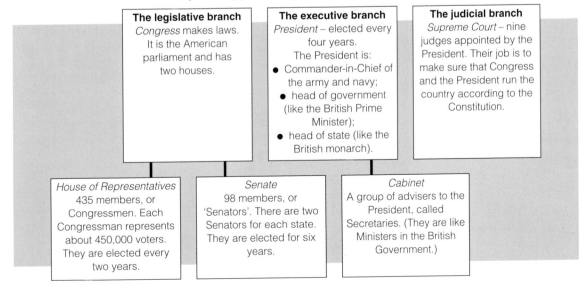

The system of federal government, 1919–1959

The legislative branch
Congress makes laws. It is the American parliament and has two houses.

The executive branch
President – elected every four years.
The President is:
● Commander-in-Chief of the army and navy;
● head of government (like the British Prime Minister);
● head of state (like the British monarch).

The judicial branch
Supreme Court – nine judges appointed by the President. Their job is to make sure that Congress and the President run the country according to the Constitution.

House of Representatives
435 members, or Congressmen. Each Congressman represents about 450,000 voters. They are elected every two years.

Senate
98 members, or 'Senators'. There are two Senators for each state. They are elected for six years.

Cabinet
A group of advisers to the President, called Secretaries. (They are like Ministers in the British Government.)

5.1 *Why was immigration restricted in the USA between 1919 and 1924?*

The United States of America had long followed the policy of 'the Open Door' on immigration. Throughout the 19th and early 20th centuries, millions had emigrated from Europe. On the Statue of Liberty, in New York harbour, Emma Lazarus's words proclaimed:

> 'Give me your tired, your poor
> Your huddled masses yearning to breath free.'

Even at the height of immigration, in the late 19th century, the 'foreign born' only constituted 15% of the US population.

Although the USA had welcomed immigrants from across Europe, there had always been native opposition to the 'foreign born'. In the 1850s, the 'Know Nothing' Party opposed Irish Catholic immigration. In 1882, four years before the Statue of Liberty was unveiled, the Chinese Exclusion Act was passed. In 1907, Congress set up the Dillingham Commission into immigration. It recommended literacy tests for non-English-speaking immigrants.

However, it was the First World War that resulted in the calls for a restriction on immigration reaching national prominence. There were fears over the loyalty of new immigrants, particularly those from the Central Powers (Germany and Austria-Hungary). As part of the officer selection process, the US Army introduced Stanford–Binet tests. These discriminated against non-English speakers. But they reinforced growing hostility to central and eastern Europeans. In 1917, Congress overrode President Wilson's veto to pass the Immigration Act. This Act excluded immigrants who could not read or write English.

By the end of the First World War, opposition to immigrants was reinforced by the creation of a communist state in Russia. Many Americans feared the spread of socialist and communists ideas to the USA. This was seen by the outbreak of bitter industrial disputes during the economic recession of 1920–1922. The Red Scare of 1919 and the Palmer Raids of January 1920 confirmed the belief that the USA was under threat from new immigrants, bringing with them dangerous and un-American political ideas.

Anarchists: People who do not believe in any ruling power; they set out to upset settled power.

From 1920 to 1927, fears of new immigrants and left-wing ideas centred on the Sacco and Vanzetti trial in Massachusetts. These two Italian-Americans were **anarchists**. They had also avoided conscription into the

Sacco and Vanzetti arriving at court on 19 April 1927.

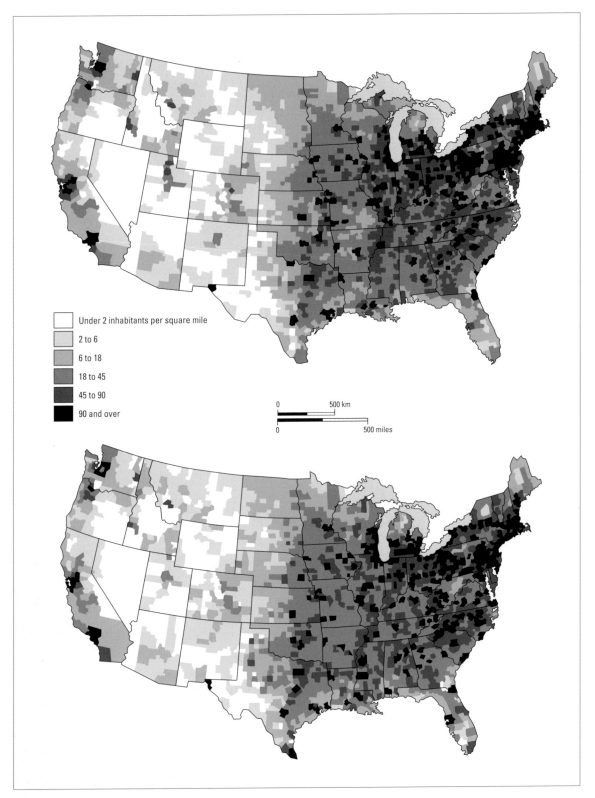

Under 2 inhabitants per square mile
2 to 6
6 to 18
18 to 45
45 to 90
90 and over

0   500 km

0   500 miles

Population density of USA in 1920 (top) and 1930.

armed forces. Nicola Sacco and Bartolomeo Vanzetti were accused of the murder of a postmaster. The trial divided the American nation because the judge showed considerable prejudice against the two defendants. Supporters of Sacco and Vanzetti believed they were scapegoats. However, evidence now suggests that Nicola Sacco was guilty. Opponents believed Sacco and Vanzetti epitomised all that was wrong with the new immigrants.

In 1921, Congress passed the Emergency Immigration Act. For the first time, a limit was placed on immigration. This restricted new European immigration to 3% of the total number of that particular origin already living in the USA, as shown in the 1910 census. This greatly favoured emigrants from the British Isles and western Europe.

Restrictions on immigration were made permanent in 1924 with the Johnson–Reed Immigration Act. This set new **quotas** of 2%, based on the 1890 census. The effect was to close the USA to emigration from eastern Europe because there had been little immigration from those parts in 1890. However, it did not apply to Hispanic Americans from Mexico who were an important labour source for Californian farmers. By 1929, Congress laid down that only 120,000 immigrants could enter per year based on 'the national origins of the American people of 1920'.

In signing the 1929 law President Coolidge claimed that, 'America must be kept American'. By this he meant WASP America. The restrictions on immigration confirmed White Protestants as the top social and political group. The defeat of Catholic Alfred Smith in the 1928 presidential election confirmed this position.

The impact of the loss of immigration was varied. It removed competition for jobs from would-be immigrants, in particular during the economic recession of 1920–1922, but more importantly during the great economic depression from 1929. On the other hand, it had a limiting effect. In 1972 the Nobel Prize Winner for Literature, Saul Bellow, gave a lecture in Chicago Public Library on 'The City in Historic and Philosophical Context'. He noted:

'Diversity made immigrant Chicago vivid 50 years ago The immigration laws of the 1920s stopped the flow of labourers, shopkeepers, confectioners, upholsters, cabinet makers, cooks and waffle wagon drivers who once filled the streets of Chicago. As time has deprived the city of its culture, so has it stolen its individuality.'

It was only with the relaxation of immigration laws, in the 1960s, that this racial and ethnic diversity began to return to the big cities of the USA.

Quotas: Limitations on numbers of immigrants officially allowed entry into a country during a given period. It can also refer to quantities of goods or services imported into a country.

1. What do you regard as the most important reason for the introduction of restrictions on immigration? Explain your answer.

2. To what extent had the United States been a land open to immigration from around the world?

The Harding Administration, 1921–1923: leading posts

President:	Warren Harding
Vice President:	Calvin Coolidge
Secretary of Treasury:	Andrew Mellon
Secretary of Interior:	Albert Fall until 1923, then Hubert Work
Secretary of Agriculture:	Henry C. Wallace
Secretary of Commerce:	Herbert Hoover
Secretary of Labor:	James Davis

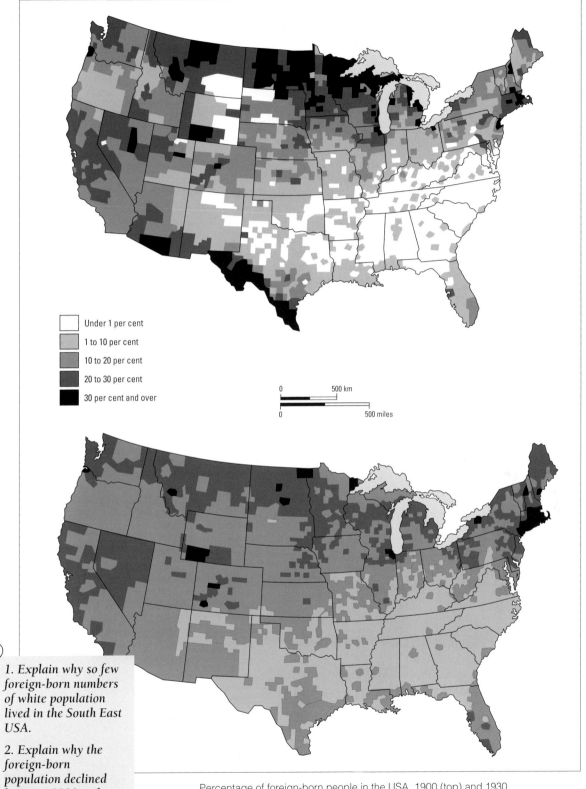

Under 1 per cent

1 to 10 per cent

10 to 20 per cent

20 to 30 per cent

30 per cent and over

0   500 km

0   500 miles

1. Explain why so few foreign-born numbers of white population lived in the South East USA.

2. Explain why the foreign-born population declined between 1900 and 1930.

Percentage of foreign-born people in the USA, 1900 (top) and 1930.

5.2 What impact did national prohibition have on the USA between 1920 and 1933?

The Eighteenth Amendment of the Constitution declared illegal the manufacture, sale and consumption of intoxicating liquor. The definition of what constituted 'intoxicating liquor' was made by the Volstead Act of 1920. This defined 'intoxicating drinks' as those containing at least 0.5% alcohol. This prohibited beers, wines and spirits.

Known as 'The Noble Experiment', national prohibition proved to be a failure. In 1933, Franklin D. Roosevelt proposed a new amendment of the Constitution, the Twenty-First, which reversed the Eighteenth Amendment. Since then, prohibition has been a state, not a federal, matter.

The campaign for national prohibition was long, and involved a variety of pressure groups. The Women's Christian Temperance Union (WCTU) supported prohibition because intoxicating drink was seen as a threat to family life. Men would waste money on drink and/or engage in wife or child abuse as a result of drunkenness. Drink was seen as responsible for many crimes and acts of violence. In the 1870s, the WCTU was able, through their agitation, to force Kansas to become the first state to introduce prohibition.

The WCTU campaign was later supported by the Anti-Saloon League in the 1890s. Under the effective leadership of Wayne Wheeler, this pressure group supported pro-prohibition political candidates. By the outbreak of the First World War, many mid-western and western states had become 'dry'.

The First World War provided the basis for the proposal of the Eighteenth Amendment. How could the war effort be effective if people were allowed to drink? Why should valuable grain be used for alcohol at a time of war? These economic arguments were added to the moral and religious arguments which had been put forward since the 1870s.

Prohibition poster

Warren G. Harding (1865–1923)
29th President of the USA (1921–23), a Republican. According to historian Patrick Renshaw, 'Every ten years American historians place past presidents in rank order. Harding always fills last place.' During his Presidency, the Administration was involved in a number of major corruption scandals. The most notorious was the sale of federal oil reserves at Elk Hills and Teapot Dome. However, during Harding's Administration the federal government was reorganised with the creation of the Office of the Budget. This enabled the President to produce the annual budget more effectively. This was an important development in increasing the power of the President.

'Booze': A slang word for alcoholic drink.

Prohibition was patriotic in another way. Most of the big brewers were of German origin: Budweiser, Pabst, Schlitz. Also, drink was closely associated with immigrant groups which WASP, small-town America disliked: Catholic Irish, Germans and East Europeans. In 1918, it took only three days' debate to pass the Eighteenth Amendment through Congress. Like restrictions on immigration, it represented another triumph for 'nativist' Americans against new immigrants.

Of all the laws passed in the USA, national prohibition was the most widely ignored. President Harding had alcoholic drinks delivered to the White House. Across the country, thousands of illegal drinking places (speakeasies) appeared. By the late 1920s, women who had been so prominent in supporting prohibition now began to campaign for its repeal. The Association against the Prohibition Amendment claimed that national prohibition encouraged crime and undermined the morals of America. It was supported by the Dupont family, who were prominent chemicals manufacturers.

National prohibition also had the effect of splitting the Democratic Party between 'wets' and 'drys': the 'dry' Democrats came from the rural areas of the South and West; the 'wets' represented the immigrant communities of the urban North and East. Divisive debates on prohibition affected the Democratic National Conventions of 1924 and 1928. In the latter, a north-eastern urban 'wet', Alfred Smith, was chosen as presidential candidate.

Prohibition failed on a national scale for a wide variety of reasons. One was the continued availability of alcoholic drink. '**Booze**' was still available in Canada and Mexico. With thousands of miles of land borders, it would have taken a considerable number of men to enforce compliance. At its height, the Treasury Department had about 3,000 prohibition agents to enforce prohibition nationwide. These agents were paid, on average, $2,500 a year. They could be easily bribed by those involved in the billion-dollar 'bootlegging' industry.

(above) Inside a speakeasy (illegal drinking establishment); (right) 'society' women in a New York speakeasy.

Distilleries: Places where whisky and similar strong alcoholic drink is made by a process of distilling.

Bootlegging: Engaging in the illegal manufacture and sale of alcoholic drink.

1. Explain why national prohibition was introduced.

2. How far was the involvement of organised crime responsible for the failure of national prohibition?

In addition to limited enforcement, the availability of industrial alcohol and the existence of illegal **distilleries** all over the country meant that the USA was still able to produce its own supplies without imports. Chicago proved the ideal centre for the distribution of 'booze'. It was near Canada and at the centre of a nationwide network of roads and railroads (railways).

What made national prohibition virtually unworkable was the involvement of organised crime. Such criminals had existed in the USA before national prohibition. They were heavily involved in prostitution and gambling. However, the manufacture and sale of 'booze' proved to be highly profitable. To ensure lack of interference of federal and state authorities, gangsters bribed and intimidated officials. The most celebrated gangsters were based in Chicago. The most effective were Italian-Americans, notably Al Capone. In the St Valentine's Day (14 February) Massacre of 1929, Capone removed his main rivals in Chicago. These were Irish and Jewish Americans associated with the gangster Dion O'Banion. Even when Capone was finally arrested and imprisoned in Alcatraz Jail, in San Francisco Bay, he was convicted for tax evasion, not murder or **bootlegging**. The Treasury Agent mainly responsible for Capone's capture, Elliott Ness, was an alcoholic!

President Hoover established the Wickersham Commission to investigate prohibition. Although it favoured the continuation of prohibition, it also claimed it was impossible to enforce.

When Franklin Roosevelt became President, in March 1933, one of his first acts was to get Congress to pass the Beer Act. This amended the definition of intoxicating liquor made in the Volstead Act. It allowed the production of beer, which created jobs. To many Americans, FDR's campaign song, 'Happy days are here again', welcomed the return of 'booze.'

National prohibition had failed partly because the federal government had underestimated the money and personnel required for its effective enforcement. It also failed because it attempted to force one moral view of society on all Americans. To many immigrant groups, such as the Irish, Germans and Italians, drink was an essential part of their culture – which they were reluctant to give up.

On the negative side, the failure of the 'Noble Experiment' reduced respect for law and encouraged the involvement of organised crime in politics. On the positive side, it did alter American drinking habits. While it was in force, national prohibition proved a boon for the sales of firearms, motorboats and fast cars – and produced a lot of work for undertakers!

Alphonse Capone (1899–1947)

Most celebrated gangster of the 1920s, known as 'Scarface'. Rose to prominence as assistant to Johnny Torrio's Chicago gang in the early 1920s. In November 1924, Capone eliminated a major rival Dion O'Banion. This began a gang war in Chicago, which lasted until the St Valentine's Day Massacre of 1929 when Capone had seven of O'Banion's men gunned down in a garage. In 1927, Capone's 'business empire' was worth an estimated $27 million – coming from bootlegging, prostitution and gambling. Based in Cicero Park, Chicago, Capone controlled local politicians including the Mayor of Chicago, Big Bill Thompson. He was finally arrested and imprisoned in 1931 for tax evasion. During the trial he tried to bribe the jury but was eventually found guilty and served 11 years in jail. After his release in 1939, Capone suffered a long period of ill health, allegedly brought on by syphilis (a sexually transmitted disease).

5.3 Why did the Ku Klux Klan at first revive and then decline rapidly in the 1920s?

The strongest example of WASP intolerance in their attempts to maintain their dominance in US society was the reappearance of the Ku Klux Klan (KKK). Originally, the organisation aimed to protect white Southerners during the years of Reconstruction after the Civil War. Along with other white supremacist groups, such as the Knights of the White Camelia, the KKK terrorised the African American community in the former Confederate states. However, following the establishment of white supremacist state governments in the Old South, the KKK had declined.

It reappeared, in 1915, as a result of the work of William J. Simmons, a former Methodist preacher. Two important influences resulted in the reformation of the KKK: the book *The Clansman* by Thomas Dixon and the film 'Birth of a Nation' directed by D.W. Griffith. Both of these works portrayed the KKK as an heroic organisation defending WASP America against forces which were trying to destroy it. In the 1860s and 1870s, these forces were African Americans, carpetbaggers and scallywags (see page 91) who were exploiting the Old South. From 1915, Simmons and the new KKK added Catholics, Jews, bootleggers and atheists.

Apart from the example offered by *The Clansman* and 'Birth of a Nation', the KKK grew rapidly for a variety of reasons. Firstly, the First World War led to a rise in patriotism and opposition to 'alien influences' associated with non-Anglo-Saxon immigrants. It was also aided by the fear in many southern communities of the return of African American servicemen who had fought in France. The 'Red Summer' of 1919 saw major race riots across America. In East St Louis, returning African American servicemen were singled out for **lynching**.

Lynching: What happens when an angry crowd of people kills someone by hanging them without a trial, because they believe that the person has committed a crime.

Fundamentalism: The belief of religious groups that events described in the Bible or other sacred texts are literally true and should not be questioned.

Attorney General: The chief law officer who advises the government.

Impeach: To charge someone with committing a serious crime. Used especially in the USA when a senior official or politician is charged with a crime in connection with their job.

Although it was William J. Simmons who refounded the KKK, the two individuals most responsible for its rapid rise were Edgar Young Clark and Elizabeth Tyler. Using public relations techniques learned in raising funds for Liberty Bonds and the Red Cross during the War, Clark and Tyler appealed to Protestant **fundamentalism** and traditional moral values to 'sell' the Klan across America. With a $10 joining fee and an emphasis on robe wearing, cross burning and elaborate ceremonial, the Klan rose to a national membership of four million by the time of Elizabeth Tyler's death in 1924.

The Klan's rise also involved increased political influence. When the **Attorney General** of Maine, W. Pattangall, denounced the KKK at the 1924 Democratic National Convention he was defeated in the November elections of that year because of Klan opposition. The Klan also claimed it controlled the Governor of Colorado. It was able to **impeach** an anti-Klan Governor in Oklahoma. Klan members also became state assemblymen, sheriffs and judges. They even included a future US Supreme Court justice, Hugo Black of Alabama. By 1925 'Klaverns' of Klan members stretched across America to Oregon, Maine and Vermont, as well as to the Old South and the 'Bible Belt' of the Mid-West and West.

The rapid rise of the Klan was mirrored by its rapid decline. A major cause for decline was the actions of 'Indiana Grand Dragon', David Curtis Stephenson. In 1925, Stephenson was convicted of the rape and murder of a 28-year-old secretary. This severely damaged the claim that the Klan defended traditional moral values. The Klan was also affected by corruption and intimidation scandals in Pennsylvania.

The Klan's decline was also the result of the efforts of Imperial Wizard, Hiram Wesley Evans, to turn the organisation into a sort of social club. He even attempted to ban the wearing of masks in public.

1. *Explain why the Ku Klux Klan grew rapidly between 1915 and 1924?*

2. *To what extent was the rapid rise and decline of the Ku Klux Klan due to the actions of individuals?*

The combined effect of scandal and the efforts of Evans had reduced Klan numbers to 200,000 by 1929. However, its decline could also be attributed to the impact of the immigration restrictions imposed by Congress in 1919, 1924 and 1929. The Klan represented the sinister side of white supremacist views. The onset of economic depression also tended to lessen, rather than increase, tensions between different social and racial groups.

5.4 In what ways were the 1920s a period of cultural change?

Popular culture: Cultural pursuits followed by the majority of the population. Different from 'high culture', which is followed by a small number of intellectuals. Popular culture in the 1920s included reading comic books and newspapers, listening to radio and jazz, dancing the Charleston, and going to the cinema.

The 1920s were a decade of remarkable cultural change and creativity. In **popular culture** the decade was associated with the rapid growth of radio entertainment and, above all, the cinema. Hollywood became the world centre for film production. It was also the decade of mass spectator sport. Baseball and college football became national pastimes.

The changes in popular culture in America in the 1920s have been given various names. It is sometimes known as 'The Jazz Age'. This term reflects changes not only in popular music, but also in fashion and dance. The decade could also be known as the 'Age of the Flapper' to reflect the new social and cultural position of women. According to Gertrude Stein, a major literary figure of the decade, the artists and writers of the 1920s were 'The Lost Generation'. They had been disillusioned by the First World War and the 'botched' peace that ended it.

The leading literary figures of the decade included poet Ezra Pound and novelists Sinclair Lewis, F. Scott Fitzgerald and Ernest Hemingway. A leading critic of US society of the time was Baltimore journalist, H.L. Mencken.

Did the 1920s witness a 'sexual revolution' in the USA?

According to the authors of *The Enduring Vision* (1993): 'The most enduring twenties' stereotype is that of the flapper – the sophisticated, fashionable, pleasure-mad, young women.' The 'flapper' reflected important changes in the life of American women in the 1920s. New fashion and dance suggested a more carefree, pleasure-seeking lifestyle. No longer was the role of woman one of home making and child rearing. Many young women in the 1920s had the opportunity to follow an independent lifestyle, which was not dominated by the need to find a husband. Thousands of women were able to find employment as telephonists, typists, secretaries and clerks in the rapidly expanding American economy.

Quintessence: Most perfect version or example.

The individual who, at the time, symbolised these changes was the Hollywood film star Clara Bow, known as the 'It Girl'. The novelist Scott Fitzgerald called her 'the **quintessence** of what a "flapper" signifies: pretty, impudent, superbly assured, worldly-wise [and] briefly clad'. Amory Blaine, the hero of Fitzgerald's 1920 novel *The Other Side of Paradise*, 'saw girls doing things that even in his memory would have been impossible'. The decade did see the rise in the use of birth control to avoid unwanted pregnancies. It also saw the rapid growth of smoking among women.

Perhaps the most revealing development was the growth of women's cosmetics. Beauty salons appeared across America. The cosmetics industry increased its earnings during the decade from $17million to

Two flappers dancing the Charleston on the roof of the Sherman Hotel, Chicago, 1926.

How useful is this illustration to a historian writing about US popular culture in the 1920s?

$200 million per year. It helped to make Chanel, Helena Rubenstein and Elizabeth Arden household names in the USA. Previously, make-up had been associated with prostitutes. Now, women in America were taking control of their sexuality (i.e. using cosmetics, wearing shorter skirts and removing corsetry).

Like all stereotypes, the flapper reflected only one aspect of the life and role of women in American society in the 1920s. The prestigious women's college, Vassar, offered courses in 'Wife, Motherhood and the Family as an Economic Unit'. In many ways the decade was a period of unfulfilled expectation for many women. It had begun promisingly with the passage of the Nineteenth Amendment, giving women the vote. However, a distinctive 'women's' movement never really materialised. It is true that, in 1928, the League of Women Voters was able to proclaim that 145 women had won seats in 35 state legislatures and two had become governors, but these were the exceptions in the male-dominated world of politics.

Beginning in 1923 the National Woman's Party, led by Alice Paul and Rose Winslow, failed to get an Equal Rights Amendment accepted. They had wanted the Constitution to include an amendment stating that 'men and women shall have equal rights throughout the United States'. This campaign led to conflict with groups who had fought long and hard to protect women during the Progressive Era. If the Equal Rights Amendment (ERA) became law, labour laws restricting the number of hours and type of work open to women would be lost. The campaign from the political feminist movement did not reappear again until the late 1960s.

In what ways did popular music and dance change in the 1920s?

'The Jazz Age' of the 1920s saw the rise to national prominence, for the first time, of a type of music that came directly from African American culture. It reflected one of the most important movements of population in the inter-war period, that of African Americans from the Old South to the North. Chicago and the Cotton Club in Harlem, New York City, became centres for the development of jazz. It may have had its origins in the Deep South but jazz was an urban-based, northern brand of music.

New forms of popular music were accompanied by new forms of dance. Out went the waltz of the pre-war concert or dance hall. In came the 'Charleston', the 'Black Bottom' and the 'Turkey Trot'. These dances were associated with improvised steps and daring women's fashion, including dresses that only went down to the knee!

However, not all America flocked to these new music and dance crazes. Small-town and white working-class America in the South, Mid-West and West still clung to the 'hoe down' dance and country music, the forerunner of Country and Western music. The religious revival of the 1920s saw preachers, such as Billy Sunday and Aimee Semple McPherson, condemn the loose morals and sexual excesses of the decade, which were epitomised by these new musical and dance developments.

How important was mass spectator sport in American popular culture in the 1920s?

America in the 1920s is regarded as the world's first consumer society. With rising pay cheques and the development of radio and cinema, mass spectator sports benefited. The national game was baseball. However, in 1919, the national game was affected by scandal. The Chicago White Sox were accused of 'throwing' the World Series for money. Judge Kenesaw Mountain (he was named after the civil war battle in Georgia) Landis led an enquiry which banned most of the White Sox team. Professional baseball in the 1920s was dominated by the New York Yankees and, in particular, Babe Ruth – the so-called 'Sultan of Swat'. Ruth held the professional baseball 'home run' record until overtaken, in the 1970s, by Hank Aaron.

Not all spectator sports were professional. College football was very popular. The 1920s saw the emergence of the Mid-Western Catholic team Notre Dame. Under coach Knut Rockne, 'the Fighting Irish' as they were called were unbeaten in 1924. Rockne revolutionised the game by inventing the forward pass.

Mass spectator sport and the radio came together most effectively in professional boxing. KDKA, the Pittsburgh, Pennsylvania radio station went on air to broadcast Jack Dempsey winning the world heavyweight boxing title in 1919. Throughout the decade, it continued to bring live commentary of matches to a wide American audience.

What impact did radio and cinema have on American society in the 1920s?

KDKA of Pittsburgh was America's first radio station. By the end of the decade, hundreds of radio stations had spread across the country. For the first time, small towns and remote rural areas were able to hear up-to-date news broadcasts, music, radio plays and comedy shows. These broadcasts were sponsored by private companies. This meant that the growth of radio was matched by the spread of advertising.

Of even greater significance was the development of cinema. By 1919 Hollywood, a suburb of Los Angeles, had become the major production centre for the world film industry. With silent films, the issue of language was unimportant. American stars dominated the 'silent screen'. Harold Lloyd, Buster Keaton and Charlie Chaplin provided comedy. The main 'action hero' was Douglas Fairbanks Snr. He married the leading female star of the period, Mary Pickford. Together they acted like cinema royalty such was their fame.

Every small town across America had its 'picture house'. Cinema became the main form of entertainment. Film gave even the remotest part of America glimpses of life in Ancient Rome, the Wild West, the First World War and of how the rich lived. Fashions that appeared in films were copied by film fans.

Perhaps the most influential film to come out of Hollywood in the

Douglas Fairbanks Snr and Mary Pickford in the film of 'The Taming of the Shrew', in 1929

silent era was D.W. Griffith's 'Birth of a Nation', in 1915. It dealt with the Civil War and Reconstruction period. Its heroic depiction of the Ku Klux Klan helped to increase racism in America and was an important factor in the re-emergence of the KKK.

In 1927, Hollywood faced major technological change with the development of 'talking pictures'. 'The Jazz Singer,' starring Al Jolson, was the first film that contained sound. This development made films even more popular. The establishment of the Academy Awards (Oscars), in 1928, gave Hollywood an annual showcase to prove its importance in American society and world cinema, which it has not lost since.

How important were the 1920s for the development of American literature?

The 'lost generation' of writers of the 1920s laid the foundation of modern American literature and provided an important insight into life in America. Sinclair Lewis from Minnesota wrote effectively about small-town, Mid-West America. In *Main Street* (1920), he wrote about the fictional small town 'Gopher Prairie', which he described as smug and culturally barren. He added to his view of America in 1922 with *Babbit* which took a critical look at middle-class life. In Oxford, Mississippi, William Faulkner wrote about life in a fictitious Mississippi County Yoknapatowpa from the Civil War to 1902.

The two most significant writers, however, were F. Scott Fitzgerald and Ernest Hemingway. Their writing epitomised the feeling of disillusionment with 1920s society. Fitzgerald's greatest novel, *The Great Gatsby* (1925), dealt with the material excesses associated with the economic boom. Hemingway, who was an exile for much of the period, wrote about those who had been affected by their experience of world war. *The Sun Also Rises* (1926) and *A Farewell to Arms* (1929) both deal with people damaged physically and mentally by war.

An important feature of literary development was the African American cultural renaissance, centred on Harlem, New York City. This took many art forms. In 1921, an all African-American Broadway musical was produced, 'Shuffle Along'. In literature, Langston Hughes produced *The Weary Blues* in 1926, which explained the black experience. Finally, the National Association for the Advancement of Colored People used its periodical 'The Crisis' to publicise the works of young African-American poets and writers.

In spite of these cultural developments, African Americans still faced discrimination across America in jobs, housing and education. The Harlem cultural renaissance must be placed against the re-emergence of the Ku Klux Klan to provide a broader perspective of society in the 1920s.

1. How important were the 1920s for the development of music, dance sport and literature?

2. With what success did women improve their position within American society in the 1920s?

3. Why was the development of radio and the cinema so important to most Americans?

4. What do you regard as the most important cultural development in the 1920s? Give reasons for your answer.

5.5 How far did the United States experience an economic boom in the 1920s?

The Declaration of Independence, in 1776, had declared that the new state should aim to enable 'life, liberty and the pursuit of happiness'. The 1920s seemed to be the decade when this aim had been achieved, at least in an economic sense.

The 1920s were seen as a decade of unrivalled prosperity. However, the period did begin with an economic recession, from 1920 to 1922. The economic boom the USA had experienced during the First World War came to an abrupt end. The Government cancelled contracts once the war had ended. Bankruptcies and unemployment rose.

Gross national product (GNP):
This is a way of measuring the
wealth of a country and is the total
amount of production by US firms
and businesses whether in America
or abroad.

For the rest of the decade, the performance of the US economy was
impressive. The **gross national product (GNP)** rose from $73.3 billion in
1920, to $104.4 billion in 1929 (in 1929 prices). This reflected an average
growth rate of around 2% per year. Unemployment never rose above 3.7%.
Compare this with the average of 6.1% between 1911 and 1917. Inflation
never rose above 1%. The average working week in industry fell from 47.4
hours in 1920 to 44.2 hours in 1929. Real wages rose by approximately
13% between 1922 and 1929.

These economic statistics meant that the purchasing power of
Americans rose steadily. For instance, in 1922, some 100,000 radios were
produced. In 1929, this had increased to 350,000 per year. The major US
corporations saw profits increase by 62% between 1923 and 1929. The
industry that epitomised the 1920s boom was the motor car industry.
General Motors saw its earnings rise from $173 million at the start of the
decade to $1.5 billion by 1929. The 1920 census highlighted the social
changes that fuelled the economic boom. For the first time in American
history more people lived in towns than in the countryside.

What were the reasons for the economic boom of the 1920s?

(a) Size and economic wealth of the USA
In the 1920 census the population of the USA had reached 106.4 million.
This compares with 42 million in Britain in 1921. Not only was the population large, it also had considerable purchasing power. Unlike in Britain, US
manufacturers had a large domestic market in which to sell their goods.

The United States also had a very effective internal transportation
system. Since 1869, transcontinental railroads united the country. These
were supplemented by the development of a road system in the early 20th
century. Roads allowed the newly invented car to provide communication
in areas between the railroads.

To fuel economic growth, the USA possessed an abundance of raw
materials. These provided the basis for the industrial revolution that the
USA experienced from the 1850s. There were extensive coalfields in
Kentucky, West Virginia and Pennsylvania. The country had large
reserves of oil in Texas, Oklahoma and Pennsylvania. Iron ore, lead, tin,
copper and other important metals were found across the West. **Lumber**
came from the large coniferous forests of the Pacific North-West. The
South provided cotton and the Mid-West and West an abundance of
farm produce.

Lumber: North American term for
timber sawn into rough planks or
otherwise roughly prepared for the
market.

(b) The entrepreneurial spirit and the American Dream
Thomas Edison, the American inventor, once said that genius is 1% inspiration and 99% perspiration. America had a gift for both of these. 'Yankee
ingenuity' had resulted in the invention of the electric light bulb, the sewing
machine, phonograph and telephone. Coupled with this was the 'work
ethic' of the USA – 'rugged individualism', which encouraged hard work
and thrift. Long before the 1920s, the USA had developed a strong business
class and a powerful industrial **infrastructure**. Self-made millionaires such
as Andrew Carnegie and John D. Rockefeller epitomised the 'American
Dream'. If you worked hard enough, you could be prosperous. This idea led
millions to cross the Atlantic in search of wealth. The immigrant population
provided hard-working and cheap labour which made industrialisation
such a success.

Infrastructure: The basic structure
on which a country, society or
organisation is built, such as the
facilities, services and equipment
which are needed for it to function
properly.

(c) The impact of the First World War
In 1914, the USA had become one of the world's major industrial powers. It
rivalled Britain and Germany. Fortunately for the USA, its major economic
rivals virtually bankrupted themselves fighting the First World War. By

1918, Britain had lost almost one million dead and over two million wounded. It owed the USA millions in inter-allied war loans. Germany had fared even worse. It lost over two and half million dead. After the war, it faced a bill of £6.6 billion in **reparations** to the Allies. These problems led to the virtual collapse of the German economy by 1924.

Reparations: Payments made by a defeated state to compensate the victorious state(s) for damage or expenses caused by the war.

The USA benefited from the war in other ways. The demand for armaments stimulated the growth of American industry. By 1918, the United States emerged from the First World War as the world's major industrial power.

(d) Technological progress and 'Fordism'
According to Joshua Freeman in *Who Built America?* (published in 1992):

'Taken together, a series of new methods in manufacturing, labor relations, and consumer sales perfected during and after World War One constituted a virtual second industrial revolution.'

The centre for this 'second industrial revolution' was Detroit, Michigan. It was here that Henry Ford revolutionised car manufacture. Although cars had been produced in America since the 1890s, Ford introduced new industrial methods which led to their mass production. Firstly, he took the work to the man rather than taking the man to the work. An assembly line meant that unskilled and semi-skilled workers could learn how to assemble a specific part of a car quickly and easily. The assembly line, always working at the same pace, meant that the rate of production could be set.

Secondly, Ford concentrated production, until the mid-1920s, on one car type – the Model T. He stated that: 'The way to make automobiles is to make one automobile just like another, to make them come through the factory alike – just like one pin is like another pin.' As a result, Ford boasted that customers could have a Model T in any colour they liked as long as it was black!

Finally, Henry Ford introduced the $5-a-day rate for car workers. This was substantially above rates offered elsewhere. In return, workers were not expected to join trade unions and were expected to follow the company's strict policies on assembly line working. By 1926, Ford was producing a Model T car every 10 seconds.

The scale of car production at Fords was awesome. By the end of the First World War, Henry Ford had constructed the River Rouge plant in Detroit. This employed 75,000 workers. Ford benefited enormously from economies of scale. By 1927, 15 million Model T Fords had been produced.

By 1929, the motor manufacturing industry directly employed 7% of all industrial workers and paid almost 9% of industrial wages. Indirectly, motor car manufacture created thousands of jobs in the steel, rubber, paint, lumber and electrical industries.

As historian Donald McCoy noted in *Coming of Age* (1973):

'The rise of motor vehicle manufacturing contributed to the expansion of the petroleum industry, for the use of [petrol] shot up from less than 3 billion gallons in 1919 to 15 billion in 1929. Add to all this the development of tourism, roadside advertising and merchandising, garages, automobile dealerships and various other enterprises catering to motor traffic, and it is plain that within a decade the automobile industry and related businesses had become the most important and attractive element in the American economy.'

The federal government aided the development of the industry with the Federal Highways Act of 1921. This gave the Government responsibility for building roads. During the 1920s it built, on average, 10,000 miles of road per year (up to the Wall Street Crash). In the decade, surfaced roads grew from 350,000 miles in 1919 to 662,000 in 1929.

While motor manufacture and its related industries epitomised the decade, these new manufacturing techniques affected virtually all industries.

(e) New management and selling techniques

Alongside 'Fordism' came the development of business management. Frederick W. Taylor spread the idea of 'scientific management'. Taylor's idea was that all aspects of the manufacturing process should be analysed scientifically and that an efficient system should be adopted which would get the greatest level of productivity out of workers. These 'time and motion studies' became a feature of management as the decade progressed.

However, the most important development in manufacturing management was the growth and development of the large corporation. Large corporations were able to benefit from **economies of scale** and integration. Perhaps the clearest example of this development was the electricity supply industry. A key figure in this was Samuel Insull of Middle West Utilities, a holding company. Insull's corporation owned 111 subsidiary companies by the end of the decade, with an estimated value of $3 billion. Through his control of the market, Insull was able to provide cheap electricity to middle-class Americans.

Economies of scale: The economic benefits of lower cost per unit of production that are made when large manufacturing companies are formed.

By 1929, 16 holding companies controlled over 90% of US electricity production. In that same year, the largest 200 corporations controlled 20% of the nation's wealth and almost 40% of its business wealth. These corporations were able to benefit from discount purchasing, and they engaged in research and development, which helped to produce cheaper and more efficient products. They could also staff their organisations with specialists.

The government encouraged corporate control of individual industries. Herbert Hoover, at the Department of Commerce, encouraged the growth of trade associations within an industry. The aim of a trade association was to allow firms to benefit from exchange of information, which would allow them to standardise manufacturing methods and take advantage of the latest technology. Although 2,000 trade associations already existed by 1920, hundreds more were created by 1929. Many criticised this development because trade associations acted like trusts.

Large corporations could also borrow money easily for the purposes of investment.

The 1920s was also the decade that saw the rapid growth of advertising and marketing. These were aided by the technological developments of the radio, the motor car and the cinema. New methods of high-pressure selling were pioneered by individuals such as Bruce Barton who claimed, in books such as *The Man Nobody Knew* (1926), that selling and Christianity were compatible. Barton claimed that Jesus 'would have been a national advertiser today'.

(f) Government policies

President Calvin Coolidge (1923–1929) once remarked that 'the business of the American people is business'. Throughout the 1920s the federal government, supported by Congress, helped to create the conditions for a business boom. The Republican Party, by the 1920s, was associated with *laissez-faire* economics.

Laissez-faire **economics**: The belief in free trade and that government interference should be kept to a minimum.

In fact, the Republican administrations of Harding and Coolidge, on occasion, went out of their way to aid business. In 1922, Congress passed the Fordney–McCumber Tariff Act. This placed import duties on a wide variety of goods including farm products, chemicals, textiles, chinaware and other industrial products. The Federal Trade Commission was given the power to advise the President on tariff increases up to 50%. This had the effect of protecting American manufacturers against foreign competition.

Of more importance were the tax-cutting policies of Republican administrations. Secretary to the Treasury from 1921 to 1932 was Andrew Mellon who came from a rich banking family in Pittsburgh, Pennsylvania. In a series of revenue acts 1921–1926, he cut the tax on the rich (known as surtax) from above 50% to 20%. Mellon's favourable tax policy towards the rich and large corporations encouraged the development of business. In spite of tax cuts, the rapid growth in business meant that the Treasury had a surplus in the Budget for the 1920s.

Businesses also benefited from less regulation by the Federal Trade Commission, and from State and Congressional support against trade unions. 'Yellow dog' contracts (no-strike agreements) were supported by the courts, which allowed greater management control over their work forces.

(g) Easy credit and hire purchase

New technological and management techniques allowed American manufacturers to produce more goods at a lower unit cost per item. However, an economic boom would not have taken place if there had been a lack of domestic demand to buy these goods.

Part of the answer was an increase in the average wage of Americans during the decade. Average wages rose from $1,308 to $1,716 per year in the USA in the 1920s. This was at a time of low inflation. There was also the development of hire purchase. This allowed consumers to buy goods at a small proportion of the price. They could then pay off the rest of the price, and a small rate of interest, in either weekly or monthly instalments. Encouraged by new methods of advertising, consumers bought a wide range of goods by this method – from cars to refrigerators. Between 1919 and 1929, the amount of consumer credit, outside agriculture, grew from $32 billion to $60 billion.

1. In what ways did new industrial and manufacturing methods help to create an economic boom in the 1920s?

2. What do you regard as the most important reason for the economic boom of the 1920s?

Give reasons for your answer.

Do these figures suggest the US economy was facing an economic boom in the 1920s? Explain your answer.

Consumer borrowing in the USA in the 1920s

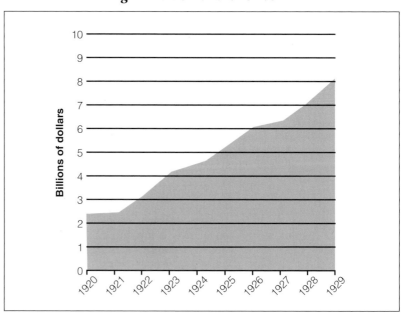

Americans plunged into debt in the 1920s in order to play the Stock Market and to buy new cars and other consumer products.

President and Congress: the separation of powers

The United States Constitution created a series of 'checks and balances' between the Government (President) and the law-making institution (Congress).

When a President nominates someone to the Cabinet, he has to get approval from two-thirds of the Senate. This is part of the Senate's 'advice and consent' powers. This also includes appointments to the US Supreme Court and heads of agencies such as the Federal Trade Commission and Federal Bureau of Investigation (FBI).

The President also needs Congressional support if he is to implement laws. Congress can either delay proposals for laws, or amend them radically. The House of Representatives has considerable power over the granting of money and the raising of taxes for the federal government.

Therefore, it is possible for the President to face either a Senate or House, or both, who are opposed to his policies. As both Senate and House are elected separately from the President they may be from the opposing party. For the Republican presidents of the 1920s, both houses of Congress had Republican majorities. President Nixon (1969–1974) and President Clinton (1993–2001) faced a Congress controlled by the opposing party.

Which groups missed out on the prosperity of the 1920s?

Farmers

While the 1920s were a boom time for US industry, they were a period of decline for farmers. During the First World War, farmers had experienced a period of rising agricultural prices and increasing demand for their producte. Prices for farm goods rose 82% between 1913 and 1917. In the same period, the number of farmers earning $2,000 per year rose from 140,000 to 1.8 million. However, by 1920, the fall in demand caused farm prices to drop. Those countries that had imported large amounts of US farm produce, such as Britain, had now begun to recover from war.

Also, the Fordney–McCumber Tariff Act of 1922 resulted in many foreign markets being closed off for US farm produce as countries began to raise duties from their own import duties on US imports. Even the introduction of national prohibition had an adverse effect on agriculture. Demand for grain from distillers and brewers simply disappeared from 1920.

Finally, US agriculture faced overproduction because of the onset of mechanisation. The use of tractors, combine harvesters and other modern farming machinery greatly increased output, further depressing prices.

In the 1920 census, for the first time, more Americans lived in towns than in the countryside. By 1929, a further 5% drop occurred in those who earned their living from agriculture. Also, between 1920 and 1930, the number of farms in the USA declined. Around 13 million **acres** (5 million hectares) of cultivated land were abandoned.

The 1920s were not the first decade in which farmers faced a crisis. In the 1880s and 1890s, farmers organised into the Granger and Populist parties to make a strong defence of farming interests. In 1915, many farmers formed the Non-Partisan League to defend farming interests. However, this had very limited impact. Instead, the dominant farmer group during that decade was the moderate Farm Bureau.

Acres: An acre is a measure of the area of land 4,047 square metres (or 4,840 square yards). One hectare equals 2.47 acres.

Nevertheless, farmers did gain some assistance from the Department of Agriculture under Secretary Wallace. The Agricultural Credits Act of 1923 gave low-interest loans to farmers. The Capper–Volstead Act, also of 1923, encouraged the creation of farm cooperatives. However, the main attempt in the 1920s to aid farmers, failed. This was the McNary–Haugen Bill. Initially introduced into Congress in 1924, it was vetoed twice by President Coolidge, in 1925 and 1927, and never became law. The aim of the Bill had been to cut supply to domestic consumers but to maintain farm incomes. The government would buy excess farm produce and sell it abroad. Historical research by Gary Koerselman of Northern Illinois University in 1971 showed that these proposals would have benefited large-scale farmers. Indeed large-scale farmers, such as the fruit growers in Southern California, fared well in the 1920s. They used cheap Hispanic-American labour.

Trade unionists

While 'big business' prospered in the 1920s, trade unionism declined. Union membership had grown during the First World War, from 2.27 million in 1916 to 5.03 million in 1920. It then declined to 3.6 million during the 1920s.

The Red Scare of 1919 and the Palmer Raids of the 1920s led many workers to avoid joining unions. Another factor was 'the American Plan', whereby non-union members would receive the same benefits as union members if made redundant.

A more important reason was the action of 'big business', which was usually anti-union. Union membership was either discouraged or employees were forced to sign 'yellow dog' contracts in which employees agreed not to strike.

Big business was supported by both the government and the judiciary. Attorney General Daugherty broke the 1922 railroad strike by getting a federal judge to declare union action illegal. Also, between 1922 and 1925, the US Supreme Court passed several anti-union judgements making it difficult both for unions to strike and for the creation of a minimum wage.

Trade unions did not help themselves. The American Federation of Labor (AFL) was interested only in skilled labour. It made no attempt to unionise the semi-skilled and unskilled workers.

African Americans

During the decade, most African Americans continued to live in the Old South. There they led a poverty-stricken existence, mainly as **sharecroppers**. They occupied the lowest economic position in a relatively poor region of the USA. The existence of **segregation** and, as a result, poor

Sharecroppers: Farmworkers who work for a share of the crops they grow, instead of a wage.

Segregation: The practice of keeping apart people of different racial or religious groups, or of different sexes.

The Coolidge Administration, 1923–1929: leading posts

President:	Calvin Coolidge
Vice President:	Charles Dawes
Secretary of Treasury:	Andrew Mellon
Secretary of Interior:	Hubert Work until 1929, then Roy West
Secretary of Agriculture:	Henry C. Wallace until 1924, then Howard Gore to 1925, then W. Jardine
Secretary of Commerce:	Herbert Hoover until 1928, then William Whiting
Secretary of Labor:	James Davis

1. For what reasons did different social and economic groups miss out on the economic prosperity of the 1920s?

2. 'The 1920s were a decade of economic prosperity for the mass of the American people.'

Explain why you agree or disagree with this statement.

education reinforced the poor social and economic position of African Americans.

However, during the decade approximately 850,000 African Americans migrated North to cities such as Chicago and New York. By 1930, African Americans were beginning to occupy industrial and manufacturing jobs. Even in the North they tended to get the worst-paid jobs. This was due to a mixture of racism and the poor education received by the majority of African Americans, which was an aspect of the former.

5.6 Why, and how, did economic depression affect the United States from 1929?

Did the Wall Street Crash of October 1929 cause the Depression?

The economic depression, which first hit the United States and then the world, began with the collapse of share prices on the New York Stock Exchange in October 1929. The Bank of England raised British interest rates to 6.5% in order to attract capital from the United States. As a result, many European investments were up for sale on the New York Stock Exchange. This resulted in a fall in the value of shares, which created an atmosphere of uncertainty among shareholders who began to sell their stocks. On Thursday 24 October 1929 (known as Black Thursday), 12.8 million shares changed hands. By the end of that day, overall share values had fallen by $4 billion.

On the following Tuesday, 29 October (Black Tuesday), a record 16 million shares changed hands at very low prices. By the end of November 1929, $30 billion had been wiped off the value of shares.

The share collapse caused panic. On the trading floor of the Stock Exchange, fist fights broke out. Prices were so low that a messenger boy bid $1 for a share in the White Sewing Machine Company and, as a result, became a major shareholder! The President of the Union Cigar Company committed suicide by leaping to his death off the Beverly Hotel in Manhattan, New York.

The prices of shares in ten US companies

	3 March 1928	3 September 1929	13 November 1929
American Can	77 ¢	182 ¢	86 ¢
Anaconda Copper	54 ¢	162 ¢	70 ¢
Electric Bond and Share	90 ¢	204 ¢	50 ¢
General Electric	129 ¢	396 ¢	168 ¢
General Motors	140 ¢	182 ¢	36 ¢
New York Central	160 ¢	256 ¢	160 ¢
Radio	94 ¢	505 ¢	28 ¢
United States Steel	138 ¢	279 ¢	150 ¢
Westinghouse E & M	92 ¢	313 ¢	102 ¢
Woolworth	181 ¢	251 ¢	52 ¢

Speculation: The purchase of land or shares in order to make a quick profit. A person who engages in share speculation is a stag.

Bull Market: A bull market occurs when share prices in a stock market are rising. A bear market occurs when share prices are falling.

According to the historian Michael E. Parrish, in *The Anxious Decades* (1994), 'The collapse of the stock market did not "cause" the terrible economic depression that followed.' Nevertheless, **speculation** in shares and land did contribute to US economic instability in the 1920s.

In 1925–26, a preview of the problems associated with share speculation had been apparent in land dealings in Florida. With promises of large financial returns on investment, thousands bought land and property in the 'Sunshine State'. One woman who bought Florida land for $25 in 1900 sold it for $150,000 in 1925. Areas such as Coral Cables and Biscayne Bay, near Miami, became some of the most sought after properties in the USA. The most notorious example of spurious land advertising was for plots of land near the prosperous town of Nettie, which had never existed.

The Florida Land Boom collapsed by 1926 for several reasons. Swindlers, such as Charles Ponzi, conned potential purchasers out of their money. Builders failed to meet construction deadlines. The lack of railroads impeded development. In 1925, the Internal Revenue Service began taxing profits made on property speculation. Finally, a severe hurricane on 18 September 1926 caused devastation in south Florida.

Speculation in land was replicated in share speculation. The 'Great **Bull Market**' on the New York Stock Exchange saw the number of shares listed rise from 500,000 in 1925 to 1,127,000 by October 1929. Using easy credit facilities offered by banks, thousands bought shares 'at the margin'. They offered to pay 10% of the share value as a down payment. These would be paid off when profits were made from the sale of these shares at a later date. This system worked well when share prices continued to rise, but it collapsed dramatically when share prices fell. By October 1929, share prices had leaped ahead of the real business values. Sooner or later, an adjustment was bound to take place. On 5 September 1929, business analyst Roger Babson stated:

'Sooner or later a crash is coming, and it may be terrific. Factories will shut down, men will be thrown out of work, the vicious circle will get in full swing and the result will be a serious business depression.'

However, as historian Donald McCoy notes in *Coming of Age* (1973):

'The stock-market crash did play an important role, but its larger significance was as a trigger and as a dramatic symptom of deeper and more complicated national and international causes of the depression.'

Stock markets are inherently unstable. Even during the 1920s, the price of shares occasionally dropped, although there was an upward trend across the decade. In both the late 1980s and late 1990s, the New York Stock Exchange witnessed large falls in the value of shares. But, on both occasions, no economic depression followed.

The causes of depression must therefore be found elsewhere.

Underconsumption and overproduction

According to the historian Joshua Freeman, in *Who Built America?* (1992), underconsumption was the major cause of the depression. Throughout the 1920s, businesses had benefited from Treasury Secretary Andrew Mellon's low tax policies. Part of the result of this was that the bottom 40% of the population received only 12.5% of the nation's wealth. In contrast, the top 5% owned 33% of the nation's wealth.

This maldistribution of wealth had unfortunate consequences. Domestic demand for goods never kept pace with production. The problem of underconsumption was masked by the growth of easy credit and hire purchase. By 1929, it was becoming clear that mass consumption in the USA had reached a point where consumers were reluctant to take on more credit to sustain demand. Overseas demand was affected by the high tariff policies operated by many states in response to the Fordney–McCumber Tariff Act of 1922.

International economic problems

According to President Herbert Hoover (1929–1933), America's economic problems after 1929 could be traced to international, rather than domestic, causes. The world economy of the 1920s faced severe economic

? *How far do these statistics and graphs suggest that the Wall Street crash caused the Depression?*

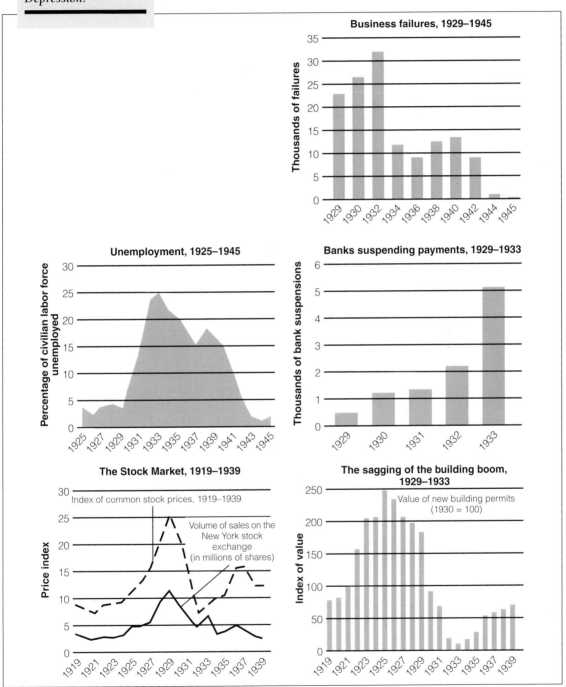

Graphs showing the statistics of hard times in the USA.

Collapse of stock market prices
on New York Stock Exchange
and other stock exchanges
across the USA.

Loss of savings, the collapse of
banks and loss of business
confidence results in closure of
factories leading to sharp rise
in unemployment.

Fall in domestic demand.
Exports hit by high foreign
tariffs and the spread of
economic depression world
wide as fall in US stock
markets leads to fall in stock
markets across the world. The
withdrawal of US investment
from Germany causes very
severe economic depression.

More factories closing. Banks
close because of loss of loans
as companies become
bankrupt.

Endemic: Peculiar to a people or to a district.

1. Explain the ways in which historians, economists and people at the time have disagreed over the main cause of the economic depression.

2. How important was the Wall Street Crash in causing economic depression from 1929?

problems as a result of the First World War and the peace treaties which followed it. Allied powers, such as Britain, France and Belgium, owed the USA millions of dollars in inter-allied war loans. Germany, as a result of the Treaty of Versailles, had to pay the Allies £66 billion in war reparations. These financial burdens created economic instability. To raise money all European states, except Britain, placed tariffs on imported goods. They also raised taxes. These had the effect of cutting demand, especially demand for US goods. Therefore, the US economy could not expand its foreign markets as rapidly as it could increase its production. Manufacturing output increased 50% in the USA, between 1920 and 1929, but exports rose only 38% in the same period.

In addition, political unrest helped to destabilise other parts of the world. Political unrest was **endemic** in China. The establishment of communism in Russia excluded a large overseas market. In South America, Paraguay and Bolivia fought the Chaco War.

Government policy

The economist J.K. Galbraith is critical of the economic policies of Republican Administrations in contributing to the Depression. In the 1920s, there had been too little regulation of business by the Government. Wartime controls had ended as soon as the Wilson Administration had left office. Low taxes made the maldistribution of wealth greater. Also, failure to aid farming helped to perpetuate the depression in agriculture, which lasted the whole decade. Low capital gains tax encouraged share speculation, which resulted in the Stock Market crash.

To encourage business, stock exchanges such as Wall Street requested little investigation into firms who had placed their shares for sale. In hindsight, it is easy to criticise Republican governments for their *laissez-faire* economic philosophy. However, it was an economic policy followed by most western, capitalist economies when not faced by war.

The weakness of the US banking system

If the Government can be criticised it is over the regulation of banks. Only one-third of US banks were under the jurisdiction of the Federal Reserve Board, the USA's central bank. Even here the Federal Reserve's powers were limited to dealing with short-term loans. Instead, the USA had a banking system made up of hundreds of small, state-based banks. If a crop failure in one state led to the collapse of a bank, it could lead to a 'run' on other banks resulting in a banking collapse. Between 1921 and 1928, 5,000 banks went out of business. In 1929 alone, 659 banks suspended operations.

The collapse of share prices had a devastating effect on banking. The resulting banking collapse led to the closure of thousands of businesses and farms. As historian Michael Parrish has noted:

'The stock market debacle [mess] dealt Americans both a financial and an emotional body blow … Within one year, GNP declined from $87.8 billion to $75.7 billion. The slide into economic chaos had begun, and the Great Crash had played something more than a minor role.'

How was the United States affected by economic depression from 1929 to 1933?

The most obvious effect on the lives of Americans was the sharp rise in unemployment. Before the Crash, unemployment had been rising in the coal and textile industries. On the eve of the Crash, unemployment had been 1.5 million. By March 1930, it rose to 3.25 million. By the time

Franklin D. Roosevelt became President, in March 1933, the figure had risen to 13 million (24.9% of the work force).

As economic activity collapsed, the gross national product fell from $103 billion in 1929 to $55 billion in 1933. Average weekly earnings fell, over the same period, from $25 to $17. Income from agriculture, forestry and fishing fell from $8.3 billion in 1929 to $3.3 billion in 1933. The number of banks operating fell from 25,500 in 1929 to 14,700 in 1933.

Taken together, the effects of these economic statistics were to plunge the United States into the biggest domestic crisis since the Civil War. As millions lost their jobs, thousands of men left home in search of work. Using railroads to travel, these hobos became a feature of American life in the depression. Farms were repossessed by banks. Soup kitchens, run by churches and charities, were to be found in every major town and city. Society was transformed from one based on confidence in the economic future into one based on disillusionment and despair.

The strain on society began to show. The suicide rate rose 14% between 1929 and 1932. The number of marriages fell 10% between 1929 and 1932, and with it the birth rate. Those who were affected particularly badly were children who suffered poor diet, clothing and education as the economic crisis worsened. Small-scale farmers, African Americans and Hispanic-Americans suffered more than any other socioeconomic group.

Faced with such a crisis, many Americans began to look for someone to blame.

Using the information above, draw a spidergram to illustrate how the USA was affected by economic depression between 1929 and 1933.

How useful is this picture as evidence of economic conditions in the USA in the 1929–1933 period?

Unemployed men walking the road in search of jobs, mocked by the poster for train travel – California, 1938.

5.7 *Herbert Hoover*
A CASE STUDY IN HISTORICAL INTERPRETATION

**Herbert Hoover
(1874–1964)**
31st President of the USA
(1829–33), a Republican.
Before the First World War he
travelled widely as a mining
engineer. After the War, he
organised relief work in
occupied Europe. Food
Administrator for the USA
(1917–19), before becoming
Secretary of Commerce
(1921–28). Defeated Democrat
Al Smith in 1929 presidential
election. However, Hoover lost
public confidence when he
opposed direct government aid
for the unemployed in the
Depression. **Shanty towns**, or
Hoovervilles (see page 151),
sprang up around large cities –
evidence of Hoover's failure to
cope with the effects of the
Depression and to prevent the
decline of the economy.
F.D. Roosevelt succeeded him
in 1933. Hoover was later
called upon to administer the
European Food Programme
(1947) and in the 1950s he
headed two commissions into
reforms in government
structure and operations.

Shanty towns: Areas where poor
people live. The dwellings are small,
rough huts built from tin, cardboard
and other flimsy materials.

The case against Herbert Hoover

President Hoover has been a figure of ridicule for both people at the time and for historians since. The shanty towns of the homeless were called Hoovervilles. A newspaper covering a homeless person was referred to as a 'Hoover blanket'. The Broadway musical, and subsequent Hollywood film of the 1980s, 'Annie' was set in 1932. One of its more notable songs was 'We'd like to thank you, Herbert Hoover'. It is sung by homeless people in New York City. It ends with the verse:

> We'd like to thank you, Herbert Hoover
> For really showing us the way,
> You dirty rat, you bureaucrat,
> You made us what we are today.

To critics of Hoover, he always did too little too late. Historian Donald McCoy stated, in *Coming of Age*:

> 'What he [Hoover] and his administration did either was insufficient to combat the deep and long-extended economic crisis or came too late, and Congress did little to help. It is plain in retrospect that Hoover was too cautious.'

In dealing with the Depression, Hoover thought the main role of the federal government should be to coordinate private, state and local issues, rather than take direct action himself. Under the US Constitution, states, rather than the federal government, had responsibility for welfare. By the time of the Depression, only eight states had any kind of unemployment compensation. Instead the poor had to rely on the help of private charities. Support for 'voluntaryism' was a major feature of Hoover's early attempts at dealing with the depression. It coincided with his belief in 'rugged individualism' and the American tradition of independent action. Hoover argued that relief was a local responsibility; federal involvement would strike at the 'roots of self-government' and would destroy 'character'. Hoover did have some initial success in persuading business to help. Some companies froze wages to prevent further hardship, but this had limited success. By 1931, a major corporation, US Steel, introduced a 10% wage cut.

In his reluctance to use the federal government directly in aiding the poor, Hoover was supported by important members of his Administration. Treasury Secretary, Andrew Mellon, declared that as a result of the depression 'people would work harder, live a more moral life' and, therefore was

---

The Hoover Administration, 1929–1933: leading posts

President:	Herbert Hoover
Vice President:	Charles Curtis
Secretary of Treasury:	Andrew Mellon 1929–32, then Ogden Mills
Secretary of Interior:	Ray Wilbur
Secretary of Agriculture:	Arthur Hyle
Secretary of Commerce:	Robert Lamont until 1932, then Roy Chapin
Secretary of Labor:	James Davis until 1930, then William Doak

'not altogether a bad thing'. It was up to individual, local politicians to take action. Elected in 1930, Mayor Frank Murphy of Detroit created food stations for 14,000 unemployed. In New York State, Governor Franklin Roosevelt successfully organised relief for the unemployed and poor, which gained him a national reputation.

Instead of looking for the causes of the depression within the United States, Hoover argued that international economic conditions were the root cause of problems. The breakdown in international trade and the economic crisis in Europe were more important than a lack of federal government involvement.

Hoover was president, though, when Congress passed the Hawley–Smoot tariff in June 1930, which raised import duties on the Fordney–McCumber tariffs on average by 30%. Historian Michael Parrish claims that:

> 'as the stock market crash helped dry up the springs of international credit, the Hawley–Smoot tariff choked off international trade and compounded economic misery from Boise [Idaho] to Berlin, from San Diego [California] to Singapore.'

An episode which seemed to display the heartlessness of the Hoover Administration was the Bonus Army march of 1932. In May and June, First World War veterans marched on Washington DC demanding full payment of their veterans' bonus immediately, instead of having to wait until 1945 when it due to be paid.

Following the Senate rejection of this demand, the Administration used the army, under General Douglas MacArthur, to remove the 21,000 remaining veterans and their families from a shanty town on Anacostia Flats. Millions of Americans were horrified by the sight of tanks and cavalry, and by the use of tear gas, as troops destroyed the shanty town.

By November 1932, Hoover had become the most hated man in America. Hitch-hikers carried signs stating that if they did not receive a lift, they would vote for Hoover. Having won a landslide victory in 1928, Hoover was defeated by another landslide in November 1932. The American electorate of that year had given their verdict on Hoover's efforts.

The case for Herbert Hoover

According to British historian Hugh Brogan, in the second edition of *The Longman History of the United States of America* (1999):

> 'Hoover saw the peril [of the depression] and acted to avert it. During the rest of his Presidential term he was to act incessantly, doing more than any previous President had done in any previous economic crisis.'

Hoover's problem was that he faced an unprecedented economic situation. Depressions had occurred before, most notably in the 1890s and 1920–22. It was seen as a normal part of the business and trade cycle. Although we now know how deep this depression was to become, Hoover did not know this in 1929 and 1930.

Nevertheless, he did take action. In agriculture, even before the Wall Street Crash, he called a special session of Congress, in April 1929, to help farmers. The Agricultural Marketing Act established a nine-man Federal Farm Board with funds of $500 million to create farming cooperatives. In 1930, Hoover created the Grain Stabilisation Corporation, which bought surplus wheat from cooperatives as a way of stabilising grain prices. However, these attempts were destroyed by the world collapse in grain prices. By 1932, the Federal Farm Board had failed.

Moratorium: A legally authorised delay in the performance of a legal duty or obligation. From the Latin *mora* – delay.

To try to boost international trade, Hoover introduced a **moratorium** on inter-Allied war debts, in June 1931. This meant the USA would delay collecting debts for 18 months. Unfortunately, it came too late to save Europe from severe depression.

Hoover placed great hope in an international economic conference to be held in London in early 1933. However, F.D. Roosevelt (FDR) refused to cooperate with other countries, claiming that America's economic ills were caused by domestic rather than international problems.

Although an initial opponent of direct federal aid, Hoover did change his policy once he became aware that voluntaryism and cooperation were failing. The first significant departure in this direction was the creation of the Reconstruction Finance Corporation (RFC). This was approved by Congress, in January 1932. It had the power to lend up to $2 billion to rescue failing banks and insurance companies. Ninety per cent of loans went to small- and medium-sized banks. When he became president, FDR continued to use the RFC as part of his economic policy towards the depression.

Direct federal help for the unemployed came with the passage of the Emergency Relief and Construction Act on 21 July 1932. To receive aid, state governments had to declare that they had run out of money to help the unemployed. The corporation that was set up by the Act had the authority to lend up to $1.5 billion to states to fund public works for the unemployed.

In July 1932, Congress also passed the Federal Home Loans Act. Federal home loan banks were created to provide up to 50% assistance for those persons who could not pay off their mortgages.

Taken together, these measures were as far as Hoover was willing to go to involve the federal government directly. They were introduced only after voluntaryism and state action had failed. They were also the result of consistent Congressional pressure from Senators such as Robert Wagner of New York, Robert La Follette Jr from Wisconsin and Edward Costigan of Colorado.

Verdict?

Historian Martin L. Fausold, in *The Presidency of Herbert C. Hoover* (1985), claims:

> 'It has been said that the jury on the Hoover presidency is still out – that scholars who seek to assess American presidents react differently depending upon their sources of information, their times and their values.
>
> The jury consists of three important constituencies:
> - Hoover's close associates at the close of his presidency
> - the majority of Americans throughout the half century following his presidency
> - historians at the half-century mark after his presidency.
>
> [They all] agree that the Hoover presidency was a failed one.'

1. Why do historians and people at the time have such varied views of the role of Herbert Hoover in the depression from 1929–1933?

2. How far do you agree with Martin L. Fausold's verdict of Hoover's presidency in dealing with the Depression?

Increasing numbers of historians, including this author, see Hoover's many qualities. It is regrettable that, as the 21st century begins, many of the nation's citizens continue to see in Herbert Hoover what he himself saw in his presidency: 'the dark side first'. Given the emphasis that is placed on the presidency in public affairs, it is improbable that this assessment will ever change.

Study the figures in the table.

(a) What trends in voting behaviour can be made from studying these figures?

(b) Why do you think some counties of Georgia voted against Democrat candidate Alfred Smith in the 1928 election?

Presidential elections, 1920–1932

	Popular vote	Electoral College vote
1920: Warren Harding, Republican	16.1 million	404
James Cox, Democrat	9.1 million	127
1924: Calvin Coolidge, Republican	15.7 million	382
John Davis, Democrat	8.3 million	136
1928: Herbert Hoover, Republican	21.4 million	444
Alfred Smith, Democrat	15.0 million	87
1932: Franklin Roosevelt, Democrat	22.8 million	472
Herbert Hoover, Republican	15.7 million	59

Source-based questions: The US economy in the 1920s

SOURCE A

Economic growth in the USA 1919–1929

	Gross national product (in billions of dollars)	Income per head (in dollars)
1919	78.9	755
1920	88.9	835
1921	74.0	682
1922	74.0	672
1923	86.1	769
1924	87.6	768
1925	91.3	788
1926	97.7	832
1927	96.3	809
1928	98.2	815
1929	104.4	857

SOURCE B

We in America today are nearer to the financial triumph over poverty than ever before in the history of our land. The poor man is vanishing from among us. Our workers with their average weekly wages, can today buy two or even three times more bread and butter than any wage earner in Europe. Today we demand a larger comfort and greater participation in life and leisure.

From Herbert Hoover's acceptance speech as Republican Party Presidential candidate, June 1928

SOURCE C

Depression? Most Americans had come to assume during the 1920s that there would never be another depression. This misguided optimism proved to be an important factor in generating an economic freefall after 1929. Throughout the 1920s the idea grew that American business had entered a new era of permanent growth. Such naïve talk helped promote an array of foolhardy get-rich-quick schemes. Speculative mania fuelled the Florida real-estate boom.

From America by George Tindall and David Shi, 1984

Source-based questions: The US economy in the 1920s

SOURCE D

During the 1920s the gap between the well-off and the not-so-well-off widened greatly. Between 1922 and 1929 wages rose an average of about 40%, but in the latter year the 36,000 wealthiest families received as much as the 12 million poorest.

From Who Built America? *by Joshua Freeman, 1992*

1. Study Sources A and C and use information from this chapter.

Explain the meaning of:

(i) 'Gross national product' (Source A)

(ii) 'speculative mania' (Source C).

2. Study Sources A and B and use information from this chapter.

Of what value are these two sources to a historian writing about the US economy of the 1920s?

3. Study Sources C and D and use information from this chapter.

What do these sources suggest were problems facing the US economy in the 1920s?

4. Study Sources A–D and use information from this chapter.

'The growth of the US economy during the 1920s benefited the few rather than the many.'

Explain why you agree or disagree with this view.

6 FDR and the New Deal, 1933–1945

Key Issues

- How successful was FDR as president in domestic affairs between 1933 and 1945?

- How important was opposition to the New Deal?

- Did the New Deal bring fundamental change to the United States?

Framework of Events

1932	(8 November) FDR wins presidential election: receives 22.8 million votes and wins 472 electoral college votes against Hoover's 15 million votes and 59 electoral college votes
1933	(6 February) Twentieth Amendment of Constitution
	(4 March) FDR is inaugurated as president
	(March–June) First 100 Days of New Deal
	(8 November) Civil Works Administration established under Harry Hopkins
1934	(January) Gold Reserve Act
	(June) Securities and Exchange Commission is created
	Silver Purchase Act
	(November) Coughlin forms National Union of Social Justice
	Mid-term elections give Democrats majority of 45 in Senate and 219 in House of Representatives
1935	(April) Emergency Relief Appropriations Act creates Works Progress Administration
	(May) Resettlement Administration is created
	Rural Electrification Administration is created
	(27 May) Black Monday, when Supreme Court invalidates Farm Mortgage Act and NIRA
	(June) National Youth Administration is formed
	(July) National Labor Relations or Wagner Act is passed
	(August) Banking Act; Revenue Act; Social Security Act; Public Utility Holding Company Act
	(September) Huey P. Long assassinated
1936	(January) Supreme Court invalidates AAA
	(June) FDR nominated as Democrat candidate for presidency
	(November) Landslide victory for FDR over Landon (wins 46 out of 48 states)

1937	(February) FDR submits 'Court Packing' bill to Congress
	(March) In 'West Coast Hotel v Parrish', Supreme Court upholds Washington state minimum wage act
	(April) Supreme Court upholds Wagner Act and Social Security Act
	(June) Roosevelt Recession begins
1938	(February) Second Agricultural Adjustment Act
	(June) Fair Labor Standards Act
1939	(April) Executive Office of President is created by Executive Order 8248
1940	(November) FDR re-elected for unprecedented third term as president
1941	(December) USA enters Second World War
1942	(January) Emergency Price Control Act sets maximum prices
	Creation of War Labor Board and War Production Board
	(February) Japanese Americans removed from west coast
	(April) Creation of War Manpower Commission and Office of Price Administration
	(October) James Byrnes is placed in control of Office of Economic Stabilisation
	(November) Mid-term elections bring big gains for Republicans
1944	(November) FDR wins fourth term as President
1945	(12 April) FDR dies at Warm Springs, Georgia.

Overview

THE period when Franklin D. Roosevelt (FDR) was president was one of the most monumental in the history of the United States. When he became president, in March 1933, the USA faced the worst economic crisis in its history. Twenty-five per cent of the workforce was unemployed and the banking system was on the verge of collapse. When FDR died in office, in April 1945, the United States had recovered from economic disaster to become the world's greatest economic power.

The period began with FDR's attempts to get America out of economic depression. His first 100 days in office (March–June 1933) was a period of frantic law-making activity in the US Congress. No less than 14 major Acts were passed, establishing government agencies that dealt with different aspects of economic activity. The First New Deal of 1933–35 brought the economic decline to an end. However, it took the Second New Deal of 1935–37 to bring major change to the social and economic structure of the USA. Legislation – such as the Wagner Act, the Revenue Act and the Social Security Act, all in 1935 – helped to lay the foundations of the American '**welfare state**'.

For all its achievements, the New Deal received criticism. At the time, criticism came from both the right and left of US politics. The Liberty League accused FDR of trying to introduce **socialism**. Huey Long of Louisiana, as well as **socialists** and **communists**, believed FDR had not gone far enough in bringing about social and economic change.

The most serious challenge to the New Deal came from the US Supreme Court. In a series of judgements in 1935 it declared large parts of the New Deal unconstitutional. Fortunately for FDR, the Supreme Court changed its views towards New Deal legislation from 1937, following the resignation of the more conservative justices.

FDR stated that 'Dr New Deal' had saved the US economy from collapse. It

'Welfare state': Provision by the state of a basic level of income and services for all citizens: health services, housing, education and, ideally, maintenance of full employment.

Socialism: The extension of the role of the state in the economy, with the intention of creating a more equal society.

Socialists: People who believe in the principles of socialism.

Communists: People who believe in communism – the political belief that the state should own and control the means of producing everything, so that all levels of society can be made equal. In this way, everyone should do as much as they can and get as much as they need.

took 'Dr Win the War' to bring about complete economic recovery. Even in 1941, on the eve of US entry into the Second World War, the country was affected by serious labour disputes. However, the drive to aid the Allies, from 1939, and then to win the War, made the USA the 'arsenal of democracy' (see page 203).

The end of economic depression was the result of unprecedented federal intervention in social and economic affairs. FDR's Administrations exploited the phrase in the US Constitution which gave the federal government the right 'to promote the general welfare'.

Once the USA had become involved in the war, in 1941, the federal government took over large sections of US industry. By 1945, the federal government had intervened in the lives of ordinary Americans, which would have been unthinkable in 1933.

The New Deal era also brought about important changes in politics. In 1932, FDR had won the election by bringing together a range of different groups in a 'New Deal' **coalition**. This helped the Democratic Party dominate Congress and the presidency until the late 1960s. The coalition was made up of southern whites, **blue-collar workers** in trade unions, northern liberals, African Americans, Catholics and Jews.

The year 1932 can be seen as a 'turning point', or 'watershed', in US history, or for many reasons. One of the most important was that it marked the end of '**WASP**'-dominated America. From 1933, large numbers of Irish, Italian and Jewish Americans entered national government for the first time.

FDR's period in office also saw the rise of the 'Imperial Presidency'. Under FDR, the power of the president increased considerably. This was due, in part, to the growth of the federal government. It was also due to FDR's style of presidential politics. His 'fireside chats' on the radio brought the US President in direct verbal communication with the US public for the first time. FDR's personal charm and 'patrician' style made him widely popular. By 1939, presidential government had grown so much that the Executive Office of the Presidency was created to include all the presidential advisers. The US involvement in the Second World War merely accelerated a trend which was already apparent in the 1930s.

Certain social groups within the USA clearly benefited from the 'New Deal' years. The Agricultural Adjustment Acts of 1933 and 1938 laid the foundations of modern US farm policy. Together with other New Deal initiatives – such as rural electrification – farmers faced a more stable, prosperous future. In industrial America, some of the beneficiaries of the New Deal were the trade unions. Legal recognition and the right to strike were firmly established by the end of the 1930s. Also, the rapid growth of the Congress of Industrial Organisations gave FDR and the Democrats an important **voting bloc**.

Less certain was the impact of the New Deal on African Americans. They clearly benefited from agencies such as the Works Progress Administration (WPA), which provided much-needed jobs. However, very little progress was made in civil rights. Attempts to make lynching a federal offence came to nothing. FDR was too sensitive to southern white opinion within the Democratic Party to make any radical changes, especially in tackling segregation in the South. Nevertheless, FDR's wife, Eleanor Roosevelt, took a personal interest in assisting the social, political and military advancement of African Americans.

Similarly, women's rights did not develop significantly in the New Deal years.

Coalition: A government containing representatives of more than one party or group. In the USA in 1932, the 'coalition' was made up of representatives of southern whites, **blue-collar workers** in trade unions, northern liberals, African Americans, Catholics and Jews.

Blue-collar workers: People who do manual jobs – as opposed to white-collar workers in offices.

'**WASP**': Stands for 'White Anglo-Saxon Protestant'.

Voting bloc: The supporters of a particular political party who come from different regions and different social and ethnic groups.

New Left historians: This term is used for historians from the 1960s who have studied the 1930s from the perspective of socialists. They contend that FDR should be criticised for defending socialism, rather than for being more radical.

1. In what ways did the New Deal change the economy in the USA?

2. What do you regard as the most important area of change brought about by the New Deal:

(a) the economy

(b) the lives of women and African Americans

(c) politics?

Give reasons for your answer.

In 1933 Frances Perkins, the Secretary of Labor, became the first woman Cabinet member. However, the traditional role of women as the 'home minder' remained. It took the major manpower shortage caused by the Second World War for women to enter blue-collar jobs in large numbers for the first time. Even here, the increased female involvement in the workforce was seen as temporary due to the wartime emergency.

Historians are divided about the impact of the New Deal years on US politics and society. To **New Left historians** the New Deal was conservative, helping to preserve capitalism. Others, such as William Leuchtenburg, believed the New Deal brought fundamental change. It greatly increased the power of the presidency and federal government. It also laid the foundations of a national system of social welfare. To other historians, such as Peter Clements and Tony Badger, many New Deal agencies overlapped and worked inefficiently with contradictory aims. The National Recovery Administration – one of the central agencies of the First New Deal – had achieved little by the time it was declared unconstitutional by the Supreme Court. Other agencies, such as the Civil Works Administration (1933–34) and the Works Progress Administration (1935–42), brought genuine relief to millions.

6.1 Why did Franklin D. Roosevelt win the 1932 Presidential election?

The 1932 elections were a turning point in US political history. They brought Republican control of the federal government and of the Congress to an end. They also saw Democrats replace Republicans across America in state governorships and state legislatures.

The central triumph was the election of Franklin D. Roosevelt (often referred to as 'FDR') as president in a landslide victory against Herbert Hoover. Roosevelt had been Assistant Secretary for the Navy under Woodrow Wilson during the First World War. In 1920, he was Democrat

Franklin D. Roosevelt (1882–1945)

32nd President of the USA (1933–45), a Democrat and a lawyer. Educated in Europe and at Harvard and Columbia universities. Elected to the New York State Senate in 1910. F.D. Roosevelt (FDR) was Assistant Secretary for the Navy (1913–21). He suffered from polio in 1921 but returned to politics, winning the governorship of New York State in 1929.

Became President in 1932. With a group of experts around him, he launched his reform programme. The 1936 presidential election was won by FDR entirely on the record of his New Deal policy. In 1938 he introduced measures for farm relief and for the improvement of working conditions in the USA. Soon after the outbreak of the Second World War, FDR launched a vast

rearmament programme, introduced conscription and provided arms to the Allies on a 'cash-and-carry' basis. FDR was re-elected for a third term as President in 1940. From the point at which the USA entered the War on 7 December 1941, Roosevelt concerned himself solely with the conduct of the war. He was re-elected President for a fourth term in 1944, but died the next year.

An American cartoon of the 1936 Presidential election. Only two states, Vermont and Maine, did not vote for Roosevelt in the election.

Vice-Presidential candidate when James Cox lost heavily to Warren Harding. However, his political career seemed to come to an abrupt end, in 1921, when he contracted polio.

For the rest of his life FDR lost the use of his legs. What was remarkable was the fact that FDR did not appear in public in a wheelchair or using crutches. He kept up the pretence of being able to walk by using steel leg braces and by using his son and other helpers to lean on so that he appeared to walk.

FDR's political comeback came in 1928 when he won the governorship of his home state of New York by a small margin. During the early depression, his state administration received a reputation for acting decisively to aid the poor and the unemployed. When he was chosen as Democrat candidate for the presidency in the summer of 1932, FDR was a popular political figure. This popularity was enhanced by his campaign call for bold government experimentation to end the economic crisis. This stood in marked contrast to Hoover's Administration, which was perceived as incapable of dealing with the crisis.

Although FDR had many fine attributes, it was Hoover and the Republicans who lost the election. Faced with the worst economic crisis in US history, the Republicans were slow to act. Believing that it was the 'business cycle' and economic system which had brought prosperity in the 1920s, they hoped that the economic downturn would be short. By late 1931, the Hoover Administration began to act more decisively – but this was seen as too little too late.

By November 1932, the presidential election result had become a foregone conclusion. It was only the scale of Democratic victory that was in question. The Democrat Vice-Presidential candidate, John Nance Garner, stated that FDR was successful because he was able to put together a coalition of different groups that would allow the Democrats to dominate national politics for a generation. The coalition included

Presidential election results,
USA, 1936

1. What do you regard as the most important reasons for FDR's win in the 1932 Presidential election?

Give reasons for your answer.

2. To what extent did Herbert Hoover lose the election, rather than FDR winning it?

traditional Democrat groups, such as southern whites. The 'Solid South' remained loyal to the Democrats until the 1960s. They were also supported by immigrant groups such as Irish, Italian and Jewish Americans. These groups were not attracted by the Republicans' 'WASP' leadership and support for racial and religious reasons. In addition, trade unionists and blue-collar workers formed an important source of support. These had suffered under the pro-business policies of the Republicans. They were also unimpressed by Hoover's limited attempts to deal with the economic crisis.

For the first time, the majority of African Americans voted for the Democrats. During the 1920s, tens of thousands of African Americans had migrated north to industrial cities such as Detroit and Chicago. Freed from the oppression of segregation, they no longer feared the WASP-dominated Democratic Party.

6.2 How successful was the First New Deal in dealing with the effects of the Depression?

FDR was inaugurated as President on 4 March 1933. His acceptance speech has rightly been regarded as one of the most important in US history. On that date, most of the banks across America were closed. One in four of the workforce was unemployed. Faced with such a crisis, FDR's speech was a rallying cry to the American people. He called for a 'New Deal' to rebuild the US economy. He also called for wide, sweeping powers to meet the economic crisis and he stressed that the only thing Americans needed to fear was fear itself. Followed shortly afterwards by his first radio 'fireside chat', FDR gave the American people hope.

However, between his election in November 1932 and his inauguration in March 1933 – known as the 'lame duck' period – FDR did nothing to stop the economic collapse. He gave no real indication of what he planned to do once he became president. Also, he refused to take up President Hoover's offer to work together during this period. As a result, the economic crisis became worse over the winter of 1932–33. Hoover was already discredited, FDR had yet to offer leadership.

When it came, FDR's leadership was decisive. Calling a special session of Congress, FDR launched the '100 Days' of frantic legislative activity. The 100 Days brought an end to prohibition, reformed the banking and financial system, and began the first steps on the road to 'Relief, recovery and reform'. This meant:

- *relief* from the effects of the economic depression

- *recovery* from economic depression

- *reform* of the economic system to prevent further depressions in the future.

Reforming the banking and financial system

Emergency Banking Act, March 1933
FDR acted quickly to end the crisis in banking and finance. He used the Trading with the Enemy Act, which had been introduced by President Woodrow Wilson during the First World War. This allowed him to proclaim a national bank holiday from Monday 6 March to Thursday 9 March. In this period, he persuaded Congress to pass an Emergency Banking Act. It did so in just seven hours. The aim of the Act was to restore confidence in the banking system. It gave the Treasury power to investigate all banks threatened with collapse. This was supported by the Reconstruction Finance Corporation, which took over bank debts. To gain public support, FDR made his first 'fireside chat' on national radio on 12 March.

The effect of the bank holiday and the Act was to save US banking. FDR had relied on advice from the banking community. He had no other choice, given the crisis he faced. The banks did not encourage the development of branch banking. This had prevented major bank closures in Canada. Nevertheless, one of FDR's 'brains trust' advisers, Raymond Moley, claimed that FDR had saved American capitalism in just eight days.

Glass–Steagall Act, June 1933
In order to bring reform to the banking system, the Glass–Steagall Act prevented commercial 'high street' banks from taking part in investment banking. This had been a major cause of bank collapse following the Wall Street Crash of 1929. The Act also created the Federal Deposit Insurance Corporation (FDIC). This federal agency guaranteed all bank deposits up to $5,000.

Between them, the Emergency Banking Act and the Glass–Steagall Act stabilised US banking. Although the division between state and federal banking remained, FDR's first two terms as president (1933–41) saw less bank closures than any previous Administration. For the first time in almost 60 years, no national banks collapsed in 1936.

Interest rates: The price of borrowing money to purchase things.

Farm Credit Administration, March 1933
Even though a banking collapse was averted, FDR still had to deal with the debt problem faced by farmers. By Executive decree on 27 March, he created the Farm Credit Administration (FCA). This helped farmers to meet their mortgage repayment by offering lower **interest rates**.

Home Owners' Loan Act, 13 June 1933
This Act created the Home Owners' Loan Corporation (HOLC), which gave urban householders similar financial aid to that offered to farmers under the FCA.

The Federal Securities (Truth in Securities) Act, May 1933
To limit share speculation, this Act stated that all new share purchases had to be registered with the Federal Trade Commission. However, it took until June 1934 for the creation of the Securities and Exchange Commission (SEC) to regulate the share and stock market. Between 1934 and 1941, the SEC's budget rose from $1.5 million to $5.3 million and it had control over 20 stock exchanges across America.

The London Economic Conference, July 1933
On 19 April 1933, the USA left the Gold Standard. This standard had been the basis of international trade for over a century. It also meant that the values of separate currencies were kept stable. The USA was not alone in leaving the Gold Standard. Britain had left at the height of the economic crisis in 1932.

President Hoover had always claimed that the causes of economic depression were worldwide and not unique to the USA. He had placed great faith in the major industrial countries working together to solve the world economic depression. As a result, a world economic conference was held in London on 6 July 1933. FDR, in contrast, believed that the solutions to the USA's economic problems were domestic. He supported the idea of lowering the value of the US dollar against other currencies. Other countries wanted currencies stabilised. As a result, FDR brought about the collapse of the London Conference by announcing the devaluation of the US dollar. According to Paul Conkin, in *The New Deal* (1967):

> 'Roosevelt completely bungled the affair by reversing himself, betraying his own delegates, misleading other countries, and revealing his ignorance of the principal issues involved.'

The Gold Reserve Act, January 1934
This Act accepted the new devaluated value of the US dollar. The dollar was set at $35 per ounce (28.35g) of gold. This would make imports dearer and exports cheaper. FDR hoped that it would raise prices, aiding economic recovery

The Silver Purchase Act, June 1934
FDR also hoped to raise prices by increasing the amount of silver in the coinage. He increased federal silver stock until it reached an equivalent of 30% of the gold reserves.

However, the attempt to use monetary policy and changes in the money supply to bring about economic recovery had little impact. If economic recovery was to take place, it had to be brought about by increases in output and not changes in the currency.

Overall, FDR's attempts to reform the banking and financial systems of America were essentially conservative. He wanted to preserve the economic system, not to transform it.

> ### The 100 Days of the First New Deal (March–June 1933): major developments
>
> **9 March**   Emergency Banking Act
>
> **20 March**   Economy Act
>
> **22 March**   Beer and Wine Revenue Act
>
> **31 March**   Unemployment Relief Act creates Civilian Conservation Corps (CCC)
>
> **19 April**   USA leaves the gold standard
>
> **12 May**   Federal Emergency Relief Administration (FERA) is created
>
> Agricultural Adjustment Administration (AAA) also created
>
> **18 May**   Creation of Tennessee Valley Authority (TVA)
>
> **27 May**   Federal Securities Act
>
> **13 June**   Home Owners' Refinancing Act
>
> **16 June**   Glass–Steagall Banking Act
>
> Farm Credit Act
>
> National Industrial Recovery Act created:
>
> ● Public Works Administration (PWA)
>
> ● National Recovery Administration (NRA)

Getting America back to work

In his inauguration address of 4 March 1933, FDR had stated that the 'greatest primary task is to put people to work'. In the 100 Days and the First New Deal, the Roosevelt Administration tried a number of different initiatives to reduce unemployment. These initiatives became known as the 'alphabet agencies'. You will see why in the following section.

The Civilian Conservation Corps (CCC), March 1933

This 'alphabet agency' aimed to give work to young men aged 18 to 25 years. Under the direction of the army, three million young men were given the opportunity to work in developing the national and state park systems, building roads, felling trees and engaging in conservation. They earned $30 a month, of which $25 was sent back to their families. Initially for two years, the CCC lasted until 1942. It helped in developing literacy and in ending, at least temporarily, the problem of unemployment. However, once young men left the CCC there was no guarantee that they would get a job.

The Federal Emergency Relief Administration (FERA), May 1933

This 'alphabet agency' was placed under the control of Harry Hopkins, a social worker by profession. It aimed to give relief to the unemployed. However, aid was given through states. A 'FERA' office was created in each state. With a budget of $500 million, FERA organised relief programmes. It supported state construction of over 5,000 public buildings, 7,000 bridges and various schemes to aid the poor and disadvantaged, such as literacy schemes.

Harry L. Hopkins (1890–1946)
Close confidant of FDR who began his career as a social worker. Head of Federal Emergency Relief Administration (1933–35). Then became head of Works Progress Administration (1935–38). Helped the unemployed with ambitious programmes of public work. Head of Lend–Lease from 1941.

According to historian Tony Badger, in *The New Deal, The Depression Years 1933–1940* (1989):

> 'By the end of 1933 [Hopkins] was a key figure in the development of New Deal strategy. His relief programmes were the key to the success of Roosevelt's short-term efforts to alleviate mass distress.'

Hopkins spent much of his time trying to force reluctant state governments to implement relief programmes. Governor Tallmadge of Georgia and Governor Martin of Oregon prided themselves on not offering direct aid to the poor. To force states to comply, Hopkins threatened to cut off federal funding. In six states, Hopkins had to take over relief programmes directly because of local resistance.

The Civil Works Administration (CWA), November 1933

Even with the FERA, relief for the poor and unemployed failed to deal with the huge problems of the economy as winter approached in 1933. As a result, Hopkins was able to gain support for direct federal involvement in relieving economic hardship. The CWA was given a budget of $400 million. Within weeks of its launch, the CWA was providing work for nearly one million. By Christmas, three million were employed on its projects, rising to 4.2 million by 18 January 1934. Although most jobs were for manual labour, almost 10% of jobs created were in the white-collar, clerical sector.

For all its success, FDR was concerned at the vast expense of the agency. It was costing around $200 million a month, compared with $60 million for FERA. Under the advice of the conservative Budget Director, Lewis Douglas, the CWA came to an end on 31 March 1934.

The Public Works Administration (PWA), June 1933

This agency was created by the National Industrial Recovery Act and was placed under the control of Secretary of the Interior, Harold Ickes. It was given a budget of $3.3 billion to help stimulate economic growth. However, Ickes took a completely different view from Hopkins in helping America to get back to work. Hopkins wanted to give hope back to the unemployed by giving them any type of job. He was accused of creating 'boondoggle' jobs. These had no real purpose other than providing some form of employment. Ickes was determined to use his agency's monies wisely. While Hopkins spent $5 million of FERA's budget within two hours of taking office, Ickes had spent only $110 million of the PWA's budget in the first six months.

Demanding that all money be spent on worthwhile projects, the PWA was eventually responsible for building some 13,000 schools and 50,000 miles of roads. However, it failed to offer sufficient support to reduce unemployment to any significant extent. In this respect, it stood in marked contrast to the work of the CWA under Hopkins.

Reforming business

The National Recovery Administration (NRA), June 1933

The most well-known alphabet agency of the First New Deal was the NRA. Its 'Blue Eagle' sign was seen across America. It was led by General Hugh Johnson, whose energetic leadership added to the NRA's high profile.

The NRA made many changes. As stated by one of FDR's advisers, Raymond Moley, the NRA represented a major step away from the economic philosophy of *laissez faire* which had been followed by the Republicans before 1933. It aimed to provide codes of practice for industry. These aimed to ensure fair competition, and to lay down wage rates and hours of work. Child labour under the age of 16 was made illegal. It also aimed to help workers. Under Section 7(a) of the National Industrial Recovery Act, it gave

---

Harold L. Ickes (1874–1952)
Progressive Republican who backed Theodore Roosevelt in 1912 presidential election. Made Secretary of Interior in 1933. Given control of Public Works Administration (PWA) budget of $3.3 billion in 1935. Criticised for using PWA too slowly and too cautiously. Served in FDR Cabinet (1933–45).

employees the right to bargain 'collectively' for wages. This had been the call from American trade unions for generations. The NRA also had $3.3 billion to spend on public works projects over two years.

During its lifespan – 1933–1935 – the NRA drew up 557 different codes of practice for different industries. Once these codes were accepted, firms could display the Blue Eagle sign of the NRA. Unfortunately, many of these codes proved to be unworkable. This was mainly due to the speed with which they were adopted. The NRA also excluded agricultural workers and domestic servants. These were areas which contained large numbers of African Americans. According to historian Tony Badger, in *The New Deal*:

> 'to radical critics the National Recovery Administration epitomised the capture of a regulatory agency by the special interests who were supposed to be regulated. The effect of business control of the NRA was to dash the hopes of all the groups whose ideas had influenced the Recovery Act.'

Businessmen played a key role in drafting the Act and in its implementation. The NRA did not deal, either, with trusts that controlled whole industries. This led to price fixing, which disadvantaged small firms. By the time the NRA was declared unconstitutional by the US Supreme Court in 1935, it was becoming unworkable.

Nevertheless, the NRA had helped with economic recovery. Hugh Johnson proved to be an effective head of the agency – a skill he transferred to leading the Works Progress Administration (WPA) from 1935. Also, while Harold Ickes at the PWA was reluctant to spend money, the NRA helped with relief in 1933–34.

Helping farmers

The Agricultural Adjustment Administration (AAA), May 1933
Under the leadership of Secretary for Agriculture, Henry A. Wallace, the AAA laid the foundations for modern farming policy. Throughout the 1920s, farming had been in crisis. Overproduction had resulted in low farm prices. The Act that created the AAA gave Wallace the power to deal with farm problems. As a result, the AAA helped to reduce supply and to

Does this poster suggest the New Deal was not successful in dealing with the effects of the Depression? Explain your answer.

Poor blacks line up for government relief alongside a billboard in 1937 – part of a national advertising campaign to encourage business in America.

stabilise farm prices. The AAA was based on a 'domestic allotment' plan. Farmers agreed either to reduce the area they cultivated or to reduce production. The plan affected major commodities such as wheat, cotton, pigs, corn and milk. Thousands of piglets were slaughtered, milk was poured away and crops were ploughed up. Reduction in crop yields was also aided by the drought of 1933.

By 1935, over 75 million acres (30 million hectares) had been removed from cultivation. Farm incomes rose from $4.5 billion in 1933 to $6.9 billion by 1935. The historian Arthur Schlesinger, in *Coming of the New Deal*, stated that this policy 'assigned the federal government the decisive role in protecting farm income'. These federal payments greatly aided farmers. However, with a reduction in production less farm labourers, such as sharecroppers and migrant workers, were needed. It took the Resettlement Administration of 1935 to deal with this problem.

For all its benefits, the US Supreme Court declared the AAA unconstitutional, in January 1936, in the case of 'United States versus Butler'. It took another Agricultural Adjustment Act of 1938 to restore many of the features of the first act. However, the benefits which farmers received during the New Deal were not solely the result of the AAA.

According to historian M.J. Heale, in *Franklin D. Roosevelt* (1999):

1. What do these two images show about the plight of agricultural workers in the 1930s?

2. How successful was the New Deal in tackling problems in American agriculture?

'Farm prices rose although it is unclear how far production controls themselves were responsible. More helpful to farmers was the credit made available by New Deal programmes. Late in 1933 the Commodity Credit Corporation was established to provide loans on stored crops like cotton and corn.'

Also important was the creation of the Farm Credit Administration, mentioned above.

Two images of the USA in 1936 (the year of the dust bowl): (left) a government poster for the Resettlement Administration by Ben Shahn; (right) a photograph by Dorothea Lange for the Farm Security Administration entitled 'Migrant Mother, Nipomo, California', which appeared in newspapers throughout the country in March.

Regional development

The Tennessee Valley Authority (TVA), May 1933

The Tennessee Valley Authority provided a model for regional planning in a traditionally poor part of the Upper South, which contained two million people and covered around 40,000 square miles in seven states. It was also a major area of support for the Democratic Party. Its aims were flood control, agricultural regeneration and cheap electric power. Under the chairmanship of Arthur Morgan, the TVA faced opposition from private business. However, by 1945 it had established a network of dams, which regulated the flow of the Tennessee river. This prevented flooding and soil erosion. It also had a major impact on the provision of electricity. In 1933, only 2% of the Tennessee Valley farms had electricity; by 1945, the number had risen to 75%.

According to historian James T. Patterson, in *America in the Twentieth Century* (1989):

'Critics complained that the TVA was state socialism. But Roosevelt thought not. The TVA he said was "neither fish nor fowl but it will taste awfully good to the people of the Tennessee Valley".'

Historian Paul Conkin, in *The New Deal*, believes that: 'the TVA proved the efficiency, flexibility and social concern possible in government-owned, non-profit corporations. Of all the New Deal programs, the TVA had the most impact on foreign countries.'

The First New Deal faced many critics. On the left, many thought it had not gone far enough. Instead of changing the economic system it had merely prevented it from collapsing. However, by February 1934, the FERA, PWA and CWA had offered work to 20% of the workforce. Yet millions were denied relief by reluctant state governments.

To others, the New Deal had gone too far. It had introduced either a form of **fascism** or a form of socialism to the United States of America.

Fascism: The beliefs of nationalists, which started in Italy in 1919 in opposition to Communism. As part of the *partito nazionale fascista*, under the leadership of Benito Mussolini (1833–1945), the fascists controlled Italy from 1922 to 1943.

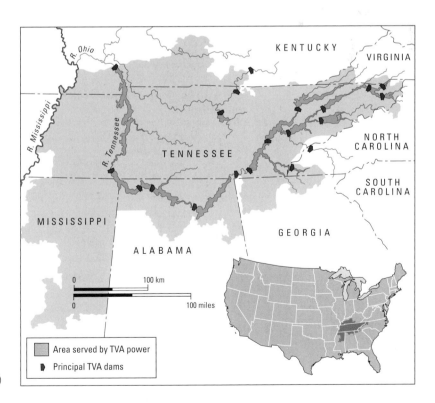

The area administered by the Tennessee Valley Authority (TVA)

1. *In what ways did the First New Deal bring 'relief, recovery and reform' to the USA?*

2. *How successful was the First New Deal in:*

(a) aiding the unemployed

(b) reforming the banking and financial system

(c) helping farmers?

Give reasons for your answers.

The historian Peter Clements, in *Prosperity, Depression and the New Deal* (1997), questioned the coherence of the First New Deal. Some New Deal agencies overlapped in their areas of operation; some had contradictory aims. However, as FDR stated before he took office, he would engage in bold experimentation. If one plan failed, he would try another. The First New Deal is evidence of this approach. Its plan was to get America back to work by whatever means.

Whatever the verdict of some critics at the time and historians since, the First New Deal was popular with the US electorate. In the mid-term elections of 1934, the Democrats increased their majority in both the Senate and the House of Representatives. As FDR stated: 'Everyone is against except the voters!'

6.3 How significant were the reforms of the Second New Deal of 1935–1937?

The American political commentator Walter Lippmann called the Second New Deal 'the most comprehensive program of reform ever achieved in this country in any administration'.

The Second New Deal went much further than the First. This was due, in part, to a reaction by FDR to his critics on the left of American politics. Individuals such as Louisiana Senator Huey P. Long, Catholic priest Charles Coughlin and Francis Townsend had called for more radical reform. Following the mid-term elections of 1934, the 75th Congress contained more radical elements who wanted to bring permanent change to US society.

The result of all these pressures was the Second 100 Days of 1935. The combined effect of these reforms was to lay the foundations of an American welfare state in which the federal government played a central part.

The Works Progress Administration (WPA): help for the unemployed

Created by the Emergency Relief Appropriation Act on 8 April 1935, the WPA became the most significant relief agency in the New Deal. Under the direction of Harry Hopkins, it received $4.8 billion from Congress.

As historian Michael Parrish notes, in *The Anxious Decades* (1992):

'from its creation until its official demise in 1943, the WPA spent over $11 billion on work relief and ultimately employed eight million Americans, about one-fifth of the nation's entire workforce. In seven years they built 2,500 hospitals, 5,900 schools, 350 airports, 570,000 miles of rural roads and 8,000 parks.'

The WPA was particularly significant in helping white-collar professionals, women, artists, young people and African Americans. For instance, in 1936 the WPA ran camps along CCC lines for 5,000 women. Although they were paid, they also received education.

● Federal Project One aided musicians and actors.

● The Federal Writers' Project aided writers, especially African Americans.

The Second New Deal (April–August 1935): major legislation

April 1935 Emergency Relief Appropriation Act created the Works Progress Administration (WPA)

May 1935 Resettlement Administration

Rural Electrification Administration

June 1935 National Youth Administration

July 1935 Wagner National Labor Relations Act

August 1935 Public Utility Holding Company Act

Social Security Act

Banking Act

Revenue Act

Guffey–Snyder Coal Act

● The Theatre Project employed 11,000 performers and workers in 22 production centres. Film stars such as Orson Welles and John Huston benefited from WPA money to fund their productions.

● The Music Project funded 38 symphony orchestras.

● The Public Work Art Project employed artists to decorate federal buildings.

In four years, the WPA spent $46 million aiding unemployed artists.

Of particular significance was the creation of the National Youth Administration (NYA), which encouraged education and provided part-time jobs for students. The NYA Division for Negro Affairs was headed by African American Mary McLeod Bethune, who ensured that African Americans benefit from NYA and WPA initiatives.

As a result, the WPA stands out as the most significant relief agency in the whole New Deal period.

The Wagner National Labor Relations Act, July 1935: a 'new deal' for labour

According to historian Tony Badger, 'The 1930s saw the largest ever growth in union membership in a single decade. Trade union membership trebled. The gains were decisive and permanent.'

Trade unionists were some of the most enthusiastic supporters of FDR's first two administrations. By 1932, some progress had been made in defending trade union rights. In that year the Norris–La Guardia Act outlawed court injunctions which upheld 'yellow dog' (no strike) contracts. However, it was not until the New Deal that substantial headway was made. Section 7(a) of the National Industrial Recovery Act gave unions the right to bargain with employers collectively. NRA codes helped to raise wages and to improve working conditions in many industries.

The centrepiece of trade union legislation was the Wagner Act of 1935. It helped to make up for the loss of the NRA (which was declared unconstitutional by the US Supreme Court in May 1935). However, the main drive for legislation did not come from FDR himself. He had always been

Collective bargaining: Talks that a trade union has with an employer, which are intended to settle what the workers' pay levels and/or conditions should be.

reluctant to get involved in labour relations. Instead, it came from those Democrats in Congress who supported organised labour.

The Wagner Act confirmed the right to **collective bargaining**. It also allowed workers to join unions of their own choice through secret ballot. To ensure that both employers and unions acted correctly, a three-man National Labor Relations Board was created.

The Act did not bring labour disputes to an end. The January–February 1937 sit-down strike by United Auto Worker Union members at General Motors plant in Flint, Michigan was a success which further helped union growth; as was the creation of the Congress of Industrial Organisations (CIO), mainly through the efforts of Al Lewis of the coalminers in November 1935.

Other legislation was also important. The Guffey–Snyder Act of 1935 and the Guffey–Vinson Act of 1937 enabled a national coal commission to set minimum prices for coal and, more importantly, to ensure fair labour standards in the coal industry.

Finally, the Wagner Act benefited from the change in view of the US Supreme Court which took place in 1937–38. Unlike the NRA, it survived a challenge in the Court which upheld the act in the case of 'National Labor Relations Board versus McLaughlin Steel, 1937'. According to the historian M.J. Heale, 'the Act did represent a major step in the mutually supportive accord that was forged between the New Deal and organised labour'.

The Act may have aided organised labour, but trade unions still faced attack. Members of the House Committee on Un-American Activities (HUAC), set up in 1938, attacked the National Labor Relations Board as pro-communist. In 1943, the Smith–Connally War Labor Disputes Act gave the President power to seize strike-bound factories and made it a crime to encourage strikes.

The Social Security Act, August 1935: an American 'welfare state'?

While the Works Progress Administration dealt with the immediate problem of giving relief to the unemployed, the Social Security Act attempted to provide long-term permanent assistance.

The Act introduced federal-funded old age pensions and unemployment benefit (the dole). The Progressives had advocated pensions since 1912. In 1932, the state of Wisconsin introduced its own scheme of unemployment assistance. More recently, FDR had faced criticism on these issues from the left. Upton Sinclair, in his 'End Poverty in California' campaign, and Francis Townsend's 'Old Age Revolving Pension Plan' pressured the Administration for change. When this Act was introduced, it fell far short of their expectations.

The Social Security Act was financed by contributions from employers and workers. However, federal/state relations complicated it. The federal government provided the pension scheme, while the states administered the unemployment insurance programme. This development was due, in part, to FDR's fear that the US Supreme Court might declare the act unconstitutional if he did not include a role for the states.

Pensions were to be paid out at a rate between $10 and $85 per month, according to the degree of contribution. Unemployment benefit was to be paid at a maximum of $18 per week for 16 weeks only.

The Act provided the basis for welfare for decades to come. However, from the outset, it excluded millions of workers who pursued occupations not covered in the act. Also, pensions were not to begin until 1940.

The Revenue Act, August 1935: 'soaking the rich' or a 'raw deal'?

Franklin Roosevelt had always been a conservative in matters of tax and finance. He had found it difficult to accept a deficit budget to help get the economy working again during the First New Deal. Although he may have engaged in **Keynesian demand management of the economy**, he did not do it knowingly. Already, in 1934, a Revenue Act had been passed, mainly because of the pressure of radicals in Congress on those Americans who earned over $9,000 per year.

To help pay for the New Deal reforms, taxation had to be raised. This was achieved with the Revenue Act of 1935. It raised the top levels of income tax from 63% to 79%. It also increased **estate taxes**. An undistributed profits tax was introduced in order to force large companies (corporations) back into the Stock Market to raise money for investment.

These changes, as one might expect, were not popular with 'big business' and the wealthy. The newspaper magnate, William Randolph Hearst, termed it the 'soak the rich' act. Big business was particularly upset by the undistributed profits tax. Yet only 10% of US families earned over $3,200 per year! Less than 5% of Americans paid federal income taxes throughout the 1930s.

However, paying for the New Deal reform was only partly the reason for the Act. FDR also wanted to silence critics on the left of US politics. Louisiana's Huey P. Long ('The Kingfish') had launched the 'Share Our Wealth' campaign, which demanded a major redistribution of income. Long was planning to run for the Democratic Presidential ticket in 1936. Also, FDR had to pay for the veterans' bonus in 1936 rather than waiting until 1945. This had been the demand of the 'Bonus Army' in 1932. Finally, the US Supreme Court had declared the agricultural processing tax unconstitutional.

The Resettlement Administration and The Rural Electrification Act, 1935: aiding poor farmers

The Agricultural Adjustment Administration during the First New Deal helped to regulate agricultural prices by reducing output. Part of the impact of this policy was to reduce demand for farm labourers. In addition, the mid-1930s saw the developments of the **'Dust Bowl'** in areas such as Oklahoma, the panhandle of Texas and southern Kansas. The combined result of these developments was increased poverty in rural areas.

The aim of the Resettlement Administration was to relocate over 450,000 poor farming families away from the worst affected areas. This would involve the federal government buying more suitable farming land, as well as educating people to move and to develop better farming skills.

In the end, under 5,000 families moved to 'green communities' in states such as Wisconsin and Ohio. This was due, in part, to the cost of the operation and the reluctance of families to move.

In 1930, only 10% of farmers had electricity. Most power companies thought it too expensive to provide power lines to rural areas. Already, under the Tennessee Valley Authority, cheap electricity was provided for rural areas in the Upper South.

In 1935, the Rural Electrification Act created the Rural Electrification Administration (REA). The REA granted low-interest loans to rural **cooperatives** so that they could provide electricity. Partly as a result of the Act, 417 cooperatives were providing electricity for over 250,000 homes by 1939. By 1945, 40% of American farms had electricity.

Keynesian demand management of the economy: Ideas associated with the British economist John Maynard Keynes. He criticised the traditional views that government intervention in economic matters should be kept to a minimum. This was known as *laissez-faire* economics (see page 167). Instead, Keynes believed the government could, and should, intervene in economic matters to get an economy out of depression. He suggested that, through government spending, demand would be increased. This would have the 'knock on' effect of creating more employment, and then more demand. The use of government spending to get economies out of depression occurred in Germany and Britain, as well as the USA.

Estate taxes: Property taxes due when someone dies.

'Dust Bowl': Flat grasslands that were ploughed in order to grow cereals were hit by prolonged drought followed by high winds. In many areas, the topsoil blew away. In the Tennessee valley, it was washed away – producing poor growing conditions.

Cooperatives: Factories, shops or farms that are owned by the people who run them.

The Banking Act, 1935: a modern banking system?

Although the 1933 Banking Act had helped to save the US financial system from collapse, it still left the federal and state banking systems intact. By 1935, the head of the Federal Reserve Board (the American equivalent of a federal central bank) wanted to increase federal control over the system.

The 1935 Banking Act created the Federal Reserve Board, in which governors were chosen by the President, with Senatorial advice and consent. The new Federal Reserve Board had direct control over the 12 regional branches.

As historian M.J. Heale states, in *Franklin Roosevelt: The New Deal* (1999):

'The measure served to enhance the authority of the federal government and to centralise the power of the Federal Reserve System over monetary policy. Very belatedly in the western world, the United States had a central banking system.'

Public Utility Holding Company Act, 1935: a replacement for the NRA?

A holding company owns several other companies which are actually involved in trading and manufacturing. As a result, a small number of holding companies can control large parts of the industry. This was particularly true of the power generation industry in the USA in the 1930s. The practice led to the high cost of electricity for industry. According to historian Tony Badger, in *The New Deal*:

'The top holding company secured lucrative management fees and dividends from its subsidiaries, hindered improved service and effectively escaped state and federal regulation.'

The Public Utility Holding Company Act aimed to end these practices. Under the Act, all holding companies had to register with the Securities and Exchange Commission (SEC). The SEC was also given power to control the issue of shares of holding companies on the stock market. All holding companies more than two stages away from the production of goods or services were to be prohibited.

Although FDR wanted to end the practice of holding companies altogether, the Act was a compromise following extensive pressure on Congress from holding companies.

The Second New Deal: a verdict

According to P. Boyer *et al*, in *The Enduring Vision* (1993):

'By September 1935, the Second New Deal was complete. A set of laws had been enacted promoting the interests of the jobless, the elderly, the rural poor and the blue-collar workers; regulating major business enterprises more strictly; and somewhat increasing the taxes paid by the wealthy.'

The Second New Deal helped to divert some of the criticism FDR had faced from radicals in Congress and from the left of US politics around the country, such as Francis Townsend, Huey Long and the socialists. It could also be regarded as providing the basis for modern American trade unionism. Historian Michael Parrish describes the Wagner Act as labour's **Magna Carta**. The Social Security Act laid the foundations for a federal welfare state system which lasted until the 1980s.

Magna Carta: The document by King John granting English freemen basic rights in 1215.

However, FDR's aim was never to destroy the US economic system, but to strengthen it. This was to be done by distributing the benefits of the economic system more fairly. Many of the reforms passed were compromises between the views of radicals and pressure from business interest groups.

In drafting the Democratic Party manifesto for the 1936 elections, one of FDR's advisers, Samuel Rosenman, declared that the basis of the New Deal was 'that the government in a modern civilisation has certain inescapable obligations to its citizens among which are:

(1) protection of the family and the home.

(2) establishment of democracy of opportunity for all the people

(3) aid to those overtaken by disaster.'

The Second New Deal clearly went a long way towards achieving these ideals.

To prove the popularity of the Second New Deal one does not have to go beyond the 1936 elections. As historian Hugh Brogan points out, FDR's re-election was as certain as George Washington's. On election day, FDR received 27,750,000 votes. The Republican candidate, Alfred Landon of Kansas – known as the 'Kansas Coolidge' for his quiet, unassuming manner – polled a mere 16,600,000 votes. In the electoral college, FDR won 46 states (523 votes to 8). Only the small north-eastern states of Vermont and Maine voted for Landon.

In Congress, the Democrats won a landslide. In the House of Representatives they outnumbered the Republicans 331 to 89, and in the Senate 76 to 16. The 1936 elections proved to be the 'high tide' of the New Deal.

1. In what ways did the Second New Deal help workers and the unemployed?

2. What do you regard as the most important reform of the Second New Deal? Give reasons for your answer.

3. Compare the reforms of the Second New Deal in this section with the reforms of the First New Deal in the previous section. What do you regard as the most significant period of reform: the First New Deal or the Second New Deal? Explain your answer.

6.4 How serious was opposition to the New Deal?

The New Deal attracted critics from both left and right of the American political scene. To many socialists and communists the New Deal did not go far enough. It was seen as helping to preserve, rather than destroy, the capitalist economic system. This was FDR's plan all along. On the right, FDR was seen as a dangerous radical. His Administration had abandoned *laissez-faire* economics and had used the powers of the federal government in a way not seen in peacetime. Even FDR recognised, in a newsreel broadcast in 1935, that he had been accused of being either a fascist or a communist. Many of the critics of the New Deal from the left of American politics helped to push FDR in a more radical direction than he wished to go. Other critics from the right forced FDR and his Administration to compromise on many reforms.

How important was opposition from the US Supreme Court?

The US Supreme Court is held in high esteem by the vast majority of Americans. It is regarded as the 'watchdog' of the US Constitution. Under the Constitution, the Supreme Court is the highest court of appeal for all state law and federal law cases. It also has the power to declare unconstitutional: acts of state governments, the federal government or Congress. The President, with the **advice and consent** of the Senate, nominates Supreme Court judges. Once nominated, they are in office until they decide to resign or are impeached. So far in US history, no Supreme Court justice has been impeached. When FDR took office, judges appointed by Republican presidents dominated the US Supreme Court. Under the Chief

Advice and consent: Under the US Constitution, several Presidential appointments must receive two-thirds support in the US Senate if they are to be legal. These appointments include the Cabinet and all US Supreme Court justices.

**Charles Evans Hughes
(1862–1946)**
Republican Presidential
candidate against Woodrow
Wilson in 1916. Made Chief
Justice of the Supreme Court in
1930. Hughes was in favour of
judicial restraint, which resulted
in declaration of major New
Deal legislation as
unconstitutional in 1935.
Resisted FDR's 'court packing'
plan of 1937. Retired in 1941.

Justiceship of Charles Evans Hughes, the Supreme Court proved to be the most formidable opponent of the New Deal.

In 1935, the Court virtually wrecked the main reforms of the New Deal. The Court declared the National Industrial Recovery Act to be unconstitutional in 'A.L.A. Schechter Poultry Corporation v United States' in May 1935. Known as the 'sick chicken case', a New York firm of Jewish poulterers were accused of selling diseased chickens, thereby breaking a NRA code. The Court declared that the federal government had exceeded its powers by interfering in intra-state commerce, which was a state matter. Part of the problem for FDR was the fact that the National Recovery Administration was introduced very quickly and had not been properly drafted. As historian Hugh Brogan points out, 'the NRA was a premature experiment in a fully planned economy conducted with inadequate tools'.

In fact, the Schechter Corporation received financial support for bringing the case to court by the owners of US Steel in order to challenge the NRA's right to regulate commerce.

In January 1936, the Court, in 'United States v Butler', also declared the Agricultural Adjustment Administration (AAA) unconstitutional for similar reasons to the Schechter case. In a private memorandum, FDR wrote: 'The decision virtually prohibits the President and Congress from the right, under modern conditions, to intervene reasonably in the regulation of nationwide commerce and nationwide agriculture.' In all, the Court declared 11 New Deal laws unconstitutional, including the Farm Mortgage Act. Up to 1933, the Court have vetoed 60 federal acts. This places in perspective the amount of opposition from the Court to the New Deal.

Fortunately for FDR and his Administration, many of the features which had been in the NRA and Agricultural Adjustment Act were later incorporated into the Second New Deal and the Agricultural Adjustment Act of 1938. Nevertheless, FDR was determined to thwart any further attempts by the Court to damage the New Deal.

Following his landslide victory in 1936, FDR began his second term as President with a direct attack on the Court. In spite of his enormous popularity, this attack proved to be FDR's major mistake in domestic affairs in his long tenure as president. It lost him valuable support in Congress and the nation.

In February 1937, FDR submitted a bill (The Judicial Procedures Reform Bill) to Congress which, if passed, would have forced all justices over the age of 70 to retire. Although this applied to the whole federal judiciary, it was clear where FDR was aiming his attack. In 1937, six of the nine US Supreme Court justices were over 70 years old. It would also give the President power to appoint up to six new justices, thus increasing the number of justices to 15. If passed, the Act would have given FDR enormous power as President. He would have had the right to 'pack' the court with his own nominees. It also brought to a head the criticism that FDR was amassing too much political power. Since 1933, federal government powers and, in particular, the powers of the President had grown considerably. FDR's plan was rejected in the Senate by 70 votes to 20.

What also undermined FDR's planned reform was a change in attitude in the Court. On 29 March 1937, the Supreme Court upheld a minimum wage act passed by the state of Washington. Six months earlier, it had invalidated an almost identical act from New York State. This 'switch in time that saved nine' took away many of FDR's criticisms of the Court. To the shock of most of the country, on 12 April, the Court upheld the Wagner Act of 1935.

Finally, the most conservative justice, Willis van Devanter, announced his retirement in 1937. This allowed FDR to nominate his own justice.

As a result of all these changes, the Second New Deal did not face the same fate as the First New Deal at the hands of the Court. However, FDR's reputation had suffered a major knock. Never again would he be able to command such support in the Congress for his domestic reforms. The 'Third' New Deal – of 1937–39 – was a pale shadow of the other two. A new Agricultural Adjustment Act and a Fair Labor Standards Act were the only two notable reforms. The period was also one of increased unemployment – known as 'The Roosevelt Recession'.

Two cartoons on the quarrel between Roosevelt and the US Supreme Court: (left) an American cartoon by Clifford Berryman which appeared in 'Washington Star', 23 April 1937; (right) a British cartoon from 'Punch', June 1935.

What impact did opponents from the left have on the New Deal?

Huey P. Long (1893–1935)
Democrat. Governor for Louisiana 1928–31; US Senator for that state from 1931 to his death. Under the slogans 'Every man a king' and 'Share our Wealth', he became a major critic of the First New Deal. Private polls conducted by FDR's adviser James Farley suggested Long could have won around 10 million votes if he had run as a third-party candidate in the 1936 presidential election. However, he was assassinated in September 1935 in Baton Rouge, state capital of Louisiana, by a deranged doctor.

Socialists and Communists
The most extreme opponents of the New Deal from the left of US politics were socialists and communists. Both wanted to see the destruction of the capitalist economic system, which they regarded as beyond reform. However, even in 1932, these groups had little impact on national politics. In the presidential election of that year, Norman Thomas, the socialist, received 883,990 votes, compared with FDR's 22.8 million. William Foster of the Workers' Party polled just 102,000 votes. In 1935, Thomas's vote dropped to 187,000, while Earl Browder, the Communist presidential candidate, received a derisory 79,000 votes.

Huey P. Long ('The Kingfish')
Of greater significance was opposition from the Louisiana Democrat Huey P. Long. He launched the 'Share Our Wealth' campaign in February 1934. He was a serious and voluble critic of FDR from within his own party. Long wanted to guarantee to every American family a 'homestead allowance' of $5,000 and a minimum annual income of $2,500. To finance such a grand scheme, Long planned to increase income and inheritance taxes to a point where no individual could earn over $1.8 million a year.

Although personally opposed to 'big federal government', Long's own proposals would have led to an increase in government involvement in people's lives.

Long's plans were popular. By early 1935, there were 27,000 chapters of the 'Share Our Wealth' campaign across America with over eight million members. By the summer of 1935, Long was taken seriously as a possible presidential candidate for 1936. However, Long was gunned down in September 1935 by a disgruntled supporter. Nevertheless, support for schemes such as Long's helped to push the FDR Administration further to the left during the Second New Deal.

Charles E. Coughlin, the radio priest

By 1930, Father Coughlin had over 35 million regular listeners to his radio programme 'The Golden Hour of the Little Flower'. Coughlin regularly blamed American and British bankers for the depression. Initially, he supported the New Deal, stating that 'The New Deal is Christ's Deal'. Yet, in 1934, he formed the National Union of Social Justice, which was an alternative to the New Deal. Father Coughlin claimed that FDR had become influenced by the banking community. He advocated monetary reform, including the introduction of silver coinage and the encouragement of inflation. Those in debt welcomed his support for inflation. However, by 1935, his attacks on the New Deal were becoming more **anti-semitic**, with criticism levelled at Jews in the Administration – such as Henry Morgenthau and Felix Frankfurter.

Anti-semitic: Against Jews or the Jewish religion (Judaism).

Francis Townsend and the Old Age Revolving Pension Plan

A retired doctor from Long Beach, California, put forward a plan for old age pensions in 1933. Under the plan, all those over 60 years would receive a government pension of $200 a month, as long as they spent all the money within 30 days of receiving it. Townsend hoped that it would prevent poverty in old age and would stimulate domestic demand at the same time. By 1935, over 500,000 old people had joined Townsend clubs across the country. In January of that year, a bill was submitted to the House of Representatives based on Townsend's plan and supported by a petition of 20 million signatures.

It seems clear that the pressure from these various groups helped to push the FDR Administration into more radical legislation during the Second New Deal. However, the political threat they posed was marginal. Following Long's assassination in September 1935, the supporters of Long, Coughlin and Townsend got together to support a presidential candidate for the 1936 election, William Lemke of the Union Party. Lemke polled 892,000 votes, compared with FDR's 27.7 million.

Communism: The political belief that the state should own and control the means of producing everything, so that all levels of society can be made equal. Then everyone should do as much as they can and get as much as they need.

A popular joke against the New Deal during the 1930s

Socialism: If you own two cows you give one to your neighbour.

Communism: You give both cows to the government and the government gives you back some milk.

Fascism: You keep both cows but give the milk to the government who sells some of it back to you.

New Dealism: You shoot both cows and milk the government.

How important were opponents from the right to the New Deal?

The New Deal was opposed by a large number of groups on the right of US politics. Most notable was the Republican Party. However, for most of this period the Republican Party was largely ineffective against the New Deal. In the 1936 election, Alfred Landon of Kansas proved to be a poor opponent. In 1940, when FDR decided to run for an unprecedented third term as president he was faced with a more formidable opponent, Wendell Wilkie. This time, the Republicans polled 22.3 million votes against FDR's 27.2 million. However, the Republicans won only 82 electoral college votes against FDR's 449, the Democrat carrying 38 of the 48 states.

Outside national politics, the New Deal found opponents in local state governments who were reluctant to introduce the new reforms. This was most notable in states such as Mississippi, even though the Democratic Party controlled the state.

Much New Deal legislation was opposed by 'big business'. They fought individual New Deal measures by putting pressure on Congress. This was true of the Public Holding Utility Act of 1935. They also took the FDR Administration to court, as in the 'sick chicken case' of 1935.

The most notable opponent on the right was the Liberty League. Formed in the summer of 1934, it drew support from various anti-FDR groups. These included Alfred E. Smith, the Democrat candidate for the presidency in 1928 and former Governor of New York State. The aim of the League was 'to defend and uphold the Constitution and to foster the right to work, earn, save and acquire property and to preserve ownership and the lawful use of property'.

However, to see the Liberty League as representing all American big business is wrong. The New Deal did have support from several big industrialists, such as movie **mogul** Jack Warner of Warner Bros. and Walter Teagle of the Standard Oil (Esso) corporation. Many businessmen were advisers to the Administration. This was particularly true during the First New Deal when FDR relied heavily on the banking community for his banking and financial legislation.

Mogul: An important, rich and powerful businessperson, especially one in the movie (film) or television industry.

1. In what ways did opponents influence New Deal legislation?

2. Why was the US Supreme Court such a formidable opponent of the New Deal between 1935 and 1936?

3. How significant was opposition to the success of the New Deal?

6.5 What impact did the Second World War have on the domestic history of the USA, 1941–1945?

What impact did the War have on the economy?

'Dr Win the War', as FDR termed it, did what 'Dr New Deal' had failed to do. It brought economic prosperity back to the USA. By 1942, the USA was enjoying full employment as the country developed a war economy. However, ever since the outbreak of European War, in September 1939, the USA had benefited from the demand for armaments by Britain and France. Even after France was defeated, the USA remained 'the arsenal of democracy' by providing weapons through the **Lend–Lease programme** of early 1941. Gross national product almost doubled between 1939 and 1942.

The Second World War had a significant impact on taxation and government spending in the United States. The Revenue Act of 1942 brought large numbers of Americans into the federal income tax system for the first time. In 1939, less than four million paid federal income taxes. This had risen to almost 43 million by 1945. In 1940, total federal revenue was $7 billion. By 1944, it had risen to $51 billion. The increased revenue was needed to pay for war expenditure. However, even the rise in taxes could not provide enough money. The rest was made through borrowing. Much money was raised through selling **war bonds**. Famous Hollywood film

Lend–Lease programme: An American policy introduced during the Second World War by which military aid was given to Britain, and other allied countries, with the aim of acquiring payment for such aid after the war.

War bonds: A form of loan to the US government. These were government certificates sold during the Second World War to raise money for the war effort. Individuals were encouraged to buy them. Once the War was over, the government planned to repay the purchaser.

stars such as Bing Crosby and Bob Hope went on fundraising tours selling war bonds.

All this extra spending had a major impact on economic growth. In 1938, the GNP was $85.2 billion. This had risen to $100 billion by 1940. By 1945, it had reached $213.6 billion. Even allowing for inflation, the US economy grew a staggering 73% during the War.

These changes had a huge impact on US industry. Corporate profits rose from $6 billion in 1939 to $10.5 billion in 1945 as companies benefited from government contracts. Usually, large firms received defence contracts and this led to mergers and the growth of larger firms. By 1943, 100 large firms were providing 70% of manufacturing output. In achieving these changes, the US economy provided the backbone of Allied armaments against Germany, Italy and Japan. During the war, the USA produced over 300,000 aircraft, 100,000 tanks and 93,000 ships. Most of the Red Army was transported to Berlin in US trucks.

The War also saw a major increase in the powers of the federal government. From December 1941, the federal government took a major role in the direction of the economy. The Office of Price Administration (OPA) controlled prices. In October 1942, the Office of Economic Stabilisation replaced it. The War Production Board oversaw defence production. The War Manpower Commission allocated labour between industries. In May 1943, these were subordinated to a super ministry, the Office of War Mobilisation, which ran the US economy on a war footing.

The most awesome task of the federal government was to mobilise men for the armed forces. The USA had, traditionally, a small volunteer army numbering just over 250,000 in 1939. By 1945, over 12 million men (12% of the population) were in uniform.

What impact did the War have on US society?

With 12 million men in uniform by 1945, and the economy growing at a rapid rate, the shortfall in workers had to be made up by women. In all, hundreds of thousands of women became involved in the war effort. Many served in the armed forces as telephonists, car drivers and secretaries. Many more worked in war industries doing blue-collar jobs. 'Rosie the Riveter' became a **propaganda** character to represent women in the aircraft manufacturing industry.

The War also presented new opportunities for African Americans – serving in the forces and working in industry. If black people could fight for freedom from oppression for others, then why not for themselves? This period, 1941–43, saw a rise in racial tension across America. Major race riots occurred between whites and African Americans in Detroit in 1943. Riots also occurred in many northern cities. The armed forces were not immune. The USA still segregated white and African American troops. Fighting occurred in several locations overseas between these racial groups. Nevertheless, FDR issued presidential Executive Order 8802 in 1941, which banned discrimination against African Americans in federal employment and the defence industries. It also established the Fair Employment Practices Commission to supervise the labour market. The number of African Americans in federal employment rose from 3% in 1942 to almost 10% by the end of the war.

The most notorious example of racism during the War was made against Japanese Americans, most of whom lived on the west coast. In February 1942, FDR's Administration authorised the relocation of all Japanese Americans to camps away from the coast. It was believed they might cooperate with a possible Japanese invasion. In all, 112,000 Japanese Americans were forced to leave their homes and businesses despite the fact that none were arrested for espionage.

Propaganda: Information, often exaggerated or false, which is spread by political parties, governments or pressure groups in order to influence others.

1. In what ways did the Second World War change the lives of ordinary American men and women?

2. What do you regard as the most significant development in US economy and society between 1941 and 1945? Give reasons for your answer.

1. How successful was the New Deal in bringing about economic recovery from 1933 to 1940?

2. What impact did the Second World War have on US economic prosperity?

Unemployment and manufacturing output in the USA, 1928–1944

Year	% Unemployed	Index of Industrial Output (1926 = 100)
1928	4.4	104
1930	8.7	96
1932	23.6	60
1934	21.7	78
1936	16.9	110
1938	19.0	92
1940	14.6	132
1942	4.7	220
1944	1.2	260

1. Explain why the National Debt rose during the period 1910–1920 and again between 1930–1940?

2. Do the figures suggest that the US economy was in difficulty between 1930–1950?

Explain your answer.

US National Debt, 1900–1950

Year	National Debt	Debt per person
1900	$1,263,417,000	$17
1910	$1,146,940,000	$12
1920	$24,299,231,000	$228
1930	$16,185,310,000	$132
1940	$42,967,352,000	$325
1950	$257,357,352,000	$1,697

6.6 Did the New Deal bring fundamental change to the USA?

A CASE STUDY IN HISTORICAL INTERPRETATION

Since the 1930s, the New Deal has received a wide variety of assessments. In 1992, in *The Anxious Decades*, Michael Parrish declared:

'Franklin Roosevelt and the New Deal failed the American people: in six years of effort, economic prosperity had not returned and the Depression lingered. Nearly 10 million citizens, over 17% of the labor force, remained out of work in 1939. A much larger percentage remained in 1939 as in 1936 "ill housed, ill clothed, ill nourished".'

To many conservative critics of the New Deal, these development were easy to explain. Roosevelt had introduced too much reform and there was too much regulation of the US economy. As a result of government interference, the economy had not recovered. Far too many of the New Deal 'alphabet agencies' had unclear goals. Many of the agencies had overlapping areas of responsibility. Some were in competition with each other.

In a study of economic statistics, the New Deal failed in one of its main aims – 'to get America back to work'. As historian Paul Conkin stated in *The New Deal* (1967): 'From almost every perspective, the New Deal solved a few problems, ameliorated [solved] others, obscured many and created unanticipated new ones.'

From this perspective, FDR's achievements seem shallow. Although critics might accept that he was charismatic, eloquent and flexible in approach, he was nothing more than a con artist who hoodwinked the American people into believing 'Happy days are here again' – as his campaign song stated.

Compared with other western economies, the US economy took longer to get out of depression than any other. Yet to others, FDR did not go far enough. To left-wing critics, he failed to nationalise the banking system, refused to pass laws banning lynching and did little to provide affordable public housing. Even where reforms were made, such as the Social Security Act of 1935, it fell far short of similar measures in Britain, Australia and New Zealand.

To the left in America, FDR's greatest crime was in helping to preserve the capitalist economic system. Instead of being the enemy of 'big business', he helped to save it. Far from bringing fundamental economic change, FDR prevented it from taking place.

Even where advances were made for working people in the USA, FDR and his Administration did not get the credit. In 1992, the American Social History project published *Who Built America?* It stated that:

> 'In the last half of the 1930s, working people made America a more democratic nation. By organising, protesting, sitting-in, and voting as a **progressive bloc**, they forced the federal government to begin acting as a guarantor of workers' rights to organise, bargain collectively, and earn a decent wage.'

Progressive bloc: Those members of Congress who supported the involvement of federal government in social welfare.

Yet FDR and the New Deal did achieve much. Tony Badger, in *The New Deal,* contrasts FDR with Hoover's efforts of 1929–33. In industry, agriculture and banking, FDR made considerable strides. He helped to put the unemployed back to work, he aided farmers, he prevented a complete banking and economic collapse. FDR restored hope to people who had grown fatalistic.

When assessing FDR's performance, the obstacles he faced must be taken into consideration. He had to work within a federal system which had given state governments considerable authority in social and economic matters. He had to win the support of Congress for his reforms. He also had to battle against a US Supreme Court which almost destroyed the First New Deal in 1935–36. From a position of serious crisis, in March 1933, FDR had laid the foundations for economic recovery. As historian Hugh Brogan writes, in *The Longman History of the United States* (1999):

> 'Thanks to Franklin Roosevelt, in short, six years (1933–1938) transformed America from a country which had been laid low by troubles which in its own incompetence had brought on it, and which it was quite unable to cope with, to a country superbly equipped to meet the worst shocks that the modern world can hurl at it. It was enough.'

In addressing Congress, in 1938, FDR defended his own record:

> 'Government has a final responsibility for the well-being of its citizenship. If private cooperative endeavour fails to provide work for willing hands and relief for the unfortunate, those suffering hardship from no fault of their own have a right to call upon the Government for aid; and a government worthy of its name must make a fitting response.'

In FDR's own words, the New Deal did bring a fundamental change in American thinking about distress and in the government's role in dealing with it.

It is clear that the New Deal years left a profound mark on the USA. Nowhere more so than in the role of the federal government. By the outbreak of war, in 1941, the federal government's role had expanded out of all recognition. With it had grown the role of the President. The creation

1. Why do historians have differing views on the success of FDR and the New Deal?

2. In what ways did the New Deal bring fundamental change to the USA?

3. Which was more significant in bringing about social, economic and political change:

(a) the New Deal years 1933–1940

(b) the Second World War years 1941–1945?

Explain your answer with reference to
(i) social,
(ii) economic and
(iii) political change.

of the Executive Office of the Presidency, in 1939, underlined this change. What the New Deal had started, the war years finished. By 1945, the 'Imperial Presidency' had been created with the federal government playing a dominant role in the lives of virtually every American.

The New Deal years also brought about a political realignment, which lasted until the 1970s. The coalition of southern whites, African Americans, blue-collar workers, Catholics and Jews meant that the Democrats dominated the presidency and Congress for over a generation. Democrat dominance was also reflected in the control of state governorships and state legislatures.

However, the New Deal brought little change in the plight of women or African Americans. What the New Deal had failed to do was provided by the huge social changes brought about by the Second World War. Any assessment of the New Deal is complicated by the fact that it was immediately followed by a period of considerable social and economic change.

Source-based questions: FDR and the New Deal

SOURCE A

In this nation I see millions of families trying to live on incomes so meagre that the threat of family disaster hangs over them day by day.

I see millions whose daily lives in the city and on the farm continue under conditions labelled indecent by so-called polite society a half-century ago.

I see millions denied education, recreation and the opportunity to better their lot and the lot of their children.

I see millions lacking the means to buy the products of farm and factory and by their poverty denying work and productivity to many other millions.

It is not in despair that I paint you a picture but in hope – because the nation, seeing it and understanding the injustice in it, proposes to paint it out. The test of our progress is not whether we add more to the abundance of those who have much, it is whether we provide enough for those who have too little.

From a speech by President Roosevelt on his inauguration as President, 20 January 1937

1. Study Source A.

What problems does Roosevelt identify as facing the United States in 1937 and what attitude does he reveal to the solving of these problems?

2. Use your own knowledge.

Why, and in what ways, did the Supreme Court oppose the New Deal in the years 1933–1936?

3. Use your own knowledge.

How successful was the New Deal in promoting the recovery of agriculture and industry in the United States in the years 1933–1941?

7

US foreign policy, 1890–1945

Key Issues

- How far did US foreign policy change between 1890 and 1945?

- How important were the US presidents in the conduct of foreign policy?

- Why did the USA emerge as one of the world's major powers between 1890 and 1945?

Framework of Events

1898	Spanish–American War
	Annexation of Hawaii
1899	Boxer rebellion
1902	Roosevelt Corollary
1906	Building of the Panama Canal starts
1907–1909	Voyage of the 'Great White Fleet'
1914	Start of First World War
1915	Sinking of the 'Lusitania'
1917	American entry into First World War
1919	Paris Peace Conference
1922	Washington Naval Conference
1924	Dawes Plan
1932	Japan invades Manchuria
1935–1937	Neutrality Acts
1939	Start of Second World War
1941	Attack on Pearl Harbor
1945	Dropping of atom bomb and end of Second World War.

Overview

UP until the 1890s, the United States of America (USA) had largely kept out of the affairs of other countries. Its own inward expansion, followed by the Civil War and Reconstruction gave the USA little concern for foreign affairs. But this changed towards the end of the century. There was a growing body of opinion that the United States should take a fuller role in world affairs generally, and in those of Latin America in particular. Though there were as many arguments to counter this view, the two decades between 1890 and 1910 saw America take a more prominent role on the world stage, and even saw it acquire colonies of its own in the Caribbean and Pacific.

Over the turn of the century, Presidents Roosevelt and Taft consciously expanded America's role in the world. Theodore Roosevelt believed that the USA had a duty and a right to take a more prominent role in international affairs. Under his administration, the so-called 'Roosevelt Corollary' stated explicitly that the USA had the right to interfere in the affairs of the states of Latin America. Roosevelt also increased American involvement in the Far East – a policy continued by Taft with his encouragement of American financial investment in China.

When war broke out in Europe in 1914, many felt it was an argument between the 'old powers' and was of no concern to the United States. However, once it affected American liberties – such as the freedom to travel and to trade – the President, Woodrow Wilson, became more concerned. German naval attacks eventually forced America into the War, where its role in providing extra equipment and a supply of fresh soldiers was instrumental in the final Allied victory. But the losses of the War and the disappointment of the peace conference made Americans cynical about playing a world role and they retreated into **isolationism**.

Isolationism: A policy by which a state (e.g. the USA in the early 1930s) pursues its own domestic interests, in isolation from the wider considerations of international politics.

Even though the 1920s and 1930s are seen as the great period of isolation, American financial connections with Europe made it impossible for the United States to remove itself from the affairs of the continent. Likewise, an internal desire for cuts in spending meant the USA took an important role in international arms control. It was only really in Latin America that the American governments of the period pulled back.

The Great Depression of the 1930s turned American attention firmly to domestic affairs. Even while trouble bubbled in Europe, Congress passed a series of Neutrality Acts in an attempt to ensure that the USA was not pulled into another European war. But even then, they gave support to the British cause, due to the destructive nature of the Nazi regime and a belief by Roosevelt that a German victory would be bad for American security. What finally brought America into the Second World War was the attack on Pearl Harbor – itself a culmination of rivalry in the Pacific going back half a decade. With American manpower and economic might, victory was assured in 1945 and the United States emerged from the War as the most powerful nation on earth. From then on, there could be no return to the isolationist policies of the past.

Throughout the period 1890–1945, the United States of America had both a desire to increase its role in world affairs, yet at the same time not to get too involved in them. In fact, this period saw a fairly steady growth in American involvement overseas.

Latin America continued to be seen as an area of legitimate American interest for both strategic and economic reasons. The level of direct interference simply varied depending on the particular policies of the Presidents or events in Latin America itself. The US attitude to Europe was more mixed. As the majority of American citizens were descended from Europeans they were affected by events on the continent, but as refugees who had left Europe's problems behind they were reluctant to get involved. However, the ties of history and its economic power meant the United States found itself drawn into European affairs through two world wars. It was perhaps in the Pacific and the Far East that one can see most clearly a definite growth in American influence.

In 1945, the USA was a world power. The desire for focusing only on its own interests was still there, but the USA's economic and military might meant its role in the world had changed dramatically. In 1890 the USA was potentially very powerful: it had a large population, a strong economy and an important geographical position, but its political influence in the world was not as great. By 1945, the United States had become, quite simply, the world's most powerful nation.

7.1 Why were the 1890s a turning point in US foreign policy?

Throughout much of the 19th century, when the European powers were extending their empires and embarking on the so-called 'scramble for Africa', the Americans stood above it all in an attitude of superiority. As a former colony, they condemned the **imperialism** of the Old World. Yet, in the last two decades of the century, America also embarked on colonial expansion in the Pacific and Caribbean, and interfered extensively in the affairs of Latin America.

Imperialism: The control of one country by another, usually by military and political occupation. It can also be by economic control.

The growth of imperialism

In the 1880s and 1890s, support for an imperialist foreign policy grew inside the USA for political, economic, social and even religious and racial reasons.

Since the 1840s, Americans had recognised the concept of 'Manifest Destiny', the idea that it was the destiny of the United States to dominate the northern half of the continent of America. This had encouraged the expansion westwards beyond the Mississippi and the Rockies. By the 1890s, the West had been settled and the British had made it clear that they had no intention of giving up Canada. Therefore, some argued that 'Manifest Destiny' could, and should, be extended to Latin America and even beyond. It was the duty of America to spread its civilisation. The United States had extended as far as it could across the continent, it was now time to look outwards for expansion.

This argument, unfortunately, had racial overtones. The Social Darwinism that became popular in Europe at the end of the 19th century (see page 129) also had supporters in the USA. American democracy and capitalism were clearly superior to the monarchies and the backward economies that existed in many parts of the world, so it was the duty of the USA to extend its power over these areas for their own good. Americans, in effect, were superior to other races and, therefore, were morally obliged to extend their influence in the world. This kind of thinking was famously illustrated by William McKinley when he referred to natives of the Philippines as America's 'little brown brothers' and talked of America's duty to 'uplift, civilise and Christianise' them, ignoring the fact that the vast majority of Filipinos were Roman Catholics. Yet it must also be said that in extending its 'civilisation' the USA did expand education, public health and democracy in many of the places it went to, and that many Christian missionaries acted out of a genuine desire to care for others.

However, there were also more practical political and economic motives for the support of imperialism, which were not much different from the justifications used by the European powers for their empires. America's industrial economy had grown rapidly in the 1870s and 1880s with gross national product (GNP) growing by 4% annually but, by 1893, it was experiencing a downturn that began a four-year depression. There was a

William McKinley (1843–1901)
25th President of the United States (1897–1901). McKinley was a lawyer who entered politics as a Republican. He was a member of the House of Representatives from 1877 and Governor of Ohio from 1892. He was elected for two terms, but was shot and killed by an anarchist in 1901. It was under his presidency that the USA fought and won the Spanish–American War.

fear that the domestic market had been saturated, so overseas outlets had to be acquired. Asia, and China in particular, was seen as a potentially massive market for American goods. Also, overseas possessions would provide American manufacturers with access to cheap raw materials. Outward expansion would also relieve the labour tensions and unrest that had grown during the depression.

The USA was also concerned that, as European empires grew and extended further across the world, American power would be diminished. In effect, they were being left behind. Between 1875 and 1914, a quarter of the world was claimed as colonies by various powers: if the USA did not get into the imperial 'club' now it never would and the **balance of power** could shift against it.

An influential book was Alfred Thayer Mahan's *The Influence of Sea Power on History* (published in 1890). In it, Mahan argued that the powerful nations of history had always been sea powers. With two coasts, the USA needed to become a major naval power and that required the acquisition of colonies as supply bases around the world. Mahan also argued for a canal connecting the Atlantic and Pacific Oceans, and emphasised the importance of the Caribbean in protecting that canal. The need for the USA to become a naval power was accepted and acted upon. By 1900, the US navy was the third largest in the world – after Britain and Germany. Clearly, the United States was increasingly seeing itself as a world power.

Arguments against imperialism

Although the voices in support of imperialism were getting louder in the 19th century, there was also a vocal and important minority arguing against it. In 1898, this minority formed the Anti-Imperialist League. Among its members were the writer Mark Twain, the steel magnate Andrew Carnegie and the lawyer and politician William Jennings Bryan.

As the historian Anders Stephanson points out, in *Manifest Destiny* (1995), the anti-imperialists had a range of arguments to counter the calls for expansion. When others talked of America's mission to civilise alien races, they pointed out that the USA did not have a record of treating its own minorities, such as African and Native Americans, particularly well. They argued that there were no massive new markets in Asia, that expansion would lead to further entanglements, possibly war, and that, unlike Britain, the USA had neither the manpower nor expertise to run an empire. They were, on the whole, correct. From a moral standpoint, the anti-imperialists argued that trying to dress up expansion as some kind of modification of 'Manifest Destiny' was deceitful and that it was nothing more than European-style imperialism. Far from enhancing America's position in the world it could weaken it because by acting like the other Great Powers the USA would lose its unique role as a powerful, democratic nation that respected the freedom of others. Above all, the anti-imperialists condemned those who forgot America's past: how could a colony that had fought a war for its freedom now enslave others?

Although the anti-imperialist movement had powerful friends and many supporters, it was moving against the tide of the era. Ultimately, it failed to prevent successive American administrations from building what was, in effect, an American empire.

The beginnings of expansion

European interference in the American continent had been condemned as far back as 1823 by the **Monroe Doctrine**, so when the British government fell into a border dispute with Venezuela over British Guiana in 1895, the Americans stepped in. The Americans urged **arbitration** of the dispute,

Balance of power: The view that the important nations of the world should be roughly equal in terms of power and influence, otherwise there would be instability and war.

Monroe Doctrine: Statement made by President James Monroe in 1823 that the continent of America was independent and the European powers could not consider re-colonising it. An attack on these independent states could be viewed as an attack on the USA.

Arbitration: The judging of a dispute between nations or states by someone not involved, whose decision both sides agree to accept.

which was accepted eventually and the matter settled. But Congress had granted President Cleveland the authority to use force if necessary. America had little direct interest in the dispute but it showed a renewed willingness to assert its authority on the continent.

Likewise in the Pacific, the Unites States found itself taking on a more active role as islands across the Ocean were viewed as vital links in maintaining and developing trade in Asia. For example, in 1889 a **joint protectorate** was established with Britain and Germany over the Samoan Islands.

The Hawaiian Islands had long been a destination for American missionaries and planters, and in 1887 the USA was granted exclusive use of Pearl Harbor (see map on page 221). In 1890, the island's right to export duty free sugar into the USA was abolished, leading to a fall in demand and a collapse of prices by 40%. The Hawaiians and the plantation owners worried for their livelihoods and anti-foreign sentiment grew, led by the islands' Queen Liliuokalani. In 1893, American settlers and US marines toppled Queen Liliuokalani and set up a pro-American government, which requested annexation by the USA. President Cleveland was reluctant to do this, but in 1898 McKinley granted the request. This began a process which would culminate in Hawaii being granted full statehood in 1959.

It was clear that, in this decade, American attitudes to empire were changing significantly. The war with Spain was to see the United States taking on colonies in the Philippines and establishing what was, in effect, a colonial relationship with Cuba.

Joint protectorate: Where stronger nations agree to share the protection of a smaller, less powerful nation. This is usually done to keep out a rival power, rather than benefit the under-developed nation being 'looked after'.

1. **What were the arguments for and against an American Empire in the period 1890–1896?**

2. **How far was American expansion in the period 1890–1896 governed by economic factors?**

7.2 Why did the USA go to war with Spain in 1898?
A CASE STUDY IN HISTORICAL INTERPRETATION

Since 1492 when Columbus found the New World, large parts of America and the Caribbean had been settled by Spain. Between 1811 and 1830, the majority of Spanish colonies in South America had gained their independence, and the Cubans wanted theirs. Revolts against the Spanish broke out in 1868 and 1879; the third attempt, in 1895, was to be ultimately successful.

The revolt against Spanish rule began in 1895. In December, the Spanish dispatched 98,400 troops to crush the rebellion, joining the 63,000 already on the island. Although they were outnumbered, the rebels had many successes with the support of the ordinary people and by 1897 were declaring their independence. Initially, the Americans seemed keen to keep out of the conflict, but in February 1898 with the sinking of the 'Maine' they entered the war. Why did the Americans go to war? Was it the sinking of the 'Maine' or, as many claim, had the United States intended all along to replace Spanish control of Cuba with its own? In one sense, the Americans were simply putting the Monroe Doctrine into action and showing support for a fellow nation trying to win its freedom from a ruling kingdom thousands of miles away – just as they themselves had done a century before. But there were more complex motives for their action. Cuba roused the feelings of the nation and it had both strategic and economic importance to the USA.

When the war broke out, it was closely followed in the American press, notably the so-called '**yellow press**' of William Randolph Hearst and Joseph Pulitzer. These two men were locked in a circulation war over their

'Yellow press': Style of journalism that was deliberately sensationalist so as to attract a mass readership.

respective newspapers, the 'New York Journal' and 'New York World'. They competed to tell the most sensational stories from the war, some of which were clearly untrue but all of which were ferociously anti-Spanish. Hearst's stories, in particular of the concentration camps of the 'butcher' General Weyler where as many as 200,000 died, provoked the Americans. In fact, there were atrocities on both sides, but the American people were genuinely outraged by the way the Spanish treated their rebel prisoners and the Cuban people. The historian Maldwyn Jones, in *The Limits of Liberty* (1995), sees this as an important factor and states that '[the] conflict was as much the product of idealism as a desire to assert American power'.

What ultimately pushed America into joining the war was the explosion in Havana harbour, in February 1898, which blew up and sank the 'USS Maine', killing 260 American sailors. Hearst immediately blamed Spain and urged the government into war with the battlecry 'Remember the Maine'. Investigations at the time blamed mines for sinking the ship, most probably laid by the Spanish. An investigation, in the 1970s, claimed that the explosion was most likely the result of sparks igniting ammunition in the hold and that it was simply an accident. Whatever the cause of the explosion, the effect was to push the United States towards war with Spain. Even then, McKinley took until 11 April to get approval from Congress to send troops to expel the Spaniards. He hoped for a negotiated settlement, but was unable to get Spain to agree to acceptable terms. McKinley didn't want war but knew the mood of the people was for intervention. The anti-Spanish hysteria had not been helped by the publication of a letter from the Spanish Ambassador in Washington, Dupuy de Lôme, criticising the President. In the end, with public opinion as it was and with the deaths of the sailors, McKinley had little choice but to declare war.

Congress debated Cuba for over a week. The anti-imperialists were concerned to show that the USA had no intention of throwing the Spanish out and of taking over Cuba themselves. The **Teller Amendment** made this clear by stating that the United States believed that 'the people of the island of Cuba are, and of right ought to be, free and independent', and that 'the United States [rejects any] intention to exercise sovereignty, jurisdiction or control' over the island. This would seem to support Maldwyn Jones' view

Teller Amendment: On 18 April 1898 a resolution for war with Spain was passed by Congress. This amendment to the resolution was intended to show that the USA had no desire to take over Cuba.

How useful is this cartoon in explaining the causes of the Spanish–American War?

THE BIG TYPE WAR OF THE YELLOW KIDS.

that the Spanish–American War was fought for noble motives. Although the Teller Amendment is good evidence of admirable intentions, the historian Louis Perez argues, in *The War of 1898* (1998), that it was passed in an atmosphere of pro-Cuban hysteria and masked America's real intention which was to take over the island.

Long before 1898, the Americans had shown an interest in acquiring Cuba. As early as 1854, they had offered to buy the island from Spain for $130 million. In 1881, the US Secretary of Defence, James G. Blaine wrote that 'If ever ceasing to be Spanish, Cuba must necessarily become part of America'. And in 1897, J.C. Breckenridge, Under-Secretary of War, wrote of Cuba: 'our policy must be to support the weaker against the stronger, until we have obtained the extermination of them both, in order to annex the Pearl of the Antilles [Cuba]'.

Cuba's strategic and economic position made it attractive to America. It controlled the Gulf of Mexico, the Caribbean and from there trade with South America. Also, if the Panama Canal were to be built, which seemed imminent in 1898, this would only increase Cuba's strategic importance. There were even those who argued that 'Manifest Destiny' extended to Cuba: just over 200 kilometres from the American coast it clearly should form part of the USA. The United States had $50 million invested in Cuba, primarily in sugar and tobacco, and 86% of all Cuban exports went to the USA. If the Cubans were to become independent, this could damage American property and trade, whereas a Cuba under US control would create more markets and opportunities for American business. Blaine had talked about Cuba being 'part of the American commercial system'. It may be that it was the sinking of the 'Maine' which was the reason for war, or that the Americans genuinely wanted to help the Cuban people. Clearly, other motives also played their part, and the fact that America did take control of Cuba after the war would indicate that these factors were important.

Why did the USA win the War so easily?

The first American attack was in May 1898 in the Philippine Islands, which were a Spanish colony in the Pacific. The American navy, led by Commodore Dewey, attacked the Spanish fleet there, sinking ten ships and killing almost 400 sailors. On 13 August, they took the capital Manila.

In Cuba, too, there was a naval engagement at Santiago Bay where almost 500 Spanish sailors died when they tried to run the American blockade of the harbour. Earlier, in June, 17,000 troops had landed on Cuba itself. There were American victories at El Caney Hill and more famously at San Juan Hill where Theodore Roosevelt's 'Rough Riders' led the charge against the Spanish guns. In July, Santiago fell and on 12 August an **armistice** was signed. The historian Hugh Brogan, in *The Pelican History of the United States of America* (1985), calls it 'a short, businesslike affair' and Secretary of State John Hay called it 'a splendid little war'. But the United States had entered the war with Spain completely unprepared. The army at the time consisted of only 28,000 men and was dependent on local organisation, rather than on the federal government, for supplies and equipment. Needless to say, these were frequently inadequate. The United States lost 379 men in the fighting (100 of those at San Juan Hill) but lost another 5,000 to disease. It was as much due to luck and to the weariness of the Spanish that they won.

Under the Treaty of Paris, the USA acquired the Philippines, Guam and Puerto Rico. Cuba was recognised as independent, but American troops stayed on the island for another four years and an American 'governor' was

Armistice: Agreement between countries who are at war with one another to stop fighting for a time and to discuss ways of making a peaceful settlement.

put in charge. The justification was that Cuba needed help with establishing stability after the war, and with writing its constitution. As a nation that had been through a similar process of fighting for independence and setting up a new state with a new constitution, American advice might have been helpful.

The real reason, suggested by the Platt Amendment 1901, was to maintain some element of control over Cuba. This amendment to the Cuban constitution gave the United States the right to intervene to maintain the independence and stability of Cuba, and it asserted that Cuba could not make treaties that would impair that independence. It was America who would decide what did and did not impair Cuban independence. The constitution also granted the USA the right to maintain a base at Guantánamo Bay. American troops were withdrawn from the island in 1902 and a new government was set up and run by Cubans. America had, and indeed still has, the base at Guantánamo, and US companies continued to dominate the Cuban economy until the revolution led by Fidel Castro in 1958. Clearly, whether or not the USA had fought the war to guarantee Cuban freedom from Spain, the Treaty of Paris gave America a large say in Cuban affairs.

1. How did the USA defeat the Spanish in Cuba?

2. Why, and how far, do historians differ in their explanations of American reasons for going to war with Spain in 1898?

What does this map show about the important role played by the navy in winning the war?

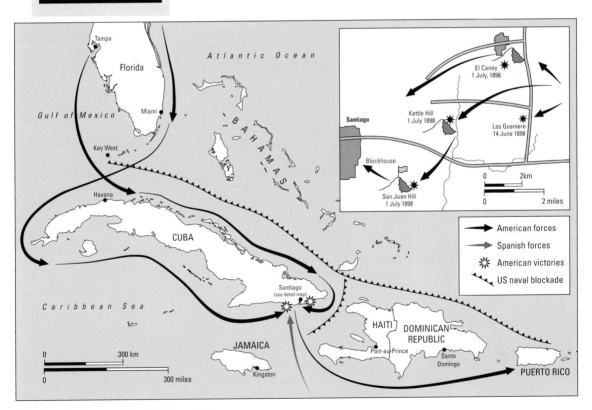

The Spanish–American War in Cuba, 1898

7.3 How successful was Theodore Roosevelt's foreign policy?

When President McKinley was shot in 1901, his Vice-President, Theodore Roosevelt (TR), became the youngest president of the United States. At only 42, he already had a long record in public office. He was Assistant Secretary of the Navy when the Spanish–American War broke out and he resigned his post to join the cavalry, being nominated for the Congressional Medal of Honour for the Battle at San Juan Hill. It was Theodore Roosevelt who finally seemed to move America onto the world stage to take its place as one of the Great Powers.

'Teddy' Roosevelt served as President from 1901 to 1909, being elected in his own right in 1904. His Administration was marked by an era of progressive reform (see Chapter 4). To an extent this concern for domestic reform meant that the public and Congress would not always support his actions. It also meant that he was left to get on with the business of running foreign affairs very much in his own way. His skill in international relations is frequently contrasted with Woodrow Wilson's. Where Wilson was naïve, TR understood when to threaten force and when to act behind the scenes; where Wilson believed in self-determination and the rights of all nations, TR believed the world was divided into the civilised and the barbaric. It was the duty of the civilised, Christian nations – such as the USA – to help those countries that were backward and lawless, even if that meant using force. This view of the world as two halves also had a racial component since the civilised nations were, on the whole, white, western and Christian. The Japanese, as an orderly and industrial nation, were also included in TR's definition of 'civilised'. Roosevelt hoped that the Japanese would exert an orderly influence in the eastern hemisphere as America did in the western hemisphere.

TR also believed that an active foreign policy would be good for the nation. Like many men of his time, he worried about the lazy nature of modern society. He saw virtue in the hardship of struggle and war. Of his own experiences in Cuba, he said: 'It makes me feel as though I could now leave something to my children which will serve as an apology for my having existed.' With these views it was likely that Theodore Roosevelt would pursue an active foreign policy.

The Panama Canal

As Alfred Thayer Mahan pointed out in *The Influence of Sea Power on History* (1890), the USA was unusual among the Great Powers in being both a Pacific and Atlantic power. As a result of the Spanish–American War, the United States became a Caribbean power with its temporary acquisition of Cuba. This brought the long-discussed plans for a canal through the Isthmus of Panama much higher up the political agenda.

Does this photograph have any use to the historian trying to explain Theodore Roosevelt's views on America's world role?

Theodore Roosevelt (1858–1919)

26th President of the USA (1901–09), a Republican. 'Teddy' or 'TR', as he was often known, was Assistant Secretary of the Navy (1897–98) and during the Spanish–American war he commanded a volunteer force of 'rough riders'. As McKinley's Vice-President he took over as President when McKinley was assassinated in 1901. At only 42, he was the youngest president. He already had a long record in public office, having been a Civil Service Commissioner, Police Commissioner and Governor of New York. When in office, he became more liberal. In 1906 he was awarded the Nobel Peace Prize for his part in ending the Russo–Japanese war. He wrote several historical works, including *The Naval War of 1812* (published in 1882) and *The Winning of the West* (1889–96). The 'teddy' bear gets its name from this US President.

The Panama Canal

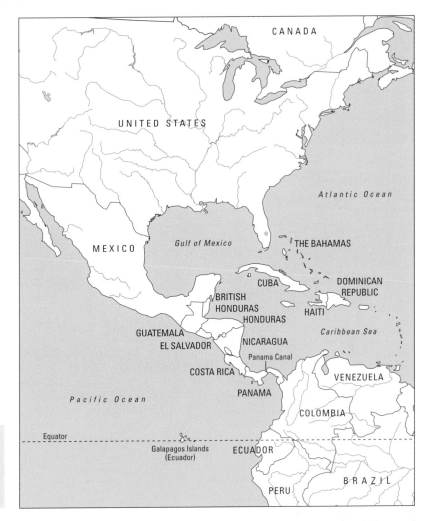

What does this map show about the strategic importance of the Panama Canal?

Ferdinand de Lesseps, the man who built the Suez Canal, had obtained a lease on Panama from the Colombian government but had gone bankrupt trying to get the canal built. In 1889, he offered the canal project to the American government for $109 million, but was refused, partly because the price was too high and partly because the British had an equal interest in the area under a treaty of 1850. Both of these problems were overcome. The Hay–Paunceforte Treaty 1901 gave the Americans exclusive control over the proposed area and, when de Lesseps lowered his price to $40 million, the agreement went forward. A 99-year lease was agreed with the Colombian government in 1903, but the Colombians then delayed, wanting to negotiate new terms once the agreement made with de Lesseps ran out the following year. The American government was not prepared to wait and so end up with less favourable terms. In November, a Panamanian revolution broke out against Colombian rule. In fact, the 'revolution' had been organised by an employee of the Canal Company, Philippe Bunau-Varilla, helped and supported by the Americans. Roosevelt sent the cruiser 'Nashville' to prevent the Colombians from re-taking control of Panama. The Americans recognised the rebel government and then negotiated with them for control of a strip, 10 miles wide, across the Isthmus of Panama. The USA was granted control of the Canal Zone forever for the price of $10 million and $¼ million rent per year. Work began in 1907 and, in 1914, the Canal opened to traffic.

Roosevelt boasted that he had taken the Canal Zone while Congress talked. There was much support for his methods within the United States, since there had been previous attempts by Panamanians to gain their independence from Colombia. In Latin America, however, the methods he had used caused dismay and much mistrust. This was not to be the last time that the United States would encourage trouble in Latin America for its own ends.

Theodore Roosevelt acted decisively in foreign affairs. Under the Constitution, the President has control of foreign policy, but McKinley had ensured that he had congressional approval before going to war with Spain. Roosevelt acted much more on his own initiative. He acquired the Panama Canal for the United States without much reference to Congress. As America's role in the world grew, so did the importance of foreign policy: and as the President controls foreign policy this meant a growth in the power of the presidential office.

The Roosevelt Corollary

With the USA now having a much greater interest in Latin American affairs through its possessions in Cuba and Panama, Roosevelt felt that its right to intervene in order to maintain stability in the area and to protect US interests must be upheld. The crisis came in 1902 when the government of Venezuela defaulted on debts to Europe. A combined fleet from Britain, Germany and Italy blockaded the Venezuelan coast. The USA feared that the Europeans would use this excuse to take bases or to land in the area – a fear heightened when the Germans began to bombard Venezuelan ports. Any attempt by the Europeans to establish themselves in Latin America would be a clear violation of the Monroe Doctrine. But TR went further and issued an amendment to the Doctrine, which became known as the 'Roosevelt Corollary'.

In the Roosevelt Corollary he stated that to preserve order the United States had the right to intervene in the affairs of other countries on the continent in cases of 'chronic wrongdoing or impotence'. What exactly constituted 'wrongdoing' was for the Americans to decide. It was used to justify their taking over the finances of the Dominican Republic in 1905, when it defaulted on its debt. 'Wrongdoing' was also used to explain military intervention some years later, in Nicaragua in 1912 and Haiti in 1918.

Far from being an isolationist power, America was now declaring to the world that the Western Hemisphere was its sphere of influence. Yet it would be misleading to equate this simply with European empire-building. It cannot be denied that the United States was interfering in the internal affairs of sovereign nations for its own ends, but Roosevelt thought it was crucial to maintain stability in Latin America. If some level of stability were not maintained, the European powers themselves might seek to interfere. Although US marines remained in the Dominican Republic until 1924, and in Nicaragua and Haiti for a further decade, when they left it was because the American government withdrew them. In many of Europe's colonies, imperial forces were only withdrawn after long and bloody fights for independence. Although the USA might interfere, TR had successfully preserved Latin American independence from Europe, and in several cases American involvement did improve financial stability.

Japan

Under President Roosevelt, American interest and involvement in the Far East continued to grow. The Russo–Japanese War of 1904–05, it was feared, would create instability in the area. But the swiftness and ease of the Japanese victory, rather than calming American fears, increased them as they saw the balance of power in the Far East shifting in Japan's favour. Roosevelt worked hard to bring the two powers together to establish peace. Under the Treaty of Portsmouth 1905, Japan gained Korea, South Sakhalin and the southern part of Manchuria. In spite of Roosevelt gaining the Nobel Peace Prize for his mediation of the treaty, Japanese–American relations worsened. America feared the growth in Japanese power in the Far East, while Japan resented American racism as schools in San Francisco proposed to **segregate** Japanese children.

To ease relations, Roosevelt got the school boards to back down. Then, in 1907, he sent the 'Great White Fleet' on a tour of Pacific ports to underline America's interest in the area. The fleet received an invitation and friendly welcome to Japan. This was followed by the 1908 Root–Takahira Agreement recognising the status quo in the Far East and Pacific. The potential breakdown had been averted but its signs for the future were ominous. Japanese power in the Pacific was growing and its own needs for new markets were pushing it to expand, while at the same time America's needs drew it into a more active world role and expansion in the Far East. With the defeat of Russia and the decay of China, there was little to check Japanese ambitions. The foundations for Pearl Harbor were being laid. In the short term, TR had vastly improved relations in the area and, in his own words, performed 'an important service … to peace.'

'In office Roosevelt actually performed on the whole with consummate skill and prudence in the foreign arena,' wrote Anders Stephanson in *Manifest Destiny* (1995). Roosevelt had expanded American power considerably in Latin America, through the Roosevelt Corollary and through the building of the Panama Canal. He had helped bring peace to the Far East, and through the two-year voyage of the 'Great White Fleet' he had signalled America's power and presence to the world. Most of this had been achieved through diplomacy. Though he was not averse to threatening force when necessary, TR largely kept America out of conflict. If his aim had been to increase the influence and role of the Americans in world affairs, he had undoubtedly been successful.

Segregate: To keep apart usually because of race, sex or religion. In this instance, Japanese students in schools in San Francisco were deliberately separated from other children because of their ethnic origins.

1. What was the purpose of the 'Great White Fleet' voyage?

2. How far would you agree that in foreign policy Theodore Roosevelt performed with 'skill and prudence'?

7.4 How far had an 'American Empire' been created by 1917?

Both before and after Theodore Roosevelt, American power in the world had been expanding. Under McKinley, Taft and Wilson, the involvement of the United States in world affairs grew. Their methods and motives might have differed, but the effect was the same. By 1917, the USA had interests around the globe.

Why did the USA get more involved in China?

American politicians and businessmen alike eyed China with avarice. With 3.5 billion square miles and a population three times the size of the USA, the potential markets for American trade were huge. The crumbling political system within China had allowed the European powers to dominate China's politics, and successive American administrations feared that they might be squeezed out. To prevent this, McKinley's Secretary of State, John Hay, sent a note to the European capitals asking for an **'open door'** policy with regard to trade in China. In fact, the European powers virtually ignored the letter, but Hay announced that they had accepted it. The historian Alan Brinkley, in *The Unfinished Nation* (1993), points out how the USA was building an informal empire rather than directly colonising areas, as Europe had done. America used its economic power to extend its influence not its military might. The rivalries between the

'Open door': The idea that all nations should have free and equal access to trade with China.

Europeans themselves meant they could not make any attempt to prevent American penetration into Chinese affairs.

However, foreign involvement led to military involvement. In June 1899, the Society of the Harmonious Righteous Fists (often referred to as 'Boxers' by western journalists) began a revolt against foreign domination of China. They murdered several hundred Europeans and Chinese who had converted to Christianity. By 1899, they had surrounded the diplomatic residential section of Peking. A year later, a multi-national force was sent to crush this so-called 'Boxer Rebellion' and the USA contributed 2,500 troops. When the revolt was over, Hay once again committed America to the open door policy in China. The other powers now accepted this and the area was kept open to American trade.

The importance of free trade to American expansion and influence in the world can be seen running from the open door policy through Wilson's Fourteen Points (see page 227) and even to the anti-globalisation protests against McDonald's in the 1990s. In fact, under William Taft the idea of using American financial and economic power as a way of gaining influence became overt and was known as 'dollar diplomacy'. Railway workers and bankers, for example, were encouraged to invest in areas like Manchuria and Latin America. US external investment increased seven-fold between 1860 and 1914.

The Philippines, 1898–1901

Emilio Aguinaldo (1869–1964)
Politician and soldier. Fought against the Spanish in 1896 and then led the fight for Philippine independence against the USA.

Guerrilla war: A plan of campaign fought against a regular army by small bands of armed men and women.

Francisco Indalecio Madero (1873–1913)
Revolutionary and reformer. Overthrew the government of President Díaz. Madero was President of Mexico from 1911.

Victoriano Huerta (1854–1916)
Military and political leader. Toppled Madero's government but was forced from office because of his oppressive rule.

Venustiano Carranza (1859–1920)
Politician and rival of Huerta. President of Mexico, 1914–1920. Introduced new constitution in 1917.

Constitutionalist: Person who organises or governs a country according to a constitution.

Further eastwards, as a result of the Spanish–American War, the USA had also gained the Philippines. It was initially seen as a stepping stone to the Far East, but quickly became a liability. Having had no say in their transfer from Spanish to American control, the Filipinos revolted demanding independence. They were led by Emilio Aguinaldo. It took three years and 70,000 soldiers to crush the rebellion and to capture Aguinaldo. Some 4,300 Americans died and the American treatment of their 'little brown brothers' was no better than the treatment the Spanish had handed out to the Cubans, and which had been so widely condemned in the United States. In many ways, the frustration of the soldiers fighting a **guerrilla war** so far from home, leading to anger, frustration and subsequent atrocities, more resembles Vietnam than Cuba. There were killings of prisoners-of-war (POWs), executions and destruction of crops. It is estimated between 20,000 and 50,000 Filipinos died in the three-year war. Although the Filipinos often refer to their colonial past as '200 years in a convent followed by 50 years in a whorehouse', American rule brought significant improvements with the building of schools, hospitals, roads, sewage systems etc. An American governor-general governed the islands, but there was also an elected assembly and the promise of self-rule. There was never the support for annexation, either within the islands or in the USA, that there was in Cuba or Hawaii. Independence was eventually gained shortly after the end of the Second World War.

Mexico

Woodrow Wilson was very critical of policies such as 'dollar diplomacy' and the interference of the United States in other countries, yet he too sent American troops into Latin America. It was Wilson who sent the marines into Haiti and increased control over the Dominican Republic, and in Mexico he involved the USA in a civil war.

In 1913, the government of Francisco Madero was toppled by Victoriano Huerta and Madero was murdered. Wilson referred to Huerta's men as 'butchers' and refused to recognise them. Instead, he sent arms and support to **constitutionalist** rebels led by Venustiano Carranza. Seven

Francisco 'Pancho' Villa (1877–1923)
Mexican revolutionary. The son of a peasant, he became a military commander in the 1910 revolution. His actions brought American involvement in Mexico, but after their withdrawal he continued to oppose Carranza until 1920. Villa was assassinated in 1923.

thousand soldiers were sent to the port of Vera Cruz to prevent Huerta getting his own arms supplies from the Germans. The tactic appeared to have been successful. Huerta's government fell and Carranza took power.

Yet Woodrow Wilson's support for Carranza had been half-hearted. At the same time, the Americans had been hinting that they would support the soldiers led by the nationalist 'Pancho' Villa. When the Americans recognised the Carranza government, Villa was furious and launched two raids over the border killing 35 American citizens. Thousands of US soldiers were sent to hunt him down, unsuccessfully. But the danger of America getting bogged down in the confused and violent politics of Mexico was clear. With the war in Europe increasingly taking his attention, Wilson negotiated with Carranza. A new constitution was issued and American troops withdrew.

As several writers show, for all he said about self-determination Wilson was as prepared as Roosevelt or McKinley to use troops to protect what he believed to be America's interests. He might disapprove of the Roosevelt Corollary but when American security or business interests, or even his own views on what constituted a democratic government, demanded it he acted in accordance with its principles.

From the Philippines to Mexico, it is clear that in the two decades before the First World War America had changed its attitude to the outside world. It had gained possessions in Hawaii, Guam, the Philippines, Samoa, the Virgin Islands, Puerto Rico and several other Pacific islands, and had been directly involved in the affairs of Cuba, Mexico, China, Nicaragua,

How far could the USA, by 1914, be regarded as a Pacific power?

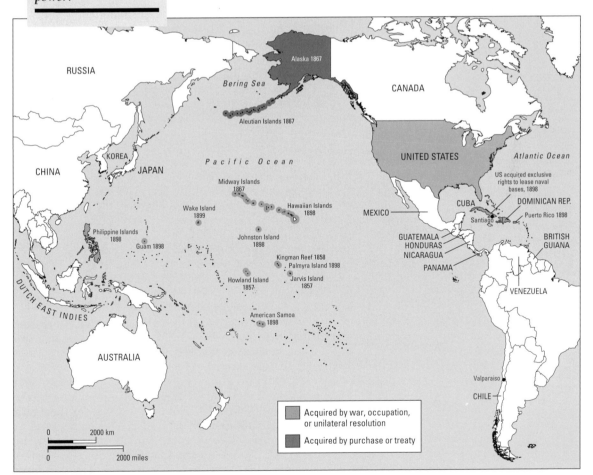

US territorial expansion in the late 19th century

Haiti and several other Latin American countries. Yet the United States could not be said to be an imperial power in the way that Britain or France was. There was no colonial office set up at home, no civil service trained to run the 'colonies', no attempt to make their new possessions part of an American Empire ruled by Washington. Americans were still suspicious of colonialism and while there was support for a more active foreign policy, there was also a strong desire for the USA simply to look after its own economic and strategic interests and not become involved in empire-building. Yet there is a contradiction here. Looking after American interests required involvement in foreign affairs, and though America did not control vast areas of the world like Britain, it did take over some areas as its own, such as Hawaii. It also used its economic power to control the affairs of other areas, such as Cuba. America's colonial past, and its desire to play a part in the world fitting its status, meant that its attitude towards empire was contradictory. This contradiction can be seen in American foreign policy through both world wars and into the Cold War and beyond.

1. Why was influence in China considered important?

2. How far was American expansion between 1896 and 1914 a result of the Spanish–American war?

7.5 Why did the USA become involved in the First World War?

In August 1914, war broke out in Europe between Britain, France and Russia on one side, and Germany and Austria-Hungary on the other. Over the next three years the war spread, dragging in many of the other European nations. Even the Japanese joined the war, on 23 August 1914. The war would last four years and cost the lives of 18 million people.

The eight million Americans of German descent were sympathetic to the so-called Central Powers. Irish-Americans were also sympathetic due to their resentment of British rule in Ireland, as were many Jews and Poles who had fled to America to escape Russian persecution. But support for the Allies was stronger. Ties of language, culture and history meant that the majority of Americans supported Britain. There was also a long friendship with France going back to the War of Independence. With the exception of autocratic Russia, the Allied Powers were seen as the decent and democratic nations defending Europe from the unprovoked aggression of the **militaristic** Germans. This attitude was encouraged by very effective British propaganda which emphasised German 'atrocities', particularly against the defenceless Belgians.

Militaristic: Aggressive, heavily relying on military force.

There were some in America who thought that the United States should take part in the War. Ex-president Theodore Roosevelt thought staying out was cowardly. Others, including some in the Administration, felt that America needed to be prepared to defend democracy. They formed groups such as the National Security League. President Wilson himself was appalled by the German attack on neutral Belgium. However, he felt, as the vast majority of Americans did, that the war was a European affair and they did not want to be dragged into it. Wilson urged the people to be neutral in thought and deed, to show by example that Americans were somehow 'better', that there were other ways to resolve issues. The American public might be sympathetic to the Allied cause, but it was not their fight and, above all, they wanted to keep out of it.

Being neutral, however, proved more difficult than the Americans had imagined. They had an economic involvement in the War long before their military involvement. The First World War created a boom in American industry and agriculture with sales of goods and supplies to both sides. Money was loaned to enable the Europeans to pay for the goods they bought. By 1917, the USA had loaned over $2 billion to the Allies and $27 million to the Germans. Understandably, the Germans complained that this was hardly neutrality, but even before the War the

United States had done a great deal more trade with Britain than with Germany. This led some to believe that America got involved in the war for financial reasons. Clearly, an Allied victory was preferable in order to protect American investment and it was probably a contributory factor to the decision to enter the War in 1917. Public opinion and American security also favoured an Allied victory and may have affected the Senate's decision. But it was the war at sea that was the ultimate cause of US entry into the First World War.

Early on in the war, Britain had used its naval strength to blockade the German coast and to stop and search vessels believed to be taking goods to the Central Powers. Some shipping lanes were also mined. America protested when its own ships were stopped or goods seized, but for Britain the blockade was an effective weapon. By 1915, the blockade was already causing shortages in Germany.

The Germans responded with submarine warfare to try and sink British ships and starve Britain into surrender. In February 1915, they announced that Allied ships would be sunk without warning. Though this made sense militarily, it went against accepted 'rules' of warfare. In the USA, it was seen as barbaric and as an infringement of the freedom of the seas. The American government protested. Some proposed banning US citizens from travelling on Allied vessels, but Wilson felt that this limited American freedoms. Then, on 7 May, the Germans sank the British passenger liner the 'Lusitania'. Of the 1,200 who died on the ship, 128 were Americans. In fact, the ship had been carrying ammunition. The Germans knew that Britain used liners for that purpose and saw the ship as a fair target, but public opinion in America was incensed. When two more Americans were killed on the 'Arabic' in August, the Germans seemed to back off in the face of American anger. In 1916, more Americans were hurt when the 'Sussex' was sunk. Wilson made it clear to Germany that if they continued to endanger American lives there would be serious consequences. The Germans were anxious to keep the Americans out of the War and they abandoned the U-boat (German submarine) campaign.

The crisis seemed to have been averted and Wilson went to the polls in 1916 on the slogan of having kept America out of the war. He won by a narrow victory of 277 electoral college votes to 254. Throughout 1916, Wilson had worked to avoid war. He proposed a peace conference to Edward Grey, the British Foreign Secretary, indicating that, if the Allies accepted the conference and the Germans did not, the USA might join the war against Germany. It came to nothing, as neither side really believed America would join. It is doubtful if Wilson could have carried Congress with him had he proposed it seriously. He knew that the public still did not want war.

Wilson also realised that, should war come, America needed to be more prepared than it was. He asked Congress for an increased army and navy. The army was increased to over 200,000 men and the National Guard to 400,000. (Just how unprepared America was is illustrated by the fact that General Haig was able to field 200,000 British soldiers at the Battle of the Somme alone.) A massive naval building programme was also embarked on which would soon see the American navy as one of the two most powerful in the world. This build-up caused criticism, with accusations that Wilson was getting America ready to join the War. Wilson did not want war, but as President, and Commander-in-Chief, he knew that he had to be ready if it came.

By the 'turnip winter' of 1916–1917, Germans were suffering severe hardship and hunger due to the British blockade. In January, in an effort to end the war, they announced the resumption of unrestricted U-boat warfare. After the agreement over the 'Sussex', the Germans knew they

Autocracy: Political system in which the ruler has total power and is answerable to no one.

1. In what ways did the United States have an interest in the outcome of the First World War before 1917?

2. 'It was the U-boat campaign of 1917 which brought America into the First World War.' How far would you agree with this view?

were risking bringing the United States into the conflict, but they felt they had to take the risk. They gambled that the Americans might not fight, or that if they did it would take too long for them to mobilise, by which time the Germans would have won. In both of these, they were wrong.

Although the January announcement led to a break in diplomatic relations, Congress was not yet ready to declare war. They even refused Wilson's request to have American merchant ships armed. Two events strengthened Wilson's hand. Firstly, the February Revolution in Russia ended the **autocracy** and brought in a Provisional Government promising democratic reforms. This meant that the Allied cause could now be seen as thoroughly democratic. Secondly, the British presented the Americans with a copy of the 'Zimmerman Telegram'. The British had intercepted the telegram from the German Foreign Minister, Arthur Zimmerman, to the German ambassador in Mexico. It suggested to the Mexican government that if they joined the war against the USA, Germany would ensure that in the end they got back New Mexico, Texas and Arizona, which they had lost to America in the 1840s. This was a violation of the Monroe Doctrine and put America and Germany on a collision course. The further loss of American lives at sea, in February and March of 1917, finally turned public opinion. Although there were a few Mid-Western Congressmen and Senators who held out, when Wilson asked Congress for a declaration of war in April it was granted by 82–6 votes in the Senate and 373–50 in the House of Representatives. He promised to make the world 'safe for democracy', and on 6 April the United States declared war on Germany.

7.6 How successful was Wilson's foreign policy 1917–1919?

America and the First World War

When America declared war, it was expected that its contribution would be primarily economic, but by 1917 the Allied forces were exhausted and their economies in collapse. In the first few months of the year, almost two million tons of shipping had been lost, 340,000 British soldiers had been killed or wounded in the mud of Passchendaele and the French Army was in mutiny. Americans had not been prepared by Wilson for the necessity of sending their young men to fight in Europe, but American troops were vital to the war effort.

The Selective Services Act introduced conscription in May 1917. Initially, men aged 21–30 were called up, though this was later extended to men aged 18–45. During the course of the War, 3.5 million men were drafted, with an additional 1.5 million who volunteered, including 260,000 African-Americans. Over half of these men eventually served on the Western Front, and over 100,000 would give their lives to the War.

Training and equipping these men took time and, by March 1918, only 84,000 American soldiers had arrived in Europe. When they arrived in Europe the American soldiers wore British helmets, as America was not producing its own. A War Industries Board was set up to organise supplies and raw materials. Wilson put financier Bernard Baruch in charge, and although there continued to be many inefficiencies and mistakes it was soon supplying the needs of the military. It taught a useful lesson, for those involved the in Second World War, of the need for government control of the economy. However, it was late summer before there were significant numbers of US soldiers ready to fight, by which time they were needed to help defend Paris.

US soldiers leaving for France in August 1917.

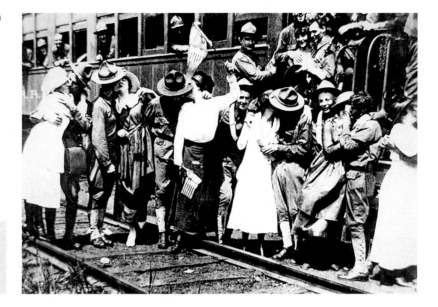

Does this picture tell us anything about attitudes to the War?

Why was the victory at *Château-Thierry* important?

In October 1917, Lenin's Bolsheviks had carried out the second Russian Revolution. The world's first communist government was set up and it immediately condemned the War and announced its intention to back out, which it did in March 1918. This freed up a million German soldiers from the Eastern Front. General Ludendorff launched a spring offensive, hoping to take Paris before the Americans arrived in force. The gamble almost succeeded and the Germans got to within 40 miles of the French capital.

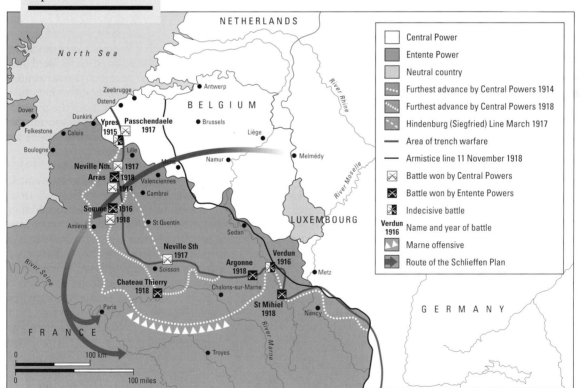

The Western Front

General John Joseph Pershing (1860–1948)
American army officer. Commanded soldiers in the Mexican War and led American Expeditionary Force in the First World War.

Vladimir Illyich Ulyanov, 'Lenin' (1870–1924)
Russian revolutionary and leader of the Bolshevik or Communist Party. Along with Leon Trotsky, he organised the communist seizure of power in November 1917. He was leader of Russia until his death in 1924.

Ferdinand Foch (1851–1929)
French soldier and Chief of the General Staff in 1917. In 1918 he was put in overall command of the Allied armies on the Western Front.

American forces were under the command of General John J. Pershing, a veteran of the Cuban and Mexican wars. As an 'Associate' power rather than an Allied power, American forces were not integrated into the Allied army under General Ferdinand Foch, but they formed an important part of his counter-offensive launched in the summer. Pershing's men halted the German advance at Château-Thierry and at Bellau Wood. By September, American soldiers were arriving in large numbers. More important, was the psychological effect they were having on both sides. Their youth, enthusiasm and the resources on which they would eventually be able to call breathed new life into the Allied cause. As for the Germans, they knew that if Ludendorff's gamble failed they had lost the War. In September, Foch launched the Argonnes Offensive. The French and Americans defeated the German army at St Mihiel, and the Germans were pushed back. The Ludendorff Offensive had failed and Paris was saved. In October, a new German government was set up under Prince Max von Baden and they asked for an armistice. The War ended on 11 November.

The Americans also contributed to the victory in other ways. When they joined the War in April 1917, Allied shipping losses for that year were already two million tons. With the American navy joining the campaign against German U-boats, Allied losses fell by two-thirds by the end of the year. In addition, American shipyards embarked on a building programme which meant that they could replace any ship the Germans sank, and more. By the start of 1918, the war at sea had been won. The strength of the American economy was vital. Altogether, they had spent around $35 billion on the war, and their supplies and loans to the Europeans between 1914 and 1917 had been crucial in enabling the Allies to maintain the fight. The Americans may only have been in the First World War for 19 months and their losses may have been low, compared to those of the other powers, but their contribution to victory was as important as that of any of the Allies.

Peacemaking and the Treaty of Versailles

When the Germans asked for peace it was to the Americans that they went, not the British or French. They believed that the Americans would be more lenient. This belief was partly due to the fact that the Americans had not been fighting for so long nor on their own territory, as the French had. They also understood that Wilson's Fourteen Points (see opposite) would form the basis of the peace treaty. In all, there were five treaties with each of the Central Powers which made up the Versailles Settlement of 1919, but by far the most important was the Treaty of Versailles itself with the Germans. The Treaty is generally considered to have been a failure, given that war broke out again between its signatories just 20 years later. Woodrow Wilson is given much of the blame for this failure.

President Wilson was an academic, a history professor who moved into politics in his 40s. He was very bright and, like many presidents, had a great interest in foreign policy, as it is one area of American Government over which the Administration had undoubted control. Wilson believed in America's role as an influence for good in the world. Its power would spread the ideals of liberalism, democracy and capitalism. He was a deeply religious man and is frequently referred to as an idealist. He was an idealist in that he believed in the good in people and had a desire to improve the world, but he was not a fool and he was not weak. His willingness to send troops into Mexico, as well as his support for the Allies in the first three years of the War, showed an understanding of the necessity of force in politics. Like Roosevelt, he used the power of his office to full effect.

Even before US entry into the War, Wilson had a desire to influence the peace. For example, his insistence that American citizens be allowed to travel freely in spite of the dangers from German submarines illustrates one of his foreign policy goals, freedom of the seas for all. As the War was coming to a close in 1918, he outlined his aims for the post-war peace, in common with other leaders. These aims were most clearly laid out in a speech to the Senate on 8 January and became known as the 'Fourteen Points'.

The causes of the First World War are complex and widely debated, but Wilson believed that if one identified the causes of the war and removed them, this would guarantee peace for the future. For example, he believed the network of secret treaties and the arms build-up in the years preceding 1914 had created an atmosphere of mistrust, which was sparked into war by the assassination in Sarajevo. Hence, points 1 and 2 would prevent a recurrence. Likewise, the clauses on **self-determination** would address the issue of Serbian nationalism. Self-determination also embodied Wilson's own belief in democracy and in the American anti-imperialist tradition. By giving as many people as possible a say in their own future, Wilson hoped the causes of conflict would be removed.

Self-determination: The right of people to decide their own future.

In this sense, Wilson was too idealistic. The clauses on Poland illustrate the difficulty of putting things into practice. The peacemakers had to balance the ideals of self-determination with the practical issues of security and economics. Without access to the sea, Poland would be severely weakened, but giving it access meant putting a large area of German territory under Polish rule. However, the practicalities of re-drawing the map of Europe were the least of Wilson's problems. It was the ambitions and desires of the other powers that drove him to distraction and even illness.

When Wilson arrived in Paris, he was greeted as a saviour. European people were grateful for the American contribution to ending the War and believed the ideals Wilson spoke of would, as he said, 'make the world safe for democracy'. But France had fought Germany twice in the previous 40 years, and the First World War had cost them 1.4 million lives. Britain had been bankrupted by the War and had lost 900,000 men. They wanted

---

Summary of Wilson's 'Fourteen Points'

1 Open covenants openly arrived at
2 Freedom of the seas
3 Free trade
4 Disarmament
5 Impartial adjustments of all colonial claims
6 Evacuation of Russia by the Germans and self-determination for the Russian people
7 Evacuation and restoration of Belgium
8 Return of Alsace-Lorraine to France
9 Re-adjustment of Italian frontiers based on nationality
10 Self-determination for the people of Austria-Hungary
11 Evacuation and restoration of Romania, Serbia and Montenegro
12 Self-determination for the peoples of the Turkish Empire
13 Establishment of an independent Poland with access to the sea
14 Establishment of a League of Nations (see next page) with mutual guarantes of independence and security.

Points 1 and 4 were an attempt to address the European causes of the War, and for the Americans it was Point 2. Wilson's belief in free trade was emphasised in both Points 2 and 3. Points 5–13 show how important the idea of self-determination was to the President. He felt that if the principle could be applied as widely as possible, then the causes of much conflict would be reduced. Point 14 was an attempt to bring about peace through cooperation.

The 'Big Four' at Versailles – Lloyd George, Orlando, Clemenceau and Woodrow Wilson

How far did these men share common goals?

to make Germany pay. The arguments between the 'Big Four' – Wilson, Britain's Prime Minister Lloyd George, France's Premier Georges Clemenceau and Italy's Prime Minster Orlando – were fierce. The Europeans were determined to have their territorial and reparation demands met. Some were valid and easy to accomplish, such as the return to France of Alsace-Lorraine, which had been taken by the Germans in 1871. Others, such as Italy's claims in the Adriatic, were considered too extravagant. Arguments over the issue had Orlando in tears. Compromises had to be made. Wilson could never have hoped to gain all that he set out to achieve. Whether the claims of the other Allies were just or not, the fact remains that they did have claims. Having fought the War for four years, the Allies would not let Wilson and America dictate terms to them.

However, Wilson did make many mistakes in his handling of the negotiations. He was dead set against imposing reparations on Germany, believing that this would cause resentment and future conflict. But France and Belgium insisted on reparations in order to rebuild the devastated towns and villages of the Western Front. Wilson was forced to give in and accept these demands. Had the Americans not insisted on repayment of the money they had loaned to Europe, the European nations may have been more willing to listen to him. As it was, the Reparations Commission in 1921 saddled Germany with a debt of $33 billion, which they were to pay to the Allies who in turn would use part of it to repay the Americans. The economist John Maynard Keynes resigned from the Conference in protest at the reparations issue and called Wilson 'incompetent'. Given the economic costs of the First World War, it was unlikely the Europeans would ever have agreed to a peace without some form of financial settlement.

Another mistake was Wilson's insistence on having the **League of Nations** as part of the Treaty. Building on an idea that had originated in Britain during the War, Wilson proposed an organisation of nations at which issues and problems could be talked through, instead of resorting to war. The members would also promise to protect each other in the event of an attack, thus making war less likely. This concept was known as 'collective security'. This was so important to Wilson that instead of having a separate agreement, he wanted it written into all five of the

League of Nations: Association of self-governing states created as part of 1919 Peace Treaty 'to promote international cooperation and to achieve international peace and security'. The USA did not join, and the association's failure to deal effectively with outbreaks in Japan, Italy and Germany in the 1930s meant that it had lost its relevance by the outbreak of the Second World War. It was subsequently replaced by the United Nations (see opposite).

treaties. It was written into all five treaties, but it allowed the other powers to use it as a bargaining chip to have their demands met. It was also to cause problems at home.

It was in the domestic arena that Wilson made his most serious errors with regard to Versailles. Firstly, in the mid-term elections of November 1918 he made the forthcoming peace conference a party issue, hoping to give himself a strong Democratic Congress. The plan completely backfired and the Republicans gained control of both Houses. Wilson also made no real attempt to work with the Republicans to gain their support.

'Round-robin': A letter signed by several people indicating agreement. No single person is seen as the author.

When he returned from Paris to present the Treaty to Congress, 39 Senators signed a letter – a **'round-robin'** – refusing to accept the Treaty as it stood. There were some objections to the Treaty itself, but the main objection was to the League of Nations and Article Ten of the Covenant (the clause on collective security). For many Americans this would involve their being dragged into Europe's wars, which were really none of their concern. Wilson made some changes but Article Ten continued to be the sticking point. In an effort to raise support in the country for the Treaty and the League, Wilson went on a speaking tour. Already ill from the stress of the Conference itself, the tour proved too much and Wilson suffered a severe stroke, which was to leave him infirm for the rest of his life. The Treaty was amended in the Foreign Relations Committee, so when it went to the Senate to be voted on Wilson insisted that the Democrats vote against it. He would not accept the Treaty with the amendments. The Treaty failed to get the necessary two-thirds majority vote for **ratification**. A peace was signed with Germany, but for all Wilson's efforts and insistence that the League of Nations be written into the treaties, the United States never joined.

Ratification: Vote in the Senate giving legal recognition to a treaty. The vote must have a two-thirds majority to pass.

United Nations: Organisation formed after the Second World War. It tries to encourage international peace, cooperation and friendship.

Had Wilson handled the Republicans better, or been more willing to compromise, he might have got the League of Nations accepted. Undoubtedly, the absence of the United States was fatal to the League, but America's presence would no more have been a guarantee against war than its presence in the **United Nations** has been. The Treaty of Versailles had many faults:

● Self-determination set up the weak 'successor states' in Eastern Europe which would fall to the Nazis in the 1930s.

● The 'mandates' allowed powers like Britain to maintain imperialist control of areas like the Middle East, but under a different name.

● The treaty overall created a fierce resentment in Germany and a determination among all political parties to see it destroyed.

However, Wilson did achieve many of the Fourteen Points. The Treaty of Versailles was, of necessity, a compromise between the conflicting demands of the victorious powers. Most historians agree it was a bad treaty: harsh enough to create resentment but not harsh enough to prevent a resurgence of German power. Yet Wilson is not wholly to blame for this. He made mistakes, but so did Lloyd George, Clemenceau and Orlando. The collapse of the settlement was as much an outcome of the events of the 1920s as of the Treaty itself.

The Wars of Intervention

One result of the First World War had been two revolutions in Russia. November 1917 had seen the Bolsheviks take control and pull Russia out of the War. But rather than returning to peace, Russia was plunged into civil war between the Bolsheviks and their enemies. British and French troops were sent to Russia, partly to reclaim supplies they had sent to an ally who had now pulled out of the fight, but also because they supported the anti-Bolshevik cause. The Japanese also sent troops to Vladivostok. In March 1918, Wilson sent 7,000 American troops to Russia, from where they were not finally removed until 1920. They had little effect on the civil war, so why did Wilson send them?

1. In what ways did the USA contribute to the Allied victory in the First World War?

2. How far did President Wilson achieve his aims at the Paris Peace Conference?

One reason was to support his Allies. The British and French had felt betrayed by Russia's withdrawal and wanted to help defeat the Bolsheviks and possibly bring Russia back into the War. Wilson was showing his support for them by backing their efforts. There was also concern that the Japanese might use the 'Wars of Intervention' to gain territory in the East and Wilson wanted to prevent this. It may also have been, as Lenin had suggested, that the capitalist nations wished to crush Communism at birth. Whatever Wilson's motives, it led to many hundreds of American casualties for no perceptible gain to the USA. More damagingly, it left the Russians with a mistrust of the Americans that was to continue right through to the Cold War.

Source-based questions: President Wilson and the First World War

SOURCE A

The people of the United States are drawn from many nations, and chiefly from the nations now at war. It is natural and inevitable that there should be the utmost variety of sympathy and desire among them with regard to the issues and circumstances of the conflict. Some will wish one nation, others another, to succeed in the momentous struggle. It will be easy to excite passion and difficult to allay it. Those responsible for exciting it will assume a heavy responsibility, responsibility for no less a thing than that the people of the United States, whose love of their country and whose loyalty to its government should unite them as Americans all, bound in honour and affection to think first of her and her interests, may be divided in camps of hostile opinion, hot against each other, involved in the war itself in impulse and opinion if not in action.

Such divisions amongst us would be fatal to our peace of mind and might seriously stand in the way of the proper performance of our duty as the one great nation at peace, the one people holding itself ready to play a part of impartial mediation and speak the counsels of peace and accommodation, not as a partisan, but as a friend.

President Wilson's Declaration of Neutrality, 19 August 1914

SOURCE B

Unless the Imperial Government should now immediately declare and effect an abandonment of its present methods of submarine warfare against passenger and freight-carrying vessels, the Government of the United States can have no choice but to sever diplomatic relations with the German Empire altogether.

President Woodrow Wilson to the German government, 19 April 1916

SOURCE C

On the first of February we intend to begin submarine warfare unrestricted. In spite of this, it is our intention to endeavour to keep neutral the United States of America.

If this attempt is not successful, we propose an alliance on the following basis with Mexico: That we shall make war together and together make peace. We shall give general financial support, and it is understood that Mexico is to re-conquer the lost territory in New Mexico, Texas and Arizona. The details are left to you for settlement.

Note from the German Foreign Minister, Zimmermann, to the German Minister to Mexico, 19 January 1917

Source-based questions: President Wilson and the First World War

SOURCE D

We have loaned many hundreds of millions of dollars to the Allies in this controversy. While such action was legal and countenanced by international law, there is no doubt in my mind but the enormous amount of money loaned to the Allies in this country has been instrumental in bringing about a public sentiment in favour of our country taking a course that would make every bond worth a hundred cents on the dollar and making the payment of every debt certain and sure. Through this instrumentality and also through the instrumentality of others who have not only made millions out of the war in the manufacture of munitions, etc., and who would expect to make millions more if our country can be drawn into the catastrophe, a large number of the great newspapers and news agencies of the country have been controlled and enlisted in the greatest propaganda that the world has ever known to manufacture sentiment in favour of war.

Speech by Senator George W. Norris in opposition to Wilson's War Message, 1917

SOURCE E

The committee finds, further, that the constant availability of munitions companies with competitive bribes ready in outstretched hands does not create a situation where the officials involved can, in the nature of things, be as much interested in peace and measures to secure peace as they are in increased armaments.

While the evidence before this committee does not show that wars have been started solely because of the activities of munitions makers and their agents, it is also true that wars rarely have one single cause, and the committee finds it to be against the peace of the world for selfishly interested organisations to be left free to goad* and frighten nations into military activity.

Report of the Special Committee on Investigation of the Munitions Industry (The Nye Report), 24 February 1936

*goad = provoke

1. Read Source A. What reasons does President Wilson give for the need for Americans to remain neutral in the War?

2. Read Source B. What had led President Wilson to issue this warning to Germany?

3. Read Sources D and E. What support is there in Source D for the view of the Nye Commission on the role of the arms industry in the outbreak of war?

4. How valuable are Sources D and E to a historian studying the causes of the First World War?

5. Using all the sources and your own knowledge, assess the extent to which submarine warfare led to American entry into the First World War.

7.7 How far was the USA 'isolationist' between the two world wars?

By 1920, Wilson was ill and had failed to gain American approval for his aims to create a new world order. In the 1920 presidential election, the uninspiring James Cox represented the Democrats. The Republicans comfortably regained control of Congress and the White House, under Warren G. Harding. Both Harding and his successor, Calvin Coolidge, believed America's role in the world was primarily economic, not political. This led to the foreign policy of the inter-war years being called 'isolationist'. While it is certain that the American people and governments of the 1920s and 1930s desired to stay out of European affairs, America's economic influence and its interests in Latin America and the Far East meant that it continued to be a player on the world stage, albeit a reluctant one.

Isolation in the 1920s

America's turning in on itself can be seen in several of the policies it pursued in the 1920s. Immigration restrictions, such as the Quota Act 1921 and the Johnson–Reed Act 1924, reflected Coolidge's view that 'America must be kept American'. Although the legislation was primarily a response to domestic pressure, it was indicative of the mood of the times that the rest of the world was not really of concern to America. Likewise, tariff polices reflected this new mood. The Fordney–McCumber Act 1922 introduced the highest **import tariffs** in US history in order to protect American goods from foreign competition.

Import tariffs: Taxes on goods coming into a country.

While legislation of this kind was motivated by domestic considerations, it does indicate that in the inter-war period the United States was looking inwards rather than outwards. Also, these measures affected its foreign policy. The immigration laws, particularly the clauses cutting Asian immigration, were interpreted as racist. They worsened relations with Japan. The high tariffs made it difficult for European economies to grow by cutting off the American market to their goods. Both of these problems were to worsen significantly in the 1930s. (Even when Hitler came to power and began persecuting Jews, the American government refused to relax the immigration laws, letting in only 60,000 Jewish refugees between 1933 and 1938.)

Yet even in the Republican era of the 1920s, the United States could not be said to be totally isolationist. Although American observers refused to join the League of Nations, they attended more than 40 meetings of the assembly, and the USA supported much of the work done by the League in areas such as health. The USA was a member of the International Labour Organisation, which monitored labour conditions throughout the world and worked to improve them. However, proposals for full membership of the World Court were defeated in the Senate in 1935.

Economic considerations meant the USA could not fully retreat from world affairs. In some ways, they did not want to. All three Republican Presidents of the decade – Warren Harding, Calvin Coolidge and Herbert Hoover – believed that a strong world economy, governed by free trade, was the best guarantee of peace. Ironically, their own protectionist policies made this more difficult.

The United States emerged from the First World War with the strongest economy in the world and a larger share of world trade. The economies of Europe, on the other hand, were devastated by four years of fighting and they owed enormous sums, principally to the USA. The Senate estimated that America was owed $22 billion dollars. To pay this back, the European nations needed to expand their trade, but American tariffs made this difficult. There was a feeling among some European countries that, as an ally in the War, the Americans should have written off this money, but the feeling in America was very different. For one thing it was a vast amount. As Coolidge said, 'they hired the money didn't they'. There was also a fear that if the debt was written off the money would simply be used to buy arms. However, the need to pay back the loans meant the Allies had to press hard on Germany for reparations.

In 1922, the Germans had announced that they could not pay the next instalment of the $33 billion they owed. This led, the following year, to an invasion by the French and Belgian armies of the heavily industrialised Ruhr area of Germany in an attempt to get the coal and steel they felt they were owed. The German government responded with a policy of 'passive resistance', where they refused to cooperate with the invaders. Production shut down and **hyperinflation** resulted. The crisis was causing the collapse of the German economy and relations between the French and

Hyperinflation: Extremely severe price rises.

Belgians and the German people threatened to break into violence or all-out war the longer the occupation went on. No one wanted to see a resumption of the war, least of all America, so a conference was organised in 1924 to sort out the problem.

The conference was presided over by Charles Dawes, a Chicago banker. The solution it came up with was to reschedule Germany's repayments. The USA was to grant $200 million in loans to Germany in order to help them rebuild their industry and enable them to pay the reparations. Secretary of State Charles Evans Hughes made a tour of European capitals to encourage support for the Plan. It was accepted and the crisis came to a peaceful end. (Four years later a further conference, again presided over by the Americans, came up with the Young Plan, which cut reparation payments to $9 billion to be paid over 59 years.) Even though the issue was primarily economic and the loans were made by private bankers not by the US government, these ties meant that though the Americans might like to believe they had removed themselves from European affairs it was not so simple.

Disarmament was another area in which the USA played a world role. After the War, disarmament was popular with the populations of most of the combatant countries as a way of avoiding another war. For the Republicans it also had the advantage of allowing them to cut military spending and, therefore, cut taxes. At the Washington Naval Conference 1921–1922, three agreements were signed. The first set limits on naval capacity regarding battleships. There was to be a ratio of $5:5:3:1\frac{3}{4}:1\frac{3}{4}$ for the navies of the United States, Britain, Japan, France and Italy respectively. In fact, the American navy was still considerably smaller than the British, so they were encouraging others to cut their capacity while not having to cut their own. A further conference, in London in 1930, made a similar agreement over cruisers and destroyers, with ratios of $10:10:7$ and $10:10:6\frac{1}{2}$ for America, Britain and Japan.

Also at Washington a Four-Power Treaty was signed between the USA, Britain, Japan and France agreeing to consult on matters in the Pacific. A further Nine-Power Treaty was signed, in which the signatories agreed to respect the territorial position of China.

These agreements were popular and allowed the Republicans to cut military spending. They also prevented a naval race of the kind that, it was believed, had led to the First World War. To some extent, they also eased tensions in the Pacific where Japanese expansion was a concern. But again Japan resented the way it had been put in an inferior position to the other powers. Also, none of the agreements had enforcement clauses. When the Nine-Power Treaty was broken in the 1930s, the Americans did nothing.

The problem of enforcement lay at the root of America's reluctance to get too involved in world affairs. In 1927, a conference in Geneva attempted to negotiate arms limitations for land armies, similar to those in the Washington Treaties. It was one thing for the French to agree to cuts in their navy, but quite another to agree to cuts in their army and without any guarantees of security against another German attack. Having rejected the League of Nations, the American Congress was hardly likely to give such a guarantee – and the conference broke up. But the desire for peace was real.

In 1928, the French Foreign Minister Aristide Briand and US Secretary of State Frank B. Kellogg signed an agreement renouncing war. The Kellogg–Briand Pact condemned 'recourse to war for the solution of international controversies and [renounced] it as an instrument of national policy'. Two million people signed petitions supporting the Pact and 62 countries signed it. Yet for all its popularity, it meant little. It had no mechanism for enforcement and, before the Senate gave it its 85–1 approval, they made it clear that signing the Pact would have no effect on

Repudiated: Disowned, saying
something no longer applies.

Clark Memorandum: State
Department document issued in
1930 laying out America's policy
towards Latin America.

the Monroe Doctrine or on America's self-defence. The principles behind
the agreement were commendable, but it was no more than an expression
of hope for a peaceful world. In practice, it had no effect whatever.

One area of the world where the Americans took a more active interest was Latin America. Yet the 1920s saw a change. Between 1922 and
1925, American troops were withdrawn from Cuba, the Dominican
Republic and Nicaragua. In 1921, Colombia was paid $25 million
compensation for America's role in the Panamanian revolution. Hoover
made a goodwill tour of Latin America in 1930 and the Roosevelt
Corollary (see section 7.3) was officially **repudiated** in the **Clark
Memorandum**. When revolutions broke out or debts were defaulted on,
Hoover took no action. Yet this was only part of the policy of 'isolation'.
America's chief concern in 1930–31 was the worsening Depression, not
Latin American revolts. In some areas those revolts produced governments more to America's liking, such as Trujillo's dictatorship in the
Dominican Republic in 1924 and Samoza's in Nicaragua in 1925. Some
historians argue that the United States could afford to interfere less
politically in Latin America because they had established American
economic power in the area so effectively. For example, in the 1930s,
two-thirds of Cuban sugar production was owned by American
companies, as was half of all Venezuelan oil production. As shown by
David Ryan, in *US Foreign Policy in World History* (2000), by 1929
American investments in Latin America were worth $3.52 billion.

America responded to the experience of the First World War with a
determination to stay out of the entanglements of other countries. To an
extent they succeeded, though their economic power and ties still gave
them enormous influence. In the 1930s, the Great Depression encouraged
them to be even more inward looking at a time when the deteriorating
international situation meant they had to take more notice of the outside
world.

Franklin D. Roosevelt's foreign policy

Understandably, FDR's first few years were focused on domestic issues.
With 25% of the workforce unemployed, the Great Depression was the
worst domestic crisis faced by any American government. The Depression
was a worldwide phenomenon and might have been tackled internationally.
Instead the United States pursued its own interests. In 1930, Congress had
passed the Smoot–Hawley Tariff Act, increasing tariffs even further than the
1922 Act. This discouraged international trade when it needed to be
increased. Rather than help the USA, it meant Europeans could not buy up
American agricultural surpluses. A world economic conference, in 1930,
collapsed when Roosevelt announced that the United States would pursue
its own tariff policy. To an extent, he was responding to the Ottawa
Conference of the year before where Britain had made an agreement that
gave preference to trade within its own Empire. This economic isolationism
encouraged still further American political isolationism. In 1934, however,
the Trade Agreements Act allowed the signing of tariff agreements with 18
countries, mainly in Latin America.

Roosevelt largely continued the Republican policy of reducing American
involvement in Latin America. In 1933, at a conference in Montevideo,
Roosevelt signed an agreement not to interfere in the internal and external
affairs of other Latin and South American states. The following year, the
Platt Amendment was finally removed, giving control of their own state
back to the Cubans.

As before, this new mood had its limits. When the radical Cuban
government of San Martín was replaced by the Batista regime, it was with

the active support of the American ambassador and an American warship. Fulgencio Batista's government trampled on the rights and freedoms of the Cuban people, but it was supported because it encouraged American investment.

The new mood also had no effect on the Monroe Doctrine, which continued to be American policy. However, by the late 1930s, the Americans had reason to be worried by European intervention on the continent. The **fascist** governments of both Italy and Germany made no secret of their desire for influence in South America. To improve ties, therefore, a Pan-American Conference was held in Lima in 1938. It was agreed that all 21 republics of the continent would consult in the event of a threat to any of them. So, although many Nazi war criminals may have fled to South America after the War, at no point was American influence in the Western Hemisphere seriously threatened.

From 1933, the real danger spot as far as Roosevelt was concerned was Europe. There was support in the USA for the Nazi Party and its succession to power, notably from the **German-American Bund**. However, most Americans saw it as being none of their concern who ran Germany. The public mood continued to be strongly isolationist. As Nazi aggression increased tension in Europe throughout the 1930s, Americans became more determined than ever to ensure they were not dragged into conflict as they had been in 1917.

The publication, in 1934, of the report of the Nye Committee into the causes of the First World War increased this determination. The Committee blamed the War on the lobbying of arms manufacturers keen to increase their profits. In a poll, 70% of Americans said that looking back they should never have joined the War. In 1936, half a million American students took part in a boycott of classes as part of a 'peace strike'. But the Americans were not the only ones hoping for peace. In a debate in the Oxford Union, British students voted to support a motion that 'this house will in no circumstance fight for its King and country'.

In the 1936 election, Roosevelt promised to keep the United States out of any war, but Wilson had made similar promises so Congress passed a series of neutrality acts in the 1930s in an attempt to prevent a repeat of the circumstances that led to American involvement. The 1935 Neutrality Act provided for an **arms embargo** on any warring nations and allowed the President to warn Americans against travelling on their ships. The 1936 Neutrality Act prohibited loans to **belligerents** and in 1937 Americans were banned from travelling on the ships of belligerent nations. The economic ties to the Allies in the First World War, as well as the role of the 'Lusitania', were clearly on the minds of the legislators.

In the meantime, the situation worsened in Europe. In 1935, the Nazis re-introduced conscription and announced a rearmament programme. The following year, the Rhineland was re-occupied. All of this was in breach of the Versailles Treaty. No one in Europe was inclined to take action any more than the Americans were. In 1936, the fascist nations of Germany, Italy and Japan came into alliance through the Anti-Comintern Pact. American economic interests in Europe and the Pacific could be threatened by the spread of fascism. When Roosevelt suggested, in 1937, the '**quarantining**' of warring nations, the reaction was very hostile and he backed down. The depth of isolationist feeling is illustrated by an attempt by Congressman Louis Ludlow to introduce a constitutional amendment requiring a **referendum** before the President could declare war. Roosevelt argued forcefully that such an amendment would completely tie a president's hands in the conduct of foreign policy, but it was only defeated by a narrow majority of 209–188 in the House.

Roosevelt realised the growing danger of war. In the spring of 1938, the

Fascist: Nationalistic political ideology, which aims to overthrow democracy and replace it with a dictatorship. Central to such groups is the heroic leader and the extensive use of propaganda.

German-American Bund: A pro-Nazi organisation made up largely of Americans descended from German immigrants.

Arms embargo: Political action in which pressure is placed upon other states to stop fighting by banning the sale of arms (weapons) to them.

Belligerents: Nations, states or groups waging war on others.

Quarantining: Cutting someone off from usual trade and relationships as if they were infected.

Referendum: A form of political consultation in which the electorate is asked for its response to a specific measure proposed by the government.

Appeasement: The policy of giving in to someone's demands in the hope that it will satisfy them and discourage further demands.

? *Why was isolationism popular with the American public in the 1920s and 1930s?*

Ed Murrow (1908–1965)
Respected journalist in radio and later in television. Reported from Europe in the 1903s and during the Second World War. After the War, he was a critic of the anti-communist hysteria and of McCarthy (see Chapter 11).

Nazis were 'invited' into Austria and it was clear Czechoslovakia was next. The President asked Hitler for a guarantee not to attack certain countries, but Hitler responded by making a joke of the request in a speech in the German parliament. A proposal to Britain for a conference to discuss the international situation was rejected. Britain, too, was anxious to avoid war but believed **appeasement** was the answer. The British Prime Minster, Neville Chamberlain, went to Munich and an agreement was reached with Germany gaining a large area of Czech territory, the Sudetenland. But Chamberlain knew that the 'piece of paper' Hitler had signed would not prevent war: it had merely bought time. Early in 1939, the German army took the rest of Czechoslovakia.

War in Europe was now on the cards. Roosevelt wanted to prepare America for the worst. He believed that the security of Europe was crucial to the security of America. He was able to persuade Congress to approve the Naval Expansion Act allowing a 20% increase in the US navy (although this would only take it up to the equivalent size of the German and Japanese navies). In 1939, he got an extra $525 million for air defence. At the start of the Second World War, however, the American army still only numbered 185,000.

Why did the USA become involved in the Second World War?

When Britain declared war on Germany, in September 1939, American sympathy was strongly on its side. Unlike Wilson, FDR made no attempt to appear neutral in attitude. Like him, many Americans felt that what happened to Britain could affect American security, and they set up groups such as The Committee to Defend America by Aiding the Allies. As in the First World War, there was still no desire among the general public to join in – as shown by the America First Group. To give some help, a neutrality act was passed allowing the British to buy American goods. But these had to be carried on British ships – hence the nickname the 'cash and carry' act – and America would grant no loans. The supplies were important to the Allied war effort, but they could not prevent the fall of France in 1940.

The speed with which the German army overran Western Europe shocked the American public. By June 1940, the Nazis were in control of Norway, Denmark, Holland, Belgium and France. Through the summer and autumn, the Battle of Britain was fought, with Britain and its Empire standing alone against the Nazi threat. The broadcasts of journalist Ed Murrow from London during the Blitz did much to communicate to Americans the intensity of the struggle taking place.

A Europe controlled by Nazi Germany would not only be bad for American trade, it also represented a strategic threat. The USA now began to step up its defensive preparations. The army was expanded in September under the Selective Service and Training Act, which introduced America's first peacetime conscription. It required all men aged 21–36 to register. The air force was also increased and the National Defence Research Committee was set up to produce new weapons, beginning a process that would culminate in the development of the atom bomb. Although America was preparing itself, it was Britain who needed aid. Roosevelt wanted to help but the Neutrality Acts and the forthcoming election prevented him. He managed to get around the terms of the various Neutrality Acts in order to swap 50 old First World War destroyers for naval bases in British colonies. The move was criticised on many sides. To Americans, Roosevelt was evading Congressional legislation while, to the British, he had taken advantage of their plight. Nevertheless, Roosevelt had provided 50 more ships for Britain.

Warmonger: Someone who encourages people to expect war, or someone who tries to get a war started.

Wendell Willkie (1892–1944)
Lawyer, businessman and politician. Willkie started out as a Democrat but later became a Republican. A popular man, he supported FDR's government during the War. He spoke out and wrote in favour of international cooperation.

Tyranny: Cruel and unjust rule by a person or small group of people who have absolute power over everyone else in their country or state.

In the 1940 election, both Roosevelt and the Republican candidate Wendell Willkie supported the British in the War. Both were aware of public opinion. Willkie presented Roosevelt as a **warmonger** and Roosevelt responded by promising not to send American soldiers to fight in Europe. Willkie was a popular candidate and he did very well, but he was running against an even more popular man who, many believed, had rescued America from the Depression. Roosevelt was elected for an unprecedented third term.

In March 1941, Roosevelt was able to persuade Congress of the importance to America of helping Britain. The Lend–Lease Act allowed the United States to lend or lease arms, supplies, food etc. to any nation if it was felt that country's defence was necessary for the defence of America. Congress voted for the Act 317–71 in the House and 60–31 in the Senate. Even at this stage there was no desire among the American public to join the War, but there was a feeling that this was different from the First World War. The Nazi regime was clearly destructive, if not evil, while Britain could still call on the ties of history, language and friendship with America. When Hitler attacked the Soviet Union in June 1941, lend–lease was immediately extended to the Russians. There is no doubt that American aid was a crucial factor in Britain's survival.

Step by step, throughout 1941, Roosevelt increased support for Britain, especially at sea. His critics accused him of trying to take America into the war by stealth. While he may not have been guilty of this, there is no question he was giving as much help as he could short of entering the war. In April, the western half of the Atlantic was declared a neutral zone allowing American ships to patrol it and pass on information to the Royal Navy about German shipping. This was later extended to cover routes as far as Greenland and Iceland. When the Germans fired on the 'Greer' on 4 September, Roosevelt responded by ordering German U-boats to be sunk on sight. The stakes were raised, in October, by the sinking of the 'Kearney' and the 'Reuben James', killing 126 Americans. Congress voted 212–194 and 50–37 to repeal the Neutrality Acts and allow merchant ships to be armed. The closeness of the vote shows the unease among many congressmen and senators. It also showed the fear that, just as in 1917, the United States was being sucked into a war 2,000 miles away due to its naval policies.

The British Prime Minister, Winston Churchill, still hoped to persuade the Americans to join the fight. He and Roosevelt met on a ship off the Newfoundland coast in August. Roosevelt would not declare war, but he did promise to help the fight against **tyranny**. The two men also agreed on a set of war aims, which became known as the 'Atlantic Charter'. Like Wilson's Fourteen Points, the Charter talked of self-determination, free access to trade, freedom of the seas and disarmament. It included clauses on economic collaboration and freedom from want. They were, in fact, laying the foundations of the United Nations.

By the end of the year, America had joined the War. Hitler declared war on the USA in support of his allies, the Japanese. They were at war with the United States because of their attack on Pearl Harbor.

Pearl Harbor

Relations with Japan had been deteriorating since the 1920s; in the 1930s, they worsened. In 1931, the Japanese invaded Manchuria. In fact, they already had many links to this part of China through investments and control of the South Manchurian railway. Like America, Japan was suffering the effects of Depression, and the pressure from its rapidly growing population meant that it was looking for expansion in Asia. However, the invasion broke the nine-power agreement to respect the territory of China

Puppet-state: Control of one state by the government of another (i.e. someone else 'pulling the strings').

and the Covenant of the League of Nations. The League was found to be fatally weak, but the Americans took no action either other than refusing to recognise the **puppet-state** of Manchukuo (formerly Manchuria) which the Japanese had established.

China was in no state to defend itself against Japanese expansion. They had their own internal conflicts and by 1937 had descended into civil war. The Japanese took advantage of the chaos to attack. The Americans were keen to support China but were no more anxious to go to war in the Far East than they had been in Europe. Likewise, the Japanese did not want to draw the United States into a war. When they sank the US gunboat 'Panay', they apologised immediately and paid an indemnity. Roosevelt protested about the invasion but took no action. As the Japanese made further inroads, the American government worried for its trade and the open door policy. In 1938, they loaned $25 million to the Chinese, and increased it to $250 million two years later.

Japanese ambitions went beyond China. They spoke of creating a Greater East Asia Co-Prosperity Sphere while expanding into the Dutch East Indies and French Indo-China. When they formed a military alliance with Germany in 1940, Roosevelt took action. He feared that if America found itself in the War it would not have a big enough navy to fight in both oceans. Trying to make the Japanese pull back, America banned a number of exports and only allowed the sale of oil with a licence. Rather than have the desired effect, however, it made relations worse.

In July, Roosevelt froze all Japanese assets in the USA and closed the Panama Canal to Japanese shipping. The turning point came in August, when they banned oil exports. Without access to foreign oil, Japan could fight for no more than 18 months. On both sides there were real attempts to

Does this picture tell you anything about America's ability to fight Japan after Pearl Harbor?

Pearl Harbor, 7 December 1941

negotiate a peace. Japan offered to withdraw from South East Asia if the Americans would unfreeze their assets, allow oil to flow and cease their aid to Chiang in China. Roosevelt refused. If he agreed it would leave China extremely vulnerable and he was not prepared to do this. In spite of this failure, many in the government in Tokyo wanted to continue the search for a peaceful settlement but, in October, Tojo became Prime Minister and the voice of the military was now the loudest. They believed that if Japan were going to have to fight America, then their only hope was a surprise attack.

If Japan was to fight the USA it would be a war at sea, in the Pacific. Pearl Harbor in Hawaii was America's most important Pacific base. The Japanese hoped that the surprise attack would destroy the power of the US navy and thereby weaken America's ability to fight.

On 7 December 1941 – which Roosevelt famously called 'a day that will live in infamy' – 350 planes launched from six carriers attacked the US naval base at Pearl Harbor. In fact, the American military had cracked the Japanese codes in November and knew an attack was imminent, but they did not know where. They expected it to be in the Philippines. When the young radar operator on duty spotted the planes, they were believed to be American B-17s. As luck would have it several US Navy ships, including aircraft carriers, were out of port that Sunday morning on exercise. This saved hardware, which was to prove vital in the War. Even so, eight battleships, three cruisers and three destroyers were sunk. Hundreds of planes were bombed as they sat on the airfields and more than 2,000 Americans were killed. The following day, with only one dissenting voice, the US Congress gave Roosevelt the authority to declare war on Japan. Three days later, on 11 December 1941, Hitler declared war on the United States.

1. In what ways did Japanese–American relations worsen between 1937 and 1941?

2. Why did the United States enter the war in 1941 and not in 1939?

7.8 What role did the USA play in achieving Allied victory in the Second World War?

The United States had been supporting Britain in various ways for over a year, but they were not ready to take a full part in the War. The War Powers Act 1941 gave the President wide-ranging powers and he used them to mobilise the American population and economy for total warfare. Boards were set up to control labour, production and prices. In 1943 the Office of War Mobilisation was set up under James Byrne, who did a similar job to that done by Baruch and the War Industries Board in the First World War. The Second World War saw a massive growth in federal government and federal power.

When America entered the War, this time as an ally, things were not going well. The Germans controlled most of Europe – from the Atlantic coast to the Balkans – and were occupying large areas of the Soviet Union and North Africa. In the East, the Japanese expansion was rapid. By May 1942, they had taken Guam, Wake Island, the Dutch East Indies, Singapore, Hong Kong and the Philippines. Roosevelt knew the American public wanted to focus on Japan and take revenge for Pearl Harbor, and it was in the Pacific theatre that the **Axis**' advance was stopped. However, Churchill was able to persuade the President that the military focus should be on defeating Hitler in Europe.

Axis: The name given to the alliance between Germany, Italy and Japan during the Second World War.

The War in Europe

There were many arguments between the Allied political and military leaders during the War. At the beginning, they focused on tactics. As well as arguing for the concentration on Europe, Churchill also argued for an attack in the Mediterranean and not in France. The Russian leader, Joseph

Stalin, was keen for the Allies to open a 'second front' in the West to take pressure off the Red Army. But Churchill persuaded Roosevelt that any second front would take a long time to plan fully. In the meantime, an attack on Italy, the weakest Axis power, would be more effective. (This delay in organising the second front was to cause much suspicion between the Great Powers but, given how close the D-Day landings were to failure, an early attack might have delayed victory even longer.)

In October 1942, the first important Allied victory of the War occurred when Montgomery's troops defeated the Germans at El Alamein and began to push them out of Egypt. In November, General Dwight D. Eisenhower led Allied landings in North Africa at Oran, Algiers and Casablanca. The weakness of American preparation was clear, but they soon learned and they had talented leadership under General 'Blood and Guts' Patton. With American and British soldiers advancing from the West and the British Eighth Army advancing from the East, the Germans and Italians were trapped. In May 1943, around 250,000 Axis soldiers in Tunisia surrendered.

Controlling North Africa both allowed the Allies to maintain control of the Suez Canal and gave them a launching point for the attack on Italy. Sicily was attacked from the sea and the air in July, and fell quickly. From there they moved on to the Italian peninsula itself, taking Naples in October 1943. It seemed the victory would be quick and easy but, though the Italians surrendered in September, the German army moved in to take control. They proved to be a more effective adversary. The Americans had heavy fighting around Monte Cassino and it was not until 1944 that Rome finally fell and Italy was taken.

1943 was a crucial year in the War. Not only were there victories in North Africa and Italy, but the Battle of the Atlantic had turned. The 'wolf packs' of German U-boats had been very effective in sinking Allied shipping. However, superior technology such as radar (developed by Britain), sonar, depth charges etc., and above all the ability of American shipyards to replace ships as fast as they were being sunk, kept the supply lines of the Atlantic open. This kept Britain fed and allowed the build-up of men and equipment ready for D-Day.

1943 was also the year of the victory at Stalingrad. This was easily one of the worst battles of the war: at its height, life expectancy of the soldiers involved was three days. The Soviet victory in February began the retreat of the German army from the East.

In the West, little could be done until the Allies were prepared for the invasion. The bulk of the fighting in Europe until 1944 had fallen on the Russians. Allied air forces, however, played their part with the continuous bombing campaigns of Germany. The actual effect of these campaigns is debatable. They probably had little effect on German morale while costing the loss of 10,000 planes. A question frequently asked is why none of these bombing raids was conducted against the death camps of the **Holocaust**. The Allied leaders argued that bombing places like Auschwitz would take effort away from the main targets in Germany and the extra distance to Poland was difficult to manage. These arguments may have some truth, but there is little doubt that bombing the camps might have saved thousands of lives in the long run.

By 1944, the invasion was ready. On D-Day, 6 June 1944, it was launched. Over the next two weeks, over one million men were landed on the beaches of Normandy, but it was July before General Bradley's men finally broke through the German lines at St Lô. From there they advanced quickly and, in August, American soldiers liberated Paris. Then the Germans rallied and the Ardennes Offensive pushed the Americans back, echoing Ludendorff's gamble a quarter of a century earlier. At the

Holocaust: The mass murder of Jews by the Nazis (members of the Nationalist Socialist Workers' Party in Germany, led by Adolf Hitler) during the Second World War. The term was introduced by historians during the 1950s, as an equivalent to the Hebrew *hurban* and *shoah* meaning 'catastrophe'; but contemporary references to the Nazi atrocities as a 'holocaust' (meaning 'great slaughter') have overtaken the earlier meaning.

so-called Battle of the Bulge, the Americans lost 55,000 killed or wounded.

By 1945, the Allies were again on the advance and, in January, crossed into Germany. Tragedy came in April, but not on the battlefield. On 12 April, Franklin Roosevelt died. He had been elected for a fourth term just five months earlier, but his struggle against the Depression and the tyrannies of Japan and Germany had finally taken their toll. He was by no means a perfect leader in either peace or wartime and he made a lot of mistakes. In negotiations during the War he could be too idealistic and naïve, particularly regarding political and diplomatic issues. But any man who could work with, and stay on good terms with, such individuals as Churchill and Stalin, not to mention egos, was no fool. Roosevelt deserves much of the credit for keeping the Grand Alliance together during the Second World War. He managed to defend American interests, occasionally at the expense of the wider picture, but his support of Britain before 1941 was crucial to

---

Timeline of the USA and the Second World War

1941 (August) Meeting between Franklin Roosevelt and Churchill off Newfoundland, leading to signing of **Atlantic Charter**, which condemned aggression and proposed self-determination and collective security.

(December) Pearl Harbor and German declaration of war

1942 (January) UN Declaration putting forward proposals for new international organisation

(May) Battle of the Coral Sea

Surrender of the Philippines

(June) Battle of Midway Island

(November) Allied landings in North Africa

1943 (July) Allied invasion of Sicily

(November) **Tehran Meeting** between FDR, Churchill and Stalin, agreeing to post-war division of Germany and neutrality of Austria

1944 (June) D-Day landings

Fall of Rome

(July) **Bretton Woods conference** to discuss post-war economic settlements. Eventually leads to establishment of International Monetary Fund and World Bank.

(September) US soldiers land in Philippines

(December) Battle of the Bulge

1945 (February) Capture of Iwo Jima

Yalta conference – discussion of reparations from Germany, free elections in Poland and USSR agrees to join war against Japan

(April) Fall of Berlin

(May) German surrender

(July) **Potsdam conference** – meeting between Truman, Stalin and Attlee. Further discussion of German settlement.

(August) Dropping of atom bombs

(September) Japanese surrender.

Military campaigns in Europe, 1939–1945

UNION OF SOVIET SOCIALIST REPUBLICS

Caspian Sea

IRAN
25 August 1941

IRAQ
Pro-German Coup
April 1941
10 May 1941

SYRIA (France)

PALESTINE (British Mandate)
Tripoli · Beirut · Haifa · Jerusalem

TRANS-JORDAN

EGYPT
Alexandria
El Alamein Nov 1942
22 June 1941

LIBYA
Tobruk April 1941

TURKEY

Cyprus

Crete
20 May 1941

Mediterranean Sea

Black Sea

Azov
Nov 1942
Dec 1941

UKRAINE
Kiev Dec 1943

Crimea · Yalta · Odessa

Moscow · Stalingrad

Nov 1942
Dec 1942
Dec 1941

Leningrad Nov 1942
June 1944

ESTONIA · LATVIA · LITHUANIA

Minsk
22 June 1941
Late June 1944

ROMANIA
Ploesti

BULGARIA

GREECE
6 April 1941
27 April 1941

Ionian Sea

HUNGARY
Budapest Dec 1944

YUGOSLAVIA
Zagreb 6 April 1941

CZECHOSLOVAKIA
Dec 1944

POLAND
Warsaw
1 Sept 1939

Berlin

Adriatic Sea

ITALY
Salerno · Taranto 9 Sept 1943
Rome June 1944
Anzio 22 Jan 1944
3 Sept 1943

Sicily 10 July 1943
9 Sept 1943

Malta (British)

Corsica

Sardinia

TUNISIA
Tunis Nov 1942

ALGERIA (France)
Algiers 8 Nov 1942

MOROCCO (Spain)
Tangier · Gibraltar

MOROCCO (France)
Casablanca 8 Nov 1942

SPAIN

PORTUGAL

Balearic Islands

FRANCE
Paris 22 June 1940
Rouen 11 June 1940
Bordeaux
Marseilles 15 August 1944
11 June 1940

SWITZERLAND

GERMANY
Frankfurt Dec 1944
Hamburg 10 May 1940
10 May 1940

NETHERLANDS
Amsterdam
Brussels 11 June 1940

DENMARK
9 April 1940

NORWAY
British Landings in Norway April 1940

SWEDEN

Baltic Sea

UNITED KINGDOM
London
Edinburgh
6 June 1944

EIRE

North Sea

Atlantic Ocean

Bay of Biscay

Legend:

- Maximum extent of territory under Axis control
- Territory that remained under Soviet control
- Territory under Allied control by Dec 1942
- Neutral state
- Oil well and pipeline

▲▲▲ Soviet advance by date shown
▲▲▲ Western Allied advance by date shown
→ Allied advance with date
Axis advance by date shown
⇧ Axis advance with date

1000 miles
1000 km

Britain's ability to continue the fight. He left many complex issues for his successor, Harry Truman, to deal with, but Roosevelt is without doubt one of the greatest and most important presidents in America's history.

Roosevelt did not live to see the victory he had done so much to bring about but, on 7 May, the Germans surrendered. Full attention could now be turned to defeating the Japanese.

War in the Pacific

Although Germany fell first, the US Navy brought initial American victories in the Pacific. In May 1942, the Battle of the Coral Sea stopped the rapid Japanese advance and secured Australian safety. The Battle of Midway Island, the following month, resulted in the sinking of four Japanese carriers and the destruction of more than 300 planes. From then on, the Japanese were on the retreat. Coral Sea was a battle fought entirely by aircraft carriers, and illustrates the importance of luck in war. Had the American carriers not been out at sea when Pearl Harbor was attacked, the whole Pacific War could have been different.

Although the British took a major role in the war in the East on land (e.g. in Burma), the Pacific War was largely an American affair. The Americans launched a two-pronged attack across the Ocean led by Admiral Chester Nimitz in the North and General Douglas MacArthur in the South. They 'island hopped' their way to Japan. In August, American marines landed at Guadalcanal. But it took six months for the island to fall into their hands. Throughout the next year they fought for and captured islands including Tarawa and Saipan, the latter putting them within 1,500 miles of Japan itself. From there, air force B-29s launched firebombing raids on the Japanese mainland. Further naval battles in 1944 effectively destroyed the Japanese navy. The Battle of Leyte Gulf, in October 1944, was the largest naval battle in American history. It seemed that the war in the Pacific was to be the story of hard, but steady, advance.

The brutality and difficulty of the battles worried the American military. Guadalcanal had taken six months to capture. When the marines took control of Iwo Jima, they had more than 25,000 casualties and 21,000 Japanese were killed. Taking Okinawa cost even more. Japanese 'kamikaze' pilots had sunk more than 30 ships. It was believed the Japanese would fight equally hard to protect their homeland, meaning that their defeat would take at least another 18 months as well as cost an additional million lives. In July, Truman warned the Japanese that if they did not surrender unconditionally the Americans would unleash on them a new weapon. Atomic bombs were dropped on Hiroshima on 6 August and on Nagasaki three days later. Five days later Japan surrendered, the formal ceremony taking place on 'USS Missouri' on 14 September.

The decision to drop the bomb has been the subject of controversy ever since. The main argument has been that it was unnecessary and was done to stop Russian advances in the East. There is little doubt that Truman was influenced by a desire to contain Russia. It had been agreed at Yalta in February 1945 (see Chapter 8) that in return for its declaration of war on Japan the USSR would gain territory in Sakhalin and the Kurile Islands. It was feared that once war started it would advance quickly and capture not only Japanese territory, but also occupied areas such as Korea. If the Russians then held on to these areas it would upset the balance of power in the East. Russia declared war on 8 August and a second bomb, argued to be unnecessary by Truman's critics, was dropped the following day. Even Secretary of State James Byrnes admitted that the bomb would 'make Russia more manageable'. Though it was a factor, this had not been Truman's primary motive.

'Kamikaze': Suicide pilots who flew bomb-laden aircraft at American ships.

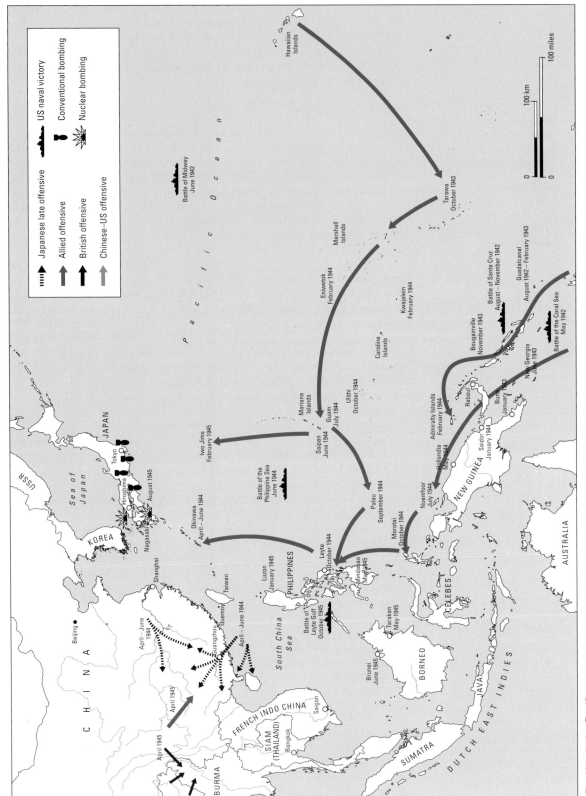

The Manhattan Project had spent $2 billion developing the bombs – among many new weapons developed during the Second World War to make victory more likely. It was hardly likely that given this investment they would not use the weapon once it had been tested successfully. The USA was in a race. Had the Germans developed the atomic bomb first there is little doubt that they would have used it.

It has sometimes been claimed that the United States had a racist motive for dropping the bombs on Japan. Even though their previous treatment of Asian peoples is hardly a record to be proud of, the atom bomb was initially developed for use against Germany. That it was ready for use only after the fall of Europe was simply a matter of timing.

The cost of taking the islands, and the perceived cost of taking Japan, was Truman's main motive. The War, as already stated, was expected to cost at least a million American lives and last another year. The use of the atom bomb was to end the War with the loss of as few American lives as possible. Even after the bombs had been dropped, it was five more days before the Japanese finally surrendered. Few soldiers in the Pacific at the time would have criticised Truman's decision.

1. With reference to the maps on pages 242 and 244, explain the contribution of the USA to the Allied victory.

2. Explain the reasons why Truman dropped the atom bombs on Japan in August 1945.

7.9 Why had the USA become a superpower by 1945?

Throughout the Second World War, the United States had been a full member of the Grand Alliance. They took part in the political and strategic discussions at Casablanca, Cairo and Tehran in 1943, at Yalta and at Potsdam. Unlike in the First World War, they were full Allies. But this time round, American involvement did not stop with the end of the war. The United States of America emerged from the Second World War as the world's leading nation, playing a full role in international affairs. Why was this so?

Firstly, the American contribution to the War had been crucial in the victory. It has been said that Britain provided the time, the Russians provided the blood and the Americans provided the money – there is some truth in this. The sheer size of the American economy and productive capacity was incredible. Fifteen million men and women served in the War; America produced 86,500 tanks, 300,000 aeroplanes and six million tons of bombs. The list goes on. Sixty per cent of the world's oil production and 50% of the world's steel production was American. Its GNP had doubled and the value of its agricultural land had increased by $2 billion. Rather than fall back into Depression, as many feared, the ending of the War saw the American economy continue to grow. By the end of the Second World War the USA was the economic superpower of the world.

The economy was also technologically advanced thanks to the new developments of the War. There were new military technologies, such as radar, but also others such as the development of synthetic fuels and fabrics. And, of course, there was the atom bomb, which for the moment was an American monopoly.

This pre-eminence was added to by the destruction of Europe and Asia which the war had brought. Thirty million people had been killed (an incredible half of whom were Russian). There were more than 20 million refugees. Hundreds of cities and factories and acres of farmland throughout Europe and Asia had been destroyed. The economies of the European powers had been bankrupted by the cost of the War and their people were starving. The great European empires were also being lost.

The devastation left a **power vacuum** in the world, into which the Americans stepped. The crucial point was that this time round they were willing to do so. Even before the end of the War, the Atlantic

Power vacuum: A term used to describe a region in which no state exercises effective control. Such areas are always liable to be occupied by expansionist powers.

1. What do you understand by the term 'superpower'?

2. Why do you think the USA was regarded as a superpower by 1945?

Charter indicated a change of mood. When the United Nations was set up in 1945 at the San Francisco Conference, the Senate voted 89–2 to accept the Charter and American membership. Americans were worried by worldwide commitments and there continued to be an isolationist pull on their foreign policy, but their view of themselves and of their position in the world had changed. They had fought a war in which they were clearly the 'good guys' and now their power would enable them to shape the new order in their own image. Whether or not they would succeed, where Wilson had failed, remained to be seen. But there was no question that, in 1945, the United States was *the* superpower.

8 The USA and the Cold War in Europe, 1945–1991

8.1 Why did the Grand Alliance break down?

8.2 Historical interpretation: How far was Truman responsible for the development of the Cold War?

8.3 Why was Germany central to the Cold War in Europe?

8.4 How far did American–Soviet relations in Europe improve under Eisenhower?

8.5 How effectively did Kennedy pursue the Cold War in Europe?

8.6 How successful was Nixon's policy of *détente*?

8.7 How far did *détente* continue under Carter?

8.8 Why did the Cold War in Europe come to an end?

Key Issues

● Why did a Cold War develop between the United States and the Soviet Union?

● How did the USA attempt to contain the Soviet Union in Europe?

● How did US policy help bring about the end of the Cold War?

Framework of Events

1945	(February) Yalta Conference
	(July) Potsdam Conference
1947	Truman Doctrine
	Marshall Plan
	National Security Act
1948–1949	Berlin Blockade and Airlift
1949	North Atlantic Treaty Organisation
1955	(14 May) Warsaw Pact
	(July) Geneva Summit – Eisenhower meets Khrushchev
	Austrian State Treaty
	German re-armament
1956	Hungarian Revolution
1957	Launch of 'Sputnik'
1958	Berlin Crisis
1960	Paris Summit
	U-2 crisis
1961	Vienna Summit – Kennedy meets Khrushchev
	Berlin Wall Crisis
1969	Strategic Arms Limitation Talks begin in Helsinki
1972	Moscow Summit
	SALT I
1975	Helsinki Agreements
1979	SALT II
	Soviet invasion of Afghanistan
1980	Solidarity Movement begins in Poland
1982	Strategic Arms Reduction Talks (START) in Geneva
1986	Reykjavik Summit
1987	Intermediate-range Nuclear Forces (INF) Treaty
1989	(November) Fall of the Berlin Wall
	Velvet Revolution in Czechoslovakia
1990	Germany Re-unified
	Communists overthrown in Romania
1991	Collapse of Soviet Union.

Overview

T the end of the Second World War, the alliance between East and West, which had been so successful against the Nazis, began to break down. Fears and suspicions surfaced, creating a climate of mistrust between the United States and the Soviet Union. The imposition of communist governments on to eastern European states made the Americans fear for the freedom and security of Western Europe. As this would affect their trade and security, a policy of **containment** was established. It was the aim of the United States to halt the spread of communism throughout the world. The Soviets saw this as unnecessarily aggressive. The Second World War had cost the Soviet Union as many as 27 million lives. They were determined that they would not be attacked again from the west. To ensure their protection they established friendly, communist governments on their borders. This fear and hostility was not simply a product of events at the end of the War: the two superpowers had conflicting **ideologies** and world views, and both came to the conclusion, in the late 1940s, that the two ideologies could not live side by side. The next 45 years would be a struggle to win this conflict. In an age of nuclear weapons, conflict could not be allowed to become a war – so the Cold War was fought through propaganda, through the exercise of economic power, particularly by the Americans, and through the build-up of military strength in an arms race. Occasionally, the Cold War would turn 'hot' in some part of the world, but the Soviets and Americans never faced one another over a battlefield.

Containment: American policy for much of the Cold War, aimed at limiting the spread of world communism (see page 202). It was put forward by President Truman in April 1947 as the Truman Doctrine.

Ideologies: These are sets of beliefs about the world and how it works (e.g. communism; nationalism).

In 1947, President Truman set the tone for the Cold War with the Truman Doctrine and the Marshall Plan, which established the policy of containment in Europe. The following year, when the Soviets blockaded Berlin in an attempt to get the Allies to withdraw from the city, Truman successfully enacted his policy forcing the Soviet Union to back down. Containment was tried and succeeded again, though somewhat less successfully, two years later and 5,000 miles away in Korea (see Chapter 9).

When Eisenhower entered the White House in 1953, there was something of a change of policy. Though containment continued, the Americans took on a more aggressive tone, talking about 'rolling back' the borders of communism and liberating people from its grasp. However, in a world that now had the hydrogen bomb as well as the atom bomb, the stakes in the Cold War, and its costs, had been raised. The Americans also tried to pursue a policy of 'peaceful co-existence'. If the opportunity arose, they would try to free people from communism but, at the same time, make an effort to get on better with the Soviet Union and avoid possible conflict which could lead to nuclear war. Meetings at Geneva and Camp David went a long way to improving relations, but the bloody crushing of the Hungarian uprising by the Red Army in 1956 and the shooting down of an American spy plane in 1960 soured relations once again. When Kennedy became President in 1961, the Cold War was very tense.

Kennedy was determined to stand up to the Soviet Union as Truman had done. He did so by embarking on a massive arms build-up, and by responding to the Russian space programme by promising to put an American on the moon. Yet he also wished to continue the work begun by Eisenhower. Kennedy, too, travelled to Europe to meet the Soviet leader, Nikita Khrushchev, face to face in Vienna. After the building of the Berlin Wall in 1961, conflict over Europe had lessened notably. For Kennedy's successor, Lyndon Johnson, it was events in Vietnam, not in Europe, that took his attention.

By the time Nixon came to office in 1969, the danger of war in Europe seemed to be a thing of the past. The Cold War was by no means over, but the two sides had long had two alliance systems – NATO and the **Warsaw Pact** – protecting their interest and making war unlikely. Behind these two systems had been a massive build-up of arms. While in no way abandoning its hostility to communism, the American government launched a policy of *détente*. This looked back to Eisenhower's policy of peaceful co-existence, but this time was centred around talks to reduce nuclear weapons. It was a successful policy in that in the 1970s it produced SALT I and SALT II, the first agreements by the superpowers to limit nuclear weapons.

Many Americans, though, remained deeply suspicious of communism and believed that the Soviets were not abiding by their promises. Old fears of Soviet expansion were revived when they invaded Afghanistan in 1979. America's President Carter tried to take a firm stance, but there was little he could do beyond boycott trade and forbid American athletes from attending the Moscow Olympics. Ronald Reagan, the Republican President who took office in 1981, took a much firmer stance and embarked on the biggest arms build-up the world has ever seen. America's allies became very nervous that relations between East and West seemed worse than at any time since the 1940s. But things were different. Although he was determined to be strong, Reagan was also willing to talk to the Soviets and the 1987 Intermediate-range Nuclear Forces (INF) Treaty was the first arms agreement which actually dismantled some weapons rather than just limiting build-up. It was a very small change, but it was a start. The Soviet Union had a new leader, Mikhail Gorbachev, who knew that his country could not afford to compete against the Americans in another arms race. To do so would cause their economy to collapse. He also wanted to bring real change and openness to the Soviet Union, so improving relations with the United States was part of his policy. These policies led to demands for change throughout Eastern Europe, which were encouraged by the West. By 1989, these demands had become so strong that the Berlin Wall was torn down and communism throughout Eastern Europe collapsed. The Americans, it was claimed, had won the Cold War.

Warsaw Pact: The military alliance of Eastern bloc states created in 1955. It came into being one week after West Germany was allowed to join NATO.

Détente: Relaxation of tension between countries. Also characterised by increased cooperation and cultural exchanges, such as overseas tours by Soviet athletes and ballet companies, particularly to the USA.

Secretaries of State during the Cold War

Truman's Administration:	Edward R. Stettinus Jr (1945)
	James F. Byrnes (1945–47)
	George C. Marshall (1947–49)
	Dean Acheson (1949–53)
Eisenhower's Administration:	John Foster Dulles (1953–59)
	Christian A. Herter (1959–61)
Kennedy's Administration:	Dean Rusk (1961–63)
Johnson's Administration:	Dean Rusk (1963–69)
Nixon's Administration:	William P. Rogers (1969–73)
Ford's Administration:	Henry A. Kissinger (1973–77)
Carter's Administration:	Cyrus R. Vance (1977–80)
	Edmund Muskie (1980–81)
Reagan's Administration:	Alexander M. Haig Jr (1981–82)
	George P. Schulz (1982–89)
Bush Senior's Administration:	James A. Baker III (1989–92)

8.1 Why did the Grand Alliance break down?

What agreements were made at Yalta?

During the Second World War, the Americans, Soviets and British worked well together in their common fight against the Nazis. The friendship of the three greatest powers in the world was known as the 'Grand Alliance'. However, there were old suspicions and hostilities between the three and the leaders had to work hard to maintain cooperation. Roosevelt set great store by personal contact and throughout the War there were face-to-face meetings between the 'Big Three'. At their meeting in Yalta on 4–11 February 1945, Stalin, the Soviet leader, agreed to help the Americans in the East against Japan and to put pressure on the Chinese communists to end their civil war. Roosevelt also got Stalin's promise to support the setting up of the United Nations. In return, the Soviets demanded reparations for their losses in the war, a weakened Germany and land in Asia. Not everything was agreed to, but it was accepted that Germany would be divided between the Grand Alliance and the French, until its fate was decided. It was also accepted that each of the 'Big Three' would have a **sphere of influence**: the Union of Soviet Socialist Republics

Sphere of influence: An area of the world considered to be under the protection and control of a more powerful nation. That nation does not rule or own that area but has an accepted influence there so other nations should keep out.

Winston Churchill, Franklin Roosevelt and Josef Stalin at the Yalta Conference, February 1945

Josef Stalin, real name **Josef Vissarionovich Dzhugashvili (1879–1953)** Communist revolutionary; leader of the USSR (1928–53). He was responsible for modernising Russian industry and building up its military power so that it was able to fight when the war came. His continued build-up of military power and the control he established over Eastern Europe after the War meant Stalin turned the USSR into a superpower. He was also a ruthless dictator. To enforce his agricultural polices, thousands were sent to labour camps and he allowed no opposition: those who did criticise also went to the camps. In the 1930s and again after the war, Stalin launched a series of 'purges' where his enemies – real or imagined – were removed. Millions of people died in this terror, killed on the orders of their own leader.

Harry S. Truman (1884–1972)
From a Missouri farming family. He served in Europe during the First World War and entered local politics in the 1920s. Elected to the Senate in 1935, where he served for 11 years. Appointed Vice-President to Roosevelt in 1944 as a compromise man, someone who would offend no one: he was neither a **northern liberal** nor a **southern conservative** and was considered a moderate on most issues. On Roosevelt's death in 1945, Truman took office as President, serving for seven years. Truman was regarded by many in the Democratic Party as hard working but somewhat colourless.

Northern liberal: Liberals tend to be in favour of change and reform. In the USA, the North-East is more closely identified with this kind of view than other parts of the country.

Southern conservative: Conservatives tend to favour things the way they are. In the USA, although the Democratic Party was strong in the South, many there disliked the Party's liberal tendencies over certain issues, notably civil rights. They were suspicious of anything that seemed too left wing or tending towards giving the federal government too much power. Southern Democrats were also against segregation.

George Kennan (1904–)
US diplomat who worked extensively in Eastern Europe and USSR in the 1920s and 1930s. In 1946, he wrote the memorandum for President Truman advising the policy of 'containment' with regard to Soviet Communism – a view which he later rejected. Though he served as US Ambassador to the USSR briefly (1951) and Yugoslavia (1961–63), after 1949 he was primarily a lecturer and historian.

(USSR) in Eastern Europe, the United States in Western Europe and Britain in Greece. Roosevelt and Churchill were criticised for this. However, the fact was that the Red Army already controlled much of Eastern Europe, and the 'Big Three' could not afford to fall out while Germany and Japan still remained to be defeated.

Despite the agreements reached at Yalta, cracks in the Alliance had begun to appear, particularly over Poland. In 1944, the Red Army was close to liberating Warsaw, the Polish capital, so the Poles rose up against the Germans expecting aid from the Red Army. Instead the Russian advance halted and tens of thousands of Poles were killed by the Nazis, including many supporters of the Polish government-in-exile in London. This allowed Stalin to establish a pro-Soviet government there instead. At Yalta, though, he promised to allow free elections for the Poles. Many in the West doubted he would keep that promise, and he did not.

How did policy change when Truman came to power?

In April 1945, Russian and American troops met on the banks of the River Elbe and, within weeks, the Germans surrendered unconditionally. However, it was not Roosevelt who celebrated the victory but the new president, Harry S. Truman. As Roosevelt's Vice-President, he took office when FDR died on 12 April. According to historian William Chafe, in *The Unfinished Journey* (1986), 'few people were less prepared for the challenge of becoming president'. Even Truman himself said he felt as though the moon, stars and planets had fallen on him. Under Truman, American policy towards the Soviet Union became much tougher. When the 'Big Three' met in Potsdam in July and August 1945, little was agreed. It was determined that Japan had to surrender unconditionally, and more details about the division of Germany were discussed. Exactly what to do about Germany was a real problem (see section 8.4), but the changes in personnel made the discussion tense. (Churchill was also replaced when a general election in Britain put Clement Attlee in Downing Street.)

Truman was determined not be seen to be soft on communism. Anti-communism in the USA had subsided during the War but it quickly resurfaced, and Truman could not afford to ignore it. There had been criticism that FDR was too soft with Stalin. Truman did not want to suffer the same accusation. When Churchill made his famous speech in Fulton, Missouri, on 5 March 1946, saying that an iron curtain had descended across Europe, Truman was by his side nodding approvingly.

The desire to stand up to Stalin was encouraged by a 16-page memorandum written by George Kennan, a diplomat in Moscow. Kennan was a leading authority on the USSR so when Truman found himself having to deal with Stalin, he asked Kennan to give him some background and advice. Kennan said that conflict between the two powers was inevitable so there was no point in trying to get along. Instead, he advised a policy of containment (i.e. the United States should stand up to the USSR when they tried to expand aggressively). He also wrote an anonymous article in 'Foreign Affairs' magazine, in July 1947, in which he argued that 'the main element of any United States policy towards the Soviet Union must be that of a long-term patient but firm and vigilant containment of Russian expansive tendencies'. Many years later, Kennan said that he had been wrong and cooperation should have been tried, but at the time it was a popular view. Many Americans believed that given the chance the communists would try to take over Europe, so it was up to the USA to keep them to the areas they controlled already.

A 'Punch' cartoon of 1947. 'Punch' is a British political magazine.

?

1. What message is the cartoon trying to make about Stalin's policy in Eastern Europe?

2. Is the USA portrayed in a positive way in the cartoon? Explain your answer.

Totalitarian: Not allowing criticism or opposition. There is usually one party in control and people are rarely allowed to vote. The press and media are usually controlled and censored. Nazi Germany was a totalitarian state.

What other factors damaged the Grand Alliance?

Ideological thinking also affected the relationship between the USA and Russia. Truman saw communism as a **totalitarian** ideology. Communism was the opposite of what he believed in, which was American democracy and capitalism. The two were incompatible – a view which Stalin seemed to share. In a speech in 1946, he said that the two ideologies could not live side by side.

Economics were also a factor in the break-up of the Alliance. Truman believed that a communist-dominated world would be closed to American trade. American economic power at the end of the Second World War was as strong as its military power, but the United States feared slipping back into the Depression of the 1930s, so trade with Europe was essential. Although it had been involved in the War for four years, America had come nowhere near the extent of its industrial strength and had lost 405,400 men. The Soviet Union had lost 25 million people and more than 25% of their property. At the end of the War, the Americans gave loans of $3.75 million to help the Poles re-build their land, but nothing to the Soviets. Exploiting the resources of Eastern Europe was equally essential to the USSR for rebuilding its shattered economy. Both nations feared that the other wished to squeeze them out of Europe economically.

A major factor in the continued tension between the Soviet Union and the United States after the War was atomic power. America had decided on the dropping of the atom bomb on Japan in August 1945 without any reference to its allies. Stalin now believed that with this power the Americans could do just as they liked and would not abide by any agreements they made. Truman knew the Soviets were working on their own atom bomb. He did not want to get into an arms race, so the Baruch Plan was proposed in 1946. The proposal was for an international authority to control atomic power, together with the agreed destruction of existing nuclear weapons in stages, with the USA giving its up last. Unsurprisingly, the Soviets rejected it.

What was the Truman Doctrine and how did it come about?

This was the situation in 1946. The Grand Alliance was already in trouble and the USA were worried by the spread of communism in Eastern Europe to Poland, Hungary, Romania, Bulgaria, Yugoslavia and Albania. The Soviets had also taken direct control of the Baltic States – Latvia, Estonia and Lithuania. They also appeared to have their eye on the Mediterranean and on oil lands in the Middle East. In Iran, it had been agreed that all the allied armies there would leave within six months of the end of the war. The British did, but the USSR held on because they knew Britain and the USA had negotiated rights from the Iranian government to drill oil and they wanted the same rights. In the end, the Red Army was forced to leave and the Soviets failed, but to Truman it seemed yet more evidence of Soviet aggression.

In Greece, there was a civil war between monarchists and communists. Britain had been helping the monarchists but, in February 1947, they told the Americans that they could no longer afford to be involved. Truman believed the Greek communists were backed by the USSR. He felt the Americans had to prevent communist expansion in Greece and in Turkey (where the Soviet Union had soldiers stationed on the border). In fact, Stalin was abiding by the Yalta agreement and was not interfering in Greece, but the affair allowed Truman to make containment official American policy.

In a speech to Congress in May 1947, Truman said 'it must be the policy of the United States to support free peoples who are resisting **subjugation** by armed minorities or by outside pressures'. In other words, the United States was promising to help any country to fight communism, whether it was from internal revolution or from outside attack. This promise is known as the Truman Doctrine.

Subjugation: Conquest; being taken over by force.

In this speech to Congress, what reasons does Truman give for providing financial help to the Greek government?

Extract from Truman's speech to Congress

'The gravity of the situation which confronts the world today necessitates my appearance before a joint session of the Congress. The foreign policy and the national security of this country are involved.

The United States has received from the Greek Government an urgent appeal for financial and economic assistance.

The very existence of the Greek state is today threatened by the terrorist activities of several thousand armed men, led by Communists, who defy the government's authority at a number of points …

Meanwhile, the Greek Government is unable to cope with the situation. The Greek army is small and poorly equipped. It needs supplies and equipment if it is to restore the authority of the government throughout Greek territory. Greece must have assistance if it is to become a self-supporting and self-respecting democracy.

The United States must supply that assistance.

The peoples of a number of countries of the world have recently had totalitarian regimes forced upon them against their will.

At the present moment in world history nearly every nation must choose between alternative ways of life. The choice is too often not a free one.

One way of life is based upon the will of the majority, and is distinguished by free institutions, representative government, free elections, guarantees of individual liberty, freedom of speech and religion, and freedom from political oppression.

The second way of life is based upon the will of a minority forcibly imposed upon the majority. It relies upon terror and oppression, a controlled press and radio, fixed elections, and the suppression of personal freedoms.

I believe that it must be the policy of the United States to support free peoples who are resisting attempted subjugation by armed minorities or by outside pressures.

I believe that we must assist free peoples to work out their own destinies in their own way.

I believe that our help should be primarily through economic and financial aid, which is essential to economic stability and orderly political processes.

It is necessary only to glance at a map to realise that the survival and integrity of the Greek nation are of grave importance in a much wider situation. If Greece should fall under the control of an armed minority, the effect upon its neighbour, Turkey, would be immediate and serious. Confusion and disorder might well spread throughout the entire Middle East.

I therefore ask the Congress to provide authority for assistance to Greece and Turkey in the amount of $400,000,000 for the period ending 30 June 1948. In addition to funds, I ask the Congress to authorise the detail of American civilian and military personnel to Greece and Turkey …

The free peoples of the world look to us for support in maintaining their freedoms.

If we falter in our leadership, we may endanger the peace of the world – and we shall surely endanger the welfare of our own nation.'

To enforce the Truman Doctrine and to help Greece and Turkey, Truman asked Congress for $400 million. The Republican Congress was reluctant to spend this kind of money even to fight the communists, so Truman had to play up the communist threat. (This was an important factor in the rise of McCarthyism – see Chapter 11.) It worked. Congress approved the money and the communists in Greece were defeated. The Truman Doctrine was the basis of American foreign policy for the next 40 years.

In what ways was the Marshall Plan also part of containment?

After the First World War, America had insisted that countries which were still weak repaid money owed to them. This had been one of the contributing factors to the Depression, as economically weak nations could not trade. After the Second World War, this did not happen. The United Nations Relief and Rehabilitation Administration and the World Bank poured $9 billion into the shattered European economies. For economic, moral and political reasons, the United States also gave money to help

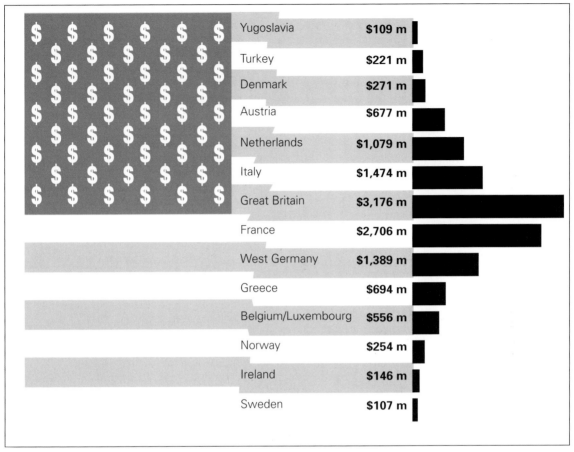

Marshall Aid to Europe
1947–1952

Europe recover. This was known as Marshall Aid. Seen as the economic counterpart of the Truman Doctrine, the idea came from George Marshall, the US Secretary of State.

Under the Marshall Plan or European Recovery Programme, the United States gave money to European states to rebuild their economies (see diagram). Over the next five years, $13.5 billion was paid out to 16 countries through the Organisation of European Economic Cooperation (OEEC). Aid was given in cash and in goods, some of which the USA controlled. For example, the OEEC asked for 67,000 tractors but got only half because American farmers feared European competition. In return for aid, recipients had to share some information about resources.

Why did Britain, France, West Germany and Italy receive the most money under Marshall Aid?

Marshall Aid was also offered to Eastern European countries including the USSR, but the Soviets would not accept it and would not allow their allies to accept. The Americans knew the USSR would never share economic information, so it was clear that they never wanted them to get Marshall Aid. George Marshall said the Plan was aimed against 'hunger, poverty, desperation and chaos'. Although he denied it, there was an element of anti-communism in it. Strengthening Western Europe would help it to stand up to the Soviet Union.

Truman was also concerned for US trade. As European states were trading with each other, Truman was afraid America would be kept out of

1. What agreements were made between the USA and the USSR at Yalta?

2. Explain the reasons why the Grand Alliance had broken apart by 1947. Which factors do you think were most important? Give reasons for your answer.

European markets. A third of the world's exports, in 1947, were from America: if Europe had more dollars to spend they might use them to buy more US goods. In fact, it became a condition of receiving aid that a certain percentage would be spent on American goods. Congress clearly agreed with him as the Economic Cooperation Act, which set up the Marshall Plan, was passed easily in both Houses of Congress (69–17 votes in the Senate and 329–74 in the House of Representatives).

The USSR retaliated with its own economic bloc, Cominform (the Communist Information Bureau). It was a propaganda effort more than anything because, in reality, they could not afford to give much to their allies. Marshall Aid was very important to Europe in helping the recovery from the Second World War. It also helped American trade. The aid was also about containing communism. Truman called the Marshall Plan and Truman Doctrine 'two halves of the same walnut'. By 1951, 80% of American aid to Europe was military.

8.2 How far was Truman responsible for the development of the Cold War?
A CASE STUDY IN HISTORICAL INTERPRETATION

During the Cold War itself, writers in the West blamed the Soviet Union for the disintegration in relations between East and West. It was argued that the USSR was aggressive and determined to build an empire in Europe, therefore the West had to stand up to them. There was a fear of Soviet expansion in both the USA and in Western Europe. Stalin had imposed communist governments on Eastern Europe. Also, the Red Army was the largest army in the world and, unlike the American army, had not been demobilised at the end of the war. This fear was also influenced by the Kennan memorandum and by American experience of the Second World War. Stalin was seen as the new Hitler. As Hitler had tried to do, Stalin would take over Europe if the United States did not stand up to him. The lesson many Americans learned from the war was that they must not appease dictators. Instead, they must be confronted and contained.

The collapse of communism, in 1991, and the opening up of Soviet archives have led many historians to see a pattern of aggression in Soviet behaviour in Europe. They argue that it was this aggression and America's response to it which created the Cold War. For instance, John Lewis Gaddis, a historian from Yale University, argues that Truman understood Russia's need to protect itself. He accepted that it should have a sphere of influence in Eastern Europe, but that Soviet behaviour increasingly convinced the President and the American people that the USSR could not be trusted. (See 'Soviet Unilateralism and the Origins of the Cold War' in *Major Problems in American History Since 1945* [2001] edited by Robert Griffith and Paula Baker.) The failure of the Soviet Union to help the Poles in Warsaw in 1944 shocked the American people. They were further disturbed by Stalin's behaviour in Eastern Europe and other parts of the world, such as Iran. Even if the USSR did not intend to attack the West, its behaviour was aggressive and untrustworthy so it must be restrained.

Gaddis also points out that one of the reasons for the Cold War was that the American people disliked communism, which they, like Truman, saw as totalitarian. The Soviet Union and the Americans had a history of mistrust going back to the 1917 Russian Revolution. Their two political systems were virtually opposites. In 1919, the Americans had – along with the French, British and Japanese – sent troops to fight against the communists during the Russian Civil War (see Chapter 7). This War of Intervention meant that the Soviets believed America wanted to destroy communism.

Popular front: In this instance, a joining together of all kinds of governments and parties to oppose to the Nazis.

This belief was encouraged, in the 1930s, when Stalin proposed a 'popular front' to fight against the rise of Nazi Germany. The West refused, so Stalin responded by signing the Nazi–Soviet Pact in 1939, where the USSR and Germany agreed to split Poland between them and not to fight each other. The Pact was greeted with shock in the West. Both sides thought, therefore, that the other could not be trusted. Even though they worked together successfully after 1941, these suspicions never went away and, as soon as the common enemy was removed, they resurfaced.

Historian Ralph B. Levering accepts, in *The Cold War, 1945–1987* (1988), that the Soviets believed the USA wanted to destroy communism, and that the two opposing world views were elements in the Cold War. He also points to the domestic pressure on Truman as an important factor. Levering quotes newspapers from the 1940s, which printed many anti-Russian articles and editorials. In a survey conducted in September 1945, almost 50% of the American public said that although Russian friendship was desirable the government should not make too many concessions to it. Almost 10% wanted as little as possible to do with the USSR. Anti-Russian groups, such as Polish-Americans and German-Americans, also put pressure on the Administration. Above all, the Republicans in Congress criticised Truman for being 'soft on communism'. Given the other problems he had with the unions, inflation and with McCarthyism, Truman could not afford to be seen as weak when dealing with Stalin.

Even though there was pressure on Truman at home, he did deliberately play up the threat of communism to get support for his policy in Greece and to get the the Truman Doctrine passed. He and Secretary of State, Dean Acheson, exploited the Soviet threat as they wanted the United States to take a more active and forceful role in the world. This included 'getting tough with Russia', as Truman put it in 1946. It was time he said to 'stop babying the Soviets'. The fact that only the USA had the atom bomb allowed Truman to be hostile, not caring that this only made the USSR more fearful and therefore less likely to cooperate. So, although FDR had expressed worries about Stalin's trustworthiness just before his death in April 1945, there is no doubt that American foreign policy took a much tougher stance once Truman took over. This worsened relations between East and West.

However, perhaps the fundamental problem was one of understanding. The USSR failed to understand that in a democracy an American President had to take note of voters and opposition parties. Stalin also refused to see how his behaviour in Eastern Europe worried and dismayed the West. On the other hand, the Americans did not fully understand what the Second World War had cost the Soviet Union and why they were so determined to protect themselves. Americans also had a tendency to blame all communist activity, such as in Greece, on the Soviet Union, when far more frequently it was a product of local influences.

Dean Gooderham Acheson (1893–1971)
A lawyer who first worked for FDR in the Treasury Department. He was Secretary of State (1949–53), helping to develop the Truman Doctrine and the Marshall Plan. Acheson was a strong supporter of NATO and of America's support for the Nationalist Chinese. He returned to practising law after the 1953 presidential election but was an advisor on foreign policy to succeeding presidents.

1. What reasons did the USA and the USSR have to mistrust each other?

2. How far do historians agree on who was to blame for the Cold War?

'The confrontation between the United States and the Soviet Union derived from differing post-war needs, ideology, style and power of the two rivals and drew on an historical legacy of frosty relations. Each saw the other, in mirror image, as the world's bully.'

(*American Foreign Relations: a history since 1895* by Thomas G Paterson et al [2000])

8.3 Why was Germany central to the Cold War in Europe?

Does this map show any potential problems in the settlement for Germany in 1945?

○ Berlin and Vienna were each divided into four occupation zones

Now part of Poland

British Zone

○ Berlin

GERMANY

Russian Zone

French Zone

US Zone

Vienna ○ Russian

US

French

British

AUSTRIA

Divided Germany: occupation zones immediately after the Second World War.

Unilaterally: Done without consultation. In this case, it had been agreed that any change in Germany would be agreed by the occupying powers jointly, but America changed its policy on reparations without consulting the Soviets.

Between 16 July and 2 August 1945, Truman, Stalin and Churchill, accompanied by Attlee, met at Potsdam, to discuss what to do with Germany now that it had surrendered and Hitler was dead. The problem was whether or not to punish Germany and, if so, how severely. They did not want to repeat the mistakes of 1919 when it was believed Germany had been punished enough to create resentment but not severely enough to prevent it starting another war. Henry Morgenthau, the Treasury Secretary, put forward a plan in 1944, which proposed removing industrial facilities and reducing Germany to a purely agricultural economy. This plan was initially approved, but later rejected, by Truman. There were also those who felt it would be useful to build Germany up as a barrier against Soviet expansion in Europe. (Truman himself had said in July 1941, about the war in Europe, 'if we see that Germany is winning we should help Russia, and if Russia is winning we ought to help Germany.') There were fierce arguments about which policy to pursue.

In the end, it was agreed that Germany would be divided into four zones, each administered by one of the Big Three plus France. Berlin, in the Russian zone, would be divided into four sectors. All decisions regarding the sectors and zones were to be made jointly and all of the powers would be able to take reparations from their zone. The country was also to be de-Nazified – that is, the Nazi leaders removed and many put on trial, and an Allied Control Commission (ACC) set up to administer German affairs.

At first, the West punished Germany, and they took reparations. As this was a drain on the US economy, having to feed the thousands of German refugees, it was decided to start giving aid instead. America decided on this change in policy **unilaterally**. Secretary of State Byrnes simply announced the change of policy in a speech in Stuttgart, in September 1946. This was only the beginning of the change in American policy towards Germany. By 1948, Marshall Aid was pouring into the western zones and the Allies were secretly discussing a new government and constitution for their zones, which they planned to join together.

In some ways, these actions were no more than an acknowledgement of reality. Britain, France and the USA had been working together, administratively and politically, and they all knew that the economic recovery of Germany was essential to the economic recovery of Europe. However, there were also Cold War considerations at work. The Americans believed a weak Germany could be infiltrated or taken over by communism. Conversely, a strong Germany was felt to be a barrier against Soviet expansion into Western Europe. By creating a single, strong western Germany they would be able to preserve democracy and capitalism at the centre of Europe.

How did the Berlin Airlift come about?

The Soviets knew of the secret talks being held by the Allies and were angry. The Americans failed to understand Soviet fears of a German military revival or the sense of betrayal that they felt at these secret negotiations, which went against the principles laid down at Potsdam. In March 1948, the Soviet delegation walked out of the ACC talks.

In June, the Allies joined their zones together and introduced a new currency, the Deutschmark. A few days later, it was extended into the Allied zones of Berlin. They also planned to introduce a democratically elected council into the western half of the city. In retaliation, the Soviets blocked all access from western Germany to Berlin by closing all roads and railways. This cut off two million West Berliners from the rest of Western Europe.

Stalin was hoping that this would force the Allies to leave the city: he argued that he could not see why the Allies would want to stay now they were creating their own West German state. But Truman felt that the United States could not abandon Berlin. Not only would this present the Soviets with a terrific propaganda coup, but it would also see his policy of containment fail at the first hurdle. Stalin's actions confirmed Truman's belief in communist expansionism. That same year the Soviets had forced a communist government on Czechoslovakia and, in China, the communists were on the verge of winning the civil war (see Chapter 9). Truman felt that to back down would be like Chamberlain's capitulation (surrender without much of a fight) to Hitler in the 1930s.

There were some in the Democratic Administration who advised the President that Berlin was not worth fighting for, but others saw the city as having a crucial role in the Cold War. Berlin was the only frontier where Soviet and American troops faced each other directly. For many, this alone was enough reason to stay. The overriding factor was to contain Soviet expansion. If the Allies did not stand up to the Russian threat here, where would be next?

General Clay, the American military commander in Berlin, said:

'When Berlin falls, western Germany will be next. If we mean to hold Europe against communism we must not budge … If we withdraw, our position in Europe is threatened. If America does not understand this now … then it never will, and communism will run rampant. I believe the future of democracy requires us to stay.'

Truman himself put it more simply: 'We are going to stay, period.'

Clay felt that the army should fight its way into Berlin if necessary, but Truman and the British believed this was too risky. So Ernest Bevin, the British Foreign Secretary, suggested that they should supply Berlin by air.

Under 'Operation Vitals', British and American planes took off every three minutes. They carried 2,000 tons of supplies to the city each day. At the height of the Airlift, this rose to almost 10,000 tons. Two million Berliners were fed and supplied from the air for the next 11 months. By any measure, it was a tremendous military achievement.

In May 1949, Stalin called off the blockade. The Allies joined their zones together to create the Federal Republic of Germany (FDR). The Soviets responded by creating the German Democratic Republic (DDR). Germany was divided into two separate countries for the next 40 years.

Containment had worked and the Americans had won. Yet Truman had risked war with Russia. If the USSR had shot down an American plane either by accident or by design, the United States would have had to respond. Truman felt that backing down would have been worse. Besides, would the Soviets risk war when the Americans had a monopoly of atomic weapons? To ensure the Soviets understood how serious he was, Truman had stationed B-29 bombers in Britain. Everyone knew that these planes carried nuclear weapons. The crisis had enabled America to strengthen its military position in Europe, and this was to be strengthened still further with the creation of NATO.

1. What message is the cartoon trying to make about the Berlin Airlift Crisis of 1948–49?

2. How useful is this cartoon to a historian writing about the early Cold War between 1945–49?

A 'Punch' cartoon, July 1948

'**Eastern bloc**': The countries in the east of Europe and in the Soviet Union that had communist regimes in the post-Second World War period.

The victory for Truman's policy of containment, however, did not solve the 'problem' of Berlin. While, for the West, it continued to be a beacon of democracy in the '**Eastern bloc**', for the Soviet Union it continued to be a thorn in their side. Crises were to arise again over the city in 1958 and 1961.

Why was NATO created?

The Berlin Blockade convinced the United States of the need to strengthen Europe against the Soviet Union. In March 1948, Britain, France, Belgium, Holland and Luxembourg had signed a mutual defence treaty. Acheson was able to build on this to create the North Atlantic Treaty Organisation (NATO) in April 1949. Given the success of the Airlift and the seeming success of Truman's containment policy, the Senate approved the signing of the NATO agreement by 82 votes to 13.

NATO was the first peacetime military alliance in US history. It consisted of 13 European states plus the USA, Canada and Iceland. Under its terms, an attack on one member was an attack on them all. However, the United States and Europe interpreted it differently. The United States saw it mainly as a 'nuclear umbrella' for Europe (i.e. America's nuclear weapons would give Europe all the protection it needed). Truman told the American public that large numbers of US soldiers would not be sent to Europe. But the Europeans and many of Truman's critics believed the USA was committing itself to protecting Europe militarily. When the Soviets exploded their own atom bomb in September, NATO was strengthened and the USA soon stationed soldiers in bases throughout Europe, backed by $1.5 billion in military aid.

In 1952, NATO was extended to include Greece and Turkey. As early as 1950, the Americans had wanted to bring Germany into NATO in order to strengthen its position within the western sphere of influence. They were also concerned that, with the outbreak of the Korean War, American troops would be stretched too far. They hoped that a rearmed Germany would lift some of the burden in Europe. Needless to say, the French, the British and the Soviets were very unhappy when Acheson announced his proposals to create ten German divisions. To ease European fears, the French Prime Minister René Pleven proposed that West Germany should be rearmed as part of a European army, where it could be controlled. So the European Defence Community was established in 1952, consisting of France, Italy, Germany, Belgium, Holland and Luxembourg.

However, this solution satisfied no one and the Americans continued to press for West German entry into NATO. To forestall this, the USSR even proposed a united, neutral Germany but this suggestion was never taken seriously. Continued pressure from the Eisenhower Administration finally led to West Germany joining NATO on 9 May 1955. In response to what they saw as a renewed military threat, the Soviet Union brought together its Eastern European allies into the Warsaw Pact five days later. It seemed that Germany had once again divided Europe into two armed camps.

Although the USSR feared a German military revival, it did not do as much damage to the new policy of peaceful co-existence which Eisenhower and Khrushchev were entering into, as it might have done. Just a few weeks after the creation of the Warsaw Pact, the Geneva Summit took place. The Soviet attempt to prevent West German entry into NATO had produced agreement over Austria.

Austria, like Germany, had been occupied by the four powers at the end of the Second World War. The Soviet Union had always insisted that a final agreement over Austria must go hand in hand with agreement over

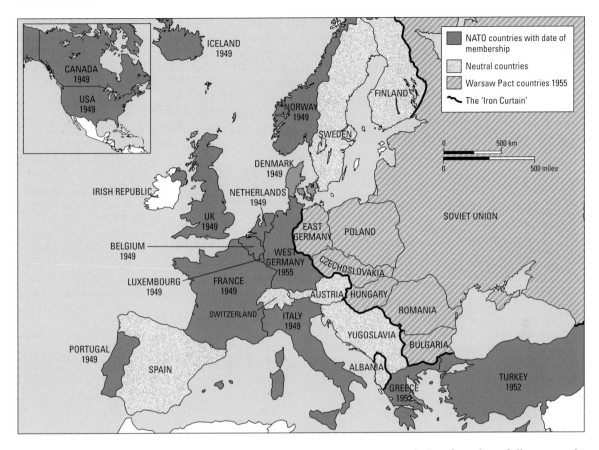

NATO countries with date of membership

Neutral countries

Warsaw Pact countries 1955

The 'Iron Curtain'

North Atlantic Treaty
Organisation (NATO),
4 April 1949

Germany. To show their moderation and therefore, hopefully, persuade the Americans to give way over Germany, the Soviets dropped their demand. This led to the signing of the Austrian State Treaty, which ended the ten-year occupation and created an independent, neutral Austria. Both sides could present this as a 'victory' as it kept Austria out of both NATO and the Warsaw Pact. The agreement helped the improving relationship between the USA and the USSR. However, it did not prevent West Germany joining NATO, as the Soviets had hoped, and it did not stop Germany being a problem for the two powers.

What was NSC-68?

From the late 1940s, Truman's advisors were saying that the United States would need to change its defence policy. The new demands of the Cold War and the commitments of the Truman Doctrine meant that the organisation of the American military and its security system needed to be updated. The 1947 National Security Act created a Department of Defense to oversee all the armed forces, instead of having separate departments for the different services. It also set up the National Security Council to advise the President on defence and security issues, and the Central Intelligence Agency (CIA) to gather information. This was primarily an administrative measure, but it illustrates how far the United States had moved from the isolation of the inter-war years, and how important foreign policy now was.

Along with the Truman Doctrine and NATO, the USA would be spending much more on defence. In 1950, the National Security Council passed a resolution, NSC-68. This document analysed the international situation given the explosion of the Soviet bomb and the 'fall' of China to communism the year before. According to NSC-68, the Soviet Union was intent on spreading communism throughout the world – as China had shown – so it was up to the United States to prevent them. This would mean massively increasing military spending. When the Korean War broke out later that year, it seemed to confirm what the National Security Council was saying. The US defence budget rose rapidly from around $13 billion per year in the 1940s to $50 billion in 1953.

The professionalisation of the Defence Department and the increase in military spending under NSC-68 had important domestic effects on America. Companies involved in arms production throughout the USA now had far greater opportunities to gain government contracts. The aerospace industries of the south-western states, for example, saw their production levels and profits rise rapidly. The politicians from these states tried to ensure that continued to be the case. This growth in the defence industry's wealth and influence worried some people: they referred to it as the military-industrial complex and felt that no one area of industry should be so politically and economically powerful. When he left office in 1961, it was one of the things Eisenhower warned the American public about.

Some critics, including George Kennan, argued that the government was wrong and had exaggerated the Soviet threat. Others worried about the amount of money and effort that was now going into fighting the Cold War. By stressing the communist threat, NSC-68 unintentionally gave a boost to McCarthy's anti-communist campaign (see Chapter 11). What NSC-68 had done was to confirm and strengthen containment of communist expansion as America's number one foreign policy priority.

1. Why did Truman refuse to back down to the Russian blockade of Berlin in 1948?

2. How far had American military influence in Europe increased between 1945 and 1950?

? *Source-based questions: Containment in Europe, 1947–1949*

SOURCE A

The Marshall Plan was an economic extension of the Truman Doctrine. American Secretary of State George Marshall produced his European Recovery Programme (ERP) which offered economic and financial help wherever it was needed. 'Our policy,' he declared, 'is directed not against any country or doctrine but against hunger, poverty, desperation and chaos.'

From Mastering Modern World History *by Norman Lowe, 1982*

SOURCE B

Most of the countries of Europe and Asia today are in a state of physical destruction or economic dislocation or both ... two of the greatest workshops of Europe and Asia – Germany and Japan – upon whose production Europe and Asia were to an important degree dependent before the war have hardly been able even to begin the process of reconstruction ... unforeseen disasters – what the lawyers call 'acts of God' – have occurred to the crops of Europe. For two successive years unusually severe droughts have cut down food production ...

Your Congress has authorised and your government is carrying out a policy of relief and reconstruction today chiefly as a matter of national self-interest. For it is generally agreed that until the various countries of the world get on their feet and become self-supporting there can be no political or economic stability in the world and no lasting peace or prosperity for any of us.

From a speech by Dean Acheson on 8 May 1947 (Department of State Bulletin, 18 May 1947)

Source-based questions: Containment in Europe, 1947–1949

SOURCE C

Certainly there is no 'precedent' for today's worldwide cleavage [deep split] between democracy and communism. Perhaps, however, there is something of a parallel in remembering what occurred prior to a similar cleavage between democracy and Nazism when we surely learnt that we cannot escape trouble by trying to run away from it and when 'appeasement' proved to be a fatal investment. Of course we shall never know if history would have been different if we had all stood up to the aggressor at Munich. But at least we know what it cost to 'lie down'.

Senator Arthur J. Vandenberg Jr, March 1947 (from the 'Private Papers of Senator Vandenberg', 1952)

SOURCE D

My objection, then, to the policy of containment is not that it seeks to confront the Soviet power with American power, but that the policy is misconceived, and must result in a misuse of American power ... [It] commits this country to a struggle which has for its objective nothing more substantial than the hope that in ten or fifteen years the soviet power will, as a result of long frustration, 'break up' or 'mellow'.

Walter Lippmann writing in 1947, from The Cold War: A Study in US Foreign Policy Since 1945 *by Walter Lippmann (1973).*

SOURCE E

Soviet power, unlike that of Hitlerite Germany ... does not work by fixed plans. It does not take unnecessary risks. For this reason it can easily withdraw – and usually does – when strong resistance is encountered at any point. Thus, if the adversary has sufficient force and makes clear his readiness to use it, he rarely has to do so. If situations are properly handled there need be no prestige-engaging showdowns ...

Many foreign peoples, in Europe at least, are tired and frightened by experiences of the past, and are less interested in abstract freedom than in security. They are seeking guidance rather than responsibilities. We should be better able than the Russians to give them this. And unless we do, the Russians certainly will.

From George Kennan's telegraphic message from Moscow of 22 February 1946, published in Kennan's Memoirs, 1925–1950 (1967).

---

1. Study Sources A and B.

How far do the sources agree on the motives for Marshall Aid to Europe?

2. Study Source A and use your own knowledge.

What was the Truman Doctrine?

3. Study Source D.

How useful is this source to an historian studying the origins of the Cold War?

4. Study all the sources and use your own knowledge.

Why did the United States develop the policy of containment in 1947?

8.4 How far did American–Soviet relations in Europe improve under Eisenhower?

Republican Dwight D. Eisenhower won the 1952 presidential election in the USA with 55% of the vote. 'Ike' was a famous soldier who had been commander of the Normandy invasions and head of NATO. He was widely liked by people of all parties and by Congress, and was very popular with the public. 'Ike' talked about a new kind of Republicanism and introduced some new ideas into foreign affairs. Even though he was the first Republican president since Hoover in 1932, there was never any attempt to go back to the Republican isolationism of the 1920s; the world had changed too much for that. In many ways, Eisenhower was to continue what Truman had done, but he also added some new elements.

The world situation was more promising under Eisenhower than at any time since the Second World War. In some ways, it seemed that he might be able to build an easier relationship with the Soviet Union than Truman had been able to do. In 1953, Stalin died, the Korean War ended and Eisenhower was concerned to improve international relations. Yet the world was getting more complex and as communism spread to other areas there was more potential for conflict.

During the election campaign, 'Ike' and his Secretary of State, John Dulles, criticised Democratic foreign policy, saying that Truman did not do enough to stand up to communism. Containment was criticised as 'negative, futile and immoral'. Instead of merely containing the communists, Dulles talked about 'rolling back' the frontiers of communism and 'liberating' people from communist rule. As events were to show, this was not a realistic possibility. Without war the USSR was hardly likely to give up its influence in Eastern Europe, and Eisenhower was not prepared to go to war to remove them. In many ways, the Eisenhower Administration simply continued Truman's policy of containment.

What was the 'New Look'?

As a Republican, 'Ike' was committed to cutting government spending, including the defence budget which was around $40 billion per year. At the same time, lack of success in Korea showed the limitations of US ground forces. Eisenhower, therefore, wanted an effective way of fighting wars that was also cheap. The **Joint Chiefs of Staff** came up with the Radford Plan, or 'New Look'.

The 'New Look' proposed cutting conventional forces; therefore the USA would be more dependent on nuclear weapons. This would be cheaper than conventional forces. However, nuclear weapons, especially the hydrogen bomb, would be just as threatening to America's enemies – if not more so. As it was crudely but simply expressed, they were going to get 'more bang for the buck [US dollar]'.

Cutting defence spending could send the wrong signal and make the United States look weak, so it had to be clear that it was not worth anybody's while starting a fight with the America. In fact, Dulles said that other powers should realise that, if they took on the USA, they would 'be made to suffer ... more than [they] can possibly gain', that there would be 'massive retaliation'. In other words, if anyone attacked the USA then the USA would strike back with far more force than the original attack deserved. The problem, as historian Stephen Ambrose sees it, was that 'since it was his only weapon, Dulles had to flash a nuclear bomb whenever he wanted to threaten the use of force'. This made every conflict a potential nuclear war and encouraged the spread of nuclear weapons. By 1956, the USA had 1,400 planes capable of dropping hydrogen bombs on the Soviet

Legend:
- Annexed to USSR
- Satellite States
- ----- 1938 Frontiers

NORWAY

SWEDEN

FINLAND

Oslo

Stockholm

Helsinki

Porkkala
(Russia 1945–56)

Viborg

Leningrad

Novgorod

ESTONIA

Riga

LATVIA

Smolensk

LITHUANIA

North Sea

Baltic Sea

DENMARK

Copenhagen

USSR

Lübeck

Gdansk

Hamburg

Bremen

EAST GERMAY

Berlin
(4 power control)

Warsaw

Brest-Litovsk

NETHERLANDS

WEST GERMANY

Leipzig

POLAND

Kiev

BELGIUM

Bonn

Prague

LUX

CZECHOSLOVAKIA

Krak

Lvov

Paris

Munich

Liechtenstein

Vienna

Bratislava

AUSTRIA
(Neutralised)

Budapest

HUNGARY

BESSARABIA

Odessa

FRANCE

SWITZERLAND

Lyons

Milan

Zagreb

Trieste
Fiume

ROMANIA

Bucharest

Marseilles

Monoco

ITALY

YUGOSLAVIA
(Independent communist state)

Belgrade

Sarajevo

Sofia

BULGARIA

Black Sea

CORSICA
(France)

Rome

ALBANIA

Salonika

Istanbul

SARDINIA
(Italy)

CORFU

GREECE
(Communist revolt
suppressed)

TURKEY

Mediterranean Sea

SICILY

Athens

CRETE

0   400 km

0   400 miles

Central Europe, 1955

Union. In a world so dangerous, Eisenhower also pursued a better relationship with the Soviet Union to make sure that he never had to practise massive retaliation.

How successful was the Geneva Summit of 1955?

The 'New Look' was only part of Eisenhower's foreign policy. His aim was not just to go round the world threatening people, he also believed in personal diplomacy in working with other powers and trying to remove the sources of conflict. Luckily, the Soviet leadership was also willing to talk. Nikita Khruschev had replaced Stalin and, like Eisenhower, he wanted to cut military spending. If relations with the West were better, there should be less need for troops to be stationed in Europe. In 1953, Khruschev talked about 'peaceful co-existence' with the West. The idea of 'peaceful co-existence' was also attractive to the Americans because the Warsaw Pact had just been formed as the Russian counter-balance to NATO, and the USSR was catching up with American nuclear technology.

Given this desire on both sides for an improved relationship, a **summit** meeting was arranged between the USA, the USSR, Britain and France in Geneva. They gathered in the Swiss resort from 18–23 July 1955.

At the summit, 'Ike' proposed free communications between the two countries, and agreements on the peaceful use of atomic power and on disarmament. He also proposed an 'open skies' policy, whereby the two superpowers would exchange information on military installations and then be allowed to fly over each other's territory to check. The Soviet Union rejected this idea, but the Americans started spy flights anyway – a policy that was to end in disaster five years later.

In fact, the summit achieved almost nothing concrete. Yet it was a great success for Eisenhower personally, and journalists spoke of the 'spirit of Geneva'. The same year, an agreement was finally reached allowing for the removal of occupying forces from Austria, and guaranteeing the country's neutrality. Also, the Soviets officially recognised the Federal Republic of Germany. It seemed as though a new era in East–West relations might be beginning.

In 1958, Khrushchev became the first communist leader to visit the United States. Crowds gathered, sometimes in virtual silence, to glimpse a real, live Russian Communist. Vice-President Richard Nixon paid a visit to Moscow the next year, where he engaged Khrushchev in the so-called 'kitchen debate' at a trade fair. The two men argued the merits of their nation's technology. However, by 1959, there were already clouds darkening this new horizon.

Why did Cold War tensions continue after Geneva?

During the 1956 presidential election campaign, Dulles again talked about 'roll back' in Europe. He said there was little support among ordinary people for communism in the countries where it existed. Dulles believed, mainly correctly, that people living under communism did not want it and that, where possible, the USA should liberate people from its grip. The frontiers of the communist world should be 'rolled back'.

In October 1956, a revolt broke out against the communist government in Hungary. The revolt had been sparked by a speech made by Khrushchev in February of that year. It had also been encouraged by CIA broadcasts on Radio Free Europe. These broadcasts encouraged the Hungarians to believe, wrongly, that they would get American support. The revolt spread quickly. It led to the withdrawal of the Red Army and the establishment of a new government under Imry Nagy. 'Ike' made a speech sympathising with the

Nikita Khruschchev (1894–1971)
From a peasant family, he joined the Communist Party and Red Army, fighting with distinction in the Second World War. Eventually, he succeeded Stalin as leader in 1958. He pursued policies of reform at home, or peaceful co-existence with the West and tried to ease tensions with Eastern Europe. Failures in agriculture and foreign policy led to his removal in 1964.

Summit: A diplomatic meeting between the leaders of the foremost nations, especially the United States and the Soviet Union.

Imry Nagy (1895–1958)
Communist politician who wanted to reform the system in Hungary. He intended to maintain a communist system, but his intention to leave the Warsaw Pact was seen as a security threat to the USSR. He was arrested after the Hungarian Revolt and taken to the Soviet Union where he was shot two years later.

1. *What message is the cartoon trying to make about Soviet policy in Eastern Europe in the 1950s?*

2. *Does the cartoon portray an accurate view of Soviet policy? Explain your answer.*

A 'Punch' cartoon published during the Hungarian Uprising of October 1956.

revolt and Dulles expressed admiration for the rebels taking on the Red Army. In November, when the Hungarians talked of leaving the Warsaw Pact, the Red Army returned and crushed the revolt. Seven thousand Soviets and 30,000 Hungarians died; a further 200,000 were made refugees. The last message out of Budapest was a plea for help from the West. The USA allowed 25,000 refugees to come to America, but did no more. They knew that, geographically, there was little they could do to help. More importantly, they accepted the political reality that Eastern Europe was a Soviet sphere of influence. The Hungarian Revolt graphically illustrated the unrealistic ambition of liberation as a policy in the Cold War.

Berlin also continued to be a focus of tension between the two superpowers. Thirteen years after the War, there had been no peace treaty signed with Germany and the situation was pretty much the same as it had been left in 1949. The western sectors had developed and grown, as American aid continued to flow into the city, while progress in the Soviet-controlled half was very slow. This not only made the USSR look weak, there was also a constant stream of people fleeing to the West looking for a better life – many of whom were skilled people who were desperately needed in the East. Therefore, in November 1958, Khrushchev gave the Americans an ultimatum: there should be a peace treaty and American troops should leave Berlin by May the following year, or the USSR would sign its own treaty with East Germany. If America accepted Khrushchev's demands they would have to recognise East Germany, accept the permanent division of Germany, end the post-war occupation and leave Berlin.

There was pressure on 'Ike' to send troops, but he did not want to push Khrushchev into a corner. At the same time, he made it clear America would not leave Berlin.

The deadline passed and nothing happened. Khrushchev came to America in September 1959 and, at talks at Camp David (the US President's summer home in Maryland), the Soviets appeared to back down. The two leaders agreed to hold a summit in Paris in 1960, where the matter would be discussed. The crisis had passed away with nothing changing in Berlin, but it showed how the city remained a problem and continued to be central to the Cold War in Europe.

Why did the Paris Summit of 1960 fail?

Because of the relative success of Geneva and of Khrushchev's visit to the USA in 1958, a second summit was arranged between 'Ike' and Khrushchev in Paris, in May 1960. The summit also came about as a result of arguments about Berlin in 1958. On the eve of the conference, the USSR announced it had shot down a U-2 spy plane.

The build-up of the Soviet military and the failure of the 'open skies' proposal had led the USA to increase its spying with U-2 fights over Russia. They denied the plane was theirs, then said that it was a research plane which had gone missing. The Soviets then produced the pilot, Francis Gary Powers – alive and well. The summit broke up as American lies were exposed and, when 'Ike' left office a few months later, US–Soviet relations were at a very low ebb.

How did the space race contribute to the Cold War?

One aspect of the Cold War was propaganda. In one particular area in the 1950s the USSR took a big lead over America, scoring a massive propaganda victory: that was in space. However, the space race also had military implications as rocket and missile technology are so closely linked.

On 4 October 1957, the Soviet Union launched 'Sputnik', the world's first man-made satellite. This was followed by 'Sputnik II' the following year. The Americans were shocked by the launches and immediately stepped up their own space programme and spending on science education (see Chapter 11). 'Explorer I', America's own satellite, was launched in January 1958. The National Aeronautics and Space Administration (NASA) was created later in the year. Although it was part of the propaganda fight in the Cold War, NASA was put under civilian control, not military.

In August 1957, the Soviets also launched the first inter-continental ballistic missile (ICBM). This meant the USSR could now hit Western Europe with nuclear weapons. It would only be a matter of time before they would be able to hit America itself. The USA soon had its own ICBMs, but the myth of American technological superiority was over. The Gaither Report showed that the USA still had a military lead, but urged an arms build-up.

Also, the USSR was financing the arms and space programmes from economic growth of 7% – twice that of the USA. In spite of this, Eisenhower refused to get into an arms race. His Republican economic views led him to want to keep defence spending low. He also feared that an arms race would intensify the Cold War and make it more dangerous.

Although 'Ike' refused to join an arms race in the way in which Kennedy would later, the USA did continue to develop its weapons programme

1. *What were the aims of Eisenhower's foreign policy in Europe?*

2. *How far did Eisenhower's policy differ from Truman's?*

3. *How successful was Eisenhower's foreign policy in Europe?*

(e.g. Polaris submarines). By the end of his presidency, 'Ike' had warned about the growth of what he called the 'military-industrial complex'. Too much of the economy was tied into defence spending. This meant the military and industries involved in defence production had little interest in peaceful co-existence; it was in their economic interests for the Cold War to continue. Politicians were involved too: if you represented a state or area where the main industry was defence, such as southern California, then the pressure was there from the defence companies in the area and from your constituents. Kennedy ignored this warning and built up America's arms production massively.

8.5 How effectively did Kennedy pursue the Cold War in Europe?

John F. Kennedy was a decorated war hero and an anti-Communist who voted for the Truman Doctrine. During the presidential election campaign in 1960 he had accused the Republicans of letting things 'drift', saying that the Communists were winning the Cold War. In Cuba, Indo-China and West Africa it seemed as though communism was on the increase, and the U-2 crisis had humiliated the United States. Coming from a very competitive family, Kennedy was determined to 'win' the Cold War.

When he became President in 1961, his inauguration speech was entirely about foreign policy. His intention to take a forceful stand in the Cold War was made clear when he said:

> 'Let every nation know, whether it wishes us good or ill, that we shall pay any price, bear any burden, meet any hardship, support any friend, oppose any foe, in order to assure the survival and the success of liberty.'

One way Kennedy wanted to 'ensure liberty' was to build up America's nuclear deterrent. The fact that the U-2 flights showed it not to be true did not stop Kennedy from asserting that there was a 'missile gap' between the East and West, which must be made up. Consequently, he embarked on the biggest military build-up in US peacetime history so far. The defence budget was increased in 1961 by 15% and Kennedy introduced a policy of 'flexible response', which would enable the USA to fight any kind of war. This entailed the building up of conventional forces, special forces such as the Green Berets and, of course, nuclear weapons. The number of ICBMs, for example, rose from 63 in 1961 to 424 in 1963. The irony of this policy was that the Soviet Union had to respond and build up its own arsenal. So rather than establish American superiority, Kennedy started an arms race making the world less secure.

John Fitzgerald Kennedy (1917–1963)
35th President of the USA (1961–63), the first Roman Catholic and the youngest person to be elected US President. He came from a very wealthy Boston Catholic family. His father Joseph had been ambassador to Britain just before the Second World War and 'Jack', as family

and friends called him, had an upbringing steeped in politics. Educated at Harvard and briefly at the London School of Economics. After serving in the US Navy during the War, he entered Congress in 1946. In 1952, at only 34 years of age, he became one of the youngest Senators ever. In 1953, he married

Jacqueline Lee Bouvier (1929–1995).
'JFK' made his name as a supporter of civil rights legislation and as a prominent internationalist. During his presidency, Kennedy did not succeed in carrying through any major domestic legislation. However, he did create the Peace Corps (volunteers who give health,

agricultural and educational aid overseas). It was in foreign affairs that his presidency was most notable.
On 22 November 1963, during a tour of Texas, JFK was shot while driving through Dallas. He died shortly afterwards. His death caused worldwide grief.

How did the Berlin Wall affect Soviet–American relations?

The most potent symbol of the Cold War era was the Berlin Wall. Built in 1961, it was a massive propaganda victory for the West. In many ways, though, it stabilised the Cold War in Europe.

Ever since the War, West Berlin had continued to get richer because of its links to the western economies, while East Berlin remained poor. By 1961, 4,000 people a day were crossing from East to West through the city. This was both a propaganda problem for the Communists and a genuine economic issue, as most of those leaving were skilled and educated, and East Germany could not afford to lose its best minds.

Khrushchev had put pressure on Eisenhower to do something. Then, when he met with Kennedy at the Vienna Summit, in June 1961, he raised the matter again. Kennedy refused to stop this movement of people. Khrushchev then resurrected the 1958 proposals, but Kennedy took the same stand as Eisenhower: there would be no change in the status of Berlin.

In an attempt to halt the flow of people, the East Germans threatened to cut off the city entirely. JFK sent 40,000 troops to Europe, called up the **reserves** and asked Congress for $3.25 billion for military spending. Kennedy had just had a disaster in Cuba with the failure at the **Bay of Pigs** so he needed a foreign policy victory. It was also about enforcing containment. Just like Truman and Eisenhower, Kennedy believed the United States had to maintain its presence in Berlin or it would lose influence in Europe as a whole.

Then, on 13 August 1961, the Germans sealed West Berlin off from the East with wire fences, which they then replaced with a 30-mile wall with just four crossing points. This wall cut the city in half, dividing streets and families. General Clay sent tanks to the Wall and, for a while, Soviet and American troops were face to face waiting for the other to move. The military advised Kennedy to destroy the Wall by force, but he was not prepared to go to war with the USSR over a wall which they had built in their own sector of the city. He spoke to Khrushchev and both sides backed off.

Reserves: Military forces which are not permanently ready for action but which can be used in emergencies.

Bay of Pigs: In 1961 the Americans backed an invasion of Cuba by CIA-trained Cuban exiles. The aim of the invasion was to topple the communist government of Fidel Castro, but it failed and most of the exiles were arrested. It was a humiliation for Kennedy. The fear of another invasion led Castro to invite the Russians to build missile bases on the island. When the Americans discovered the missile sites in October 1962, it started a crisis which took the world to the brink of nuclear war. The US navy blockaded Cuba and the Soviets were forced to remove the missiles.

President John F. Kennedy stands on a platform looking over the Berlin Wall into the Eastern sector.

1. In what ways was the Berlin Wall a failure for both the Americans and for the USSR?

2. Had the Cold War in Europe eased under Kennedy? Explain your answer.

The Wall stopped the flow of refugees to the West, allowing the East to rebuild its economy. In reality, there was nothing the Americans could do about it. For the Soviet Union it was a practical solution. For the West it provided powerful propaganda, showing to the world that under communism people had to be walled in.

It might not have been a solution either side liked, but the building of the Wall did ease tensions. Berlin ceased to be a major issue in the Cold War for the next 30 years. In fact, after the Wall went up the focus of the Cold War moved away from Europe. For Kennedy, Cuba took up far more of his time – with the failed Bay of Pigs invasion in 1961 and the Missile Crisis of 1962. Increasingly for Kennedy and particularly for President Johnson, American involvement in Vietnam was their major foreign policy concern. While the superpowers had their eyes fixed on South East Asia, their relations in Europe remained steady.

8.6 How successful was Nixon's policy of détente?

When Richard Nixon became president in 1968, the United States was still trying to achieve a victory in Vietnam. Johnson had focused what little interest he had in foreign affairs almost totally on the war, but then made a start with the Soviets on exploring the possibility of arms limitation. It was to be Nixon who would see this through.

Richard Nixon was hard working and intelligent. He was also suspicious, resentful and ruthless. In foreign policy, his best and worst traits were shown. He could be manipulative and dishonest, and he could also be **pragmatic** and adaptable.

Pragmatic: Dealing with things in a practical way; accepting things the way they are.

Although William Rogers was the Secretary of State, a much more important figure was Henry Kissinger, Nixon's National Security Advisor (NSA). Kissinger had taught international relations before he entered politics, and so was considered an expert on world affairs. As NSA, and later as Secretary of State for President Ford, Kissinger travelled all over the world talking personally to leaders of many nations. As early as 1969, Kissinger began secret meetings with Anatoly Dobrynin, the Soviet Ambassador to the United States. These so-called 'back channels' allowed Kissinger to do much of the preparation for Nixon's visits to the Soviet Union and China in 1972. Kissinger was prepared to pursue whatever policies he felt necessary to benefit the United States' position in the world. This led to criticism from the right, who felt that arms limitation and talking to the Soviets was being soft on communism.

Richard Milhous Nixon (1913–1994)
37th President of the USA (1969–74), a Republican. He entered Congress in 1947. Nixon attracted attention as a member of the Un-American Activities Committee (1948). He was Vice-President to Eisenhower (1953–61). As President, he was responsible for US withdrawal from Vietnam, and the improvement of relations with Communist China.

Nixon was the only president ever to resign from office – on 9 August 1974, over his involvement in the Watergate scandal. He was threatened with impeachment (trial for serious offences whilst in office) on three counts:
● obstruction of the administration of justice in the Watergate investigations;
● violation of the rights of citizens (e.g. attempting to use the Internal Revenue Service, FBI

and CIA as weapons against political opponents);
● and failure to produce 'paper and things'. President Ford granted him a pardon in 1974.

Henry Kissinger (1923–)
A German Jew born in Bavaria, he fled to the USA in 1938 to escape the Nazis. Appointed National Security Advisor (1969) by President Nixon, and was Secretary of State (1973–77). His missions to

the USSR and China improved US relations with both countries. He also took part in negotiating US withdrawal from Vietnam (1973) and in Arab–Israeli peace negotiations (1973–78). Joint winner of the Nobel Peace Prize in 1973.

Criticism from the left, however, was stronger. Kissinger's secret negotiations made him untrustworthy; his willingness to support dictators made him a poor spokesman for American freedom and democracy; and his strong support for the bombing campaigns in Vietnam aroused great hostility. However, he was an important figure and, throughout the period of *détente*, Nixon and Kissinger worked closely together.

Nixon and Kissinger believed in maintaining America's position and influence in the world, and that meant continuing to contain Soviet power. However, the world had changed in the 20 years since the Truman Doctrine. The Soviet Union had far more weapons and America's moral leadership had suffered badly because of the Vietnam War. Nixon's response was a policy he called 'the Grand Design'. This consisted of *détente* (i.e. building a better relationship with the Soviet Union) and the Nixon Doctrine (i.e. getting America's allies to take on more of the burden of fighting communism themselves rather that expecting the USA to do it for them). Although the Nixon Doctrine was primarily aimed at South East Asia, many Republicans also felt that it was about time the NATO countries contributed more to the protection of Western Europe. As a Republican himself, Nixon hoped that *détente* would ease tensions sufficiently to enable him to afford cuts in military spending.

Kissinger also talked about 'linkage'. He argued that if closer economic, political and strategic ties were built between the USA and the USSR there would be less room for conflict. Linkage also meant that they could not build an agreement with the Soviets in one area while disagreeing in another, so the two should be linked. What this meant in practice was that Nixon and Kissinger would negotiate arms reduction with the Soviet Union while, in return, they wanted Soviet help in pressurising the North Vietnamese to end the war.

How did Nixon pursue arms reduction?

Between 1968 and 1973, the American armed forces were cut by 1.2 million. This was partly due to withdrawing from the war (see Chapter 9), but it was also to signal to the USSR that America was serious about arms reduction. In 1969, talks about reducing arms got under way in Helsinki, but the whole policy nearly fell apart when the Soviet Union and America backed opposing sides in the 1971 war in Bangladesh. They continued, however, and to encourage the Soviets further Nixon visited China in 1972. As well as hoping to improve American relations and trade with China, Nixon and Kissinger were shrewdly exploiting the mutual fears of the two communist powers. They knew that the USSR feared a friendship between China and the USA: it would leave the Soviet Union very vulnerable. The visit produced the desired result and, in 1972, a summit meeting was held in Moscow. The result was the Strategic Arms Limitation Treaty (SALT), signed on 26 May.

Under the SALT agreement, there were limits on certain types of nuclear weapons and systems. The number of ICBMs was frozen at 1,607 for the USSR and 1,054 for the USA, while SLBMs (see panel opposite) were limited to 740 and 656 respectively. This seemed to favour the Soviet Union, but there were no limits on the numbers of bombers or on MIRVs (a missile with several, independently-targetable warheads). In both of these categories, the USA had more than double the number held by the Soviets. Neither were there any restrictions on the development of new weapons systems, such as Polaris submarines or Cruise missiles.

In a sense, SALT was a failure. It was to last only five years. It left out major categories of weapons and those categories that did have limits were fixed at higher levels than had previously existed. In other words, the two

Human rights: Belief that every individual has certain rights which must be respected by their government whatever its political beliefs and system. They include such things as freedom of religion, freedom of speech, the right to a fair trial etc.

The Arms Race: some terms

Atom bomb: A nuclear bomb. The part of the bomb that explodes and does the damage is the warhead. The missile or plane it is launched from is the delivery system.

Hydrogen bomb: A thermonuclear bomb, though usually also referred to as nuclear, equivalent to 750 atom bombs.

Strategic weapons: Long-range weapons, controlled in the USA by the US Air Force Strategic Air Command. Strategic weapons were sited in the USA and in US bases in Europe, such as in Turkey.

Strategic bombers: Planes capable of delivering nuclear weapons (e.g. B-52s).

ICBM: Inter-continental ballistic missiles with a range of over 3,000 nautical miles (e.g. Titan II).

SLBM: Submarine-launched ballistic missiles (e.g. Polaris).

Cruise missiles: Low-flying missiles that can be launched by air, land or sea.

Tactical weapons: Also known as theatre nuclear weapons. These are ones that are short range and for use on the battlefield.

MIRV: Multiple independently targetable warheads – one missile can carry several warheads, each of which can be aimed at a different target.

SDI: Strategic Defence Initiative; nicknamed 'star wars'. A theoretical defence shield that can detect missiles and destroy them in space before they hit.

countries could build up to those limits. The agreement did nothing to halt weapons production. In fact, this continued to increase over the next five years. However, SALT was a recognition by the superpowers that the arms race was getting out of control and, at the very least, it had to be slowed down. Further agreements were to follow: the negotiations for SALT II beginning in 1977, as soon as SALT I was starting to run out.

Perhaps even more important was that, like the Geneva summit in 1955, *détente* produced a new spirit in the Cold War in Europe. The same year that it was signed, the two Germanies formally recognised each other and exchanged ambassadors. There was a general recognition of the boundaries of Europe which had been in place since 1945. Three years later, the Helsinki Accords were signed, in which 35 countries formally recognised the post-war settlement and promised to respect **human rights**.

As well as the arms limitation treaty, the two sides also signed an agreement, in 1972, on the basic principles of relations between the USSR and the USA. This contributed to *détente* as the two sides were basically agreeing to work together to prevent conflict and to promote peaceful co-existence. Kissinger thought this was more important than SALT itself. However, the dangers to peaceful co-existence and *détente* were brought vividly to life the following year with the Arab–Israeli War.

The USA and the USSR had been backing different sides in the ongoing conflict in the Middle East – the Americans backing Israel and the Soviets backing the Arab nations and Egypt. Nixon and Kissinger saw this situation as part of the Cold War struggle but, when Egypt and Syria launched an attack on Israel in October 1973, they saw the danger of being dragged into a war themselves. To support his ally, Nixon sent arms to Israel. Kissinger was sent to Moscow to work with the Soviet Union on creating a truce and saving *détente*. A truce was agreed but when the Israelis refused to abide by it the Soviet Union proposed that it should be enforced militarily by the two superpowers. For Nixon this was unacceptable. Jewish voters at home would not stand for it and, more importantly, it would encourage a Soviet military presence in the Middle East. When the USSR said they would go it alone if necessary, the Americans were alarmed. To make their opposition clear, Nixon put the country and all its bases abroad on nuclear alert. Within a year of SALT, it all seemed to be falling apart. However, both sides were desperately keen to avoid war. The USSR dropped its proposals and the Americans put more pressure on Israel. A truce was agreed in 1973, backed by the United Nations, and a final settlement agreed in 1975.

As the Middle Eastern conflict had shown, the basic underlying suspicions between the two countries had not gone away and the Cold War was not over. When Nixon was forced to resign in August 1974, his Vice-President, Gerald Ford, succeeded him (see Chapter 12). The continued presence of Henry Kissinger meant there was some continuation in policy (e.g. the arms reduction talks continued). However, the USSR's failure to abide by the Helsinki Accords and the fall of Saigon in 1975 (see Chapter 9), led to an increase in anti-Communist feeling in the USA and there was a noticeable cooling in the policy of *détente*.

The arms build-up

Strategic bombers	1956	1960	1965	1970	1975	1979
USA	560	550	630	405	330	316
Soviet Union	60	175	200	190	140	140

ICBMs	1960	1964	1968	1970	1974	1979
USA	295	835	630	1,054	1,054	1,054
Soviet Union	75	200	800	1,300	1,587	1,398

SLBMs	1962	1965	1968	1972	1975	1979
USA	145	500	656	655	656	656
Soviet Union	45	125	130	497	740	989

Warheads	1945	1955	1965	1975	1985	
USA	6	3,057	31,265	26,675	22,941	
Soviet Union	0	200	6,129	19,443	39,197	

8.7 How far did détente continue under Carter?

**James Earl Carter
(1924–)**
39th President of the USA
(1977–81), a Democrat. Jimmy
Carter served as a physicist in
the navy, before taking over the
family peanut business.
Entered the Georgia State
Senate in 1962 and was
elected governor eight years
later. In 1976 he defeated
Gerald Ford in the presidential
election, becoming the first
southern president since the
American Civil War. During his
presidency, control of the
Panama Canal Zone was
returned to Panama, an
amnesty programme for
deserters and draft dodgers of
the Vietnam War was
introduced, and the Camp
David Agreements for peace in
the Middle East were drawn
up. Defeated by Ronald
Reagan in 1980.

Dissidents: Those who oppose or
criticise the government. Especially
applied to the USSR in the 1970s
when groups of intellectuals and
writers criticised the Soviet
government for signing the Helsinki
Accords on human rights but denied
free speech to their own citizens.

Democratic President Jimmy Carter wanted an ethical foreign policy.
Nixon had left office in disgrace and Carter was determined to pursue a
more honourable conduct in world affairs. Yet this presented a problem.
On the one hand, he was keen to reduce arms but, at the same time, he
was very critical of the Soviet Union for its treatment of **dissidents**,
which the Soviets resented. He was very inexperienced in foreign affairs,
and so depended heavily on the advice of his Secretary of State, Cyrus
Vance, and Secretary of Defense, Zbigniew Brzezinski. These two men
had very differing views on how to handle the USSR. All this meant that
Carter's policies were frequently inconsistent. For example, he removed
American missiles from South Korea to show good faith to the Soviets,
but then sent Brzezinski on a visit to China, which angered and worried
the Soviet government.

Arms reduction talks continued into 1978 and 1979, but this atmosphere of uncertainty made them difficult. It was also hard as Carter kept
trying to link arms reduction to human rights issues. The Soviets saw this
as the United States trying to interfere in Soviet internal affairs. However,
an agreement was finally reached in June 1979 (SALT II). There was to be
a limit on delivery vehicles (i.e. missiles and bombers) of 2,400, falling to
2,250 by 1982. There was also to be a limit on the number of warheads
per vehicle. The measure was limited but important, as it actually seemed
to introduce a reduction, not just a halt, in the arms build-up. In fact, both
the USSR and the Americans carried on installing new missiles in Europe,
such as the Pershing and the SS-20. SALT II was also widely criticised at
home. The left felt it did not go far enough, while the right felt it gave too
much away to the Soviets. Carter himself admitted that it was little, but it
was better than nothing. In the end, the arguments were irrelevant as the
USSR invaded Afghanistan in December 1979 and the Senate refused to
ratify the SALT treaty.

How did the USA react to the war in Afghanistan?

From the Russian point of view, the invasion of Afghanistan was to protect
themselves from Islamic fundamentalism and to support a friendly, neighbouring government. To the Americans, it was more proof of the basic

aggression of communism: nothing had changed since 1945. Carter announced the 'Carter Doctrine' – extending the Truman Doctrine to the Middle East – but, in reality, there was little the Americans could do. They were certainly not prepared to go to war to protect the Afghans and military support was virtually impossible in this land-locked, mountainous region.

As well as abandoning SALT II, the American government stopped exports to the USSR and increased their defence budget by $17.1 billion. The President also boycotted the Olympics held in Moscow in 1980, but many athletes went ahead and competed, ignoring their president's wishes. Carter tried to get America's European allies to join in the trade and sports boycotts but, though there was little support for the invasion in Europe, there was also little support for a trade boycott of Russia. Europe did not see the issue as that important and felt that Carter was over-reacting, especially with America's own record in Vietnam. In the end, what removed the Red Army from Afghanistan in 1988 was their own realisation that, after eight years, they were not going to win.

> 1. Why did The USSR and America pursue détente in the 1970s?
>
> 2. How far had relations between the superpowers improved between 1968 and 1980?

8.8 Why did the Cold War in Europe come to an end?

Ronald Wilson Reagan (1911–)
40th President of the USA (1981–89), a Republican with strong anti-communist views. He was a Hollywood actor before becoming governor of California. Reagan defeated Carter in the 1980 presidential election. During the 1980s, he launched the biggest peacetime military build-up in US history. Supporter of the 'star wars' initiative. However, from 1985 he negotiated with Soviet leader Gorbachev towards reducing nuclear weapons in START (strategic arms reduction talks). He was wounded in an assassination attempt in 1981. Re-elected in 1984, in a landslide victory.

Between 1979 and 1986, a new Cold War was emerging. The Soviet invasion of Afghanistan had increased the belief in the USA that the USSR had not changed after 30 years and was still intent on establishing its power over other countries. American deployment of new weapons in Europe – such as Cruise missiles – made the Soviets feel threatened once more. Third World conflicts also affected relations between East and West, particularly in the Middle East and in Latin America. Another factor was that new leaders had emerged in both countries. Leonid Brezhnev died in 1982 and was followed in rapid succession by Yuri Andropov and Konstantin Chernenko. Both men were old and ill and their unexpected deaths following so quickly created instability both in the USSR itself and in relations with the USA. The United States, too, had a change of leader in the election of 1980, which had a great impact on the Cold War.

Carter's indecisive and weak foreign policy, not just in Europe but around the world, gave way to the patriotic and aggressive foreign policy of Republican President Ronald Reagan. He believed the USA should support its friends, even if they were dictators, oppose their enemies and be prepared to use military force where necessary. He referred to the Soviet Union as the 'evil empire' and said that all the troubles in the world could be traced back to the USSR, a country bent on world domination.

How much Reagan really believed that the USSR was an evil empire is debatable. His supporters argue that he knew the Soviet Union was getting weak internally, its economy was in bad shape and the war in Afghanistan was putting more strain on it and on Russian society. Therefore, by putting the Soviet Union under further pressure, Reagan would force it to negotiate over arms and to begin reforming the USSR.

Others feel that Reagan did believe the USSR was behind most of the world's troubles. He was a fervent capitalist who detested the communist system. The Soviets had been increasing their influence in Africa and Latin America, so Reagan was convinced they were trying to take over the world. Whatever the truth, Reagan certainly pursued an uncompromising Cold War policy.

How far did Reagan pursue arms reduction?

The United States, under Ronald Reagan, embarked on the biggest arms build-up in its history. In the 1980s, $550 billion a year was being spent on conventional and nuclear weapons. New systems were being developed, such as the stealth bomber and the neutron bomb (the Soviets called this the capitalist bomb as it was supposed to destroy biological matter, such as people, but not property). In 1983, Cruise missiles were shipped to bases in Europe. This made those areas targets. It sparked several protests, including a seven-year protest by women at Greenham Common, in Britain. In spite of this phenomenal build-up, Reagan was also prepared to talk about arms control. He believed that America had to negotiate from a position of strength, otherwise it would be seen as weak and would be vulnerable to attack.

In 1982, the Strategic Arms Reduction Talks (START) began in Geneva but they failed to produce an agreement. The basic problem was that the two sides did not trust each other. During the talks, the Soviet Union clamped down hard on 'Solidarity', a democratic trade union movement which had developed in Poland. In 1983, they shot down a Korean passenger plane killing 269 people. As far as Reagan was concerned, this was typically aggressive communist behaviour. The Soviets had equal reason to be mistrustful of the Americans. During negotiations, the American side refused to discuss the possibility of including NATO in arms reduction and seemed to be asking for more than they were willing to give up. In March 1983, Reagan announced the development of the Strategic Defence Initiative (SDI), nicknamed 'star wars'. This programme was supposedly a defence shield which would destroy any missiles fired at the USA while they were still in space. In fact, most scientists believed it was unworkable. However, if it did work it would mean that many Russian missiles were effectively useless, while leaving the USSR still open to attack. To them, it seemed that the USA was talking about peace but its actions were very different.

How did Gorbachev affect the Cold War?

In 1985, Mikhail Gorbachev became the new Soviet leader and set about a new programme of reform in the USSR. This raised fears in the United States that the reforms would strengthen the USSR and improve its position in the Cold War. Although Britain's Prime Minister, Margaret Thatcher, said she could 'do business' with him, early encounters between Reagan and Gorbachev did not go well. Meetings in Geneva in 1985 and Reykjavik in 1986 produced no real agreement on arms. They argued about the types of weapon to be limited and whether current agreements were being abided by, but the real stumbling block continued to be SDI. In 1987, they signed the Intermediate-range Nuclear Forces Treaty (INF). This was a major achievement as, for the first time, there were to be actual reductions in weapons. Intermediate-range weapons were to be dismantled and there were to be inspections to ensure that each side was fulfilling its obligations. The first weapons were dismantled in 1988.

Why had this improvement happened? Many credit Reagan's military build-up with forcing the USSR into a position where it simply could not afford to carry on trying to keep up with the United States. The build-up had also worried both America's allies and the general public about the sheer number of nuclear weapons now in existence. This concern about nuclear proliferation was increased in 1986 with the accident at the Chernobyl nuclear reactor in the Ukraine, which contaminated the land and atmosphere as far away as Wales. A major factor was that the relationship between Reagan and Gorbachev had become very productive. Reagan realised that Gorbachev was genuinely looking for a better relationship with the West, and Reagan himself was more willing to compromise than his talk about the 'evil empire' implied.

Mikhail Sergeivich Gorbachev (1931–)

Son of a peasant family, he became a law graduate and joined the Communist Party in 1946. He rose through the Party to become Secretary for Agriculture in 1978 and at 41 the youngest member of the Politburo, the USSR's governing body, in 1980. In March 1985, he was elected General Secretary of the Politburo, making him in effect the leader of the USSR. He wanted to modernise the country and make it more efficient but soon realised that to do this there had to be serious reform of the Soviet system. He embarked on policies of *perestroika* (restructuring) and *glasnost* (openness), which ended in creating a democratic system in the Soviet Union. His work to democratise the USSR and the freedoms he introduced into Eastern Europe won him the Nobel Peace Prize in 1990.

Relations continued to improve with a visit by Reagan to Moscow in 1988. Yet the INF treaty only cut out one class of missile. The build-up Reagan had instigated meant there were still thousands of nuclear weapons in the East and West pointed at each other, and he had taken the USA into enormous debt to pay for them.

Why did communism in Eastern Europe collapse?

The true roots of the collapse of communism in the USSR and Eastern Europe lay in Soviet and Russian history, but the Cold War was a contributing factor. By maintaining a policy of containment for 40 years, the USA had ensured that the Soviets had to spend a lot of money on arms – money they were not able to spend improving conditions for their people. Reagan's spending made this even worse. To execute his planned reforms, Gorbachev had to reduce the Russian military. This gave encouragement to Eastern European states that they could also reform and that the Red Army would not stop them this time. From 1989, change began to happen rapidly. The border between Austria and Hungary was opened up, allowing people to travel from East Germany to the West, through Hungary and Austria. The numbers of people passing through became a flood. Gorbachev advised the East Germans to open the Berlin Wall and allow direct travel from East to West.

On 9 November 1989, the East Germans opened up the Berlin Wall. Citizens of the city, who had been divided from friends and family for four generations, poured through. All over the world, millions watched the events unfold on television, knowing that they were witnessing a turning point in history. The end of the Cold War had begun.

What was the US response to events in Europe?

The new President, George Bush, reacted slowly to events in the East. There were some who advised him to move quickly, especially when the Warsaw

What does this celebration on top of the Berlin Wall tell historians about the collapse of the Wall and the end of the Cold War?

Protesters on the Berlin Wall on 9 November 1989.

George Herbert Walker Bush (1924–)
41st President of the USA (1989–93), a Republican. Director of the CIA (1976–81) and Vice-President (1981–89). As President, sending US troops to depose General Noriega of Panama was popular at home. Success in the 1991 Gulf War against Iraq further raised his standing. However, despite signing START I (July 1991) and reducing US nuclear weapons, Bush's popularity at home began to wane. Defeated by Democrat Bill Clinton in the 1992 Presidential elections.

Pact collapsed at the end of 1989. An intelligent and well-travelled man, George Bush felt that, as the situation in the USSR and Eastern Europe was changing so rapidly, it was best for the USA to move slowly and avoid making any costly errors. The Warsaw Pact might have ended, but the USSR still possessed its nuclear weapons and one of the largest armies in the world.

Meetings were arranged throughout 1989 between Secretary of State James Baker and Russian Foreign Minister Eduard Shevardnadze. They discussed the ongoing changes in the Soviet Union and the East, and raised the possibility of beginning the START talks again. This time, the Soviets made it clear they would accept America's development of SDI, thus removing one of the major obstacles to an agreement.

In June 1990, Bush and Gorbachev met in Washington. They agreed to cuts in both chemical weapons and long-range nuclear weapons. This was made formal in July under START I, which limited both countries to 1,600 nuclear delivery vehicles (i.e. bombers, submarines etc.) and 6,000 nuclear devices. As with the INF treaty, this represented a reduction in the number of weapons and allowed for verification (checking by the other side). The two men also agreed to greater contacts between the two countries and to increased trade.

The situation in Europe continued to develop rapidly. In the spring of 1990, the Baltic States of Latvia, Estonia and Lithuania declared their independence from the USSR, followed by the Ukraine. All over the East – in Romania, East Germany and elsewhere – Communist dictators were being pressured by the people into resigning and were being replaced by democratic governments. In the USSR itself, Gorbachev was a victim as he was too closely identified with the old regime. Boris Yeltsin replaced him in December 1991 and the Union of Soviet Socialist Republics became the Commonwealth of Independent States. On Christmas Day 1991, the red flag bearing the hammer and sickle was removed from the Kremlin (central government building).

Perhaps the most important change of all came in Germany. Once the Berlin Wall was opened, demands for re-unification began. In July 1990, a new West German Chancellor, Helmut Kohl, was elected promising to re-unite his country. Bush and Gorbachev discussed the situation at their meeting in June and afterwards. America wanted the new united Germany to be a member of NATO, but Gorbachev was reluctant to accept this and wondered what NATO's purpose was now that the Cold War was over. Some other states were also concerned by the re-unification of Germany, having suffered two world wars in the 20th century which were both, arguably, due to German militarism. The Americans and Germans worked to remove these fears by pledging that the latter would not have nuclear or biological weapons and that their army, which now numbered 1.8 million, would be held in check by membership of NATO.

In September 1990, the armies of occupation were removed from Germany. In October, the Federal Republic and the Democratic Republic were joined together, re-uniting Germany 45 years after Potsdam. Perhaps Truman's policy of containment had held the line and maintained peace in Europe for all this time. Perhaps Kennan was right when he looked back in the 1960s and said that he had been wrong and that America should have tried to find a way of working with the USSR. The Cold War in Europe had cost the United States billions of dollars and decades of tension. Yet it was only after its end, in the former Yugoslavia, that NATO troops had to be sent into the field to contain a war on European soil.

1. In what ways was SDI threatening to the Soviet Union?

2. How consistent was President Reagan's arms policy?

The USA and the Cold War in Asia, 1945–1973

Key Issues

● Why did the Cold War spread to Asia after 1945?

● With what success did the USA contain the spread of communism in Asia, 1945–1975?

● How far did US policy towards Asia change, 1945–1975?

Framework of Events

1945	US occupation of Japan begins
1946	Truce in Chinese Civil War
1948	China Aid Act
	Two separate governments set up in North and South Korea
1949	Communist victory in Chinese Civil War
1950	USSR and China sign mutual defence pact
	(June) Outbreak of war in Korea
1951	US–Japanese treaty
	US treaty with the Philippines
1952	US occupation of Japan ends
1953	End of Korean War
1954	Fall of Dien Bien Phu
	Geneva Accords on French Indo-China
	Defence Pact between USA and Taiwan/Formosa
	(September) Signing of SEATO
1955	First Formosa/Taiwan Crisis
1958	Second Formosa/Taiwan Crisis
1962	Neutrality of Laos agreed in Geneva
1963	(2 November) Assassination of President Diem of South Vietnam
	(22 November) Assassination of President Kennedy
1964	(August) Gulf of Tonkin Incident
1965	(February) Attack on US military base at Pleiku
	(March) Marines land at Da Nang in South Vietnam
	Anti-war protests by Students for a Democratic Society
1968	(January) Tet Offensive in South Vietnam
	(16 March) My Lai Massacre
1969	(May) Paris peace talks begin
	(15 October) March Against Death
1970	(30 April) Invasion of Cambodia
	(4 May) Students killed in protest at Kent State University
1972	Linebacker bombing campaigns
	(22 February) Nixon visits China

1973	(27 January) Paris Peace Agreement
	(March) Americans withdraw from South Vietnam
1975	(April) Fall of Saigon.

Overview

WHILE President Truman focused his attention on Europe after the end of the Second World War, there were those in government who argued that equal attention needed to be paid to the East. After all, it was the attack on Pearl Harbor by the Japanese that had brought the Americans into the War and the USA had a long history of friendship with the Chinese going back to the 1890s. As America also got rubber and oil from the East and had bases in the Pacific, the Far East was also strategically important. These 'Asia-firsters' argued that Europeans could take care of themselves and that the government should pay more attention to the East. But as the chief adversary in the Cold War was the Soviet Union, Europe tended to play a larger role in American foreign policy. At times, events in Asia forced themselves to the forefront.

At the end of the Second World War, the Americans took on the role of main occupiers in Japan, hoping to turn it into a democratic and peaceful power. It was to be weakened so that it would never again threaten America's interests in the Pacific. Events in China forced a change of attitude. When China 'fell' to communism in 1949, Japan was turned into the United States' foremost ally in the region and was built up to be a balance against communist expansion in Asia. By 1951, the Americans had a formal alliance with their recent enemy.

The threat of the world's most populous nation falling to communism led to the extension of the Truman Doctrine to the Far East. However, geographical, as well as political, realities prevented the USA from helping the Nationalist forces in China to halt the advance of Mao's Communists. By continuing to back Chiang Kai-Shek and the Nationalists, the Americans found themselves on the verge of war with China in 1955, and again in 1958. The disagreements were over the fate of the islands of Formosa (now known as Taiwan), to which the Nationalists had fled in 1949. Disputes over the islands have continued to damage American relations with China ever since.

The policy of containment, embodied in the Truman Doctrine in 1947, could be said to have prevented war in Europe for 40 years, yet that same policy found the Americans getting into a war in the Far East in 1950. At the end of the Second World War, Korea had been divided into a Communist North and a Democratic South, led by Kim Il Sung and Syngman Rhee respectively, who both wanted to re-unify their nation. In 1950, the North Koreans invaded the South to do just that. President Truman, supported by the United Nations, decided to take a stand. An army from 16 countries went to Korea to throw out the invaders. Rather than achieving a quick and easy victory, American arrogance led to the Chinese entering the war and a two-year stalemate resulted. The war finally ended in 1953, with Korea still divided.

Even more damaging was the American involvement in Vietnam. When the former French colony of Indo-China attempted to gain its independence, in 1945, they hoped the Americans, as former colonials themselves, would help.

Instead the Americans chose to back their NATO ally in their unsuccessful attempt to hold on to power. After the French defeat at Dien Bien Phu, Indo-China was divided into four areas, with Vietnam divided, like Korea, into a communist North and a non-communist South. Unlike Korea, however, there was widespread support in Vietnam – North and South – for the Communist leader Ho Chi Minh. As in Korea, the Americans tried to enforce containment. The so-called 'Domino Theory' convinced them that, if South Vietnam were allowed to fall to communism, then the rest of Asia would follow.

Over the next two decades, American involvement in South Vietnam was gradually increased. By 1965, combat troops landed at Da Nang, the first marines sent abroad to fight since Korea: America was again at war. This time though they were fighting a jungle war, with no clear enemy in a different uniform, and they were fighting without the support of the majority of the population or of their allies. The conduct of the war in Vietnam and American losses led to an anti-war movement at home which actively opposed the governments of Johnson and Nixon. The war divided American society like no other since the Civil War. It was a war which the country was not winning. Finally, in 1973, a peace treaty was agreed and the United States pulled its troops out of Vietnam. The 'fall' which they had tried so hard to prevent happened just two years later with a North Vietnamese invasion followed by the unification of the country under Communist leadership.

American conduct of the Cold War in Asia was far less successful than its policy in Europe. In many ways, containment was an inappropriate response to events in the Far East. It assumed that the Soviet Union was behind all communist movements and, when China became communist, it was assumed the two powers acted as one. In both these assumptions, the Americans were wrong. The Soviet Union was undoubtedly involved in the spread of communism to Asia, and it did sometimes work hand in hand with China. More often the rise of communism was the result of local conditions. Revolutionary groups such as the Vietcong were frequently more nationalist than communist. This failure to understand the Far East was affected by the McCarthyism of the 1940s, which saw the removal of many experts from the State Department because of accusations of communist sympathies. It was also due to seeing policies work in Europe and falsely believing that they could be applied elsewhere. Some argue it was also due to American racism going back to the 19th century which underestimated Asian peoples. The USA did have some successes in the Far East, in fact they achieved their aims much of the time. It was the disaster in Vietnam which was the major weakness in US policy in the Far East during the Cold War.

9.1 How successful were US policies towards Japan, 1945–1952?

After the surrender in August 1945, the United States occupied Japan in order to establish a new, democratic government. As in Germany, there was a council of the four powers to discuss Japanese issues, but only US troops occupied the country. The USA also took control of several Pacific islands including the Marshall Islands, the Marianas and the Carolinas (see map on page 244). They also occupied the islands of Okinawa and Iwo Jima which they had fought so hard to capture during the War. This American dominance angered the Soviets but, as they had entered the war against Japan so late, they could do little more than protest. In respect for

**Douglas MacArthur
(1880–1964)**
Professional soldier who
served in France during the
First World War and in the
Philippines in the 1930s. He
commanded US forces in the
Pacific during the Second
World War and after a retreat
from the Philippine Islands he
organised the 'island hopping'
campaign which helped to
recapture the Pacific. He was
in command of UN forces in
Korea until removed by
Truman.

Feudalism: A system of organising
society based on land ownership and
obligation. In return for protection
and being able to farm the land, the
peasant gives obedience and service
to the landowner. This system had
been widespread in Europe but had
died out in the 18th and 19th
centuries. A type of feudalism had
continued in Japan, and the
Americans believed it held Japan
back from developing democratic
institutions. Also, because it
emphasised obedience, it had
allowed the military to lead Japan
into war. The Americans hoped that
abolishing it would speed up Japan's
modernisation.

their contribution to the war and for their strategic concerns in Asia, they were given a role in the occupation of Korea instead. The USA did as much as possible to limit Soviet and, therefore, communist influence in the Far Eastern settlement.

General MacArthur, the American commander in Japan, was given almost dictatorial power to turn Japan from a militaristic state into a democratic one. Communists were banned from government posts, the military was drastically reduced and **feudalism** was ended. MacArthur encouraged reform with votes for women, legalisation of trade unions, a democratic constitution that outlawed war, and a democratically elected government. The kind of democracy the Americans wished to create in Japan between 1945 and 1952 was very much in their own image. Communists were banned from government positions or from posts in the universities where they might influence future leaders, and restrictions were placed on trade unions. While trade links with other Asian states were encouraged, the Americans did not wish to see Japan regain its former position. It would be taught by the USA to be democratic and peaceful and content within its own islands.

Chinese troops march through Beijing in 1949. The soldiers on the lorry are holding up a photograph of Mao Ze-dong and a propaganda poster.

Why did American policy towards Japan change?

Originally, the USA had seen China as its main trading and military partner in the Far East, but 1949 changed that. When the communists won the civil war in China, it became important to build Japan back up as a strong power to counter-balance 'Red' China. Building up the Japanese economy would also have the added benefit of providing a market for US goods now that much of the former trade with China was lost. Also, as in Europe, there was the fear that if Japan remained a poor country it would be more susceptible to communism itself. All these factors turned American policy towards Japan around. It would continue to be developed as a democratic nation, but from 1950 onwards there would be help and support for its rapid economic redevelopment. The occupying forces did much to rebuild Japanese industry and Congress gave $500 million in aid. America's allies in the East – Thailand, the Philippines and Indonesia, for example – were encouraged to trade with Japan and open up their markets to Japanese exports. The Americans were determined that as the old colonial powers lost their influence in Asia, America would not lose its and it would not see communism take over. In the words of historian Richard Crockatt, in *The United States and the Cold War 1941–1953* (1989), 'Japan became the keystone of containment in Asia.'

The decision to strengthen Japan was given added urgency in 1950 when war broke out in Korea between the communist North and the western-backed South. Japan could now be useful as a base from which to run operations in Korea and as a place for 'R and R' (rest and recuperation away from the war) for American soldiers. To reinforce the new friendship a treaty was signed, in 1951, formally ending the war between the USA and Japan. The occupation ended on 28 April 1952. Also, in September 1951, a Mutual Security Treaty was signed allowing the USA to maintain military bases and troops on Japanese territory. Japan was allowed to develop an army of 110,000 men for its own defence.

Although they had been part of the war against Japan, the Soviets refused to sign the treaty. Relations between the USA and the Soviet Union had deteriorated badly in Europe since 1945 and conflicts in the East made things worse. Understandably, they took differing positions with regard to the revolution in China and the war in Korea. The USSR also resented the way it had been edged out of all decisions relating to Japan. The Soviets felt that they had a valid interest in the area. (Japan and Russia had fought a war, 1905–06, and had several historical disputes over territory.) They knew that Japan was being built up as part of American containment policy and, to the USSR, it looked as if they were being encircled.

The Soviets were not the only ones less than happy with these developments. Those countries which had suffered Japanese attack during the War were very uneasy and, within Japan itself, there were several demonstrations against the American bases. In 1954, anti-American riots forced Eisenhower to cancel a proposed visit to Japan.

In spite of the concerns, Japan quickly became economically powerful and was one of America's strongest allies in the East. Continued support and aid built Japan up from a defeated nation to one that was competing economically with the United States itself by the 1960s. The constitution which the USA had given it meant that they never supplied military help to the Americans in places such as Korea or Vietnam but, ironically, this also meant that they spent their money on economic growth not war. The thriving capitalist economy was a stronger protection against communist infiltration than any number of US bases.

1. In what ways was the political system of Japan changed under the Allied occupation?

2. Why was the USSR excluded from the Japanese settlement?

3. Why and how did American policy towards Japan change?

9.2   Why did the United States fail to prevent a Communist victory in China?

What was American policy towards the Chinese Civil War, 1945–1949?

* Chinese names can be spelled a number of ways. Chiang Kai-Shek is sometimes seen as Jiang Jei-shi and Mao Ze-dong as Mao Tse-Tung.

In 1927 a civil war broke out in China between the Nationalists, led by Chiang Kai-Shek* and the Communists, led by Mao Ze-dong. The USA had ties of trade and immigration with China going back into the 19th century and China was therefore seen as culturally and economically important to the USA. Their isolationist policies of the 1920s meant they watched with interest but took no real part in events. When the Japanese attacked China in 1937, the various groups in the civil war put aside their differences to fight the invader. At Yalta, Roosevelt had persuaded Stalin to support Chiang and to keep Mao under control so that they could focus on defeating Japan. However, conflict broke out again in 1945.

Clearly, the Americans did not want the Communists to win. A communist victory, they felt, would endanger the 'open door' trade policy which they had fought so hard to establish in China decades before. There was also a danger of communism spreading to Japan, where the USA was working hard to establish a democratic government. On the other hand, State Department officials warned Truman of the danger of identifying the Americans too closely with Chiang who was both corrupt and unpopular. Ideally, what Truman wanted was a negotiated peace which would allow the Nationalists a part in government, as well as remove the need for US intervention. An American-backed conference between Chiang and Mao, in 1945, failed to find a solution. Chiang refused to make concessions, particularly over the industrialised area of Manchuria, which both sides wished to control. Truman sent 50,000 US troops to try to help Chiang establish control once the Soviets had pulled out. This encouraged Chiang to believe that he would have American support for whatever policies he chose.

Collectivisation: The bringing under state ownership and control of farms and factories. The usual method is to combine a number of small firms or factories into lone larger one.

The following year, President Truman sent George Marshall to try and find a solution. He managed to negotiate a truce in January 1946, but it fell apart within three months when Chiang's forces attacked Manchuria after the Soviets had pulled out leaving Mao in control of the area. American support failed to help the Nationalists take the province and as

---

Chiang Kai-Shek (1887–1975)
The son of a middle-class family who became a professional soldier in 1906. While in the military he became a republican and revolutionary. When the empire fell apart, Chiang joined Sun Yat-sen's Nationalists who were trying to re-unite China. Jiang went to Moscow in 1923 to study the Soviet system, but in 1927 he threw the communists out of the Nationalist Party. In 1928, he established a government in Nanking, but it was in conflict with the

communists and then the Japanese. When Chiang lost the civil war in 1949 he took his forces to Taiwan where, with the backing of the USA, he established an economically successful state.

Mao Ze-dong (1883–1976)
Born into a peasant family, he studied at Beijing University and worked for a while as a primary teacher. Mao was a founding member of the Chinese Communist Party (CCP) in 1921. He worked on labour organisations.

Unlike most communists, who said that the urban working classes were the foundation of the revolution, Mao argued that the peasants were also potential revolutionaries. When Chiang threw the communists out of the Nationalist Party (1927), Mao and his followers began to organise the peasants in the countryside. In 1934, he led the 'Long March' during which his followers fled 6,000 miles across China to escape attack by the Nationalists. Under

Mao's leadership, the CCP grew to over a million strong by 1945. During the 1950s, Mao attempted to modernise China with the 'Great Leap Forward' programmes of industrialisation and **collectivisation** of agriculture, but they produced much hardship for the Chinese people. As rivalry for the leadership of world communism intensified, Chinese relations with the USSR deteriorated in the 1960s, while in the 1970s friendship with the USA grew.

Albert Coady Wedemeyer (1897–1989)
A professional soldier, Wedemeyer served in China and Germany between the wars and spoke Mandarin Chinese. During the Second World War he worked with General Marshall (see Chapter 8) and helped to plan the Normandy landings. In 1944, he was sent again to the Far East and advised support for the Nationalists in China. He retired in 1951.

China lobby: Politicians, businessmen and others who tried to pressure the government over their policy on China. They were usually the 'Asia-firsters' (see page 291) but included others who wanted the government to do more for China.

popular resentment against Chiang grew, it was also turned against the United States. In 1946, the Americans started to withdraw.

In the USA, Truman was criticised, especially by the Republicans, for not applying the principles of containment to Asia. General Wedemeyer advised giving further financial support to the Nationalists and, in 1948, the China Aid Act gave $400 million to Chiang, bringing to $3 billion the amount of aid given by the US since 1945. However, the aid was having little effect. Even as the Act was being passed, the Communists were moving towards victory. The outbreak of the crisis in Berlin meant that American attention was focused firmly on events in Germany. By October 1949, the Communists had won and Chiang Kai-Shek and and his two million followers had fled to the island of Formosa/Taiwan. The Americans refused to recognise the communist government of the People's Republic of China. Instead they continued to refer to Taiwan and its government as Nationalist China.

Why did the USA not intervene in China?

When General Wedemeyer gave his advice to President Truman, he said that the USA should send another 10,000 troops to help Chiang, but Truman refused. Secretary of State, Dean Acheson, pointed out that sending advisors or military chiefs would lead to more troops being sent and America had neither the men nor the desire to get into a land war in China. The defeat was also happening at the same time as problems were increasing in Berlin, so the government did not want to tie up troops in the Far East when they might be needed in Europe.

Acheson also had to admit that it was largely Chiang's own fault that he had lost. The Nationalist leader was corrupt and undemocratic, so support for Mao was strong among the poor in China. The Nationalists refused to support land reform and therefore failed to gain the support of the peasants, who made up 80% of the population. They even lost middle-class support by letting inflation run at 700%, wiping out people's savings and businesses. In 1945, Chiang had an army of 2½ million, outnumbering the Communists five to one but, by 1949, the Nationalist forces had halved through defections to the Communist side.

American political sympathies might have been with the Nationalists, but nothing either Truman or the **China lobby** could say or do would alter the realities of the situation. The USA simply could not send tens of thousands of men across an ocean to face an enemy of several millions, or do this in support of a government which was unpopular among many of its own people. As Acheson wrote, in the so-called 'China White Paper' published in 1949, 'Nothing this country did or could have done within the reasonable limits of its capabilities would have changed the result [of the civil war].'

The geographical and political realities did not stop Truman's critics from accusing him of 'losing' China. To many Americans, it seemed that communism was indeed spreading. The signing of a mutual defence pact between China and the USSR, in 1950, confirmed the belief that the Soviet Union was bent on world domination and had now added the world's most populous country to its sphere of influence. Together the USSR and China formed a massive bloc, cutting off a huge market for US trade and spreading communist dominance into the Far East.

What was the effect of the 'loss' of China on US policy?

John Dulles called it 'the worst defeat the United States has suffered in its history'. In many ways the United States over-reacted to the events in China. Firstly, for all the politicians might argue, China had not been

America's to 'lose' – as many historians have pointed out. Acheson was right when he acknowledged that there was nothing the USA could have done to affect the outcome of the Civil War. It was a fight over which they had no control and which was about China, not about the Cold War as they believed (a lesson America might well have learned before Vietnam). The Americans also overestimated the strength of the bonds between China and the USSR. They might have signed an alliance, but there were deep-seated rivalries over territory in Manchuria and over the nature and leadership of worldwide communism. The USA assumed that the two communist states acted together, and in this they were frequently wrong. However, the 'loss' was very damaging for Truman and did affect both foreign and domestic policy.

The Republicans blamed Truman for the fall of China to communism. It helped to fuel the rise in McCarthyism as they accused spies in the State Department of being responsible. Their accusation of spies in the government was given added weight when the Soviet Union exploded its own atom bomb the same year that China fell. This not only cost many State Department officials their jobs, losing valuable expertise on far Eastern affairs, but also meant that Truman had to respond to the criticism by being seen to be equally tough on communism – which fuelled the anti-communist hysteria still further.

In spite of an early attempt by Mao Ze-dong to build a relationship with the United States, the Truman Administration refused to see Communist China as anything other than a Soviet puppet. Internationally, they tried to weaken Mao's position. They blocked the entry of the People's Republic into the United Nations and tried, largely unsuccessfully, to persuade their allies not to recognise Mao's government. They continued to give financial and moral support to the Nationalists in Taiwan. This support was to cause continuing problems for Eisenhower in the 1950s.

American policy in Asia was deeply affected by the loss of China. It led to a complete turn around in its conduct towards the Japanese, who now became the United States' most valued ally in the region. It also meant that, when Truman was faced with further communist aggression in Korea, he could not afford to back down.

1. In what ways did President Truman support the Nationalist Chinese?

2. How successful was American policy towards China in the years 1945 to 1949?

9.3 How and with what consequences for foreign policy in Asia did the USA get involved in war in Korea?

During the Second World War, Korea had been occupied by the Japanese. As a result of agreements at Potsdam, the Soviet Union had joined the war against Japan and helped to liberate Korea. Consequently, the country was divided at the end of the war into two zones, occupied by the Americans and the Soviets, with the border being the 38th Parallel (see map on page 290). As in Germany, the division was meant to be temporary and elections were to be held to unify the country. However, when the Americans submitted the issue to the United Nations in 1947, the USSR refused to go along with it. The Americans decided to go ahead and hold elections in

Syngman Rhee (1875–1965)
Korean nationalist who was imprisoned by the government in his youth for his political activities. He studied in the USA, returning briefly to Korea before Japan occupied it in 1912. He returned to the USA to campaign for Korean independence. He was elected president of South Korea four times between 1948 and 1960. Although in theory South Korea was a democracy, Rhee's rule was very dictatorial. Student-led protests in 1960 led to his resignation and exile.

Kim Il Sung (1912–1994)

As a young man he fought in the guerrilla movements against Japanese occupation. In the 1930s, he went to train in the USSR and during the Second World War he served in a Korean unit in the Red Army. He became the Soviet-backed leader of North Korea in 1948. After the war he made North Korea into a one-party dictatorship. Even after the fall of communism in Europe in 1989, North Korea remained firmly **Stalinist**. He remained leader of the country until his death in 1994, when his son succeeded him.

Stalinist: A political system based on the type of communism developed by Stalin in the USSR 1929–53. It is highly centralised, the leader has great authority, and there is widespread use of terror.

their zone the next year. The two superpowers then pulled their troops out, leaving a divided Korea with Syngman Rhee leader of a democratic South and a communist-backed North under Kim Il Sung.

The Soviets had opposed the elections, as they believed Korea would vote to be a capitalist democracy. The USSR wanted to extend their power into the Far East, so a united, non-communist Korea was not in their interests. With China about to fall under communist control, Korea would add to the strength of communism in the area and extend Soviet influence. For similar reasons, the Americans did not want a united Korea if it were under communism. So, when the Soviet Union refused to go along with the elections, the Americans just held elections in their own zone. Though they wanted free elections they were not prepared to fight the USSR over the issue, especially when Berlin and China were of more immediate concern.

How did the war break out?

On 25 June 1950, North Korean troops invaded the South. Almost 100,000 men, equipped with Soviet-made tanks and aircraft, poured into the South capturing Seoul (the southern capital) and most of the country down to Pusan. The attack came without warning and was totally unexpected by the USA. In fact, diplomats heard the news first from journalists and refused to believe it. The South Koreans turned to America for help.

Truman felt he had no choice but to take a stand. Morally, the South Koreans had suffered an unprovoked attack and deserved aid from their allies. On a domestic political level, he had to take action. He was low in the opinion polls and there were mid-term elections coming in November. Truman had already been heavily criticised by McCarthy and by the Republicans for 'losing' China: he could not afford to lose Korea too. He also believed in the need for containment. He was convinced that the Soviet Union was behind the attack and, if the United States did not stop them in Korea, they would 'swallow up one piece of Asia after another'.

Two days after the attack, Truman ordered military supplies to be sent to South Korea from the American bases in Japan and ordered US planes and ships to the area. The 7th Fleet was sent to the China Sea to ensure the Chinese did not take advantage of the situation and attack Taiwan. Truman had decided that America would fight but, to avoid lengthy debate in Congress, he went to the United Nations for support for his action. He asked the UN Secretary General for a meeting of the Security Council. The UN Charter said that all the members would support any fellow member who suffered an unprovoked attack. It seemed that South Korea was in that position so the United Nations authorised the USA to organise and coordinate military action by 16 member nations against the North Koreans to get them out of the South.

Of the 11 members of the Security Council, only Communist Yugoslavia voted against the Korean operation. The Soviets could have exercised their veto in the Security Council to prevent the action, but the USSR was boycotting the UN at the time in protest at America blocking Communist China's entry to the organisation, so the vote passed. They did not make this mistake again.

How effectively did the UN pursue the war?

In July 1950, the first American troops landed in Korea. The counter-attack began in September when UN troops under General Douglas MacArthur landed at Inchon, behind the North Korean lines. The invasion quickly collapsed and by 8 October they had forced the North Koreans back behind the 38th Parallel. At this point, the Americans had achieved containment.

The United Nations
Set up in 1945 in San Francisco to remove sources of conflict and to preserve peace.

The General Assembly	**The Security Council**	**The Secretariat**
Each member state has a representative. It meets once a year and debates issues and allocates the budget.	It has five permanent members – Britain, USA, USSR, France and China – and originally had six non-permanent members. These are elected for two years by the Assembly, and the number has increased as the UN has grown. The permanent members have a veto over Council decisions.	This is the UN civil service and does the day-to-day work. In charge of it is the Secretary General, elected for five years by the Assembly. He (there has been no female Secretary General yet) is the face of the UN and can bring any matter to its attention.

The UN also has many agencies which deal with specific issues, such as the UNHCR for refugees, UNESCO for education and culture, WHO for health etc.

The UN has only twice organised peace enforcement operations: Korea in 1950–53 and the Gulf War in 1992.

They had done what the UN had authorised them to do (i.e. get the invaders out of South Korea). Instead of calling a ceasefire, the American-led forces invaded the North and, by October, had captured the northern capital, Pyongyang. With victory seeming so easy, the Americans decided to try and retake the initiative in the Cold War and regain some territory from the Communists.

An invasion of North Korea would be seen by the Chinese as a threat to their security. Urged on by Stalin, they warned the Americans not to invade North Korea. Neither the Americans nor their allies took the warning seriously. As American troops neared the Yalu River, the border between Korea and China, the Chinese invaded. On 19 October, 250,000 Chinese troops poured over the border. The UN forces were completely overwhelmed and within four months they had been pushed back and Seoul was once again in Communist hands. The Americans and the UN forces stood their ground and pushed northwards once again and, by late spring, the fighting settled around the 38th Parallel and got bogged down – almost like First World War trench warfare.

How was the war brought to an end?

Neither power wanted the war to spread to an all-out fight between America and China, nor did they want to involve the Soviets. Yet neither side wanted to back down. The Chinese knew the Americans would continue to support Chiang in Taiwan and that if they also controlled the Korean peninsula it would threaten Chinese security. While the Americans would not pull out of Korea, leaving it all in communist hands, containment meant they had to protect the South. Two years of attrition was the result.

To break the deadlock, General MacArthur wanted Truman to 'unleash Chiang' (i.e. to support an attack on the People's Republic by Nationalist forces from Taiwan). The British urged the Americans to be cautious about extending the boundaries of the war. Any direct attack on Chinese territory ran the risk of bringing the Soviet Union in to protect China. The danger was a third world war, and the British knew full well that the Soviets would probably launch an attack in Europe. The United Nations had only given them a mandate to remove the invaders from South Korea; they had not given permission for an attack on Communist China. President Truman knew that at home the people were growing tired of a war which had seemed to promise a short and easy victory, but had so far dragged on for over a year with no end in sight.

MacArthur, however, continued to press his arguments and even suggested that Truman use the atom bomb on China. In the spring of 1951, when Truman refused to see things his way, MacArthur complained to Joseph Martin, a Republican Congressman. Martin then went to the press and made public the disagreement over policies. In spite of the popularity of MacArthur, Truman had no choice but to sack him. A military commander could not be allowed to flout the will of the President and dispute his orders in public. MacArthur was replaced. The Joint Chiefs of Staff fully supported Truman's decision, but MacArthur was welcomed home as a hero. His dismissal did nothing for Truman's falling popularity.

It was obvious, even before 1951 was out, that the war was not going to be over quickly. Negotiations for an armistice began in Panmunjon but they dragged on for two years, while the fighting continued to claim lives from each side and from among the Korean civilian population. Then, in 1953, world circumstances changed, allowing for progress in the war. Stalin died and Eisenhower became President of the USA. During the election, 'Ike' had promised to end the war. Stalin's death meant the Soviet Union also had an excuse to improve relations with the USA and with a new government which genuinely wanted the war to end.

During the 1952 presidential election campaign, 'Ike' had promised to go to Korea personally to end the war. The death of Stalin meant that there was a more sympathetic attitude in the Soviet Union and a willingness to put pressure on China for a settlement. The negotiations, however, were not smooth. Twice nuclear war was threatened by Dulles who wanted to ensure the Chinese knew America was serious about ending the war one way or another. He threatened a second time when China stalled the talks because Syngman Rhee had released 25,000 prisoners when it had been agreed that the UN would do all prisoner repatriation. In order to get negotiations going again, Dulles threatened China with nuclear weapons, and they backed down.

A ceasefire was finally agreed in 1953, with the border being the 38th Parallel, where it remains today between communist North Korea and democratic South Korea. A de-militarised zone keeps the two sides apart.

The three-year war had ended with the situation pretty much as it had been before the war started. With the new border, the South Koreans gained 1,500 square miles of land. The cost of those 1,500 square miles was two million lives. During the course of the Korean War, 54,246 American soldiers died – only 4,000 fewer than in the 12-year conflict in Vietnam – and another 106,000 were wounded. The financial cost has been estimated as, at least, $20 billion. Containment in Asia was proving to be very expensive.

What were the effects of the Korean War on US policy?

Apart from the millions of dead and wounded, as well as the damage done to the villages and people of Korea, the war had important domestic and foreign policy effects on the United States.

Initially, the war had **bipartisan** support in Congress, but it quickly turned to criticism of Truman. The dragging out of the war after 1951 began to raise serious questions at home, which once again fuelled McCarthyism (see Chapter 11). The United States was the most powerful

Bipartisan: Supported by both parties. The parties put aside their differences for a while (e.g. in a war or over a piece of legislation on which they both agree).

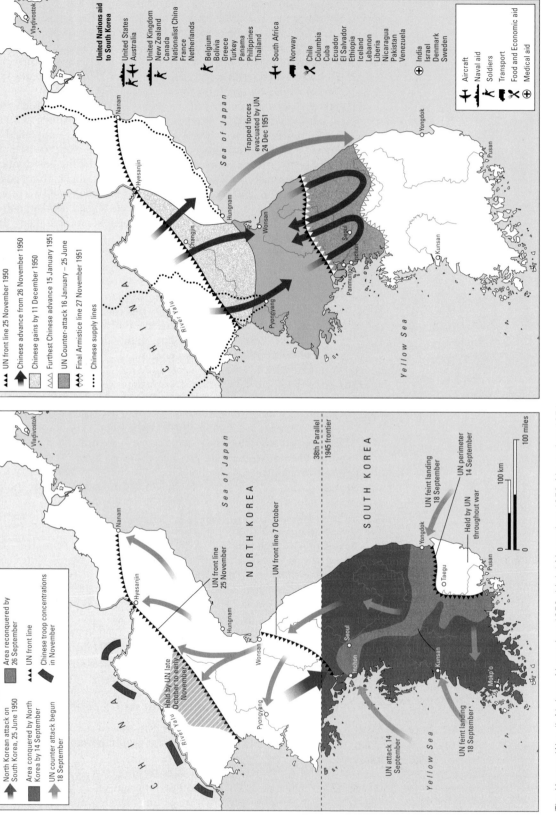

nation in the world and it was fighting, along with 15 other nations, a small Asian state. Why had they not won easily? Even when the Chinese entered the war, many Americans still could not understand their failure to secure victory against a country far less developed than theirs. Rather than look for real causes in the nature of the fighting or in the fact that a country of two billion people could absorb massive losses in battle, they looked for a scapegoat. Many found it by continuing to believe that traitors in the State Department and in government were to blame.

Many Republicans also blamed Truman for the war happening in the first place. The 'Asia-firsters' maintained that, if he had shown more resolve over China, Communist expansion would have been halted before it even reached Korea. They were still assuming that the Democratic Administration could have affected the Chinese civil war. Since Truman had proclaimed his Doctrine, the USA had been faced with having to decide whether or not to enforce it in Berlin, in China and in Korea. In the first it had succeeded, in the second it had not really been attempted, and in the third situation it had in fact succeeded by getting the North Koreans and the Chinese out of South Korea. But, as far as many Republicans were concerned, Truman's containment policy was failing in Asia.

When President Truman bypassed Congress and went to the United Nations to get support for a military operation in Korea, he was not going beyond his powers. As a member of the UN and signatory to the Charter, the USA could be expected to help a fellow member. As Commander-in-Chief of the US armed forces, Truman could send soldiers to fight abroad. Taking military action without fully consulting Congress was a further growth in Presidential power which began under Roosevelt and was to develop still further under Kennedy and Johnson with regard to Vietnam – and with more dire consequences.

The Korean War also had a serious impact on foreign policy. Korea had shown Truman the necessity of strengthening America's military position in the Far East. Truman set about forming treaties to put this right. Two defence treaties were signed in 1951, with Japan and with the Philippines. The same year, a defence pact was signed between Australia, New Zealand and the USA – the ANZUS Pact. This meant the USA was now more closely involved in Asian affairs. The Truman Doctrine, it seemed, was going to be applied to the East as well as to Europe. Although to Truman himself, Europe would always be more important, America built up bases and friendships in the East. Both military and economic aid was sent to its allies in Japan, the Philippines and Thailand.

The experience of the Korean War led the United States to be more active in its pursuit of containment in Asia. Not only did America build a system of alliances throughout the region, but there was a much firmer approach to crises in the area. When emergencies arose in Taiwan and when the French found themselves facing communist-led rebellion in Indo-China, the American position was firm. It seemed that military action was no longer ruled out. In fact, the military was deployed more frequently in Asia during the Cold War than in Europe.

President Truman not only strengthened America's military position in the Asia, he also strengthened NATO and built bases in North Africa. Eisenhower extended the system of treaties and bases creating the South East Asian Treaty Organisation (SEATO) and the Baghdad Pact in 1954. According to historian Stephen Ambrose, in *Rise to Globalism* (1997), 'Truman extended American bases around the world, hemming in both China and Russia.' The result of this containment was massive military spending. The defence budget, in 1953, was $52.6 billion. Kennan had thought of containment in primarily political and economic terms, but it was now firmly a military policy.

1. Why did the Korean War last three years?

2. General Omar Bradley famously said of MacArthur's plan to attack China that it would be 'the wrong war, in the wrong place, at the wrong time, against the wrong enemy'. How valid is this view when applied to US involvement in the Korean War?

9.4 Why did the Korean War take place?
A CASE STUDY IN HISTORICAL INTERPRETATION

The Korean War is often referred to by veterans as the 'forgotten war'. Sandwiched between the slaughter of the Second World War and the nightmare of Vietnam, its importance and its costs are often overlooked. In some ways, it is a simple war to explain: the North launched an unprovoked attack on the South; the UN came to the defence of the South and threw out the armies of the North. The intervention of the Chinese was a mistake. Unfortunately, it meant the war took longer than it should have.

The issues of the Korean War are much more complex than that. Whose fault was the war? Some blame Truman for not backing the South more forcefully, while others blame the South because there were many border incidents caused by the South which could have led to war. The North Koreans invaded, but would Kim Il Sung have dared to start a war without consulting Stalin?

Coming as it did just after the 'fall' of China, many people at the time saw the Korean War in the context of the Cold War in Asia. Many on the right, such as the 'Asia-firsters', blamed Truman for the war, arguing that his policies encouraged it. Firstly, they argued that by removing American troops in 1948 he had left South Korea defenceless against the Communists. Secondly, they pointed out that Secretary of State, Dean Acheson, had made a speech in January 1951 saying that Korea was outside the US 'defence perimeter' (i.e. the parts of Asia important to US defence). This encouraged the North Koreans and the Soviet Union to believe that South Korea was not important to America and it would not fight to defend it: a belief encouraged by America's unwillingness to fight in China.

The historian Stephen Ambrose also blames Truman, but for very different reasons. He is critical of American foreign policy and argues strongly that Truman wanted to 'sell' NSC-68 to the people and to Congress, and the Korean War was perfect (see Chapter 8). Ambrose also maintains that the President wanted to increase US involvement in Asia and that his rapid reaction to events was evidence of this policy.

James Patterson, in *America in the Twentieth Century* (1994), is much more sympathetic to the US government. He points out that Truman's military advisors, including MacArthur, had recommended removing troops from Korea. It had little strategic value and the military needed the resources being used in Korea to strengthen NATO. If Truman had conveyed the message that South Korea did not matter to the USA it was certainly not his intention and he should not take the blame for a war. Patterson also argues that although the military might suggest higher spending through NSC-68 they would hardly want a war to get it. The war did, in fact, enable a massive build-up in the US military with spending rising from $14 billion in 1949 to $52.6 billion in 1953 – 60% of the federal budget. (Though this fell again after the war.) Patterson also points out the obvious fact that it was the North who invaded the South. Therefore, whatever else might be said, they had started the war.

Gary Reichard, in *Politics as Usual: the Age of Truman and Eisenhower* (1988), looks at the personalities of the men involved as well as their policies. He agrees that Truman did react quickly when the invasion occurred, but says that this rapid reaction was simply typical of his quick, and even unthinking, response to crises.

The Americans themselves clearly believed that the Soviets were behind the attack. Kim Il Sung had visited Moscow in April 1950 and it now seems clear from the Soviet archives which have been opened recently to western historians, that Stalin did give his backing for the invasion. In May and June, the Soviets sent military supplies to North Korea, including 150 T-34 tanks. As has been pointed out – see Thomas G. Paterson et al, *American Foreign Relations: A History Since 1920* (2000) – the Soviet support was half-hearted, particularly once the war had started. It seems likely that the USSR gave its support to Kim Il Sung hoping for a quick victory in Asia after the failure in Berlin. Once the Americans made their position clear and the war began, the Soviets backed off. They were not willing to go to war with the United States in order to fulfil Kim's dream of a united Korea.

Perhaps some of the blame should go to Syngman Rhee, the South Korean leader. It may be argued that he was aggressive in his behaviour and attitude to the North, and he made no secret of the fact that he wanted to unite Korea. He encouraged border incidents hoping to bring about a war so that the USA would come to his defence and unite Korea under his leadership.

Peter Lowe's study, *The Origins of the Korean War* (1997), looks at how all the major players had an influence in the events leading to the war. He analyses each one of them in turn. Both the Americans and the Soviets played their roles. Lowe points out that Korea needs to be seen in the international context of the Cold War. In other words, the USA, the USSR and China each hoped to improve their international position by the stand they took in Korea. However, Lowe points out that what must not be forgotten is the Korean context. As well as a Cold War conflict, Korea was also a civil war and, at its heart, were the desires of Kim Il Sung and Syngman Rhee.

Inflammatory rhetoric: Speeches and statements made deliberately to annoy and anger, in this case, the North Koreans.

Although the UN investigation just after the war found that Rhee was not to blame for the invasion, it was only looking at immediate events. There was a history of border skirmishes, harassment and **inflammatory rhetoric**. Rhee had constantly looked to the United States for aid and support, and believed that he had it. Though he might not have started the war, he did welcome it.

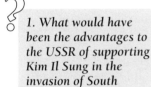

1. What would have been the advantages to the USSR of supporting Kim Il Sung in the invasion of South Korea?

2. How far and for what reasons do historians differ on their interpretations of the causes of the Korean War?

Both Lowe and Paterson agree on the central role of Kim Il Sung in events. Like Rhee, he also wanted to unite the two Koreas, but he is the one who did something about it. The visit to Moscow, in 1950, was to secure Soviet support for his plans. Kim misled Stalin over how easy the victory would be to ensure his backing and to get the necessary supplies. If Stalin had refused, he would have gone to Mao to try and secure the backing of the Communist Chinese. As Paterson puts it: 'The initiative, and probably the timing, of the war came from Pyongyang not from Moscow or Beijing.'

9.5 What problems did China/Taiwanese relations pose for the United States after 1949?

When Eisenhower became President in 1953, the Nationalist Chinese still held Taiwan, as well as the neighbouring islands of Quemoy, Matsu and Tachen. American support for the Nationalists had continued after 1949, and had been increased after the Korean War as the USA put more emphasis on its Asian alliances. Aid to Taiwan was averaging $250 million per year. The US 7th fleet, sent by Truman in 1950, was still blockading Taiwan in order to keep the peace between the Nationalists and the Communist Chinese. In 1954, Secretary of State John Dulles signed a treaty promising US protection to defend Taiwan and its islands.

At home, 'Ike' was under great pressure from the 'Grand Old Party' (as the Republican Party was nicknamed) to continue to support Chiang and not recognise communist China. The Republicans and the 'Asia-firsters' did not want another victory for Mao. Partly because of this pressure and partly because of the need to force China to negotiate over the Korean armistice, 'Ike' removed the fleet in 1953 to 'unleash Chiang'. Nationalists

---

Timeline of Sino(Chinese)–USA relations

1949   US Ambassador in China refuses invitation to meet Chinese Communist Party (CCP) leaders in Beijing

1950   USA pledges itself to defend Taiwan against the CCP and recognises Guomindang (GMD) in Taiwan as official Chinese government

   Chinese attack US troops on North Korean border

1950s   USA and China on very bad terms: supported opposite sides during Korean War (1950–53); US citizens forbidden to buy anything from China

1960s   Relationship still very poor: worsened by Vietnam War (1965–73) – support opposite sides again

1964   China tests first nuclear weapon; alarms the USA

1971   US advisor secretly visits Beijing

   Communist China allowed into the United Nations

1972   President Nixon visits China

   USA allows China to purchase a wide range of non-military goods.

---

raided the coast of China, so in retaliation the Chinese bombarded Quemoy and Matsu and invaded the Tachen islands. Nationalist raids on the coast of China were a common occurrence and the Communists used this opportunity to retaliate. They were also keen to test how strong the defence treaty of 1954 was.

In fact, the Republican Administration in America saw Quemoy as crucial to the defence of Taiwan, and Taiwan as crucial to US security in Asia. So, in January 1955, 'Ike' got approval from Congress to deploy troops to the area as he saw fit under the 'Formosa Resolution'. This was the first 'area resolution' which gave the President almost unlimited authority to use US forces in a certain area of the world. It passed both Houses of Congress with healthy majorities of 83–3 in the Senate and 410–3 in the House of Representatives. This was a very important extension of presidential power. As Dulles pointed out, at least 'Ike' was getting Congressional approval for his actions, unlike Truman in Korea.

As Eisenhower was now operating the 'New Look' policy with its doctrine of massive retaliation, the Americans threatened to use the atom bomb if China continued the bombardment. He also got the USSR to put additional pressure on China, and it finally backed down. As historian Stephen Ambrose says, '**Brinkmanship** held the line. In the process, however, it scared the wits out of people around the globe.' The United States was again enforcing containment and standing by its alliances. If Mao had been testing the defence treaty he had been given his answer.

Brinkmanship: This means taking arguments to the very brink to convince opponents you are serious, hence brinkmanship. Part of the problem with massive retaliation as a policy was that the enemy had to believe you were serious about using atomic weapons.

Why did problems between China and Taiwan arise again in 1958?

In 1958, a crisis over Quemoy rose again. Chiang had increased the Nationalist army on the islands to 100,000 men, which the Chinese saw as provocative. Once again China commenced a bombardment and, once again, Chiang turned to the Americans for help. Eisenhower sent ships to the area to escort Nationalist ships in safety, but he resisted pressure from

Republicans at home and from Chiang to use nuclear weapons. Dulles made it clear to the Communists that Chiang still had American support. He also made it clear to Chiang that the USA was under no obligation to help him every time he chose to provoke Mao. The USA would have fought for Taiwan itself, but did not want to get dragged into a war over Quemoy. Once again, timing was important.

In the same year, another crisis arose over Berlin. Khrushchev was paying a visit to the United States so the added problem of conflict in Asia was to be avoided. In October 1958, Chiang removed some of the troops and China ceased the bombardment.

What Taiwan showed, as did events in Korea and Indo-China, were the limitations on brinkmanship. It also showed how the USA was losing patience with Chiang who seemed to think the Americans would automatically help out no matter what he did. Eisenhower and Dulles had no intention of getting into a war with China for Chiang's sake. Like Truman, they also realised the growing importance of Asia as a Cold War arena and the need to build up American strength in the area.

The South East Asia Treaty Organisation (SEATO) was set up in September 1954. This organisation laid down that:

● all parties would consult if they felt threatened;

● they would act against aggressors if all agreed;

● and a separate protocol would guarantee the freedom of Cambodia, Laos and South Vietnam (the former French colony of Indo-China).

The USA, Britain, Australia, New Zealand, France, Thailand, Pakistan and the Philippines signed SEATO. It was different from NATO in that it was only a promise to consult, not a promise to act. Unlike NATO, SEATO had no permanent organisation or military force. Yet, although Dulles assured Congress that SEATO was only about consultation, at the same time he told the Cabinet that the USA would act in Asia if necessary to protect American interests, even if that meant acting alone. The USA was committing itself to containment in Asia under Eisenhower just as much as it had under Truman.

1. In what ways did Eisenhower use American military power in his policy towards the Far East?

2. How effective was Dulles' policy of brinkmanship?

9.6 Why did the USA become increasingly involved in South East Asia, 1945–1965?

Ho Chi Minh (1890–1969)
As a young man he travelled and worked in Europe. A strong nationalist, he campaigned unsuccessfully for Vietnamese independence at the Paris Peace Conference in 1919. He joined the Communist Party and trained in Moscow. Before returning to Vietnam, Ho worked in the USSR and China. He led the Vietminh to success against the French but then as leader of North Vietnam he fought against the Americans and the South Vietnamese for the rest of his life, never living to see an independent Vietnam.

The area of South East Asia which now covers Vietnam, Cambodia and Laos was taken over by the French Empire in the 19th century. In 1930, Ho Chi Minh formed the Indo-Chinese Communist Party, the Vietminh, to fight for independence from France. During the Second World War, the Vietminh, helped by the Allies, fought against Japan. When the war ended, they resumed their fight against France. As they had helped America against the Japanese, and since America was anti-colonial, Ho Chi Minh hoped the Americans would help them to get independence for Vietnam, but that did not happen.

Why did America support the French in Indo-China?

Even though the USA was anti-imperialist, Truman supported France financially, spending $2 billion which, at its peak, was 78% of France's costs. He also gave $50 billion in economic aid to the region. Truman saw the conflict in Vietnam in Cold War terms. He believed the Vietminh were taking orders from Stalin, so supporting France was enforcing containment and the Truman Doctrine. This was especially important to Truman after 1949 as he was still being criticised for the 'loss' of China and did not want another communist country in the East. He had to show he was still tough on communism.

Many State Department officials pointed out that Ho was more of a nationalist than a communist. There were many Vietnamese who were not communists, but nevertheless supported Ho Chi Minh. Dean Acheson said this was irrelevant. However, by ignoring the fact that Ho was fighting for his country's independence, the Americans always continued to see Vietnam in Cold War terms – meaning that they dangerously misunderstood the nature of the war.

Historian Vivienne Sanders, in *The USA and Vietnam, 1945–1975* (1998), quotes a far-sighted Defence Department official, who said in 1950 about Truman's continued support for the French:

> 'We are gradually increasing our stake in the outcome of the struggle … we are dangerously close to the point of being so deeply committed that we may find ourselves completely committed to direct intervention. These situations, unfortunately, have a way of snowballing.'

Even though Truman gave financial aid to the French, he did not want military involvement or to send troops to South East Asia. He was more concerned with European affairs in the 1940s and Korea in the 1950s.

How did American involvement increase under Eisenhower?

By 1953, the Vietminh had 250,000 regular soldiers and a militia of nearly two million. Also, their promises of education, healthcare and land did much to win over the ordinary people. They were also getting supplies from the Chinese. The Vietminh were numerous, popular and well-supplied.

By 1954, France was losing the battle at Dien Bien Phu where the Vietminh surrounded their forces. There was debate in the US government about what to do and whether Vietnam mattered to US security. Dulles and Vice-President Nixon wanted to bomb the Vietminh, but 'Ike' refused. He had been elected partly on his promise to end the war in Korea, so the American public would not stand for US troops being sent to another war in Asia so soon after the ceasefire. Congress made it clear they would not support involvement and, when 'Ike' sounded out America's allies, he found that they also refused to back the idea of intervention.

Eisenhower, though, worried that if Indo-China fell to communism the surrounding countries would also fall, like a row of dominoes. He believed the USA had to give some support to the French. Therefore, he continued Truman's policy of financial support but he also sent 300 US personnel to help France as the Military Assistance Advisory Group. This put the first American personnel in South East Asia.

In spite of American help, in May 1954 the French surrendered with 7,200 dead and 11,000 taken prisoner. A peace settlement was agreed between the involved powers at Geneva. Under the Geneva Accords 1954, Indo-China was split into four: Laos, Cambodia, and North and South Vietnam, which were divided along the 17th Parallel.

It was intended to hold elections in all four countries in 1956 and to reunite the two Vietnams, but the USA was afraid if they held elections Ho Chi Minh would win. 'Ike' admitted in his diary that Ho Chi Minh would probably get 80% of the vote. Therefore, the USA refused to sign the Accords and backed Ngo Dinh Diem as leader of South Vietnam, with North Vietnam being led by Ho Chi Minh. The USA invited South Vietnam to join SEATO and stepped up the amount of aid to $500 million a year. More advisors were sent, in contravention of the Geneva Accords. By 1960, there were more than 1,500 US personnel in South East Asia. As the anonymous diplomat had warned, the USA was gradually increasing its stake in Vietnam.

Diem was not a popular Prime Minister and even the USA admitted he was only the best of a bad bunch. He was Catholic in a country of Buddhists and gave jobs to his family. He made no attempt to win peasant support, as Ho did. Corruption and torture of prisoners became routine. 'Ike' urged Diem to introduce land reform to gain the support of the people, but Diem ignored him.

Many people in South Vietnam demanded the elections they had been promised and actively opposed the government of Diem. The opposition to Diem consisted of many groups and was known as the National Front for the Liberation of South Vietnam, or NLF. The Communists largely formed the military wing of the NLF, as they were the strongest group. These South Vietnamese communists were known as the Vietcong (VC). They were supported and equipped by Ho Chi Minh who, in turn, received support and help from the Chinese and the Soviet Union.

This communist backing convinced Eisenhower that this was, indeed, a Cold War conflict. His belief in the Domino Theory persuaded him that it was necessary to support Diem. Above all, Ho and the NLF were Vietnamese nationalists. They had not fought the French and the Japanese, and the French again, simply to come under American control. This misunderstanding of the nationalist nature of the Vietnam conflict was fatal for Eisenhower and his successors.

Why was the involvement in South East Asia intensified under Kennedy?

Under President Kennedy, foreign policy was very much controlled from the White House. He was more interested in foreign than domestic affairs. Military spending grew dramatically and Kennedy believed he also had to take a firm stand in South East Asia, for both foreign and domestic reasons. Having made Republican 'weakness' an election issue, he could hardly do less than they had, but his own views on the Cold War led him to increase American involvement.

Like Eisenhower, Kennedy also believed in the Domino Theory, especially in places like Vietnam. He believed that Third World areas were where the Cold War would now be fought. He was a strong supporter of the policy of containment, having entered Congress in 1946 and voted in support of the Truman Doctrine in his first days as a politician. In his own inauguration speech, in January 1963, he promised to 'bear any burden, support any friend and oppose any foe' to ensure liberty: Vietnam was an arena to put this into practice. JFK's advisors also encouraged further involvement in Vietnam. Robert McNamara, Secretary of Defence, was convinced that US military superiority would win and he advised sending 40,000 troops. Dean Rusk, Kennedy's Secretary of State, and National Security Advisor McGeorge Bundy also felt the USA should stand up to communism in South East Asia, as did the Joint Chiefs of Staff. No one was seriously suggesting to Kennedy that he might pull back from Eisenhower's position.

Like Eisenhower, Kennedy did not want to get the USA militarily involved in Vietnam, so he refused even though he was under pressure from the army to send troops. More money and more advisors were sent to help Diem so that, by 1963, 23,000 US personnel were in the country. Simply by being there it meant the US personnel were likely to get more involved.

Kennedy initially found himself involved in the affairs of Laos, where a civil war had also broken out, partly due to American backing for anti-government forces in the country. Kennedy sent some military supplies

Ngo Dinh Diem (1901–1963)
Aristocratic and catholic politician who served in the French-backed governments until 1933. He rejoined politics in 1954 as Prime Minister. In 1955, he declared himself President but refused to hold the elections as proposed at Geneva. His American-backed government was corrupt and dominated by his family. His failure to reform led to his assassination in 1963.

through Thailand, and sent advisors to Laos itself. An agreement, reached at Geneva in 1962, established a neutral government in Laos, but the USA continued to send arms and supplies as they felt that strengthening anti-Communist forces in Laos would improve their position in Vietnam.

How did military strategy increase involvement?

One of the difficulties preventing success against the NLF and VC was that the Army of the Republic of Vietnam (ARVN) and their American advisors were fighting a war against guerrillas. To combat the terrorist tactics used by the NLF and the VC, Kennedy wanted a policy of 'flexible response'. This entailed using several different methods of fighting, not just one, with particular emphasis on Special Forces such as the Green Berets. They were to train the South Vietnamese in counter-insurgency (i.e. how to defeat terrorists).

One policy used was 'strategic hamlets'. This entailed rounding people up and putting them into villages fortified and protected by the military to isolate them from the VC. However, this created resentment against the government and these hamlets could be infiltrated or taken over by VC guerrillas without the ARVN being aware.

Bombers and helicopters were sent to help, but the American crews often ended up doing the fighting.

The policies being pursued by the ARVN and the Americans were not very effective in military terms or in terms of gaining support from the people of South Vietnam. The VC, on the other hand, treated the people well, paying them for any supplies they took. Like Eisenhower, Kennedy failed to get Diem to appreciate the need to win the support of the people. In May 1963, there were widespread protests against Diem, including one by a Buddhist priest who set himself alight to show his opposition to the Diem regime.

In the same year, a plot to assassinate Diem was hatched by men within his own government. The CIA knew the plan, as did the American ambassador in Saigon, but they saw him as a liability so did not stop it. Diem was murdered just a few weeks before Kennedy himself was assassinated in Dallas. General Westmoreland, the American military commander in Vietnam, said that this involvement in assassination made the USA morally obliged to stay in the country to sort out the mess.

By 1963, there were 16,700 Special Forces troops and advisors in South Vietnam. There were American helicopters, planes and boats. The number of US personnel killed in 1963 was 489. Step by step, three presidents had increased American involvement in the war in South Vietnam.

Why did Vietnam become a military conflict under President Johnson?

The death of Kennedy provided a perfect opportunity for America to withdraw from the conflict. Instead, the new president, Lyndon Johnson (LBJ), immediately increased the number of personnel in South Vietnam by 30%. Why?

The attitude of the Johnson Administration towards the growing involvement in Vietnam was made clear when Secretary of State, Robert McNamara, said: 'We want an independent, non-communist Vietnam.' To a strongly-held belief in the Domino Theory, Johnson added the belief that the USA had to stand by its allies such as South Vietnam because, if it did not, no one would trust it again. A retreat from Vietnam would send a signal to the world of American retreat elsewhere.

Johnson's own interest was really in domestic policy and the creation of the 'Great Society' (see Chapter 11). He believed that the United States

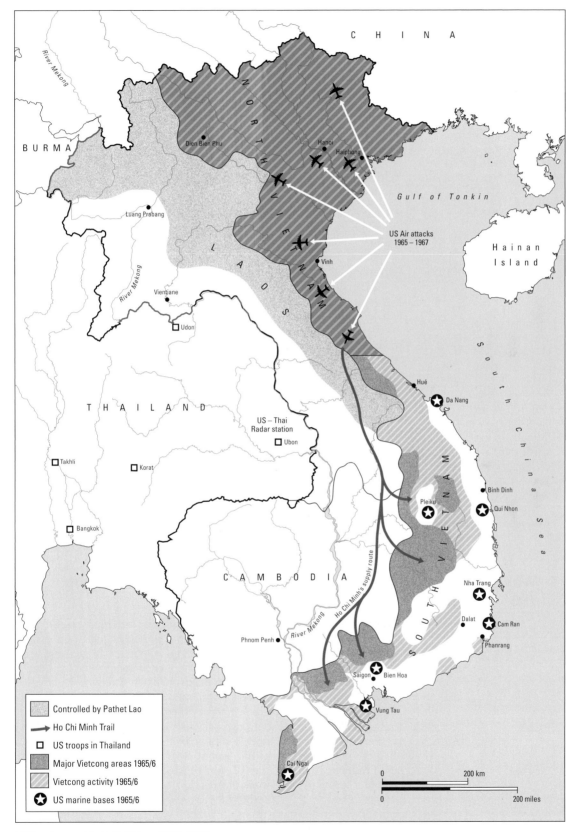

US involvement in Indo-China, 1965–1967

could free South Vietnam from the Communist threat and then reform it just as he was reforming America. The reality, on the ground, was that the Vietcong controlled 40% of the Vietnamese countryside and they were not going to give this up without a fight.

Having inherited Kennedy's Cabinet, Johnson also inherited Kennedy's advisors. They continued to support a military solution to the problem of South East Asia. Even when some cabinet members started to have second thoughts in the mid-1960s about American policy, LBJ's personality discouraged opposition. They were afraid to tell him the truth or disagree when he said he did not want to be 'the first president to lose a war'.

What was the impact of the Tonkin Incident on US policy in Vietnam?

At first, Johnson continued JFK's policies of sending aid and advisors, although the numbers increased greatly. In 1964, things changed. On 2 August, North Vietnamese patrol boats fired on the 'USS Maddox' while it was on patrol in the Gulf of Tonkin, but planes from the carrier 'Ticonderoga' drove them off. Two days later, the 'Maddox' and the 'C. Turner Joy' were again patrolling (a **euphemism** for spying on North Vietnamese coastal installations) when they reported being fired on by the North Vietnamese. They returned fire, but later investigations were unclear whether they had been attacked or had been mistaken. The incident gave Johnson the perfect opportunity he had been waiting for to escalate American involvement in the war.

In response to his request, Congress passed an area resolution. The Tonkin Resolution allowed LBJ to take 'all necessary steps including the use of military force' in South East Asia to protect US interests. It also allowed him to take the war to the North Vietnamese who were supplying the VC. By Johnson emphasising the attack and not the provocative patrols, the resolution easily passed both Houses (416–0 and 88–2).

The war now began to escalate dramatically. A US base at Pleiku was attacked, in February 1965, killing eight American servicemen and leading to air strikes on North Vietnam. In March 1965, US marines, the first combat troops sent to Vietnam, landed at Da Nang. The USA was slowly but surely taking over the fighting from the South Vietnamese. (By the end of 1965, there were 184,000 US military personnel in Vietnam.)

Euphemism: A polite word or expression which you can use instead of one that might offend or upset people (e.g. 'to pass on' is a euphemism for 'to die').

1. Why did Truman and Eisenhower support the French in Indo-China?

2. According to the 'Quagmire Theory', the USA got sucked into the conflict in Vietnam almost without realising it was happening. How far would you agree with this explanation of Kennedy and Johnson's increasing involvement in Vietnam 1961–1965?

9.7 Why did the USA fail to defeat communism in South East Asia, 1965–1973?

The number of American soldiers in Vietnam rose steadily from 200,000 in 1965 to 543,000 by 1969. Even though America largely took over the fighting from the ARVN, the war did not go any better. In fact, the way in which the war itself was fought often meant even greater involvement: if a policy failed they had to do more to make up losses. Therefore the intensity of the war increased. The desire to close down the Ho Chi Minh Trail, along which supplies were fed from North to South, led to Operation Rolling Thunder, a bombing campaign against North Vietnam. Although between 1965 and 1968 more bombs were dropped on North Vietnam than all the bombs dropped in the Second World War, they failed to have a significant effect. In the cities of North Vietnam production was moved out of Hanoi and spread around the country so that the raids did minimal damage. On the Trail, the North Vietnamese and Vietcong simply built another road in another part of the jungle.

Free-fire zones were designated, in which anyone could be a target. New technologies were brought into the fighting. For example, **defoliants**

Defoliants: Chemicals used on trees and plants that make all their leaves fall off. This made it harder for guerrilla fighters to hide in the forests.

Napalm: A type of petroleum jelly which is used to make bombs that burn and destroy people and plants.

such as Agent Orange were sprayed to try and destroy the jungle cover of the VC, and **napalm** was used in raids. There was a policy of 'pacification' which meant that, where a village was suspected of helping the VC, it was destroyed. Because they were not fighting an easily identifiable enemy, success began to be measured by 'body count' and 'kill ratio'. A dead Vietnamese was presumed to be a dead VC, whether they were or not.

Understandably, rather than winning the 'hearts and minds' of the Vietnamese peasants, these kind of policies turned many of them against the Americans and pushed them into support for the Vietcong. Young American soldiers, drafted into the war, could not understand how they were not welcomed as liberating heroes as their fathers had been in Europe. Morale in the American army worsened, with drug taking and desertions becoming serious problems. Violence against civilians worsened most horrifically at My Lai in 1968 where 347 unarmed men, women and children were killed by American soldiers (see panel).

The My Lai Massacre

On 16 March 1968, soldiers from the 11th Infantry brigade entered the village of My Lai as part of a search and destroy mission in Vietcong-held territory. During the raid, the men of 'C' company killed over 300 men, women and children, including 70 who were gathered into a pit and shot. Soldiers shot or bayoneted children as young as two years old. For over a year, the army covered up the massacre. Then it was leaked to the 'New York Times' and an investigation and trial were launched. Thirteen soldiers were charged with war crimes, but only the platoon commander, Lieutenant William Calley, was convicted. He served three years of a ten-year sentence, then he was pardoned.

The average age of the American soldiers in Vietnam was just 19. One soldier spoke of the war 'wearing us down, driving us mad, killing us'. In spite of this and in spite of the fact that the majority of soldiers did not commit atrocities, the My Lai Massacre had a profound effect on the war at home. American people were revolted by it and thought the sentences were far too lenient. Many were angry at the military cover-up. Others saw it as simply part of the madness of the war. It contributed significantly to the growing divisions in the United States over the war in Vietnam.

Murdered women and children at My Lai, 1968

Yet all the time the generals were telling the President, and the President was telling the public, that they were winning the war and that victory was just around the corner. This fiction was dramatically exposed in January 1968, when the North Vietnamese Army (NVA) and the Vietcong launched the Tet Offensive.

NVA troops and the VC mounted a coordinated attack in 36 of the 44 provincial capitals throughout the South, hoping to spark off a mass uprising against Saigon. It was the largest engagement of the war. The death toll consisted of 58,400 Communists, 4,000 US troops, more than 2,000 ARVN and 14,300 civilians. The US Embassy itself was attacked. Four embassy staff were killed. It took three weeks to re-take Saigon. In military terms, Tet was a failure for the NVA. Their losses were massive, far more devastating than the Americans realised, and they had failed to launch an uprising against the South Vietnamese government. However, psychologically, it was a turning point for the Americans. Seeing the television pictures of VC in the embassy compound brought home to the public that, in spite of what the government was telling them, they were not winning the Vietnam War.

Despite their superior technology and money, it seemed the United States could not win this war. The Americans were still backing an unpopular corrupt government that lacked the support of the majority of the people. With the help of the peasants, the VC and NVA could use the jungle and the country villages to hide out and continue their guerrilla warfare. Many military men at the time and since have argued that part of the problem was that the wrong approach was used to meet this challenge. After Tet, the army asked for a further 206,000 men. To defeat the Communists, the American government had to commit itself to total war and fully use the resources of the world's most powerful nation, as they had in the Second World War. But Johnson was not prepared to do this. Vietnam was already taking finance away from his beloved Great Society programmes and by 1968 the government was $25.3 billion in debt. There were already half a million men in Vietnam and it is doubtful if the American public would have allowed him to raise the money and manpower necessary to achieve a complete military victory. In fact, the American public was increasingly turning against the war, especially after the 1968 Tet Offensive.

While the majority of Americans had supported government policy throughout the war, an increasing number were questioning why they were in Vietnam. It was among students that the anti-war movement started, with the first 'teach-in' at the University of Michigan in 1965. The anti-war movement then spread among students, organised by Students for a Democratic Society (SDS). Their protest was about the morality of the war as much as its effectiveness. It was taking money away from Johnson's poverty programmes. In their view, the United States had no right to tell other countries how to run their governments. The students organised protest marches, burned draft cards, held debates, broke up classes etc. During the March Against Death in 1969, 300,000 filed past the White House in silence for 40 hours each carrying the name of a dead soldier or a destroyed village. At Kent State University, in 1970, four students were killed and 11 injured when National Guardsmen opened fire on a protest against Nixon's invasion of Cambodia.

Opposition was not just from students. The growing 'credibility gap' between what the government was telling people about the war and what was actually happening concerned many Americans. Among liberals especially, hostility to the war increased in the 1960s. President Kennedy's brother, Robert Kennedy, came out against the war in 1968 when he decided to run for the Democratic presidential nomination against another

> Look at the picture here, the photograph on pages 301 and Source B on page 309. How do these events help to explain why so many people in the USA opposed US involvement in South East Asia?

A student screams in horror. Soldiers shot dead four students at Kent State University who were part of a protest against the Vietnam War in 1970.

anti-war candidate, Eugene McCarthy. The architect of containment himself, George Kennan, was also a critic of the war. There were also protests in other countries and much criticism of US policy. Whether the anti-war movement had any real impact on the conduct of the war is an area of current debate. It is doubtful that the protests in themselves forced the government to make peace but, in a democracy, no government can ignore totally the protests of a large and growing section of the population.

There had been a halt in bombing as early as 1965 in order to explore peace talks, but the USA would not accept any Communists as part of the government of Vietnam so they failed. By 1968, President Johnson realised that the war had to end. Opposition was increasing at home and abroad, the war was costing billions of dollars and thousands of lives, and Tet had shown them they were not winning. The opposition and failure to make any headway in the war led Johnson to announce on television to the American public that the USA would be seeking peace talks. He also made the surprise announcement that he would not be seeking re-election in 1968. Peace talks began in May 1968 in Paris. Nothing was agreed before Johnson left office.

Why did Nixon take action between 1969–1973 to end the war?

Nguyen Van Thieu (1923–)
A soldier who for a while fought with the Vietminh but then sided with the French. He served under Diem and then under his successor Nguyen Cao Ky. Thieu was involved in Diem's assassination in 1963. He was elected President in 1967, a post he held until the fall of South Vietnam in 1975. His rule, like Diem's, was undemocratic and corrupt.

When Nixon came to office, in 1969, he wanted to end the war for the same reasons as Johnson. But Nixon also had other foreign policy aims, especially building friendship with China, which demanded peace in Vietnam. He formulated the so-called 'Nixon Doctrine': the USA would give aid to countries facing internal revolt but not ground troops. This meant withdrawal from South East Asia and no more Vietnams. Nixon felt that he could not just pull out, as this would look like a defeat. He wanted 'peace with honour'. Nixon hoped for a Korean-style solution with Thieu in charge of South Vietnam. In the meantime, while negotiations were going on, US troops had to be removed without South Vietnam collapsing. The solution was the policy of Vietnamisation (i.e. getting the ARVN to take back the responsibility for the fighting).

TNT: Abbreviation for the most famous high explosive: trinitrotoluene.

Khmer Rouge: Communist guerrilla forces in Cambodia whose leader was Pol Pot, a man of mystery who fought in jungles for five years before 1975 without making any clear statement of his political intentions. For more on the actions of the Khmer Rouge and Pol Pot see page 307.

1. What message is this cartoon making about Nixon's policy?

2. Do you think the cartoonist believed that Nixon's Vietnam policy was likely to be successful? Explain your answer.

Historian Stephen Ambrose says that this 'proved to be a disastrous choice, one of the worst decisions ever made by a Cold War president'. The policy bought the Americans time for negotiation and withdrawal, but it worsened the situation on the ground. The US troops saw little point in fighting when it was clear they were going to leave and the ARVN felt betrayed. Desertions increased in both armies. At the same time, the USA had to pour more supplies into Vietnam in order to equip them to fight the NVA; so the costs of the war increased.

To put more pressure on North Vietnam in the peace talks, and to cover the withdrawal of US troops, the bombing intensified. For example, Operation Linebacker I dropped 155,000 tons of **TNT** on North Vietnam in 1972. Nixon's bombing campaigns were part of his 'mad man' strategy: he wanted North Vietnam to believe he was mad enough to use an atom bomb if they did not negotiate. In 1969, the secret and illegal bombing of neighbouring Laos and Cambodia began, followed in April 1970 by an invasion to try and destroy the Ho Chi Minh Trail and communist bases in these countries.

When the 'New York Times' leaked the story about Cambodia, there were forceful protests at home and abroad. Congress reacted by repealing the Tonkin Resolution and passing the Cooper–Church Amendment cutting off any military aid that was being used against Cambodia. Nixon backed off, but the damage to Cambodia was immeasurable. The destabilisation of the country allowed the **Khmer Rouge** to seize power in 1975. The murderous regime, led by Pol Pot, wiped out a quarter of the entire population before it was stopped in 1979, by the Vietnamese.

Cartoon by Nicholas Garland, which appeared in 'Daily Telegraph' on 3 April 1970, entitled 'The good samaritan ...'.

Throughout 1968–1972, negotiations took place, but with little success. The USA wanted North Vietnam to accept Thieu in the South, but it refused. As the negotiations dragged on so, therefore, did the war. An attack by the North Vietnamese, in March 1972, led Nixon to launch Linebacker II – a ten-day bombing raid so fierce that the Swedish Prime Minister likened it to the crimes of the Nazi death camp at Treblinka.

In the end the negotiation, the continued fighting and pressure from the Soviet Union and China, who also wanted an end to the war, finally worked. The peace treaty was signed in Paris on 27 January 1973. Under its terms, the USA would withdraw from South Vietnam, all prisoners of war were to be returned, and there were to be negotiations to decide the future of North and South Vietnam. A Committee of National Reconciliation was to organise free elections, which included representatives of the South Vietnamese, the Communists and neutrals. In effect, Nixon had got a treaty which he could have had in 1968. Each side had made compromises but, in the intervening four years, 20,553 more Americans and half a million more Vietnamese had died.

Paris Peace Agreement, 27 January 1973

● US troops to be withdrawn from Vietnam, Laos and Cambodia.

● Establishment of a National Council for Reconciliation in South Vietnam which would include the Communists and which would organise free elections in the South.

● An international commission to oversee the ceasefire.

● Full exchange of prisoners.

The USA continued to give aid to the government of South Vietnam after 1973. They had withdrawn their troops, but had not given up hope of seeing South Vietnam remain non-communist. CIA advisors, as well as military personnel, remained behind. In 1974, Congress voted $700 million in aid for Thieu's government. But the North Vietnamese had no more intention of abiding by the ceasefire agreement than the Americans. In 1975, they launched an attack which quickly over-ran the country. The ARVN collapsed, with thousands deserting or changing sides. Thieu's government fell and, in April, Saigon was captured. Vietnam was united under communist leadership.

What were the effects of the Vietnam War on the USA and on South East Asia?

The social and psychological costs of the Vietnam War were enormous, as were the costs in people and material. The USA had spent at least $150 billion on the war, taking badly needed resources away from social policies at home. Eighty thousand Americans and at least two million Vietnamese were killed. Added to this were hundreds of thousands wounded and disabled in the USA and in Asia. The social problems of veterans returning home having lost a war they were expected to win were ignored for decades.

More bombs were dropped on Vietnam, Laos and Cambodia during the war than had been dropped in the entire history of the world. The physical damage to these countries caused suffering for many years afterwards. Thousands were disabled, thousands more developed cancer from the defoliants used by the Americans. The rebuilding of the economies and infrastructures of South East Asia would take years.

The American government and its political system were also affected badly by the war. The politicians were shown to have consistently lied to the public (e.g. over troop numbers and over the bombing of Cambodia). After the war there was a lack of faith in government. (This was made much worse by the Watergate scandal happening shortly after – see Chapter 13.)

Congress was also very concerned about the way they, too, had been misled. They also worried about the way succeeding presidents had increased America's commitments in Vietnam largely through their own office rather than through consulting Congress. JFK had used executive power to send Green Berets; LBJ also did the same and lied about the numbers of soldiers sent. The Tonkin Resolution extended presidential power in South East Asia, and Nixon illegally bombed and invaded Cambodia. To reassert its authority, Congress passed the War Powers Act in 1973 requiring that it be consulted before the President sends US forces into a war or consulted within 48 hours in an emergency. The President also had to get Congress' approval for continuance of a war beyond 60 days. In fact, the War Powers Act has never been invoked, but it symbolised how far Congress thought the Executive had sidelined them during the war.

There was disillusionment with the United States' world role among both the public and politicians, at home and abroad. The Americans were no longer the 'good guys' in the Cold War. Their role as 'world's policeman' was questioned and their willingness to act militarily was severely undermined in case it became 'another Vietnam'.

Truman had extended the policy of containment from Europe to Asia. Eisenhower's belief in the domino theory had convinced him to follow Truman's lead. Kennedy and Johnson had increased American involvement to the level that it became an all-out war to determine the political future of Vietnam. What the Americans never understood was that Vietnam was not about the Cold War: it was a nationalist war about Vietnam finally getting its independence from colonial or occupying powers in order to determine its own future. The Americans also consistently underestimated how much punishment the Vietnamese were willing to take to get that independence. When they did finally realise in 1968 that they could not win, they got out. But their determination to try not to make it look like the defeat it was kept the war going for an unnecessary five more years, at immense cost to both sides.

> 1. In what ways did the fighting intensify between 1968–1973?
>
> 2. Why were the Americans unable to win the 'hearts and minds' of the Vietnamese people?
>
> 3. How successful was Nixon's policy of Vietnamisation?

9.8 What impact did the Nixon presidency have on US policy towards Asia?

What was the impact on Laos and Cambodia?

As well as presiding over the American withdrawal from Vietnam, the military policies pursued by the Nixon government affected the states bordering Vietnam. The NVA sent supplies to the South through Laos and Cambodia. They had bases in both countries from which they operated. To destroy these lines of communication, both countries were bombed and invaded. In Laos, the ARVN was put into the field and it performed very poorly, being defeated by Laotian troops. The bombing of the country, however, caused much damage and cost many lives.

The effects in Cambodia were much more serious. In March 1969, the Cambodian ruler, Prince Norodom Sihanouk, was toppled in a **coup** by military leader Lon Nol. Sihanouk had tried to maintain neutrality in the war in Vietnam in spite of the Ho Chi Minh Trail passing through Cambodian territory. Nixon saw the coup as an opportunity. The

Coup: An attempt by a group of people, often army officers, to get rid of the ruler or government of a country and to seize power for themselves.

Cambodian government had its own problems with the Khmer Rouge. Nixon believed that he could join with Lon Nol in the crusade against communism and that the Cambodians would, in turn, close down Vietnamese operations in Cambodia. The American invasion, however, destabilised the country and when the USA pulled out of South East Asia they also pulled out of Cambodia, allowing the Khmer Rouge to take power in 1975.

Under the leadership of dictator Pol Pot, the Khmer Rouge set about building a new society in the renamed country of Kampuchea. This involved wiping out all opposition, all intellectuals, all those corrupted by western influences etc. Over the four years of the Khmer Rouge terror, a quarter of the Cambodian people were killed, including almost all the country's doctors, nurses, teachers and engineers. In 1979, the Vietnamese army invaded and removed Pol Pot, setting up a pro-Vietnamese government. The Americans were not to blame for the genocide of the Khmer Rouge but their interference in Cambodia, while it tried to stay out of the war, was a major factor in creating the conditions which allowed the Khmer Rouge to take over. What was just as damaging was that the American vote in the United Nations stopped UN aid going to Cambodia for many years because it had a Vietnamese-backed government. In many ways, the suffering of Cambodia was worse than that of Vietnam.

How did Nixon and Kissinger attempt to improve relations with China?

In July 1971, President Nixon shocked the American public by announcing his intention to visit the People's Republic of China. Henry Kissinger had arranged the visit secretly a few months before and it turned out to be a tremendous success.

Nixon had decided, on taking office, that he would modify US policy towards China. He would be able to do this in a way no Democrat could, because as a Republican and with his background of support for McCarthy no one could accuse him of being soft on communism. He could count on the support of his Republican colleagues while, at the same time, getting the endorsement of Democrats who desired better relations with China. That this would gain him votes in the 1972 presidential election was certainly a factor in his policy. He ensured that the television coverage of the visit was extensive and extremely favourable.

However, the election was only one factor in Nixon's change of strategy. A major factor was the war in Vietnam. Better relations with China might encourage the Chinese to reduce their aid to the North Vietnamese. In this he was unsuccessful as communist aid continued to flow into Vietnam. Though when peace talks started, they did have more support from the Chinese than they might otherwise have had.

A visit to China would also have the added advantage of worrying the Soviets. Where Truman had seen communism as **monolithic**, in fact relations between the USSR and China had always been tense. By 1969, the split had come out into the open. Nixon believed he could play the two states off against each other. Both would fear the other making an alliance with the United States, leaving them isolated. The longer he could keep them guessing, the stronger America's position would be. It would also make them each more likely to cooperate with his policy of *détente*. For China and Russia the advantage of friendship with the US was obvious, as it would strengthen their position against the other.

In the early 1970s, Nixon pursued a policy of *détente* towards the USSR (see Chapter 8), by which Nixon and Kissinger were able to build much better relations with the Soviet government. This led to a visit by the

Monolithic: Like a single, large block.

What impact did demonstrations like the one shown in this photograph have on US policy towards Vietnam?

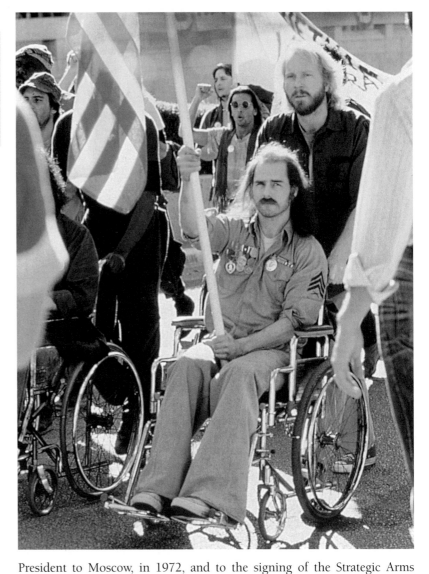

From the film 'Born on the Fourth of July', starring Tom Cruise as Vietnam veteran Ron Kovik.

Recession: A temporary decline or setback in economic activity or prosperity.

President to Moscow, in 1972, and to the signing of the Strategic Arms Limitation Treaty (SALT). Through the policy of *détente* and 'triangular diplomacy' between the USA, USSR and China, President Nixon was able to achieve two things. Firstly, he was reducing the amount of support available to the North Vietnamese. The Soviet Union would not stop supporting its ally altogether, but the new relationship with the USA would encourage it to limit that support. For example, when Nixon launched the Linebacker operations the Soviets did not respond directly as they did not want to damage *détente*. Secondly, Nixon was able to play the Soviets and the Chinese off against each other. Each was fearful of isolation. That also gave Nixon more support and freedom of action in Vietnam.

The state of the economy was also a factor in Nixon's calculations. In the early 1970s, the world was entering a deep **recession**. As it had for a century, China promised new markets for American goods.

The Americans made steps towards improved relations early on in the Administration with the lifting of restrictions on trade and travel to China. Nixon also gave permission for the American table tennis team to visit the People's Republic. Although this led to many jokes about 'ping-pong diplomacy', it was an important step in improving relations. The actual visit lasted seven days and was a great success. There were meetings between Nixon, Kissinger, Mao and the Chinese premier Zhou En-lai. There were banquets and visits to the Great Wall – all broadcast throughout the world.

The visit produced only a slight change in policy in Vietnam, notably pressure from China on the North Vietnamese delegation in Paris to come to an agreement. It was another six years before the Chinese and Americans resumed full diplomatic relations, but it did have some important effects. Trade between China and the USA increased to $700 million by 1973 and, just after Nixon's visit, the People's Republic was granted the Chinese seat in the United Nations. Both Japan and Taiwan were concerned by the growing friendship between the USA and the Communists so, to ensure that they were not left behind, both countries made their own efforts to build closer ties with Communist China. The problems had not gone away. Taiwan's fate remained a problem for the two countries and the two political systems were still opposed, but Nixon's trip had done much to increase understanding between the two nations and to ease some of the tensions of the Cold War.

? *Source-based questions: Opposition to the Vietnam War*

SOURCE A

A poster entitled 'Cooperation in battle. Shoot down any enemy aircraft in order to launch the offensive.' It was produced in North Vietnam in 1972

SOURCE B

Newspaper picture of 8 June 1972. The nine-year-old South Vietnamese girl, Kim Phuc, was the victim of a napalm attack.

Source-based questions: Opposition to the Vietnam War

SOURCE C

Generally … the media were instinctively pro-war and only shifted when sharp elite divisions had already become apparent. Undoubtedly, the famous photographs and film footage of napalm and bomb damage did have an impact. Analysis of television and press coverage, however, does not support Nixon's charges of anti-war bias. White House communication failures … were more damaging to the Administration cause than any activities of crusading journalists.

From Vietnam: American Involvement at Home and Abroad *by John Dumbrell, 1992*

SOURCE D

By the end of February [1968], the most respected figures of American journalism had placed themselves on record in opposition to the administration policy, creating in the process [approval for opposition to] the war that would ultimately compel the government to reassess its position.

From The Unfinished Journey *by William H. Chafe, 1986*

SOURCE E

Traditional history portrays the end of wars as coming from the initiative of leaders – negotiations in Paris or Brussels or Geneva or Versailles – just as it often finds the coming of war a response to the demand of 'the people'. The Vietnam war gave clear evidence that at least for that war (making one wonder about the others) the political leaders were the last to take steps to end the war – 'the people' were far ahead. The President was always far behind.

From A People's History of the United States *by Howard Zinn, 1980*

SOURCE F

I remember sitting on this wretched outpost one day with a couple of my sergeants … This one sergeant of mine, Prior was his name, said, 'You know Lieutenant, I don't see how we're ever going to win this.' And I said, 'Well Sarge, I'm not supposed to say this to you as your officer – but I don't either.'

Philip Caputo, quoted in Cold War *by Jeremy Isaacs and Taylor Downing, 1998*

---

1. Study Source A.

Explain what is meant by the term 'propaganda'.

How might this photograph be used as propaganda?

2. Study Source B.

What impact did images such as this have on the anti-war movement?

3. Study Sources C and D.

How far do they agree on press support for the war?

4. Using all the sources and your own knowledge, assess the importance of domestic opposition on America's withdrawal from the Vietnam War.

Civil rights, 1865–1992

10.1 How important was the Reconstruction period (1865–1977) for the development of African-American civil rights?

10.2 Why were the Southern states able to introduce segregation in 1877–1919?

10.3 What did African Americans do to improve their position in US society, 1877–1945?

10.4 How successful were African Americans in their attempt to gain civil and political rights, 1945–1968?

10.5 Historical interpretation: The role of Dr Martin Luther King Jr and the civil rights movement

10.6 How important was the federal government in the achievement of African-American civil rights, 1945–1992?

10.7 How far did African Americans achieve full civil rights by 1992?

10.8 In what ways did the civil rights of Native Americans change, 1865–1992?

10.9 How far did civil rights for Hispanic and Oriental Americans improve, 1865–1992?

Key Issues

● *What role did African Americans play in the achievement of political and civil equality in the USA?*

● *How significant was opposition to the achievement of full civil rights for African Americans?*

● *How important was the federal government in the development of African-American civil rights, 1865–1992?*

● *In what ways did the civil rights of Native, Hispanic and Oriental Americans change, 1865–1992?*

Framework of Events

1865	Freedman's Bureau is established
	Civil War ends
	13th Amendment of the Constitution
1866	Civil Rights Act
	Freedman's Bureau Act
	Ku Klux Klan founded
	Riots in southern cities against African Americans
1867	Reconstruction Act
	Howard University founded
1868	President Johnson impeachment trial
	14th Amendment of Constitution
	President Grant is elected
1870	15th Amendment to Constitution
	First Enforcement Act
1871	Second Enforcement Act
1872	Ku Klux Klan Act
1875	Civil Rights Act
1877	End of Reconstruction
1883	Civil rights cases in Supreme Court
1887	First Jim Crow laws passed in Florida
	Dawes Severalty Act
1895	Booker T. Washington's Atlanta Compromise Speech
1896	'Plessy v Ferguson' case in Supreme Court
1898	'Williams v Mississippi' case in Supreme Court

1909	NAACP founded
1915	Ku Klux Klan refounded at Stone Mountain, Georgia
1917	UNIA founded by Marcus Garvey
1919	Race riots across America in 'Red Summer'
1924	All Native Americans made US citizens
1934	Indian Reorganisation Act
1938	Supreme Court case of 'Missouri ex rel. Gaines v Canada'
1942	Congress on Racial Equality founded by James Farmer
1948	US armed forces desegregated
1954	'Brown v Board of Education' case
1955	Montgomery Bus Boycott begins
1957	Southern Christian Leadership Conference founded (September) Central High, Little Rock
1960	Lunch counter protests; SNCC founded
1961	Freedom Rides by CORE
1963	Birmingham demonstrations; March on Washington
1964	Civil Rights Act; Poll Tax amendment
1965	Selma to Montgomery March; Voting Rights Act Malcolm X is assassinated Rise of Black Power Riots in Watts District of Los Angeles
1966	Black Panther Party founded by Newton and Seale
1968	Martin Luther King is assassinated American Indian Movement founded Race riots across USA
1969	'Alexander v Holmes County' case AIM activists occupy Alcatraz
1971	'Swann v Charlotte Mecklenburg Board of Education' case
1974	Indian Self-Development Act
1978	Bakke case on affirmative action
1984	Jesse Jackson runs for Democratic nomination for President
1988	Jesse Jackson again runs for Democratic nomination for President
1992	Rodney King riots in South Central Los Angeles.

Overview

THE issue of civil rights is essential to understanding the establishment and development of the United States. The idea appears in the Declaration of Independence (1776), when the Founding Fathers declared:

'We hold these truths to be self-evident, that all men are created equal, and that they are endowed by their Creator with inalienable rights, that among these are Life, Liberty and the Pursuit of Happiness.'

When the Constitution was produced in 1787, many states refused to ratify it until civil and political rights were incorporated in it. In 1791, the first ten amendments – known as the Bill of Rights – were included. These allowed the Constitution to be accepted by all 13 states. Included in the Bill of Rights were freedom of speech, freedom of religion and the right to trial by jury.

Since its creation, the United States of America (USA) has faced the continuing problem of civil, political and social equality. Even though the Constitution included the Bill of Rights, from 1791, it also allowed slavery. The only time slaves are mentioned in the Constitution is for the purpose of calculating state representation in the House of Representatives. For this purpose, a slave was calculated to be worth three-fifths of a free man.

The issue of slavery eventually split North and South to create the conditions which led to the outbreak of Civil War in April 1861. Although the war began on the issue of a state's right to secede from (leave) the USA, by 1862, President Lincoln transformed the conflict into a moral crusade to end slavery. The Emancipation Proclamation of September 1862 (see page 95) declared that, from 1 January 1863, slaves would be 'forever free'.

Even though the Civil War may have brought an end to slavery, it did not bring civil, political and social equality for African Americans. From 1865 to 1992, a central feature of US society was the struggle of African Americans to achieve these rights. For most African Americans, the Northern victory in the Civil War proved to be a false dawn. It would take another 100 years before they could achieve civil and political equality. White opposition in the South, where most African Americans lived, was able to regain control of state government by the end of the Reconstruction period (1877).

Once in control, they were able to force African Americans into a position of second-class status. This was achieved by a variety of methods. **Jim Crow laws**, passed by the government in Southern states, introduced segregation. This created separate public facilities for blacks and for whites. African Americans were also barred from voting by a variety of methods. These actions received support from the US Supreme Court, which upheld segregation in a number of court cases in the 1890s.

These actions were supplemented by the use of terror and intimidation. White **vigilante groups**, such as the Ku Klux Klan, engaged in general acts of violence against African Americans. By the 1920s, African Americans had become the invisible men of US society and politics. Disenfranchised, forced to use separate facilities and to occupy low-paid jobs, they were the racial underclass of America.

Faced with this predicament, African Americans reacted in a number of ways. The leading African-American spokesman in the South in the last quarter of the 19th century was Booker T. Washington. Born a slave, he advocated social advancement at the expense of civil and political equality.

Criticised for accepting segregation, the sociologist Gunnar Myrdal, in *The American Dilemma* (published in 1944), stated:

'For his time, and for the region where he worked and where nine-tenths of all Negroes live, his policy of abstaining from talks on rights was entirely realistic.'

However, Washington's views were challenged by a leading northern African American, W.E.B. Du Bois. As the first African American to receive a Doctor of Philosophy (PhD) degree from Harvard, he dismissed Washington's acceptance of civil and political inferiority. In 1910, he helped found the National Association for the Advancement of Colored People (NAACP). The NAACP fought, primarily through the legal system, to gain full civil rights.

By the 1920s, another leading African American advocated a different course. West Indian-born Marcus Garvey supported the development of a strong black identity. This would be achieved through separate development from whites and through support for the African heritage of black Americans. Garvey's 'black nationalism' was a forerunner for the Black Muslims of the Nation of Islam, Malcolm X and the Black Panthers.

However, for the vast majority of African Americans political action had little

Jim Crow laws: 'Jim Crow' was a music-hall character invented by Thomas D. Rice in the 1820s. Dressed in rags and with his face blacked up, 'Jim Crow' came to represent a white view of happy-go-lucky blacks; his name was later applied to the laws regulating the lives of black Americans in the South.

Vigilante groups: These are formed when people join together to catch and punish anyone who they think is doing wrong or breaking the law. Such groups are unofficial, and often form when the people concerned think the police are not keeping order properly

Legal segregation: The deliberate creation by law of separate facilities for Whites and African Americans, mainly in the former Confederacy states.

impact or support. Instead, the most attractive way to avoid the **legal segregation** of the South was to migrate North. The Great Migration, in the first three decades of the 20th century, saw thousands of African Americans move north to cities such as Chicago, Detroit and New York. Nevertheless, they still lived in poor segregated housing.

A major turning point for African Americans was the Second World War. Thousands worked in war industries. Large numbers served in the armed forces in the defence of democracy against German and Japanese tyranny. They fought for democracy and freedom but faced second-class status on their return from military duty.

From 1945, the civil rights movement began to take shape across America. In 1948, President Truman desegregated the armed forces. In 1954, the NAACP successfully brought public school segregation to an end by taking the 'Brown versus Board of Education' case to the Supreme Court. Within the South, African American and civil rights bodies fought segregation in a wide variety of places and in a number of different ways. In Montgomery, Martin Luther King led a campaign to end bus segregation. In the 1960s in North Carolina, students of the Student Non-Violent Co-ordinating Committee (SNCC) helped to end lunch counter segregation. In 1961, students of the Congress for Racial Equality helped to bring an end to inter-state bus segregation.

Through their own efforts, African Americans challenged legal segregation and won. However, to achieve civil and political equality they needed the support of the federal government. The Supreme Court provided legal support by declaring segregation unconstitutional. The President and Congress passed laws that enforced civil rights and guaranteed voting rights. In jobs, they established the principle of **affirmative action**.

Affirmative action: Policies introduced by the federal government from J.F. Kennedy's Administration (1961–63) onwards, for people and for firms employed by the government. The aim was to reserve a certain number of jobs for people from ethnic minority backgrounds, such as African Americans and Oriental Americans.

By 1970, legal segregation had come to an end. However, unofficial segregation still existed in the North because of the creation of ethnic neighbourhoods. Enforced bussing and affirmative action proved a controversial way of redressing decades of discrimination. Nevertheless, by the 1980s, African Americans had achieved full civil and political equality. Many had also achieved social equality. Unfortunately, many more still lived in relative poverty in inner-city **ghettos** in the North or in rural poverty in the South. This bifurcation of African-American society still created major problems in US society, as the Rodney King riots in South Central Los Angeles in 1992 proved.

Ghettos: Areas in a city or town where poor people or people of a particular race, religion or nationality live in isolation.

Although African Americans stand out as the largest ethnic group to have faced sustained discrimination and denial of civil rights over a long period of US history, they are not alone. Native Americans faced similar problems. By 1865, Native Americans east of the Mississippi river had been defeated by the USA and either forced westward into Indian territory or into reservations (see Chapter 2).

Between 1865 and 1890, the remaining Native Americans west of the Mississippi were defeated and also forced into reservations. The Dawes Act of 1887 helped to transform Native-American society. Under the Act, collective tribal ownership of land came to an end and Native Americans were to be educated along Christian, western lines. This helped to destroy Native-American culture. In 1924, all Native Americans became US citizens.

By the 1960s, most Native Americans on reservations faced poverty, unemployment and alcohol and drug abuse. On the back of the black civil rights movement, an American Indian Movement was formed in 1968 to fight for Native-American rights. Using direct action and the courts, Native Americans began to gain civil and social equality from the 1970s onwards.

Similarly, Oriental Americans faced discrimination and social inequality over the same period. Although large numbers of Chinese labourers were used to construct the transcontinental railroad, they faced discrimination. In 1882, the Chinese Exclusion Act drastically limited Chinese immigration. Most Oriental Americans lived on the West Coast of the USA. These comprised Chinese, Japanese and, more recently, Korean and Vietnamese Americans.

The most notorious act of discrimination against Oriental Americans came in the Second World War, when the entire Japanese-American population was placed in concentration camps.

Like other ethnic minorities, Oriental Americans have benefited from the broader civil rights movement since the 1950s. In particular, they have benefited from affirmative action programmes.

Hispanic Americans have comprised some of the more historic and recent waves of non-white immigration into the USA. In the border states, Hispanic Americans faced social discrimination. In the 1960s and 1970s, their cause was championed by the Hispanic-American union leader Cesar Chavez. However, Hispanic American illegal immigration has become a major issue in the USA since the 1960s.

The historian Maldwyn A. Jones entitled his study of US history from 1607 to 1992 *The Limits of Liberty* (published in 1995). For much of the period 1865 to 1992, large parts of US society faced civil, political or social inequality. Yet the underlying theme of the period has been the achievement of civil and political equality for the vast majority of US citizens.

1. What are civil and political rights within the context of US history?

2. What factors limited the development of African-American civil rights between 1865 and 1992?

3. Explain why Native Americans, Oriental Americans and Hispanic Americans have faced discrimination within the USA between 1865 and 1992?

10.1 How important was the Reconstruction period (1865–1877) for the development of African-American civil rights?

The end of the Civil War should have been a major turning point in the history of African Americans. The North's victory brought an end to slavery. In addition, the three Civil War Amendments – the Thirteenth, Fourteenth and Fifteenth (see page 317) – seem to have guaranteed African Americans full civil and political equality.

However, the end of the Civil War and the beginning of the Reconstruction era (1865–1877) proved to be a false dawn for the four million slaves in the former Confederacy and border states. During this period, attempts were made to improve the civil, political and social position of the former slaves.

In March 1865, before the end of the Civil War, the Freedman's Bureau was created by the federal government to give food, shelter, medical aid and land to ex-slaves. In 1866, a Freedman's Bureau Act was passed, over President Johnson's veto, which extended the work of the Bureau. It also included the right of military courts in the South to hear cases of **racial discrimination**. Although poorly resourced, the Freedman's Bureau did help the creation of schools for African Americans. It was aided in this task by charity workers from the North and by religious organisations. In 1865, 95% of ex-slaves were illiterate. This had dropped to 81% in 1870 and to 64% by 1890. African-American education was enhanced further with the creation of higher education institutions, such as Howard University and Fisk University in 1866–67.

Racial discrimination: Actions which deliberately penalise a person because of their racial background.

Vagrancy: A way of life in which someone goes aimlessly from place to place and does not have a home or a job, or who often begs or steals in order to live.

Homesteaders: The people who claimed land for free in the West, following the 1862 Homestead Act. They were also called 'sodbusters' because many used eastern farming methods which did not work in the climate of the West.

African Americans also benefited from the Civil Rights Act of March 1866. This gave them citizenship and outlawed racial discrimination. However, the most important reforms were the three Civil War amendments – 13, 14 and 15.

Nevertheless, attempts to improve the position of African Americans in the former Confederacy faced considerable opposition. In 1865 and 1866, all the former Confederate states had passed 'black codes' which replaced the old slave codes. Although their content varied from state to state, the underlying aim was to keep the freed slaves in a second-class position. The most oppressive 'black code' was against **vagrancy**. Homeless freedmen were fined and imprisoned. To counter the black codes, Congress passed the Civil Rights Act of 1866.

A more sinister form of white opposition came in the form of vigilantes and the use of violence. In 1866, ex-Confederates in Pulaski, Tennessee formed the Ku Klux Klan (KKK). The KKK used violence and intimidation against African American and white supporters of Reconstruction governments in the South. In May 1866, white crowds in Memphis, Tennessee, attacked African Americans who had served in the Northern Army, killing 46. In Mississippi, Klansmen mutilated a leading black Republican. In 1870, in Georgia, the Klan murdered three scallywag Republicans.

Congress reacted to the rise of white vigilante groups by passing a series of acts between 1870 and 1872. In May 1870, the First Enforcement Act protected black voters. In February 1871, the Second Enforcement Act provided federal supervision of southern elections. Finally, in 1872, the Third Enforcement Act gave federal troops the power to suspend habeus corpus and arrest suspected KKK members. The combined result of this federal action was to remove the threat, albeit temporarily, of white intimidation of African Americans.

The Reconstruction era has been portrayed, in the past, as a period of African-American domination of southern politics. In some ways, this is true. The Reconstruction Acts of 1867 and 1868 completely altered the electorate in the former Confederacy. In the 1868 presidential election, the Republican candidate, Ulysses Grant, won by 300,000 votes. It is clear that, without the 700,000 African-American votes from the South, he would not have achieved a majority of votes.

Yet within the Southern states, black political control was a fiction. Only one African American became a Lieutenant (Deputy) Governor of a state, Pinckney Pinchback of Louisiana. Two blacks became US senators, both from Mississippi: Hiram Revels and Blanche Bruce. Fourteen blacks became Congressmen. Even when 600 blacks were elected to state legislatures, they did not always work together.

A greater failing of the Reconstruction period was in social matters. As the African-American leader Frederick Douglass noted, the former slaves were 'left free from the individual master but a slave of society'. Without education, money or property, the ex-slave faced a new type of social inferiority. Only 4,000 freed slaves gained land under the Southern Homestead Act of 1866. During the Reconstruction period, work on the plantation was replaced by sharecropping (see Chapter 5). With very high rates of interest for borrowing money, African-American sharecroppers were kept in a cycle of poverty and dependence upon whites. Following the economic crash of 1873, their position deteriorated further.

A development which became a recurrent feature of African-American life was the desire to leave discrimination and intimidation in the South by moving North and West. During the 1870s, over 15,000 African Americans left the South and moved to the Free State of Kansas to set up as **homesteaders**. When they arrived, they still faced racial discrimination. As long ago as the 1830s, the French political observer Alexis de

Civil War Amendments to the US Constitution passed during Reconstruction		
Thirteenth Amendment	Ended slavery in the USA	Became law in December 1865
Fourteenth Amendment	Provided equal protection under the law for all citizens Extended right to due process of law to the individual states	Became law in July 1868
Fifteenth Amendment	Guaranteed right to vote to all citizens irrespective of race, colour or previous condition of servitude (slavery)	Became law in March 1870

White supremacists: Whites who believe that the white race was superior to all other races. In particular, they regard African Americans as biologically and intellectually inferior.

1. In what ways did the lives of African Americans change during Reconstruction?

2. How did Southern Whites oppose Reconstruction?

3. To what extent did Reconstruction fail?

Tocqueville noted: 'race prejudice seems stronger in those states where slavery no longer exists'.

Although African Americans faced the most severe discrimination in the Old South, it did not mean that there was racial tolerance elsewhere.

In 1877, Reconstruction came to an end with the Compromise of 1877. To get elected president, Republican candidate Rutherford B. Hayes needed southern electoral college votes. To acquire these, he abandoned Reconstruction. This allowed **white supremacists** in the Democratic Party to gain control of all of the Old South, inaugurating a new 'dark age' for African Americans.

10.2 Why were Southern states able to introduce segregation in 1877–1919?

Radical Republican: Member of the Republican Party, more than likely in Congress, who wanted to bring about fundamental change in the Southern states following the Civil War. Radical Republicans were responsible for the impeachment of President Johnson in 1968.

White opposition to civil and political equality for African Americans is a major theme in the history of civil rights in America. Even though the Confederacy lost the Civil War, the changed status of African Americans was accepted with extreme reluctance. The black codes of 1865–66, and the formation of vigilante groups such as the Ku Klux Klan, were ways in which Southern Whites attempted to maintain their superiority in politics and society.

Even before the end of Reconstruction, in 1877, the rights of African Americans in the former Confederacy were being eroded. By 1876, **Radical Republican** governments existed in only three Southern states: South Carolina, Florida and Louisiana. In spite of restrictions placed on former officials of the Confederacy in the Fourteenth Amendment, white supremacist governments were already appearing. This was the result of the 1872 Amnesty Act, which had restored the political rights of all but a few hundred former Confederates.

Northern support for Reconstruction had clearly faded before the Compromise of 1876. The Senate rejected the 1875 Enforcement Bill, against southern white vigilantes. The Civil Rights Act of the same year, which guaranteed equal rights in theatres and other public places, was never enforced.

What was of considerable significance was the role of the US Supreme Court on the issue of civil rights. In the 'Slaughter House Cases' of 1873, the Court declared that the Fourteenth Amendment rights only covered national citizenship. This covered issues such as inter-state travel. The Court declared that the federal government did not safeguard civil rights against violation by individual states.

In 1875, in the 'United States versus Cruikshank' case, it was decreed that the civil rights in the Fourteenth Amendment did not protect African Americans against discrimination by individuals, only by state governments. In the following year, in the 'United States versus Reese' case, the Court refused to put on trial officials in Kentucky who had prevented African Americans from voting. Taken together, these actions show that northern politicians and the Supreme Court had abandoned African Americans to their own devices before 1877.

However, the Compromise of 1876 is significant in that it shows clearly that, in return for control of the national government, the Republican Party was willing to abandon the South to the white supremacist Democratic Party. From the 1870s until the 1960s, the former Confederacy became the 'Solid South' of the Democratic Party.

Once whites were in control of southern state governments, African Americans faced the creation of a society which placed them firmly in a position of inferiority. Beginning in Florida, in 1887, laws were passed which created legal segregation of the races. The Florida law created separate accommodation on railroad carriages. Similar laws in Mississippi in 1888, Texas in 1889, Louisiana in 1890 and Alabama, Arkansas and Georgia in 1891 followed this. Known collectively as 'Jim Crow laws' (see panel), they created a segregated society not dissimilar to apartheid in South Africa – which existed from 1948 to the early 1990s.

Examples of Jim Crow laws across the USA

Alabama	**Buses**: All passenger stations shall have separate waiting rooms for the white and coloured races.
Florida	**Education**: The schools of white children and the schools of Negro children shall be conducted separately.
Georgia	**Burial**: The officer in charge shall not bury any coloured persons upon ground used for burial of white persons.
Louisiana	**The blind**: The Board of Trustees shall maintain a separate building on separate ground for the care and instruction of all blind persons of the black race.
Mississippi	**Inter-marriage**: The marriage of a white person with a Negro or person who shall have one-eighth or more Negro blood, shall be unlawful.
North Carolina	**Textbooks**: Books shall not be inter-changeable between white and coloured schools, but shall continue to be used by the race first using them.

In introducing Jim Crow laws, the southern states were accused of violating the civil rights of African Americans under the Fourteenth Amendment. However, in a number of Supreme Court cases, the highest legal authority in the USA upheld these developments. In 1883, in three civil rights cases, the Court threw out the 1875 Civil Rights Act on the grounds that the Fourteenth Amendment applied to governments not individuals.

Of greater significance was the 1896 case of 'Plessy versus Ferguson'. Homer Plessy, a person of mixed race, challenged the legality of the Louisiana railroad company which had created separate railroad cars for whites and for blacks. The Court declared that Louisiana had not violated the Fourteenth Amendment because it had created 'separate but equal' facilities for the races. In 1899, in 'Cumming versus the Board of Education', the separate but equal principle was extended to schools. These cases laid the foundation for legalised segregation, which lasted until the 1950s and 1960s.

The loss of civil rights was not limited to the Fourteenth Amendment rights of 1868. African Americans were also denied voting rights which had been guaranteed under the Fifteenth Amendment of 1870. In 1890, Mississippi became the first state to impose new voting qualifications which had the effect of taking the vote away from most African Americans in that state. These voting restrictions included literacy tests and residential qualifications. They also included **poll taxes**, which disenfranchised poor whites. However, it also took the vote away from large numbers of African Americans. In 1898, in 'Mississippi versus Williams', the US Supreme Court

Poll taxes: These were taxes, introduced first in Mississippi, which had to be paid if someone wanted to vote. Poor whites became disenfranchised, as did large numbers of African Americans.

A Ku Klux Klansman, 1947

After being accused of murder, these two young African-American men were taken from the county jail and lynched in the public square in Marion, Indiana, on 9 August 1930.

upheld these new voting regulations. Later, states such as Louisiana, introduced the 'grandfather clause' into voting regulations. This declared that a person could vote only if his grandfather had the vote. This excluded the vast majority of African Americans, whose grandfathers had been slaves. Texas also introduced the 'whites only' primary election. In a state where Democrats always won the election, this effectively removed African Americans from the political system.

The effect of these new regulations on African-American voter registration was dramatic. In Louisiana, for example, there were over 130,000 African Americans registered to vote in 1896. Within four years, by 1900, the figure had fallen to just 5,300.

To reinforce legal segregation and disenfranchisement, whites also engaged in the use of terror. Although the Ku Klux Klan had declined, attacks on African Americans increased. Between 1890 and 1899, 187 African Americans were lynched on average each year. The vast majority of these were in the Old South. Between 1887 and 1917, a total of 2,734 African Americans were lynched. There were also outbreaks of serious race riots. In 1917, in East St Louis, Illinois, African Americans were murdered by white mobs.

By 1919, the position of African Americans in the Old South had changed little since the end of the Civil War. In political and civil rights, African Americans faced legal segregation, violence and intimidation. This latter aspect of life was exemplified by the re-founding of the Ku Klux Klan at Stone Mountain, Georgia, in 1915 by William Simmons.

In social terms, most southern African Americans lived in poverty. Most worked as sharecroppers or in menial, low-paid jobs. Outside the Old South, the plight of African Americans was only slightly better. Jim Crow laws also existed in states such as Oklahoma and Kansas.

African Americans who lived in northern cities such as Chicago and New York faced unofficial segregation. This occurred mainly in jobs and housing, but also included schooling. In Chicago, for instance, in 1919, Irish-American and Polish-American workers, in league with the police, attacked African Americans. It would seem that nowhere in the United States did African Americans achieve full civil rights.

The inferior position of African Americans was reinforced by academic views about racial superiority. The popularity of social darwinist thinking suggested that academics, such as Carl Brigham and Luther Burbank, attempted to use biological science to prove African-American inferiority.

Even in the White House, President Woodrow Wilson seemed to sympathise with opponents of African-American rights. He attempted to segregate the federal civil service during his presidency (1913–21). He also applauded D.W. Griffth's film 'The Birth of a Nation' and had the film screened at the White House. The film had an enormous effect on the American public. It portrayed the Civil War and Reconstruction period, showing the Ku Klux Klan in a heroic light and African Americans as incapable of acting responsibly.

Within this hostile political and social environment, African Americans did attempt to improve their position.

1. In what ways did the federal government undermine the civil and political rights of African Americans between 1877 and 1919?

2. What do you regard as the most important reasons for the deterioration in the position of African Americans within US society 1877–1919?

Give reasons for your answer.

10.3 What did African Americans do to improve their position in US society, 1877–1945?

During the period 1877 to 1945, African Americans attempted to improve their civil, political and social position within US society. For the majority of African Americans, life involved poor living and working conditions in the Old South. They faced the daily problem of legal segregation, as well as the possibility of violent retaliation from the white community if they challenged the status quo.

In such conditions, three leading African Americans offered differing ways of dealing with the situation. In the last quarter of the 19th century, the dominant black voice was a former slave, Booker T. Washington. In the first decade of the 20th century, his views were challenged by a northern-educated academic W.E.B. Du Bois. In the 1920s, black nationalism was supported by Jamaican-born Marcus Garvey. He supported the idea of black separateness in US society. In the 1930s and 1940s, A. Philip Randolph, an African American trade union leader, became an important voice in the search for greater rights. During the New Deal era (1933–45), important gains were made in federal employment by African Americans.

Perhaps African Americans made the most significant development. Beginning with the First World War, the 'Great Migration' of African Americans began. Tens of thousands left the Old South to move north. By 1945, cities such as Philadelphia, Chicago and New York had large African-American populations.

How important was Booker T. Washington in the advancement of African-American rights?

Booker T. Washington had been born a slave in 1856. For the first nine years of his life, he lived on a plantation in Virginia. He came to represent the hopes and aspirations of southern blacks who had been freed because of the northern victory in the Civil War. Until his death in 1915, Booker T. Washington was widely regarded as the leading voice in the African-American community. He was the first black to receive an honorary degree from Harvard University. He was also the first black person to be invited for a meal with the President at the White House.

For all his high profile, Booker T. Washington was a controversial figure. To many African-American activists at the time, and since, he has been portrayed as someone who accepted the inferior status of African Americans in US society. He represented the hopes and aims of the majority of southern blacks after the Civil War. In an era of 'rugged individualism', he advocated self-help, self-reliance and social advancement.

He was aided, during the Reconstruction period, by the efforts of northerners to improve African-American education in the South. From 1872 to 1875, Booker T. Washington attended the Hampton Normal and Agricultural Institute, in Virginia, which had been founded in 1868 by Samuel Chapman Armstrong.

For the rest of his life, Washington actively supported attempts to improve the education of African Americans in the South. However, this education was to be practical and vocational rather than academic.

The crowning glory of Washington's educational efforts came after 1881 when he was made Principal of Tuskegee Institute in Alabama. Tuskegee specialised in practical subjects such as wagon-making, wheel-making and learning to be a blacksmith or a good housekeeper. It also helped to develop studies in new agricultural techniques. Later, in the 1890s, the Tuskegee Institute developed extension courses in the area around the college.

Washington reached national prominence, in 1895, at the Atlanta International Exposition. In what became known as his 'Atlanta Compromise' speech, Booker T. Washington laid out his vision of the African American in US society. He told the African Americans in the audience that:

'Our greatest danger is that in the great leap from slavery to freedom we may overlook the fact that we shall prosper as we learn to … glorify

Booker T. Washington (1865–1915)
Black educator and leader. Born into slavery in Virginia. Attended Hampton Institute in 1860s. Became first Principal of the black Tuskegee Institute in 1881. Washington was a supporter of black self-help and self-reliance. His aim was to improve black education, which would lead to social advancement. He avoided openly campaigning for equal civil and political rights. His 'Atlanta Compromise' speech of 1895 contains his main aims and vision for the African American in US society.

common labour. No race can prosper till it learns that there is as much dignity in tilling a field as in writing a poem.'

He went on to stress the opportunities for African Americans in economics, rather than mention the lack of civil and political rights. He called on African Americans to:

'cast down your bucket where you are – cast it down in making friends … of the people of all races by whom we are surrounded. Cast it down in agriculture, mechanics, in commerce, in domestic service, and in the professions.'

The speech reflected the views of the vast majority of African Americans in the Old South. They wanted to improve their social and economic position within the framework of white supremacy and segregation.

It was Washington's implied acceptance of white supremacy which made him an influential African-American leader accepted by white America. White newspapers applauded his 'Atlanta Compromise' speech across America. It also enabled Washington to get white supporters for African-American education. It allowed him to become adviser on African-American affairs to Presidents McKinley and Theodore Roosevelt. In 1896, on a visit to Europe, he even met and had tea with Queen Victoria in Britain.

Yet, for all his national and international fame, Washington lived in an era of increasing persecution and discrimination against African Americans. From the 1890s until his death in 1915, Jim Crow laws were passed across the South, the US Supreme Court upheld segregation and thousands of blacks were lynched. While he was adviser to Theodore Roosevelt, the Brownsville affair occurred in 1906. Black troops stationed

Does this map show how the 'Great Migration', beginning at the time of the First World War, had little impact on the geographical distribution of the black population?

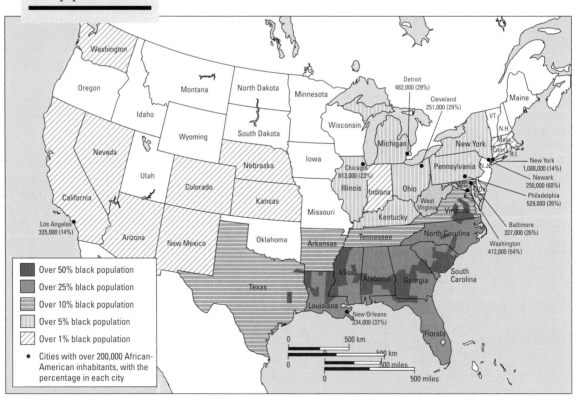

Legend:
- Over 50% black population
- Over 25% black population
- Over 10% black population
- Over 5% black population
- Over 1% black population
- Cities with over 200,000 African-American inhabitants, with the percentage in each city

Detroit 482,000 (29%)
Cleveland 251,000 (29%)
Chicago 813,000 (23%)
New York 1,088,000 (14%)
Newark 250,000 (60%)
Philadelphia 529,000 (26%)
Baltimore 327,000 (35%)
Washington 412,000 (54%)
Los Angeles 335,000 (14%)
New Orleans 234,000 (37%)

African-American population in the USA, 1965

Court-martialled: To be tried by a military court. Martial law – the law governing the armed forces – is stricter than either civil or criminal laws that affect civilians.

in Brownsville, Texas, were accused of rioting. Washington could not prevent a whole black regiment from being **court-martialled**.

Privately, Washington financially supported attempts to bring court cases to challenge segregation. However, he was unwilling to jeopardise his relationship with white America by adopting a radical stance. Such a strategy would have created a violent white backlash, which could have had serious consequences for African Americans, particularly in the Old South.

Booker T. Washington was heavily criticised, by later generations of African-American activists, as a person who seemed to turn a blind eye to civil and political rights. However, Washington was a realist. As Gunnar Myrdal stated, in *The American Dilemma* (1944):

'For his time and for the region where he worked and where nine-tenths of all Negroes lived, his policy of abstaining from talks of rights and of "casting down your buckets where you are" was entirely realistic.'

Washington's practical approach to improving the economic position of African Americans was the central feature of his adult life. In 1900, he helped found the National Negro Business League to encourage business skills and to show what African Americans had achieved in commerce and the economy. In 1911, the National Urban League was created. This organisation campaigned for equal conditions and opportunities in industry and commerce for African Americans. This approach reflected Booker T. Washington's approach to the position of African Americans in a society dominated by whites.

How did the views of Du Bois differ from the views of Booker T. Washington?

W.E.B. Du Bois (1868–1963)
Black historian, sociologist and civil rights leader. Professor of Latin and Greek at Wilberforce University, Ohio (1894–96); Professor of Sociology at Atlanta University, Georgia (1897–1910). Founder of the NAACP in 1909. Editor of 'The Crisis', NAACP magazine (1910–34). Left NAACP in 1948 because of its lack of radicalism. Joined the American Communist Party in 1961.

W.E.B. Du Bois came from a completely different background to Booker T. Washington. Born in Massachusetts in 1868, he was brought up in the North in a middle-class family. He received a PhD degree from Harvard University – the first African American to do so. His thesis was entitled 'The Suppression of the Atlantic Slave Trade to the United States 1638–1870'. Du Bois was also a socialist who wanted to see radical social and economic change in America. In later life, he joined the American Communist Party. It was whilst at Atlanta University that he had published, in 1903, *The Souls of the Black Folk* – a study of African Americans.

Initially, Du Bois supported Washington's efforts to raise the economic position of African Americans. He regarded the 'Atlanta Compromise' speech of 1895 as a 'phenomenal success – it was a word fitly spoken'. Later, he criticised Washington's views as narrow and pessimistic. This was due primarily to Washington's acceptance of the lack of civil and political rights for African Americans.

In 1905, Du Bois directly challenged Washington's position with the creation of the Niagara Movement. Du Bois led a group of African-American activists in demanding full civil and political rights for African Americans. Initially, they met in Buffalo in upstate New York. However, they were forced to move to the Canadian side of Niagara Falls to found their movement.

The Niagara Movement had paved the way for the formation of the National Association for the Advancement of Colored People (NAACP) in 1909. The aim of the organisation was to campaign peacefully for full civil and political rights. These would be achieved through educating the public, but mainly through the courts. By 1914, the NAACP had 6,000 members. In 1915, it achieved its first court success. In 'Guinn versus the United States', the 'grandfather clause' used as a voting qualification in Oklahoma was declared unconstitutional. In 1917, in 'Buchanan versus Warley', segregationist housing regulations were also declared unconstitutional.

Du Bois was an elitest. As editor of the NAACP publication 'The Crisis' from its inception in 1910 until 1934, he campaigned for the top 'talented tenth' of the African-American population to lead the campaign for full rights. In his autobiography, Du Bois claimed that 'if "The Crisis" had not been a personal organ and expression of myself, it could not possibly have attained its popularity and effectiveness!'

Du Bois' greatest contribution to the development of African-American rights was his role as a propagandist, using 'The Crisis' to highlight discrimination and black achievement. However, his lasting contribution was the creation of the NAACP, which played such an important role in the achievement of civil rights in the 1940s and 1950s.

What impact did Marcus Garvey have on the development of African-American society?

Throughout his career, Du Bois kept his distance from ordinary African Americans. His campaigns for better rights fell far short of a mass movement. Yet, in the 1920s, Marcus Garvey, under the banner of 'black nationalism', was able to achieve a mass following in the northern cities of the USA. In his study of the USA from 1920 to 1941, entitled *The Anxious Decades* (1992), Michael Parrish calls Marcus Garvey 'the black Messiah'.

Although brought up in the British West Indies, Garvey is closely identified with African Americans in northern cities such as New York. On the eve of the First World War, he founded the Universal Negro Improvement Association (UNIA). This supported the creation of a strong, independent economic base for African Americans. This was followed, in 1919, by the creation of the Negro Factories Corporation. It reflected the views of Booker T. Washington to some degree. Garvey's aims were to reclaim Africa from the white man. In this sense, he was one of the first effective black critics of European colonialism. Garvey supported black nationalism and a separate black identity. He declared integration, as supported by the NAACP, as 'the greatest enemy of the Negro'. Under the UNIA, a black star shipping line was created. Its shares were available only to African Americans. By 1920, the UNIA had over two million members.

Marcus Garvey (1887–1940)
Jamaican political thinker and activist. Formed the Universal Negro Improvement Association in 1914, and moved to the USA in 1916, where he established branches in New York and other northern cities. He was an early advocate of black nationalism. He led a 'back to Africa' movement for black Americans to establish a black-governed country in Africa. The cult of Rastafarianism is based largely on his ideas.

Study the aims of the UNIA.

a) In what ways are they similar to the ideas of Booker T. Washington?

b) In what ways do they different from Washington's views?

The aims of the Universal Negro Improvement Association

1 To champion Negro nationhood by the liberation of Africa from colonial rule

2 To make the Negro race conscious

3 To breathe the ideals of manhood and womanhood into every Negro

4 To advocate self-determination

5 To make the Negro world-conscious

6 To print all the news that will be interesting and instructive to the Negro

7 To instil racial self-help

8 To inspire racial love and self-respect.

An address made by Marcus Garvey in New York City:

'The white man of the world has been accustomed to deal with the Uncle Tom cringing Negro. Up to 1919 he knew no other Negro than the Negro represented through Booker T. Washington. Today, he will find a new Negro is on the stage. Every American Negro and every West Indian Negro must understand that there is but one fatherland for the Negro, and that is Africa.'

Garvey's black nationalist and separatist views were opposed by the NAACP. They also brought the UNIA under FBI investigation. In 1923, Garvey was convicted of mail fraud. He was fined $1,000 and sentenced to five years in prison. When he left prison in 1927, he was deported as an undesirable alien.

Yet, in his short career, Garvey had created a mass following and had laid the foundations for the black nationalism of the 1960s which would be associated with the Nation of Islam and the Black Panthers.

What contribution did A. Philip Randolph make to African-American rights?

A. Philip Randolph's contribution was primarily in the field of labour relations. In 1925, he was the founding president of the African American Brotherhood of Sleeping Car Porters on the railroad. In 1938, he took his union into the Congress of Industrial Organisations – a new national union structure. Randolph did so because he disliked the segregationist views of the other national union organisation, the American Federation of Labor.

Randolph's greatest triumph was his planned March on Washington in early 1941, as a means to force President Franklin D. Roosevelt (FDR) to make concessions to African Americans. As he stated in January 1941: 'We loyal Americans demand the right to work and fight for our country.'

The march on Washington movement was an all-black protest. It was a forerunner of the type of protest associated with the civil rights movement in the 1950s and 1960s. But the planned march never took place. Instead, FDR issued Executive Order 8802, in June 1941. It outlawed racial discrimination in the defence industries. This enabled tens of thousands of African Americans to gain employment during the Second World War.

Inspired by Randolph's action, James Farmer founded the Congress of Racial Equality, in 1942. The aim of this organisation was to engage in non-violent protest in order to help gain civil and political rights for African Americans. In 1943, this involved a 'sit-in' protest at a Chicago restaurant which had refused to serve African Americans.

How important was the 'Great Migration' for African Americans?

While leaders such as Du Bois, Garvey and Randolph helped to devise strategies to improve the position of African Americans in US society, individual blacks 'voted with their feet' to improve their lives. As a result of the outbreak of the First World War in Europe, in 1914, European immigration dropped sharply. In its place came the migration of African Americans from the Old South northward. Between 1915 and 1925, 1.25 million African Americans sought employment in the North. Between 1925 and 1940, a further one million migrated north. From 1910 to 1930, the African-American population of Chicago rose from 44,000 to 234,000. In New York, over the same period, the population rose from 91,000 to 328,000.

A. Philip Randolph (1889–1979)

Black trade unionist. Socialist Party candidate in early 1920s. In 1925, he founded the Brotherhood of Sleeping Car Porters – an African-American union. Got union to join Congress of Industrial Organisation (CIO) in 1938. In 1940–41 Randolph organised the March on Washington Movement to campaign for civil rights. The march was called off following the President's decision to end discrimination in the defence industry. In 1948, Randolph helped to persuade President Truman to end segregation in armed forces. In 1955, became Vice-President when the CIO merged with American Federation of Labor to form the AFL/CIO.

Most African Americans moving north were forced to live in black ghettos. In Chicago, blacks lived on the South Side in places such as Calumet City; in New York they lived in Harlem and in Philadelphia on the north and west of the city.

This large-scale population movement had important cultural consequences. It led to the development and growth of jazz. Black singers and musicians became known nationally. In the Cotton Club, in Harlem, New York singers such as Cab Calloway and band-leaders such as Duke Ellington were given their opportunity. African-American musicals appeared on Broadway, such as 'Shuffle Along' in 1922, and 'Blackbirds' from 1926–28. The two most prominent black artists in the period were trumpet player and singer Louis Armstrong and singer-actor Paul Robeson. These performers helped to raise the national profile of African-American culture.

It was these groups which were most receptive to Marcus Garvey's crusade for black nationalism and A. Philip Randolph's call for black membership of trade unions.

However, the arrival of large numbers of African Americans in northern cities also increased racial tension. In 1919, race riots occurred across America in 25 cities. In 1942, a major race riot in Detroit led to the deployment of troops to restore order.

How far had the position of African Americans changed within US society by 1945?

By 1945, the geography of African-American society had changed drastically. No longer were they concentrated in the Old South, engaging in subsistence agriculture. African-American education had expanded dramatically. Black schools, agricultural colleges and universities were firmly established across the Old South. However, for the vast majority of African Americans, social advancement was segregated from whites.

Nevertheless, the foundations of what was to become the civil rights movement had been laid. Beginning in 1915, the NAACP had successfully reversed discriminatory legislation in the Supreme Court. In 1938, in the case of 'Missouri ex rel. Gaines versus Canada', the Supreme Court made its first attack on the 'separate but equal' interpretation of the Fourteenth Amendment when it declared that Missouri had failed to provide law school places for African-American students.

In addition, during the New Deal, FDR had begun to offer government positions to African Americans. In the Second New Deal (1935–37), Mary McLeod Bethune was appointed director of the Division of Negro Affairs of the National Youth Administration. During the Second World War, Robert Weaver was made an adviser to the Department of the Interior. Eleanor Roosevelt, the President's wife, supported civil rights. She resigned from the Daughters of the American Revolution when they refused to allow African American Marian Anderson to sing in Constitutional Hall, Washington. During the Second World War, Eleanor Roosevelt gave active support to the creation of the African American 90th fighter group based at Tuskegee.

The NAACP, the National Urban League and the Congress for Racial Equality had all been created by 1945. Between 1940 and 1947, African-American voter registration in the Old South had increased from 2% to 12%.

When tens of thousands of African-American servicemen returned from the Second World War, hopes were high for greater civil, political and social rights.

1. Explain in what ways Booker T. Washington and W.E.B. Du Bois differed in their views on the improvement of the position of African Americans in US society?

2. Why do you think Marcus Garvey's views were popular with northern African Americans?

3. Who do you regard as the most important influence on the development on African-American rights between 1877–1945: Booker T. Washington, W.E.B. Du Bois, Marcus Garvey or A. Philip Randolph?

Explain your answer.

10.4 How successful were African Americans in their attempt to gain civil and political rights, 1945–1968?

The years 1945 to 1968 represent the most significant years in the movement for African-American civil and political rights. During this period, thousands of African Americans across the USA took it upon themselves to fight for an improvement in their position. Their efforts placed African-American civil rights at the centre of US politics.

The quest for greater equality must be seen against the background of the Cold War. From 1945, the USA and its allies were engaged in a global ideological and military struggle with communism. The USA portrayed itself as the defender of the Free World against communist tyranny. It was also a period of rapid decolonisation by the European powers, most notably Britain and France. As the former colonies received independence, they became a battleground in the conflict between East and West. Against this backdrop of world events, the existence of legal segregation in the Old South seemed to be a major embarrassment for the United States' position in the world.

Also during this period, a revolution occurred in the mass media. The development of television and, in particular, television news, brought the issue of civil rights into every American living room. No longer could the African American be regarded as America's 'invisible man', suffering discrimination in silence.

In their struggle for full civil and political rights, African Americans used a variety of methods and worked through a variety of institutions. Already in existence was the National Association for the Advancement of Colored People (NAACP), founded in 1909. It used legal challenges in the courts to overturn discrimination. In 1941, A. Philip Randolph had used the threat of a march on Washington to force the federal government to take action on behalf of African Americans in employment. In the following year, the Congress for Racial Equality was founded by James Farmer. It supported the non-violent political protest put forward by the Indian nationalist leader, Mahatma Ghandi.

These groups had to fight against legal segregation in the Old South backed up by violence and intimidation by groups such as the Ku Klux Klan. Elsewhere in America, African Americans faced discrimination in jobs and housing. In 1947, the Brooklyn Dodgers Baseball team caused a sensation by playing an African American, Jackie Robinson, in major league baseball for the first time. In Hollywood films and popular novels, African Americans were usually portrayed as poorly educated, doing menial jobs and always in a supporting role. The first African American to win an Oscar was Hattie McDaniel, as Scarlett O'Hara's African-American maid in 'Gone With the Wind', in 1939.

In popular cartoons, the only part of an African American to appear were the legs of a maid in the 'Tom and Jerry' cartoons. Even though the USA had fought to defend freedom against Nazi Germany and Japan, it had done so with segregated armed forces. In 1945, the obstacles to African-American equality seemed enormous.

The NAACP, the US Supreme Court and legal challenges to segregation in education

The challenge to legal segregation was rooted in the US Constitution. Under the Bill of Rights of 1791 and the Fourteenth Amendment of 1868, African Americans were guaranteed equal civil rights. However, the Supreme Court had interpreted the Constitution in such a way as to allow legal segregation. The most important Supreme Court judgements had been 'Plessy versus

Ferguson' of 1896 and 'Cumming versus the Board of Education' in 1899. These established the principle of 'separate but equal' facilities.

However, the interpretation of the Constitution was dependent upon the composition of the Supreme Court. In the late 1930s and early 1940s, FDR had appointed justices, such as Felix Frankfurter, who were sympathetic to black civil rights. A turning point was the appointment of Earl Warren, former Republican Governor of California, as Chief Justice in 1953. President Eisenhower later claimed that this was 'the biggest goddam mistake I ever made'. Warren was to lead the Supreme Court into its most liberal, radical phase between 1953 and 1969.

The 'Brown versus Board of Education' case, 1954

On 17 May 1954, the Supreme Court declared separate but equal educational facilities unconstitutional, in a 9–0 unanimous decision. In 'Brown versus the Board of Education, Topeka, Kansas', the Supreme Court declared that 'separate but equal' educational facilities were not of equal standard and that African-American children had been psychologically affected by such a system. The case had been brought to the Supreme Court by the NAACP legal team, headed by Thurgood Marshall, in 1953. It was the culmination of a series of cases which had been brought before the Court since 1945. For instance, in the 'Sweatt versus Painter' case in 1950, the Court had already demanded a $3 million upgrading of the African-American Prairie View University in Texas, because its facilities were inferior to those of white colleges in the state.

What was also significant about the Brown case was the fact that legal segregation had taken place in a state outside the former Confederacy. In 1955, in what became known as the 'Brown II' case, the Supreme Court demanded the integration of all public schools 'with all deliberate speed'.

Although the NAACP had won over the Supreme Court, it faced massive resistance from whites in the Old South. White citizens' councils were created across the South to oppose integration. State governors such as Ross Barnett in Mississippi actively supported these councils. Faced with possible integration, states such as Virginia merely closed down the public school system. In 1955, 100 southern Congressmen signed 'The Southern Manifesto' declaring that the 'Brown case' was a 'clear abuse of judicial power'. By the end of 1956, not one school had been integrated in the 'Deep South'.

Central High School, Little Rock, 1957

In September 1957, matters were brought to a head at Central High School, in Little Rock, Arkansas. A moderate southern state with a moderate governor, Orval Faubus, Arkansas refused to allow school integration. When nine students attempted to enrol at Central High, a white mob surrounded the school. It was only when President Eisenhower sent 1,000 members of the 101st Airborne Division that the students were able to attend school.

James Meredith and 'Ole Miss.', 1962

Another crisis over educational integration occurred when African American James Meredith attempted to enrol in the all-white University of Mississippi in Oxford. Opposed by Governor Ross Barnett and the state citizens' council, Meredith was only admitted after President Kennedy sent in hundreds of US **marshals** and thousands of troops to maintain order. Meredith was admitted to university, but was later wounded in a shooting (see photo opposite).

Marshals: Police officers in the USA who control and organise a particular area or district.

'Alexander versus Holmes County', 1969

Even after Earl Warren had retired from the US Supreme Court in 1969, the Court continued to champion the cause of school integration. In the

James Meredith lying on a Mississippi highway, 6 June 1966, after being shot by a sniper.

De facto: [Latin] Existing in fact, whether legal or not.

1969 case of 'Alexander versus Holmes County', the Court declared that all public schools should be desegregated immediately. The claim was that the Brown II case had demanded 'all deliberate speed' in 1956, and no further delays could be tolerated by 1969. Between 1969 and 1974, the proportion of African-American schoolchildren in the Old South who were educated in segregated schools, dropped from 68% to 8%.

'Swann versus Charlotte Mecklenburg Board of Education', 1971

Although legal segregation of public schools was being brought to an end following the Brown decision of 1954, schools were still divided into black and white elsewhere in America as a result of segregated housing. In the 'Swann' case, this *de facto* segregation of schools was to end.

This case led to the need to bus black and white students across urban areas in order to integrate schools racially. In the North, this involved bussing black students from inner-city ghettos into white suburbs, and vice versa. This created widespread resistance. Serious rioting occurred in Boston, Massachusetts, in 1974. It became part of a nationwide campaign called ROAR (Restore our Alienated Rights). Opposition led a more conservative Supreme Court, in 1974, to moderate its position on compulsory bussing in 'Milliken versus Bradley'.

Ending the reign of 'Jim Crow' in the Old South, 1955–1965

While the NAACP had fought a long campaign to persuade the US Supreme Court to end segregation in education, the campaign to end segregation in transportation produced new organisations and new African-American leaders.

The Montgomery bus boycott of 1955–1956

The Montgomery bus boycott is of great significance to the civil rights movement for several reasons. It saw:

● the creation of an important grassroots African-American organisation – the Montgomery Improvement Association (MIA);

● the rise to national prominence of a young Baptist minister, Dr Martin Luther King Junior;

● the growth of a concerted, well-organised and successful, peaceful resistance by African Americans to bus segregation in the heart of the Old South. (Montgomery, in 1861, had been the Confederate capital for a brief period.)

The person who sparked off the boycott was Mrs Rosa Parks, a NAACP activist, when she was arrested in March 1955 for not giving up her seat to a white man while sitting at the front of a bus. Bus boycotts had occurred before across the South, in places such as Baton Rouge, Louisiana. Rosa Parks had previously refused to give up her seat, but this was the first time she had been arrested. Local members of the NAACP, such as E.D. Nixon, wanted to use the Parks case to launch a campaign to end bus segregation in Montgomery and, ultimately, across the South.

The choice of Martin Luther King to 'front' the protest proved prophetic. A supporter of non-violent political protest, King was influenced by the example of Mahatma Ghandi, the Indian national leader. King was an excellent speaker. As a minister, he reflected a central feature of African-American leadership in the South. Using their churches, ministers had led the way in protesting against segregation and discrimination. At the Dexter Avenue Baptist Church in Montgomery, Alabama, King preached his non-violent political message. Before him, the Reverend Vernon Johns had used his position to highlight injustices against blacks.

As an outsider, as a minister and as an effective speaker, Martin Luther King was able to forge links between different African-American groups into the MIA. Initially, the MIA did not want an end to bus segregation. Instead, it wanted a more humane enforcement of segregation. For instance, it wanted drivers to be more polite to African-American customers.

However, due to white intransigence and the almost universal acceptance of the boycott by African Americans, bus segregation was brought to an end on 21 December 1956.

The Montgomery bus boycott was successful only partly because of King's leadership. The boycott also received considerable sympathy from the white press, in particular outside the Old South. It was also made possible because on 13 November, in 'Browder versus Gayle', the US Supreme Court had declared bus segregation unconstitutional in Montgomery.

The successful boycott, in the face of widespread white opposition, encouraged further action by African Americans. In 1957, the Southern Christian Leadership Conference (SCLC) was formed in Atlanta, Georgia. Martin Luther King became its leader and spokesman. The SCLC reflected the importance of African-American ministers as the focal point of opposition to discrimination. It also planned to be an **umbrella organisation** providing central direction to different civil rights groups and organisations.

SNCC and the lunch counter protests, 1960

Martin Luther King and the SCLC may have had a powerful national profile, but the civil rights movement was a broader, more diverse affair. In *Bearing the Cross: Martin Luther King Jr and the Southern Christian Leadership Conference* (1986), David Garrow quoted African-American activist Jo Ann Robinson about the nature of the movement. She states:

> 'The amazing thing about our movement is that it is a protest of the people. It is not a one-man show. It is not a preachers' show. It's the people.'

To prove this point, on 1 February 1960, a group of African-American students entered the Woolworth's department store in Greensboro, North Carolina and sat down at the 'whites only' lunch counter waiting to be served. This sparked off a wave of non-violent lunch counter protests in 54 cities across nine states in the Old South (see photo). In April 1961, at Shaw University, Raleigh, North Carolina, black activist Ella Baker founded the Student Non-violent Co-ordinating Committee (SNCC). The aim of the organisation was to give a voice to African-American students. Martin Luther King encouraged SNCC, hoping that it would be a student wing of the SCLC. However, the students stayed independent of the SCLC.

Martin Luther King (1929–1968)
US civil rights campaigner, black leader and Baptist minister. Born in Atlanta, Georgia. First came to national attention as leader of a bus boycott in Montgomery, Alabama (1955). He was a brilliant and moving speaker. Target of intensive investigation by federal authorities, chiefly the FBI under J. Edgar Hoover. Luther King was one of the organisers of the march of 20,000 people on Washington DC (1963) to demand racial equality. Awarded the Nobel Peace Prize 1964. Assassinated in Memphis, Tennessee on 4 April 1968.

Umbrella organisation: An organisation which tries to unite a variety of different organisation under its leadership.

A Caucasian (white) woman bars the way as African Americans are about to enter the lunch counter of a department store in Memphis, Tennessee, on 10 June 1961.

The sit-in protests were reported in the national press. Attacks by whites on sit-in protestors were seen on television. Student involvement was central to the protests against discrimination. The success in desegregating lunch counters laid the foundation for greater student protest. Joining with students from CORE, the Congress for Racial Equality, SNCC activist engaged in the Freedom Rides of 1961.

CORE and the Freedom Rides of 1961

The Freedom Rides, on inter-state buses through the South, reflect an important feature of the civil rights movement. The aim was to shame the federal government into action which would safeguard African-American rights. As James Farmer, founder of CORE, stated:

> 'We planned the Freedom Rides with the specific intention of creating a crisis. We were counting on the bigots of the South to do our work for us. We figured that the government would have to respond if we created a situation that was headline news all over the world, and affecting the nation's image abroad. An international crisis that was our strategy.'

All CORE planned to do was to find out if the law against segregation on inter-state bus travel really existed in the South. Already in two decisions – in 1946 in 'Morgan versus Virginia' and in 1960 in 'Boynton versus Virginia' – the Supreme Court had outlawed segregation on inter-state bus travel.

On 4 May 1961, four white and four African-American students took inter-state buses from Virginia to Mississippi to test the law. At Anniston, Alabama, the **Greyhound bus** in which they were travelling was fire-bombed. Other freedom riders were attacked by a mob in Birmingham, Alabama, and in Jackson, Mississippi.

Greyhound bus: A bus company providing long-distance travel services across the USA.

The media coverage of these events had the desired effect. It forced the Inter-state Commerce Commission and the Justice Department, under Attorney General Robert F. Kennedy, to enforce segregation on inter-state transportation.

What the lunch counter protests and the freedom rides achieved was to add a new dimension to civil rights protests. Although professing non-violence, the students of SNCC and CORE forced Southern whites into violent retaliation by their actions. They had actively encouraged violent white resistance to highlight their case to American and world public opinion. In doing so, they forced the Kennedy Administration to act.

Birmingham and the march on Washington in 1963

The need to emulate the success of African-American and white students of SNCC and CORE was not lost on Martin Luther King. Following his success in the Montgomery bus boycott of 1955–56, he had experienced mixed success. An attempt by SCLC to double the level of black voter registration in the 'Crusade for Citizenship', between 1958 and 1960, had limited success. Also, during 1961–62 King had become involved in civil rights protests in Albany, Georgia. However, the white Police Chief, Laurie Pritchett, avoided violence and forced King to abandon his campaign in August 1962.

In 1963, King was able to find the confrontation he required in Birmingham, Alabama. The Police Chief, Eugene 'Bull' Connor, played into the hands of the civil rights demonstrators who wanted to end segregation in the city. Using schoolchildren as demonstrators, the civil rights organisers were able to provoke Connor into using police dogs and water cannon – all filmed and shown on primetime television.

In August 1963, A. Philip Randolph's dream of a march on Washington took place. Over 250,000 civil rights supporters met at the Lincoln Memorial to hear Martin Luther King make the keynote speech. In his 'I have a Dream' speech, King put forward his own vision of an integrated, tolerant society. It confirmed him in the position of both leader and conscience of the civil rights movement. It also propelled him into the centre of the international stage and led, in 1964, to his being awarded the Nobel Peace Prize.

Freedom summer and the Mississippi Freedom Democratic Party, 1964

In the summer of 1964, SNCC organised communities across the South to develop local civil rights groups to campaign for greater equality. SNCC members, both white and black, faced considerable white opposition. Several were murdered. These events formed the background for the 1988 film 'Mississippi Burning', starring Gene Hackman and Willem Dafoe.

When SNCC organisers could not register black voters through normal methods, they encouraged African Americans in Mississippi to form the Mississippi Freedom Democratic Party (MFDP), as an alternative to the white-dominated state party.

At the Democratic National Convention in August 1964 in Atlantic City, New Jersey, both the official state Democratic Party and the MFDP demanded to represent the delegation from Mississippi. Lyndon Johnson and his aides were able to offer a compromise by allowing the MFDP two representatives at the Convention. Johnson's action led to the official state delegation leaving the Convention in protest.

The incident at the Democratic National Convention made many SNCC members disillusioned with the Johnson government and helped force them towards a more radical stand in 1965.

Selma and the Voting Rights Act of 1965 – the high tide of Martin Luther King's influence?

King's ability to pressure federal government into action is illustrated by his participation in the Selma to Montgomery peace march of 1965. His actions came after the failure of black activists during Freedom Summer of 1964 to increase African-American voter registration.

Deliberately marching through the most racist part of Alabama, the marchers faced violent reaction from state troopers and white protestors at Pettus Bridge, Selma. Known as 'Bloody Sunday', the incident on 7 March

1965 forced President Johnson to intervene. He placed state troopers under federal control. They allowed the march to continue to Montgomery. The publicity created sufficient pressure to help Congress pass the Voting Rights Act of 1965, which guaranteed the voting rights originally provided by the Fifteenth Amendment of the Constitution in 1870. As a result of the passage of the 1964 Civil Rights Act, the Twenty-Fourth Amendment and the Voting Rights Act of 1965, legal segregation was brought to an end in the United States. The civil and political rights first granted to African Americans in the Civil Rights Amendments of 1865 to 1870, now became a reality.

After Selma, Martin Luther King's authority as the spokesman for African-American civil rights declined. In August 1965, serious rioting by African Americans in the Watts district (now South Central) of Los Angeles left 34 people dead. In July and August, King attempted to lead a civil rights campaign in Chicago. However, attempts to desegregate the Gage Park housing district led to massive white resistance and King was forced to call off his campaign.

The 'March against Fear' was organised in June 1966. The event was to commemorate James Meredith's admission to the University of Mississippi in 1962. Early in the march, Meredith was wounded by a sniper and had to withdraw (see photograph on page 329). However, when the SCLC and SNCC became involved, splits about tactics and aims began to appear. The 'March against Fear' represents the beginning of a split within the civil rights movement, which saw the end of Martin Luther King's dominance.

In 1967, Martin Luther King made the momentous decision to speak out openly against American participation in the Vietnam War. His criticism of the Johnson Administration ended his links with the federal government, which had led to the passage of the civil rights legislation of 1964 and 1965.

1. Which states had the lowest African-American voter registration before the Voting Rights Act of 1865? Give reasons.

2. Which state displayed the greatest increase in African-American voter registration after the passage of the 1965 Voting Rights Act?

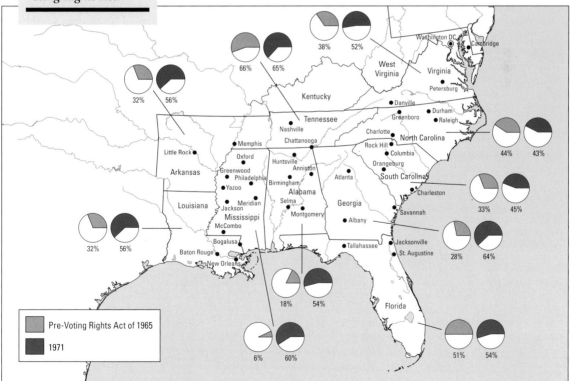

Map showing the major cities of the southern civil rights movement and the percentage of black voting-age population registered.

Civil rights legislation, 1964–1965

The Civil Rights Act, 1964

● Discrimination on the basis of race was outlawed in all places of public accommodation including restaurants, theatres, motels, sports stadia, cinemas and concert halls.

● The Attorney General of the USA was given power to start federal court action against any violation.

● The federal government had the power to withhold federal funds from any state not complying with the Act.

● It set up the Equal Employment Opportunities Commission with powers to outlaw job discrimination.

Twenty-Fourth Amendment to the Constitution, 1964

● Outlawed the use of poll taxes in federal elections.

The Voting Rights Act, 1965

● Banned literacy tests for voter registration.

● Appointed federal examiners to ensure voter registration.

In the same year, Martin Luther King broadened his campaign beyond civil and political rights. His 'Poor People's Campaign' aimed at achieving social equality. This change in direction led to a fall in support from white, middle-class liberals. When King was assassinated in Memphis, in April 1968, he was speaking in support of the sanitation workers' strike. Yet by that date, the civil rights movement had begun to fracture, revealing more radical and militant groups and aims.

The rise of radical black activism, 1965–68

Throughout its existence, the civil rights movement had been a loose coalition of groups. For a period up to 1965, Martin Luther King had acted as national spokesman. However, by then, the coalition had begun to fall apart. More radical voices than Martin Luther King's began to appear.

Malcolm X
Born in 1925, Malcolm X continues to be a figure of controversy. He presented a completely different vision of the position of the African American in US society from that of Martin Luther King. From excerpts of speeches they made, compare the views of these two figures.

Malcolm X (1925–1965)
Born Malcolm Little in Nebraska. Black radical who joined Nation of Islam. Split with Nation of Islam in 1964 and was murdered in Harlem by Nation of Islam supporters.

> **Martin Luther King's 'I have a Dream' speech, August 1963, encapsulates his philosophy:**
>
> 'I have a dream that one day this nation will rise up and live out the true meaning of its creed "We hold these truths to be self-evident, that all men are created equal."
>
> I have a dream that my four little children will one day live in a nation where they will not be judged by the colour of their skin but the content of their character ...
>
> Let freedom ring. When we let freedom ring ... we will be able to speed up that day when all God's children, black men and white men, Jews and Gentiles, Protestants and Catholics, will be able to join hands.'

> **From a speech by Malcolm X to the Northern Negro Leadership Conference, Detroit, November 1963:**
>
> 'The white man knows what revolution is. He knows that the black revolution is worldwide in scope and in nature. The black revolution is sweeping Asia, is sweeping Africa, is rearing its head in Latin America.
>
> Revolution is bloody, revolution is hostile, revolution knows no compromise, revolution overturns and destroys everything that gets in its way.
>
> Whoever heard of a revolution where they lock arms, singing "We shall overcome"? You don't do that in a revolution. Those Negroes aren't asking for a nation – they're trying to crawl back to the plantation.'

King's speech is optimistic and tolerant, looking forward to an integrated society. Malcolm X, on the other hand, supports black revolution. It is intolerant and threatening.

Part of the difference comes from the fact that Malcolm X was brought up in a northern ghetto. He was from a poor background and had spent time in jail for drug offences. King came from a middle-class Southern background.

By 1963, Malcolm X had become a member of the Nation of Islam, the Black Muslims. He supported black nationalism. As a result, he had more in common with Marcus Garvey (see section 10.2) than with Martin Luther King. Malcolm X wanted to go beyond mere civil and political rights. He supported social revolution.

In November 1963, Malcolm X decided to split from the Nation of Islam and establish his own organisation. From then until his death, in February 1965 at the hands of Nation of Islam assassins, Malcolm X began to moderate his views on whites, but maintained his support for revolutionary movements in Africa and Latin America.

Unlike King, Malcolm X had virtually no influence outside the ghettos of the North. However, he did represent a more intolerant, radical view which found expression in other groups.

Stokely Carmichael (1941–2000)

West Indian-born, radical black activist. Emigrated from Trinidad to USA in 1951. Joined SNCC at university. Was a freedom rider in 1961. Chairman of SNCC in 1966. Became supporter of Black Power. Left SNCC in 1968 and opposed the Vietnam War. Later helped found the All-African People's Revolutionary Party and changed his name to Kwame Toure.

Huey P. Newton (1942–1989)

Co-founder in 1966 with Bobby Seale of Black Panther Party in Oakland, California to protect blacks against police brutality and racial discrimination. Convicted of the manslaughter of a policeman in 1967. Conviction was later overturned. Fled to Cuba in 1974 to avoid a murder charge, but returned to USA in 1977. Murdered in Oakland (1989).

Explain why posters like this would attract African Americans to support 'Black Power'?

'Power to the People' poster produced by the Black Panthers, 1960s

Black Power and the Black Panthers

Malcolm X is less important for what he personally achieved than for his influence on other black radicals. Floyd McKissick became chairman of CORE in January 1966. In SNCC, Stokely Carmichael became chairman later in the same year. Both figures supported liberation movements in the Third World. They also wanted to adopt a more radical approach to civil rights. The idea associated with both chairmen was Black Power. It emerged from a growing belief and pride in being African American. Opposition to the Vietnam War also affected it. By 1967, Carmichael and McKissick had rejected the tolerant, non-violent strategy used by Martin Luther King. Instead, they sought solidarity with Africa and the development of a separate and distinct black identity. An offshoot of the development of Black Power was the adoption of the Afro hairstyle by many northern blacks.

The most extreme manifestation of Black Power was the Black Panther Party for Self-Defense. This was founded in October 1966 in Oakland, California, by Huey Newton and Bobby Seale. The Black Panthers identified more with Cuban revolutionary Che Guevara than with Martin Luther

King. Their demands included reparations to the black community for the discrimination faced by African Americans since their arrival as slaves. They also wanted blacks to be exempt from military service. Wearing distinctive black berets, black leather jackets and black gloves, the Panthers represented the most extreme phase of the civil rights movement.

The high point in the publicity for Black Power came with the Mexico Olympics in 1968. At the 400 metres men's final award ceremony, African Americans Tommy Smith and John Carlos made the Black Power salute with black leather gloves. After the demonstration, neither athlete represented the USA again. In 1969, 27 Black Panthers were shot by the police and 750 were arrested. By 1970, FBI infiltration had broken the back of the Black Panther leadership. Never numbering more than 5,000 members, the Black Panthers gained publicity far greater than their real influence deserved.

How far had African Americans gained their civil and political rights by 1968?

By the time of Martin Luther King's assassination, legal segregation was rapidly coming to an end in the Old South. However, *de facto* segregation of schools still existed across America because of racially separated housing areas. Although African Americans could now vote freely, many still faced severe economic hardship. Poorly educated compared with whites and living in poor housing, African Americans still faced far greater social and economic problems than the majority of the white population.

Instead of being a year of triumph for African Americans, 1968 became a year of riots in almost every major city across the USA.

1. What methods did African Americans use to advance their case for civil rights?

2. Why was legal segregation brought to an end by the mid-1960s?

3. How far was the achievement of civil rights due to actions of African Americans?

10.5 The role of Dr Martin Luther King Jr in the civil rights movement
A CASE STUDY IN HISTORICAL INTERPRETATION

The case for King

To many people, both within and outside the United States, Martin Luther King personified the civil rights movement. Today, his memory is celebrated in the USA by a national holiday on the day of his birth. In the Auburn District of Atlanta, the Martin Luther King National Historic Site has been created. It has, as its centrepiece, a history of the civil rights movement.

When King was assassinated by a lone, white gunman, he instantly became the martyr of the civil rights movement. His funeral in Atlanta, on 9 April 1968, was attended by political leaders from around the world and across America. After all, it was an election year. In his funeral oration to Dr King, Benjamin Mays, his former teacher, claimed that King had:

'contributed largely to the success of the student sit-in movements in abolishing segregation in downtown establishments. His activities contributed mightily to the passage of the civil rights legislation of 1964 and 1965.'

Later, in 1977, when King received the posthumous award of the Presidential Medal of Freedom, the citation stated: 'Martin Luther King Jr was the conscience of his generation. A Southerner, a black man, he gazed upon the great wall of segregation and saw that the power of love could bring it down.'

Clearly, Dr King had a large impact on how the civil rights movement was perceived by other Americans and by people around the world. His ability to speech eloquently and thoughtfully gave him a high profile in the age of television. His speeches during the Montgomery bus boycott maintained morale among the local African-American community. His 'I have a Dream' speech in August 1963 is widely regarded as one of the finest speeches in US history.

However, it was not just the delivery of speeches that made King so significant, it was also the message. His support for non-violent, peaceful protest was the only realistic strategy open to African Americans at the time, if they were to achieve their civil and political rights. Any other strategy would have resulted in a more violent backlash. King's strategy elevated the civil rights cause to a high spiritual and religious level. As a Baptist minister, he turned the civil rights cause into a religious movement in the way Lincoln had transformed the conflict between the states into a moral crusade into end slavery in the Civil War.

King's strategy was effective because African Americans, in theory at least, already had equal civil and political rights. These had been guaranteed by the three Civil War amendments of 1865–70. What King and his supporters were able to do through their peaceful protests was to shame America into recognising that fact. Through the use of the media and by linking the civil rights cause directly with the Declaration of Independence and the Constitution, King occupied the high moral and political ground.

In many ways, King was fortunate in facing opponents who, themselves, reflected the intolerance of which he spoke. In 1955, during the Montgomery bus boycott, African Americans were attacked and churches bombed. Then Emmet Till, a young African-American boy from Chicago, was brutally murdered by two white men in Money, Mississippi, for the crime of having talked to a white woman. His mother demanded an open casket funeral back in Chicago, where the nation's media photographed Till's badly mutilated body.

Martin Luther King delivers his 'I Have a Dream' speech in front of the Lincoln Memorial during the Freedom March in Washington DC, 28 August 1963.

From a media point of view, Eugene 'Bull' Connor, the police chief of Birmingham, Alabama, offered the most striking example of white intolerance, in the full glare of national publicity at the civil rights demonstrations of 1963. Arresting schoolchildren and pregnant women, brutally attacking the demonstrators with dogs and water cannon, Connor was the personification of everything that was wrong with legal segregation in the South.

King's contribution was also important in organisation. In 1957, he was elected president of the Southern Christian Leadership Conference. King used the organisation as an umbrella organisation to unite the various civil rights groups across the South. From 1957 to 1965, King was the unofficial leader of the civil rights movement.

He also inspired others to participate in the movement. His non-violent protest strategy inspired the lunch counter protesters of 1960, which led to the formation of SNCC. King also inspired liberal whites to take part in the civil rights cause. His moral, non-violent stance helped to create this fragile coalition of interests.

Due to his high media and national profile, King was able to act as the link between the civil rights movement and the White House during the Kennedy and Johnson years. King met Kennedy twice during the presidential campaign of 1960. It was Robert F. Kennedy, the brother of the presidential candidate, who helped get King out of an Atlanta jail after he had been arrested for the first time during a voter registration drive. These events helped to forge a link between King and the Kennedy White House, in particular with Robert Kennedy, the Attorney General. During the Kennedy Administration (1961–63), Robert Kennedy intervened decisively on a number of occasions to help the cause of educational integration in the South.

During and after the Montgomery bus boycott, King served as a catalyst of increasing symbolic and charismatic significance. He was able to direct attention onto, and support for, protests started by others.

Until the emergence of the Black Power slogan, King, through his prestige and force of personality, was able to hold together an obviously fragmenting civil rights coalition. In this respect, he served as the vital centre of the movement, standing between the 'conservatism' of the NAACP and National Urban League, and the 'radicalism' of SNCC and CORE.

A testimony to King's role in the civil rights movement is to assess what happened to the SCLC after his assassination. Under the Reverend Ralph Abernathy and then the Reverend Jesse Jackson, the organisation declined rapidly in significance.

The supporters of Black Power, who criticised King's campaign strategy, achieved far less for African Americans. It is significant that many historians conclude their studies of the civil rights movement in 1968 with King's death.

The case against Martin Luther King

Ella Baker, a former staff member of the SCLC and a founder of SNCC claimed that 'the movement made Martin rather than Martin making the movement'. It is clear that the civil rights movement, in its broadest sense, was already in existence by the time Dr King became actively involved. The NAACP had already won the historic Brown case in the US Supreme Court in 1954. King was not involved in the events surrounding the enrolment of nine black students at Central High School, Little Rock in 1957, nor was he involved in James Meredith's application to attend the University of Mississippi in 1962. In fact, on the whole issue of desegregation in education, Martin Luther King had played a marginal role.

When he was asked by E.D. Nixon to front the Montgomery Improvement Association during the bus boycott of 1955–56, he was chosen because he was an outsider and a person not associated with the civil rights struggle in Montgomery.

Andrew King, a member of SCLC and, later, Mayor of Atlanta claimed that:

> 'everything [Martin Luther King] did he was pushed into. He went to Montgomery in the first place because … he wanted a nice quiet town where he could finish his doctoral dissertation … and got trapped into the Montgomery Improvement Association. It wasn't until the time of Birmingham [1963] that he kinda decided that he wasn't going to be able to escape.'

King was more a spokesman than a leader of a wide and diverse movement. The lunch counter protests of 1960 and the Freedom Rides of 1961 were devised and executed by students outside his control. King's attempts to make the SNCC the student wing of SCLC came to nothing. From 1960 to 1965, SNCC and CORE had an uneasy relationship with King and the SCLC.

Unlike the students of SNCC and CORE, King faced a number of embarrassing failures as leader of SCLC. The campaign for increased voter registration, from 1958 to 1960, had virtually no impact. His attempt to desegregate Albany, Georgia, in 1961–62 also came to nothing. When faced by a shrewd police chief, like Laurie Pritchard in Albany, who avoided violent confrontation, King's tactics did not work.

Above all, King's area of influence was the Old South. The SCLC had its headquarters in his home town of Atlanta. In the North, King's role was marginal. On the few occasions King became involved in the civil rights movement in the North, he faced failure. In 1966, King went to Chicago to lead a demonstration against slum housing, *de facto* school segregation and poor employment opportunities for African Americans. He came across hostile reaction from Polish Americans in Cicero who stoned his march. King was injured by a brick thrown during his attempt to march through the white housing area of Gage Park.

It seems clear that King's influence was centred on the South in the years 1955–66. After that date, SNCC and CORE became detached from King's control. They looked for inspiration from the writing of Malcolm X and the lure of black nationalism. King also lost support from the Johnson White House when he began to speak out openly against the Vietnam War. This was made clear in a speech, on 4 April 1967, at Riverside Church, New York City, when he claimed:

> 'We have supported the enemies of the peasant of Saigon. What do they think as we test our latest weapons on them, just as the Germans tested out new medicine and new tortures in the concentration camps of Europe?'

Also in 1967, King began to lose white, middle-class support when he embarked on 'The Poor People's Campaign'. Having gained civil and political equality for African Americans, King was attempting to gain social equality. Through support for Third World revolutionary movements and social justice at home, King had ceased to be a liberal and was perceived to be a socialist.

King did not help his alienation from white, liberal America. He kept as a close aide a known communist, the white Stanley Levinson. This made King and the civil rights cause vulnerable to attacks from FBI chief J. Edgar Hoover, who always contested that King was a communist sympathiser.

1. What do you regard as Martin Luther King's main contribution to the civil rights movement? Explain your answer.

2. Why do you think there are so many differing interpretations of Martin Luther King's role in the civil rights movement?

Martin Luther King has come to symbolise the civil rights years of 1955–68. The nature of his death elevated King to a national hero. However, as King's own sister, Christine Farris, noted: 'My brother was no saint [but] an average and ordinary man.'

SNCC activist, Diane Nash, claims that:

'If people think that it was Martin Luther King's movement, then today they – young people – are more likely to say, "gosh, I wish we had a Martin Luther King here to lead us today." If people knew how the movement started, then the question they would ask themselves is, "What can I do?"'

10.6 How important was the federal government to the achievement of African-American civil rights, 1945–1992?

The federal government occupies a central role in the achievement of full civil rights for African Americans. It was the federal government, during the Civil War, that freed the slaves. However, from the end of Reconstruction, in 1877, the federal government turned a blind eye to the introduction of legal segregation in the Old South.

The federal government in the USA comprises the President, the Congress and the US Supreme Court. Each branch of the government has played a different role in the achievement of civil rights.

In the Congress, the dominance of the Democratic Party in the Old South, from 1877 to the late 1960s, meant that important committees were run by Southern Democrats, who were completely opposed to full civil rights for African Americans. Southern Democrats proved to be an obstacle to the introduction of effective civil rights legislation up to the 1960s.

The Presidency has also had a mixed role in the achievement of civil rights. Democrat Presidents Truman, Kennedy and Johnson all played an important role in the advancement of civil rights. However, they faced opposition from within their own party. On two occasions – in 1948 and again in 1968 – Southern Democrats put forward their own anti-civil rights presidential candidate, to stand against the official Democrat candidate.

Finally, the US Supreme Court played a central role in the achievement of civil rights. As the highest judicial body in the land, its power to interpret the Constitution was central to the ending of legal segregation in the South.

A fair deal for African Americans under Truman, 1945–1953?

During FDR's long presidency (1933–45) very little was done at federal level to aid African Americans. Attempts to make lynching a federal offence failed in the Congress. During the New Deal, alphabet agencies did aid poor African Americans. In the Youth Administration, Mary McLeod Bethune, an African American, became director of the Negro Affairs Department. However, in the Second World War era, African Americans benefited from FDR Executive Order 8802, which forbade racial discrimination in the defence industry.

Although Truman came from the border state of Missouri, he had earned a reputation for fairness during the Second World War. When peace came, Truman put the Fair Employment Practice Commission on a permanent, peacetime footing. Truman also met members of the National Emergency Committee against Mob Violence in September 1946. The Committee highlighted the extent of legal segregation in the South and of discrimination against African Americans.

In the 1948 election, Truman made civil rights an issue. In Executive Order 9980, Truman ended racial discrimination in federal employment. This order created the Fair Employment Board. In August 1948, in Executive Order 9981, he desegregated the US armed forces.

All of these actions helped to alienate Southern Democrats. In retaliation, they put forward Senator Strom Thurmond as a states' rights ('Dixiecrat') candidate for the presidency.

Truman made tentative steps towards providing better rights for African Americans. He was aided by two Supreme Court decisions – one, in 1946, which outlawed segregation on inter-state buses. He was also supported by the liberal Democrat pressure group, Americans for Democratic Action. However, he was bitterly opposed by Southern Democrat and Republic Congressmen. This group dominated the 80th Congress of 1947–49.

Reluctant player: Dwight D. Eisenhower, 1953–1961

The election of a moderate Republican, in 1952, did not augur well for the civil rights movement. Eisenhower was loath to upset the conservative coalition which had brought him to power. However, his appointment of Earl Warren as Chief Justice of the Supreme Court in 1953 helped to bring about a revolution in that institution. Under Warren's leadership, the Supreme Court became a proactive force in bringing about full civil rights. In the Brown Case of 1954, it declared unconstitutional the 'separate but equal' interpretation of the Fourteenth Amendment.

In response to this development, Eisenhower declared that:

> 'I am convinced that the Supreme Court decision set back progress in the South at least 15 years. It's all very well to talk about school integration – if you remember that you may also be talking about social disintegration.
>
> We can't demand perfection in these moral things. All we can do is keep working toward a goal and keep it high. And the fellow who tries to tell me that you can do these things by force is just plain NUTS!'

However, Eisenhower was forced to act, in September 1957, when Governor Orval Faubus opposed school integration and a white mob attempted to prevent the enrolment of black students. The 1,000 troops from the 101st Airborne Division were sent to enforce integration.

Attempts to aid African-American voter registration were made during Eisenhower's second administration. In the first civil rights acts since Reconstruction, the 1957 and 1960 Acts attempted to give federal judges more power in enforcing black voter registration. However, Southern Democrat resistance in Congress made both Acts ineffectual.

Kennedy and the New Frontier, 1961–1963

John F. Kennedy (JFK), like Martin Luther King, has gone down in history as a martyr – gunned down in his prime, promises unfulfilled. However, the Kennedy Administration had no strategy on civil rights when it entered office. For most of his presidency, JFK displayed a reluctance to get involved in civil rights, an attitude which mirrored the views and actions of his predecessor.

Kennedy was also hampered by the fact that he had won the narrowest of victories over Nixon in the 1960 election, gaining 49.5% of the vote. He also faced a hostile Congress in which a coalition of Southern Democrats and Republicans blocked much of his legislative programme.

Like Eisenhower, Kennedy was forced to act because of actions by African Americans. The lunch counter protests of 1960, the Freedom Rides of 1961 and James Meredith's attempt to enrol at the University of Mississippi forced federal action. Attorney General, Robert F. Kennedy (RFK), proved to be the most active member of the Administration. Through his actions, lunch counters were desegregated and the Supreme Court ruling on inter-state bussing was enforced. The Justice Department under RFK also helped to desegregate the universities of Mississippi and Alabama.

The intensity of African-American protest and the adverse publicity it gave at the height of the Cold War forced JFK to introduce a Civil Rights Bill, in 1963, to end legal segregation. However, there was little chance of its passing through Congress. JFK's assassination, in November 1963, changed all that.

Johnson and the end of legal segregation, 1963–1969

Ironically, it took a Southern President, from Texas, to bring legal segregation to an end. On the wave of emotion following JFK's assassination and by using his excellent powers of persuasion, Lyndon B. Johnson (LBJ) was able to pass through Congress the Civil Rights Act of 1964 and the Voting Rights Act of 1965. Together with the Twenty-Fourth Amendment of 1964, these enforced the civil and political rights which had been promised to African Americans in the Civil War amendments of 1865–70. The 1968 Omnibus Housing Act helped to end racial discrimination in housing.

In addition, LBJ's 'war on poverty' brought much needed federal aid to inner city areas. The education, medical and social reforms of the Great Society (see Chapter 11) gave many African Americans a chance for social and economic advancement.

However, the Johnson years also witnessed the riots of 1965 in Watts and of 1968 across the USA, as African Americans living in the ghettos of northern cities showed their frustration at decades of discrimination and social deprivation.

Nixon, Ford and Carter, 1969–1981 – a return to conservatism?

Richard Nixon won a narrow election victory over his Democrat opponent Hubert Humphrey in 1968. He was aided by the entry into the race of Alabama Governor, George Wallace, as the American Independent Party candidate. Wallace won the Old South. However, Nixon also received considerable votes in the area. During his presidency, he adopted the 'Southern strategy' of winning the 'solid South' away from the Democratic Party to his own Republican Party.

As part of his plan, he nominated but failed to get appointed two southern conservatives to the Supreme Court, C. Harold Carswell and Clement F. Haynsworth. However, when Chief Justice Earl Warren retired in 1969, he was able to replace him with the conservative Warren E. Burger. Although supposedly more conservative, the Supreme Court under Nixon expanded the scope of school desegregation. In 'Alexander versus Holmes County', school integration in the Old South was speeded up. In 1971, in 'Swann versus Charlotte Mecklenburg Board of Education', bussing was ordered across America to end *de facto* school segregation.

In addition, Nixon greatly reduced direct federal aid to inner cities. Instead, he introduced 'creative federalism' in which federal money was given directly to the states.

Nevertheless, beginning in 1969 with the Philadelphia Plan, Nixon

344 Civil rights, 1865–1992

extended the affirmative action programme on federal-funded projects. He wanted firms on government contracts to put aside 26% of their jobs for ethnic minorities within four years. By 1972, affirmative action was extended to embrace over 300,000 firms. In taking this action, Nixon wanted to split the New Deal coalition. He hoped to benefit African Americans and to damage the power of the AFL/CIO trade union movement. In 1971, the Supreme Court upheld Nixon's right to insist on affirmative action in 'Giggs versus Duke Power Company'.

Jimmy Carter's one-term Democratic Administration (1977–81) made little impact on the plight of African Americans. For much of Carter's Presidency, the USA faced economic recession. However, Carter did appoint 14 African Americans as ambassadors. The most high-profile appointment was that of SCLC's Andrew Young to be US ambassador to the UN.

The most significant developments in the Carter years involved legal defence of affirmative action. In the Bakke case of 1978, the Supreme Court retreated on the issue – upholding a white student's right to enter the University of California. Nevertheless, in 1980, in 'Fullilove versus Klutznick' the Court upheld the need to allocate 10% of jobs to ethnic minorities.

The New Conservatism of Reagan and Bush, 1981–1992

During the Reagan years (1981–89), serious attempts were made to limit federal government support for civil rights programmes and legislation. Reagan limited the power and authority of the US Commission on Civil Rights by appointing more conservative personnel. He did the same in the federal judicial system. In his two terms, he appointed around 25% of the federal judiciary. However, his most significant appointment was that of the conservative William Rehnquist as Chief Justice to the Supreme Court in 1986.

In 1982, Ronald Reagan supported the segregated Bob Jones University in the South in its attempt to get tax exemption status. In 1988, Reagan also vetoed the Civil Rights Restoration Bill which aimed to enforce federal support for affirmative action. However, Republicans and Democrats united in Congress to override his veto. In addition, Reagan opposed the renewal of the Voting Rights Act of 1965.

Perhaps the most significant action by Reagan was his attack on the welfare state, which had been established under the New Deal in the 1930s. 'Reaganomics' (see Chapter 12) saw dramatic tax cuts and cuts in federal programmes to aid the poor. An example was the 1988 Family Support Act, which forced people on welfare to do community service work or to take part in government training schemes. These changes in welfare hit African Americans particularly badly. In 1980, African Americans comprised 11.7% of the population but made up 43% of those receiving welfare under Aid to Families with Dependent Children, 34.4% of those in subsidised housing and 35.1% of those using food stamps.

During the Reagan and Bush years, the Supreme Court became more conservative. In 1971, following the retirement from the Court of former NAACP member, Thurgood Marshall, George Bush nominated the conservative African American, Clarence Thomas. In addition, under both presidents, the Justice Department took a hostile stance towards affirmative action programmes. In 1992, in 'Freeman versus Pitts' the Supreme Court weakened school desegregation orders. By the time of Bill Clinton's election as President in November 1992, many of the gains of the civil rights years of 1954–70 were under threat.

1. Which branch of the federal government was most supportive of African-American civil rights?

Explain your answer.

2. Was the US Presidency more of a hindrance than a help to the cause of African-American civil rights?

Explain your answer.

10.7 How far did African Americans achieve full civil rights by 1992?

In his study *Black America, 1992, An Overview* (published in 1993), John E. Jacob, President of the National Urban League, declared:

'I would categorise the state of Black America in 1992 as one of bleak despair countered by fresh hope.

The despair was rooted in the effects of a long, debilitating recession that drove many black families deeper into poverty and diminished already stagnating employment opportunities.

The hope was based on the election of a new administration pledged to chart a different course for the nation.'

Many African Americans faced a life of poverty. On average, they earned 61% of what white families received. Proportionately larger numbers of African Americans were on welfare and in prison.

The feeling of discrimination and desperation came to a head in South Central Los Angeles, in the Rodney King affair. An African American, Rodney King, was videoed being brutally attacked by members of the Los Angeles Police Department. When the police were acquitted, a riot ensued in which 54 people were killed, 2,400 injured and 17,000 arrested. Ten thousand businesses were destroyed, with the loss of 50,000 jobs. Other outbreaks of rioting occurred in Atlanta, San Francisco and Madison, Wisconsin.

The Rodney King affair shows that African Americans still had not received full civil rights. However, there had been major changes in US society. Legal segregation had gone by the end of the 1960s in the Old South. Desegregation in schooling outside the Old South was brought to an end with bussing during the 1970s. Affirmative action programmes had enabled tens of thousands of African Americans to get jobs and places at university. In the 1994 mid-term election, over 40 African Americans were returned to Congress. The number included the first African-American woman to be elected to the Senate, Carol Brown of Illinois. African Americans had become mayors of large cities, such as Tom Bradley in Los Angeles and Marion Barry in Washington DC. In 1991, the Commander of the US armed forces in the Gulf War was Colin Powell, who later became Secretary of State under George W. Bush in 2001.

In popular culture, African Americans have developed a much higher profile. On television, Oprah Winfrey has hosted one of the most popular 'chat shows'. In the cinema, actors such as Eddie Murphy, Morgan Freeman and Denzel Washington have became major stars. In popular music, Tamla Motown became an avenue for many black artists to gain national fame, such as Diana Ross and Michael Jackson.

It seems clear that many African Americans have benefited from the advancement in civil and political rights. In 1978, African-American sociologist William J. Wilson published *The Declining Significance of Race*. In this study, Wilson points out that a new black economic and social elite had appeared.

However, in the 1990 US Census nine out of 31 million African Americans lived in households with an income less than $35,000 per year. What had taken place was the bifurcation of African-American society into rich and poor.

The civil rights struggle had benefited many African Americans. Unfortunately, it had still left a large number living in poverty. In the third edition of *The Unfinished Journey* (1995), American historian William Chafe notes:

'one of the primary consequences of this process was the increasing bifurcation of black America into a two-class society. While 35 to 45 % of black families succeeded in achieving a middle-class lifestyle during the 1970s, another 30% of the black population experience a steady decline into ever deeper poverty.

As a consequence of bifurcation, the lives of inner-city blacks became a montage of unmitigated blight, depression and hopelessness.

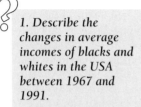

1. Describe the changes in average incomes of blacks and whites in the USA between 1967 and 1991.

2. Do the data suggest that the economic position of blacks had improved between 1967 and 1991? Explain your answer.

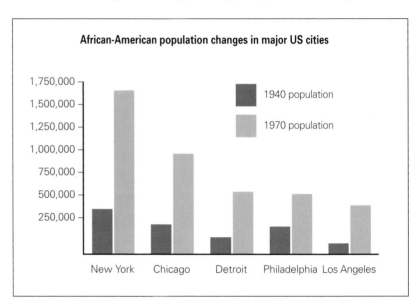

African-American population changes in major US cities

Average income of persons with income, by race and sex (1991)

	Male			Female		
	Black	**White**	**B/W**	**Black**	**White**	**B/W**
1991	$12,962	$21,395	60.6	$8,816	$10,721	82.2
1990	13,409	22,061	60.8	8,678	10,751	80.7
1989	13,850	22,916	60.4	8,650	10,777	80.3
1988	13,866	22,979	60.3	8,461	10,480	80.7
1987	13,449	22,666	59.3	8,331	10,199	81.7
1986	13,630	22,443	59.9	8,160	9,643	84.6
1985	13,630	21,659	62.9	7,945	9,312	85.3
1984	12,385	21,586	57.4	8,080	9,109	88.7
1983	12,335	21,092	58.5	7,615	8,912	85.4
1982	12,591	21,011	59.9	7,498	8,501	88.2
1981	12,851	21,611	59.5	7,412	8,343	88.8
1980	13,254	22,057	60.1	7,580	8,187	92.6
1979	14,019	22,648	61.9	7,358	8,085	91.0
1978	13,844	23,110	59.9	7,480	8,307	90.0
1977	13,560	22,850	59.3	7,446	8,622	86.4
1976	13,719	22,785	60.2	7,791	8,268	94.2
1975	13,475	22,538	59.8	7,530	8,288	90.9
1974	14,397	23,235	62.0	7,385	8,180	90.3
1973	14,754	24,392	60.5	7,352	8,146	90.3
1972	14,519	23,970	60.6	7,497	8,025	93.4
1971	13,639	22,870	59.6	6,778	7,736	87.6
1970	13,709	23,121	59.3	6,803	7,473	91.0
1969	13,603	23,386	58.2	6,361	7,543	84.3
1968	13,432	22,641	59.3	5,957	7,511	79.3
1967	12,554	21,935	57.2	5,478	6,960	78.7

In middle-class America Martin Luther King's "dream" of August 1963 seems to have come true. For African Americans living in inner city areas their social and economic position deteriorated in the 1970s and 1980s.'

David Swinton of Jackson State University sums up the problem in 'Economic Progress for Black Americans in the Post Civil Rights Era' published in *US Race Relations in the 1980s and 1990s* (1990):

'The civil rights strategy focused on the development of laws and programs to eliminate discrimination. The basic decision in these policies was to ignore differences in wealth and ownership. This strategy contains the assumption that individual black initiative is sufficient to eliminate racial inequality within a reasonable period of time.'

Unfortunately, individual black initiative benefited only a minority of African Americans.

1. Explain the meaning of the 'bifurcation' of African-American society.

2. To what extent did the civil rights movement fail to get full civil rights for African Americans by 1992?

10.8 In what ways did the civil rights of Native Americans change, 1865–1992?

Plains Indians: A collection of tribes which lived between the Mississippi river and the Rocky Mountains. The most notable being the Sioux and the Cheyenne.

In 1865, Native Americans were divided into over 250 tribes, speaking 35 major languages. At no time in American history to that date did Native Americans provide a united ethnic group. Many Native Americans remained outside government jurisdiction. Around 250,000 **Plains Indians** occupied the West. Many of the larger tribes in the East had been transported westward in the 1830s to occupy Indian territory which was later to become the state of Oklahoma in 1907.

To many in the US government in 1865, the Plains Indians were an obstacle to national development. It was the 'manifest destiny' of the US government to dominate the continent. Native Americans were seen as a primitive branch of humanity who needed the benefits of Christianity and western civilisation if they were to progress.

Between 1865 and 1890, the Plains Indians were defeated by US armed forces. The basis of US policy towards Native Americans was embodied in the Dawes Severalty Act of 1887. The Act aimed to end the nomadic life of the Plains Indians. They were given land and US citizenship. With the latter came the civil rights of all US citizens. In 1901, US citizenship was extended to the five civilised tribes living in Indian territory – Creek, Choctaw, Chickasaw, Seminole and Cherokee (see Chapter 2). In 1924, all Native Americans became US citizens.

In reality, the Dawes Act helped to destroy Native-American culture. Children were educated to become US citizens. Property and land speculators were able to buy Indian land. By 1934, the total land area given to Indians in 1887 had been reduced by two-thirds. Much of what remained for Native Americans was poor farm land. This placed Native Americans in a **cycle of poverty** in which most would remain. Riven by disease, the Plains Indians population had fallen to 100,000 by 1900.

At federal level, the white-dominated Bureau of Indian Affairs dealt with Native-American issues. Generally, Native-American views were ignored. It took until the New Deal for changes to be made. Under a new Commissioner for Indian Affairs, John Collier, the Dawes Severalty Act provisions were abandoned. In the 1934 Indian Reorganisation Act, Native-American culture was safeguarded for the first time. Tribes were reorganised into self-governing bodies which could adopt their own legal systems, police and constitution.

In spite of these changes, 75 of the 245 Indian tribes opposed the Act, including the largest tribe, the Navajo of Arizona and New Mexico.

Cycle of poverty: The social and economic position in which people cannot get out of poverty no matter how hard they try.

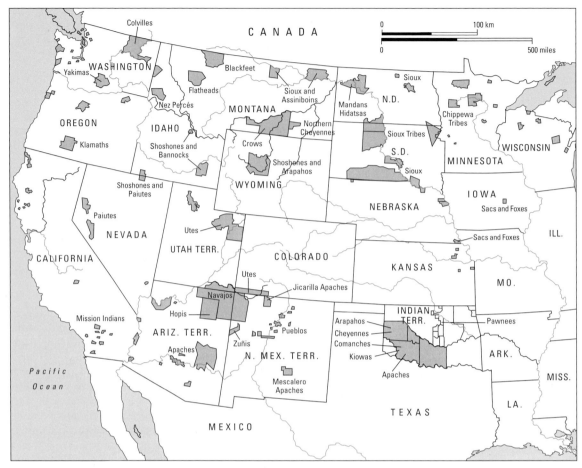

Western Indian reservations,
1890

Collier also ensured that Native Americans benefited from New Deal agencies such as the Civilian Conservation Corps (CCC) and the Public Works Administration (PWA).

Even with these changes under the New Deal, most Native Americans lived in abject poverty. It was not until 1944 that they began to organise a campaign to gain greater equality. In that year, the National Congress of American Indians (NCAI) was founded. It was the first organisation to include all Indian tribes. During the Eisenhower Administration (1953–61), the NCAI helped prevent the President ending Indian rights on reservations. Like the NAACP, the NCAI used the courts to protect Native-American rights.

In 1972, a landmark Supreme Court decision was made in 'Passamquaddy versus Morton'. The Passamaquaddy Indians of Maine received substantial damages from the US government for having broken the treaty of 1790 between the tribe and the US government. In 1980, the Sioux nation received $107 million for land taken away from them illegally in South Dakota in the late 19th century. In 1988, the tiny Puyallup tribe of Washington state was given $162 million in compensation for land taken away by the city of Tacoma in the 1850s.

Since that time, Native-Americans have used their position as 'independent nations' within the United States to introduce gambling from which they have benefited financially. However, decisions on gambling have not been welcomed by all Native Americans. The issue led to a major split within the Mohawk nation in upstate New York in the late 1980s.

Like the African-American civil rights movement, the Native-American rights movement produced its radical wing. In 1968, the American Indian Movement (AIM) was founded in Minneapolis, Minnesota. One of the founders, Dennis Banks, explained why it was created:

> 'We started because of the slum housing conditions, the highest unemployment rate in the whole of this country; police brutality against our elders, women and children.'

AIM activists made headline news in 1969, when 14 members occupied the derelict Alcatraz jail in San Francisco Bay. In 1972, AIM militants occupied the Wounded Knee battle site in South Dakota. At the same time, the actor Marlon Brando refused to accept in person his Oscar for Best Actor in the film 'The Godfather'. Instead he sent an Indian princess to Hollywood to pick up the award.

Militant action seemed to work when the federal government passed the 1974 Indian Self-Determination Act. This granted tribes control over federal aid programmes on reservations, as well as control of their schools.

1. How far have Native-American civil rights changed between 1865 and 1992?

2. Why do you think it has taken so long for Native Americans to gain full civil rights?

10.9 How far have the civil rights of Hispanic and Oriental Americans improved, 1865–1992?

Cesar Chavez (1927–1993)
Leading trade union organiser for Mexican-American migrant farm workers. Born in Arizona. Chavez was able to force producers to agree to trade union contracts after nationwide grape and lettuce boycotts in 1960s and 1970s.

For much of the period from 1865 to the end of the Second World War, Hispanic Americans formed a minority of the populations of California, Arizona, New Mexico and Texas. They were divided from mainstream American society by their language, Spanish, and their religion, Catholicism. The vast majority of Hispanic Americans worked as agricultural labourers. During the Depression, the Hispanic workers in California formed the CUCOM (Confederation of Unions of Mexican Workers and Farm Labourers) to fight for better conditions. Strikes occurred across southern California and in the Salinas valley of central California. Again in the 1960s and 1970s, Cesar Chavez led the Hispanic farm workers in a series of strikes in order to improve their working conditions.

From 1945, increasing numbers of Hispanic Americans arrived in northern cities from Mexico, Puerto Rico and Central America. Like African Americans, they were forced to lived in ghettos and to work in low-paid jobs. In New York City, Spanish Harlem began to rival African-American Harlem.

The Leonard Bernstein musical 'West Side Story', first performed in the 1950s, used Hispanic-American gang warfare in New York City as a modern interpretation of the Shakespeare play 'Romeo and Juliet'.

As European immigration has declined in the USA, Hispanic immigration has increased greatly. Driven by economic hardship, Hispanic Americans have entered the USA both legally and, increasingly, illegally.

The rapid increase in Hispanic immigration has created tension, particularly in the states that border Mexico. In 1970, the Hispanic population stood at nine million. By 1990, it had risen to 20 million but it is hard to calculate the number of illegal immigrants. Spanish has become the second language of the USA. It is predicted that by the middle of the 21st century Spanish speakers may well outnumber English speakers in many states. In 1990, almost 20% of Mexican Americans and 30% of Puerto Rican Americans lived below the poverty line.

Oriental Americans were also economic migrants to the USA. Initially,

Resident population distribution for the USA by race and Hispanic origin

	1990 Number	%	1980 Number	%	Change (+)
Total population	248,709,873	100.0	226,545,805	100.0	9.8
White	199,686,070	80.3	188,371,622	83.1	6.0
Black	29,986,060	12.1	26,495,020	11.7	13.2
American Indian, Eskimo or Aleut	1,959,234	0.8	1,420,400	0.6	37.9
Asian or Pacific Islander	7,273,662	2.9	3,500,439	1.5	107.8
Other race	9.804,847	3.9	6,758,319	3.0	45.1
Hispanic origin	22,354,059	9.0	14,608,673	6.4	53.0

1. Describe the changes in ethnic make-up of the USA between 1980 and 1990.

2. Does the data above suggest that ethnic problems have got worse between 1980 and 1990? Explain your answer.

1. In what ways has Hispanic immigration to the USA changed between 1865 and 1992?

2. How have Hispanic and Oriental Americans been discriminated against between 1865 and 1992?

they were centred on the Pacific coast but eventually most large cities had a 'China town'. San Francisco possessed the largest China town outside Asia. It also has its own distinctive 'Japan town'.

Chinese labourers formed the backbone of the workforce on the western part of the transcontinental railroad in the 1860s. However, by 1882, opposition to Oriental immigration had grown so much that Congress passed the Chinese Exclusion Act.

The greatest violation of civil rights faced by Oriental Americans came in the Second World War when the entire Japanese-American population, numbering 400,000, was forced into concentration camps for the duration of the war. It took until the Presidency of George Bush Senior (1989–93) for the federal government to make a public apology for the treatment which Japanese Americans received in the War.

Since the 1960s, Oriental immigration has included Koreans and Vietnamese. In the Rodney King riots of 1992, African-American rioters attacked stores owned by Korean Americans, as well as attacking the police.

Both Hispanic and Oriental Americans have benefited from federal government affirmative action programmes since the 1960s. In politics, Oriental-American Congressmen have been elected from California and Hawaii, where Oriental Americans form the majority of the population.

Source-based questions: The civil rights movement in the 1960s

SOURCE A

We affirm the ideal of non-violence as the foundation of our purpose and the manner of our action. Non-violence seeks a social order of justice permeated by love. Integration of human endeavour represents the crucial first step towards such a society.

Through non-violence, courage displaces fear; love transforms hate. Acceptance dissipates prejudice; hope ends despair. Peace dominates war; faith reconciles doubt. Justice for all overthrows injustice.

Love is the centre of non-violence. Love is the force by which God binds man to himself and man to man.

By appealing to conscience and standing on the moral nature of human existence, non-violence nurtures the atmosphere in which reconciliation and justice become actual possibilities.

The Student Non-violent Coordinating Committee (SNCC) Statement of Purpose, 15 April 1960

SOURCE B

Let us continue our triumph and march to the realisation of the American dream. Let us march on segregated housing, until every ghetto of economic depression dissolves and Negroes and whites live side by side in decent housing.

Let us march on segregated schools until every vestige of segregated and inferior education becomes a thing of the past and Negroes and whites study side by side in the socially healing context of the classroom.

Let us march on poverty until no starved man walks the streets of our cities.

Let us march on ballot boxes, until we send to our city councils, state legislatures and the United States Congressmen who will not fear to do justice, love mercy and walk humbly with their God.

For all of us today the battle is in our hands. The road ahead is not altogether a smooth one. There are no broad highways to lead us easily and inevitably to quick solutions. We must keep going.

'Our God is Marching On' – a speech made by Dr Martin Luther King Jr on the steps of the Alabama State Capitol in Montgomery at the conclusion of the Selma to Montgomery Civil Rights March, 25 March 1965.

SOURCE C

White America will not face the problem of color, the reality of it. The well-intended say: 'We're all human, everybody is really decent, we must forget color.' But color cannot be 'forgotten'. White America will not acknowledge that the ways in which this country sees itself are contradicted by being black. Whereas most of the people who settled in this country came here for freedom, blacks were brought here to be slaves.

Our vision is not merely a society in which all black men have enough to buy the good things in life. When we urge that black money go into black pockets, we mean the communal pocket. We want to see money go back to the community and used to benefit it. We want to see black ghetto residents demand that an exploiting storekeeper sell to them, at minimal cost. The society we seek to build among black people is not a capitalist one. It is a society in which the spirit of community and human love prevail.

'What We Want' – an essay by Stokely Carmichael, elected Chairman of SNCC in May 1966, writing in September 1966.

---

1. Use Source B.

How do the language and style of Martin Luther King's speech suggest he supports an integrated tolerant society?

2. Use Sources A and B.

In what ways do these two sources put forward similar aims?

3. Use Source A and information from this chapter.

How useful is this source to a historian writing about the methods used by the civil rights movement in the 1960s?

4. Use Sources A and C.

How have the aims of SNCC changed between its formation in 1960 and 1966?

5. Use all the sources and information from this chapter.

'The use of non-violent protest had only limited success in improving the position of African Americans in US society during the 1960s.'

Assess the validity of this statement.

US domestic history, 1945–1969

Key Issues

- How far was this period one of social and political change?

- How strong was the US economy in this period?

- How far did the power and role of federal government increase in this period?

11.1 What problems did Truman face in his first administration of 1945–1949?

11.2 How far did Truman build on the New Deal in social policy?

11.3 What impact did McCarthyism have on the USA?

11.4 How far did Eisenhower continue the policies of his Democratic predecessors?

11.5 How far were the 1950s an 'Age of Affluence'?

11.6 Why did Kennedy achieve so little in domestic reform?

11.7 Why did Johnson embark on the Great Society?

11.8 Historical interpretation: How successful was the Great Society?

Framework of Events

1945	Truman becomes president
	GI Bill
1946	Price Control Act
1947	Taft–Hartley Act
	House Un-American Activities Committee hearings start
1948	Truman defeats Dewey in presidential election
1949	Truman proposes Fair Deal
1950	McCarthy's speech at Wheeling claiming there were 57 Communists in the State Department
1951	Twenty-Second Amendment to the Constitution
1952	Eisenhower elected first Republican president since Hoover
1954	McCarthy is censured by the Senate
1958	National Defence Education Act – first federal money for education
1961	Kennedy takes office
1963	Kennedy talks about a 'war on poverty', but is assassinated before putting it into action
1964	Johnson wins landslide election and launches the Great Society
	Economic Opportunity Act
1965	Elementary and Secondary Education Act
	Medical Care Act
1966	Demonstration Cities and Metropolitan Development Act
	Clean Water Restoration Act
1967	Air Quality Act
1968	Wild and Scenic Rivers Act

Overview

By the end of the Second World War, in 1945, the United States had been through tremendous change. The Depression had seen millions of Americans lose their jobs, their savings and their homes. The economy had almost collapsed. Franklin Roosevelt (FDR) and his New Deal policies had seen federal government take on a new role in running the economy to try and bring the country out of the slump. They made fundamental changes to the welfare structure to ensure that no crisis like it could happen again. The coming of war in Europe brought jobs to American people, and its own entry into the war in 1941 finally ended the Great Depression. Federal power, particularly the power of the President, had been further extended by the needs of the Second World War. Once peace returned, two questions arose:

- Would the American economy return to depression?
- Would federal government return to the *laissez-faire* attitudes of the 1920s?

Laissez-faire **attitudes**: The belief that federal government should interfere as little as possible in the economy, but leave business to get on with it.

Although the Second World War had brought the United States out of the Depression, once the War was over the Depression did not return. Far from returning to Depression, the USA experienced massive economic growth and the majority of Americans saw living standards rise steadily through the 1950s and the 1960s. New technologies were a major factor in this growth but, unlike the 1920s, federal government also worked hard to build economic wealth. The business of American government was business. Both Democrats and Republicans now routinely used tax and spending policies to control economic growth.

However, this growth in government power worried many. Congress felt that its power had declined relative to that of the Executive. President Truman was to have many battles as Congress tried to reassert its authority. There was even the Twenty-Second Amendment to the Constitution, added in 1951, to ensure that no future president could have the amount of power which FDR was believed to have had. But there could be no return to the 1920s. In spite of constraints, Truman attempted to build on and develop the New Deal. Even when the Republicans returned to power in 1953, Eisenhower accepted many of the social changes the Democrats had made. Later on, in the 1960s, both Kennedy and particularly Johnson would extend and develop the idea that federal government should protect and care for those in need.

While the majority of Americans saw their living standards rise, there were also millions who did not. It was estimated that a quarter of Americans lived in poverty. Although there was no direct crisis such as in the 1930s, Kennedy declared a 'war on poverty' as part of his New Frontier programmes. He began a programme of measures concerning welfare, health and education, but conflict with Congress and his untimely death meant he was able to achieve little. His successor, Lyndon Johnson, was a man who had served under FDR and was determined to go further than Roosevelt had done in ending poverty in America. The Great Society was the biggest programme of social legislation in US history. Its success is disputed, but it was unquestionably an attempt to use the power of federal government to achieve improvements in the lives of millions of Americans.

Politically, the Democrats continued to hold power for most of the decade, with a Republican administration for eight years – 1953–1961. Their hold on both houses of Congress was just as strong. However, there were conflicts between the various branches of government and within the parties themselves, especially in the Democrats, which limited the achievements of the Presidents. The 'conservative coalition' of Southern Democrats and Republicans was to prove a particular problem.

The biggest political crisis of the era – apart from civil rights (see Chapter 10) – was the anti-Communist hysteria that became known as McCarthyism.

The quarter century that followed the Second World War saw the United States experience economic growth and political conflict. It also saw the growth of federal government and a real attempt to deal with poverty and injustice.

11.1 What problems did Truman face in his first administration of 1945–1949?

Truman's Administration: leading domestic posts

Secretary of the Treasury:	Henry Morgenthau Jr (1945) Frederick Vinson (1945–46) John W. Snyder (1946–53)
Attorney General:	Francis B. Biddle (1945) Thomas C. Clark (1945–49) J. Howard McGrath (1949–52)
Secretary of the Interior:	Harold L. Ickes (1945–46) Julius A. Krug (1946–49) Oscar L. Chapman (1950–53)
Secretary of Agriculture:	Claude R. Wickard (1945) Clinton P Anderson (1945–48) Charles F. Brannan (1948–53)
Secretary of Commerce:	Henry A. Wallace (1945–46) William Averell Harriman (1946–48) Charles Sawyer (1948–53)
Secretary of Labor:	Frances Perkins (1945) Lewis B. Schwellenbach (1945–48)

In April 1945, the strains of fighting the Great Depression and the Second World War finally took their toll and Franklin D. Roosevelt, America's longest-serving President, died. His Vice-President, Harry S. Truman, succeeded him.

Truman's job was not going to be easy. Although he had experience in Congress and as Vice-President, he had not been prepared for the office of President. When he unexpectedly found himself in the Oval Office (US President's official work place) he said that he felt as though the moon, stars and planets had fallen in on him. Not only did he have to follow the greatest president the 20th century had produced, but the **political machine** of Kansas City, in the state of Missouri, was known for its corruption. Many felt that they were going to get another Harding. Others, who knew him from Congress, liked and respected him.

Being from a poor background, and having worked with Roosevelt, Truman wanted to build on the New Deal to take social reform into new areas, particularly healthcare. He also knew that the American public was weary of change. After the upheavals of the Depression and of the Second

Political machine: The various party committees, groups and individuals that control elections in a certain area. Often associated with corruption.

World War, the public craved stability, in domestic politics at least. In fact, under Truman, there was conflict between the White House and Congress, conflict in industry and conflict over communism. It was to be a far from tranquil Administration.

Why did Truman have problems with Congress?

Although the Republicans controlled Congress from 1946 to 1948, for much of his time in office Truman had a Democratic Congress, yet they were by no means a united party. There were 'New Deal liberals' who wanted Truman to continue the work of his predecessor. They blamed him when things went wrong, conveniently forgetting the problems FDR had with Congress in 1938. There were the Southern Democrats, frequently referred to as 'Dixiecrats', who disliked Truman's stand on civil rights, and who had more in common with the Republicans over issues such as union rights. They frequently voted with the Republicans in Congress. This meant that, although Truman had a Democratic Congress for much of his Administrations, he did not have an easy job getting legislation through. For example, one of his first actions was to put forward a 21-point programme calling on Congress to pass a series of social reforms. They were almost all rejected. Not only was Congress concerned about the potential cost of the proposals, they also resented the way Truman was demanding so much so soon. FDR had been granted 'broad executive power' in a time of crisis: Truman was going to have to work much harder for his policies to be passed.

The mid-term elections of 1946 only made the situation worse as, for the first time since 1930, the Republicans had a majority in Congress. They held 246–188 seats in the House of Representatives and 51–45 in the Senate. The Republican Party had not been in control of Congress since Herbert Hoover was in the White House and they were determined to make the most of their opportunity.

The economic problems caused by the War, particularly inflation and the increasing number of labour disputes, had encouraged people to turn against the Administration. The Republican slogan of 'Had enough?' captured the mood of many disillusioned voters and the Democrats did badly everywhere outside the South. This was largely a protest vote, rather than a real turning away from the Democrats. It can be illustrated by the fact that both Houses returned to Democratic control in 1948. However, in the meantime, Congress did much to block several of Truman's measures.

One measure which the Republican Congress did manage to get through was the Twenty-Second Amendment to the Constitution, which limited a president to two terms. The fact that this was passed by Congress and ratified by the states shows that there was real concern over how much the power of the President had increased under FDR in the 1930s and 1940s. The determination of Congress to re-assert its power to pass or reject legislation made life hard for the Truman Administration and made relations between the two very difficult. In seven years, the President vetoed 250 bills passed by Congress and they, in turn, **overrode** 12 of those vetoes. It was one of the worst records of conflict over legislation in American history.

Overrode: If the President vetoes a bill, Congress can still pass it into law if two-thirds of the members of each house agree. This is called overriding.

How serious were the economic problems facing Truman?

At the end of the War, Truman was afraid that the USA would slide back into depression. His polices were aimed at preventing that and at encouraging real growth.

Firstly, he wanted a slow de-mobilisation of the military, because he was afraid of the effect on the economy of 12 million men suddenly flooding the job market. He also felt that given the developing Cold War it was important for the USA to keep a credible armed force. Clearly, this would be unpopular with the families who wanted their men home as quickly as possible. As the mid-term elections were approaching, the soldiers and their families used political influence to get home. There was a campaign of sending postcards to the White House with the slogan 'No boats, no votes!' The threat worked. The army was reduced from 12 million, in 1945, to 3 million within a year, and was halved again over the next year. Although there was a lot of short-term unemployment, the feared recession did not return. Unemployment never rose much above 4% during the Truman presidency.

Businessmen and the public also wanted a quick return to normality. So plants were returned to peacetime production and government-controlled factories were privatised. With all these men returning home, there would be a demand on goods and it would take time for the factories to produce enough. The economic effect, therefore, was 25% inflation in 1945–46, made worse by Congress's $6 billion tax cut. Truman's fear had been realised, and this high level of inflation was one of the reasons the Democrats lost support in the 1946 mid-terms.

To deal with this and to try and stabilise prices, the President wanted to continue the Office of Price Administration (OPA) which had controlled prices during the War. However, the **conservative coalition** in Congress wanted to abolish the OPA and return to letting business have more say over its own affairs.

Conservative coalition: The voting or working together of conservative Democrats and Republicans in Congress.

Truman proposed a price control bill, in 1946, to extend the life of the OPA. However, when the Bill reached Congress it was amended and watered down so much that the OPA would have been powerless, and so Truman vetoed the amendments. His supporters in Congress warned him that the Bill was the best he could get, and he was eventually forced to accept it. Congress had, effectively, ignored his veto and had made Truman accept an Act in which he had no faith. Although some prices, such as rents, rose dramatically, by the end of 1946 the economy was stabilising and the OPA was no longer needed.

In 1946, Congress did accept Truman's proposal for a Council of Economic Advisors (CEA). The CEA's job was to watch the economy and recommend government action, if necessary. Congress also passed an Employment Act, which gave a commitment to maximum employment and productivity. It required the President to give an annual report to Congress on the state of the economy, with recommendations. However, the Employment Act did not go as far as Truman wanted. He had hoped for a bill demanding 'full' employment, but it showed that America now accepted more government involvement in the economy and that it would not go back to the *laissez faire* of the 1920s. It was the job of the government to exercise a guiding hand, at the least, to the economy of the country.

With 12 million soldiers returning home, there would be a need for housing and for jobs to prevent a recession such as that which followed the First World War. Truman hoped to provide housing through the Federal Housing Agency, which provided government-backed mortgages at good rates of interest. However, he was unable to get money from Congress for more public housing, and construction companies were keener to build commercial properties than homes. Nevertheless, the construction boom that followed the Second World War did provide many jobs for the returning men.

GI: Stands for 'government issue'; a GI is an American serviceman who wears government issue clothes and carries government issue weapons.

Of more help was the 'GI Bill', passed by Congress as compensation for those who had served their country. Ex-servicemen were allowed 52 weeks' unemployment relief if needed; loans were given for education, farms, housing and business. Between 1945 and 1955, $20 billion was given out to help 7.8 million veterans.

By the end of the 1940s, the economy began to pick up. In 1947, half the world's manufacturing output was from the USA. By the mid-1950s, America would be experiencing massive economic growth. As industry got back into peacetime production it was able to meet demand, and demand was high. The GI Bill and wages from the War meant that the returning soldiers had a lot of money to pump into the economy. A baby boom created a massive market for domestic products. Even the outbreak of the Korean War in 1950 was also an impetus to growth, as was new technology. So although the first few years of Truman's Administration were not economically successful, the last couple of years were and the growth would continue into the following two decades.

What problems did the Truman Administration face with organised labour?

By the 1940s, trade unions were much stronger than they had been in the 1920s and 1930s. The Wagner Act of 1935 had encouraged union growth, and the need for labour during the War increased the power of the unions dramatically. By 1945, 15 million workers belonged to trade unions – approximately 36% of the non-agricultural work force.

There were two major labour organisations in the USA in the 1940s – the American Federation of Labor (AFL) and the Congress of Industrial Organisations (CIO).

The AFL was formed in 1886. It represented unions of mainly skilled workers and craftsmen. It did little for women or the less skilled workers of the factories, so in 1935 the leader of the United Mine Workers, John L. Lewis, broke away to form the CIO. Lewis did a great deal to encourage union membership among industrial workers.

In 1955, the two organisations merged into the AFL–CIO to fight for workers' rights, education, beneficial legislation etc.

The high inflation after the War meant that the trade unions began demanding wage rises. In 1946, there were strikes in most major industries. A government-organised conference, in November 1945, did little to bring management and unions together. The President mediated the strikes, but at the cost of 19% price rises and 18–19% wage rises, which all worsened the inflation problem.

For Truman this was a political problem – for when workers got pay rises management put up prices to pay for them, which only encouraged further inflation. Truman knew that the unions were vital to Democratic Party finances. He also knew that there was widespread public hostility to union demands and, within the party, the Southern Democrats were also hostile. The President was caught in the middle.

In April 1946, a coal strike began involving 400,000 miners and looked like spreading to other areas. The railwaymen then came out. Such a widespread strike in these areas would have severely damaged American industry. So, to prevent it, Truman asked Congress for emergency powers to use troops in the dispute and even to draft strikers into the army. Congress sensibly refused. Truman had overreacted and risked a major crisis in industry, far worse than the one he was trying to resolve.

Although Congress held Truman back in this instance, the Republicans and conservative Democrats were increasingly anti-union, and they took measures to reduce union power. In 1947, the Republican Congress passed the Taft–Hartley Act.

The Taft–Hartley Act of 1947

● Listed various 'unfair' labour practices

● Outlawed the **closed shop**

● Required union officers to sign non-communist oaths

● Allowed bosses to sue unions under certain conditions

● Authorised the President to demand an 80-day 'cooling-off' period before strikes.

Closed shop: The right of a union to prevent non-union members being hired by the company. It protects the union members from being outnumbered by non-union workers and therefore losing their power to protect their members.

Needless to say, the unions were furious and wanted the Act repealed. What the unions wanted were federal guarantees for the closed shop and free collective bargaining (i.e. the right to represent their members and their interests). Truman vetoed the Act, but Congress again overrode the veto. Truman felt the Taft–Hartley Act was vindictive, even though he had had his own quarrels with the unions. However, under the American Constitution, Congress passes the laws even if the government does not want them.

Executive Privilege: The right of the President to take action in an emergency.

Truman's problems did not end there, even though the power of the union was reduced. In April 1952, a strike was threatened in the steel industry where the workers demanded an increase in wages because of increased production caused by the Korean War. Because he did not want to appear weak and he was concerned about a strike in wartime, Truman seized control of the mills under Executive Order, claiming **Executive Privilege**. Although they did not want the strike, the steel companies did not want the government taking control of their factories either, so they challenged the President's authority to do this in the Supreme Court. The Court agreed with the mill owners. Truman had to hand the mills back. A seven-week strike followed, resulting in shortages and higher steel prices. Yet again, when Truman tried to act tough, he had ended up backing down and looking weak.

1. Why did Truman have poor relations with Congress in his first administration?

2. How successfully did Truman handle labour issues in his first administration?

11.2 How far did Truman build on the New Deal in social policy?

Why did Truman win the 1948 presidential election?

Truman had had many problems with the Republican-controlled Eightieth Congress, particularly over labour issues and the economy. There had also been conflict over the race issue and over social reform. The Democratic Party itself continued to be split, especially over race, and it was not enthusiastic about re-nominating Truman, the 'accidental president'. Therefore, when the elections came everyone, including the Democrats, expected the Republicans to win. Yet Truman surprised everyone and gained a victory with 49.5% of the vote.

The Democratic Party went into the election badly divided. So much so that there were, in effect, three Democratic candidates: Henry Wallace from Iowa ran as a progressive candidate and J. Strom Thurmond ran as a states' rights candidate. Wallace was a New Dealer disappointed by the lack of social reform from Truman. He was a well-respected man with wide political

The 1948 Presidential Election results

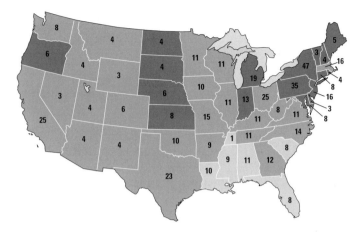

		Electoral vote	Popular vote	Percentage of popular vote
Democratic Harry S. Truman		303	24,105,812	49.5%
Republican Thomas E. Dewey		189	21,970,065	45.1%
States' Rights Strom Thurmond		39	1,169,063	2.4%
Minor parties		–	–	1,442,667	3.0%

Study the map.

Explain why Truman was able to win the election even though he won a minority of states.

Thomas E. Dewey (1902–1971)
Lawyer and US attorney who gained prominence prosecuting gangsters, successfully convicting 72 of them. He was Governor of New York for three terms between 1943–55. Chosen as presidential candidate by the Republican Party in 1944 and 1948. He was a well-liked and competent man. Failing to win the White House, he continued as Governor of New York and then returned to practising law. He was offered a Supreme Court job by Nixon, but turned it down due to his age.

experience as Secretary for Agriculture under FDR, and Vice-President before Truman (1940–44). It was feared that he could take sufficient liberal votes away from Truman to give the election to the Republicans. In the end, Wallace took less than 2.5% of the vote. Thurmond, Governor of South Carolina, led the Southern Democrats who disagreed with Truman's positive civil rights stand in the election. Like Wallace, he polled less than 2.5% of the vote but, as his votes were concentrated in the South, he managed to win four states, and tied with Truman in Tennessee. In fact, having these two candidates worked in Truman's favour, as he was able to present himself as the moderate in between Wallace on the left and Thurmond on the right.

So why, in spite of a divided and unenthusiastic Party, did Truman win? Firstly, organised labour and 'blue collar' working-class Americans supported him, in spite of the problems of 1946, because they did not want the Republicans to win. Unions had been a strong foundation of Democratic support for over 20 years and they were not now going to turn to the Party that had given them Taft–Hartley.

Likewise, black support for the Democrats remained strong. If anything, Truman's stand on civil rights tied African Americans more closely to the Democrats than the New Deal had. The votes of northern blacks more than made up for the losses to Thurmond and, on the whole, the South remained fairly solidly Democrat.

Truman's standing up to Russia in the Cold War was also popular. Throughout the election, he stressed the anti-Communist theme and the need to continue his policy of containment. Events in Berlin and Czechoslovakia added to the President's warnings and enhanced his reputation for handling foreign policy (see Chapter 8).

Elections are not only won, they are also lost. There is no doubt that Truman's victory was in part due to the poor showing by the Republicans. The Republican candidate was Thomas E. Dewey, a moderate but rather dull candidate. Dewey criticised the government for inaction and called for unity, but the Republican Party could offer little in the way of real policies. Like the Democrats, they too were divided. Many Republicans

Clark Clifford (1906–1998)
Lawyer. Served in navy during the Second World War. Special advisor to Truman, he helped formulate the Truman Doctrine and helped Truman win the 1948 election. Clifford worked for Kennedy as advisor during JFK's time in the Senate and the White House, and he was Johnson's Secretary of Defense 1968–69. He was also an advisor to Democratic president Jimmy Carter.

would have preferred Senator Robert Taft of Ohio as their candidate, but he was considered too conservative. Taft was an isolationist in foreign policy which, at the height of the Cold War, was not a popular position. There were also divisions in the Party as to how far, or even whether, they should try to reverse the New Deal. These divisions meant that they could offer little to the electorate that was positive and that they had no real strategy for victory. Truman, on the other hand, travelled 22,000 miles around the country putting across his message. That message was largely designed by his special advisor Clark Clifford.

Clifford encouraged Truman to appeal to the various groups who might support the Democrats, particularly ethnic groups. Blacks and Jews were singled out as large minorities who could win the election for them. Truman's insistence on action on civil rights forming part of the Democratic platform was undoubtedly influenced by Clifford, as was the Administration's decision to recognise the newly established state of Israel. (Though, in both cases, Truman was also taking decisions he believed to be right.) The strategy was extremely successful and both groups contributed significantly to Truman's victory.

Truman also emphasised that he was on the side of the 'people' against the 'special interests', such as the corporations. Being a Missouri farm boy he found the role of the 'little man' taking on the 'big guys' an easy one to play. But, as with civil rights and Israel, Truman was also taking policy stands in which he believed. He called for action on housing, healthcare, education and the minimum wage. Truman accused the Republican Congress of blocking progress, calling it the 'do nothing Congress'. It was especially successful as the Republican election programme contained many measures which Truman had wanted but which Congress had refused to pass. He challenged them to a special session in July 1948, saying that if they were serious about social reform they would get their chance to pass the measures. The bluff worked and the Republican promises of social reform from then on seemed hollow.

In addition to winning against all predictions, the Democrats also regained control of Congress, 54–42 and 263–171. Truman believed that this gave him a mandate for the social reform he had attempted in 1945.

How successful was the Fair Deal?

When Truman had presented his 21-point programme to Congress after the War, it was clear that he wanted to build on the New Deal, protecting the vulnerable in society. In his State of the Union address to Congress in January 1949, he said that:

> 'the foundations of a healthy economy cannot be secure so long as a large section of our working people receive substandard wages' and he asked for 'comprehensive housing legislation … [and] a national health programme to provide adequate medical care for all Americans'.

To pay for all this, he asked for a $4 billion tax increase. Both the Democratic and Republican Congresses rejected his proposals. Now he was no longer just the man who succeeded FDR, but had been elected in his own right, he returned to what became known as the Fair Deal. In his State of the Union address, he also called for:

Social security: A system by which the government pays money regularly to people who have no other income or only a very small income.

● an increase in the minimum wage

● repeal of the Taft–Hartley Act

● the expansion of **social security**

- the setting up of public works schemes

- and a healthcare programme.

All of this was to be paid for out of taxation.

In some areas, Truman was successful. Social security was extended to one million more Americans and the minimum wage went up from 40¢ to 75¢ an hour. Farmers benefited from measures for soil conservation, flood control and rural electrification. To deal with the housing shortage, the National Housing Act 1949 provided for the building of 810,000 subsidised, low-income homes over six years, though only about half the proposed number were, in fact, built. It also included measures for slum clearance and urban renewal. Congress also set up the National Science Foundation in order to encourage research and development in science which, although motivated by Cold War considerations, was a boost to education. But many of Truman's proposals were still rejected; notably, measures for federal healthcare and education – two crucial areas which FDR and the New Deal had not touched.

Truman proposed a national health insurance system based on a tax of 4% on the first $6,300 of a person's income. The proposal was attacked in Congress not only as a tax-raising measure, but also because it was felt that it was not the job of the federal government to tell people how to arrange their own healthcare. The American Medical Association, which represented doctors, attacked the proposal as 'socialised medicine'. It saw any attempt by government to interfere in this area as little short of communism. A Hospital Construction Act was passed, but it benefited the building industry more than medicine. It was to be almost 20 years before a federal healthcare programme would be passed.

Likewise, little was done in education in spite of increasing evidence of the poor state of American schools. Education was seen as a state issue, not a federal one. Democratic Congressmen knew that any attempt to interfere would run into problems, especially in southern states, because of the issue of segregation. Like healthcare, it would be the Johnson Administration that would eventually provide federal support for education.

Although Truman's relations with Congress had improved, they still blocked his measures. Conservative Democrats and Republicans worked against him on many major issues and he was no Roosevelt who could inspire Congress to agree with his wishes. Truman had a background in congressional politics but he had little tact when dealing with Congress, which was increasingly concerned with issues like Communist subversion and, from 1950, the war in Korea. To get support on these issues, he had to give up the Fair Deal.

Given these problems, Truman's Fair Deal had little chance of being enacted. For many, the New Deal had done enough and they did not want to take federal government into these areas of policy. Truman was trying to push further than either Congress or the public was prepared to go. There were some 'New Deal liberals' who saw FDR's policies as only a beginning. They had faith in the power of federal government to effect real change in people's lives and in society. But this was being replaced by a new 'Cold War liberalism' which, although it supported federal government's role, also felt that Roosevelt had tackled the most serious problems. The key now was to consolidate what they had, rather than go further. It was this mood that held the American public. So, although Truman achieved much in strengthening measures like social security, he was unable to take the Fair Deal further.

Why did the Democrats lose the 1952 election?

When the 1952 election came, the economy was picking up and Truman had had a few successes with the Fair Deal. But in election year there were crises, which damaged the chances for the Democrats. The steel strike, the war in Korea (see Chapter 9) and the difficulties with McCarthy all pointed to a poor election showing. To add to Truman's problems, hearings began in 1951 into corruption in the Reconstruction Finance Corporation and the Internal Revenue Service. Stories of bribes and 'gifts' came out involving friends of the President. These hearings were televised and did much damage to Truman's Administration.

Given these circumstances, the Democratic Party did not want Truman to stand again and was relieved when he announced his retirement. It chose the intellectual Adlai Stevenson as their candidate to take on Eisenhower. However, he was no match for the popular war hero and, for the first time since 1932, there was a Republican in the White House.

It is easy to see only the negative side of the Truman Administration. There can be no question that, domestically at least, he was not one of the more successful presidents of the post-war era. He was in constant conflict with Congress, whether it was controlled by the Republicans or by his own party. On at least two occasions he collided head-on with the unions, who were natural supporters of the Democratic Party. His Administration ended amid charges of corruption. Above all, he contributed to the rise of the anti-Communist hysteria of the period which was so damaging to the United States. Yet Truman did preside over the relatively calm transition from war to peace and, in spite of Congress, handled the economy successfully. Though he came nowhere near to achieving all he wanted, he was able to extend the social provisions of the New Deal to millions more Americans. Truman's presidency was not a shining success domestically, but neither was it one of abject failure. Like Truman himself, it could be said to have been moderately successful.

1. Why did Truman win the 1948 election?

2. How successful was Truman in domestic affairs in the years 1945 to 1953?

11.3 What impact did McCarthyism have on the USA?

Subversion: The destruction or overthrow of a government.

According to historians such as William Chafe, there is a traditional intolerance in America which surfaces periodically, such as in the early 1920s (see *The Unfinished Journey*, published in 1991). Chafe sees the rise in anti-communism of the late 1940s and early 1950s as an example of this 'seasonal allergy'. Some historians, however, view the episode as a reaction by conservatives to the New Deal and all it stood for. Others stress a fear of enemies all around which grew up as a result of the Second World War and the Cold War, coming together with a fear of internal **subversion**. Some historians see it more in psychological terms, as America coming to terms with a period of massive and frightening change and looking for someone or something to blame for their fears. Whatever the reason, the anti-Communist hysteria of the Truman and Eisenhower administrations witnessed a massive attack on the civil liberties of American people and it is looked upon as a black period in American history. What started it and what was going on?

How did the development of the Cold War affect the domestic history of the USA?

Although the United States and the Soviet Union had been allies in the Second World War, by the late 1940s there was a growing fear of Communism and its expansion. A raid, in 1945, on the offices of 'Amerasia', a Communist magazine, revealed several documents from the US State

Department and one from an official in the US navy. Shortly afterwards, the Canadian government uncovered a spy network operating in America, which was sending information to the Russians. Americans knew that communism preaches the overthrow of other political systems. Given that the Russians had established Soviet governments in most of Eastern Europe, a real fear grew that there was a danger of Communist subversion inside the USA. In 1945, the Communist Party of the United States had only around 80,000 members, in a country of 140 million, but it did take money and directions from Moscow.

The passing of the National Security Act in 1947 (see Chapter 8) further increased fears of Communism and of the USSR. The Act set up a Department of Defence by joining together the Departments of the Navy, Army and Air Force. It created the National Security Council to advise the president on security issues. That the Administration felt the need for such action created a fear that there really were weaknesses in American security. To get the Act through Congress, Truman had played on this fear, making it more real.

Truman received a letter from the Director of the Federal Bureau of Investigation (FBI), J. Edgar Hoover, saying there was a real problem with Communist conspiracies in America and that the government had to act. In March 1947, Truman issued Executive Order 9835, which established Federal Loyalty Boards.

The Order allowed for the removal of federal employees if 'reasonable grounds exist for belief that the person involved is disloyal to the government of the United States'. Although the Order did contain safeguards, these did not seem particularly effective. Individuals could be 'considered' a threat if they were members of any group which the Attorney General named as subversive. People's beliefs could get them fired as much as any actual activity and the principle of innocent until proven guilty seemed to have been abandoned. Estimates vary, but between 1947 and 1951 up to 3,000 employees were forced to resign and 300 were fired. No evidence of actual subversion was ever uncovered.

The 'Amerasia' case had clearly worried the government, and the President had no reason not to believe the head of the FBI when he warned him of danger. But Truman had set the tone for the next five years, in which accusations of Communist sympathy would do as much damage to a person as being found guilty of any actual activity.

States and cities followed the government's lead and employees had to take loyalty oaths or lose their jobs. In Massachusetts, a person could be imprisoned for even allowing a Communist to use their premises for a meeting. Other states passed their own anti-subversion laws. There were 39 by 1952.

The development of the Cold War, in the period after the Second World War, further increased the growing fear of communism within America. The tension was heightened by a series of events that served to demonstrate the increasing might of the Soviets (see Chapter 8):

- explosion of the first atom bomb by the Soviets in 1949

- fall of China to communism in the same year

- start of the Korean War in 1950

- race between the USA and the Soviet Union to develop the hydrogen bomb.

John Edgar Hoover (1895–1972)

Director of FBI from 1924 until his death. He trained as a lawyer and worked for Attorney General A. Mitchell Palmer during the 'Red Scare' of 1920. Hoover is credited with developing the FBI into an efficient and effective criminal investigation organisation in the 1920s and 1930s. A fanatical anti-Communist, he used the powers of his office to spy on Martin Luther King Jr and President Kennedy, among others. He is accused of using the information the FBI had to maintain himself in power.

How important were the House Un-American Activities Committee hearings in the development of McCarthyism?

The House Un-American Activities Committee (HUAC) had been set up in 1938, when there was a very tense situation in Europe. The job of the Committee was to monitor activities of extremist groups of both left and right, which might present a danger to the United States. Even from its early days, it was used more against Communists than against Nazis. To deal with the new supposed threat, the Committee was revived and began to hold hearings to investigate those suspected of subversive activities. These began in 1947.

Witnesses were called before the Committee and asked questions about their beliefs and actions. The question frequently asked was: 'Are you now or have you ever been a member of the Communist Party?' If someone was shown to have Communist connections, even in the past, they could be in trouble. They would also be expected to 'name names' (i.e. give the Committee the names of other Communists).

One of the most famous attacks – and the one that brought HUAC's activities much more to the notice of the general public – was the investigation of Hollywood between 1947 and 1951. According to Hoover, the Communists had been targeting Hollywood since 1935. In 1947, he wrote that 'Communist activity in Hollywood is effective and is furthered by Communists and sympathisers using the prestige of prominent persons to serve, often unwittingly, the Communist cause. The Party is content and highly pleased if it is possible to have inserted a line, a scene, a sequence conveying the Communist lesson.'

When the hearings began, those who refused to answer the Committee's questions were **cited for contempt**. The playwright Arthur Miller was interrogated by the Committee about meetings of Communist writers which he attended nine years before. When he refused to name other people present, he was cited for contempt, fined $500 and given a suspended prison sentence. This experience prompted Miller to write *The Crucible*, a play about the witch-hunts in Salem, Massachusetts, in 1692. In all, 12 actors and writers were sent to prison. For others, their careers were finished and they were **blacklisted** by Hollywood, even when they had not been convicted of any offence. Merely being called before the Committee could finish a career. Of course, some people named names; for example, a young actor called Ronald Reagan.

People called before the Committee believed that their rights would be protected by the Constitution. The First Amendment guarantees the right

Cited for contempt: Found guilty of not respecting the court and its authority. This usually carries a jail sentence.

Blacklisted: Put on a government list, which contains the names of people or organisations who they think cannot be trusted or who have done something wrong.

J. Parnell Thomas, Chairman of HUAC (right), administers witness oath to Robert Taylor (left), Hollywood film star. Taylor testified that a number of his fellow actors were communists and were a 'disrupting' influence in the motion picture industry.

How useful is this 1947 photograph to a historian writing about the impact of the HUAC hearing?

to free speech and free assembly but, in 1948, in the case of 'Dennis versus the United States', the Supreme Court held that First Amendment rights could be cut off by Congress if national security was at stake. In other words, people could be sent to prison for things they said. Some pleaded the Fifth Amendment, which says that no one has to implicate himself or herself in a crime (i.e. the right to silence), but the Committee usually treated 'taking the Fifth' as an admission of guilt. With the support of the three branches of government, HUAC was eating away at the constitutional rights of American citizens. The hearings seemed also to confirm that there were spies operating in the United States.

Alger Hiss was a worker at the State Department. He had been a New Dealer, had been with FDR at Yalta (see page 250) and had been an aide to Secretary of State Dean Acheson. He was suspected of treason when another witness named him as having belonged to a subversive organisation in the 1930s. He was convicted of perjury (lying to a court) and sentenced to five years in prison, in January 1950. The following month, the British arrested Klaus Fuchs for spying. He confessed and named others who worked at the Los Alamos project, where the atomic bomb had been developed; including a man called David Greenglass. He, in turn, named his sister and brother-in-law, Ethel and Julius Rosenberg, who were arrested and convicted of spying and passing secrets to the Russians. Throughout the trial they protested their innocence but, in spite of the fact that they never admitted the crime, and in spite of having young children, the couple were sentenced to death and were executed in 1953.

It now seems from the decoding work done by the Venona Project that both Hiss and the Rosenbergs were working for the Soviets, though many at the time and since have been convinced of their innocence. These high-profile cases convinced Congress that more needed to be done to protect America from the Communist threat.

In 1950, Congress passed the McCarren Internal Security Act. All Communist organisations had to register with the Attorney General; no Communist could be employed in a defence plant. A further Act, in 1952, strengthened its terms so that Communists could be denied passports, foreigners suspected of subversion could be deported and, in a national emergency, the authorities could detain anyone they classed as subversive. Truman felt that the Act was going too far and vetoed it but, when it returned to Congress, only 58 people in either House supported him. The fear and determination to take action was now widespread. Yet Truman must take his share of the blame. He had begun government sanctions against Communists and had played up the threat in order to get support for both the Truman Doctrine and the Marshall Plan (see Chapter 8). Both the Republicans and Democrats had emphasised their commitment to root out and remove Communist spies in order to help their election prospects. They had stirred up a process which was moved on by others, notably Joe McCarthy.

Why did Joseph McCarthy have such an impact?

Senator Joseph McCarthy was looking for an issue with which to make his name, and the anti-Communist crusade that America seemed to have embarked on suited his purposes. He did not start the 'Second Red Scare'. It may be that he really did have information about spies in government which the Venona Project has confirmed existed, but McCarthy was also a liar, a drunk and a bully who took the anti-Communist hysteria to new levels. He ruined people's lives, damaged the reputation of his country and gave a new word to the English language – **McCarthyism**.

The impact of McCarthy was enormous. The Republicans could make

Joseph Raymond McCarthy (1908–1957)
As a young man he served in the Second World War, before changing his politics to Republicanism and entering the Senate in 1946. In February 1950, McCarthy caused a sensation by claiming to hold a list of 205 Communist Party members working in the US State Department. (This number was reduced to 57, over a number of speeches.) McCarthy continued a public witch-hunting campaign against members of the Truman Administration. When it was shown that he and his aides had been falsifying evidence, President Eisenhower renounced him. However, by this time, many people in public life and the arts had been blacklisted as suspected Communists or Communist sympathisers. McCarthy died of liver disease brought on by excessive intake of alcohol.

McCarthyism: Fear of internal subversion, aggravated by genuine fears from the Cold War. This created a 'Red Scare' far larger in scale and far more damaging to society than that of the early 1920s.

the Democrats look bad with accusations of treason, so they encouraged his charges. They had been out of power for 20 years and had now found an issue on which to attack the Democrats. In response, the Democrats had to show that they were just as tough on Communism and subversion by denouncing it just as forcefully. By playing party politics with the issue, both parties gave credibility to McCarthy and must take their share of the blame for his activities.

McCarthy also found support among the public. America was not doing as well in the Cold War as Americans felt they should, especially in Korea, so there had to be an explanation: enemies in government gave them a reason. Certain groups, such as the Catholic Church, gave McCarthy their support not only because he was a Catholic, but also because Communism is atheistic. They supported McCarthy's 'religious' crusade to root it out.

McCarthy found support among ethnic groups, too. Poles, for example, had no love for the Russians, many of them having come to America to escape Russian oppression. McCarthy was a skilled politician and manipulator of the media, but he had a willing audience for his message.

He also had his critics. In 1950, the Tydings Committee looked into his accusations and called them 'a fraud and a hoax'. Studies have shown that for all McCarthy's skill in gaining and maintaining press attention, the majority of the press was critical of him. Yet the HUAC investigations continued and McCarthy's net spread wider. People were afraid to confront him in case they found themselves accused and brought before the Committee.

When the 1952 election brought Eisenhower to the White House, many hoped that he would stop what had now become known as the 'witch hunts'. But Eisenhower refused 'to get down in the gutter with that guy', believing that, if he ignored McCarthy, he would fade away. The new President seemed to be a little afraid of McCarthy: in 1953, he dropped a paragraph from a speech he was about to make in which he would have defended McCarthy's latest target, George Marshall. Eisenhower had let down a personal friend, an action he later regretted bitterly. Ike was worried what an out-and-out attack might do to the Republicans in Congress, many of whom supported the Senator. He did not want to divide his Party. In a sense he was right to leave McCarthy alone because, as his accusations grew wider and more extravagant, he began to be taken less seriously.

George Catlett Marshall (1880–1959)

Soldier and diplomat. Served in the Philippines and in Europe during the First World War. As Chief of Staff in the Second World War, he organised the expansion, training and equipping of the army and air force to enable America to fight the Nazis and the Japanese. In 1947, he became Secretary of State under Truman and was responsible for the Marshall Plan to help European recovery. In 1950, he became Secretary of Defense. He was awarded the Nobel Peace Prize in 1953.

What does this extract tell us about McCarthy's views?

'… this is not a period of peace. This is the time of the "cold war". This is the time when all the world is split into two vast, increasingly hostile camps …

The reason why we find ourselves in a position of impotency is not because our only powerful potential enemy has sent men to invade our shores, but rather because of the traitorous actions of those who have been treated so well by this nation. It has not been the less fortunate or members of minority groups who have been selling this nation out, but rather those who have had all the benefits that the wealthiest nation on earth has had to offer – the finest homes, the finest college education, and the finest jobs in Government we can give.

This is glaringly true in the State Department. There the bright young men who are born with silver spoons in their mouths are the ones who have been the worst … In my opinion the State Department, which is one of the most important government departments, is thoroughly infested with Communists.'

Why did McCarthyism decline by the mid-1950s?

By the mid-1950s the Red Scare was over and McCarthy was finished. He had become an embarrassment at home and abroad. His friends, Roy Cohn and David Schine, toured US embassies in Europe searching out 'leftist' books, which held the United States up to both fear and ridicule even among its allies. Now they were in the White House, the Republicans had no further use for him.

McCarthy was essentially responsible for his own downfall. He attacked the widely respected institutions, such as the Supreme Court and the army, which was too much for many Americans. When he began to accuse decorated soldiers, in 1954, Congress had had enough and went on the attack. The televised hearings showed the public what a bully McCarthy was.

When the Senate finally censured McCarthy, by a vote of 67–22, he was finished. It had taken them four years to pluck up the courage to do so and, even then, it was primarily the Democrats who voted against him.

Although McCarthy was finished by 1954, the HUAC hearings continued for several years and loyalty oaths remained in place in the states for a long time. In the same year as its censure, Congress also passed the Communist Control Act, which banned any Communist from holding any office in any labour organisation. It also banned 'Communist infiltrated' organisations from the National Labor Relations Board (NLRB).

What impact did McCarthyism have on the USA?

The damage done to ordinary people by the anti-Communist hysteria was massive. Hundreds lost their jobs due to the blacklists or for having been called before the Committee; for example, 300 teachers lost their jobs in New York City alone. Firms could be blacklisted as well as people, damaging their ability to conduct business. Between 1950 and 1952, 117 people were cited for contempt of Congress and jailed – more than in the whole of the previous century.

A person did not need to be a Communist to suffer. Anyone who was radical could be accused, a problem which continued in the USA long after the hearings ended. Traditionally left-wing organisations like unions dropped demands for social change and concentrated on being mere pressure groups. Politicians who called for a radical agenda were accused of being 'red'.

It could be argued that within government itself the damage was worse. The State Department which – according to historian Hugh Brogan – contained some of the most talented men in US history at the time, lost hundreds. The loss of these men meant that policies were followed that were not necessarily the best for America. For example, the 'Asia desk' lost most of the people knowledgeable about the area, which was to have devastating consequences for American policy towards Vietnam. The government simply had no one who really knew the country.

Even outside the United States, the effects of McCarthyism were felt. European youth became very anti-American, as their actions seemed to confirm a lot of what the USSR had said about America and Americans.

1. *In what ways did the development of the Cold War affect America internally between 1945 and 1953?*

2. *Why was Joseph McCarthy so successful in his anti-Communist campaign between 1947 and the mid-1950s?*

11.4 How far did Eisenhower continue the policies of his Democratic predecessors?

Politicians of both parties admired 'Ike' Eisenhower. In fact, Truman had once offered to help him achieve the presidency, and both parties considered him as a candidate. He chose to go with the Republicans as they more suited his own views, but the fact that he was considered by both gives some indication of the moderate nature of his political views.

During his Administration, 'Ike' was a very popular president. He was well liked by the voters. Part of this popularity was due to his success as a general during the War. This gave him the advantage of fame and meant he was not linked to any particular political faction. On the other hand, it also meant he had unrealistic expectations about what politicians can achieve. Many of the plans and promises he made turned out to be unrealistic once he was in office.

Eisenhower, personally, also had far more interest in foreign affairs than domestic, so he often gave more attention to external issues. He did have major domestic issues to deal with as well, notably:

● Joseph McCarthy

● the growing importance of the civil rights issue

● the economy

● whether to continue Truman's social reforms.

Why did Eisenhower win the 1952 Presidential election?

In 1952, Truman decided not to stand again (he was exempt from the provisions of the Twenty-Second Amendment limiting a president to two terms). The Democratic candidate was Adlai Stevenson, a bright but rather shy man. Few believed he would win against Eisenhower, the genial and popular war hero. Eisenhower's popularity was a major part of the Republican victory, but there were many reasons why the Republicans retook the White House after 20 years.

The choice of Richard Nixon as Republican vice-presidential candidate was astute. He was an experienced politician, where 'Ike' had little experience. So the combination gave the impression of stability. Nixon had made a name for himself in the anti-Communist crusade, so voters felt the Republicans would deal effectively with the Communist threat at home and abroad. In fact, Truman's foreign policy had many major successes but, when the election came, the USA was bogged down in war in Korea which seemed to be going nowhere and achieving nothing. 'Ike' promised to end the Korean War, if necessary by going there himself. His background as a soldier gave people confidence in his ability to handle the Cold War threats. The Republicans cleverly played on these weak areas for the Democrats and on the financial scandals that blew up, with the slogan 'K1C2', signifying Korea, Communism and Corruption.

One aspect of the election which was pointing towards the future was the use of television. The Republicans broadcast several effective advertisements focusing on Eisenhower's honesty and integrity, to contrast with the scandals in which the Democrats were embroiled. In 1960, television was to play a crucial role in the presidential election and its importance would continue to grow alarmingly.

One reason for Republican victory may have been that people were ready for a change. Eisenhower received 33.9 million votes (55%), taking 39 states, including five in the South. Stevenson polled 27.3 million votes, but this gave him a mere nine states. On the back of Eisenhower's popularity,

How useful to historians are buttons such as this?

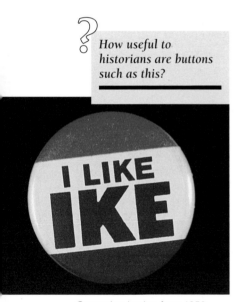

Campaign badge from 1952. Campaign badges or buttons are a popular feature of American elections.

the Republicans also retook Congress with narrow majorities of 48–47 in the Senate and 221–213 in the House of Representatives.

How successful was Eisenhower in dealing with Congress?

Capitol Hill: The US Congress, the Senate and the House of Representatives all meet in the Capitol Building on Capitol Hill, Washington DC. The expression 'Capitol Hill' is often used as a nickname for Congress.

Republican control of Congress did not last long and the Republicans did badly in the 1954 mid-terms, mainly because of the recession which had been caused by Eisenhower's cut in defence spending (see below). However, 'Ike' got on reasonably well with the Democrats on **Capitol Hill**, particularly as he interfered little in legislation, certainly far less than Truman had. But faced with a Democratic Congress – 48–47 in the Senate and 232–203 in the House – he was convinced that the Republicans needed to broaden their base of support and be careful not to be seen as extreme.

In some ways, the 1956 presidential election was a re-run of 1952, and with a similar result: Eisenhower took 35.6 million votes and Stevenson took 26 million. 'Ike' was still very popular and, though he had not achieved a great deal, there had been good relations with Congress, which the public liked. The country was stable and prospering, and many black people voted Republican because of what 'Ike' was doing for civil rights.

In foreign policy, the President also seemed to be successful. He had improved relations with the USSR, while the Democrats seemed confused over whether to applaud or criticise him for this. When two crises broke out, in Hungary and Suez, during the election campaign it worked in Eisenhower's favour, encouraging the desire for the President who had made peace in Korea.

In spite of Eisenhower's victory, Congress remained Democratic (49–47 in the Senate and 234–201 in the House of Representatives). This might indicate how much of Eisenhower's victory was due to his personal popularity.

In the final mid-terms of the Eisenhower years, there were large Republican losses in both houses: 64–34 and 282–154. These were mainly due to the second 'Eisenhower recession', as well as his failure to achieve a meaningful Civil Rights Act. The new Congress contained a lot of young, liberal Democrats and relations between them and 'Ike' were not as good as before. This new generation wanted more action as they went into the new decade – the 1960s.

Throughout his years in office, although Eisenhower did not get everything he wanted, he did get much of his legislative programme passed: 73 of the 83 bills he sent to Congress. This contrasted sharply with the difficulties Truman had had with Congress. While Truman had problems even with his own Party, 'Ike' was able to work equally well with a Republican or a Democratic Congress.

What was 'Eisenhower Republicanism'?

Fiscal conservative: Belief in low taxation and low federal spending, and balancing the budget.

One of the reasons 'Ike' got on so well with people of differing political views was that he was a moderate. He did not hark back to the days of Coolidge and Hoover, but asserted a new brand of Republicanism. He referred to his political beliefs as 'dynamic conservatism' or 'the middle way'. By this, Eisenhower meant that he was a **fiscal conservative** who promised to balance the budget and to lower taxes. He also said that he would end the 'creeping socialism' of the Democratic administrations. Like many Republicans, 'Ike' wanted to reduce the role of federal government. Yet, he did accept that the world had changed. He knew he could not, and did not want to, undo all that the Democrats had done in the previous decades. Eisenhower accepted that business needed to be regulated and that some level of welfare was now a feature of the American system. In his own words, Eisenhower was 'conservative when it comes to money and liberal when it comes to human beings'.

When he appointed his Cabinet, Eisenhower's support for big business was clear. Three members of the Cabinet had been executives at General Motors, and several had been Wall Street lawyers. The Democrats joked that the Cabinet was eight millionaires and a plumber (union leader Martin Durkin was Secretary of Labor, but lasted only a year.)

Eisenhower appointed, to federal commissions and other offices, people who thought the way he did about reducing the role of government; for example, Ezra Benson, the Agriculture Secretary, wanted to cut farm subsidies. However, their aims of reducing federal spending were not as easy to put into practice as they hoped.

Eisenhower's domestic administration (1953–1961): leading posts

Secretary of the Treasury:	George M. Humphrey (1953–57)
	Robert B. Anderson (1957–61)
Attorney General:	Herbert Brownell Jr (1953–57)
	William P. Rogers (1957–61)
Secretary of the Interior:	Douglas J. McKay (1953–56)
	Frederick A. Seaton (1956–61)
Secretary of Agriculture:	Ezra Taft Benson (1953–61)
Secretary of Commerce:	Sinclair Weeks (1953–58)
	Lewis Strauss (1958–59)
	Frederick H. Mueller (1959–60)
Secretary of Labor:	Martin P. Durkin (1953)
	James P. Mitchell (1953–61)
Secretary of Health, Education and Welfare:	Oveta Culp Hobby (1953–55)
	Marion B. Folsom (1955–58)
	Arthur S. Fleming (1958–61)

How successful was Eisenhower in economic affairs?

Gross domestic product (GDP): This is a measure of a country's wealth.

Eisenhower was fortunate in being president when the economy was doing extremely well. **Gross domestic product (GDP)** grew from $355 billion in 1950 to $488 billion in 1960, while rising wages and falling hours meant that the average worker had a real income twice that of a worker in the 1920s. Per capita income rose from $1,720 in 1940 to $2,699 in 1960. Why was there such growth?

Spending had risen after the Second World War (e.g. the spending on the GI Bill and savings amassed during the War). By the 1950s, the cumulative effect was being felt in economic growth. Businesses, as well as individuals, had been spending after the War, and investment in plant and equipment had risen to $10 billion a year. The public sector, too, experienced growth (e.g. spending on the military was almost $40 billion a year). Technology advanced, with new goods such as televisions having the kind of impact that the radio had had 30 years before. The continued growth of car ownership and the availability of credit helped to fuel a consumer boom even bigger than that of the 'roaring twenties'.

However, there were massive inequalities in the country, with as much as 22% of the population living below the poverty line. Even those who bought the new consumer goods often went into debt to do so. The very real problem of poverty in America was not tackled until the 1960s.

The economic policies of the Eisenhower Administrations show both his fiscal conservatism and the fact that he had accepted some of the changes the Democrats had brought. As a Republican, 'Ike' wanted to reduce the role of federal government, which the Republicans felt had grown far too much in the previous 20 years. This would, in turn, cut federal spending and allow him to reduce taxes, which were indeed cut by $7 billion.

The Reconstruction Finance Corporation – which was started by the Republican President Herbert Hoover but which had played such an important role in the New Deal – was finally abolished. There was also a desire to abolish that other renowned New Deal agency the Tennessee Valley Authority (TVA), but the TVA was widely supported in the South so abolishing it would be unpopular. However, federal subsidies to the TVA were slashed from $185 million, in 1952, to $12 million in 1960. 'Ike' felt that the production of power was a function of private business and not the role of government. So, as well as reducing aid to the TVA, he sold off atomic power plants to private industry and vetoed a plan for hydro-electric power production in Hell's Canyon.

A more important measure was the Submerged Lands Act 1953. Until this Act, the sale of rights to drill for offshore oil along the US coast, especially in the Mexican Gulf, were controlled federally. This meant that the whole country benefited from the sales. Eisenhower's Administration gave the rights to offshore oil deposits to the states, which meant that the money would only benefit that area. Truman had twice vetoed bills like this. But support for business and a desire to reduce federal power saw it passed now.

Although the Office of Price Administration had effectively finished by the end of 1946, the Korean War had seen inflation rise and more controls introduced. Now the war was over, they were not needed so any remaining price controls were abolished. Yet Eisenhower also vetoed a bill to abolish the Council of Economic Advisors set up by Truman, accepting that the USA had changed and that federal government now had an economic responsibility which it had never had under Hoover.

Eisenhower hoped that this reduction in federal interference in the economy would allow him to cut federal spending. In fact, over the period 1953–61 federal spending rose by 11%. Much of this was spent on arms and the space programme, but spending in some areas could not be cut as easily as the government hoped. Continuing agricultural overproduction meant that subsidies rose from $1 billion, in 1951, to $5.1 billion by 1960. American farmers simply produced too much (e.g. a beef cow cost $179 in 1952 and $90 in 1956), so if prices were allowed to fall to their true market value then millions of farmers would go out of business. The Administration had no choice but to continue the subsidies. The Soil Bank was set up, in 1956, to get farmers to cut production. It paid $750 million to farmers to put land into the 'bank', in other words not to farm it, and $450 million was spent on conservation measures. Farmers, however, tended to put the worst land into the bank, which meant that production barely fell. The Republicans might not like the fact that government was subsidising agriculture, but the 1920s and 1930s had shown that there really was no alternative.

Why did the 'Eisenhower Recessions' take place in 1953 and 1957–1958?

As a Republican, Eisenhower wanted to reduce spending. The ceasefire in Korea and the New Look policy (see Chapter 8) allowed cuts in military spending in 1953, but this put 3.7 million people out of work. In fact, the recession ended quite quickly and 'Ike' did not have to resort to New Deal-style measures. However, it did damage the Republicans in the 1954 mid-term elections.

There was a second recession in 1957–58 with five million unemployed and production falling by 14%, again largely due to cuts in government spending. Unemployment remained high until the election. In fact, there were more people in work in 1960 than in 1952, but the second recession in a decade helped John F. Kennedy to power. It damaged the reputation of the Republican government for managing the economy. Even though 'Ike' had promised to balance the budget, while he was in office there had been a total $20 billion deficit. Eisenhower had wanted to reduce spending but there were not that many areas where money could be found. Foreign policy considerations led to spending on education as well as on the space programme and, though he was a Republican, Eisenhower had social concerns. These led him to continue some of the work of the Democrats and even, in some cases, extend it.

How successful was Eisenhower's social policy?

With regard to social policy, 'Ike' did not go so far as the Democrats. He had criticised the 'creeping socialism' of their policies, yet he accepted that the federal government did have a responsibility to the poor and weak in society. This is shown in the creation of a government Department of Health, Education and Welfare – a Cabinet-level post.

As well as increasing the minimum wage from 75¢ to $1 an hour, 'Ike' helped the poor by extending social security to cover 10.5 million more Americans. There was also $1 billion for low-cost housing. All of these measures built on the work of Roosevelt and Truman. Republicans now largely accepted the responsibility of the federal government towards the poor. As 'Ike' said, 'The banishing of destitution and cushioning the shock of personal disaster on the individual are proper concerns of all levels of government.' In spite of this, Eisenhower was no New Dealer. He also said that 'If all Americans want is security, then they can go to prison.'

Republican transport policy also seemed fairly liberal entailing, as it did, massive government spending. The Republicans cooperated with the Canadians to build the Great Lakes–St Lawrence seaway, and the 1956 Highways Act built 41,000 miles of interstate highways with federal government putting up 90% of the money to the states' 10% at a cost of $30 billion. Although both of these measures were to increase trade and business, their aim was not to create jobs. Even so, the Highways Act was a massive boost to the economy providing thousands of jobs not only in construction but also in related areas such as motels, garages, diners etc.

Providing healthcare had been an aim of the Truman Administration but, while 'Ike' opposed most of the Fair Deal, he did pass measures for health. The Kerr–Mills Bill gave matching federal money to states that set up their own healthcare for the elderly poor. In fact, this was not very effective, as most states did not take up the challenge. More successful was a $30 million polio vaccination programme. Although it was a year before there were sufficient vaccines to meet demand, it was an important step in eradicating the disease.

An important measure passed by the government was the National Defence Education Act (NDEA) 1958, which gave $887 million for science and language teaching, as well as student loans for science-related courses. A similar measure had first gone to Congress in 1955, but had failed to pass because it was opposed by Catholics who wanted

Parochial schools: In this case, religious schools.

help for **parochial schools** and by civil rights activists who tried to add a de-segregation amendment.

What got this Act passed was the launch of 'Sputnik' by the Russians on 4 October 1957. The USSR successfully launching a space satellite long before them, shook the Americans' faith in their technological superiority and panicked them into taking action. The NDEA was as much, if not more, about foreign policy than about education, as was the creation of the National Aeronautics and Space Administration (NASA) the same year.

The 'middle way', 'constructive conservatism', 'Eisenhower Republicanism' – whatever one chooses to call it – was clearly different from the Republicanism of the inter-war years. The New Deal and the Second World War had changed America far too fundamentally for it to go back. Eisenhower knew and accepted this. He was an extremely popular President who seemed able to pursue his aims of a basically conservative economic policy while, at the same time, accepting and even extending the social welfare programmes developed by the Democrats. This steering of the 'middle way' initially led historians to see the Eisenhower presidency as somewhat dull and lacking leadership. Later, historians realised that, in fact, 'Ike' had made much progress. He was simply subtler and less confrontational than his predecessor or successors. As the historian Paul Boyer puts it, in *Promises to Keep* (1999):

> 'rarely in our history has a president better fit the national mood than Dwight David Eisenhower. By 1953, Americans had endured a quarter-century of upheaval – first a stock-market crash and crippling depression, and then a world war and a menacing Cold War. Americans craved peace and stability. This is what Eisenhower delivered.'

? 1. What was 'Eisenhower Republicanism'?

2. Was Eisenhower a successful president in domestic affairs? Explain your answer.

11.5 How far were the 1950s an 'Age of Affluence'?

The term 'The Affluent Society' was coined by economist J.K. Galbraith as the title for a book about the 1950s. It has since come to be used to describe the decade almost as frequently as 'roaring' has been used to describe the 1920s. Were the 1950s really an age of affluence? Some did not think so. Journalist William Shannon said that the decade was 'one of flabbiness and self-satisfaction and gross materialism … The loudest sound in the land has been the oink and grunt of private hoggishness … It has been the age of the slob.' But American GNP grew from $318 billion, in 1950, to $488 billion by 1960 and average incomes were twice those of the 1920s. The decade was not one of continuous growth and wealth. There were recessions in 1953 and 1957–58, unemployment reached 7.6% and the national debt rose to $290 million by 1960. Yet, for the majority of Americans, the 1950s were a prosperous decade.

As in the 1920s, higher wages brought material comforts. By 1960, 60% of Americans owned their own homes, 75% owned cars and 87% owned at least one television. The spread of the use of electricity allowed more people to have washing machines, dishwashers, freezers, stereos etc. There were more homes for them to put their goods in. Between 1945 and 1950, five million houses were built. This created demand for furnishings, decorating materials and repairs. People's lives at home became more comfortable.

At work, too, lives got easier. Wages rose and hours fell; meaning that **real wages** rose 10% over the decade. Labour-saving machinery and automation were also introduced in factories. There was a shift in jobs from the production line to the office. Over the 1950s, the number of industrial workers fell from 39% to 36% of the work force, while the

Real wages: What can be bought with money earned, while taking into account inflation (see page 90).

number of clerical workers rose from 40% to 46%. In some industries automation brought fewer jobs but, in others, it meant easier conditions with greater productivity and higher pay. These factories turned out a whole range of new goods, from ballpoint pens to transistor radios. New types of music, notably rock and roll, and the rise of the 'teenager' created a mass market for records and record players. There was also an amazing range of goods made from the new materials, such as plastics. Many of these goods were bought on credit. The first credit card was issued in 1950, but this meant that by 1960 consumer debt was $2 billion.

Pastimes continued to grow. Sport was now televised, increasing its popularity. The massive growth in car ownership meant that people continued to travel and visit new places. With the development of the aeroplane and jet engine in the Second World War, travel took people to far more places. Communications across America became faster and easier.

One medium that began to suffer in the 1950s was the cinema. Competition from television forced the studios to come up with new innovations, such as 3-D and the production of lavish musicals, which television could not reproduce. Films such as 'The Robe' and 'Seven Brides for Seven Brothers' were great box-office successes, but the cinema began a decline which continued well into the 1980s and which only reversed when the coming of video made films widely popular again. The growth of television in the period was massive. In 1949, approximately one million households owned a television set; by 1960, it was 49 million. Between 1945 and 1955, $15 billion was spent on television sets and repairs. To millions of people it opened up the world, giving access to sports, news and entertainment. It was important in **homogenising** the United States. Television and advertising helped to sell goods; they also encouraged a culture of **materialism**. More money was spent in America on advertising than on education and more money was spent on television sets than on school buildings.

Although the spread of car ownership created thousands of jobs in production and related industries, it also brought a rise in accidents and deaths and an increase in pollution. It also encouraged the flight to the suburbs. People could live outside the cities and drive in for work. This meant that the cities were left to those who could not afford to move out, so less was spent on them, thus creating ghettos.

Homogenising: Creating a shared set of experiences and values.

Materialism: Valuing goods and possessions more highly than personal virtues such as honesty. Being more concerned with what you have than what you are.

A family in the United States watching the television at home in 1955.

Is this picture useful in telling us about family life in the 1950s?

A family in the United States watching the television at home in 1955.

Straight after the War, the GI Bill pumped $20 billion into the American economy. Both Truman and Eisenhower increased expenditure on social security, education, housing and airports. Spending on roads alone had pumped $2.9 billion into the economy by 1960.

Half of all federal spending was on defence. The launch of 'Sputnik', in 1957, led President Eisenhower to introduce the NDEA and to set up NASA. The arms and space programmes put money into the economy and created thousands of jobs, particularly in the South-West. In Texas, Nevada and California, new industries such as computing brought work and people to the areas. They were based around defence plants and became known as the 'sun belt' industries. The space programme also brought new products on to the market, such as Teflon, transistors, electronics and home computers. Along with the jobs, this military spending created a large section of the economy with an interest in maintaining the Cold War. In his final speech before leaving the White House, Eisenhower warned about this development of what he called the 'military industrial complex'.

Oligopoly: Control of an industry by a small group (e.g. the car industry being dominated by the three corporations of Ford, General Motors and Chrysler).

As in the 1920s, the 1950s saw the spread of **oligopoly**. In cars, steel, aluminium, oil, aircraft, chemicals and electrical goods, a few companies controlled the bulk of the industry. In the 1950s, companies who made different things combined into conglomerates or multi-nationals (i.e. they bought up companies all over the world making a variety of goods). This created many new job opportunities, but it also cut down competition and choice. It made some of these corporations very powerful.

The decline in farming continued with more people moving to the towns and cities. Now only 15% of the population lived and worked on the land. As in industry, it was small farms that went out of business with more and more of agriculture becoming 'big business' subsidised by the government.

In what ways did living standards rise in the 1950s?

How far was federal spending responsible for the economic growth of the 1950s?

Disneyland opened in 1955, symbolising much of the affluence of the 1950s. Disney was a corporation that made films, but had now moved into tourism. The theme park at Anaheim was easy to reach by car, and afforded by families with more money and more spare time in which to spend it. The family could marvel at the technology of the rides and spend their money on plastic souvenirs.

Although the majority of Americans did very well out of the 1950s, this was not the case for everyone. Poverty in America was to be a problem tackled by Eisenhower's successors.

11.6 Why did Kennedy achieve so little in domestic reform?

John F. Kennedy's presidency, personality and private life are still the subject of much debate, but did he actually achieve very much?

John Fitzgerald Kennedy (1917–1963)
35th President of the USA (1961–63), the first Roman Catholic and the youngest person to be elected US President.
He came from a very wealthy Boston Catholic family. His father Joseph had been ambassador to Britain just before the Second World War and

'Jack', as family and friends called him, had an upbringing steeped in politics. Educated at Harvard and briefly at the London School of Economics. After serving in the US Navy during the War, he entered Congress in 1946. In 1952, at only 34 years of age, he became one of the youngest Senators ever. In 1953, he

married Jacqueline Lee Bouvier (1929–1995).
'JFK' made his name as a supporter of civil rights' legislation and as a prominent internationalist. During his presidency, Kennedy did not succeed in carrying through any major domestic legislation. However, he did create the Peace Corps (volunteers who give health,

agricultural and educational aid overseas).
It was in foreign affairs that his presidency was most notable.
On 22 November 1963, during a tour of Texas, JFK was shot while driving through Dallas. He died shortly afterwards. His death caused worldwide grief.

Deliberately echoing the New Deal, Kennedy talked about how his Administration would bring a 'new frontier'. Kennedy spoke of how the 'torch [had] been passed to a new generation of Americans' and he emphasised how the New Frontier would 'get America moving' again. In foreign policy, it meant taking a strong stand against the Russians and Cubans in the Cold War and, in domestic affairs, it meant reform. Kennedy wanted to do something about civil rights, about poverty, about education, about health and about the economy. To do this, he wanted to harness the enthusiasm of the American people, especially the young. As he so eloquently put it in his inauguration speech, 'ask not what your country can do for you, ask what you can do for your country'.

Why did Kennedy win the 1960 Presidential election?

Robert Francis Kennedy (1925–1968)
Brother of President John F. Kennedy. Lawyer. Served in US Navy during Second World War, then worked on his brother's Senate campaign. He also worked for HUAC. Robert helped to organise JFK's 1960 presidential election campaign, where he earned a reputation for ruthlessness. Appointed Attorney General in 1961, where he fought to convict corrupt union boss Jimmy Hoffa and defended civil rights. Elected Senator in 1964, he spoke out against Vietnam. Robert was assassinated while campaigning for Democratic nomination in 1968, which many believe he would have won.

As a result of the elections, Democratic control of Congress remained strong with 64–36 seats in the Senate and 263–174 in the House of Representatives. However, the 1960 presidential election was one of the closest in American history, with JFK winning 49.9% of the vote to Richard Nixon's 49.6%. Kennedy's youth and energy were popular with younger voters, especially when contrasted with Nixon, the Republican candidate. Richard Nixon had been Eisenhower's Vice-President and, though the two men were not that far apart in age (Nixon was just four years older than Kennedy), they seemed to be of different generations. This was emphasised in the televised debates of September 1960. Nixon came across particularly badly because he was tired, recovering from a knee operation and suffering from flu. Kennedy, on the other hand, was well prepared and fresh having flown in on his private jet. He gave the image of youth and vitality. The four debates attracted an audience of 61–70 million and such debates have since become a feature of American elections.

Kennedy's campaign criticised the Republicans for 'drift' in foreign and domestic policy. The recession seemed to support this charge with regard to the economy. The U-2 incident during the run-up to the election (see Chapter 9) did not help the Republicans either when they were caught out lying. JFK accused them of not standing up to the Communists. He talked of a 'missile gap' that the Republicans had allowed to develop. (Which was not, in fact, the case.) Kennedy also made an issue of civil rights. Although Congress had passed two Civil Rights Acts, it was weak. JFK scored a victory when his brother Robert helped to get Martin Luther King Jr out of jail. The black vote which this gained was crucial to Kennedy's victory.

However, many liberal Democrats were not confident in Kennedy. His voting record in Congress was not especially good and he had friends on the far right. Although his Catholicism worried many voters, notably in the South, the choice of the moderate, Protestant Lyndon Johnson as vice-presidential candidate helped to deliver the votes of the South. Combined with the black vote and the votes delivered by the cities, Kennedy polled enough to become the 35th and youngest US President.

Like FDR, Kennedy surrounded himself with intellectuals and bright young men (but not women). These included his brother Robert, Theodore Sorenson, and Arthur Schlesinger. The White House became known for its culture and glamour, earning the nickname 'Camelot', where people were informal and hard working. Contemporaries talked of the 'buzz', but this has been criticised as creating a sense of crisis about everything and giving the appearance of work as a substitute for real action. Kennedy made a strong inauguration speech, which helped to create a sense of change and optimism. He talked of 'the torch [passing] to a new generation of Americans' and told the people to 'ask not what your country can do for you, ask what you can do for your country.'

Consciously reflecting FDR, Kennedy's Administration was known as the New Frontier. The newspaper columnist Walter Lippman said that Kennedy was:

'a man of the centre ... far removed from the social struggles of the New Deal. Although he had a liberal image his past record and his first two years in office supported this view, disappointing many who had voted for him.'

Kennedy's Administration (1961–1963): leading domestic posts

Secretary of the Treasury:	C. Douglas Dillon
Attorney General:	Robert F. Kennedy
Secretary of the Interior:	Stewart L. Udall
Secretary of Agriculture:	Orville L. Freeman
Secretary of Commerce:	Luther H. Hodges
Secretary of Labor:	Arthur J. Goldberg until 1962, then W. Willard Wirtz
Secretary of Health, Education and Welfare:	Abraham A. Ribicoff until 1962, then Anthony J. Celebrezze

---

Why did economic growth take place during JFK's presidency?

During the presidential campaign, JFK made much of the need to 'get America moving again'. He made economic growth his domestic priority. 'Ike' had inflation running at 3.5%, while unemployment was 6.5% when he left office. To Kennedy, a strong economy was not only essential for the USA itself, but also to strengthen its position in the world. In fact, in spite of the recession, the economy was basically strong, but it had weaknesses which needed addressing.

More in common with Eisenhower than with FDR, Kennedy believed tax cuts would get the economy moving. Although the Democrats had a majority in Congress, Kennedy did not feel he could ask for a tax cut too soon. He had the same problem that Truman had with the conservative coalition, particularly the Southern Democrats. He saw little point in sending legislation to the House which he knew would fail. He felt this would make him look ineffective. It was 1963 before his $10 billion tax cut was put to Congress, but it was to be passed by Johnson.

Kennedy was very concerned about the rise in unemployment and pursued several policies to try and create jobs. The 1962 Trade Expansion Act cut tariffs to encourage trade and, although he didn't cut personal tax, he was able to reduce taxes for business under the Revenue Act, which gave $1 billion in tax credits for new equipment and investment.

Kennedy's increases in defence and space spending were done more for foreign policy reasons than to help the economy. However, the 20% increase in spending on defence and the space programme, which amounted to more than $25 billion, encouraged internal prosperity. They were a major factor in the sustained economic growth which America experienced in the 1960s. By doubling NASA's budget, Kennedy was able to fulfil his promise to put a man on the moon by the end of the decade – a promise fulfilled by Neil Armstrong in July 1969.

Kennedy also used the power of his office to encourage further growth through federal spending. States were encouraged to apply for, and spend, federal grants for housing, school building, highways etc. He was not allocating new money, but encouraging both federal and state authorities to spend what they could as soon as they could to create employment. Whether it was due to Kennedy's spending or not, unemployment did start to fall and was down to 5.3% by 1964.

In his attempts to create jobs while keeping inflation low, Kennedy found himself in conflict with one of America's largest corporations, US Steel. JFK had asked for price rises and wage increases to be in line with increased productivity. The steel industry had 3% productivity and the workers accepted a rise of 2.5%. US Steel then raised its prices, followed by other steel companies. Steel was vital to the automobile industry and to defence. Price rises for steel would have a knock-on effect and worsen inflation.

Kennedy was furious that US Steel was breaking their agreement. He threatened investigations by the FBI and the denial of government contracts. He also put pressure on other steel manufacturers not to follow the price rise. Faced with the threats from the government and the threat from being undercut by their competitors, US Steel backed down and inflation remained below 1.3%.

How successful was Kennedy's social policy?

When he became president in 1961, a great deal was expected of Kennedy because of his rhetoric and because he was a young liberal. The problem was that, in an era of such wealth and growth, many Americans lived in poverty. Kennedy did little about the poor in the first few years of his Administration. However, by 1962, he was starting to act particularly after reading Michael Harrington's *The Other America*, which said that 40 million Americans were living in poverty.

Poverty was defined as a family of four on an income of less than $3,000 per year, and there were millions more living on incomes just above the poverty line. A Senate report, in 1960, estimated that eight million old people had incomes lower than $1,000 per year. The military had also found that a third of draftees (service men and women entering the forces) were medically unfit for service, largely due to poor living conditions having caused poor health. In 1959, it was estimated that the average rural wage was less than 50¢ an hour. The poor were not confined to one area or to one racial group: the rural Deep South, the inner cities, areas of high immigrant populations, Native-American reserves – all suffered deprivation. The causes of poverty were also complex: old age, racism, unemployment and poor education all contributed. Kennedy was especially concerned by 'structural unemployment' (i.e. unemployment created not by a recession but by permanent changes in the economy such as automation). Tackling all this was a massive problem.

JFK believed that his improvements in the economy would help the poor, but he also needed to tackle the problem directly. To some extent he continued the work of Truman and Eisenhower, with increases in social security and the minimum wage. The minimum wage (now $1.25 an hour) was also extended to more professions including retail, which was a great help to women. The Manpower Development and Training Act 1962 provided $435 million for school and job-based training, especially for those who had lost their jobs due to automation. Two hundred thousand people went through the schemes. JFK also proposed a $2 billion public works programme, but Congress rejected it.

The Area Redevelopment Act 1961 gave grants and loans for training, development, community facilities as well as help for depressed areas such

Kennedy delivering his inauguration speech, 20 January 1961.

as Appalachia. The government spent more than $500 million on various schemes and programmes. The Area Redevelopment Act was criticised for not providing sufficient jobs considering the money spent and for some of the schemes it financed. For example, federal money was used to help build two luxury hotels in Oklahoma. The Administration argued that the hotels would create jobs and encourage further development and further jobs in the area.

In practical terms, JFK probably achieved little. The Housing Act, for example, helped property developers more than the poor. However, his speeches raised awareness when he talked about the need to make 'war on poverty', and how there had to be aid, training and education for the poor. His economic advisors, such as the Council of Economic Advisers (CEA), had already begun to formulate programmes that Johnson would adopt.

Although JFK was the first president since Hoover not to have a woman in the Cabinet, he did set up a presidential commission on the status of women, headed by Eleanor Roosevelt. The commission opposed an Equal Rights Amendment seeing it as a product of middle-class ambition. They argued that practical issues such as poverty, healthcare, education and childcare were much more important. In 1963, an Equal Pay Act was passed. It did not cover all women and had no powers of enforcement, but 171,000 women benefited. The Act passed through Congress without much opposition, but it shows that the Kennedy Administration was moving into new areas of policy.

In the 1960s, the environment also became an issue. Books, such as *The Silent Spring* by Rachel Carson, were having an impact. Kennedy was the first president to start to tackle environmental issues seriously with an advisory committee on pesticides and a Clean Air Act in 1963, which limited pollution from cars and factories. Again, this was an area on which Johnson built.

Two areas where Kennedy proved to be no more successful than Truman were health and education. Like Truman, JFK proposed a health-care scheme funded from a payroll tax, but the idea was rejected for the same reasons as it had been 15 years before. Kennedy's 1961 proposals for education were passed by the Senate but failed to get through the House. The bill proposed to give federal money to states for scholarships and buildings, with the most money going to the poorest states. There had been little spending on schools in 20 years and there was a shortage of teachers, but the Bill failed. It was opposed by those who objected to the cost, by those who objected to federal interference in education and by religious groups. Kennedy would not give aid to parochial schools in case he was accused of favouring the Catholic Church but, when he did not, his own church would not support the bill either. JFK was able to get the Higher Education Facilities Act passed in 1963, which gave $145 million grants for graduate schools in science, language and engineering. This passed through more because it was an extension on NDEA than because of the need for educational reform. Like poverty, Johnson would address health and education more successfully.

Why did JFK achieve so little in domestic affairs?

Firstly, Kennedy was more interested in foreign policy and domestic issues simply did not get as much attention. Secondly, the conservative coalition in Congress blocked many of his measures. They blocked measures on education, healthcare, transport as well as a proposal to set up a department of urban affairs, which would tackle the growing problems of the cities (crime, drugs, decay, housing, transport etc.). His relations with Congress might have been better if JFK had worked at it. Many resented, or at least disliked, his northern liberalism, his ambition and his easy charm – and he did nothing to change this perception.

Yet, although JFK was not a radical president, under him the USA experienced the longest period of continuous economic growth in its history, due largely to military spending and the space race. He did work hard to reduce unemployment. In social reform he was not much more successful than Truman, but who knows what he would have gone on to do had he lived. Kennedy believed that a solid victory in 1964 would give him a mandate for more reform so he would not do too much in his first term to damage his re-election prospects.

It is also important to remember Kennedy's impact in inspiring a generation. He laid much of the groundwork for Johnson's Great Society in terms of bringing social issues to the forefront, starting some policies moving, and in leaving a strong economy so that the Great Society could be paid for.

1. What were the aims of the New Frontier in domestic affairs?

2. How successful was the Kennedy Administration in dealing with these problems?

11.7 Why did Johnson embark on the Great Society?

When JFK was assassinated in 1963, Lyndon Baines Johnson (LBJ) found himself in a similar position to Truman in 1945. He not only had to take over the White House, he also had to deal with the country's shock and grief. He inherited a cabinet who, largely, did not like or trust him. He and Robert Kennedy particularly disliked each other. However, the presidency was a job he had worked for and wanted. The liberals in Congress were worried by LBJ's Southern background and voting record (e.g. supporting HUAC and Taft–Hartley), but they had forgotten his role in civil rights and the New Deal.

Lyndon Baines Johnson (1908–1973)
A Southerner, born in Texas. He trained and worked as a teacher. Entered Congress in 1937 as a Roosevelt New Dealer. He was a Congressman until 1948, when he became a Senator. He was Senate Majority Leader (1954–60) where, according to historian William Chafe (*The Unfinished Journey*, 1991), 'he dominated the Senate as no one had before'. He was crucial to 'Ike' in helping to get the 1957 Civil Rights Act through, and as President he was far more involved in the details of legislation than 'Ike' or JFK had been. In 1960, JFK chose him as his running mate because Johnson would bring the Southern Democrat vote to complement Kennedy's popularity in the North.

Consensus: Agreement, a sharing of aims and values.

Johnson felt the need to create **consensus** to help the country get over the assassination. He also believed that it was his job to create consensus in the country. LBJ was able to present the need for unity to the country and therefore use the national grief to force through some of JFK's measures. Ironically, in spite of his desire to create consensus, the Vietnam War and Johnson's pursuit of it, along with the race struggle, were to divide the country as it had not been since the Civil War.

To an extent, Johnson wanted to continue the work of the New Frontier. He supported Kennedy's aims in wanting to tackle poverty, to improve education and healthcare and to help African Americans. When Kennedy was killed, several of these measures were being blocked in Congress and Johnson was determined to see them through. But he wanted to go much further than that. Like Kennedy, Johnson also believed that the power of the federal government could be used to make life better for the American people. He spoke of creating a 'Great Society', which would do all that the New Frontier had set out to do, and more besides.

Why did Johnson win a landslide victory in the 1964 Presidential election?

Johnson won by the largest majority in American history up to that point. The Democrats got 61.1% of the vote; the Senate and House of Representatives had large Democrat majorities, 68–32 and 295–140 respectively (though they lost 47 House seats in 1966).

Why did Johnson have such a massive victory? Firstly, he had achieved a lot in 1963 and the mood was, for a while, supportive of more reform. Secondly, Vietnam had yet to become as divisive as it would over the following years. Thirdly, and most importantly, the Republican candidate Barry Goldwater was thought to be too right wing. The Republican Senator from Arizona was fairly extreme on many issues. He opposed civil rights, opposed taxation to pay for social reform, and supported the use of nuclear weapons in Vietnam. Even many Republicans found him too far right. The Democrats were able to exploit this very effectively. Goldwater's election slogan 'In your heart you know he's right' was mimicked with 'in your guts you know he's nuts.'

Johnson felt the victory gave him a mandate for further domestic reform. However, although Johnson had a large majority, there were many Southerners and white, working-class Democrats who did not like many of his policies. He would not be able to get everything he wanted.

Why did the American economy continue to expand?

Federal deficit: The amount of money the federal government owes.

Under LBJ, the economy continued to thrive. GNP increased by 7% in 1964, by 8% in 1965 and by 9% in 1966. The **federal deficit** fell by $1 billion and unemployment dropped below 5%. Why was this so? For one thing, LBJ pushed through Kennedy's tax reduction bill, cutting taxes by $10 billion. The economy was also helped by general world economic growth. As with JFK, military spending, especially on Vietnam, helped to boost employment.

The US economy had grown almost constantly since the Second World War, but Michael Harrington's estimate of 40 million Americans living in poverty was what Johnson wanted to address.

Why did LBJ launch a 'war on poverty'?

Blue-collar jobs: Manual work, as opposed to white-collar jobs in offices.

Poverty was worst in the cities. Changes in technology meant fewer **blue-collar jobs** were available and affluence meant those who could, moved to the suburbs. At the same time as this so-called 'white flight', there was

---

Johnson's Administration (1963–1969):
leading domestic posts

Secretary of the Treasury:	C. Douglas Dillon (1963–65)
	Henry H. Fowler (1965–69)
Attorney General:	Robert F. Kennedy (1963–65)
	Nicholas Katzenbach (1965–67)
	Ramsey Clark (1967–69)
Secretary of the Interior:	Stewart L. Udall
Secretary of Agriculture:	Orville L Freeman
Secretary of Commerce:	Luther H. Hodges (1963–65)
	John T. Connor (1965–67)
	Alexander B. Trowbridge (1967–68)
	Cyrus R. Smith (1968–69)
Secretary of Labor:	W. Willard Wirtz (1963–69)
Secretary of Health, Education and Welfare:	Anthony J. Celebrezze (1963–65)
	John W. Gardner (1965–68)
	Wilbur J. Cohen (1968–69)
Secretary of Housing and Urban Development:	Robert C. Weaver (1966–69)
	Robert C. Wood (1969)
Secretary of Transportation:	Alan S. Boyd (1967–69)

---

large migration of blacks from the South to the northern cities – seven million between 1950 and 1970. The ghettos, with their high crime, drugs and welfare families, were seen as much as a race problem as a poverty problem. In 1965, 43% of black families lived in poverty and fewer than two-fifths of blacks finished high school.

There was also uneven income distribution among whites. Poverty was highest among blacks, female single-parent families, the old, the sick and the poorly educated. In areas like Appalachia the decline of traditional industries was a major cause of poverty.

If LBJ wanted to end poverty in America, he also had to bear in mind the various interest groups like corporations, unions and the professions. These groups had their own interests to protect and were not necessarily going to support welfare reform. Neither were these groups or Congress likely to want to pay for mass welfare programmes. Luckily, the strong economy meant Johnson's plans were easily affordable for the first two years.

What were the aims of the Great Society?

In spite of the difficulties, LBJ wanted to do something about poverty but he wanted to go beyond that. He talked about creating a 'Great Society'. In a speech, in March 1964, he explained what that meant:

'The Great Society is where every child can find knowledge to enrich his mind and enlarge his talents. It is a place where leisure is a welcome chance to build and reflect, not a feared cause of boredom and restlessness. It is a place where the city of man serves not only the needs of the body and the demands of commerce but the desire for beauty and the hunger for community. It is a place where man can renew contact with nature. It is a place which honours creation for its own sake and for what it adds to the understanding of the race. It is a place where men are more concerned with the quality of their goals than the quantity of their goods.'

How did the Great Society programmes attempt to deal with America's domestic problems?

Before and after the election, Johnson launched a massive legislative programme. The 89th Congress passed more than 60 pieces of legislation, including 11 conservation bills, four education bills, 10 health measures, an increase in the minimum wage and an increase in social security to two million more people. He knew he had to act quickly, before the mood for reform evaporated.

Passing JFK's tax cut encouraged continued growth and allowed the Great Society to be paid for without raising taxes. This was important as it maintained support for the President's programmes. Once the Vietnam War started to take the money and taxes were raised, support for the Great Society declined.

Some of the Great Society measures:

1964   Tax Reduction Act – cut taxes by $10 billion to encourage growth.

Manpower Development and Training Act – expanded a 1962 Act with job training for the poor.

Economic Opportunity Act – created a range of poverty programmes under the Office of Economic Opportunity.

National Wilderness Preservation Act – created 45 national parks.

1965   Elementary and Secondary Education Act – first federal money to go directly to help schools.

Higher Education Act – scholarships and loans for college students.

Medical Care Act – healthcare for the poor, the disabled and the elderly paid for from taxes and from federal funds.

Omnibus Housing Act – money to build cheap housing and provide rent aid for the poor.

Appalachian Regional Development Act – $1 billion for highways, health centres and development programmes.

National Endowment for the Arts – federal money to help and support the arts and culture.

1966   Demonstration Cities and Metropolitan Development Act – subsidies for housing, slum clearance and transport in 'model cities'.

Urban Mass Transportation Act – money to help cities develop public transport networks.

Clean Water Restoration Act – $3.5 billion to clean up rivers and prevent pollution.

Highways Beautification Act – limitations on the number of billboards beside the highways.

Endangered Species Protection Act – protection for threatened species, making such protection a national goal.

1967   Air Quality Act – limits on sources of pollution including car exhausts.

1968   Wild and Scenic Rivers Act – protection of sections of eight named rivers from development.

By far the most important measure against poverty was the Economic Opportunity Act, which set up the Office of Economic Opportunity, headed by Kennedy's brother-in-law, Sargent Shriver, to coordinate the various schemes. It set up:

● VISTA (Volunteers in Service to America)

● Head Start where children went to pre-school classes

● Job Corps to give skills to inner-city youths

● Community Action Programmes (CAP) which set up clinics, law centres etc.

Head Start had some successes with eight million children benefiting from the programme, but it and CAP especially got caught up in local politics and ethnic conflicts. These limited their effectiveness. The promise of CAP was that there would be 'maximum feasible participation' of local people but, when these people criticised local councils and city authorities, the federal government would always back the authority. What Johnson was not facing up to was that in order to tackle poverty properly there needed to be much more fundamental change in the way society was run. That would mean challenging the political system – something he was not prepared to do.

Job Corps also had problems as much of the training was done in camps, where discipline led to problems. However, some large companies like IBM did get involved in the scheme and eventually it had some success finding 10,000 jobs. Eventually, $10 billion was spent on the 'war on poverty'. However, poverty was not only an urban problem. Some of the poorest parts of America were rural, such as Appalachia in the South-East. The Appalachian Regional Development Act gave $1 billion for highways, health centres and development. But most of the schemes were short term and many contracts went to 'outsiders'. The problem was that the main industry – mining – was in decline and there were few other businesses. What Appalachia needed was jobs.

As a trained teacher, LBJ knew the importance of education in lifting people out of poverty. The Elementary and Secondary Education Act, begun by JFK, was passed giving $1 billion for poor students in public and parochial schools. Local school boards decided where the money went, so it was frequently spent on middle-class children rather than on the poor it was intended for. To get it passed by Congress, Johnson had to respect states' rights. What really mattered was that federal government was now taking a role in education. More successful was the Higher Education Act, which provided $650 million for scholarships, low-interest loans and resources for colleges, benefiting 11 million students.

The 'Great Society' went beyond material wealth. Johnson wanted to improve the environment in which people lived, both in the cities and in the countryside. To improve life in cities both housing and transport reform were supported with the Omnibus Housing Act giving $8 billion to fund three million units of low and middle-income housing as well as rent aid. The Demonstration Cities and Metropolitan Development Act gave $1.2 billion in subsidies for housing, recreation, slum clearance, transit systems etc. Johnson understood and believed that people were affected by their surroundings and improved living conditions would create a better country. Even transport was supported to make the cities cleaner, through the Urban Mass Transportation Act and the creation of the Department of Transport. Cities like Washington and San Francisco used the Act to develop clean and cheap public transport networks.

Outside the cities, Johnson wanted to create an environment 'where man can renew his contact with nature'. It was in the 1960s that people were starting to realise the dangers of pollution and the threats to the land and animals of economic development. The National Wilderness Preservation Act created 45 national parks, including Redwood in 1968, and protected nine million acres of forest. The Endangered Species Protection Act protected 833 species of plants, animals and birds. The government spent over $35 million cleaning up rivers and extending its power to control various kinds of pollution. The president of the National Geographic Society called LBJ 'our greatest conservation president'. Even America's roads were made to look better through the Highways Beautification Act, sponsored by the President's wife who also wanted to create beauty and green spaces in the ghettos. Claudia 'Ladybird' Johnson was criticised for this, but she, like her husband, believed that people had the right to live in an attractive environment whatever their wealth.

They also believed that not only the rich should have access to culture, so the National Endowment for the Arts gave money to theatres, operas and art galleries. More than 700 companies got money, but there was much criticism, then and since, that the government has no business financing art.

Johnson's commitment to improving the nation meant that the 'Great Society' tackled an immense range of issues, but perhaps the most important was healthcare. The Medical Care Act set up the first federally funded healthcare system: Medicare for the elderly and Medicaid for welfare recipients. Six and a half billion dollars were spent on hospitals, nurses, doctors, nursing care and medical tests. In fact, it was less than Truman had proposed. It did not cover most prescriptions and was to prove very expensive. For many, though, it meant access to healthcare which they had been previously denied. The United States was one of the very few developed countries that had no government healthcare. Johnson's Medical Care Act was, therefore, of major significance.

1. In what ways and for what reasons did Johnson want to introduce major domestic reforms?

2. In which areas do you regard the Great Society as having been most successful:

(a) education

(b) inner-city reform

(c) the environment

(d) healthcare?

Give reasons for your answer.

11.8 How successful was the Great Society?
A CASE STUDY IN HISTORICAL INTERPRETATION

As Johnson expected, public support for liberalism and reform did not last long. By 1966, people were tiring of change and of the liberalism which had dominated politics for the previous five years. They were also disillusioned with policies which were now seen to have weaknesses (largely because they had been rushed). Recipients of welfare resented the federal intrusion, while conservatives resented federal government moving into so many areas of people's lives. The 'Great Society' had raised expectations that could not have been met realistically, especially the 'war on poverty'. The historian William Chafe says, ' … when measured against the expectations set forth by Johnson, the war on poverty remained a disappointment'. But was the Great Society a failure?

It is probably true that the government underestimated the size and scale of the problem. LBJ wanted to achieve consensus but, in order to get real change, the existing systems and structures would have had to be challenged, which he was unwilling to do. Political scientist Ira Katznelson argues, in *Major Problems in American History Since 1945* (2001), that the problems went back as far as the 1940s. Basically, the Democratic Party was not prepared to challenge the system. It wanted to work within it and this prevented the Great Society from effecting real change.

Another problem was that, in the rush to get legislation through, much was not thought through properly and money was often spent on the wrong things (e.g. a lack of spending on sufficient teachers under Head Start). William Chafe argues that part of the problem was Johnson himself, who personalised everything and refused to compromise or make sacrifices. However, Johnson felt that if he did not rush legislation through then the national support for the Great Society would have gone. As Johnson's aide Jack Valenti said, 'Of course we made mistakes. We were doing things!'

It was estimated that the Great Society would cost $1.4 billion in 1966, rising to $6.5 billion in 1968 and $10.4 billion in 1970. In fact, they never spent more than $2 billion in a year and 20 times more was spent on the war in Vietnam than on all the Great Society programmes put together. It has been said that it substituted good intentions for cold, hard cash. Yet at the same time, Medicare was set up in a way that would see the costs to the federal government soar from $40 billion in 1965, to $125 billion in 1975 and to $400 billion in 1985.

In spite of the amount spent, many groups were left out. By emphasising opportunity, the Great Society did not help those who could not take up the opportunities (e.g. the old, disabled, single mothers etc.). Many criticised the government for trying to force middle-class values on the poor, wanting them to help themselves out of poverty when they did not have the skills to do so. Katznelson claims that the Great Society 'favoured equality of opportunity rather than equality of results'.

Historian Allen J. Matusow, in *The Great Society: a Twenty-Year Critique* (1986), claims that the 'war on poverty' was lost. The only real solution was to re-distribute wealth through taxation, which the Great Society did not do. Matusov also questions whether health improved as a result of the Medical Care Act. As he points out, the poor did have access to healthcare before the Act through charities. All the Act did was to end up paying doctors for services which they had previously given for free.

For all its shortcomings, there were successes. According to the US Census Bureau, the number of families in poverty dropped from 40 million in 1959 to 28 million in 1968 and to just over 25 million two years later. While it might be argued that the general economic growth could account for this, after Johnson left the White House the number of poor families remained almost the same and, in the 1980s, rose again above 30 million. For black people, there was also improvement with the number earning less than $3,000 a year falling from 41% in 1960 to 23% in 1968. The Administration had shown that poverty mattered and, more importantly, that it could be addressed by federal government. As Johnson's domestic affairs advisor Joe Califano said, 'We simply could not accept poverty, ignorance and hunger as intractable [difficult to remove or deal with], permanent features of American society.'

The Great Society also did the following:

- It protected 7,200 miles of river, 14,000 miles of trail and 83 million acres of wilderness.

- It increased the number of students graduating from high school.

- It introduced consumer protection and safety in cars with seatbelts.

- It saw poverty levels drop and life expectancy rise.

According to John McCormack, the Speaker of the House, the 89th Congress was 'a Congress of accomplished hopes. It is the Congress of realised dreams.' Historian Paul Boyer says that 'The Great Society made the United States a more caring and just nation.' That seems a judgement most presidents should envy.

1. According to the census, the number of families in poverty dropped from 40 million in 1959, to 28 million in 1968 and to 25 million in 1970. What do these figures tell us about the success of the 'war on poverty'?

2. How far do historians agree on the success of the Great Society?

Source-based questions: American Anti-Communism

SOURCE A

There shall be a loyalty investigation of every person entering the civilian employment of any department or agency of the executive branch of the federal government …

The standard for the refusal of employment or the removal from employment … shall be that, on all the evidence, reasonable grounds exist for belief that the person involved is disloyal to the government of the United States.

Truman's Executive Order 9835, 1947

SOURCE B

…the decision that would affect our lives was being made at the Waldorf-Astoria Hotel in New York. There, on 27 November 1947, the representatives of the motion picture industry formally decided to fire any accused worker who would not freely answer all the questions asked by the Un-American Activities Committee and could not clear himself of charges that he was or had been a member of the Communist Party.

From It's a Hell of a Life But Not a Bad Living *by Edward Dmytryk, one of the Hollywood Ten, 1987*

SOURCE C

It was the great body of the nation, which, not invariably, but in general, kept open its mind in the Hiss case, waiting for the returns to come in. It was they who suspected what forces disastrous to the nation were at work.

From Witness *by Whittaker Chambers, 1952*

SOURCE D

[1949] had brought nothing but bad news to McCarthy. He had angered prestigious senators in both parties and he had problems at home … in a crisis he would do anything … A poll of Washington correspondents had chosen him as America's worst Senator. In two years … he would be up for re-election.

From The Glory and the Dream *by William Manchester, 1974*

SOURCE E

The censure resolution avoided criticising McCarthy's lies and exaggerations; it concentrated on minor matters – on his refusal to appear before a Senate Subcommittee on Privileges and Elections, and his abuse of an army general at his hearings.

At the very time the Senate was censuring McCarthy, Congress was putting through a whole series of communist bills. Liberal Hubert Humphrey introduced an amendment to one of them to make the Communist Party illegal.

From A People's History of the United States *by Howard Zinn, 1980*

---

1. Study Source A and use your own knowledge.

Why did Truman issue the Loyalty Order?

2. Study Sources A and B and use your own knowledge

How useful are these sources to an historian studying the anti-Communist hysteria of the period?

3. Study Sources C, D and E and use your own knowledge.

Assess the extent to which McCarthy should be blamed for the anti-Communist hysteria in the decade after the Second World War.

From Nixon to Clinton: US domestic policy, 1969–1992

Key Issues

- *To what extent did domestic policy become more conservative between 1969 and 1992?*

- *In what ways did the US economy change between 1969 and 1992?*

- *Did the power of the President change in the years 1969–1992?*

Framework of Events

1968	Nixon wins presidential election
1970	Nixon proposes Huston Plan
	Environmental Protection Agency established
1971	Nixon introduces wage and price freeze
1972	Watergate break-in
	Equal Rights Amendment passed by Congress
	Nixon wins landslide in presidential election
1973	Trial of Watergate burglars
	Senate creates Special Committee to investigate Watergate
	Vice-President Agnew resigns; replaced by Gerald Ford
	'Roe v Wade' Supreme Court case
	OPEC quadruples world oil price during Yom Kippur War
1974	Supreme Court orders Nixon to release Watergate tapes
	Whip Inflation Now (WIN) program
	Indian Self-Determination Act
	House Judiciary Committee votes to impeach Nixon
	Nixon resigns; Ford becomes President
1975	Ford pardons Nixon
1976	Carter defeats Ford to become 39th President
1978	Double-digit inflation and rising interest rates
1979	OPEC doubles price of oil following Iranian Revolution
	(March) Three Mile Island Nuclear Accident
1980	Reagan is elected President
1981	Reagan survives an assassination attempt
	Major cuts in taxes and domestic spending
	Severe economic recession begins
1982	Equal Rights Amendment fails to be ratified by states
1984	Reagan defeats Mondale in landslide election victory
1986	Immigration Reform and Control Act
	Federal budget deficit rises to $221 billion

1987	Iran-Contra Scandal
	(October) Stock Market Crash
	Trade deficit with other countries reaches $170 billion
1988	Bush defeats Dukakis to become President
1989	'Exxon Valdez' oil spill in Alaska
	Supreme Court limits abortion and restricts civil rights laws
1990	Federal Clean Air Act is passed
	Bush and Congress agree five-year budget deficit reduction plan
	New recession begins
1991	Controversy over appointment of Clarence Thomas to Supreme Court
1992	Supreme Court upholds 'Roe v Wade' decision on abortion
	Arkansas Governor Bill Clinton defeats Bush in presidential election.

Overview

THE period 1969–92 was one of considerable social, economic and political change within the United States. In 1968, Nixon won a narrow victory over his Democratic Party opponent, Hubert Humphrey. His victory was aided in no small way by the split within the Democratic Party, which produced George Wallace's American Independent Party.

Nixon inherited a country riven with social and political strife. The anti-Vietnam War movement had helped to topple Johnson's Administration. The riots at the Democratic Party Convention in August 1968 were the culmination of anti-war demonstrations across the country. In addition, the country was affected by racial conflict. The assassination of Martin Luther King led to race riots in almost every major city. Social conflict continued for much of Nixon's first term.

The year 1969 was also a turning point in politics. The New Deal coalition began to fall apart. From 1932 to 1969 the Democrats had been the dominant national party because they were able to win support from blue-collar workers, Catholics, Jews, blacks, southern whites and northern liberals. The social turmoil of the 1960s had led to the fragmentation of this coalition. From 1969 to 1992, the Republicans emerged as the dominant party in presidential politics. They also greatly increased their power in Congress and in state governments.

In national government, major changes occurred in the Supreme Court. The liberal Court of Earl Warren came to an end in 1969 when the Chief Justice retired. Initially, under Warren Burger (1969–86) and then William Rehnquist (1986–92), the Court became more conservative as a result of nominations by Republican Presidents.

The period after 1969 saw major changes in the power and authority of the President. Nixon's first term was the high point of 'imperial presidency'. However, the Watergate scandal of 1973–74 temporarily destroyed presidential power. It was only with the first term of Ronald Reagan's presidency (1981–85) that presidential power regained much of its prestige. Even that was temporary. The Iran-Contra Scandal of 1987 was another blow to presidential authority.

There were also major changes in the relationship between the federal and state governments. Lyndon Johnson's 'Great Society' was the high point in federal involvement in social and welfare matters. From 1969, financial decision making in these areas was gradually handed back to the states. It began with Nixon's 'revenue sharing' with the states. It accelerated under Reagan. From 1969, both major parties came to oppose 'big government' from Washington DC.

In economic terms, the United States had experienced two decades of crisis and adjustment. The Vietnam War had placed great strain on the US economy, leading to inflation. In 1973, the OPEC decision to quadruple the price of oil plunged the world into economic recession. The Iranian Revolution of 1979 created another major oil price increase. Combined with Reagan's economic policy, the USA experienced the worst economic recession, 1981–83, since the Depression of the 1930s.

Economic crisis helped to fuel major changes in the US economy. Many old manufacturing industries, such as car manufacture and steel, shed thousands of jobs. New industries associated with information communication technology grew. Many industries relocated to the 'sun belt' of the South, leaving behind a 'rust belt' in northern states such as Michigan.

1. In what ways did the USA experience radical political, economic and social change between 1969 and 1992?

2. What do you regard as the greatest change in US domestic history in the period 1969–1992?

Explain your answer.

The civil rights years had brought gains for African Americans (see Chapter 10). However, major social problems remained. Inner-city ghettos, the rise of violence and drug abuse, together with poor education, remained important social issues. These were not confined to African Americans. Hispanic Americans also faced similar problems.

In the period 1969–92, civil rights also embraced issues such as women's rights and gay rights. Such developments resulted in a right-wing backlash. From the 1970s, the religious right gained influence in US politics. It reached the height of its influence during Ronald Reagan's presidency, 1981–89.

By 1992, the Republicans had dominated national government for over 20 years. Bill Clinton's victory over George Bush Senior started a decade of Democratic Party rule.

12.1 How far did domestic policy change under Nixon, 1969–1974?

Richard Nixon narrowly won the 1968 presidential election over Democrat Hubert Humphrey by 31.7 million votes to 31.3 million. The electoral college made the gap wider (301 to 191) because Nixon won in 32 states. Nixon claimed he represented 'Middle America' – a group he later described as the 'silent majority'.

However, Nixon had to deal with a Congress dominated by the Democrat Party. In the 91st Congress (1969–71), the Democrats controlled 58 seats in the Senate and 243 out of 435 in the House. In the 92nd Congress (1971–73), they still controlled 54 Senate seats but increased their hold on the House with 255 seats. As a result, Nixon's attempts to follow a conservative domestic policy were severely limited. Congress

Richard Milhous Nixon (1913–1994)
37th President of the USA (1969–74), a Republican. Born in Yorba Linda, South California, and brought up as a Quaker. Attended Whittier University, before serving in US Navy in

Pacific in Second World War. Nixon was elected to House of Representatives (1946) and Senate (1950). Member of Joseph McCarthy's campaign against communists in USA. Vice-President to Eisenhower (1953–61).

Lost to John F. Kennedy in 1960 elections. Lost Governor's election in California in 1962. As President, he was responsible for US withdrawal from Vietnam, and the improvement of relations with Communist

China. Only president ever to resign from office (9 August 1974) – over his involvement in the Watergate Scandal. He was threatened with impeachment (trial for serious offences committed whilst in office).

could, and did, introduce legislation that Nixon disliked. For instance, Congress passed the Twenty-Sixth Amendment in 1970, which lowered the age of voting in elections from 21 to 18. This was ratified by the states in 1971. Congress also passed the Federal Election Campaign Act in 1972.

Nevertheless, Nixon attempted to change radically the role of the federal government. He also planned to develop a new base of support for the Republican Party.

Nixon's southern strategy

Nixon's victory in 1968 had seen the end of the Democrat's control of the 'Solid South'. Nixon won southern states such as Tennessee, North and South Carolina, Virginia and Florida. The Democrats also lost states such as Mississippi and Alabama to George's Wallace's American Independent Party.

In developing a strategy, Nixon was helped by a Republican aide, Kevin Phillips, who produced 'The Emergence of a Republican Majority' in 1969. This suggested the Republicans could capture votes from the middle class, southern whites, Catholics and westerners.

During his first term in office, Nixon deliberately adopted policies that were aimed to win over the South. He opposed an extension of the 1965 Voting Rights Act. He also wanted to modify the Fair Housing Act of 1968, which would have had an adverse effect on African Americans.

Nixon also wanted to prevent any further desegregation of schools in Mississippi. However, the Supreme Court thwarted him. In 1969, in 'Alexander versus Holmes County', the Court demanded school integration with all possible speed. In 1971, in 'Swann versus Charlotte Mecklenburg Board of Education', the Court attacked *de facto* segregation. The Court advocated bussing children between black and white neighbourhoods in order to achieve racially-integrated schools. However, in 1974, in 'Milliken versus Bradley', the Court limited the amount of bussing.

These developments were slightly surprising because Nixon had nominated a conservative Chief Justice, Warren Burger, when Earl Warren retired in 1969. To make matters worse, when liberal Justice Abe Fortas retired, Nixon's attempt to appoint a conservative Southerner backfired on two occasions. In 1969, the Senate rejected his nomination of South Carolina's Clement Haynsworth. In the following year, the choice of G. Harrold Carswell of Florida was also rejected. However, by the time he resigned from office, Nixon had been successful in appointing three

---

The Nixon Administration, 1969–1974: leading members

President:	Richard Nixon
Vice-President:	Spiro Agnew (1969–73)
	Gerald Ford (1973–74)
Treasury:	David Kennedy (1969–70)
	John Connelly (1970–72)
	George Schultz (1972–74)
	William Simon (1974)
Justice:	John Mitchell (1969–72)
	Richard Kleindienst (1972–73)
	Elliott Richardson (1973)
	William Saxbe (1973–74)
Chief White House Aides (1969–73):	H.R. 'Bob' Haldeman and
	J. Erlichman

conservative justices: Harry Blackmun of Minnesota, Lewis Powell of Virginia and William Rehnquist of Arizona.

Nixon's southern strategy did show results. In 1972, he won every southern state. Also, since 1969, the South has no longer been a solid Democrat area.

The problem of radicalism

During the 1968 presidential campaign, the nation seemed to be overrun with radical groups. At the Democratic National Convention, radical groups such as Students for a Democratic Society (SDS) and the Youth International Party (Yippies) did battle with the Chicago police. In addition, the Black Panther Party and other radical black groups demanded fundamental social change. Across America, a variety of radical groups opposed the USA's continued involvement in South East Asia.

By the early 1970s, the feminist movement was demanding equality for women. Similarly, the gay liberation movement was demanding equality for gays.

Student protest against the Vietnam War reached its height in May 1970 when it was announced publicly that US troops had invaded Cambodia. The shooting of four students at Kent State University by

How reliable is this source as evidence of the Kent State University shootings of May 1970?

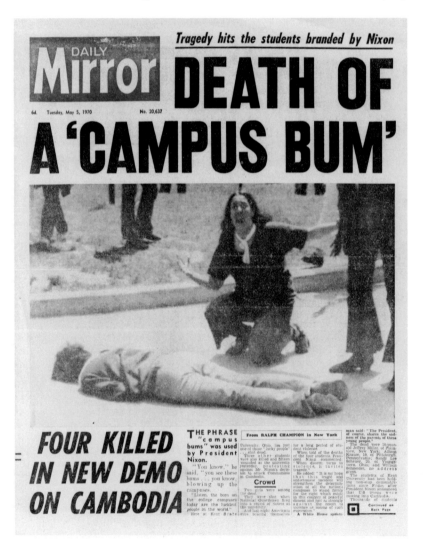

Front page of 'Daily Mirror' in the UK, 1 May 1970.

Cartoon by Mike Peters, 1982, 'Look guys, why don't we just say that all men are created equal … and let the little ladies look out for themselves?' published in 'Dayton Daily News', 1982.

1. *What point is this cartoon making about the campaign for equal rights for women?*

2. *How useful do you regard this cartoon as evidence of US opinion on the campaign for women's rights?*

Campus: Area of land which contains the main buildings of a university, such as the lecture rooms, administration offices, sports facilities, and some living accommodation for students.

Pentagon: Building in Washington DC which is the headquarters of the US Department of Defense.

Sexual equality: The idea that men and women have the same civil, political and social rights.

Abortion: When a woman ends her pregnancy and loses her baby, usually deliberately.

Ohio National Guardsmen caused national outrage. Nixon did not help matters by referring to the college students as '**campus** bums' at an informal briefing at the **Pentagon**!

Fortunately for Nixon the student protest movement split asunder of its own accord. The SDS fell apart at its national convention in 1970. A group known as the Revolutionary Youth Movement demanded violent revolution and lost support accordingly.

Beginning in 1967, the CIA (see panel on page 397) launched 'Operation Chaos' against left-wing groups. This was supported by the FBI's 'Cointelpro' programme. Both organisations amassed information on left-wing groups. In particular, the Black Panther Party was targeted for special attention. In 1969, 28 party members were killed by police. Many more were imprisoned.

By the time of the 1970 mid-term elections, Nixon had campaigned against what he called 'the rock throwers and the obscenity shouters in America'. He appealed to the great 'silent majority' of America. By that stage, the student protest movement had dissolved into attempts to find alternative lifestyles.

Of greater significance was the rise of a militant feminist movement associated with the National Organisation of Women (NOW). Founded in 1966 by Betty Friedan, the author of *Feminist Mystique,* NOW supported the campaign for **sexual equality**. This reached its height in the Nixon era. In 1972, the Educational Standards Act laid down that colleges had to set up affirmative action programmes to ensure equality of opportunity for women. In the same year, Congress passed the Equal Rights Amendment which, if ratified by the states, would have guaranteed sexual equality in the Constitution. Finally, in 1973, the US Supreme Court, in 'Roe versus Wade', legalised **abortion**.

In 1970, following police raids on gay clubs in New York City, the Gay Liberation Front was created. Almost 800 gay organisations had been established across the country by 1973.

Nixon and the environment

Superficially, Nixon's presidency seemed to be successful in environmental matters. During his first term as President, Congress passed the Water Quality Improvement Act. This attempted to control pollution caused by industry and power companies. Congress also passed the Clean Air Act,

Pollution emissions: The amount of air pollution produced by industry and private car use.

which attempted to control **pollution emissions** from cars. The Resource Recovery Act promoted the recycling of waste. At government level, the National Environmental Policy Act 1970 created the Environmental Protection Agency, which enforced federal law on the environment.

In developing these environmental laws, Nixon played an insignificant and reluctant part. Several environmental laws were passed over Nixon's veto. When forced to appoint a head of the Environmental Protection Agency, Nixon chose William Rogers who proved to be ineffectual.

Nixon's social policy

Sociologist: Someone who studies or teaches sociology – the study of human societies and relationships between groups in these societies.

In 1969, Nixon appointed a leading **sociologist** and Democrat, Daniel Patrick Moynihan, as his urban affairs adviser. The result of this development was the Family Assistance Plan. This proposed to end handouts to the poor, with a minimum annual income of $3,000 for a family of four. It was criticised by conservatives for being too radical and by liberals for its low payments. As a result, it was defeated in the Senate and dropped.

In the area of affirmative action (see page 314), Nixon introduced the Philadelphia Plan which required trade unions working on federal projects to accept quotas for African-American workers. This greatly extended affirmative action to include almost 300,000 firms by 1974. To assist this attempt to win African-American support, Nixon appointed James Farmer, the founder of CORE, as an assistant secretary in the Department of Housing, Education and Welfare (HEW).

Food stamp funding: Food stamps are given to the unemployed instead of money. They can only be used to buy food.

However, the Democratic-controlled Congress passed legislation less to Nixon's liking, such as the Occupational Health and Safety Act of 1970. Congress increased social security benefits by linking increases to the rate of inflation. It also increased **food stamp funding**.

Nixon and the economy

Stagflation: Rising inflation and rising unemployment at the same time.

Economic problems plagued the Nixon presidency. By the early 1970s, the US economy was suffering the effects of what became known as **stagflation**. Inflation stood at 3% per year in 1967. By 1973, it had increased threefold to 9%; by 1974, it had gone up another 3%. The unemployment rate was 3.3% in early 1969. By 1972, it had risen to 5.6%. This had been caused by a variety of factors.

Budget deficit: Where government expenditure is greater than government income from taxation.

Firstly, the joint costs of the 'Great Society' and the war in Vietnam had resulted in a large government **budget deficit**. In addition, the USA was facing stiff competition in world markets from Japan and West Germany.

Secondly, as the world's greatest consumer of oil the USA was vulnerable to oil-price increases. During the Yom Kippur War of 1973 between the Arabs and the Israelis, the Arab-dominated, oil-producing group OPEC (Organisation of Petroleum Exporting Countries) increased the world price of oil by 400%. This was particularly damaging to the US car industry which had a tradition of producing 'gas guzzling' cars which had a fuel consumption of 9 to 12 miles per gallon.

These factors helped to cause the 'Nixon recession' in 1971–74. In response, Nixon tried to reduce inflation. The US central bank, the Federal Reserve Board, raised interest rates. This made borrowing money more expensive. Then in August 1971, Nixon announced his 'New Economic Policy'. A freeze was made on all wages and price increases for 90 days (3 months). Later, in 1973, restraint on pay and price increases was made voluntary.

Also in August 1971, the United States abandoned the fixed exchange rate system established at the end of the Second World War. This aimed to create stability in international trading. The backbone of the system was the US dollar. However, with its economic difficulties, the USA could no longer underpin the system. The Smithsonian Agreement of 1972 saw the formal end to fixed exchange rates across the western world. As a result, the US dollar was devalued. This made exports cheaper and imports dearer. To protect the US car industry, Nixon also placed a tariff on imported Japanese cars.

These measures, along with a tax cut, did lead to some improvement in the economy. This allowed Nixon to win re-election in 1972. However, the combined effect of increased economic competition, oil price rises and a flexible exchange rate system all led to major restructuring in the US economy during the 1970s.

Summary

When Nixon came to office, in 1969, he faced social discord, a faltering economy and a Democratic-controlled Congress. He did make some important changes. Congress finally agreed to his revenue-sharing plan with the states in 1972. The liberal Supreme Court of Earl Warren was altered with the appointment of more conservative justices. However, Nixon's domestic policy and, with it, his reputation as President, was overshadowed by the Watergate Scandal of 1973–74. This became the greatest political scandal in 20th-century American history.

1. What difficulties did Nixon face in domestic affairs between 1969 and 1974?

2. How successful was Nixon in dealing with America's domestic problems 1969–1974?

12.2 *The Watergate Scandal*
A CASE STUDY IN HISTORICAL INTERPRETATION

The Watergate Scandal dominated American politics from 1973 to 1974. It destroyed the Nixon presidency. It also severely damaged the power and prestige of the office of President. The reasons for the scandal go far beyond the investigation into a burglary at the Democratic Party head-quarters in Washington DC during the 1972 presidential election campaign. Following the break-in and the trial of the burglars, Nixon was accused of obstructing investigations into the affair. He claimed executive privilege for not cooperating with a Senate investigation. He also lied about the involvement of the White House in the affair. The result was a temporary collapse of presidential power. By August 1974, he realised he would be impeached. The impact of the Watergate Scandal on the American political system is still open to debate. So, Nixon became the first President to resign whilst in office.

What were the causes of the Watergate Scandal?

(a) Nixon's personality
A long-term cause of the scandal was the personality and psychological make-up of the President. Nixon has been subject to several psycho-analytical studies. In *Richard Nixon, A Pyschobiography* (1997), Volkan, Itzkowitz and Dod point out that Nixon was an introvert with a strong sense of inferiority. His humble Quaker background in California helps to explain this. He suffered physical abuse from a strict father. He was in awe of his mother, whom he adored. He constantly referred to her throughout his life as a 'saint'. As a result of this background, Richard Nixon resented those with more privileged backgrounds, such as the East Coast liberal elite. Nixon was also suspicious of others and feared 'enemies everywhere'.

To Nixon this problem was made clear, in 1971, when a State Department official, Dr Daniel Ellsberg, released to the press 'The Pentagon Papers'. These secret documents on US involvement in Vietnam showed that the government had lied to the American people about why it had become involved. From that incident on, Nixon was determined to prevent any other leaks about the government reaching the press.

Given his psychological make-up, Nixon was almost bound to engage in actions which spied on his political opponents or anybody else he felt might threaten his position as President. He engaged in surveillance of opponents and actively plotted to discredit them. This led to a break-in of the Democratic National Headquarters during the presidential campaign of 1972. It involved bugging the offices of Democrat National Chairman, Larry O'Brien.

Watergate also involved other illegal activities. Successful attempts were made to discredit leading Democrats who could have been formidable opponents to Nixon in the 1972 election. A malicious rumour was spread that the wife of Edmund Muskie of Maine, who was a Catholic, had had an abortion. Senator Scoop Jackson of Washington was accused of having had an affair with a younger woman. The overall aim was to secure the nomination of liberal George McGovern of South Dakota as his opponent.

(b) Nixon's hopes of a landslide victory

In 1960, Nixon suffered a narrow defeat in a presidential election. He believed John F. Kennedy 'stole' the election because political supporters in Chicago had tampered with the votes, thereby securing Illinois and the election. In 1968, Nixon narrowly defeated Hubert Humphrey in a three-way contest that included George Wallace of the American Independent Party. Nixon planned to 'win big' in 1972 and ensure a second term. This would mean that he would be President during the bicentennial celebration of 1976, the 200th Anniversary of the Declaration of Independence.

To achieve this end, Nixon used any means at his disposal to ensure a victory. Like other Presidents before him, such as Lyndon Johnson, Nixon bugged the opposition to find out their campaign strategy. Nixon stated, in 1977, that Watergate emerged 'exactly how the other side would have played it'. It was 'all politics pure and simple'. As Maurice Stans, former chairman of CREEP (The Committee to Re-Elect the President) stated, 'to him [Nixon], on the political battlefield "the end justified the means"'.

(c) The Imperial Presidency

Nixon's presidency can been seen as a longer-term process, which Arthur Schlesinger identified as the rise of the 'Imperial Presidency'. By the early 1970s, the office of President had amassed enormous power. The President had the awesome power to launch an all-out nuclear war. However, within the United States, he was limited by the terms of the Constitution. This was made clear in Nixon's first term as President when he had to work with a Democrat-controlled Congress. With his power over the intelligence agencies such as the FBI, CIA, NSA and DIA (see panel), the President had, at his disposal, the power and authority to spy on others.

The White House from 1970 coordinated the work of the intelligence agencies as part of a plan to end the social disorder caused by radical and left-wing groups. Once established, this network was then used against Nixon's political opponents, the Democrats.

(d) The CIA Trap Theory

This theory comes from the belief that the CIA attempted to stop the agency falling under the control of the Nixon White House. According to supporters of this view, former CIA agents, such as James McCord, deliberately botched the bugging of the Democrat Headquarters in order to create political problems for Nixon.

At the Senate Committee hearings into Watergate, McCord, a former CIA agent and one of the burglars, wrote a memorandum which stated:

> 'It appeared to me that the White House had for some time been trying to get political control over [the] CIA. When linked with what I saw happening to the FBI – political control by the White House – it appeared then that the two agencies were no longer able [to conduct their own business].'

(e) The work of Nixon subordinates

Subordinates: Those individuals under a person's management control.

Throughout the Watergate Scandal and since, Nixon has claimed that the burglary and other supposedly illegal activities were the work of overzealous **subordinates**. Individuals, such as Gordon Liddy, were regarded as having acted on their own initiative. If the White House was involved, it was associated with Nixon aides H.R. 'Bob' Haldeman and John D. Erlichman, rather than Nixon himself. As the President he was forced, eventually, to accept responsibility for the acts of others.

According to Maurice Stans, chairman of CREEP:

> '[Nixon's] tragic downfall through Watergate was the result of excesses of loyalty, first by his campaign staff who wanted him to win an overwhelming [victory] in the 1972 election through a petty burglary unknown to him, and second, by his endorsement of a cover-up to protect his staff and through them his re-election.'

Why was Nixon forced to resign over the Watergate Scandal?

Nixon was on the verge of impeachment, in August 1974, because he was accused of using agencies such as the FBI and CIA for political purposes in order to discredit opponents. He was also accused of lying about his involvement in the scandal and of using his position as President to obstruct justice.

Throughout the scandal, Nixon consistently refused to cooperate with the Senate Investigating Committee, the Special Prosecutor into the affair and even the Supreme Court. He claimed 'executive privilege'. This meant he used the issue of national security to refuse to give evidence. It formed the basis of his refusal to hand over tapes of conversations in the White House on the affair. In ascertaining why Nixon was forced to resign, a number of issues arise.

(a) The role of two 'Washington Post' reporters

According to their book *All the President's Men* (published in 1994), Bob Woodward and Carl Bernstein, two investigative reporters working for the 'Washington Post', played a major role in linking Nixon with the Watergate break-in. On 19 June 1972, an article by the two reporters linked the burglars with Howard Hunt, a White House aide. They uncovered an illegal 'slush fund' of hundreds of thousands of dollars which had been used by CREEP for illegal activities during the 1972 presidential campaign. Later investigations highlighted the roles of Maurice Stans and other senior Republican Party officials, including Attorney General John Mitchell.

During their investigations, Woodward and Bernstein were aided by an anonymous White House official, whom they nicknamed 'Deep Throat'. In their study of the Watergate Case, called *Silent Coup: The Removal of a President* (1991), Len Coldny and Robert Gettlin believe 'Deep Throat' to be the name given to several anonymous sources used by the reporters.

At the time, and in the subsequent Hollywood Film 'All the President's Men', Woodward and Bernstein were portrayed as the driving force behind the investigations which finally led to Nixon's resignation.

Timechart of the Watergate Scandal

1972

(28 May) First break-in by Watergate burglars at Democratic National Headquarters in Washington DC.

(17 June) Second break-in which leads to arrest of James McCord and Cuban-exile burglars at Watergate Building.

(15 September) Grand Jury **indicts for trial** Gordon Liddy, Howard Hunt and Watergate burglars.

Indicts for trial: When either a law official or a grand jury makes a decision which suggests there is sufficient evidence to try a person for a crime.

1973

(8–30 January) Trial and conviction of James McCord and Gordon Liddy for Watergate break-in.

(7 February) Senate establishes Select Committee on Presidential Campaign Activities under chairmanship of Sam Ervin.

(19 March) James McCord gives a letter to federal judge John Sirica alleging that high-ranking White House officials were involved in cover-up of burglary.

(27 April) FBI Director Patrick Grey resigns after it is revealed that he destroyed evidence given to him by Nixon's legal adviser John Dean.

(30 April) Resignations of Nixon's closest White House advisers, Haldeman and Erlichman, and Attorney General Kleindienst. John Dean fired by Nixon.

(27–28 June) John Dean testifies to Senate Committee linking White House with Watergate break-in.

(13 July) White House junior official Butterfield reveals existence of tapes of all conversations made at Nixon White House.

(10 October) Vice-President Spiro Agnew forced to resign over income tax evasion.

(20 October) 'Saturday Night Massacre' – Nixon asks Attorney General to fire Special Prosecutor into Watergate Scandal, Archibald Cox. When he refuses, he is sacked by Nixon. He also sacks Assistant Attorney General, William Ruckelhaus, when he refuses to sack Cox. Eventually, acting Attorney General, Robert Bork, sacks Cox.

(1 November) Leon Jaworski becomes Special Prosecutor into Watergate Scandal.

(6 December) Gerald Ford becomes Vice-President.

1974

(1 March) Grand Jury indicts for trial former Attorney General John Mitchell, Haldeman, Erlichman and other White House aides for conspiring to hinder Watergate investigation.

(24 July) Supreme Court demands that Nixon release tapes on Watergate.

(27 July) House Judiciary Committee begins impeachment proceedings against Nixon.

(8 August) House Judiciary Committee agrees to impeach Nixon for lying and obstructing investigation into Watergate Scandal.

(9 August) Nixon resigns as President.

(b) The Congressional investigations
Although Woodward and Bernstein may have highlighted many of the links between the burglars and the White House, it was the Senate Investigating Committee that acted as the main driving force leading to impeachment. It was in front of the Committee that John Dean, the President's legal adviser, linked Haldeman, Erlichman and Nixon to the burglary and other illegal acts. It was also in front of the Committee that Alexander Butterfield announced that Nixon had installed a tape system which recorded all his conversations in the White House.

With extensive national television coverage, the Senate investigating hearings helped to build up opposition to Nixon. In the House of Representatives, the House Judiciary Committee amassed sufficient evidence to recommend the impeachment of Nixon. This decision forced the President's resignation.

(c) The role of the Supreme Court
On 24 July 1974, the Supreme Court ruled unanimously that Nixon should hand over to the House Judiciary Committee tapes of 54 conversations made during 1972. When these were published in written form they linked Nixon to the cover-up. They also revealed that the President made racist comments about other politicians, and that he swore constantly. Swear words were replaced by the phrase 'expletive deleted'. This decision brought the whole affair to a head. Within three weeks, Nixon was on the verge of impeachment by the Judiciary Committee, which forced him to resign on 9 August.

(d) Nixon's personality
In her study *Richard Nixon: The Shaping of His Character* (1991), Fawn Brodie declares:

> 'Nixon lied to gain love, to store up his grandiose fantasies, to bolster his ever-wavering sense of identity. He lied in attacks, hoping to win. And always he lied, and this most aggressively, to deny that he lied. Finally, he enjoyed lying.'

As Nixon once explained, he was not the first President to use the FBI or CIA to watch and report on political opponents. However, his compulsive habit of covering up and lying eventually undermined his position.

'Bob' Haldeman, one of Nixon's senior aides, stated:

> 'it really doesn't matter why or who ordered the Watergate break-in. What really matters is how we dealt with it after it happened, and that's where we made our fatal mistakes. I agree with Nixon's statement to David Frost [television interviewer] that, "I gave them a sword and they stuck it in me".'

What impact did the Watergate Scandal have on American politics?

(a) The increase in Congressional control of the Executive and its agencies
The Watergate Scandal led to major attempts by Congress to hold the President, federal government and intelligence agencies more accountable. It resulted in the passage of several laws on campaign finance, freedom of information and more openness in government.

Building on the Federal Election Campaign Act of 1971, Congress established limits on fundraising in elections. The law of 1974 limited individual campaign contributions to $5,000. These helped the growth of Political Action Committees (PACs), which circumvented the law.

The Privacy Act was also passed in 1974. This permitted individuals to see information kept on them in federal files. In 1975, the Hughes–Ryan

"He says he's from the phone company…"

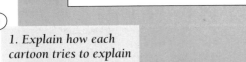

1. Explain how each cartoon tries to explain the Watergate Scandal.

2. Which cartoon do you regard as the most effective in getting its message across? Explain your answer.

3. How useful do you regard these cartoons in explaining the Watergate Scandal?

(Top) Syndicated cartoon by Jules Feiffer, 15 July 1973;
(left) cartoon by Paul Conrad, published in 'New York Times', 11 September 1972;
(below) 'Nixon in Tape Web' by Robert Pryor, 1975.

Undercover operations: Attempts to find out information in secret.

Amendment required the President to report to Congress on all **undercover operations**. In 1977, Senate and House committees were created to monitor the intelligence community.

In 1978, Congress passed the Ethics in Government Act which required all senior government officials to disclose their finances. It also established the Office of Government Ethics to monitor the process. In October of the same year, the Foreign Intelligence Surveillance Act required the CIA to obtain a court order before it could place a wiretap. In 1980, the Intelligence Oversight Act provided new requirements on the CIA to report its activities to Congress.

(b) The high-water mark of the Imperial Presidency
According to historian Stanley Kutler, in *Wars of Watergate: The Last Crisis of Richard Nixon* (1990):

> 'Watergate altered public perception of the presidency. Watergate transformed American attitudes towards government, and especially the presidency.
>
>   Watergate bestowed a new vulnerability on the presidency. Once peerless and invincible, presidential majesty seemed diminished.'

The changes in American public opinion aided the election of Jimmy Carter in 1976. It took until the 1980s, under Ronald Reagan, for the prestige of the presidency to recover – albeit for a short time. Following the Iran-Contra Affair of 1986–87, the presidency was again tainted with scandal.

(c) The Democrat and Republican Parties
The Watergate Scandal greatly aided the Democrat Party in the short run. It helped them to increase their control of the Senate and House in the mid-term elections of 1974. However, in the longer term, it led to a revitalised Republican Party, which was more conservative. In many ways, Watergate helped to lay the foundations for the Reagan Revolution of the 1980s.

1. Why are there differing interpretations about what caused the Watergate Scandal?

2. Explain why you think Nixon was forced to resign the presidency by 1974?

3. 'Watergate marked a turning point in American politics.'

Assess the validity of this statement.

Source-based questions: Richard Nixon

SOURCE A

What were Richard Nixon's main strengths and weaknesses? I'd say his strengths lay in his intellect primarily. He has a brilliant mind in the areas in which he is interested. He is like a racehorse specifically trained to run a particular race. He's running for the race to be President and that's what he lived for.

   I would say his major weakness was in interpersonal relationships. He was a fellow who at the time I knew him was very weak in family relationships and in friendships. He had no strong friendships. Some of the worst times I ever spent with him were when he tried to fire somebody. He knew he had to do it, but he couldn't do it. It was a little bit like killing the Thanksgiving turkey with a dull axe, hack away and back off and ask somebody else to do it. He was terrible at that kind of thing.

From an interview with John Erlichman in 1987. John Erlichman was a senior White House aide under Nixon and was jailed for his part in the Watergate Scandal.

SOURCE B

My appraisal of him today is as objective as I can phrase it:
   – Richard Nixon was a man from a modest, near-poverty background endowed with extraordinary ambition, and energy and drive.
   – He was an inherently timid man, uncomfortable in social settings yet dominant in political gatherings, and one of the most eloquent speakers of our time.

Source-based questions: Richard Nixon

– He was a person of broad vision, seeking to innovate in major national events rather than merely respond to them.

– He was a man with a brilliant mind; a keen student in evaluating the pros and cons of a problem; decisive when he was satisfied with the facts before him; working at his job all the waking hours; probably the most hardworking President of this century.

– He was extraordinarily sensitive to criticism; impatient with opposition; often bitter in defeat; and he was frantic over leaks.

A recollection of Richard Nixon by Maurice Stans in 1987.
Stans had been Chairman of CREEP (Committee to Re-Elect the President) in 1972.
He became Secretary for Commerce in Nixon's Administration, 1973–74.

SOURCE C

He was accustomed to rely entirely on his own perceptions; his decisions were mostly taken alone. Morally he was a shallow man; the only [views] he ever mentioned were those he learned from his Quaker mother and his football coach. The rich and honourable traditions of American Republicanism meant nothing to him by comparison. He had been poor, so he would never cease to be preoccupied with the rich, envying them, fearing them, craving to be one of them. He

lost the Presidency to John Kennedy, so the latter's good looks, wit and charm became another painful obsession. He had lost the gubernatorial [governorship] election in California in 1962, and blamed his defeat on a hostile press. 'Congratulations gentlemen,' he said ungraciously to reporters, 'you won't have Richard Nixon to kick around any more.' Within him was a darkness that he mistook for the light. Eventually it would destroy him.

From The Longman History of the United States of America *by Hugh Brogan, 1999 – assessing Nixon's character.*

---

1. Study Sources A, B and C.

How far do these sources agree about Nixon's character and personality?

2. Study Source B.

How reliable is this source as evidence of Nixon's character and personality?

3. Study Sources A, B and C and use information from this chapter.

'Nixon's fall from office was due mainly to defects in his character and personality.'

Assess the validity of this statement.

12.3 What impact did Ford's presidency have on domestic policy?

Gerald Ford (1913–)
38th President of the USA (1974–77), a Republican from Grand Rapids, Michigan. He was elected to the House of Representatives in 1949; was nominated to the vice-presidency by Nixon (1973) following the resignation of Spiro Agnew. Became President when Nixon was forced to resign following the Watergate Scandal. Ford granted Nixon a full pardon (September 1974). His visit to Vladivostock in 1974 resulted in agreement with the USSR on strategic arms limitation. Defeated by Carter in 1976 election by a narrow margin.

Gerald Ford entered the White House, in August 1974, at one of the most difficult times in US history. The Watergate Scandal had severely damaged the political system and, in particular, the office of President. In economic affairs, the country faced rising inflation and unemployment. In foreign affairs, the Portuguese empire collapsed in 1974–75 resulting in the formation of extreme left-wing governments in Portugal's former African colonies such as Angola. In 1975, Ford faced the humiliation of the fall of South Vietnam, Laos and Cambodia to communism (see Chapter 9).

When he entered the White House, Ford became the only person in history never to have been elected to the post of either President or Vice-President and yet attained both offices. Yet he had some advantages. According to the historian Hugh Brogan, in *The Longman History of the United States of America* (1999):

'Ford was a good-humoured, honest, straightforward man, who did not pretend to genius. The new President's family was attractive and reassuring: they began to exorcise the cloud of sulky secrecy which had lain over the White House for so long.'

The Nixon pardon

Within weeks of taking office, Ford faced controversy. On 8 September 1974, he gave a full pardon to Nixon for 'any and all crimes' committed during his presidency. Without such a pardon, Nixon would have faced trial and likely imprisonment for his role in the Watergate Scandal. Ford argued that he wanted to end the crisis faced by the USA as a result of the Watergate Scandal, which had taken place over 18 months.

The Ford Administration, 1974–1977: leading members

President:	Gerald Ford
Vice-President:	Nelson Rockefeller
Treasury:	William Simon
Justice:	William Saxbe (1974–75); then Edward Levi (1975–77)

Economic policy

In October 1974, Ford introduced his plan to end the economic problems facing America. In the WIN (Whip Inflation Now) programme he called for voluntary restraint on pay rises. However, this had little effect on rising prices. Ford cut federal spending. He also supported the Federal Reserve Board (the US central bank) when it raised interest rates.

Ford's failure to bring about major economic change resulted in a severe economic recession in 1974–75. The major cause of this recession was the world economic slowdown, which was accelerated by the 400% increase in oil prices made by OPEC in October 1973.

By election year, 1976, unemployment had risen to 8%. Areas such as Detroit were badly hit as the US car industry faced competition from more fuel-efficient Japanese cars.

The 1976 elections

The Democratic Party couldn't wait for the 1976 elections. With the fall of Indo-China to communism, a severe economic recession and the fallout from Watergate, the Democrats were in a very strong position. After the 1974 mid-term election, they held 61 Senate seats and 291 out of 435 House seats.

The Democrats chose a former Governor of Georgia, Jimmy Carter. He had a reputation of being an outsider untainted by Washington politics. He was also honest – a major advantage in 1976.

For all Ford's problems, he only narrowly lost the election. Carter polled 49.9% of the vote, compared with Ford's 47.9%, winning 297 against 240 electoral college votes. In Congress, the Democrats kept 61 seats in the Senate and increased their House representation by one.

1. What problems faced Ford during his presidency?

2. Given his short period in office do you regard Ford as having been a successful president?

Explain your answer.

12.4 How successful was Jimmy Carter in domestic policy, 1977–1981?

Jimmy Carter planned to offer a new style of presidency. After his inauguration, he broke with tradition and walked with his wife down Pennsylvania Avenue to the White House. He had won the presidency partly because he was an outsider from a southern state. However, his inexperience in dealing with a Democrat-dominated Congress created

Macroeconomic policy: Economic
policy that affects the whole
economy, such as the national
employment figures or inflation rate.

major problems. One commentator stated that 'Carter couldn't get the Pledge of Allegiance through Congress!'

Carter's lack of a clear policy and his lack of optimism compounded his own problems in the future. Hugh Brogan states, in *The Longman History of the United States of America* (1999), that 'The new president was inclined to view the present as one big emergency and the future as marked by a sharp diminution of promise of American life.'

Carter's economic policy

When he entered office, Carter used 'demand side' policies to stimulate the economy. These had been the basis of US **macroeconomic policy** since the Second World War. However, very high fuel prices and foreign competition had caused the severe recession facing the USA from the early 1970s. These two developments led to a rise in inflation and in unemployment at the same time, known as stagflation. Stimulating demand through increased consumer spending only helped to increase inflation as well as the purchase of imports such as foreign cars.

In the first year of Carter's term in office, unemployment dropped slightly from 8% to 7%. However, inflation kept rising, reaching 10% by the end of 1978. By 1980, inflation rose again to 13%, with interest rates at 20%.

The inflation rate was boosted in 1979 because of the Iranian revolution which led to the fall of the Shah of Iran. It also resulted in the OPEC decision to double the price of oil. On 23 October 1979, Carter was given power by Congress to introduce petrol rationing.

To make matters worse, there was a nationwide reaction against a big-spending government. In 1978, in California, a statewide referendum accepted Proposition 13, which drastically cut state taxes. This action was followed by other states.

Changes in government

Carter did have some successes. He greatly increased the number of ethnic minorities in government. The highest-profile appointment was that of SCLC's Andrew Young to the US ambassador's post at the United Nations.

Carter also created a new government department, Energy. In 1979, he divided the Department of Health, Education and Welfare (HEW) into the separate departments of Education, Health and Human Services.

Carter's Administration, 1977–1981: leading members

President:	Jimmy (James Earl) Carter
Vice-President:	Walter Mondale
Treasury:	Michael Blumenthal (1977–79); then William Miller (1979–81)
Justice:	Griffin Bell (1977–79); then Benjamin Civiletti (1979–81)

The 1980 elections

Carter became the first one-term president in the USA since the Second World War. He lost the 1980 election for a variety of reasons. In foreign affairs, he faced the humiliation of US embassy staff in Iran being held hostage. They were only released in January 1981. Carter took responsibility for a failed military mission to release the hostages. He also faced humiliation when the USSR occupied Afghanistan in 1979. Carter's decision to boycott the 1980 Moscow Olympics only added to his problems.

The presidential election of 1980

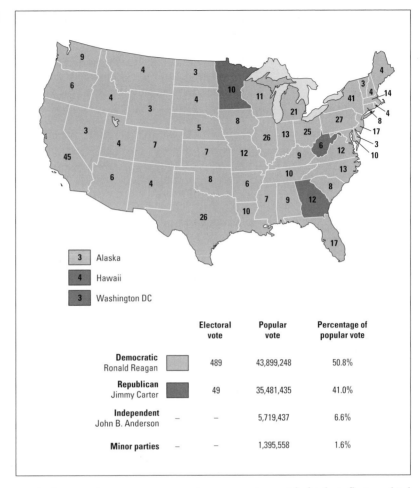

	Electoral vote	Popular vote	Percentage of popular vote
Democratic Ronald Reagan	489	43,899,248	50.8%
Republican Jimmy Carter	49	35,481,435	41.0%
Independent John B. Anderson	–	–	5,719,437	6.6%
Minor parties	–	–	1,395,558	1.6%

At home, the economy was in a recession with high inflation, high interest rates and unemployment.

Opposing Carter in the 1980 election was conservative Republican Ronald Reagan, former governor of California. Reagan supported a new approach to the economy, known as 'supply side' economics. He also had support from fundamentalist religious groups which had grown in influence during the 1970s. The most influential was the 'moral majority' pressure group run by Reverend Jerry Falwell.

Reagan also had the backing of women's groups opposed to feminism. These were led by Phyllis Schafly and the National Right to Life Committee. The latter had 11 million members by 1980.

In *The Limits to Liberty* (1995), historian Maldwyn Jones notes:

'The election was the most devastating rejection of an incumbent president since Hoover's defeat in 1932. For the first time since 1954 the Republicans won control of the Senate. They also gained 33 seats in the House. The main reason for the Republican landslide was the discontent produced by unemployment, inflation and the faltering economy. But the voters also seem to have been demanding a stronger foreign policy and more decisive leadership.'

As a result, the 1980 election – like in 1932 – brought about fundamental change in US domestic history. The two-term presidency of Ronald Reagan was aptly termed 'The Reagan Revolution'.

1. What problems faced Carter in domestic affairs?

2. Why did he last only one term as President?

12.5 To what extent was the presidency of Ronald Reagan a turning point in domestic affairs?

Ronald Wilson Reagan (1911–)
40th President of the USA (1981–89), originally a Democrat but left to become a major anti-communist Republican. He was a Hollywood actor (head of Screen Actors' Guild after Second World War) before becoming Governor of California. Defeated Carter in the 1980 presidential election. During the 1980s, he launched the biggest peacetime military build-up in US history. Supporter of the 'Star Wars' initiative. However, from 1985 he negotiated with Soviet leader Gorbachev towards reducing nuclear weapons in START (strategic arms reduction talks). He was wounded in an assassination attempt in 1981. Re-elected in 1984, in a landslide victory.

Reagan was 69 on Inauguration Day 1981 – the oldest person to become President. A former Hollywood actor, Reagan was charming and good-natured. He acquired the title 'The Great Communicator' for his ability to speak well on television.

Unlike his predecessor, Reagan had a clear view of what he wanted to achieve. He wanted to restore prestige to the office of President. He also wanted to restore the USA's standing as the world's greatest power. At home, he wanted to bring about fundamental social and economic change. In doing so, he planned to dismantle the New Deal welfare state which had existed since the mid-1930s.

'Reaganomics'

Ronald Reagan had inherited an economy that had been in difficulties for almost the whole of the 1970s. Unemployment had averaged 6.2% over the decade, compared with 4.1% in the 1960s. Inflation had reached double-digit levels.

In response, Reagan produced the 'Program for Economic Recovery'. The basis of this plan was a rejection of 'demand management' macro-economic policy. This had attempted to create low inflation and unemployment through the manipulation of the rate of direct taxation and of government spending. Instead, Reagan supported 'supply side' economics. This aimed to create economic growth through improvements in productivity and output. It was to be achieved by major tax cuts as an incentive to work and a reduction in government spending.

The first part of this economic policy passed Congress in two Acts in 1981: the Omnibus Reconciliation Act and the Economic Recovery Tax Act. To prevent a major budget deficit, the first Act aimed to cut federal government spending in over 300 programmes. The Office of Management and Budget, part of the Executive Office of the President, calculated that spending would be cut by $963 billion between 1981 and 1987. The Congressional Budget Office calculated the cut to be $1,041 billion. In the second Act, personal income tax was cut to 25%. These changes were more remarkable because the Democrats still controlled the House of Representatives.

These measures helped to bring about economic recovery. Real GNP grew by 11% by the end of 1984 – one of the fastest economic recoveries since the Second World War. Unemployment declined to 7% by 1984 and

What message is this cartoon trying to make about Ronald Reagan's economic policy?

Cartoon by Ben Sargent in 'Texas Monthly', 1983, showing Reagan as the proud rooster.

inflation dropped to 3.8% over the same period. Such developments helped to ensure a landslide victory for Reagan in 1984.

However, although Reagan had cut federal programmes, such as welfare payments, he launched the biggest peacetime build-up of the US armed forces in history. This had the effect of creating a huge federal budget deficit by the mid-1980s. The trade deficit alone was $170 billion by 1986. This led to the Balanced Budget and Emergency Deficit Control Act of 1985 (also known as the Gramm–Rudman Act). The aim of the Act was to reduce the federal budget deficit gradually until it disappeared (supposedly) by 1991. However, by the time Reagan left office, it was far from its goal.

Overall, economic recovery did create thousands of new jobs in the USA, the rate of inflation fell and economic growth occurred. According to Joseph J. Hogan, in *Reaganomics and Economic Policy* (1990):

'The overall economic performance of the United States during the Reagan era was little more than average for OECD (Organisation of Economic Cooperation and Development) countries, while the claim that this performance was the product of [Reagan's policies] is untenable.

The great federal budget deficits, the large trade deficits and their impact on converting the US into the world's leading debtor nation are the [main] legacies of the Reagan era.'

Social policy

The attitude of the Reagan Administration to social policy was affected by a number of factors. Firstly, Republicans were concerned by the growth of what they saw as a dependent underclass in US society. Martin Anderson, Reagan's first Domestic Policy Adviser, identified those on welfare programmes as having a disincentive to work. Secondly, the Reagan Administration wished to cut federal programmes as part of their new approach to economic management. Finally, Reagan wanted to develop a new relationship with the states – New Federalism – where the states would take more responsibility for their welfare.

The welfare programmes identified by the Administration included healthcare for the elderly (Medicare), healthcare for the poor (Medicaid), means-tested aid to Families with Dependent Children (AFDC) and food stamps. In 1981, around 3.7 million families received AFDC; about 20 million people received food stamps and 21.6 million received Medicaid. Approximately 20% of the African-American population participated in these programmes.

Reagan's main reform was the Omnibus Reconciliation Act of 1981. This Act cut AFDC and food stamps by around 13% between 1982–85; child nutrition programmes were cut by 28%; and Medicaid was cut by 5%. As a result, the number officially defined as 'poor' increased from 11.7% of the population in 1979 to 15% by 1982 and 13.5% thereafter.

Another important feature of the Omnibus Reconciliation Act was the attempt to reduce the dependency underclass known as 'workfare'. To receive AFDC payments, people had to do community service. By January 1987, 42 states had followed the federal government's lead and had established programmes where welfare payments were linked to some form of work. The workfare provisions in the 1988 Family Support Act reinforced this development.

In aiding the unemployed, the Reagan Administration began to work in partnership with the private sector. An example was the Job Training and Partnership Act of 1982. In *The Limits of Social Policy* (1988), Nathan Glazer notes that the Reagan Administration 'believed people could manage by themselves and had no need of federal government interventions'.

Dilys Hill, in *Domestic Policy in the Era of 'Negative' Government* (1990), states that:

> 'Where the Reagan Administration did not succeed was in cutting middle-class entitlement programmes of social security, Medicare and military and civil service pensions. The less well-defended bore the brunt of domestic cutbacks.'

New Federalism?

Linked to cuts in welfare was the plan to reduce the size of the federal government. Beginning with Nixon's revenue-sharing plans of the early 1970s, successive Republican governments had attempted to give more responsibility to state and local governments. In April 1981, Reagan set up two committees on the issue: the Presidential Advisory Committee on Federalism and the Coordinating Task Force on Federalism. Both were dominated by conservative Republicans.

In his 1982 'State of the Union Message' to Congress, Reagan announced his plan to reduce federal spending. It was to be part of his plan to bring government 'closer to the people'. Money would be given to the states by the federal government in block grants. The states had the discretion to use the money as they saw fit.

However, these plans were not passed by Congress. They also received a lukewarm response from many states. The National Governors' Association saw New Federalism as a way of simply cutting government programmes.

The federal judicial system

One of the most significant changes to occur in Reagan's presidency was in the federal judicial system. In his two terms of office, Reagan appointed 290 district and appeal court judges – about 40% of the total.

Of equal significance was Reagan's impact on the US Supreme Court. Following the retirement of Earl Warren in 1969, Presidents Nixon and Ford had appointed more conservative judges to the Court. Reagan completed the process. In 1986, when Warren Burger retired as Chief Justice, Reagan nominated the conservative William Rehnquist of Arizona as his replacement. He also successfully nominated two other conservative justices, Antonin Scalia and Sandra Day O'Connor – the first woman justice.

However, in 1987, Reagan faced embarrassment following the retirement of Justice Lewis Powell. On two occasions, Reagan failed to get his nominee accepted by the Senate. Firstly, Robert Bork and then Douglas Ginsburg were rejected. The latter revealed during the Senate hearings that he had smoked cannabis at university. Eventually, a more moderate conservative, Anthony Kennedy, was accepted.

The Reagan Court produced judgements that reflected its new conservative majority. In 'Wards Cove versus Atonio' in 1987, it provided restrictions on affirmative action. However, the Court did not go far enough to the right for Reagan's liking. For instance, it continued to uphold the 'Roe versus Wade' decision of 1973 which allowed abortions.

The decline of the Reagan Presidency in 1987

The Iran-Contra Scandal of 1986–1987

Reagan's popularity took a major blow in 1986–87 with the uncovering of the Iran-Contra Scandal. In Lebanon, in the early 1980s, several westerners

> ## Reagan's Administrations, 1981–1989: leading members
>
> | | |
> |---|---|
> | *President:* | Ronald Reagan |
> | *Vice-President:* | George Bush Senior |
> | *Treasury:* | Donald Regan (1981–85) |
> | | James Baker (1985–88) |
> | | Nicholas Brady (1988–89) |
> | *Justice:* | William Smith (1981–85) |
> | | Edwin Meese (1985–88) |

had been held hostage by militant Islamic groups – many linked to Iran. Among the hostages were American and British citizens. The latter included Terry Waite and John McCarthy. The Reagan Administration had stated consistently that it would not do deals with terrorist organisations over the keeping of US hostages. On 3 November 1986, a Beirut newspaper claimed that the USA had shipped 500 anti-tank missiles to Iran, which was at war with Iraq. In return, US hostages were released in Lebanon. The money received from the arms sales was used to help the Contra rebel forces fighting the left-wing government of Nicaragua.

In a joint Senate–House investigation of the affair in 1987, top White House aides were implicated. These included Chief of Staff Donald Regan and National Security Advisers Robert McFarlane and Admiral Poindexter. The key witness was Lieutenant-Colonel Oliver North who admitted taking part. He implicated the others.

Although no evidence was produced to link President Reagan directly with the affair, he suffered badly as a result. Later, in July 1988, Attorney General Edwin Meese was accused of corruption and forced to resign.

Black Monday, 19 October 1987

The buoyant stock market, which reflected the economic recovery from 1983, came to an abrupt halt on 19 October 1987. The **Dow Jones stock index** fell 508 points. Almost $500 billion in the paper value of American companies was wiped out. This was around 20% of the stock value of the USA.

When combined with the increase of the national debt, which had risen to $1.4 trillion, the final Reagan years were a period of considerable economic uncertainty.

Summary

According to Dilys Hill and Phil Williams, in *The Reagan Legacy* (1990):

> 'The restoration of American pride and the regeneration of American power were major achievements of the Reagan Administration.'

Yet, at home, Ronald Reagan left a nation where the gap between rich and poor had increased. '**Reaganomics**' had limited success in bringing economic recovery. The reduction in taxes and huge military expenditure merely created a vast federal debt.

However, Reagan did restore much of the prestige to the presidency, which had been lost in the 1970s. His almost monarchic style had made him popular. It had also prevented him from being implicated in policy failures of his subordinates or even directly in the Iran-Contra Scandal.

Dow Jones stock index: The listing of shares on the New York (Wall Street) Stock Market.

Reaganomics: The economic policy of President Ronald Reagan. It was based on 'supply side' rather than 'demand management' economics. It involved big cuts in direct taxation and the reduction of the federal budget.

1. In what ways did Reagan's Administration change social and economic policy between 1981 and 1989?

2. To what extent did Reagan bring about fundamental change in domestic policy?

12.6 In what ways was George Bush Senior's domestic policy different from that of Ronald Reagan?

George Herbert Bush (1924–)
41st President of the USA (1989–93), a Republican. From rich New England family, attended Yale University. Fought as fighter pilot in Pacific in Second World War. Became rich oilman in Texas. Director of the CIA (1976–81) and Vice-President (1981–89). As President, sending US troops to depose General Noriega of Panama was popular at home. Success in the 1991 Gulf War against Iraq further raised his standing. However, despite signing START I (July 1991) and reducing US nuclear weapons, Bush's popularity at home began to wane. Defeated by Democrat Bill Clinton in the 1992 presidential elections.

George Bush Senior became the first Vice-President since Martin Van Buren in 1837 to win a subsequent presidential election. In 1988, he defeated a lacklustre Democrat, former Governor of Massachusetts, Michael Dukakis. He also won because he had been associated with Ronald Reagan's presidency. Was Bush's presidency a continuation of Reagan's?

Economic policy

Bush had inherited a very large federal budget deficit. During the election he had committed himself to not raising taxes by making the statement: 'read my lips – no new taxes'.

In addition, a Democrat-controlled Congress was opposed to any further cuts in welfare. In 1991, Bush faced major expenditure when the Gulf War took place. Also, between 1990 and 1992, an economic recession reduced tax revenues. By 1992, the federal budget deficit had risen to $400 billion. This created problems because the Gramm–Rudman Act of 1986 had required the President to balance the budget by 1993.

In 1990, Bush was forced to raise taxes and to make cuts in military and domestic expenditure of $492 billion. However, these measures failed to make any impact on the recession. Interest rate cuts by the Federal Reserve Board, down to the lowest level for 18 years (3.5%), made little difference.

Bush also faced major problems with America's savings and loans companies, the equivalent of British building societies. Even before Bush became President, these companies had been facing severe financial difficulties. When he came to office, Bush produced a federal rescue plan to save these companies. The plan involved the expenditure of $50 billion. However, by April 1990, the rescue figure had risen to $325 billion. Matters were made worse when one of Bush's sons, George W. Bush, was involved in one of the savings and loans companies in difficulty.

Unfortunately for George Bush Senior, his Administration found it difficult to work out an aid package with the Democrat-controlled Congress. A Senate committee reported that George Bush Senior was the only president since Herbert Hoover who had seen the average standard of living decline while he was in office.

In spite of his triumph in the Gulf War of 1991, Bush was seen as a failure in economic matters.

Social policy

Bush Senior tried to carry on Reagan's policy but in a more conciliatory way. In education, he put forward his goals in 'America 2000' in September 1989. The aim was to raise the high school graduation rate to 90%, to improve maths education, to increase adult literacy and to improve anti-drugs education. Bush also proposed a New American Schools Development Corporation, which would be a partnership with private business to raise educational standards. However, to achieve 'America 2000' Bush had to work closely with the states and with Congress. Congressional opposition brought the proposal to an end.

On environmental issues, Bush got Congress to pass the Clean Air Act of 1990 to cut pollution. In October 1992, shortly before the election, Bush signed the Energy Policy Act. This was a major attempt to limit dependence on imported oil through energy conservation and the promotion of renewable energy.

Civil rights

A major crisis began for the Bush Administration in 1991 with the Rodney King affair. King was an African American who was brutally attacked by members of the Los Angeles Police Department, in March 1991. A passer-by videoed the event. When the police were acquitted in the spring of 1992, serious racial rioting occurred in South Central Los Angeles – an area of great social deprivation.

The Bush Administration failed to show decisive leadership in the affair. Bush and his Vice-President, Dan Quayle, blamed the riots on a failure to keep law and order and a fall in family values. Only in early May did Bush suggest that an emergency programme for the poor should be implemented. By 22 June, Bush signed the Urban Aid Supplemental Bill into law, which provided $1.1 billion aid for inner cities – a figure well below what Congress had wanted.

A minor success was the Americans with Disabilities Act, passed in July 1990, which barred discrimination against people with physical or mental disabilities. However, in October 1990, Bush vetoed the Civil Rights Act on the grounds that it established quotas for ethnic minorities. Then, in 1991, he accepted a slighted amended version of the 1990 Act.

In nominations to the Supreme Court, Bush continued the conservative policy of his predecessor. In 1990, he nominated David Souter to replace William Brennan. What proved a major embarrassment for Bush was his nomination of African American Clarence Thomas to replace the former NAACP lawyer Thurgood Marshall in 1991.

Not only was Thomas inexperienced, but a former colleague also accused him of sexual harassment. In the Senate judiciary committee hearings on the Thomas nomination, Oklahoma University law professor and conservative Republican African American, Anita Hill, claimed that Thomas had a poor record on civil rights as well as sexual harassment. On 15 October 1991, the Senate approved Thomas by 52 votes to 48 – the narrowest for a successful candidate in the 20th century.

George Bush Senior's Administration, 1989–1993: leading members

President:	George Herbert Bush
Vice-President:	Dan Quayle
Treasury:	Nicholas Brady
Justice:	Richard Thornburgh

Why did Bush lose the 1992 presidential election?

Bush's domestic record and the poor state of the economy were clearly major factors. Even with these problems, Bush looked unbeatable in 1991 following his successes in foreign policy, such as the Gulf War.

However, he had to face a young, gifted opponent in Bill Clinton who had organised an effective campaign for change. Bert Rockman, in an article in 1992 in 'Cosmos' magazine entitled 'That Elusive Quality called Presidential Leadership', claimed:

> 'Bush committed the cardinal sin of politics by implying that the status quo often is better than existing alternatives.'

Bush was also affected by the appearance of a strong third candidate, Texan billionaire Ross Perot who ran on a 'clean up national politics' ticket.

Front cover of 'New Yorker' magazine in 1993 with illustration by Edward Sorel.

Yet, Bush's failure to gain a second term might have had a deeper cause. In an assessment of Bush's presidency, Dilys Hill and Phil Williams (1994) noted:

'the failures of the Bush Administration were partly self-inflicted, they also reflected problems that go well beyond a particular presidency. The presidency is suffering above all from a gap between expectations and capability, the root of which is that Americans understand the need for power but distrust its exercise.'

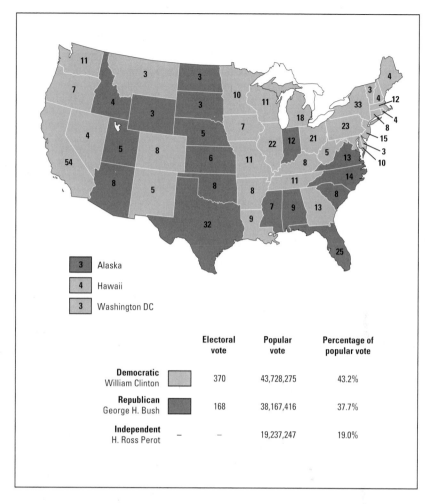

		Electoral vote	Popular vote	Percentage of popular vote
Democratic William Clinton		370	43,728,275	43.2%
Republican George H. Bush		168	38,167,416	37.7%
Independent H. Ross Perot	–	–	19,237,247	19.0%

The US presidential election of 1992

Further Reading

A selection of useful articles, texts, videos and websites on US history

CHAPTER 1   The Foundations of the United States, 1776–1803

Texts designed for AS Level students

The Enduring Vision, Volume 1, to 1865 by P. Boyer and others (D.C. Heath and Co., 1992)

America by G.B. Tindall and D. Shi (W.W. Norton & Co, 1993)

The Limits of Liberty by Maldwyn Jones (Oxford University Press, 1995)

The Longman History of the United States of America by Hugh Brogan (Longman, Second edition, 1999)

CHAPTER 2   Western expansion in the 19th century

Texts designed for AS Level students

The Enduring Vision by P. Boyer and others (D.C. Heath and Co., 1992)

Texts for A2 and advanced study

The Limits of Liberty by Maldwyn Jones (Oxford University Press, 1995)

America by G.D. Tindall and D. Shi (W.W. Norton & Co., 1993)

Bury My Heart at Wounded Knee by Dee Brown (Pan Books, 1971)

The Indian Frontier of the American West by Roger Utley (University of New Mexico Press, 1984)

Television and videos

'The Way West' – a documentary written and produced by Ric Burns (1995); shown on BBC as 'The Wild West' divided into six one-hour episodes. Covers Western expansion from the 1840s to 1890, but concentrates on 1860s–1890.

'The West' – produced by Stephen Ives and written by G. Ward and D. Duncan (1996); divided into eight one-hour episodes. Covers Western expansion during whole of 19th century. Available from DD Video, 5 Churchill Court, Station Road, North Harrow, Middlesex HA2 7SA.

CHAPTER 3   The causes and course of the Civil War, 1840–1865

Texts designed for AS Level students

The Origins of the American Civil War 1846–1861 by Alan Farmer (Hodder and Stoughton, Access to History series, 1996)

The American Civil War 1861–1865 by Alan Farmer (Hodder and Stoughton, Access to History series, 1996)

A House Divided: Sectionalism and the Civil War, 1848 to 1865 by R. Sewell (John Hopkins University Press, 1988)

Texts for A2 and advanced study

Conflict and Compromise: The Political Economy of Slavery, Emancipation and the American Civil War by R. Ransom (Cambridge University Press, 1989)

The American Civil War by P. Parish (Holmes and Meir, 1975)

The Battle Cry of Freedom by J. McPherson (Penguin, 1988)

With Malice Toward None: a biography of Abraham Lincoln by S. Oates (Mentor, 1977)

Lincoln by D. Donald (Jonathan Cape Press, 1995)

The Origins of the American Civil War by Boyd and Hilton (Longman, Origins of Modern Wars series, 1998)

Video

'The Civil War'– produced by Florentine Films, written and produced by Ken and Ric Burns (1990); divided into six one-hour episodes. Covers the causes but mainly the course of the American Civil War. Available from DD Video, 5 Churchill Court, Station Road, North Harrow, Middlesex HA2 7SA.

CHAPTER 4   'The Gilded Age' to the First World War, 1865–1919

Texts designed for AS Level students

The Enduring Vision, Volume 2 since 1865 by Paul Boyer and others (D.C. Heath and Co., 1995)

Texts for A2 and advanced study

The Limits of Liberty by Maldwyn Jones (Oxford University Press, 1995)

The Longman History of the United States by Hugh Brogan (Longman, Second edition 1999)

The Pivotal Decades, The US, 1900 to 1920 by John Milton Cooper Jr (W.W. Norton & Co., 1990)

Unity and Culture, The United States 1877 to 1900 by H. Wayne Morgan (Penguin, 1971)

CHAPTER 5   Boom and Bust: the United States, 1919–1933

Texts designed for AS Level students

Prosperity, Depression and the New Deal by Peter Clements (Hodder and Stoughton, Access to History series, 1997) – an accessible text but the sections on the Wall Street Crash are difficult to understand.

The USA 1917–1929 by Doug and Susan Willoughby (Heinemann, 2000) – a simplistic, lightweight text which covers the main issues.

The Enduring Vision by P. Boyer and others (D.C. Heath and Co., 1993) – a US-produced text which is easy to read. Contains good illustrations.

Texts for A2 and advanced study

The Anxious Decades by Michael Parrish (Norton, 1992) – a US-produced text which contains effective analysis of the main issues.

The Longman History of the United States of America by Hugh Brogan (Longman, Second Edition 1999) – highly readable, scholarly text by leading British historian of the USA.

The Twenties in America by Paul Carter (Harlan Davidson, Second edition 1975) – a short, US-produced text which offers a good overview of the decade.

The Great Crash by J.K. Galbraith (Hamish Hamilton, 1955) – still an authoritative account of the causes of the Depression by a leading neo-Keynesian American economist.

CHAPTER 6   FDR and the New Deal 1933–1945

Texts designed for AS Level students

Prosperity, Depression and the New Deal by Peter Clements (Hodder and Stoughton, Access to History series, 1997) – a readable, accessible text.

Franklin Roosevelt: The New Deal and War by M.J. Heale (Routledge, Lancaster pamphlets, 1999) – a short and very useful pamphlet which covers 1933–1945.

America by G. Tindall and D. Shi (W.W. Norton & Co., Third edition 1993) – a large history of the USA which has a useful section on the New Deal and the War.

The Enduring Vision by P. Boyer (D.C. Heath and Co., 1993) – a large but highly accessible general history of the USA which has a good section on the New Deal.

The New Deal by John A. Salmond (Frederick Warne, 1970) – succinct and readable coverage of the New Deal.

Hell in the Pacific by Jonathon Lewis and Ben Steele (Boxtree, 2001) – a revisionist account, based on the Channel 4 series, giving the vivid story of the brutality of the Pacific war,

Texts for A2 and advanced study

The Anxious Decades, USA 1920–1941 by Michael E. Parrish (W.W. Norton & Co., 1992) – a scholarly and detailed coverage.

The Longman History of the United States by Hugh Brogan (Longman, Second edition 1999) – extremely readable, scholarly work by Britain's leading historian of the USA.

The New Deal, the Depression Years 1933–1940 by Tony Badger (Macmillan, 1989) – detailed and readable text which is about the best individual text on the New Deal by a British historian.

The New Deal by Paul Conkin (Harlan Davidson, Third edition 1992) – a short but scholarly account of the New Deal.

Who Built America? Volume II by the American Social History Project (Pantheon, 1992) – an extremely good study of social history.

Franklin D. Roosevelt and the New Deal, 1932–1940 by William E. Leuchtenburg (HarperCollins, 1963) – dated but still excellent study of FDR and the New Deal.

FDR by Ted Morgan (Simon and Schuster, 1985) – a very readable but large biography.

Video

'FDR' – a video written and produced by David Grubin for 'The American Experience' series (1994); four one-hour episodes covering FDR's political life and his relationship with his wife Eleanor.

CHAPTER 7   US foreign policy, 1890–1945

Texts designed for AS Level students

The Enduring Vision by Paul Boyer and others (D.C. Heath and Co., 1993) – easy to read and well-illustrated narrative.

The USA and the World, 1917–1945 by Peter Brett (Hodder and Stoughton, 1997) – clear narrative with practice exercises and note-making guide.

A History of the United States of America by Hugh Brogan (Longman, Second edition 1999) – good introductory text.

The Limits of Liberty by Maldwyn Jones (Oxford University Press, 1995) – clear narrative account.

Texts for A2 and advanced study

The Unfinished Nation by Alan Brinkley (McGraw Hill, 1993) – easy to read and scholarly, with good maps.

The War of 1898 by Louis Perez (Chapel Hill, 1998) – a study which provides different historical interpretations.

US Foreign Policy in World History by David Ryan (Routledge, 2000) – analysis of motives behind US foreign policy.

Manifest Destiny by Anders Stephanson (Hill and Wang, 1995) – study of American expansion.

Television and video

'The World at War' – Thames TV programmes (1973) shown on BBC in 2001 in 'Second World War' series. Available from Pearson TV International Ltd on either WWW.WORLDATWAR.COM or WWW.PEARSONTV.COM.

'FDR': episode 4 – PBS/BBC

'Truman' – written and produced by David Grubin for 'The American Experience' series (1994). It is divided into three one-hour episodes: the first covers Truman's political rise and the dropping of the atom bomb on Japan in 1945; the second episode covers Truman's Administration in domestic and foreign affairs up to 1949; the third episode concentrates on the Korean War.

Useful websites

HTTP://WWW.HISTORYOFCUBA.COM – useful information and lots of documents on the Spanish–American War.

HTTP://WWW.THEODOREROOSEVELT.ORG – contains documents, speeches etc. as well as biographical detail on Theodore Roosevelt.

HTTP://WWW.AMERICANPRESIDENT.ORG – based on PBS television series; covers the US Presidents and US foreign policy.

HTTP://TLC.AI.ORG – contains lots of links to other sites on US foreign policy.

CHAPTER 8   The USA and the Cold War in Europe, 1945–1991

Texts designed for AS Level students

The Enduring Vision by Paul Boyer and others (D.C. Heath and Co., 1993) – easy to read and well-illustrated narrative.

The USA and the Cold War by Oliver Edwards (Hodder and Stoughton, 1997) – clear narrative with practice exercises and note-making guide.

The Limits of Liberty by Maldwyn James (Oxford University Press, 1995) – clear narrative account.

The Cold War by Bradley Lightbody (Routledge, 1999) – clear chapters covering whole period, with lots of source questions.

Texts for A2 and advanced study

Rise to Globalism by Stephen Ambrose and Douglas Brinkley (Penguin, 1997) – fascinating and detailed account of post-war policy, quite critical of the USA.

Major Problems in American History Since 1945 edited by Robert Griffith and Paula Barker (Houghton Mifflin, 2001) – sets of documents on major issues, followed by interpretative essays by leading historians.

American Foreign Relations: A History Since 1920 edited by Thomas G. Paterson, J. Garry Clifford, Kenneth J. Hagan (Houghton Mifflin, 2000) – detailed narrative, well illustrated.

The Truman Years 1945–1975 by Mark Byrnes (Longman, Seminar Study series, 2000)

Television and video

'The Cold War' – CNN production shown on the BBC (1999–2000). Divided into six videos: (1) Iron Curtain; (2) Reds; (3) M.A.D.; (4) Dirty wars; (5) Third World wars; and (6) Final Countdown. Available from DD Video, 5 Churchill Court, Station Road, North Harrow, Middlesex HA2 7SA.

'Truman' – a video written and produced by David Grubin for 'The American Experience' series (1994). It is divided into three one-hour episodes: the first covers Truman's political rise and the dropping of the atom bomb on Japan in 1945; the second episode covers Truman's Administration in domestic and foreign affairs up to 1949; the third episode concentrates on the Korean War.

Useful websites

The Cold War has hundreds of websites. The following are just a few.

HTTP://HISTORY1900S.ABOUT.COM – lists lots of other sites and has a quiz.

HTTP://WWW.GWU.EDU/~NSAARCHIV – the US National Security Archive containing lots of sources and the international Cold War history Project.

HTTP://WWW.EAGLE3.AMERICAN.EDU/~MM5860A/ORIGINS – description of the Cold War but also lots of links.

HTTP://WWW.CNN.COM/SPECIALS/COLD.WAR – site for CNN television series, but has interesting photographs and bits of information including some animated summaries.

CHAPTER 9   The USA and the Cold War in Asia, 1945–1973

Texts designed for AS Level students

The Enduring Vision by Paul Boyer and others (D.C. Heath and Co., 1993) – easy to read and well-illustrated narrative.

The USA and Vietnam, 1945–1975 by Vivienne Sanders (Hodder and Stoughton, Access to History series, 1999).

The Cold War by Bradley Lightbody (Routledge, 1999) – good, clear chapters covering whole period with lots of source questions.

Texts for A2 and advanced study

Rise to Globalism by Stephen Ambrose and Douglas Brinkley (Penguin, 1997) – fascinating and detailed account of post-war policy; quite critical of the USA.

Vietnam by John Dumbrell (British Association for American Studies, 1992) – an easy-to-read pamphlet covering the war 1945–1975 at home and abroad.

A Noble Cause? America and Vietnam by Gerard de Groot (Longman, 1999) – covers the military, strategic, political and cultural aspects of the war as well as looking at the legacy for both countries.

Dispatches by Michael Herr (Picador, 1991) – a journalist's account of the war from talking to soldiers that truly brings home the nightmare quality of Vietnam.

America's Longest War by George Herring (McGraw-Hill, 1996) – detailed analysis of American policy from the 1950s onwards in Indo-China.

Vietnam: A History by Stanley Karnow (Pimlico, 1991) – detailed and comprehensive analysis of the war.

The Korean War by Peter Lowe (Longman, Origins of Modern Wars series, 1997) – looks at the war from the perspective of all the countries involved.

The Limits of Liberty by Maldwyn Jones (Oxford University Press, 1995) – clear narrative account.

American Foreign Relations: A History Since 1920 edited by Thomas G. Paterson, J. Garry Clifford, Kenneth J. Hagan (Houghton Mifflin, 2000) – detailed narrative, well illustrated.

Television and video

'The Cold War' – CNN production shown on the BBC (1999–2000).

'Vietnam: A Television History' – 13-part series produced by PBS shown on Channel Four in 1982.

'Truman' – a video written and produced by David Grubin for 'The American Experience' series (1994). It is divided into three one-hour episodes: the first covers Truman's political rise and the dropping of the atom bomb on Japan in 1945; the second covers Truman's Administration in domestic and foreign affairs up to 1949; the third episode concentrates on the Korean War.

Websites

The Cold War in Asia has hundreds of websites. The following are just a few.

HTTP://WWW.GWU.EDU/~NSAARCHIV – the US National Security Archive containing lots of sources and their international Cold War history project.

HTTP://WWW.EAGLE3.AMERICAN.EDU/~MM5860A/ORIGINS – description of the Cold War but also lots of links.

HTTP://WWW.CNN.COM/SPECIALS/COLD.WAR – site for CNN televison series, but has interesting photographs and bits of information including some animated summaries.

HTTP://HOMETOWN.AOL.COM/VETERANS/WARLIB6K – websites for the Korean War.

HTTP://HOMETOWN.AOL.COM/VETERANS/WARLIB6V – websites for the Vietnam War.

WWW.YALE.EDU/LAWWEB/AVALON/COLDWAR.HTM – a site for primary documents on the Cold War in Asia.

HTTP://WWW.LBJLIB.UTEXAS.EDU/SHWV/SHWVHOME.HTML – internet project on Vietnam with images and links.

WWW.PBS.ORG/WGBH/PAGES/AMEX/VIETNAM/- – website for 13-part series 'Vietnam: A Television History' containing the scripts of each one-hour episode.

CHAPTER 10   Civil rights, 1865–1992

Texts designed for AS Level study

Race Relations in the USA by Vivienne Sanders (Hodder and Stoughton, Access to History series, 2000)

Martin Luther King Jr and the Civil Rights Movement in America by John White (British Association for American Studies, 1991)

Texts for A2 and advanced study

The Civil Rights Movement by William T. Martin Riches (Macmillan, 1997)

Black Civil Rights in America by Kevern Verney (Routledge, 2000)

Black Leadership in America from Booker T. Washington to Jesse Jackson by John White (Longman, Second edition 1990)

Sweet Land of Liberty? by Robert Cook (Longman, 1998)

Bearing the Cross: Martin Luther King and the Southern Christian Leadership Conference by David Garrow (William Morrow, 1986) – Pulitzer Prize Winner.

Parting the Waters: Martin Luther King and the Civil Rights Movement 1954 to 1963 by Taylor Branch (Macmillan, 1991)

Pillar of Fire: America in the King Years, 1963–1965 by Taylor Branch (Simon and Schuster, 1998)

Video

'Eyes on the Prize: the Civil Rights Years in the USA, 1954–1970' – PBS.

Websites

WWW.WORLDBOOK.COM/FUN/AAJOURNY – these give a good introduction to topics such as the Civil Rights Act 1964, the Equal Employment Opportunities Commission and Affirmative Action.

WWW.WATSON.ORG/~LISA/BLACKHISTORY – provides introductory coverage of topics such as school integration.

WWW.BLACKHISTORY.EB.COM/MICRO/727/78 – provides pen portraits of black leaders such as Stokely Carmichael.

INFO.GREENWOOD.COM/BOOKS/0313250 – contains encyclopaedia of African-American civil rights.

WWW.NPS.GOV/MALU/DOCUMENTS – contains information on Jim Crow laws, Martin Luther King and the civil rights issue in general.

WWW.TOPTAGS.COM/AAMA/VOICES/SPEECHES/NEGROCON – contains African-American almanac covering broad range of African-American history.

HOMETOWN.AOL.COM/KLOVE01 – contains excerpts from Martin Luther King's speeches.

HOMETOWN.AOL.COM/NOWACUMIG/BACKGRND – contains information on the American Indian Movement and Native-American civil rights.

CHAPTER 11   US domestic history, 1945–1969

Texts designed for AS students

Promises to Keep by Paul Boyer (Houghton Mifflin, 1999) – easy to read and well-illustrated narrative.

Politics as Usual: the age of Truman and Eisenhower by Gary W. Reichard (Harlan Davidson, 1988) – an easy-to-read but detailed narrative that emphasises the continuation in policy.

Texts for A2 and advanced study

The Unfinished Journey by William H. Chafe (Oxford University Press, 1991) – critical narrative with good section on Johnson.

The Truman Years 1945–53 by Mark S. Byrnes (Longman, Seminar Studies series, 2000) – has a strong narrative but also has useful sections containing primary and secondary documents, a timeline and glossary.

Promises Kept by Irving Bernstein (Oxford University Press, 1991) – dense and quite hard to read, but useful in that it argues Kennedy did a lot more than he is given credit for.

Lyndon B. Johnson and American Liberalism by Bruce J. Schulman (St Martin's Press, Bedford Series in History and Culture, 1995) – a brief biography with a very useful document section.

Websites

Most presidents have their own libraries, which are on the internet.

WWW.TRUMANLIBRARY.ORG – on the Truman Years.

WWW.EISENHOWER.UTEXAS.EDU – on Eisenhower.

WWW.LBJLIB.UTEXAS.EDU – on Lyndon Johnson.

WWW.JFKLIBRARY.ORG – on John F. Kennedy.

CSTL.SEMO.EDU/MODERNPRESIDENCY/LINKS – a site full of links to other sites so it's a good starting point.

WWW.PBS.ORG/WGBH/AMEX/PRESIDENTS/INDEX – a site from the American Public Broadcasting Corporation and has pages for all American presidents.

Television and videos

'LBJ' – four-part documentary on Johnson for PBS (1997).

'Truman' – a video written and produced by David Grubin for 'The American Experience' series (1994). It is divided into three one-hour episodes: the first covers Truman's political rise and the dropping of the atom bomb on Japan in 1945; the second episode covers Truman's Administration in domestic and foreign affairs up to 1949; the third episode concentrates on the Korean War.

CHAPTER 12   From Nixon to Clinton: US domestic policy, 1969–1992

Texts designed for AS students

The Enduring Vision, Volume 2, from 1865 by P. Boyer and others (D.C. Heath and Co., 1995)

The American Pageant, A History of the Republic by T. Bailey and D. Kennedy (D.C. Heath and Co., 1979)

Texts for A2 and advanced study

The Limits of Liberty by Maldwyn Jones (Oxford University Press, 1995)

The Unfinished Journey by William Chafe (Oxford University Press, 1995)

The Longman History of the United States of America by Hugh Brogan (Longman, 1999)

Nixon Volumes 1 and 2 by Stephen Ambrose (Simon and Schuster, 1989)

Watergate and the Myth of American Democracy by L. Evans and A. Myers (Pathfinder, 1974)

Wars of Watergate: The Last Crisis of Richard Nixon by Stanley Kutler (W.W. Norton & Co., 1990)

The Reagan Presidency, An Incomplete Revolution? edited by Dilys Hill (Macmillan, 1990)

The Bush Presidency edited by Dilys Hill and Phil Williams (Macmillan, 1994)

Films

'All the President's Men' directed by Alan J. Pakula and starring Robert Redford and Dustin Hoffman (1976).

'Nixon' directed by Oliver Stone and starring Anthony Hopkins (1996).

Acknowledgements

Every effort has been made to contact the holders of copyright material, but if any have been inadvertently overlooked the publishers will be pleased to make the necessary arrangements at the first opportunity.

Extract from Marcus Cunliffe American Presidents and the Presidency, Fontana 1970; extract from Natives and Strangers: Blacks, Indians, and Immigrants in America, Third edition by Leonard Dinnerstein, R.L. Nichols & D.M. Reimers, copyright 1997 by Oxford University Press, Inc. Used by permission of Oxford University Press, Inc.; extracts from Donald McCoy Coming of Age (1996) courtesy of W.W. Norton & Co. Inc.; Penguin UK for extracts from Coming of Age by Donald McCoy, published in 1973; extracts from Joshua Freeman, Who Built America? by permission of Pantheon (1992); Pearson Education for extracts from Longman History of the United States of America by Hugh Brogan (1999); The Presidency of Herbert C. Hoover by Martin L. Fausold published by University Press of Kansas (1985); The New Deal by Paul Conkin published by Harlan Davidson (1992); extracts from The New Deal, The Depression Years 1933–1940 by Tony Badger, published by Macmillan Press (1989); extracts from Franklin Roosevelt: The New Deal by M.J. Heale, a Lancaster pamphlet published by Routledge (1999); extracts from James T. Patterson, America in the Twentieth Century Harcourt (1999) 2nd edition; extracts from The Anxious Decades: USA 1920–1941 by Michael E. Parrish (1992) courtesy of W.W. Norton & Co. Inc.; extract from Paul Boyer The Enduring Vision © 1993 by Houghton Mifflin Company; extract from Public Papers of the Presidents, Harry S. Truman 1947 published in 1963 by the Government Printing Office, Washington; Penguin UK for extract from Rise to Globalism by Stephen Ambrose and Douglas Brinkley (1997); Thomas G. Paterson et al American Foreign Relations: a history since 1895 © 2000 by Houghton Mifflin Company; Mastering Modern World History by Norman Lowe published by Macmillan Press (1982); Pearson Education for extract from The Cold War: A Study in US Foreign Policy Since 1945 by Walter Lippmann (1973); extract from Memoirs, 1925–1950 by George Kennan (1967) reproduced by permission of Little Brown & Co.; The USA and Vietnam, 1945–1975 by Vivienne Sanders published by Hodder (1999); extract from Vietnam: American Involvement at Home and Abroad by John Dumbrell published by BAAS (1992); © Jeremy Isaacs and Taylor Downing. Extracted from COLD WAR by Jeremy Isaacs and Taylor Downing, published by Bantam, a division of Transworld Publishers. All rights reserved; extracts from The Unfinished Journey by William Chafe by permission of Oxford University Press, Inc.; Pearson Education for extracts from Black Leadership in America from Booker T. Washington to Jesse Jackson by John White (1985); Penguin UK for extracts from The Eyes on the Prize (1991); Hugh Brogan, Promises to Keep © 1999 by Houghton Mifflin Company; It's a Hell of a Life But Not a Bad Living by Edward Dmyrtyk published by Times Books (1987); The Glory and the Dream by William Manchester (1974) published by Bantam, a division of Transworld Publishers; The Balkin Agency for extracts from A People's History of the United States by Howard Zinn (1980); extracts from The Nixon Presidency, Kenneth Thompson (ed.), 1987, by permission of University Press of America; extract from Richard Nixon: The Shaping of His Character by Fawn Brodie (1991), courtesy of W.W. Norton & Co. Inc.; extract from The Limits to Liberty by Maldwyn Jones 1995 by permission of Oxford University Press; Reaganomics and Economic Policy by Joseph J. Hogan and Domestic Policy in the Era of 'Negative' Government by Dilys Hill (1990) both published by Macmillan Press; The Reagan Legacy by Dilys Hill, Raymond Moore & Phil Williams (1990) published by Palgrave; Wars of Watergate: The Last Crisis of Richard Nixon by Stanley Kutler (1990) by permission of Alfred A. Knopf; The Bush Presidency by Dilys Hill and Phil Williams published by Macmillan Press (1994); Kenneth Thompson (ed.) for extracts from The Nixon Presidency: Twenty-Two intimate Perspectives of Richard M. Nixon published by the University of Virginia (1987).

The publishers would like to thank the following for permission to reproduce pictures on these pages.

(T=Top, B=Bottom, L=Left, R=Right, C=Centre)

Bettmann/Corbis 152, 157L, 158, 270, 309B, 319R, 331, 338, 364, 379; Corbis 40, 99, 156, 192R, 216, Corbis/© Underwood & Underwood 161, Corbis/© Oscar White 321, Corbis/© Robert Maass 277, Corbis/© Baldwin H. Ward & Kathryn C. Ward 282, Corbis/© Robert Pryor 400B, Corbis/© Wally McNamee 412; Feiffer © Jules Feiffer. Reprinted with permission of Universal Press Syndicate. All rights reserved 400T; John Frost Newspapers 392; Columbia Pictures, courtesy The Ronald Grant Archive 163; Universal Pictures, courtesy The Ronald Grant Archive 308; Library of Congress, Clifford Berryman Collection/Washington Star, 1937 201L; Peter Newark's American Pictures 39, 67, 70, 85, 118, 157R, 175, 184, 191, 192L, 213, 225, 228, 238, 250, 309A, 336, 368, 374; ©1982 Mike Peters, Dayton Daily News 393; Popperfoto 303, 319L; © Punch Ltd 201R, 252, 259, 267; © Estate of Ben Shahn/VAGA, New York/DACS, London 2001 192L; Sargent © Austin American-Statesman. Reprinted with permission of Universal Press Syndicate. All rights reserved 406; © Telegraph Group Ltd, 1970/The Centre for the Study of Cartoon and Caricature, University of Kent 304; Topham/ Associated Press 329, Topham Picturepoint 301; Tribune Media Services, Inc. All Rights Reserved. Reprinted with permission 400C.

Cover picture: Three Flags by Jasper Johns (1958), The Bridgeman Art Library © Jasper Johns

Index